Mesocosm

Seto Bhairava dancing

Mesocosm

Hinduism and the Organization of a Traditional Newar City in Nepal

ROBERT I. LEVY
with the collaboration of
Kedar Rāj Rājopādhyāya

MOTILAL BANARSIDASS PUBLISHERS
PRIVATE LIMITED • DELHI

Reprint: Delhi, 2019
First Indian Edition: Delhi, 1992

ISBN: 978-81-208-1038-9

MOTILAL BANARSIDASS
41 U.A. Bungalow Road, Jawahar Nagar, Delhi 110 007
1 B, J S Compound, Kennedy Bridge, Nana Chowk, Mumbai 400 007
203 Royapettah High Road, Mylapore, Chennai 600 004
236, 9th Main III Block, Jayanagar, Bengaluru 560 011
9, Panchanan Ghosh Lane, 1st Floor, Kolkata 700 009
Ashok Rajpath, Patna 800 004
Chowk, Varanasi 221 001

Endpaper map adapted from *Société et Religion chez les Néwar du Népal* by Gérard Toffin. Paris : Éditions du Sentre National de la Recherche Scientifique, 1984

Printed in India
by RP Jain at NAB Printing Unit,
A-44, Naraina Industrial Area, Phase I, New Delhi–110028
and published by JP Jain for Motilal Banarsidass Publishers (P) Ltd,
41 U.A. Bungalow Road, Jawahar Nagar, Delhi-110007

For Upendra Rāj Rājopādhyāya and Nerys

> And my husband says the same, only I don't believe it, replied the Princess Myagky. If our husbands were not so fond of talking, we should see things as they are.
>
> Tolstoy, *Anna Karenina*

Death: Did you enjoy your reprieve?

Knight: Yes, I did.

Death: I'm happy to hear that. Now I'll be leaving you. When we meet again your and your companions' time will be up.

Knight: And you will divulge your secrets?

Death: I have no secrets.

Ingmar Bergman, *The Seventh Seal*

Contents

PART 2. THE CONSTRUCTION OF THE MESOCOSM

Maps

Figures

Preface and Acknowledgments

The many years of research and writing that resulted in this book required the support of many people and institutions. I am grateful and relieved to be able, at long last, to acknowledge them.

The years of research in Nepal were supported by grants from the University of California and the National Science Foundation. There were two one-year periods when I was providentially freed from other responsibilities and able to write at leisure. The first was made possible by a John Simon Guggenheim Fellowship, supplemented by a grant from the Social Science Research Council, and the second by a Fellowship at the Center for Advanced Study in the Behavioral Sciences at Palo Alto, once again with supplementary support from the Social Science Research Council. The Center for Advanced Study provides an incomparable setting for intellectual stimulation and for getting work done. Its Fellows are usually burdened for life with affectionate nostalgia and gratitude, as am I.

Leslie Lindzey at the Center, and Marian Payne at the University of California, San Diego, helped enormously in various stages of preparing the manuscript. Cathy Hertz of the University of California Press meticulously saved me from a multitude of errors. The ones that remain are mostly a matter of my own stubbornness. Susan Coerr carved an orderly index out of the tangled materials of the book.

I had invaluable aid in getting started on the study from Christoph von Fürer-Haimendorf, Leo Rose, the late Bhuwan Lal Joshi, and Jaya Pratap Malla. In Nepal I received much information and support from

Abner and Sylvia Hurwitz, Jacob and Patricia Crane, Gabriel Campbell, Lynn Bennett, and the staff of the United States Educational Foundation. Many departments of His Majesty's Government generously helped me with maps, statistical information, and support of various kinds. In Bhaktapur the great scholar Rāmapati Rāj Śārma gave me patient and invaluable help with my many linguistic, historical, and interpretive problems. The very many others in Bhaktapur who wish to remain anonymous helped as informants, teachers, and scribes. In the United States Devi and Gautam Vajracharya helped in the translation of masses of interview materials and acted as living reference works during the years in which the book was being written. Steven Parish had many useful comments to make on the manuscript based on his own research in Bhaktapur. Roy D'Andrade helped me through some of the more tangled patches of the material on kinship terminology.

My indebtedness to the works of contemporaries and predecessors in the study of the Kathmandu Valley is, as the following chapters will show, enormous. Among these, I am especially indebted to Niels Gutschow, whose many years of work in Bhaktapur, whose maps—including the ones he has prepared for use in this book, and whose frequent "personal communications" stimulated by his careful reading of the manuscript inform and embellish the book.

The introductory chapter tells something of what I owe to my collaborator, Kedar Rāj Rājopādhyāya. This book would have been something entirely different and very much less without him.

And, finally, to the one without whom there would have been no book, and not much of anything else, my beloved wife, Nerys.

The maps in the book were prepared by Niels Gutschow. He is also responsible for the photograph used on the jacket and as a frontispiece. Roy Porello prepared the color plates of the Nine Durgā masks. The other photographs are by Robert Levy.

In the quotations used in the book we have generally altered the transliteration of Nepali, Newari and Sanskrit terms to follow the usages of the text.

CHAPTER ONE

Introduction

THE BACKGROUND OF THIS STUDY

This book is based on a study of Bhaktapur, a Newar city in Nepal, during the years 1973 to 1976, and it is the first of two projected volumes. My central interest has been in the reciprocal relations of the public life of communities and the private worlds of their members. I began working in Bhaktapur after studies in two small Tahitian-speaking communities in the Society Islands of French Polynesia ("Piri" and "Roto") in the hope that the enormous contrasts between the ways of life of that Himalayan Hindu city and of the tiny Polynesian communities might be illuminating in some unforeseen way.

My intention at first was to report on Bhaktapur in much the same way that I had on the Society Islands communities. I would write a short section on the social and cultural context of people's lives and follow it with an extended description and discussion of some individuals' private experience and of their "mental worlds" as those small worlds were related to their larger contexts. I collected, as I had in Piri and Roto, information on the social and cultural context and, with the help of lengthy tape-recorded sets of interviews, information on private worlds. Instead of the forty pages that were required to introduce the relevant aspects of the Tahitian context, however, it has taken me this large volume to present the relevant Bhaktapurian context. That, in a way, is the central point of this study. For it is the weight and complexity of its culture and society that most evidently distinguishes public life in Bhaktapur from public life in Piri and which, in turn, powerfully affects many aspects of private experience and personal mental organization of people in Bhaktapur in comparison with people in the Tahitian communities.

But what is the relevant context? Bhaktapur is a repository of much of the cultural and social history of South Asia. What was to be studied there, and what included in this volume?[1] The decision, as always in ethnographic reports, has been somewhat uncertain and a compromise. Thus some of this book is devoted to the commonplaces of the tradition of ethnographic description—sketches of history, economy, and, more elaborately, social structure. Most of it is concerned with the elaborate "religious" life of the city, the system of symbols that helps organize the integrated life of the city so that it becomes a *mesocosm*, an organized meaningful world intermediate to the microcosmic worlds of individuals and the culturally conceived macrocosm, the universe, at whose center the city lies.

The religious organization of Bhaktapur is of central interest for the theoretical ambitions of this study. One of the most striking differences between Bhaktapur and Piri is the enormous comparative elaboration of a particular kind of symbolism (which we will call "marked symbolism") in Bhaktapur and its miniscule importance, even its suppression, in Piri. As I will propose in chapter 2, this elaboration is a crucial resource for organizing a certain *type* of community and society, a certain *type* of city—an "archaic city." Bhaktapur represents a Hindu community in its full development, a "climax community" of Hinduism, and Hinduism so viewed is a symbolic resource that once served, and still anachronistically serves in Bhaktapur, to organize many such cities.

A final reason for emphasizing Bhaktapur's symbolic organization is that the striking contrast between Piri's emphasis on what it takes to be the mundane and Bhaktapur's emphasis on the dramatic theatrics of marked symbolism is intimately and centrally connected with differences not only, as one might expect, in the intimate experience of people in the two places but also in aspects of their "mental organization." It was as an essay in comparative "mental organization" that I undertook the study, and it is here that this volume has a problem. The understanding that I began to have during the course of this study of various people's private lives, of their ways of thinking and feeling, of their consciences and their motives, often motivates and shapes the sociocultural description presented in this volume. The neurophysiologist and cybernetician Warren McCulloch once entitled a paper "What is a

Number, That a Man May Know It, and a Man, That He May Know a Number?" (1965). These intimately interdependent questions, transformed to "what is Bhaktapur that a Newar may know it, and a Newar that he or she may know Bhaktapur" serve admirably to indicate what I am mostly after, with the qualification that "know" is too limited, and would need to be expanded to "act in, be secure in, be sane in, be human in," as well as "resist, struggle against, reinterpret" or whatever words we may find for those aspects of Man (who is, of course, generic Man) that turn out to be dependent on the forms of the community in which an individual lives. However, the materials on the mind and experience of "the Newar," or, more modestly and accurately, of sample Newars, must be presented in detail elsewhere. In this volume I have had to introduce as assertions with no supporting data ideas about some of the most relevant psychological and personal "resonances" (a useful word for deferring considerations of cause and effect, of direction of the flow between individuals and community) of the symbolic order, ideas, for example, about "sophistication," symbol hunger, special qualities of "self" and "person," the implications and resonances of the "purity complex," and of the special personal force of blood sacrifice. The apologetic and hopeful phrase "We will treat this at length elsewhere" is often used in admission that the reader might be uncomfortable with one or another *obiter dictum*.

I approached Bhaktapur from Tahiti with a different set of questions and with a different kind of competence and ignorance from those of an Indologist or Himalayan expert. I must ask the Indologist's indulgence for my errors and amateurism and the use of secondary sources and translations for South Asian history and for Hindu texts. The Indologist and the anthropologist working in South Asia need much mutual forbearance on the one hand and dialogue on the other.

My choice of Nepal, the Newars, and Bhaktapur for study was originally motivated by a growing conviction that the kinds of psychological forms that I had seen and reported on in Piri and Roto (Levy, *Tahitians*, 1973) were something more than the simple consequence of an historically derived "cultural tradition." The personal experience and psychological characteristics of individuals in Piri and Roto turned out to be in many ways similar to those reported elsewhere throughout Polynesia and Micronesia. This raised questions (Levy 1969, 48):

> To what degree are the similarities artifacts of shared emphases of the common intellectual subculture of Micronesian and Polynesian specialists? To what degree are they simply a negative category, a lack of some peculiarly

> modern urban trait, turned into a pseudopositive form? To what degree are these necessary structural psychological responses of all people who live on islands, or who have semisubsistence economies based on horticulture and fishing, or who live in traditional "simple" societies of any kind? To what degree are they universal responses to encounter with vastly more powerful societies, or to prolonged colonial experience? And finally, to what degree are the reported areal psychological similarities part of a shared and historically transmitted cultural tradition, in which personality can be viewed as an historical product?

With such questions in mind and with considerable curiosity about experience in different kinds of places that were exotic to me, I looked for a community that was as different from a Tahitian village as I could find, while still being "non-Western." I chose, finally, the Newar city of Bhaktapur in the Kathmandu Valley. Piri, the Tahitian village that was the principal site of my previous study, was small (some 284 people living in fifty-four households), on a small island, with comparatively little differentiation of social and sexual roles, based on a fishing and horticulture economy, traditionally nonliterate, a variant of Polynesian culture and society, and, since the late eighteenth century, under increasing Western colonial influence. Bhaktapur was a very large community by anthropological standards, some 40,000 people living in extraordinary density in an area of less than one-half square mile; situated in a high mountain valley in the interior of a large continental area; socially highly differentiated into a hierarchical caste structure, with markedly differentiated gender roles; with an economy based on farming, crafts, and trading; traditionally highly literate, in fact, a traditional center of Himalayan and South Asian High Culture; and although under the political control of the Gorkhālis since the late eighteenth century, almost untouched by Western influences until the early 1950s. It would be difficult to find two non-Western communities that were more different from each other. The usual strategy in comparative studies is to compare two communities that differ from each other in as few dimensions as possible and to try to trace the influence of those few dimensions. A strategy of maximal contrast is a different matter. One learns something from comparing a mouse and an elephant, something about mammalian universals and about the possibilities and limits of variation, and, concurrently, about gross differences in adaptation.

In this book the comparison between Bhaktapur and Piri (and of both with "the West") is sometimes overt, but for long stretches it becomes covert, informing the point of view and the emphasis given to the possible significance of certain phenomena.

In the description of the relatively simple life of an isolated village it is possible to achieve a considerable degree of accuracy. Whenever possible, many variants of an event can be observed, many informants can be queried, small but possibly significant details can be explored, contradictions can be exploited. Bhaktapur, in contrast to such villages, is not only large in size and population—full of events, crammed with symbolic forms, and highly socially differentiated—but also has a literate tradition that many of its inhabitants know, and that in itself complexifies reports and interpretations as to what goes on. But what its inhabitants think Bhaktapur is and what this study claims it, in fact, to be in large part is a unified sociocultural system. If one is concerned with the organization of this system and its implications for those who live in it, it has to be approached in long focus, trying to keep in view the multitude of forms and events that are visible to all in the city's public urban space and time. This requires the gathering of masses of material—often necessarily based on one viewing or sometimes one glimpse, and/or on the reports of limited numbers of informants, all under pressures that often make it impossible to adequately check reliability, details, and mistakes. In short, there are undoubtedly more errors of detail in this book than would be seemly in the study of a small community.

HOW THE STUDY WAS DONE

I worked in Bhaktapur from April 1973 to April 1976, except for a six-month period starting in September 1974, during which I returned to the United States. During the first year and a-half I lived in Bhaktapur and studied primarily the public culture and social system and the Bhaktapur dialect of the Newari language. Although I had learned a little Nepali, the *linqua franca* of Nepal, before going to Nepal, I was not able to begin studying the Bhaktapur dialect of Newari[2] until I began work in that city. During the first several months I was dependent on English-speaking Newars for explanations, translations, and language instructions.

During the first year and a-half I lived in Bhaktapur. Because I would have been unable to live with any except a very-low-caste Hindu family because of my "ritual uncleanliness," and because living with a low-caste family would have made it very difficult for me to interview higher-status people, I had to establish my own household with Newar servants from Kathmandu. With the help of English-speaking assistants in the first stages I began the survey of the aspects of city life described in the report. A variety of approaches and materials—mapping of local spatial features (e.g., shrines, festival routes and locations, the residential areas of different status groups) on aerial maps, study of city documents and records, and interviews and surveys of various kinds were used to work out the skeleton of city organization. The work of other people on Nepal, the Newars, and Bhaktapur[3] provided me with essential information for orientation as well as with proposals to be checked, confirmed, or corrected. In the years during which this manuscript has slowly grown other works have appeared that have been of great use to me, particulary the recent extensive volumes of Mary Slusser (1982) and Gérard Toffin (1984).

After this first period in Bhaktapur I spent six months back at the University of California working with Kedar Rāj Rājopādhyāya in the development of interview schedules. On returning to Nepal I began interviewing in Newari. In an approach to private lives I picked eight people—six men and two women—in various positions throughout the caste system for extensive series of tape-recorded interviews. These interviews became the bases for further interviews and observations in pursuit of the differentiated experience of the life of the city to be presented, it is intended, in a second volume. With the help of two scribes (who wish to remain anonymous) all the interviews were transcribed from tapes as Devanāgarī text. The scribes were Bhaktapur Brahmans, one an expert on traditional religion, the other on history and linguistics. They were non-English-speakers, and starting at this time most of my work was conducted in Newari. The scribes soon became associates in the study, and many of the descriptions of religious procedures and of various aspects of the city's culture, often stimulated by issues or obscurities (for me) in the recorded interviews, started with their descriptions and explanations. Because of the major emphasis on secrecy and privacy in Bhaktapur the scribes and a few of the people being interviewed traveled to Kathmandu, some eight miles from Bhaktapur, to work with me. During this last year I lived in Kathmandu and traveled to Bhaktapur, where I had an office on the ground floor of an unoccupied house, to do several sets of interviews, observe festivals and various special events, and do some surveys.

Newari is a complex language of Sino-Tibetan provenance, with an enormous vocabulary derived from its complex history as the language of an ancient and complex society.[4] It has many sociolinguistic and stylistic variations, many of Bhaktapur's major social units as well as many geographic divisions of the city having distinctive pronunciations, vocabulary, and usages. Although I conducted interviews in Newari, and understood to a considerable degree what people were trying to tell me, I missed some of the sense and many of the nuances at the time of the interviews. The study of the Newari written transcripts after the interviews and again on return from Nepal helped clarify much of this. As a further and important step in clarification, however, I had all the interviews (including my own parts of the dialogue) translated into English on return to the United States. This was done mostly by two Newar scholars, Gautam, and Devi Vajracharya.

The penultimate stage in this long process, prior to the preparation of the final manuscript of this volume, was the joint reading over some months during 1979 of a draft manuscript of the sociocultural materials with Kedar Rāj Rājopādhyāya. Many corrections and amplification were made during this reading. The final manuscript is the result of the slow reworking of the corrected draft manuscript to bring our descriptions and interpretations into relation with the South Asian and wider scholarly literature relevant to the study, and to which, we hope, the study is relevant.

Kedar Rāj Rājopādhyāya is the chief Brahman priest of Bhaktapur's Taleju temple, once the temple of its Newar kings and still at the center of the city's civic religion. He is a member of a family that has held that post for many generations. The position passed to him in 1973 when his father, Upendra Rāj, died. Upendra Rāj had been chief Taleju priest for several decades and had known Bhaktapur in its time of Himalayan isolation, when upper-status people were still carried on the roads in palanquins and the forms of "medieval" Bhaktapur still flourished. Kedar participated in the work of his father and uncles and was taught by them and studied the Hindu religious tradition in a Sanskrit school in Bhaktapur. He works not only in Taleju with its Royal and Tantric activities and its various relations to wider civic religion and as a *purohita*, a family priest, with his family's traditional clients but also in the city's nascent modern sector as a member of the city's administrative council and of other urban organizations. He is fluent not only in Sanskrit, and like most upper-status people of Bhaktapur, Nepali and Newari (both Kathmandu and Bhaktapur dialects), but also English. Kedar, as he is known throughout Bhaktapur, came to believe that Bhaktapur would soon change into something else, and that an attempt had to be made to tell something about its old religious life to a wider world. He was first an informant for me, but soon came to be much more, my collaborator in this book. From here on "I" becomes "we" for this book is a product of our continuing dialogue.

This volume is concerned with the symbolic ordering of Bhaktapur, and thus of only some of the many dimensions that make Bhaktapur an interesting place. This choice was made in consonance with the theoretical concerns introduced in the next chapter, above all because of an interest in Bhaktapur itself as the locus of the experience of its citizens. We have for the most part neglected economy, social dynamics, ecological relations, material culture, and so on. One neglected topic requires comment, however. We have had to neglect Bhaktapur's relations to its traditional hinterland. This would have been a major project in itself, and it is to be hoped that others will undertake it. Much of this would have to be an historical study, as the events of the last 200 years have caused Bhaktapur to draw into itself and at the same time—especially in recent decades—to be related to a wider Nepal in the external relations it did have. However, the neglect of the hinterland leaves out what would be the essential necessary next step in the analysis of the "kind" of city Bhaktapur once was. As *polis* meant, depending on its context, sometimes the Greek city within its boundaries, sometimes that city and its hinterland, so "Bhaktapur" once meant sometimes the city, sometimes the city-state or "little kingdom" of which the city and its privileged inhabitants were the royal center. There are a few remaining ceremonial relations with the Newar villages and towns of the hinterland recalling the old relations, and a few continuing economic relations with some of those towns and more especially with the surrounding non-Newar hill peoples. Now, and in a lengthening post, however, the hinterland of the city means for the most part only the rich farmlands that immediately surround it, farmed by people who live within Bhaktapur. We cannot be sure how in the past integration into the city-state altered the indentity and experience of the Bhaktapurians of the little kingdom. We would guess that the change now is mostly for the dwellers of the peripheral towns and villages in their new self-sufficiency. But whatever the previous economic, political, and symbolic integrations of city and hinterland may have been it seems plausible—from what history and chronicles and tradition we have to guide us—that the dwellers within the main royal cities always thought that the universe was most clearly and safely represented *within* their city boundaries. The dangerous deities who stand at the boundaries and protect those boundaries against the dangerous and difficult world beyond the city have stood there since time immemorial.

One other problem requires comment—and a justifying argument. Our emphasis on the order of Bhaktapur is very liable to appear regressive, ideological, Orientalist, and various other unpleasant things in the contemporary climate of criticism of essays presenting "other" times and "other" peoples. We are, in this volume, describing a normative order, an ideal order. We have many questions to address to it—what *kind* of an ideal order is it in comparative perspective, what does it do, and what are its parts and relations and dynamics. As those questions show, we accept its "reality" as an essential focus of concern and analysis for understanding Bhaktapur. It is only against this ideal system, that our ultimate inquiry, the dilemmas, conflicts, understandings, and points of view of individuals in Bhaktapur—all of whom find themselves in vital interaction with the concrete realizations of the ideal system—can be understood. We have constructed our representations of the urban symbolic order from many sources. Much of it is from the material realizations of the ideal order in city space, the precipitate of the conceptual and building programs of past elites. Much of it is from obervations of aspects of action expressing that order, or the interface between that order and contrary problematic ones. And many parts of this book are based on the conceptions and descriptions of elite informants, specialists of various kinds, but above all Rājopādhyāya Brahmans.

The conception of a civic order is thus not just that of a sentimental Westerner, it is that of local specialists in symbolic order. The book is, in part, a presentation of *their*, their own, imagery. For Bhaktapur, that conception is not just the wishful ideological thinking and propaganda of precarious elites but a powerful force that in itself helps to create order. Whatever the untouchable, for example, thinks about it all, it is these conceptions which form the matrix of his life. Against the ordering interpretations of the elite, popular interpretations where they differ are either simply "wrong" when they are alternatives within the same sort of ideological domain, or else, when they are explanations of some radically different sort (as when a farmer, say, represents untouchability as a guarantee of social order), represent attempts at critical "demystifications" of the system, both alternatives illuminating the tensions, tasks, and dynamics of the dominating system of symbols and interpretations. How the ideal system is experienced, represented, and known by others in the city and its ontological status when "the people" are the center of our concern are the intended subject of another work.

This coherent symbolic order is a peculiar attempt to order a community. It is not in itself adequate to represent "the life of the community." That life has many aspects, levels, and kinds of order and disorder. To try to make one aspect the "real" one is to engage in ideological polemics or, worse, tendentious and covert use of the exotic. However, to neglect order where it does exist is another and peculiarly postmodern ideological move in itself.

PART ONE

Orientations and Contexts

CHAPTER TWO

Orientations

In the following chapters we will discuss those aspects of the past and present of the Newars and of Bhaktapur that will serve as context and background to our principal concerns. We must first introduce the Newars briefly and then, at rather greater length, present a collage of theoretical "conceits" that will suggest the field of discourse in which this book and its selections, arguments, and assertions is located.

BHAKTAPUR AND THE NEWARS

Traditional Nepal, an ancient Asian society with a literate high culture, was confined largely to the Kathmandu Valley. The people of this valley came in time to call their territory Nepal, themselves Newars, and their language Newari. Archaeology has not yet fully clarified their prehistory, but it seems that at an early period (perhaps the eighth or seventh century B.C.) a predominantly Mongoloid, Tibeto-Burman speaking people settled in the valley where they may have encountered an aboriginal population speaking an Austro-Asiatic language. From perhaps the first or second century A.D. a political organization emerged that was to characterize the Kathmandu Valley until the late eighteenth century. A ruling class, a king and his court of North Indian origin, speaking and writing Sanskrit for sacramental and literary purposes and a Sanskritic North Indian language (a Prakrit) for everyday purposes, was progressively woven into an underlying society and culture with Himalayan and Central Asian features. Gradually a language (Newari) and culture (Newar) arose that synthesized these elements. Although the Sanskrit culture of the priests and court persisted, it became more narrowly traditional and ceremonial. Progressively more of the larger religious, political, and literary life was expressed in Newari and Newar forms.

There were dynastic disputes and confusion, but the Newars flourished. The valley soil is exceedingly rich, the bed of an ancient lake. A complex system of irrigation works for the collection and distribution of rainwater from the slopes of the surrounding hills was inaugurated sometime prior to the establishment of the first North Indian dynasty, and the rich soil and irrigation permitted highly productive farming. The Valley in time found itself on the major trade routes between India and Lhasa, in Tibet, and trade, tolls, and services became the basis, along with the rich agriculture, for considerable wealth. This made possible (and was, in turn, developed through) a great sociocultural efflorescence.

Stimulated by Indian ideas and images throughout a very long period of time, the Newars began, perhaps from the fourth century onward, the progressive elaboration and centralization of their society and culture in urban centers. Of these, three—Bhaktapur, Patan, and Kathmandu—became variously principal or secondary royal centers. They became concentrated, bounded (walled during certain times), highly organized units, surrounded by a hinterland of farmland and villages. Finally the three cities became politically divided. The hinterlands became territories, and three small states developed, each with its own central royal city, its king, its particular customs, its dialect.

During these centuries the Newars created architecture; sculpture in wood, stone, and metal; music; drama; a multitude of beautiful crafts; and domestic goods—and above all they created a complex public religious and social drama, for which the cities became the great stages. In these Kathmandu Valley cities there was an elaboration of a particular kind of society, culture, and person. This had much to do with Hinduism (in its widest sense as a set of peculiarly South Asian understandings, images, and actions) and much to do with the structural necessities and implications of a certain kind of organized life, which I shall call here the "archaic city."

In the late eighteenth century the Newar kingdoms, divided and inward-looking, fell to the attacks of the armies of the chief of the small Indianized mountain state of Gorkhā in the western Himalayas. The Gorkhāli alliances and conquests defined the greatly enlarged territory and state of modern Nepal. The Newars were no longer *the* people of Nepal. They were only one of some seventy linguistic and "ethnic groups," and a conquered one at that. The Gorkhā alliance put its capital at Kathmandu, and the long autonomous political history of the Newars was over.

Yet, Bhaktapur, only eight often muddy miles away from Kathmandu (a long enough distance for those who walked or were carried in palanquins) was left more or less alone. It lost its Newar king (although he continued and continues to be powerfully present symbolically) but it remained relatively isolated by Gorkhāli political policy for dealing with what was in effect a conquered state. That policy, variously motivated, was to isolate Nepal from the "outside," and to isolate Newars from power within the new state. The Gorkhālis encouraged Newar traditional life, as had the previous North Indian founders of Newar dynasties. However, these latter-day rulers did not become integrated as their predecessors had into a Newar state. The conquerors' language, Gorkhāli, became "Nepali," the official language of the newly expanded country, and the Newars found themselves no longer a small nation, but in the eyes of other Nepalis (although not in their own) just one "ethnic group" among others.

Bhaktapur ran on in very much the old way, like a clockwork mechanism assembled long ago that no one had bothered to disassemble. The first serious shocks of modernity began only in the early 1950s, when, following a political revolution, Nepal opened itself to the West. Development—education; agriculture; health programs; increasing travel in and out of the country; burgeoning communications of all kinds, books, movies, radio; and internal transportation—began to alter this conservative, isolated Himalayan country.

Altered in what way? Bhaktapur had always been in history, but it had tried for hundreds of years to turn the flow of history into what might seem a timeless eternal civic order. In 1973, when this study began, the city, or most of it, was still trying. The signs of a deep transformation to another way of being in time and in history were evident and were illuminating for both what had been and what might be about to happen. This book is concerned with the struggle to order Bhaktapur, its particular way of carving out a space and time and common reality in the face of history. It describes at length things that are important in that they are aspects of that order. As the order changes, as it "modernizes," such things will be of interest for other reasons—as problems for modernization and as potsherds left over from old broken pots, clues for antiquarian enterprises.

WAYS OF LOOKING AT THE ORGANIZATION OF BHAKTAPUR

BALLET

We will make use of some interrelated ways of looking at and talking about Bhaktapur. The book will illustrate the value these "fanciful and ingenious conceptions" or "conceits," as they once could have aptly been called, may or may not have. Our collage of conceits is more fanciful, literary, and metaphorical than precise, but "marked symbolism," "ancient" and "archaic" types of cities, "axial transformations," "epistemological crises," and the like are ways of adumbrating what seem to us the important tendencies and relations that may well be lost in the mass of details that are to follow.

We may start with an assertion that in comparison with certain kinds of simple traditional communities such as Tahitian villages[1] on the one hand, and with complex modern urban communities on the other, Bhaktapur is to a very large degree characterized by the presence of a great deal of a certain kind of symbolism. We may defer for a while the questions as to what kind of symbolism and what that symbolism might do, what purposes it may serve. For now we may characterize it as "extraordinary," and of compelling local intellectual and emotional interest. That symbolism is, in large part, derived from the vast resources of South Asian "religious"[2] ideas and images, locally transformed, ordered, and put to use for Bhaktapur's civic purposes.

In the following chapters after first considering the contexts of Bhaktapur's "symbolic world," we will distinguish and discuss various aspects and elements of that world. For those who live in or are familiar with other kinds of cities, whose experience of urban symbols is of a different kind, it may be useful to think, at the start, of the civic life of Bhaktapur as something like a choreographed ballet. The city space is the carefully marked stage. Beyond the city is another sort of space, another kind of world, the wings of the civic stage. Both the civic stage and its wings are symbolically represented, the dance moves off center stage at times, but the symbols, conceptions, and emotions proper to the city stage and to its wings are quite different, although interdependent. The civic stage is separated from the "outside" by clear boundaries and is elaborately differentiated and marked out through the symbolic divisions imposed on the physical space of the city, which we will present in chapter 7. These spaces contribute their own meanings to the performances that take place on them and, in turn, take further meaning from these performances.

Distributed through this differentiated space are images of deities, shrines, and temples, many of which are semantically appropriate to the spaces they characterize. Like all our analytically separated out aspects and elements, specific deities give meaning to and take meaning from the other aspects—space, actors, time, form of enactments, and so on. We can think of the gods and shrines as the distributed, differentiated, and, above all, meaningful decor of the ballet, setting the mood and context against which the human actors dance. "Decor" is too weak for the deities' roles, however; they strain our metaphor, and their contribution is more like that of the Commandatore in Mozart's *Don Giovanni*, part decor, part singer. We introduce them in chapter 8.

Largely through descent, roles in this ballet are assigned to the city's inhabitants. There are more than 300 clan-like units (*thar*s) that in large part determine what ritual and occupational roles their members will play in the city. These are ranked in some twenty or so "macrostatus levels," in a hierarchy of statuses from king and Brahman to untouchable. Civic roles, the civic social structure, is the subject of chapters 5 and 6.

Actors, decor, and space are set into motion by the city's conventional arrangements of time, the music of the ballet, signaling various beginnings and endings, rhythms and tempos, entrances and exits, movements, and phases of performances. There are some eighty annual events[3] determined by the lunar and solar calendars. There are other times and tempos in the city. The time of the life cycle—birth, maturation, menarche, and so on—brings on stage a dozen events during life, and a large number on dying and after death (app. 6). Another kind of time, making use of the planets and, for some purposes, the moment of birth, is associated with its own deities, the astral deities (chap. 8) and is used in attempts to bring the city dance into relation with what seems from the perspective of the order of the dance to be choice, accident, chance, and luck.

If one knows what a person's surname is (the designator of his or her *thar*), his or her age and sex, what day of the lunar (for some purposes the solar) year it is, and where the person lives in Bhaktapur, one can make a plausible guess at where he or she is, what he or she is doing, and even something of what he or she is experiencing. One has come to understand "the work." This is, in part, simply to claim that there is considerable social and cultural order in Bhaktapur. This in itself is banal, but when that order is placed in comparative perspective, when the details of the ballet are worked out, when the relations between actor and role, between person and symbol are considered—then the question shifts from order to a special order, and, in part, a particular *kind* of order. Our approaches to "kind," our typological conceits include "the archaic city" and "climax Hinduism."

TYPOLOGICAL CONCEITS: THE ARCHAIC CITY

Bhaktapur, as we will see in chapter 4, is an exceedingly densely populated community containing a very large number of people (in the comparative scale of premodern communities), whose life in relation to that community is highly and complexly integrated. Their community life is such—to paraphrase a synthesizing definition of the "city" in archaeological perspective (Redman 1978, 216)—that their identity derives from their aggregation, an aggregation that is formally and impersonally organized, that the economy of the community comprises many nonagricultural activities and provides "a diversity of central services both for its inhabitants and for the smaller communities in the surrounding area."[4] This makes Bhaktapur a "city" by such criteria, but what kind of city?

In a fundamental paper on "the part played by cities in the development, decline, or transformation of culture," Robert Redfield and Milton Singer (1954) attempted a classification of types of city in historical perspective. For our purposes their types can be divided into two different sets. The first is a group of types in which cultural heterogeneity and secularity are of central importance. These are cities, in their words, where (Redfield and Singer 1954, 57):

> one or both of the following things are true: (1) the prevailing relationships of people and the prevailing common understandings have to do with the technical not the moral order, with administrative regulation, business and technical convenience; (2) these cities are populated by people of diverse cultural origins removed from the indigenous seats of their cultures. They are cities in which new states of mind, following from these characteristics, are developed and become prominent. The new states of mind are indifferent to or inconsistent with, or supersede or overcome, states of mind associated with local cultures and ancient civilization. The intellectuals of these... cities, if any, are intelligentsia rather than literati.[5]

In contrast, there are kinds of cities that they term "administrative-cultural" "which carry forward, develop, elaborate a long-established local culture or civilization. These are cities that convert the folk culture into its civilized dimension" (ibid., 57). These are the cities of the literati. They also call this kind of city "the city of orthogenetic transformation," and "the city of the moral order," in contrast to the "city of heterogenetic transformation and technical order." They claim that the first cities in early civilizations were cities of orthogenetic transformation where local culture was carried forward rather than broken down to be replaced by new means of relation and integration, familiar to us in Western urban history.

In an analysis of such early cities, Paul Wheatley (1971, 225f.) argued for the centrality of "symbolism" in their structure and function:

> Whenever, in any of the seven regions of primary urban generation, we trace back the characteristic urban form to its beginnings we arrive not at a settlement that is dominated by commercial relations, a primordial market, or at one that is focused on a citadel, an archetypical fortress, but rather at a ceremonial complex. . . . The predominantly religious focus to the schedule of social activities associated with them leaves no room to doubt that we are dealing primarily with centers of ritual and ceremonial. Naturally this does not imply that the ceremonial centers did not exercise secular functions as well, but rather that these were subsumed into an all-pervading religious context. . . . Operationally [these centers] were instruments for the creation of political, social, economic, and sacred space, at the same time as they were symbols of cosmic, social, and moral order. Under the religious authority of organized priesthoods and divine monarchs, they elaborated the redistributive aspects of the economy to a position of institutionalized regional dominance, functioned as nodes in a web of administered . . . trade, served as foci of craft specialization, and promoted the development of the exact and predictive sciences.

Bhaktapur is not an ancient city in terms of historical continuity, but its organization reflects many of the same principles that have been ascribed to otherwise differing ancient cities as members of a certain type of urban community. As a member in some respects of such a class it may well suggest, *mutatis mutandis*, something of what they might have been, and may be thought of as an archaic city.

HISTORICAL CONCEITS: THE ANCIENT INDO-EUROPEAN CITY AND THE AXIAL AGE

In his classic, once influential, and recently much criticized[6] 1864 study *La Cité Antique*, Fustel de Coulanges was (of interest for our present purposes) concerned with a transformation from one state of affairs to another, the transition to the classic cities of Greece and Rome. This work, and its echo in the idea of a transformative "axial age," give us another set of metaphors to suggest Bhaktapur's peculiarities. Fustel tried to look back through the texts of "the Greeks of the age of Pericles and the Romans of Cicero's time" for clues to an earlier urban organization of society and religion that was already ancient to Classic Greece and Rome, clues preserved in vestiges of language and ritual and legend. He added, because of his "addiction to the newfangled Aryan doctrine" (as Finley [1977] puts it) comments on what he took to be early Indian social forms based on his reading of available translations of some Sanskrit texts. He felt that the first Mediterranean European cities arose on the basis of a shared peculiarly Indo-European family organization. "If we compare," he wrote, "the political institutions of Aryas of the East with those of the Aryas of the West, we find hardly any analogy between them. If, on the contrary, we compare the domestic institutions of these various nations, we perceive that the family was constituted upon the same principles in Greece and in India" (Fustel de Coulanges 1956, 113).

According to Fustel's idealized schema the preclassical ancient city was built out of successively inclusive cellular (bounded and internally autonomous) units (ibid., 127f.).

> When the different groups became thus associated, none of them lost its individuality, or its indpendence. Although several families were knitted in a phratry, each one of them remained constituted just as it had been when separate. Nothing was changed in it, neither worship nor priesthood, nor property nor internal justice. The city was a confederation. . . . It had nothing to do in the interior of a family; it was not the judge of what passed there; it left to the father the right and duty of judging his wife, his son and his client.

There was a nesting of these cellular units—"family, phratry, tribe, city"—each level marked by its relevant gods and rituals, and in contrast to, say, a Frenchman, "who at the moment of his birth belongs at once to a family, a commune, a department and a country," (ibid., 128) the citizen of the ancient city moved via a series of *rites de passage* over many years into membership in successively more inclusive units.

Each increasingly inclusive level of structure (as expressed in Fustel's historical and temporal language) had its proper gods and cult. "In the beginning the family lived isolated, and man knew only the domestic gods. . . . Above the family was formed the phratry with its god. . . .

Then came the tribe, and the god of the tribe. . . . Finally came the city, and men conceived a god whose providence embraced this entire city . . . a hierarchy of creeds and a hierarchy of association. The religious idea was, among the ancients, the inspiring breath and organizer of society" (ibid., 132).

Each unit had its interior and its exterior, and the interior was protected by secrecy. Above all, this was true of the household. "The sacred fire . . . had nothing in common with the fire of a neighoring family, which was another providence. Every fire protected its own and repulsed the stranger. . . . The worship was not public. All the ceremonies, on the contrary, were kept strictly secret. Performed in the midst of the family alone, they were concealed from every stranger. . . . All these gods, the sacred fire, the Lares, and the Manes, were called the consecrated gods, or gods of the interior. To all the acts of this religion secrecy was necessary" (ibid., 37).

The ultimate unit to which people were related at this "stage" was the ancient city itself. There was "a profound gulf which always separated two cities. However near they might be to each other, they always formed two completely separate societies. Between them there was much more than the distance which separates two cities today, much more than the frontier which separates two states; their gods were not the same, or their ceremonies, or their prayers. The worship of one city was forbidden to men of a neighboring city. The belief was, that the gods of one city rejected the homage and prayers of any one who was not their own citizen" (ibid., 201).

What anchored and tied together this structure of cells was its rootedness in a fixed and local space. "When they establish the hearth, it is with the thought and hope that it will always remain in the same spot. The god is installed there not for a day, not for the life of one man merely, but for as long a time as this family shall endure, and there remains any one to support the fire by sacrifices" (ibid., 61). The city came to define in itself its own proper social unit and was sacred for that group within the city boundaries. Just outside the city boundary lived a special class of people, a special class of outsiders, who were placed in an essential contrast with the insiders. Those people who were "excluded from family and from the [family] worship fell into the class of men without a sacred fire—that is to say, became plebeians" (ibid., 231).

Fustel's portrait contained a deeply felt myth, that of an earthly paradise of orderly, family-based unities prior to a transformation into a larger, impersonal, and conflict-ridden state organization. This was one of a set of such myths putting a lost or distant world into contrast with the modern. It was compelling to his contemporaries and annoying to those of ours who are engaged in countermyths. The problem for a summary rejection of Fustel's vision is that the particular formal features of his "Ancient City," that we have chosen to review here are characteristic of Bhaktapur.

Let us now consider another conceit that, in fact, supplementary to Fustel's has more respectability, or at least currency. For Fustel the features he imagined to characterize the primitive stages of the Indo-European "ancient city," disappeared in the Mediterranean West in those transformations of the ancient city that had made the Athens and Rome of Fustel's classic sources into new kinds of places. That sense of an historical transformation of High Cultures, somehow fundamental for what we are now, has been characterized in various ways. It has been seen as a watershed separating us from an alien, archaic *civilized* world, stranger to us in many ways than the world of primitive peoples. For Robert Redfield the transformation represented the breakdown of the moral order that had arisen through the "orthogenetic transformation" of a still prior cultural order, the "primitive world" (Redfield 1953). A new kind of basis for urban order was required, and the city and its inhabitants begin to be transformed into their modern forms.

It has been argued (for example, Benjamin Schwartz [1975, 1], in a volume reporting a symposium on "wisdom, revelation, and doubt: perspectives on the First Millennium B.C.") that the European urban and cultural transformations were part of a worldwide wave of "breakthroughs" within the orbit of the "higher civilizations," during the first 700 or 800 years before the Christian Era in an "axial age" (the term and idea were suggested by Karl Jaspers) consisting in the "transcendence" of the limiting definitions and controls of these ancient forms. In Greece this was manifest in "the evolution from Homer and Hesiod to pre-Socratic and classical philosophy" (and, Fustel would have argued, in the changes in urban organization he discerned). For India, the "transcendence" might be seen in "the transition from the Vedas to the Upanishads, Buddhism, Jainism and other heterodox sects" (Schwartz 1975, 1).

When this argument is pushed beyond its heuristic uses toward more specific historical analysis and toward such questions—of interest to us here—as "did India undergo an axial transition" it becomes diffusely problematic. In the same symposium Eric Weil notes that those who did not participate in this transformation have simply been rejected as ancestors of the modern world. In a consideration of the political and sociological conditions necessary for the nascent "transcendent" ideas to *succeed*, he notes in passing that the lack of a politically unifying force might explain "why historical and anthropological differences were never overcome in India. There is a tendency to forget these differences in order to bring India into our own scheme of historic progress toward universality; we wish to look only at those phenomena which fit" (Weil 1975, 27). The heterodoxies that followed the preaxial Vedas—particularly the one that proved elsewhere most powerful, Buddhism, with its powerfully transcending attack on the symbolically constituted social order that were concomitant with its ontological challenges—did not prevail[7] in India. What did prevail was ultimately the static social order of Hinduism, which, whatever its peripheral inclusion in their proper place of the socially transcendent gestures of renunciation and mysticism, was hardly any kind of "breakthrough" into whatever the idea of an axial "transformation" was meant to honor.

All of which is to suggest that traditional India and Bhaktapur, in so far as it may be characteristic of traditional India, are very old-fashioned places indeed.

TYPOLOGICAL CONCEITS: KINDS OF MINDS—A CONTINENT IN THE GREAT DIVIDE

The quest for the defining "other" led in the nineteenth century to conceptions of powerful oppositions in contrast to European urban society. These oppositions, which left little place for "preaxial" civilizations, were dichotomies of two variously characterized extreme terms: simple, complex; primitive, modern; prerational, scientific; and Eden, Exile. The oppositions implied not only types of community organization but also aspects of the experience and thought of members of such communities, the "states of mind" of Redfield and Singer. "*Gesellschaft*," for example, required of its members (in presumed contrast with "*Gemeinschaft*")—as a consequence of its emphasis on contract and rationality in regard to an individual's "interests"—that "beliefs must submit to such critical, objective, and universalistic standards as [those] employed in logic, mathematics and science in general" (Loomis 1964, 286).

These dichotomies, like our various historical conceits, although they never fully characterized actual communities, have continued to haunt scholarly imagination as "ideal types" as possible tools in the quest for a clarification of aspects of social order. Paul Wheatley, in his discussion of the beginning of urban forms, uses the classical terms of contrasts. "We are seeking to identify those core elements in society which were concerned in the transformation variously categorized as from Status to Contract, from *Societas* to *Civitas*, from *Gemeinschaft* to *Gesellschaft*, from mechanical to organic solidarity, or from *Concordia* to *Justitia*" (1971, 167). In a footnote bearing directly on our view of Bhaktapur he added an amplification, the suggestion that the early city was of neither one nor the other type. "It should be noted that this transformation was *only initiated* by the rise of the ceremonial center and that . . . the society of the temple-city was neither fully *contractus*, *civitatis*, *Gesellschaft* nor organic" (ibid., 349 [emphasis added]).

The social philosopher Ernest Gellner is one of those who makes use of the dichotomy in a very strong form. Modern industrial civilization is unique and stands historically across a great frontier or divide from what went before. It is in "a totally new situation." The clarifying task is to characterize "primitive thought" in its oppositional contrast to the most powerful form of modern cognition, science. This contrast will help clarify how we are unique.

If this contrast is used as a method, then (Gellner 1974, 149f. [emphasis added]):

> One is naturally left with a large residual region between them, covering the extensive areas of thought and civilization which are neither tribal-primitive nor scientific-industrial. Hence there is a certain tendency for evolutionary schemata of the development of human society or thinking to end up with a three-stage pattern. This tendency is a consequence of the fact that the very distinctively scientific and the very distinctively primitive are relatively narrow areas, and three is a very big region in between.
>
> Nevertheless, it is my impression that the problem of the delimitation of science, and the problem of the characterization of primitive mentality, are one and the same problem. To say this is not to deny that the area between them is enormous, and comprises the larger part of human life and experience. But this middle area perhaps *does not exemplify any distinctive and important principle*. With regard to the basic strategic alternatives available to human thought, there is only one question and one big divide. . . . The central question of anthropology (the characterization of the savage mind) and the central question of modern philosophy (the characterization or delimitation of science) are in this sense but the obverse of each other.

It is the burden of this book that within this heterogeneous range of thinkers and thought between "primitive" and "scientific," and in the wide range of communities between the "simple" face-to-face community and whatever it is we have (or had) become, there is a kind of continent in the Great Divide, which has its own distinctive typological features, exemplifies its own distinctive and important principles in relation to both sociocultural organization and to thought, distinctive features that are blurred and lost in these classical oppositions. Bhaktapur and places that might have been analogous to it in the ancient world are illuminating for this middle terrain. Neither primitive nor modern, Bhaktapur has its own exemplary features of organization and of mind.

ORGANIZATIONAL CONCEITS: THE CIVIC FUNCTION OF SYMBOLISM IN BHAKTAPUR AND, PRESUMABLY, IN OTHER SUCH ARCHAIC CITIES

Shortly after arriving in Bhaktapur, I (the senior author) was standing with a Newar inhabitant of that city in a public square when a nearby man began to shout angrily at a boy. "Who are those people," I asked, "and why is the man shouting?" My friend was unable to answer either question. In Piri, the Tahitian village, the understanding of, response to, and staging of such episodes was the predominant way in which village order was known, taught, learned, rehearsed, experimentally violated, and repeatedly brought under control. Conversely, worry that one's behavior would inevitably be seen and known to others—who would always know exactly who you were and what you were doing—underlay the moral anxieties central to villagers' discourse about and attempts at self-control. In its intimacy, in the constant interplay of being watched by the whole village and watching it, through its close agreement on moral definitions and proper responses, and above all in its construction of people's sense of a "normal" reality, the village of Piri operated as what Erving Goffman (1956) once called a "total institution" with consequent implications for the "mind and experience" of its inhabitants (Levy 1973). In Bhaktapur the kind of communally shared learning from patterned, contextualized, "ordinary" events which was pervasive in Piri was limited to only certain sectors of people's experience of the community—to the bounded and isolated household unit and, sometimes, to the larger kin group or the household's immediate neighborhood. Thus, how did the inhabitants of Bhaktapur understand, learn from, and adjust themselves to the larger city, most of which was out of sight and hearing, and whose complexity, whose quantities and varieties of people and events seemed beyond any direct and intimate grasp? How did citizens understand and how were they affected by a *city* that, like Redfield's "cities of orthogenetic transformation," seemed to embody a cultural tradition in urban rather than village form? In large part, we propose, by making use of a resource for communication, instruction, understanding, and control that is not much used in Polynesian communities where culturally shaped common sense used to interpret culturally shaped face-to-face interactions and observations provides the core of community integration. Bhaktapur, in contrast, makes elaborate use of particular sorts of symbols—"marked symbols"—to solve the problems of communication induced by magnification of scale. How it does it, the extent and limits of the resource, is one of the concerns of this book.

ORGANIZATIONAL CONCEITS: EMBEDDED AND MARKED SYMBOLISM

The idea of "symbolism" in anthropological studies has become so extended that it is little more than an invitation to view *anything* in the life of a community in a certain way. A symbol in this view is "any structure of signification in which a direct, primary meaning designates, in addition, another meaning which is indirect, secondary and figurative, and which can be apprehended only through the first" (Ricoeur 1980, 245), in short, in one or another context, potentially everything.

It is useful for comparative purposes—and particularly for emphasizing an important difference between places such as Piri and places such as Bhaktapur—to distinguish two different kinds or aspects of symbol or symbolism, "embedded" and "marked." The term "embedded" implies "indirect, secondary, and figurative meanings" that are condensed and dissolved in any culturally perceived object or event so that they seem to belong to the object or event as aspects or dimensions of its "natural" meaning. Examples of such culturally shaped embedded and naturalized symbolic forms are the Hindu and Bhaktapurian complex of purity, impurity, contamination, purification, and the like, which are the subject of chapter 11. "Embedded symbolism" is associated with the cultural structuring of "common sense," the structuring of the assumptions, categorizations, and phrasings through which processes of cognition themselves are structured and through which meaning is created and selected out of the flow of stimuli generated and experienced within a community. Such culturally constructed perceptions and understanding have the experiential characteristics of "ordinary reality." They are no more (or less) questionable than any other sensations or perceptions, and the knowledge associated with them is felt to be directly derived from sensations and perceptions. Beliefs derived from or composing such knowledge are generally directly held with no epistemological problems. Faith is not at issue.

The "symbolism" of concern to recent "symbolic anthropology" has been, to considerable degree, such "embedded" symbolism.[8] However, the kind of symbolism that is strikingly elaborated in Bhaktapur is of the sort to which statements about "symbols" in ordinary discourse refer—something whose meaning must *evidently* be sought elsewhere than in what the object or event seems to mean "in itself." "Marked" symbols, in contrast to "embedded" symbols, are objects or events that use some device to call attention to themselves and to set themselves off as being extraordinary, as *not* belonging to—or as being something *more* than—the ordinary banal world. This is the symbolism of various attention-attracting, emotionally compelling kinds of human communication, whether it be art, drama, religion, magic, myth, legend, recounted dream, and so forth, which are marked in some way to call attention to themeselves as being special, as being other than ordinary reality. Most of this volume, beginning with chapter 7, is concerned with such marked symbolism and its special spaces, practitioners, messages, resources, and functions in the life of the city.

TYPOLOGICAL CONCEITS: HINDUISM AS AN ARCHAIC KIND OF SYMBOL SYSTEM AND BHAKTAPUR AS A HINDU CLIMAX COMMUNITY

Bhaktapur, the argument goes, can be considered to have interesting typological analogies with archaic cities insofar as it represents a community elaborately organized on a spatial base through a system of marked symbolism. The particular symbolic system made use of is a variant of Hinduism. When contrasted with Judaism, Christianity, Islam, and Buddhism (other than its Vajrayāna and Tantric varieties),[9] Hinduism is a peculiar contemporary religion. Ahistorical (without a heroic, that is, transcending, founder, and without a future to be obtained through some progressive struggle of faith, wisdom, or rectitude); rooted in local space, a local population, and a local inheritance; distributive of its godhead into a pantheon of meaningful and immanent gods—essential resources for the organization of space, time, and community; insisting on the inclusion of social order and social behavior within the sacred realm; insisting on the presence of the sacred in the here and now, and not restricted and banished to eschatological beginnings and endings and distant heavens—Hinduism is in many of its features, which contrast with the "world historical religions," a system for and of what we have called "archaic urban order."

Louis Dumont remarks, in a section of his study of Hindu caste treating "the territorial framework: the little kingdom," that "contemporary anthropological literature frequently stresses the fact that actual caste systems are—or rather, were—contained within a territorial setting of rather small scale. Here social anthropologists found what they were at the same time mistakenly seeking at the level of the village, a social whole of limited extent, established within a definite territory, and self-sufficient" (Dumont 1980, 154). Dumont noted the periodic absorption of these "little kingdoms" into larger political states and argued that "the compartmentalization of the little kingdom must have been at its height at periods of instability and political disintegration" (ibid., 156). That instability and disintegration characterized the larger territory, but it was a stimulus to and opportunity for the ordering of the Hindu city-states—a royal city and its hinterland—within that territory.

Whatever the shifting historical relation between caste and territorial units might have been, the conditions that allowed for the formation and development of little kingdoms allowed for the fulfillment of Hinduism's potentials for ordering a community. Such little kingdoms seem to have represented, to borrow a term from ecology, "climax communities" of Hinduism, where it reached the full development of its potentials for systematic complexity, and with it a temporary stability, an illusion of being a middle world, a *mesocosm*, mediating between its citizens and the cosmos, a mesocosm out of time.

PSYCHOLOGICAL CONCEITS: WHAT IS A NEWAR THAT HE OR SHE MAY KNOW BHAKTAPUR

Yeats put it exactly right in "Among School Children": O body swayed to music, O brightening glance, How can we know the dancer from the dance?[10]

Piri's dance and Bhaktapur's dance are greatly different. What about the dancers? The private lives of some of Bhaktapur's people, people whom we believe to be representative in some ways, will be the subject of another volume. There we will consider aspects of the city's traditional life, such as family religion and rites of passage, which are relatively neglected here, as well as what some different sorts of people experience and how they interpret and are affected by the aspects of the civic life presented here. In this volume, as we remarked in the last chapter, we will deal with such personal dimensions at only a very few points where it seems necessary for suggesting the psychological impacts and functions of some of the city's most important symbolic patterns—this is the case, for example, with the discussion of purity and of aspects of the significance to the civic audience of the Nine Durgās troupe of god-possessed performers.

The differences in scale, complexity, and kinds of resources used for community organization have, we believe, direct implications for differences not only, obviously, in people's private experience but also (*pace* Gellner) for the "mentality" of people in the two communities. These private contrasts are both dependent on differences in community organization and help maintain and motivate them. For our final orienting conceit we will sketch some of these implications, asserting in a condensed, simplified, and idealized form what will be illustrated, argued, and qualified at length elsewhere. We must now look at our contrasting communities' organization once more, but this time not in itself but as it affects and is experienced by the communities' members.

As we have asserted above, much of the psychologically significant order of a traditional Tahitian village lies in its complex construction of what was locally taken to be literal reality, resulting in what William Blake, speaking of another world, called "mind-forged manacles." The heterogeneity of the village is contained within a narrow and relatively consistent set of assumptions, values, and definitions; this, as well as the structure and limits of vocabulary in certain domains, makes critical and philosophical thought and discourse difficult. This shaped experience, reinforced by hierarchies of coherent redundant controls (Levy 1977), results in convictions of the solidity and rightness of local common sense. Incompatible understandings, motives, and feelings are relegated to an unconscious realm, which is in large part derived from dense social agreement on the unthinkable. With the conscious aspects of their understanding constructed in a comparatively simple and direct manner out of the forms of the "total institution" in which they live, Tahitians act in its terms because it is the *natural* thing to do. An outsider sees the powerful influence of the village-based construction of local reality, but villagers acting from their certainties about the nature of their world, from their solidly constructed selves, feel themselves to be very autonomous *individuals* for whom external controls or even advice on correct behavior from others in the village would be both unnecessary and oppressive.

What people know in what they take to be a trustworthy manner seems to them to be based largely on their sensory experience of their concrete world. They believe, for the most part, in what they think they see; in Tahiti, as is general in Polynesia, the word for knowing and seeing is significantly the same. The conditions of their life generate a corresponding epistemology. In contrast, if something with a claim to truth is presented to them through verbal reports or other obviously "symbolic" forms that seem disconnected or disconnectable from direct experience, they are suspicious, it is "only something that they have heard about." Even those claims of religion that are neither directly experienced nor intuitively "natural" are subjects for skepticism. Faith, a category that is essential for the Newars, is problematic for them. They are only dimly aware of differences in different people's subjective realities and have minimal interest in psychological or sociological speculation, the revolutionary viewpoints that enable a transcending insight into aspects of one's own possibly arbitrary reality and that make the very idea of "mind-forged manacles" possible. Living in their taken-for-granted common-sense reality, they are familiar to us as the kinds of people whom reflective intellectuals and sophisticated city dwellers see pejoratively as rural, provincial, naive, and unsophisticated people, rigid and unimaginative in their convictions and certainties and their dismissive encounters with other worlds.

Tahitian villagers live in a resolutely ordinary, daylight, sunny world. It is surrounded by a shadowy, poorly discriminated, and thus uncanny world, which they refer to metaphorically as the "night." They depart from the literalness of their daylight world into imaginative marked symbolic enactments, ceremonies, and rituals only on restricted occasions. Now and (as suggested in reports of the time of first Western contacts) in the past, symbolic enactments are and were used, as they are everywhere, mainly for signaling radical and usually irreversible changes of status, as digital markers of socially significant change of state—for the individual during rites of passage, and for the community for a transition from peace to war or the submission to a new chief. In these cases, where one socially defined object or person or situation is suddenly transformed into another, Tom suddenly becoming Harry, the pattern of the ordinary is not sufficient and something more than common sense is required.

The experience—and the personal consequences of that experience—of citizens of Bhaktapur is different. Like Tahitian villages, Bhaktapur is a bounded, largely self-sufficient, and highly integrated sociocultural system. But in Bhaktapur's complex organization every mature individual is involved in a great number of *different* culturally defined and validated realities and experiences calling upon and evoking quite different aspects of or even kinds of "self" as he or she moves from one to another.[11] Experience in Bhaktapur is greatly more complex; multiple points of view are not only possible but forced on people. Living systematically in shifting and contrasting worlds, many citizens of Bhaktapur are forced into an epistemological crisis, forced to the understanding that external reality, as well as self, is constructed, and in some sense illusory, or in the Hindu philosophical expression, *māyā*.[12] They are now, like Princess Myagky in our introductory epigraph, in position for a kind of skeptical and critical analysis that transcends the ideology of their culture, and they become the anthropologist's potential collaborators in the analysis of their own culture and situation, rather than, as in the case of rural village Tahitians, the passive subjects of analysis.

Able in certain special contexts and conditions to say and know such things as "gods are representations of human feelings and activities," or "we must have untouchables because without them we would lose the caste system and there would be chaos," or "it is not the behavior of others so much as people's images of themselves that makes them accept their positions [in the caste system]," or "there must be shame and embarrassment everywhere in the world, but of course, what people are ashamed and embarrassed about must vary," people, quite ordinary people, in Bhaktapur's society are "sophisticated," in its dictionary sense of "altered by education, worldly experience, etc. . . . from the natural character or simplicity." If sophistication, taken as the index and result of a profound difference from the conditions that nurtured Tahitian life and mind, characterizes the majority (as we have reason to believe)[13] of the people of Bhaktapur, there is a still further move, a characteristic response to the epistemological shift that makes knowledge problematic that, in turn, distinguishes the citizens of Bhaktapur from representative (or ideal) moderns. For Bhaktapur is precisely as Redfield and Singer characterized the genre, a city of literati (that is, enthusiasts and technicians of marked symbolism) and not of intelligentsia. The insights that the preceding quotations illustrate are generated by minds working over contradictions and contrasts in the culturally proffered certitudes of various sectors and phases of a complex culture, contradictions and contrasts that are potentially subversive to the society and in many ways problematic to the integration of the self. Rather than making the analytic pursuit of these intellectual problems an end in itself, a move that would encourage the formation of a social class of critical intellectuals, of socially destabilizing philosophers and scientists, people seek their most satisfying answers to intellectual paradoxes, mysteries, and threats to solid constructions of "self" and "other" and "reality" in the complexly ordering devices of marked symbolism, and develop, in fact, a craving for such devices, a *symbol hunger*. The crisis of complexity is met through a kind of enchantment that people accept in spite of or in tension with their common sense through a leap of faith into a commitment to the extraordinary and fascinating forms of the community's coherent and fascinating array of marked symbols. In chapter 9 and elsewhere we will present interview materials illustrating this movement in some individuals' recollections of childhood, adolescence, and maturity, a movement from simple certainties, to intellectual doubts about the family's and city's religious doctrines, to a *conversion* into "understanding," acceptance, and social solidarity—a conversion arguably associated with some of the personal implications of Bhaktapur's ubiquitous blood sacrifice.

For people living in Bhaktapur, the city and its symbolic organization act as an essential middle world, a *mesocosm*, situated between the individual microcosm and the wider universe as they understand it. This large aggregate of people, this rich archaic city, uses marked symbolism to create an order that requires resources—material, social, and cultural—beyond the possibilities and beyond the needs of a small traditional community. The elaborate construction of an urban mesocosm is a resource not only for ordering the city but also for the personal uses of the kinds of people whom Bhaktapur produces. Or at any rate has produced. Some of our acceptable cultural ancestors tried to make doubt a method, and finally succeeded in freeing us, as they believed, from marked symbolism, succeeded in making the symbolic "only" symbolic. The people of Bhaktapur are beginning to desert their continent in the great divide for familiar shores.

CHAPTER THREE

Nepal, the Kathmandu Valley, and Some History

INTRODUCTION

Bhaktapur's mesocosm was built out of the materials available to it. In this chapter we will review something of the long history that helped form the present city, and out of whose debris it tried to build a seemingly timeless structure. That history, in turn, was much affected by the setting of the Kathmandu Valley—temperate, relatively disease-free compared to the southern jungles between Nepal and India, isolated and closed in by southern hills and those jungles to the south and by the Himalayas to the north, and with an enormously fertile soil, the essential support for the civilization that came to flourish there.

NEPAL

Modern Nepal is a country of extreme geographic and ethnic diversity. At the time of our study (according to the 1971 census) 11.5 million people lived in a rectangular land some 500 miles long on its northeast-southwest axis and averaging some 100 miles in breadth. Totally land-locked, it is wedged in between India and Chinese Tibet "like a gourd between two rocks" as Pṛthvīnārāyaṇa Śāha, the Gorkhāli founder of modern Nepal, put it in a phrase that all Nepalese leaders have always in mind. Nepal rises progressively in height from south to north from the low-lying jungles and plains of the Terai borderlands with India to the giant Himalayan ranges of the northern borders. In its jungles and valleys and on the mountain slopes live a genetically, ethnically, and linguistically diverse set of peoples. There are by some accounts some seventy mutually unintelligible languages spoken, suggesting the corresponding cultural diversity of the country.[1]

Among these diverse peoples the Newars are peculiar. For they are themselves the remnants of a sort of nation, an older Nepal whose boundaries were usually the slopes of the hills surrounding the Kathmandu Valley. Hill people in the far reaches of the territory of modern Nepal still speak of the Kathmandu Valley as "Nepal." The Newars were the citizens of this now submerged polity whose arts and traditions still constitute most of "Nepalese Culture" when "Nepal" is represented in museums and in art and religious history as a South Asian High Culture. Modern Nepal began with the submerging of the Kathmandu Valley nation and the amalgamation of "over 50 principalities and tribal organizations" (Gewali 1973) into a much larger unity through the conquests of the western Nepalese Gorkhāli hill tribes and their allies under the chief, Pṛthvīnārāyaṇa Śāha, who after a number of campaigns against the Valley profited from the internal disarray and jealousies of its Newar kingdoms to conquer them in 1768 and 1769.[2]

Because we are concerned with the Newars, not with "greater Nepal," our focus is on the Kathmandu Valley, which remained even after Newar incorporation into greater Nepal and some Newar dispersal (mostly as traders and businessmen to the developing cities of the new state) the main center of Newar life.

THE KATHMANDU VALLEY

The Kathmandu Valley is a rough ellipse measuring about 15½ miles along its east-west axis and 12 miles at its greatest width, with a base area of some 218 square miles. The Valley is about 4,400 feet above sea level and ringed by hills that rise from 1,000 to 4,000 feet above the level of the Valley. Visible on the horizon to the north of the Valley in clear weather are the ranges of the high Himalayas. The Valley is the bed of an ancient lake. Its alluvial soil contains deposits of peat and of clays with high phosphate content which were traditionally dug and used as fertilizer. Now it is drained by a network of rivers that, almost dry during the dry months, swell during the rains and join in the main course of the Bagmati river which drains the Valley at its southwestern boundary. Recorded mean monthly temperatures are reported as varying between maximums of 24°C (75.2°F) in June and a minimum of 7°C (44.6°F) in January. The climate is usually temperate, and it is rare that temperatures dip a degree or two below freezing. The summers are first warm and dry, then more and more humid until the onset of the monsoon rains.

In the years 1967–1969 the Kathmandu Valley had between forty-four and sixty inches of annual rain (Central Bureau of Statistics 1974). Nearly half of the annual rainfall occurs during the monsoons of July and August, while the lowest rainfall, usually less than an inch in all, falls during November, December, and January, when the ground and air become progressively drier and dustier.

Valley farmlands, such as those around Bhaktapur, are in the flat-lands at the base of the hills and on terraces on the hill flanks. The fields are irrigated after the rainy season through a system of connecting ditches that are periodically unblocked to allow water to flow from collection basins in the hills. Various crops—rice, wheat, and a variety of vegetables (see chap. 4)—are successively raised in these fields during the course of the year.

The Kathmandu Valley, particularly the city of Kathmandu, is now the center for national government and administration. Light industry, tourism, and a multitude of commercial activities are centered there. It is estimated that about 5 percent of Nepal's people live in the Kathmandu Valley, some 600,000 people according to the 1971 census. They live[3] in the three major Valley cities of Kathmandu (150,402), Patan (59,049), and Bhaktapur (40,112),[4] a large number of secondary towns and villages, and in scattered hamlets and farms. Most of the country's ethnic groups are represented in the Valley. Census data in 1961 suggested that about half the Valley population were Newars.[5,6]

NOTES ON EARLY NEWAR HISTORY

According to D. R. Regmi (1969, 14), the first written examples of the term "Newar" to denote the people and society of the Kathmandu Valley date from the seventeenth century, but, as he remarks, the term may well have had a long usage before then. Although, as we shall see, contemporary Newars in some contexts limit the "Newars" to the "climax" society that began to form in the time of the "medieval" Malla kings, as the society and culture seems to have developed more or less continuously from its most ancient roots, we can follow Regmi in referring to the Kathmandu Valley society, culture, and language from the earliest days until its capture by the Gorkhālis in the late eighteenth century as Newar.

Local inscriptions and foreign accounts, mainly Chinese, on which a history of early Valley Nepal can be based date only from the fourth century A.D. In the absence of adequate archaeological studies, which may some day clarify and alter our conceptions of the early history, inferences about early periods are based on Nepalese chronicles and legends and on problematic allusions in Hindu epic literature.[7] There is still much debate on the interpretation of these sources for histories of political dynasties and events, and even for a correct chronology. But for the purposes of locating Bhaktapur, a provisional history can be sketched out.

The earliest written inscriptions (from the period of the Sanskrit-speaking court of the Licchavi dynasty) show that more than 80 percent of the place names in the Valley were non-Sanskritic. This supports a tradition that non-Sanskritic dynasties ruled early Nepal, perhaps from (at least) as early as the seventh century B.C. This society, referred to as "Kirata," was apparently of Mongoloid origin, speakers of a Tibeto-Burman language.[8] According to P. R. Sharma (1973, 67f. [spelling standardized]):

> Despite the lack of proof, the Kirata tradition in Nepalese history is too deeply rooted to be dismissed easily. The Kiratas are a widely mentioned tribe in ancient Sanskrit literature, especially the Epics. Many references point to the northeastern Himalayan foothills as the home of these people. The Himalayas were still an area outside the sphere of Aryan domination, and the Kiratas therefore seem to differ from them racially. The Rais and Limbus [of contemporary Eastern Nepal] claim to be the Kiratas. The features of these people distinctly betray their Mongoloid origin. The use of the term Kirata in ancient literature seems to have been wide enough to encompass all groups [in Nepal] of Mongoloid stock. . . . The matrix of Nepalese culture in the valley must have been laid by these Kiratas. The modern inhabitants of the valley, the Newars, are believed to be an intermixture of Aryan and Mongoloid strains resulting from the unions between the Kiratas and the Aryans migrating from the plains of India. The early prototype of the Newari language might have struck its first roots also during this time, as the language is considered to be basically of the Tibeto-Burmese group. The liberal assimilation of the Indo-Aryan Sanskrit into the language proceeds only from the time of the Licchavis, who were responsible for introducing Sanskrit into the land.

By the first or second century A.D., a Sanskrit-using and Prakrit-speaking court, the Licchavis,[9] had replaced the Kirata court. They were presumably related to the Licchavi rulers of Vaiśali in Bihar in North India. This was the beginning of a continuing pattern of Sanskritic courts derived from North India ruling over a Tibeto-Burman-speaking people.[10] Gradually the language and customs of the courts and the people were to blend in a Newar synthesis. Always within this synthesis, however, there were certain segments of religion and court life that followed Sanskrit models and some aspects of the life of the people that maintained residues of ancient Himalayan and Northern modes.

Irrigation of the Kathmandu Valley was developed under the Licchavis as many inscriptions attest,[11] with the construction of tanks and canals enabling farmers to husband and distribute the monsoon rains. In concord with the rich soil of the Valley, irrigation led to the kind of agricultural surplus that eventually made extensive urbanization possible.

In the later days of Licchavi rule (from the late sixth century A.D.) Tibet was developing a unified state, which was eventually to center at Lhasa. Now "Himalayan passes to the north of the Valley were opened. Extensive cultural, trade, and political relations developed across the Himalayas, transforming the Valley from a relatively remote backwater into the major intellectual and commercial center between South and Central Asia" (Rose 1974, 956). Much of the art and religion of the Newars and the Tibetans grew out of shared Indian sources, but also in mutual interchange and stimulation, and thus had many common features.

According to Prayag Raj Sharma (1973, 71):

> In the early Licchavi period, Nepal, together with India undertook the cultural colonization of Tibet. Buddhism and its concomitant art spread from Nepal to Tibet in the 7th Century A.D. According to Tibetan tradition the famous Nepali King Amshuvarman[12] married his daughter to the first historical King of Tibet, Srongtsan-Sgam-po. Brikuti is said to have carried an image of Buddha among other things as her nuptial present to her husband, and during her lifetime in Tibet knowledge of Buddhism spread far and wide. . . . From the Seventh Century to the present days, Nepal's relationship with Tibet has been continuously reaffirmed. Nepalese [that is Newar] artists, especially bronze makers, painters, and architects went to work in Tibetan monasteries and seminaries. Buddhist scriptures were taken to Tibet to be copied or translated. Ranjana, an ornately elaborate Newari script became the divine script in Tibet. . . . The different Tantric schools which overwhelmed Tibet, also found their way from Nepal as well as India.

Nepal and her princess were, of course, only one component of the influences forming seventh-century Tibet, but one of considerable importance.

Nepal during the Licchavi period reflected most of the Indian religious developments of the times. Early inscriptions and art indicate that there were sects devoted to Viṣṇu, Śiva, and the Buddha and their associated deities. Viṣṇu and his cult may have been more associated with the courts, and Śiva, in this early period, perhaps somewhat more with the non-Kṣatriya classes.[13]

Some writers, notably the Sanskritist Sylvain Lévi (1905), believed that the major popular Indian religion of Nepal during this early period, the religion of the Tibeto-Burman segment of the people, was Buddhism superimposed on old Himalayan forms, while the religion of the court aristocracy was one or another sect of Hinduism. During this period both Theravāda and Mahāyāna Buddhist monasteries were founded.

Lévi (1905, 255 [our translation]) proposed further that the first form of high Indian religion introduced into Nepal had, in fact, been Buddhism:

> Buddhism, malleable and accommodating, was able to introduce itself into the organized life of the Newars, without greatly disturbing it; it discretely sowed Indian ideas and doctrines, and let the harvest ripen slowly. But from the moment it was ripe, a brutal adversary came to dispute it. Sacerdotal Brahmanism menaced with death by the triumph of heresies had skillfully searched for refuge in popular cults; it had adopted them, consecrated them, and took up the struggle with rejuvenated gods and a renewed pantheon.

The rejuvenated Hinduism that contested Buddhism was Saivism.

David Snellgrove noted that the earliest Kathmandu Valley monuments are "definitely" Buddhist. "It is likely therefore that Buddhist communities established themselves in this valley well before the beginning of the Christian era" (1957, 93f.), which would mean that the Licchavi dynasty found themselves from the beginning in contact with a Buddhist community, adhering also presumably to local Himalayan religious forms. Whether or not Buddhism preceded "Brahmanical religion," all early evidence shows them operating side by side, Brahmanical religion presumably being that of the "foreign" court and its "foreign" Brahmans and, Buddhism, being that of the "people." These speculations, like those regarding an early courtly Vaisnavism versus a popular Saivism, reflect a scholarly conviction that the Brahmanical ideal of an intimate organic interrelation of Brahman, king, and people was still on a far horizon.

There is also evidence for the Licchavi period of Śakti worship, of the worship of the sun and other astral deities, and some indication of early Tantric forms[14] that were to become of major importance for the Kathmandu Valley, and for Lhasa beyond it. These latter were the precursors of the massive invasion of Tantrism which was to come later as a result of the dislocations produced by the Islamic invasions of India.

BHAKTAPUR'S BEGINNINGS

By the end of the Licchavi period most of the ingredients were present that were eventually to lead to the *climax community* of the royal Malla city-states, a community in which various preexisting elements developed fully, flourished, and became, for a time, related to each other in a closely interdependent and stable system.

The Licchavi dynasty fell in the ninth century, and there followed a period of historic and historiographic confusion out of which emerged the Malla dynasty. In this period Newar society and culture were to develop and flourish in its urban centers—Kathmandu, Patan, and Bhaktapur—and their dependent hinterlands. The Malla dynasty lasted in one form or another until the late eighteenth-century conquest by the Gorkhālis, which tranformed Nepal and the Newars into something different.

We must now begin to bring Bhaktapur toward the center of the scene, and consider the Malla period from its perspective. From the beginning of the thirteenth century there were a number of contesting ruling families bearing the name "Malla," interspersed with rulers who did not use this name. Eventually one man, Jayasthiti Malla, who married into the royal family of Bhaktapur and who began his reign in 1382, established an order and a dynasty that was to be remembered by the Newars as *the* Mallas, *the* Newar kings, *their* kings. His direct descendants ruled as Malla kings for more than four hundred years until the Gorkhāli conquest of the Valley.

Bhaktapur seems to have been founded as a royal city by Ānanda Deva,[15] who is believed to have reigned from 1147 to 1156 A.D. According to two early chronicles (D. R. Regmi 1965–1966, part I, p. 180), Ānanda Deva built a temple and royal palace in Bhaktapur.

According to the Padmagiri Chronicle, which substitutes Ānanda Malla for Ānanda Deva (Hasrat 1970, 49):[16]

> Having left his throne in charge of his elder brother he [Ānanda Malla] went to the western direction where he founded a new city which he called Bhaktapur, in which he erected 12,000 houses of all descriptions. When the city was built, Ānanda Malla sent for [the goddess] Annapūrṇā Devī from Benares and had the goddess settled there in an auspicious hour. . . . Afterward he built a palace in Bhaktapur . . . where he beheld the Nine Durgās whose images he placed in a temple.

The chronicle published by Daniel Wright, known as "Wright's Chronicle,"[17] adds some details. Ānanda Malla "founded a city of 12,000 houses, which he named Bhaktapur and included sixty small villages and seven towns in his territory. He established his court at Bhaktapur, where he built a Durbar; and having one night seen and received instructions from the Navadurga [Nine Durgās],[18] he set up their images in proper places, to ensure the security and protection of the town both internally and externally" (Wright [1877] 1972, 163).

The chronicles assert that the city was founded and developed as a royal center. There was something there before, however, and the attempts to construct a symbolically rationalized space that were to follow had to account for and work with preexisting structures. The most extensive work on the incorporation of previous structures into the "ordered space" of Bhaktapur is that of Niels Gutschow and his associates (Auer and Gutschow 1974; Gutschow and Kölver 1975; Gutschow 1975, Kölver 1980). They believe that the founding of Royal Bhaktapur involved a unification of a number of small villages that had developed in the area from perhaps the third century, following the development of irrigation in the Kathmandu Valley.[19]

Bhaktapur and the settlement that preceded its official Royal founding, has been referred to by a variety of names. Its early names were all Tibeto-Burman. According to the linguist Kamal Malla, its modern Newari name *Khopa* is derived from the earlier form *khoprn*, derived in turn from the Tibeto-Burman terms *kho* (river) and *prn* (field). The chronicles and inscriptions also refer to Bhaktapur as Khrpun, Makhoprn, and Khuprimbruma. The first usage of an Indic name, Bhaktagrama, dates from A.D. 1134 (Malla, personal communication). Its modern Nepali names are Bhaktapur, Bhadgaon, or Bhatgaon. Bhaktapur is taken to mean "city of devotees," the other names are said to mean "city of rice."

Bhaktapur, situated on the Hanumante river and bordered by rich farmland, was surrounded by a hinterland traversed by routes to the mountain passes to Tibet. Trade with Tibet became important for the Bhaktapur economy, and was to be of particular advantage during the periods when the Valley was divided into three semiindependent states.[20]

Bhaktapur eventually became the "metropolis of the Malla dynasty and the nerve-center of its culture and civilization" (Hasrat 1970, xxxix). The steps by which this happened can be only dimly glimpsed in records and monuments. Some historians believed that there was an early period of joint rule by the three Valley cities[21] which was sometimes peaceful, sometimes contested. But although earlier historians (e.g., D. R. Regmi 1965–1966, part I, p. 256) believed that the eventual hegemony of Bhaktapur in the Valley was not established until the later fourteenth century, later studies suggest that "since [its establishment in] the mid-twelfth century, Bhaktapur had been the capital city, *de facto* and *de jure,* and the Kings who titled themselves *Malla* continued to rule from it" (Slusser 1982, 54).

The fourteenth century marked the expansion of the empire of the Turkish Tughluq dynasty in northern India to and beyond the borders of Nepal. For the Newars the most important consequence was the dispersal of threatened Indian Buddhists and Hindus in the path of the Turks. Many of them came to the Nepal Valley where they greatly reinforced the Tantrism that was beginning to dominate and transform the earlier introduced forms of South Asian religion. The chronicles personify this movement in Harisiṃhadeva, a king of Mithilā, who was said to have been driven into exile in the Valley, where he became king of Bhaktapur, installing his *kul deveta*, or lineage goddess, Taleju, in the royal palace (Hasrat 1970, 52f.; Wright 1972, 175–177). Harisiṃhadeva's conquest of Bhaktapur is legendary, although it is generally believed in by Bhaktapur literati, and we will hear much of him, but the introduction of the Maithili deity Taleju as the Newar king's royal lineage goddess (chap. 8) along with her associated Tantric cult seems to have clearly been due to the effects of Turkish movements in northern India during this general period.[22]

Another chronicle, the Gopālarājavaṃśāvalī, only recently made generally available, is a unique witness to what seems to have been the actual relation of Harisiṃhadeva to Bhaktapur. As its editors note (Vajrāchārya and Malla 1985, xvi):

> Unlike the later chronicles which almost unrecognizably distort the truth by presenting Harisiṃha as a conqueror of Nepal and his descendants as legitimate rulers, the Gopālarājavaṃśāvalī notes that he was a political fugitive who died on his way to the valley, and his wife and son sought political asylum in Bhaktapur. Although they ultimately managed to rise to power by manipulating the local politics, the Queen and the Prince of Mithilā had entered Bhaktapur as refugees.

The Maitili queen and her son, the prince, became involved, apparently, in struggles for power. Eventually a protege of hers, Jayasthiti Malla, whose marriage had been arranged to the queen's granddaughter, was to become ruler of Bhaktapur and the remembered architect of its present order.

Nepal itself suffered an invasion in the mid-fourteenth century when

Shams ud-Dīn Ilyas raided the Valley from Bengal in 1349.[23] "The Muslim invasion shook the foundations of the kingdom, the invader having destroyed the city of Patan, laid waste the whole Valley of Nepal. He indulged in an orgy of mass destruction and incendiarism, plundered the towns and sacrileged the temples of Pasupati and Svayambhunath" (Hasrat 1970, p. xli). According to another chronicle, the Gopāla Vamśavli (folio 52[*a*], pp. 4–5), in Nepal Samvat 470 on the ninth day of the dark half of the month of Marga (January 1349), Sultan Shams ud-Dīn burned the city of Bhaktapur during seven continuous days. Petech (1958, 118–119) believed that this invasion was responsible for the disappearance of "all the monuments of ancient Nepalese architecture."[24]

Bhaktapur was now on the eve of its experiment in the construction of an ideal urban order. The partial destruction of the haphazard forms of a more ancient Nepal must have greatly facilitated and stimulated the undertaking.

JAYASTHITI MALLA AND THE ORDERING OF BHAKTAPUR

In 1355 A.D., shortly after the Muslim invasion of Nepal, Jayasthiti Malla, "a figure of obscure lineage and controversy with regard to his status as a sovereign ruler" (Hasrat 1970, xli), married the granddaughter of Rudramalla, a powerful Bhaktapur noble. After a period of shifting rulers and alliances he eventually emerged as the paramount ruler of Nepal, beginning his *de jure* reign in 1382.[25] "To Jayasthiti Malla goes the credit of saving the kingdom from the throes of disintegration and confusion. He curbed the activities of the feudal lords, brought the component units of the kingdom into submission, and with a strong hand, restored order" (Hasrat 1970, xlii).

Jayasthiti Malla was credited by some of the later chronicles—and by the present people of Bhaktapur—with the establishment of many of the laws and customs of Bhaktapur, particularly those involving caste regulations, with standardizing weights and measures, with establishing an order. Let us review some of the achievements traditionally ascribed to him. "Each caste [in Bhaktapur now] followed its own customs. To the low castes dwellings, dress and ornaments were assigned, according to certain rules. No sleeves were allowed to the coats of Kasais [butchers].[26] No caps, coats, shoes, nor gold ornaments were permitted to Podhyas [untouchables]. Kasais, Podhyas, and Kulus were not allowed to have houses roofed with tiles, and they were obliged to show proper respect to the people of castes higher than their own" ("Wright's chronicle," Wright 1972, 182f.). The chronicles credit Jayasthiti Malla with dividing the people into a large number of "castes" (sixty-four in some accounts, thirty-six in others). "The four highest castes [here *varṇa* is meant; see chap. 5] were prohibited from drinking water from the hands of low caste people, such as Podhyas or Charmakaras. If a woman of a high caste had intercourse with a man of a lower caste, she was degraded to the caste of her seducer" (Wright 1972, 186f.). According to the Padmagiri chronicle, "He constituted a fine for all such persons as follow the profession of others, as if a blacksmith follow the profession of goldsmith, he shall be fined" (Hasrat 1970, 56).

"He ordered that all the four castes of his subjects should attend the dead bodies of the Kings to the burning-ghats, and that the instrumental music of the Dipaka Raga should be performed while the dead bodies were being burned. . . . He constituted for each of the 36 tribes a separate *masan* or place for burning their dead and the corpses were decreed to be conveyed by four men proceeded by musicians" (Wright 1972, 182). Jyasthithi Malla classified houses and lands and standardized a system of measurement. "To the four principal castes, viz., the Brahman, Kshatri, Vaisya, and Sudra, were given the rules of Bastuprakaran and Asta-barga for building houses" (Wright 1972, 184). He changed the criminal laws. Previously criminals had been punished "with blows and reprimands, but this Raja imposed fines, according to the degree of the crimes" (Wright 1972, 182).

Jayasthiti Malla "made poor wretched people happy by conferring on them lands and houses, according to caste" (Wright 1972, 187). This particular aspect of reordering may explain, in part, reports of one set of laws that seem to run counter to the rigid codifying of social hierarchy and custom generally attributed to him. That is, Jayasthiti Malla "made many laws regarding the rights of property in houses, lands, and *birtas*[27] that hereafter became saleable" (Wright 1972, 182). Or as Padmagiri's chronicle has it, "He allowed his subjects to sell or mortgage their hereditary landed property whenever occasion required it." One may assume that this increased negotiability of property rights had something to do with the reforming of the status system and facilitated the economic base of the new regulations.[28]

A manuscript in the Hodgson Collection (vol. 11, n.d.) collected between 1820 and 1844 entitled "Institutes of Nepal Proper under the Newars or the Jayasthiti Paddhati" includes detailed regulations for the "four *varṇa*s and thirty-six *jāt*s" on rites of passage, and detailed regulations on such matters as payments to various specialists. It includes fines and punishments of various kinds, including those for illicit sexual intercourse. It prescribes the functions and some of the internal regulations (particularly the periods of pollution for birth and death, and whether they must purify themselves or be purified by a 'barber") of various groups, beginning with the lowest and ascending through the hierarchy.

Moreover, along with all this, it is said of Jayasthiti Malla in the chronicles that he built and repaired, established and consecrated temples and images of the gods. As the Wright Chronicle sums it up, "Thus Rāja Jayasthiti Malla divided the people into castes and made regulations for them. He also made laws about houses and lands, and fostered the Hindu religion in Nepal, thereby making himself famous" (Wright 1972, 187).

Jayasthiti Malla came to represent to Newars the Hindu ordering of Bhaktapur, an order built on an ancient plan. "In making laws about houses, lands, castes, and dead bodies, he was assisted by his five pandits. . . . Such laws were formerly in existence, but having fallen into disuse through lapse of time, they were again compiled from *Shastras* and brought into use" (Wright 1972, 183f.). Certainly, as D. R. Regmi argues (1965–1966, part I, p. 367), he built on preexisting hierarchical structures of some kind and on preexisting principles and forms of Hindu and Newar order. As Slusser notes, already during the Licchavi period "society [had been] hierarchically stratified by caste, and occupations were not only caste-determined but enforced through a special office " (1982, 38). During Jayasthiti Malla's reign (Slusser 1982, 59):

> New concepts of administration, nascent in the early Malla years, became clearly established. . . . But he cannot be credited with introducing the caste system into Nepal, nor with single-handedly infusing hierarchy into Nepalese society, two deeds on which his fame popularly rests. The Indian caste system was in effect in the Nepal Valley from at least the beginning of the Licchavi Period, as inscriptions attest. Similarly, the complex system of subcastes that ordain Valley social behavior must be viewed as the product of centuries of gradual accretion, not a sudden imposition by law. Significantly, Sthitimalla's own annals make no mention of these undertakings. . . . Nonetheless, Sthitimalla may well have codified the particular social patterns that had developed by his time, and thus given established local custom the force of law.

Jayasthiti Malla revivified, extended, and codified an order that built on preexisting forms and forced them into Hindu ideals of the proper form for a little kingdom, a city-state. Subsequent developments of this order must have been retrospectively credited to him, validated by his name. This order was the mesocosmic order of the Newar cities, which was to last in Bhaktapur for some 600 years.

FROM JAYASTHITI MALLA TO THE FALL OF THE NEWAR POLITY

Jayasthiti Malla died in 1395. There followed almost 400 years of complex and shifting relations between the three major Valley cities and their hinterland "states." "His weak and inefficient successors discovered the formulae of collegial rule and remained joint sovereigns without the division of the kingdom until 1428 A.D. But the adoption of this extraordinary mode of rule by common consent proved a dismal failure; it tended to create administrative chaos, irresponsibility and encouraged intrigue and partisanship in the councils of the government" (Hasrat 1970, xliii). The period of joint rule and, apparently, decentralization and the beginning of fragmentation, lasted some twenty years, until the rule of Yaksa Malla, the grandson of Jayasthiti Malla. Reigning from Bhaktapur he reunified the Valley and continued the special development of Bhaktapur. It was he, according to the Wright Chronicle, who began to build a moated wall around the city.[29] The inscription placed on one of its gates was said to have asserted "Yaksa Malla . . . made this fortification and ditch and a high citadel, in which to keep troops and ammunition. In building this fortification the people of the four castes willingly bore loads of bricks and earth." In part, this was for defense, but it also effected a further bounding and containment of the city at whose boundaries Ānanda Malla had long before placed protective goddesses.

At this stage Bhaktapur was the central seat of a larger Valley government; Yaksa Malla was also paramount ruler of the other major Valley cities. But when in the time of his sons the three city-states became divided, Bhaktapur, like the other Newar cities, would become in the face of growing Valley conflict even more concentrated and isolated within its boundaries.

Yaksa Malla ruled for fifty-three years. His reign, as D. R. Regmi (1965–1966, vol. 1, p. 446f.) has it, constituted a glorious chapter in the history of Nepal:

> [He was] a builder, a devotee leading a pious life, a patron of art and learning and a ruler who had given peace and stability to the hitherto strife ridden country. In his time the Rama Vardhana feudatories were liquidated, and though certain others within the confines of the Valley were yet in a position to challenge the authority of the kingdom, he was able to curb them by persuading them to accept his plan of peace. Yaksa Malla built by himself many temples and shrines. His records are the most numerous for any monarch of Nepal for the age. These extend over the entire Valley of Nepal, and commemorating as they do inauguration of the completion of many water conduits, tanks and canals they bear testimony to his efforts to make Nepal happy and prosperous. During Yaksa Malla's time Nepal witnessed [the] flourishing of art and literature. In the list of original works written in Sanskrit and Newari we find that a majority of them belong to this period.

On Yaksa Malla's death the kingdom, after a period of joint rule among his sons, eventually became divided into three small kingdoms, Bhaktapur, Kathmandu, and Patan, each comprising a royal city and its hinterland. Around them in the Valley were other vaguely bounded tiny ministates which were variously related to and incorporated into the three larger units.

Now, as Gewali sums it up, these three "kingdoms of the valley were well-developed city-civilizations. The countryside surrounding them was fertile and large and they had a lucrative trade with Tibet, inherited from the ancient Licchavi rulers of Nepal. The division of the valley into three kingdoms was, therefore, the division of wealth, or [of] the potentiality of earning wealth by trade. This led to mutual jealousies and hostilities among these kingdoms and rendered them an easy prey to the lean and hungry invaders from the western hills" (Gewali 1973, 52). This denoument, looming large in the minds of modern Nepalese historians was not to occur for some 300 years, and Bhaktapur entered on its long period of relative isolation.

The chronicles and inscriptions of those next three centuries give some dim glimpse for Bhaktapur of successions, conflicts, the introduction of new festivals, and the completion of new buildings (D. R. Regmi, 1965–1966, part II, chap. III). We hear of the introduction of a dance cycle, the Nine Durgās (which will later concern us) at the beginning of the sixteenth century, of the introduction of aspects of the festival of the solar New Year in the mid-sixteenth century, of the development of temples, including in the seventeenth century, the building of a large new royal palace and an associated temple of the royal goddess Taleju as well as of a major temple of the Tantric god Bhairava and a complementary one, Ñātāpwa(n)la, to his consort in an adjoining square. The urban religious geography of Bhaktapur continued to be developed throughout the Malla period.

The additions were variously motivated. "Bhupatindra Malla built a three-storied temple, the length of which ran north and south, and placed in it, facing west,[30] a Bhairava for the protection of the country, and the removal of sin and distress from the people" (Wright 1972, 194). Omens, dreams, desires for emulation, and desires for personal merit of the rulers, seemed to have played their part. But the additions were woven in one way or another into the ongoing present of the city.

We have one, at least, European view of Bhaktapur under the Mallas, contrasting it to the two other Valley cities in terms that would be reflected by later observers after the Gorkhāli conquest. Father Ippolitio Desideri wrote in 1722 "Badgao [Bhatgaon, Bhaktapur] stands on a hill some six or seven miles from Kathmandu. The air is much better, and with its fine houses and well laid out streets it is a much gayer and more beautiful city than the other two; it has several hundred thousand inhabitants who are engaged in trade" (as quoted in D. R. Regmi [1965–1966, part II, p. 1013]).

THE GORKHĀLI STATE, AND THE SUBMERGING OF THE NEWARS IN GREATER NEPAL

In the latter part of the eighteenth century Pṛthvīnārāyaṇa Śāha, the ruler of a tiny principality, Gorkhā, in the western part of present-day Nepal, began a series of campaigns that were to lead to the fall of the ancient Valley dynasties and a transformation of the situation of the Newars. The conquest of the Valley was a result of twenty-five years of coordinated effort. Ludwig Stiller (1973, 104f.) has delineated the "phases" of the conquest:

> Phase one, 1744–54 aimed at sealing off the northern and western passes, therby cutting off the flow of money into the Valley from Tibet. . . . Phase two, 1754–64, aimed at cutting the Valley off from the states to the south, and preventing any flow of help or supplies into the Valley. [This phase] was chiefly characterized by a stringent blockade that seriously weakened the Malla Kings and reduced the people of the Valley to a total dependence on the produce of the Valley itself. . . . Phase three, 1764–69 provided the *coup de grace* to the Malla Kings. With their isolation complete, the Malla Kings were forced to watch in morbid fascination as the Gorkhāli troops pushed their outposts right up to the walls of their capitals and finally to see them break through [to] the final victory.

The combination of careful strategy, the determination of the tough invaders, and the internal division of the comfortable, long-settled Valley kingdoms led to the fall of Kathmandu on September 25, 1768 and of Patan on October 6, 1768.

Bhaktapur held out for more than a year, and was the last of the Valley kingdoms to succumb. "On the night of 10 November 1769 the Gorkhālis burst through the eastern gate [of Bhaktapur] and poured into the city. . . . The battle for the city lasted until 12 November, with the defenders gradually withdrawing to the more protected places in the palace and the Gorkhālis edging nearer and nearer. . . . Jaya Prakash [the king of Kathmandu, who had taken refuge in Bhaktapur] had taken virtual command of the defenses and it was only after he had been wounded by a musket ball in the leg that the defense collapsed" (Stiller [1973, 129f.], taken from the Bhasha Vamsavali, 887–892).

The old Nepal, the Nepal of the Newars was now to be radically transformed. This was not, as it had been from Licchavi times, to be a new dynasty fitting into and ruling from *inside* an established community, eventually to be integrated into it. For now the Newars—Malla kings, Brahmans and all—were considered to be just another of the many ethnic groups that were to be brought together in a greatly expanded territory and ruled over by the Gorkhālis and their allies from the western hills.

The historiography of Nepal now turns to the new, larger Nepal and to Kathmandu, its national capital. It becomes even more difficult to find in the available written sources the specific history of the now submerged Newars, deprived of their kings but to a considerable degree otherwise left to get on with their affairs in the traditional manner, with the new kings of the Śāha line established (in Gorkhāli perspective, at least) as the legitimate political and ceremonial heirs of the old dynasty. The situation in Kathmandu was special, for Pṛthvīnārāyaṇa Śāha chose it as the capital of his new kingdom, and it became his royal city. The other cities, Patan, and even more so the more distant Bhaktapur, were peripheral to the events at the center.

The general policy of the Gorkhāli rulers toward the multiple ethnic and political units that made up their new state was, as Stiller (1973, 225f.) remarks, to rely on the existing structures in the annexed kingdoms:

> It has been said by historians of Nepal, and very wisely too, that the Gorkhāli conqueror did not introduce large-scale change because to do so would unnecessarily disturb the people of the conquered territories and lead to un-

> rest and possibly to uprisings. This is basically true. But the failure of the Gorkhālis to introduce such changes goes much deeper than that. For the typical Gorkhāli administrator of the time, limited as he was by his own experiences in his own tiny state, merely to grasp what was being done in other localities was an accomplishment. . . . He did not introduce changes, largely because he did not know how things could be done better, and this was true because he did not understand, at least initially, how things were done at all. The Gorkhāli was thus forced by the very magnitude of the problem to rely at the outset on local administrative structures in the areas conquered.

Those traditional forms that assured some stability were useful to the Gorkhālis. As long as they maintained order and were able to collect revenues the internal structure of the various units, even in nearby Bhaktapur, seems to have been of little concern to them. They were, however, in closer contact with the Valley Newars than with the outlying tribal and hill people. A kind of division of function took place. The Newars were the farmers, the craftsmen, and the merchants. The Gorkhālis and their old allies were the rulers, administrators, and soldiers. In time, Newars were used as advisors and in lower-level government positions. Yet, Bhaktapur, although some few of its people had some business or position in Kathmandu, remained albeit without its king, a Newar city.

We now begin to have descriptions of Bhaktapur by foreign observers during the period of the Grokhāli kings and their Rana prime ministers (who during a period of 100 years became *de facto* rulers of Greater Nepal). Colonel Kirkpatrick, on a mission to the Kathmandu Valley in 1793, noted that Bhaktapur (which he called "Bhatgaong") was the smallest of the three Valley cities[31] but "its palace and buildings, in general, are of more striking appearance, and its streets, if not much wider, are at all events much cleaner than those of the metropolis" (Kirkpatrick [1811] 1969, 163). This was faint praise for he had remarked that the streets of the "metropolis," Kathmandu, were "excessively narrow and nearly as filthy as those of Benares" (ibid., 160).

Of the Newars, after noting that they differ from the other Hindu inhabitants of Nepal in character, customs, manners, features, religious rites, and language, he writes that they were "a peaceable, industrious and even ingenious people, very much attached to the superstition they profess, and tolerably reconciled to the chains imposed on them by their Gorkhāli conquerors, although these have not hitherto condescended to conciliate them by the means which their former sovereigns. . . adopted" (Kirkpatrick 1969, 186). He also notes the stigmatization that was beginning to be applied to the Newars by their conquerors, "their courage is at present spoken of very slightingly by the Purbutties [Parbatiyās, or "mountain people"]" and, he notes, "Instances of their being employed in the armies of the state are exceedingly rare. Their occupations are chiefly those of agriculture, besides which they almost exclusively execute all the arts and manufactures known in this country" (ibid., 186).

Ambrose Oldfield, writing of Nepal in 1880, has some notes on Bhaktapur. He echoes Kirkpatrick's favorable comparison of Bhaktapur's condition with Kathmandu and Patan, which he attributed to a relative leniency of the Gorkhālis toward Bhaktapur (Oldfield [1880] 1974, vol. I., p. 132f.):

> The great majority of its inhabitants being Hindus, the Gorkhā King—himself a bigoted Hindu—appears to have respected their temples, and to have restrained his followers from committing any flagrant or open violence against the public buildings with which the city abounded. Prithi Narayan may also have felt some sympathy for the fallen fortunes of his former ally, Ranjit Mall, whose applications for assistance against the Kings of Kathmandu and Patan had been the immediate cause of bringing Gorkhās into the territories of Nipal. From these various causes the aged King of Bhatgaon was treated by Prithi Narayan with considerable leniency; his capital was respected, and though the Gorkhās . . . appropriated the entire revenues of the state, and the greater portion of those of the church, yet they fortunately spared enough of the latter to enable the Niwars to keep the majority of their temples in a state of very good repair. It is in consequence of this unusual moderation on the part of the Gorkhās that, in comparison with Patan or Kirtipur, Bhatgaon still presents a flourishing appearance; its streets and inhabitants have a cheerful aspect, and its religious edifices generally are, even at the present day, in fairly good preservation.

Nevertheless, he notes, "the ancient walls and gateways of Bhatgaon, like those of the other capital cities, are fast crumbling into ruin" (ibid., 133).

Forty years later, in the 1920s, Perceval Landon ([1928] 1976, vol. 1, p. 219f.) wrote:

> A little apart from the main traffic ways of the Valley, and busy with its own concerns, Bhatgaon has retained an individuality and an aloofness that other towns in the Valley have to some extent lost in the ever-growing influence of Kathmandu—and naturally none has lost it more than Kathmandu herself. it is commonly said that in her daily life Bhatgaon resembles the outlying and, to Europeans, unknown parts of Nepal more than does any other town in the Valley. She rests upon the fold above her curving river cliff, adjusting herself to its couch-like shape, and cultivates her well-watered fields below,

> remote—willingly remote—from her neighbors, and one of the most picturesque towns in the East.

THE 1950 REVOLUTION AGAINST THE RANA REGIME

Soon after the death of Pṛthvīnārāyaṇa Śāha the Śāha family, although continuing to be the nominal and legitimate dynastic rulers of Nepal, lost control of the governance of the new nation. A long turbulent period followed in which various families of the western mountain conquerors strove for control. In the mid-nineteenth century a family that was to take the name of "Rana" rose to power following the violent seizure of power by one of their members, Jang Bahadur Rana. The family provided the successive "prime ministers," the *de facto* rulers of Nepal for the next century. The Rana regime continued their predecessor's policy of isolation from potentially disturbing forces elsewhere in the world and of a quasifeudal rule of a decentralized nation. As the Nepali political scientist Rishikesh Saha (1975*a*, 164–166) characterized the Rana period:

> The basic objective of the Ranas was to keep the power within the family by maintaining the *status quo* in every field. Even in the sphere of internal affairs, every effort was made to insulate Nepal from the impact of Western influence and ideas, which was being felt in Asia during the latter part of the 19th and the beginning of the 20th century. In accomplishing this policy of isolation the Ranas were aided by the geographical location and topography of Nepal. Nepali people were not merely deprived of the influence of Western ideas but were also discouraged from any contact with the neighboring people of India. . . . Change of any kind was suspected of weakening the foundations of Rana rule. Educational development was very slow, and the number of high schools and colleges could be counted on one's fingers. Public works programs during the Rana period were almost non-existent and were particularly deficient with respect to transportation and communication.

In the late 1950s a complex and complexly motivated series of events led to the loss of the Rana monopoly of power and the restoration of power to the Śāha king, Tribhuvan. This "revolution" initiated experiments in modernization of the government and of the country, a series of tentative efforts at liberalization, followed by retreats, and yet again by new efforts. Old structures of political order, needs for modernization, new ideas introduced through travel and education, the need to survive the dangers and to try to make use of the rivalries of the bordering giants, India and China, all have made this period of modernization difficult and uncertain.[32]

Although during the period following the Gorkhā conquest the politics of national Nepal were Gorkhāli, as was the language, the Gorkhālis in the Kathmandu Valley began to become influenced by Newar religion and culture, which they came to think of as being to a large degree the distinctive *Nepalese* religion and culture. Kamal Malla quotes the Nepalese historian Karidar Baburam Acharya, "Pṛthvīnārāyaṇa Śāha founded a new nation by defeating Jaya Prakash Malla and other kings. But he was unable to conquer Nepali [i.e., Newar] culture. The Gorkhālis had nothing except a common language in the name of cultural heritage. . . . So being completely overwhelmed by Nepali [Newar] culture, although Pṛthvīnārāyaṇa Śāha was able to defeat an individual called Jaya Prakash, he was defeated by Nepali culture."

Both Gorkhāli and Newar began to be affected together—and to grow more like each other—in consequence of the tentative modernization of Nepal. Yet, as a major governmental development plan for the Kathmandu Valley of the Nepal government put it, Bhaktapur "has shown very little change throughout the last several decades and thus remains the purist existing documentation of historic Newar towns in the Valley" (His Majesty's Government, Nepal 1969, 76).

Which brings us to the time of our present study.

CHAPTER FOUR

Bhaktapur's Other Order

INTRODUCTION

In the later chapters of this book our central concern will be with Bhaktapur's marked symbolism. The city has, of course, another sort of life that must be described and analyzed in its own terms and whose relations to the particular sort of symbolic order we are concerned with are various. This other order is often dealt with as more real in some sense than the "merely" symbolic order—as one or another kind of "infrastructure." It includes spatial and ecological constraints, aspects of production and distribution, demography, and the like. In still other scholarly traditions "social structure" is given the privilege of a more fundamental reality. These privileged realities are set against what we call "marked symbolism," which is often degraded to epiphenomenal or "expressive" or at best to some modestly supplementary status. We will claim more for Bhaktapur's marked symbolism, but we are not reversing the ideology to argue that the other orders are unimportant or secondary. The interrelations of the realm of marked symbolism and other kinds of order (suffused with their own embedded symbolisms) are diverse. We will touch on some of this in the course of this book. For the reasons urged in chapter 2, however, marked symbolism is our centerpiece.

Bhaktapur's other orders thus become peripheral, but hardly trivial. Their presentation, the subject of this and the following two chapters, is relatively summary, and for this chapter heavily indebted to the work of others.

Figure 1. Bhaktapur, looking north to the Himalayas.

THE PHYSICAL CITY

Bhaktapur (see fig. 1) at the time of this study had not, at first sight, changed very much in appearance from nineteenth-century descriptions and aside from a general weathering and decay, probably not much from its appearance at the end of the reign of the Malla kings. Built on the sides and summit of a broad hill rising from the valley floor, the city suddenly appears, clearly demarcated from the extensive farmlands around it. The city is roughly elliptical, about one mile in length and about one-half mile in breadth, with its long axis running from west to east with a slight southwest-northeast rotation. A main road enters the city from the west and meanders along the central axis running parallel to the Hanumante River, which borders Bhaktapur to the south. This road soon becomes the bazaar, a dense conglomeration of small shops that line the street for much of its extent. At intervals the road widens out into various public squares full of temples and shrines as is the case in many Newar settlements. Its inhabitants think of Bhaktapur as consisting of a lower city to the southwest and an upper city to the northeast. The bazaar street has two prominent large squares, Ta:mārhī Square in the lower city and Dattātreya in the upper. The main axis is intersected by a number of routes that have bridged the Hanumante and entered the city from the south. It leads finally to a road leaving Bhaktapur to the east, once an important route to Tibet.

To the north of the central axis in the western part of the city is the former Malla Royal center, the Durbar square or Lāekū. At its northern side is a prominent gateway covered with golden images of gods, the entrance to a complex of courtyards, shrines, and sanctums—the temple of Taleju, the tutelary goddess of the Malla kings. Adjoining the Taleju temple is the large palace, formerly the seat of the Malla kings of Bhaktapur, now administrative offices for a new polity. Around the Durbar square are the tall, tile roofed houses of many of the Rājopādhyāya Brahmans, once closely associated with the court, as well as houses of descendants of the old court aristocracy.

In various parts of the city there are clearly differentiated neighborhoods. There is the potters' quarter with its potting wheels, its kilns and open spaces for the firing and sun-drying of pots; the dyers' quarters with various brightly colored woolen yarns hanging to dry near the dying vats; farmers' quarters with—depending on the season—rice, wheat, corn, peppers, and other crops being threshed, winnowed, dried. There are neighborhoods of Buddhists, mostly in the northern parts of the city, surrounding their old monasteries, now centers of Tantric, non-monastic Buddhism. There are other neighborhoods not so clearly marked by external contrasts, but clustered around a central square with its temples or shrines. Toward the borders of the town are generally poorer areas with lower, simpler houses. But among them there are groups of taller, more elaborate houses, those of the butchers whose low status places them toward the periphery of the city, but whose comparatively high earnings have allowed them to build larger houses than their neighbors. To the south of the city, in an area that is said to be outside its boundaries, in squalid small houses, tightly grouped together, live the untouchables.

Along the Hanumante River at a number of places are clusters of shrines and *ghāṭs* or steps leading down to the river. Here clothes are washed, and here and there are ramps for dipping the feet of a dying man into the river at his last breath. Along the Hanumante River, mostly on the far side, are cremation grounds. There is another river, the Kasan, to the north of Bhaktapur, which joins the Hanumante to the west of the city. This northern river has little to do with the life of the town.[1]

Everywhere there is a bustle of activity, of people coming and going, of processions, of music, of business, of craftsmen working. Scattered here and there are new buildings in modern styles, offices and houses for officials, modern houses for some rich merchants, schools, a hospital, a cinema.

And everywhere are dirt and foul smells, the dust and wear of centuries, the feces of animals and children in the streets, of adults in the fields and at the riverside. There are houses cracked and fallen during the last of the series of earthquakes that regularly trouble the Kathmandu Valley. The fields and streets are full of scavenging emaciated dogs and of large carrion crows. Huge fruit bats hang in some seasons in the trees, and on clear nights jackals howl in the fields outside of the city and occasionally a predatory, hungry leopard snatches off the infant of an unwary farmer in a field bordering on the forest. All this is a reminder that Bhaktapur was and is still a clearing in a yet more ancient world.

SOME DEMOGRAPHIC NOTES

According to the 1971 census report (published by the National Planning Commission of Nepal's Central Bureau of Statistics), Nepal then had a total population of 11,555,983. Of these, 618,911 lived in the

Kathmandu Valley, which was divided into three districts—Lalitpur (Patan), Kathmandu, and Bhaktapur. These districts comprised roughly the three old Newar kingdoms, each with its central city and surrounding secondary towns, villages, and scattered hamlets. Of the three districts, the Bhaktapur district had the smallest population, 110,157, in comparison with Patan's 154,998 and Kathmandu's 353,756.

Within these districts the city of Bhaktapur had a total population of 40,112 people, in comparison with urban Patan's 59,049 and urban Kathmandu's 249,563. The census for Bhaktapur conveniently distinguishes categories of prisoners incarcerated there and of military and police stationed at Bhaktapur, people who represent for the most part an "external" population. Without these two categories (133 prisoners and 918 police and military) Bhaktapur's population consisted of some 39,061 people, living in 6,484 households.

Between 1961 and 1971 the population of Bhaktapur had reportedly grown by 17 percent, somewhat less than the 22.8 percent reported for Nepal as a whole, and the 25 percent reported for Kathmandu. (Kathmandu's population increase is augmented by internal migration within Nepal.) These increases were probably due to recent improvements in public health and nutrition and, perhaps, changes in census techniques. Overall, however, there is no indication that Bhaktapur has increased in population very much since the eighteenth century; that increase is just beginning now.[2] We have noted Kirkpatrick's report for 1793, that he was told that Bhaktapur and its dependencies (approximately equivalent to the present Bhaktapur district) had some 12,000 homes. If we guess that houses had something like the present number of inhabitants, such a figure would not indicate a great increase in the population of Bhaktapur district over the past 200 years. Similarly, Oldfield writes that in the 1850s there were supposed to be about 50,000 inhabitants in Bhaktapur city itself ([1880] 1974, vol. 1, p. 131).

The age structure of the population of Bhaktapur in 1971 was that of a young population—15.3 percent of the population of the city being under five years, and some 47.7 percent of the population under the age of twenty. The figures for sex (for the nonmilitary and prisoner populations) show a slight excess of males over females of 2.5 excess males per hundred males. This sex ratio, when compared to the much larger predominance of males over females in other Nepalese cities, is an index of Bhaktapur's lack of in-migration, which for other cities was mostly male.[3] This lack of in-migration was confirmed by a sample survey by the United Nations Fund for Population Activities done in 1976, which during a period when there was an immigration into the Kathmandu Valley of about 2,000 people a year, showed a "negative migration" for Bhaktapur where there was no appreciable in-migration and a small annual out-migration of some 100 to 150 persons a year, mostly "to seek jobs in Kathmandu" (Acharya and Ansari 1980, 106).

All available indexes suggested that at the time of this study Bhaktapur's population was, and had been for a very long time, quite stable.

POPULATION DENSITY

The most significant demographic aspect of Bhaktapur for the purposes of this study besides its stability is its population density. In a pioneering study of the physical and cultural geography of Nepal, Pradyumna Karan (1960, 51) remarked that:

> Few parts of the world are more empty than the snow-covered ranges of northern Nepal; few parts are more crowded than the Kathmandu Valley. . . . In the major areas of concentration the average population densities range from 500 to 700 per square mile, and there are rural densities in a few small areas of more than 800 per square mile. Such density of rural population is hardly approached in Western Europe or North America; it is equaled only in monsoon Asia and in a few small areas of Africa and the Caribbean. Despite the many empty areas, virtually all of Nepal's space is fully used in terms of the number of people it can support with its present technology. . . . The population of Kathmandu's urban area attains a density of 47,783 per square mile, almost twice that of New York City.

Bhaktapur's density is still higher. A survey cited in Acharya and Ansari (1980, 105f.) estimates that when the open spaces are removed the concentration of people in the built-up residential areas of Bhaktapur is 110,334 people per square mile. Most of those open spaces are at the outskirts of the city, and our own estimates of the settled area give a density of some 117,000 people per square mile for the remainder of the city, including its inner open spaces. Such population density is even more striking in that the city has a considerable number of such open spaces and public squares and that, in contrast to modern inner cities, most of its houses consist of five stories or less.

Such figures are astonishing not only in themselves but also because for those familiar with "downtown" areas of New York, London, or Calcutta, Bhaktapur in no way seems *crowded*. Throughout the entire city space there is an orderly and widely distributed placement of people and of their movements. It is only during certain of the city's annual festivals when much of the population gathers together at one or another focal point or area that the great mass of population becomes apparent in an unusual concentration that in itself generates some of the meaning of the festival.

BHAKTAPUR'S DEMOGRAPHY: NEWARS AND HINDU NEWARS

We shall present in later chapters other demographic characteristics of the population of Bhaktapur—its ethnic, religious, and social composition and aspects of household size and composition. It is essential to emphasize, however, that less than sixty households among Bhaktapur's more than 6,000 households are, by criteria that we will discuss in the next chapter, *not* Newars. That is, the city is almost entirely a Newar city. It is, in addition, almost entirely a *Hindu* Newar city. In the 1971 census 92 percent of the Newar population called themselves "Hindus"; the rest, the remaining 8 percent, identified themselves as "Buddhists." It is this great preponderance of Hindu Newars who are at the center of our treatment of Bhaktapur's symbolic organization. Some individuals in the other groups are, in fact, involved in that organization—in sometimes illuminating ways—but their involvement is peripheral, and they themselves are most centrally related to other centers of community and of identity.

THE HINTERLAND

Bhaktapur district, the area containing the city of Bhaktapur and its surrounding towns, villages, and open lands, with its 110,157 people in 1971, is the most densely populated of the three valley districts. There are some seven settlements (other than Bhaktapur) in the district with more than a thousand population. Six of these ranged between 1,200 and 3,000 people in 1968. One of them, Thimi, had more than ten thousand people (His Majesty's Government, Nepal 1969, 81). The other district settlements are hamlets and small villages. Some of the Newar towns in the various Valley districts have been studied (Barré, Berger, Feveile, and Toffin 1981; Toffin 1977; Müller 1981). What remains still to be done is a study of their past and present relations with the main cities, and the systematic transformations of Newar social and cultural life illuminated by the contrast in size of the central and peripheral communities. The relation of the city of Bhaktapur to the rest of the district is for reasons given in chapter 2 only minimally considered in this present study.

RELATION TO THE CENTRAL GOVERNMENT

In the early 1970s Bhaktapur, like all settlements of more than 10,000 people in Nepal, was treated as a "*Nagar* (town) *Panchayat*." It was administered as part of a complex four-tiered system of representative councils called *panchayats*, which was an attempt to form a connection between the strong, relatively autocratic central government at Kathmandu, centered on the king and his immediate advisors and peripheral political or potentially political structures. The system starts with *village* or *town panchayats*, which, in turn, send representatives to a *district panchayat*, which is supposed to be more important for administrative purposes than the village and town *panchayats* below it or the *zonal* assembly above it made up of representatives of the various districts amalgamated into larger zones. In the early 1970s Nepal had 3,860 village *panchayats*, 16 town *panchayats*, 75 district *panchayats*, and 14 zonal assemblies. The zonal assemblies, in turn, elected some of the members of a national unicameral legislature, the *Rāṣtriya* (National) *Panchayat*. Of the *Rāṣtriya Panchayat*'s 125 members, 90 were elected by the zonal assemblies, 15 by seven "Class Organizations" (e.g., Farmers, Youth, Labor, Ex-Servicemen, and Women), and four from the "Graduate Constituency" made up of college graduates. The king nominates an additional 16 members. (For the *panchayat* system and its development, see Prachanda Pradhan [1973], Sinha [1972], K. P. Pradhan [1968], Rose and Fisher [1970], and Joshi and Rose [1966].)

Following the restoration of the Shah dynasty in 1950 there were a series of tentative oscillating experiments in the extension and retraction of decentralization and of participatory democracy. In the early 1970s the central government was strong. As Rishikesh Shaha (1975*b*, 73) wrote:

> The new Panchayat system does not reflect any real decentralization or deconcentration of political and administrative power. . . . The Village Panchayats, the Town Panchayats and the District Panchayats have been given limited taxation and administrative powers. Their administrative functions include assisting development programs, supervising and managing the village, the district or the municipality owned or controlled property, and maintaining certain records and statistics. The Village Panchayats are

> granted judicial jurisdiction in minor civil and criminal cases. The claim that the new Panchayat system represents decentralization of political power and functions is completely invalid in as much as the central government's ultimate authority is maintained intact by granting the Panchayat Ministry discretionary power to suspend or dissolve a Panchayat and replace it with a provisional Panchayat authorized to exercise the same powers.

Even within the terms of this sytem the town *panchayat* is comparatively insignificant. The village panchayat includes a Village Assembly, "a legislative body charged with the power to ventilate grievance; to question the . . . members of the executive body; . . . to move a resolution of . . . no confidence [against] the executive. . . ; to make decisions regarding taxes" (K. P. Pradhan 1968, 107). However (Pradhan 1973, 151):

> In the case of Town Panchayats no direct relation between the elected members and the town people are established. In the case of Village Panchayats, there is a Village Assembly which at least twice a year makes the Panchayat members answerable and responsible for the projects initiated by the assembly. In many ways, Town Panchayats are weak bodies. In the deliberations of the District Assembly, Town Panchayats are particularly weak and become a target of attack for the village people who have an overwhelming majority of representation in the District Assembly.

The town *panchayat* helps to identify problems of certain kinds and helps implement centrally originated decisions. Greatly limited by the funds made available to it, and by the requirements and decisions of the district and central administrations, the town *panchayat* is responsible for maintaining and developing local facilities and services.[4]

The city of Bhaktapur was divided into seventeen "wards," as they are called in official English translations, for the purposes of *panchayat* organization.[5] The wards elect the town council, the Nagar Panchayat, which, in turn, selects two of its members as executive administrators. In the early 1970s the activities initiated by Bhaktapur's Nagar Panchayat were limited, concerned mostly with repair and maintenance. The Town (Nagar) Panchayat was intended as a device for encouraging participation in centrally directed modernization, and was, as Joshi and Rose have put it for the *panchayat* system in general, "an attempt to rationalize administrative process by creating viable institutions in areas where a serious lacuna had previously existed, thus providing the basis both for a modernized administrative system and for agencies through which economic development programs could be implemented" (1966, 400).

Decisions were usually made for town projects by the Home and Panchayat Ministries of the central government, often in consultation with Bhaktapur leaders. After the decisions were made it was the responsibility of the Town Panchayat to help carry them out. The formal local political leadership of Bhaktapur could not be said to involve much power. It was minimally significant for the organization and movement of the daily life in Bhaktapur. This may well change in the future as the traditional sources of order in Bhaktapur break down and as the city becomes more "modern." For the time being, however, at the city level Bhaktapur has little effective local political control. There is plenty of politics within some of the component units of the traditional city organization, but that is another matter.

THE AGRICULTURAL ECONOMY

The economy of Bhaktapur, like that of Nepal as a whole, is fundamentally agricultural.[6] The city is ringed with farmlands. Bhaktapur's farmers, typically of Newar farmers (and in contrast to Indo-Nepalese farmers who live in isolated farmhouses on their farmlands) live within the city—where they are integral members of its urban life—and walk to their farms to work them as necessary. Some 66 percent of the "economically active" population of urban Bhaktapur worked in farming according to the 1971 census. For the rural communities, the smaller towns and villages of Bhaktapur district, the figure was 76 percent. This relatively small difference illustrates the fact that Bhaktapur and its hinterland do not represent the familiar urban–peasant polarization, which is, and has long been, prevalent elsewhere. Bhaktapur is an agricultural city surrounded by smaller agricultural towns and villages. Most of its crops are grown for local consumption, mostly for the consumption of the farming families themselves.

The main crops grown in Bhaktapur (listed in order of the amount of land devoted to their cultivation) are rice, wheat, and maize (used for animal feed), followed by crops grown in much smaller quantities—millet, potatoes, oil seed, barley, sugarcane, and a large variety of vegetable crops, such as pulses, peppers, onions, soya beans, tomatoes, and ginger.[7] The fields are irrigated, and those on the hillsides are terraced. Land use is very intense.[8] Crops are rotated between a rice crop, and, depending on the nature of the field, a wheat or vegetable crop. The fields are cultivated by means of small hand tools.[9]

Farms are worked by most able bodied members of a farming family, male and female.[10] In a study of the total income (that is, both cash and kind) of a sample of farming families in Bhaktapur, Wachi (1980) reports that for 70 percent of her sample farming accounted for more than 70 percent of their household cash income, while for 11.5 percent of the households it accounted for 50 to 70 percent of their income, and for 11.5 percent it accounted for 30 to 50 percent of their income. All of the households in her survey supplemented their crop income in various ways—by some limited sale of animal products (meat, eggs, milk), by income from various trades and crafts (such as weaving, cap-making, yogurt-making), by wage labor (construction, working for other farmers, as assistants in city offices or as laborers on city projects), and from the rental of land or, rarely, through local commerce in something other than farm products. Time devoted to other sources of income is flexible, allowing people to work on the farms at the times when most labor is needed.

Farming households were able to barter grain for some supplies and services, but they needed cash to pay land taxes, to buy goods at bazaar shops, for trips to Kathmandu, and so on.[11] That cash came from the nonfarming activities noted, and from the sale of some farm products, particularly grain, some of which is sold to intermediate merchants for the Kathmandu market.

Wachi (1980; also personal communication) reports that about 60 percent of the farming households owned some of the lands that they farmed. Only 2.3 percent of the households owned all the land that they cultivated, but another 58 percent owned some of the land they worked and supplemented it with additional rented lands. The remainder were non-land-owning tenant farmers,[12] and a very few itinerant farm laborers, working only for others. According to Wachi's study, the land rents amounted to about 25 to 28 percent of the value of their produce. The high ownership of land and the relatively low rents for tenancy are the results of a series of land reforms, or Land Acts dating from 1957, which attempted to limit and distribute the amount of agricultural land in individual possession, and to limit the rent that could be charged to tenants.[13] Furthermore, attempts were made to protect tenants against manipulation and eviction by landowners.

M. C. Regmi (1976, 208) summed up the effect of the series of Land Acts for Nepal:

> With the imposition of ceilings on landholding, the existing concentration of landownership has been broken, both through the redistribution of lands in

excess of the ceilings and through voluntary transfers in anticipation of land reform. Big landowners no longer constitute a dominant economic class in the agricultural community. . . . The land-reform program has also conferred greater security of tenure on tenants and made it possible for them to appropriate the major portion of the produce. . . . Their rights are clearly defined by law and are actually being enforced by courts in their favour. Nevertheless, the land reform program has had little impact on the [traditional] agrarian structure.

The land reforms with their resulting marked improvement in the economic and social position of the farmers in Bhaktapur has had an unintended effect. To the degree that the traditional landowning classes, the Brahmans and merchants, lost their lands and land revenues and the farmers gained them, the newly wealthy farmers have come to be the supporters and clients of much of the traditional religious system as well as important employers of Brahmans. Less educated and less open to modernization than the higher classes, this transition has helped to slow down change and to support and conserve the old system.

As we have noted, the agricultural fields are in active use during most of the year. However, one (and *only* one) part of the year's agricultural activity is fundamental for Bhaktapur's symbolic life. This is the rice growing cycle (see fig. 2), which is what we will mean in our references to the "agricultural cycle" in this volume. It is the reference and source of much of the meaning of the segment of the annual festival cycle that we treat as the "Devī cycle," and for much of the meaning of the "dangerous goddesses." Ulrike Müller (1981, 57f.) summarized the sequence briefly for the town of Thimi in Bhaktapur's hinterland in a description that will serve exactly for Bhaktapur itself:

According to the variety of rice and the locality, the farmers begin with the digging of the fields at the start of the rainy season (June). This work is done by the men with a short-handled hoe (*kodali* [Nepali], or *ku* [Newari]). . . . Whilst the fields are still being dug and whilst the women are breaking up the clods with a long-handled, wooden hammer and carefully leveling the ground, rice is already being raised in seedbeds. Two or three weeks after being sown, the rice plants are [re]planted [from the seed bed] out in the main field. . . . By the fifteenth day of the Month Sravan (the end of July) all the rice plants would be replanted. [The rains are now expected and the fields will be watered directly by the rains and by means of controlled irrigation from water catchments on the hillsides.] After the water has been drained from the fields at the end of September (or even earlier in the case of some varieties), the main harvest takes place in October and November. The rice is cut with a sickle and threshed directly in the fields. . . . The grains of

Figure 2. Jyāpu women planting rice paddy plants.

> rice are brought home, whilst the straw remains in the fields to dry. . . . After the winnowing [which takes place in the farmers' quarters within the city] the grains of rice are dried for a few days in the sun if the weather is good. During this time, streets and squares, yards and roof-terraces are full of rice, which is spread out on straw mats and turned over several times. . . . After drying, part of the rice is taken to one of the [town's water-driven] rice mills and there the husk is removed. The largest part of the harvest however, is stored with the husk still on [in special granaries in the farmer's houses].

THE NONAGRICULTURAL ECONOMY

An inventory of the small stalls and shops that crowd the bazaar street gives some idea of the variety of the supplies and of the specialists who provide them, which are necessary for the material and symbolic life of Bhaktapur. There are (in no particular order) specialized shops or market areas selling: cloth for saris and clothes; ready-made clothes; Ayurvedic medicines; modern medicines; cigarettes, tobacco, and smoking supplies; rice and other grains; mustard oil, kerosene, and other fuel oils; metal cooking pots; curds; water buffalo meat; curios for the tourist trade; books; gold and silver ornaments and small religious figures in gold and silver; wood for construction; tools and nails; house paint; hair decorations and arm bangles; caps; sweetcakes; red peppers; electric goods; fruit; betel nuts; sewing thread; fertilizer; vegetables; salt; metal sheetings for roofing; woolen blankets; religious drawings and pigments for use in rituals; brass and copper pots of various kinds; brass religious images; animal feed; goats; chickens; locally made furniture; clay pots. And there are also stalls for serving tea and soft drinks, stalls for serving alcoholic beverages, stalls for serving cooked food. The shops and stalls are owned and run by members of a socioeconomic class, the *sāhu* or shopkeepers.[14] Most of these are from the high-ranking Chathar and Pa(n)cthar groups of *thar*s (see chap. 5)—collectively referred to as "Shresṭhas" or "Śresṭhas" in some writings on the Newars—but some come from lower ranks of the traditional status system.

Besides the craftsmen, bakers, butchers, collectors and grinders of herbal medicines, spinners and weavers, blacksmiths, metal image casters, and the like who provide the goods for the shops, there are the city craftsmen—masons, carpenters, wood carvers, stone carvers, and so forth who are involved in construction and repair in the city. Finally, there are all kinds of specialized performers and providers of services—musicians of various types, ritual "dancers," barbers, medical specialists of various types, various kinds of priests and ritual specialists, midwives, cutters of umbilical cords, astrologers, tailors, fishermen, sweepers, and many more.

In contrast to the limited sample of specialists found in South Asian villages, Bhaktapur has a full panoply. They are, for the most part—as we shall see in following chapters—organized in the city's hierarchical system, and made use of for the symbolic life of the city.[15]

The 1971 census reported for Bhaktapur that 65.8 percent of the workforce was engaged in agriculture, 8.5 percent in commerce (shops and trade), and 8.2 percent in manufacturing, primarily crafts. The census also listed a small number of people engaged in electrical, gas, and water services (0.1 percent, some 20 people), in construction (0.8 percent, some 115 people, mostly house builders and masons), in transport and communication (1.1 percent, 153 people, including the mail service, an elementary telephone service, and truck drivers), and in finance and business (0.4 percent, some 53 people working mostly at a local branch of the Nepalese bank). The census also enumerated some 2,197 people, 15.1 percent of the economically active population, engaged in "personal and community services."[16] Many of these are the barbers, washermen, healers of various sorts, and so forth, who provide traditional services, often for patron families. Some of these providers of personal and community services work for the City Panchayat as sweepers and in repair and maintenance. Some work in the Bhaktapur administrative offices, some are teachers in Bhaktapur schools, and some, finally, of this group commute on buses, the electrified trolley (which was inaugurated in the early 1970s to connect Bhaktapur and Kathmandu), or occasionally by automobile or motorcycle to Kathmandu to work in one of the many offices of the Central Government's bureaucracy.

In short, the economy of Bhaktapur was at the time of this study concerned mostly with the production and distribution of goods and services for itself, most goods were produced and distributed within the city or its near environs,[17] few people were involved in administrative or bureaucratic jobs within the city itself, and much of the household income was "in kind" rather than in cash.[18]

Bhaktapur also had in comparison with many other modernized cities and towns in Nepal less differentiation of income. Compared to Kathmandu and Patan there is a "low level of income even for the rich people in Bhaktapur" (Acharya and Ansari 1980, 113). This is in part because of the importance of agricultural wealth in Bhaktapur, and the extensive ownership of land by the farmers themselves.

A SUMMARY NOTE

We have described a city that at the time of our study still retained many of the features which had long charcterized it. It had an enormously dense but stable population. It was a city that, in comparison with communities elsewhere in the world—and in much of Nepal—was relatively little related to larger economic and political networks. Its economy, which had a large nonmonetary component, was still heavily based on internal (including its bordering farms) production and exchange. For the city as a whole it was more of an administered than a political unit, the sources of power and decision were elsewhere, in the non-Newar national government at Kathmandu. That external administration was minimally disruptive, and it was certainly not innovative. It provided what support it could to the ongoing life of the city. Bhaktapur was then in both fact and ideology "self-sufficient" and turned in on itself. But this was nothing new. In its Malla days its political adventures were the affairs of kings and their armies and were to a very large degree—once a dynasty had established itself—external to the life of the city. The city was used to being a world in itself. Royal power, and in recent centuries Gorkhāli power, had taken advantage of this as a basis for stability. The proper policy, the successful policy, was to support and encourage the city's, in our case Bhaktapur's, isolated, and self-sufficient order. Bhaktapur's dense and isolated population was almost entirely Newar and almost entirely Hindu Newar. These Newars share a tradition, an identity and a culture—in both the popular and anthropological senses of the word. Bhaktapur is in contrast to Kathmandu, to European medieval and modern cities, a unicultural city.

In the presence of such conditions, what kind of internal order did the city construct? We may, or more accurately must, begin with its system of defining, organizing, and assigning social and economic and "ritual" roles. It is a system tailor-made, as it were, for the conditions of Bhaktapur's life.

CHAPTER FIVE

The Distribution of Roles: The Macrostatus System

When every one is somebodee,
Then no one's anybody!

W. S. Gilbert, *The Gondoliers*

INTRODUCTION: *THAR* AND MACROSTATUS LEVELS

Bhaktapur, like Fustel de Coulange's Ancient City, has a social organization largely constructed out of bounded, relatively autonomous units, or "cells" that are combined in successively more inclusive ones. Households with their own deities and religious practices are joined in patrilineal extended families with *their* own deities and practices. Patrilineal groups are in turn joined in wider inclusive units called *thar*s whose members have a common surname. The *thar*s are in turn organized into what we will call "macrostatus levels."

There is an essential difference between *thar* and macrostatus levels and the smaller units. The latter, household and extended families —as well as some smaller units within the family and some groupings of extended families—are all more or less alike throughout the city and provide vital nested "structural units" for the city. There is an essential difference between a certain man's role as, say, father, husband, leader of an extended patrilineal family group, that is his role *within* one of the constituent cells of the city, and his urban role as a Brahman, farmer, or untouchable, a role that is of *direct* importance to the city as a whole. Such urban roles are ascribed through membership in—that is, through being born into—a *thar*.

In contrast to smaller constituent units *thar*s and macrostatus levels are differentiated so that their outputs are elements in the pattern of the city. For the city organization it is the public functions of *thar*s—their outputs into the public city life and their external relations with and hierarchical position in relation to other *thar*s and groups of *thar*s—that is important, not their internal organization. From the point of view of the city as a whole, what goes on within the *thar*s is of no importance as long as their essential outputs of goods, services, and differentiated kinds of social persons are maintained. Internal practices and organization vary considerably from *thar* to *thar*, but as long as they produce their necessary public effects, internal matters are not only immaterial to outsiders, but unknown and in fact hidden from them. In the same way the still smaller nested units that compose the *thar*s must have *their* proper outputs into larger units, but their inner affairs are no business of others. In fact, hidden and secret knowledge, procedures, spells, and protective deities are often thought to be essential to the unit's effective output into larger units, and eventually into the life of the city.

Thus for the kind of city organization we are concerned with—the city at its own level as an organized and organizing mesocosm—the outputs and groupings and hierarchical organization of *thar*s are the relevant elements. The *internal* organization of the *thar*s, and particularly of their component kin-based units are the city forms that most closely affect the "private" experience and early education of the city's people. "Private" in Bhaktapur begins with the internal affairs of a *thar*, and takes a deeper meaning as action jumps from each unit to the next smaller—that is extended family, household, one or another internal household grouping, and finally to an individual's "self" and "inner thoughts." We will in the next chapter discuss some of the "sub-*thar*" organization. This will be necessary for discussions elsewhere of "private lives," but for the purposes of this book it will be an excursus.

We will be writing about a variant of a kind of South Asian social organization that is usually, of course, called a "caste system," a system that is said to have elements called "castes" and "subcastes" and various clusters of such units. It has seemed proper (for reasons that will follow) for our discussion of Bhaktapur's social categories to avoid such terminology and some of the assumptions that it entails and to use either local terminology, or neologistic terms. Thus we will call that aspect of the city's hierarchical organization that provides a pattern to the city as a whole the *macrostatus system*, and distinguish it from the systems of status and social organization within the smaller cellular units, the city's collection of *microstatus* systems. We have called the gross hierarchical arrangements of *thar*s that make a difference to the city as a whole *macrostatus levels*. In contrast to these there are, for example, hierarchical arrangements of the *thar*s within a *macrostatus level*, which are of no concern to people outside of that level, as there are also status rankings within the groups that constitute *thar*s.

To return to our conceit of the city as a ballet, it is *thar* membership that assigns the roles of the dancers. There are other miniballets within the *thar*s and within their component units, but they are not our present concern, although we will say something about them in chapter 6.

THE *THAR*

Newars in Bhaktapur have, in addition to their given names (usually two), a surname that is their *thar* name.[1] That name allows Bhaktapurians to place each individual exactly in the macrostatus system. In order to try to obscure their "caste" membership some Newars in the relatively anonymous, socially heterogeneous, and mobile society of Kathmandu and other Nepalese cities often change their surnames to such ambiguous and mildly honorable sounding names as Śresṭha,[2] Singh, and the like in order to try to obscure low traditional status. But the use of such names in Bhaktapur would be obvious and futile attempts to escape traditional categorizations.

The Bhaktapur Town Panchayat's registry of the city's population has about 350 *thar*-designating last names for the city's Newar population. This list is not exactly equivalent to the actual number of *thar*s because in some cases *thar* members have the option of using one of a limited number of equivalent alternate *thar* names. Furthermore, in a very few cases the same name appears at two status levels and represents two different *thar*s. This is either because some function designated by the *thar* name (e.g., Tantric priest or physician) is performed by practitioners at different status levels, or because a family segment that was outcast for some transgression (usually an improper marriage) might have kept its original *thar* name when it was reduced to a lower status level. Thus the list of *thar* names actually represents about 340 different *thar* groups (see app. 2).

"*Thar*" is a term widely used in Nepal, deriving from a Prakrit term for "collection," and is usually translated in Nepali-English dictionaries as "clan" or "tribe." The significance of "*thar*" among the Newars differs from that of other groups of Indian origin in Nepal, the "Indo-Nepalese," as we will refer to them in contrast to the Newars throughout this book. Thus Khem Bahadur Bista writes of the Indo-Nepalese Chetri that the *thar* name is no more than a family name, "equivalent to an Anglo-Saxon family name such as Brown" (1972, 31). Lynn Bennett (1977, 41), also writing of the Chetri, supports this usage:

> Although villagers sometimes refer to *thar* as if it were a clan or even lineage unit, strictly speaking, *thar* is really nothing more than a last name shared by many different descent groups. Individuals with the same *thar* may or may not be patrilineally related. Yet, because of the vague sense of the *thar* as an extended patrilineage, there is a preference to marry outside one's *thar*.

She also notes and accepts an observation of Fürer-Haimendorf's (1966, 30) that Chetri *thar*s are not ranked, that "no *thar* is inherently superior or inferior to any other Chetri clan."[3] The Newar usage of "*thar*" is different from this.

It is possible to find some groupings of *thar*s in Bhaktapur that in their internal organization resemble the Chetri *thar*s. In comparsion with Newar *thar*s, however, Chetri *thar*s are a special case, representing one kind of internal organization found among some Newar *thar*s, and lacking the external hierarchical ordering that defines much of the meaning of *thar*s (or, sometimes, of sets of equivalently ranked *thar*s) in Bhaktapur. Newar *thar*s in Bhaktapur are heterogeneous units and have (or are thought by members to have) quite different kinds of corporate origins—common descent, or some shared trade in the past, or some common historical origin prior to settlement in Nepal or Bhaktapur, or some mixture of these.[4] Some are endogamous, some few are exogamous, while in others it is optional whether one marries within or outside the *thar*. In all cases marriages out of a *thar* must be made with only a limited number of other *thar*s at the same macrostatus level.

The *thar*s are arranged in twenty distinct levels in Bhaktapur's urban macrostatus system. Those *levels*, while absolutely distinct in the minds of virtually all Bhaktapurians (although they may occasionally disagree on the membership of one or another *thar* in a particular level), do not have any local name (which is why we use a neologism "macrostatus level"). In some cases, however, a particular level or groups of contiguous levels may have a name (e.g., Brahman, Chathar, or Jyāpu), and if not, there are various local ways of indicating which level is being referred to if that is necessary.

When people in Bhaktapur talk about someone's significant position and function in the macrostatus system, they will sometimes use a *thar* name, sometimes a status-level term, and sometimes a "class designation" (see below). This depends in part on the context of the discussion, and is a matter of which social function or aspect is being emphasized and discriminated. In these discussions what the individual in question is said to "belong to" is not a *thar* or a status level but to a *jāt* (a Nepalese variant of the South Asian term *jāti*), which simply means a kind or category. Italian, bird, and crow are all a creature's *jāt* in one or another context and abstraction.

Our question in this chapter is what kinds of *jāt*s, that is, what kinds of kinds are Bhaktapur's *thar*s? What are they made to do? The same question must be asked about the macrostatus levels. There are some twenty of these levels, ranked from Brahman to untouchable, and the 340 or so *thar*s are sorted among them. Sometimes a macrostatus level contains only one *thar* (Brahmans, butchers, etc.), sometimes a group of *thar*s. These levels determine or are expressed by patterns of marriage, eating, and association and, for many groups, places of residence. In the traditional system they were—and for some groups still are—determinant of differential access to wealth and, in some cases, details of clothing, decoration, and house types. They are ranked from up (*cwe*) to down (*kwe*), and are associated, in classic South Asian ways, with theories and symbols of purity and pollution, which we will examine in chapter 11.

AN EXCURSION. CASTE, CLASS, AND VARṆA

If we take any summary definition of a "caste system," such as Bouglé's (as given in Dumont [1980, 21]), that a caste system is one that, "divides [a] whole society into a large number of hereditary groups, distinguished from one another and connected together by three characteristics: *separation* in matters of marriage and contact . . . ; *division* of labor, each group having, in theory or by tradition, a profession from which their members can depart only within certain limits; and finally *hierarchy*, which ranks the groups as relatively superior or inferior to one another,"—does Bhaktapur have a caste system? It has a hierarchical system of separated units (separated by marriage and aspects of contact), and the system ensures and controls most of the city's division of labor. It thus has a caste system by these criteria.[5] The problem with such a definition is that real local groupings, that is, *thar*s and status levels, are not necessarily characterized by all three of Bouglé's conditions and the idea of "*a* caste" as a particular group in which all of Bouglé's criteria coexist is not generally useful, although it works for *some* groups, such as Brahmans and untouchables.

Some *thar*s resemble the units that are called *jāti* in some other South Asian settings, while the macrostatus levels resemble more closely what David Mandlebaum has called "*jāti* clusters."[6] *Thar*s are not always *jātis* in Mandlebaum's sense, however. In some clusters of *thar*s constituting a status level, the *thar*s may consider themselves equal and intermarry, and the cluster of *thar*s becomes in itself something like a *jāti*, although the cluster itself is not, usually, named. In other clusters there is a disputed or agreed-upon internal hierarchy within the same macrostatus level, and *thar* members do not marry other *thar*s within the level but only within the *thar*. It is in this situation where the *thar*s are like *jāti*, and the *thar* cluster like a "*jāti* cluster."

By avoiding terms such as "caste," "subcaste," and "*jāti*" and rather discussing the variety of relations of *thar*s with occupation, marriage arrangements and macrosocial rankings, however, one can present Bhaktapur's status system without forcing it into a procrustean bed of generalizing analytic terms.

There is another kind of status designation superimposed on the system of macrostatus levels. Although many professions are *thar*-specific, there are some professions as there are elsewhere in South Asia that involve people from many *thar*s and more than one status level. The main ones in traditional Bhaktapur are farmers (*jyāpu*) and shopkeepers (*sāhu*).[7] There are other groupings that have some unity of definition, characteristics, or interests. There are craftsmen, priests, "unclean" *thar*s, and in earlier times (but still vividly represented in various symbolic enactments) the city's own royalty, court, and military.[8] Such groups are associated directly with differentiations in power, kinds of production, and differential control of resources and represent something like a "class" stratification superimposed on "caste." In recent years shifts in the economic and political system have caused the beginning of a dissociation of the relative unifications of the traditional system in which prestige, wealth, power, and purity were all controlled and ranked to reflect a common order. There has been a disruption of this unity for Bhaktapur, and a further disequilibrium produced by people's awareness of their relative poverty and low living standards in comparison to Newars and non-Newars elsewhere in Nepal—particularly Kathmandu and the towns in the relatively wealthy agricultural and industrial area along the southern border of Nepal, the Terai. Some people in Bhaktapur speak of "class," *barga* (from Nepali). Thus Brahmans and members of other upper status levels talk of themselves as "middle class," *madhyambarga,* when thinking of larger, modern Nepal and its modern upper class, the *pujipatti*, people of a wealth and power that has nothing to do with their traditional *thar* heritage.

The classical concept of *varṇa*, the ideal ancient Vedic four-level hierarchy of Brahman, Kṣatriya, Vaiśya, and Śūdra, has as elsewhere in South Asia, a vague residual existence in Bhaktapur. People occasionally speculate on the relation of the macrostatus groups to these ancient classifications and occasionally make use of them to add further metaphorical point to some status distinction,[9] but the use of *varṇa* is mostly an intellectual game, with no implications for Bhaktapur's society.

WHO IN BHAKTAPUR IS A NEWAR?

We will be concerned in this volume with the social and symbolic organization of the 99 percent of the city's population who are called by others and by themselves Newars, and, for the most part, with the 92 percent of the city's population who call themselves not only Newars but also Hindus.

The term "Newar" is used by those people whom other groups in Nepal refer to as Newars in a complex way. It is used in a general way by the "Newars" themselves to differentiate themselves from various kinds of outsiders, usually lumped as "*Khāe*(n)," the western Indo-Nepalese "invaders" on the one hand and the "*Sāe*(n)," or Mongoloid hill peoples of northern origin, the Sherpas, Tibetans, Tamang, and so on, on the other. In Bhaktapur in reference to people living in the city, the maximal use of "Newar" distinguishes those groups who "follow Newar customs," from others living in the city, whom we will introduce later in this chapter as "non-Newars." Some of those non-Newar groups have lived in Bhaktapur since the time of the Newar Kings (for example, the Jhā and Bhaṭṭa Brahmans, and the Liṅgāyat temple priests). These groups (and other "outsider" groups) are not Newars because although they have various functions in the city, they are not members of the central hierarchical and symbolically integrated system. They have not, in contrast to so many other groups over the centuries, become incorporated into the "Newar" sociocultural synthesis. Such people are simply omitted from the listings "Newars" make for themselves and for inquiring outsiders of the members of Bhaktapur's "caste system." No one including members of those outsider groups seems to have any hesitation in saying that they are not Newars, in much the same way as tourists and visiting anthropologists are not Newars.

The usage of "Newar" is further differentiated internally within the "Newar community" in certain contexts. Middle-status and upper-status people will often use the term "Newar" to refer to the upper-status "kṣatriya" and merchant *thar*s, those that were traditionally attached to the courts, in distinction to the Brahmans above them and the Jyāpu farmers and others below them. The "Newar Brahmans," the Rājopādhyāya Brahmans (below), although, in most contexts they consider themselves Newars, conform to this usage in certain contexts, and refer to those upper-status groups who were their traditional patrons in the Malla days as "Newars" in distinction to themselves on the one hand and to the remaining mass of people—that is, the farmers and all middle and lower groups—on the other. The very lowest *thar*s, for example, the Po(n) and Jugī, will also in some contexts refer to *all* the Bhaktapur's "core" *thar*s—including Rājopādhyāya Brahmans—above them as "Newars," and say that they themselves are not Newars. This may be considered perhaps as a rejection of the system in which they are disadvantaged and stigmatized, but it also reflects a hesitation by others above them as to whether they are in or out of the Newar society. They are, in fact, uniquely both. The same low-status people will refer to themselves as "Newars" in other contexts, where they are emphasizing their membership in the town system. For those groups that have been integrated into the core systems as "Newars" in the largest sense there seems to have been an historical process, where a group coming from elsewhere slowly finds a position in the system, perhaps functionally replacing or displacing another group, and slowly becomes defined as Newar, with some hesitation for decades or centuries among those people with long historical memories. These usages and equivocations should not obscure the point that there is a major difference between those who are essential role players and carriers of symbolic meaning within Bhaktapur's mesocosmic system—whatever play on the term "Newar" may be involved—and those, whatever their economic and occasional ritual contributions to the city may be, who are "non-Newars" because they are ignored by that system, not defined in or given precise symbolic value by it except in perfunctory ways as one or another kind of foreigner.

The vast majority of the Newars of Bhaktapur think of themselves—and define themselves to the census takers—as Hindu, or more precisely as Śiva *mārgī* (followers of the path of Śiva) Newars, in contrast to Buddha *mārgī* Newars. We will return later in this chapter to the fairly complex question of what it means for a Newar to be a "Buddhist" rather than a "Hindu," and the various ways that such Buddhists are related to Bhaktapur's core macrostatus system.

THE MACROSTATUS LEVELS: NEWAR HINDUS, THE CORE SYSTEM

In this and the following sections we will introduce all the *thar*s in the core system that have in themselves a differentiated macrosocial significance and the macrosocial levels into which these *thar*s are sorted. (In appendix 2 we list *all* of Bhaktapur's *thar*s, placed in their respective status levels.) We will also introduce in the following sections the Newar Buddhist groups and those non-Newar groups that are stable components of the city's population and who live within the city. We will return in much more detail to many of these *thar*s and other social units in later chapters. They are brought together here for a necessary overview of the city's social structure before we lose ourselves in the details and special issues of later discussions.

As we have noted, the list of *thar* names comes from Bhaktapur civic population records and is presumably complete. Their ranking in status levels is something else. Ranking is in the conception of individual rankers, among whom Brahmans—who represent and legislate the order that the "caste system" represents—have a privileged position. As seems to be true everywhere in complex South Asian social hierarchies, the Brahmans (and other upper-status people) are certain about the upper and lower ordering, but not sure of the details of the position of every one of the great number of middle—that is, for the most part farming—*thar*s, which are arranged in several middle-level strata. There are two bases for disagreements. One is the relative ranking of status levels—for example, are butchers higher or lower than some neighboring level? The other is the membership of a particular *thar* at one or another level. Ordering of status levels may be argued about by people in adjacent levels, but in these cases we accept the certainties of upper-status people. We have rechecked membership in the middle-ranking levels with people of similar status, however, and accepted their disagreements as more "correct" than the Brahmans' disinterested guesses about such cases. There is still some uncertainty in our lists about the membership of some *thar*s in the farming ranks.

The view of the upper reaches of the system by low-status people is significant in ways that we will discuss later. Thus members of lower-level *thar*s consistently give certain of the upper-status *thar*s with priestly functions, such as astrologers and Tantric priests, *higher* status than they are given by their near peers. Members of lower-level *thar*s also tended to simplify and collapse some of the status levels.

Middle-level and upper-level *thar*s appear to agree exactly on the number and ranking of levels, however, and to a very large degree on the membership of each level. In Malla days the *thar*s were assigned to their proper levels in written documents setting out privileges, restrictions, and sanctions, as we have noted in our discussion of Jayasthiti Malla in chapter 3. The many legalistic written orderings of the status system in Bhaktapur helped stabilize and force agreement on status ordering,[10] more so than in other South Asian communities where the order is not so anchored.[11]

We will list the macrostatus levels (numbered by roman numerals) from the top down. In later sections we will discuss the "entailments and markers," that is, the significance of the levels. We will note some of the internal differentiations within the levels when they have some general significance elsewhere in the city organization.

I. Brahmans. These are all members of one endogamous *thar*,[12] the Rājopādhyāya *thar*. They are sometimes referred to as "Dya: ("God") Brahmans" or "Newar Brahmans" in those contexts where it is necessary to distinguish them from other, "non-Newar," Brahmans in Bhaktapur itself, or from the Indo-Nepalese Brahmans of elsewhere in Nepal. There is also a lower, separate, nonintermarrying section consisting of three or four families, the "Lākhe Brahmans,"[13] with their own traditional low-status clients. We will discuss the Brahmans, along with Bhaktapur's other priestly practitioners, in chapter 10.

"Brahman"—or one of the Newari variants of the word—refers in Bhaktapur's usage to *both* the status level and the *thar*, which is (ignoring the Lākhe, as is usually done) its only member. This is characteristic of all levels with only one member *thar*. A problem in naming arises for levels that contain more than one *thar*. Most of these levels are, in fact, not named, although they are clearly understood. They may be referred to, if necessary, sometimes by the name of one of their leading *thar*s, sometimes by some characteristic of the level that is relevant to the context of the discussion. The next two status levels (II and III) contain groups of *thar*s and *do* have names; these are the Chathar and Pa(n)cthar levels.

In the literature on the Newar social and economic system these two groups are collectively referred to as *śresṭha* or *sesya*:.[14] These two terms are not used in Bhaktapur, where they are thought of as Kathmandu usages. The two groups of *thar*s are sometimes referred to as "Newars" (by themselves, by Brahmans, and by *Jyāpu*s), and sometimes, particularly by the lower levels emphasizing their most visible economic function, as *sāhu* or shopkeepers. Occasionally the lower *thar*s (who tend to separate out the two *thar*s with religious vocations in these two levels and to ascribe higher status to them) refer to the remaining secular *thar*s as *girastha*. That term, used in both Nepali and Newari, is derived from the Sanskrit term "*gṛhastha*," "householder," one of the traditional stages of life of classical Hinduism, upper-status people who had not yet renounced the life of the household.[15]

These two groups of *thar*s were traditionally the patron *thar*s who employed the Rājopādhyāya Brahmans as *purohit*s or family priests. They include the descendants of the Malla kings and the families of their advisors and administrators and also of the suppliers of various commodities required by the old court. All these families were traditionally landowners (with Jyāpus as tenants before the land reforms), and many had members who worked as government functionaries, sometimes at high Royal Palace levels in Kathmandu during the Śāha and Rana periods. These families now include most of Bhaktapur's shop owners and shopkeepers and people in various trading and business enterprises and provide many of the present-day members of the government bureaucracy in Kathmandu (to which they commute each day) as well as schoolteachers and other learned professionals. The two groups also include within them two *thars* with religious functions, astrologers, Jośi (found at each of the two levels) and Tantric priests, Ācāju, at the Pa(n)cthar level.

There are important contrasts between the two groups. Upper-level informants say that the term "*Śresṭha*" used elsewhere would properly apply only to the Chathariyā.[16] The Chathariyā are thought to be "Kṣatriya" in origin; the Pa(n)cthariyā are thought to be "Vaiśya"[17] and to have close connections in religious practices and origins with the farming *thars*.

II. Chathar. The general term "*chathar*" for the group that now includes thirty-one *thars* means the "six *thars*," and is of unknown origin to present informants. The group includes, as has been noted, descendants of the Malla kings and families closely involved with the Malla court as officials and to some limited extent as royal provisioners and is said to be of Kṣatriya origin. One segment of the Jośi or astrologers, are also included.[18] There are also several *thars* who are said originally to have belonged to level III—Pa(n)cthar—but who rose into the Chathar category at various times after the fall of the Mallas.

III. Pa(n)cthar. This is a group of thirty-five *thars* that seems to have had as a core group a set of *thars* that provided services and provisions to the Malla courts. They include one important group of auxiliary priests, the Ācājus, who specialize in Tantric procedures (chaps. 10 and 11). They also include a *thar*, Jośi, whose specialty was astrology, which is also (and mostly) represented in the Chathar, and a *thar* whose name (Baidhya) indicates that its members were, traditionally, Ayurvedic physicians. Within the Pa(n)cthar level there are thirteen *thars* (called the "Cārthar," the "four *thars*") who claim to be at a higher level within the Pa(n)cthar group, and there is some restriction of marriage between these two internal levels. As we have noted, upper-status informants say that the Pa(n)cthar is of Vaiśya origin, and that their religious customs are closer to those of the Jyāpus than to those of the Chathar. This suggests a different origin for levels II and III. The Pa(n)cthar may have been derived in part from some earlier upper stratum of Newar society, while the Chathar may have shared with the Malla kings a more recent North Indian origin.

Brahmans, Chathariyā, and Pa(n)cthariyā are considered together, in some contexts, as the dominant high "castes" or levels of Bhaktapur society. The next large status-level cluster below them are the Jyāpus or farmers. Between the high-status groups and the groups of farmers is another level, the Tini. This is one of several groups of priestly specialists scattered throughout the status hierarchy (chap. 11).

IV. Tini. This level consists of one *thar*, with the *thar* name Śivācārya, whose members have special priestly functions during the ritual sequence following death for middle-level and higher-level groups. They are also auxiliary priests in an important rite of passage for girls, the mock-marriage or *Ihī* (app. 6). The Tini also serve as family priests, *purohita*, for one of the marginally clean *thar*s at level XIII, the Bhā.

Male members of groups I to IV and of one anomalous *thar* of priests, the Jyāpu Ācāju, situated in the highest segment of farmers, have the exclusive right to wear the sacred thread upon initiation into their *thar*s, and, of very much greater importance in Bhaktapur's religious life, exclusive rights to Tantric initiation. Their families have special lineage gods, Āga(n) Gods. These rights place them in a special aristocratic sector of the city's Hindu religious life (chap. 9).

The next seven sections (levels V to XI) include the four separate levels of Jyāpu or farming *thar*s (levels V, VIII, IX, and XI).[19] Mixed with the farming *thar*s, sometimes at the same status level, sometimes at separate levels, are a number of "clean" craft *thar*s. These Jyāpu and craft levels constitute the middle range of the ranked macrostatus system. The group as a whole are often referred to collectively as "Jyāpu," although the term may be used in more restricted ways.[20]

V. Jyāpu (level 1). A group of seventy-four farming *thar*s.

VI. Tama. This level has only one *thar*, with the *thar* name "Tāmrākar." These are metalworkers in brass and bronze, makers of metal dishes, pots, small bells, and cast-metal god images and other equipment for rituals. As is the case with all *thar*s in the levels V to XII , some individuals also farm.

VII. Kumha: and *Awa:*. This section contains two *thar*s who are considered at the same level and who intermarry. They are the Kumha: or hereditary potters (whose *thar* name is Prajāpati), and the Awa: or Awāl, whose hereditary profession is masonry and tile roofing.

VIII. Jyāpu (level 2). This is a group of about 146 mostly farming *thar*s, but includes two *thar*s with occupational specialties who intermarry with other *thar*s at this level. One of the occupational groups is Kāmi (*thar* name Silpakār) who were traditionally wood carvers, one of the Newar high arts and now make furniture and do woodwork in the construction and repair of houses. The other is Loha(n)kāmi, or stone carvers.

IX. Jyāpu (level 3). This is a group of fourteen intermarrying farming *thars*.

X. Chipī. This is a group of about six *thars*, one of which uses the high-status name "Śresṭha." They are shopkeepers, in government service, and farmers.[21] There are two other *thars* considered to be at the same level that are not usually included with the Chipī, and who form a separate section at this level.

XI. Cyo (or Cya). A farming *thar*, with the *thar* name Phusikawā(n), which has some ritual functions during the death ceremonies of upper-level *thars*.

XII. Dwi(n). This level has one *thar*, Dwi(n). They farm and operate small shops and foodstalls. Their low status is now manifested in a *thar* duty to clean the courtyard of the Taleju temple.[22]

Levels I to XII are those levels that are, in ways that will be specified later, "clean" levels. Although all the hierarchical differences between status levels are associated with relative differences in purity, manifested focally in regulations regarding the consumption of boiled rice, starting with level XIII, which we call the "borderline clean *thars*," another issue, that of classes and degrees of "absolute impurity," associated with increasingly extensive avoidances and prohibitions, becomes salient. These groups can be designated not only as "less clean" than some other but also, in one or another degree and sense, as "unclean." Starting with this level whose "uncleanliness" is the concern of only Brahmans and the most orthodox individuals—that is, those who attempt to mimic Brahmans' ways of life—in the upper-status *thars*, each successively lower level is progressively more contaminating, in relation to the extent of the upper levels who are vulnerable to them, to the conditions under which they become polluting, and to the "quantities" of pollution that they can transmit.

XIII. The borderline-clean thars. This group contains ten (or in some listings eleven) *thars* who perform personal services or who engage in crafts or in "ritual"[23] activities that render them contaminating to high-status people. The *thars* at this level do not intermarry or interdine together. Each group tends to marry members of the same *thar* in other Valley towns. Each *thar* within the level tends to consider itself higher than the other *thar*s in the group. For Brahmans and for many or most individuals in the upper three or four levels, water touched by members at this level (and below) was considered polluting. In the last twenty or so years for less strict individuals in these upper levels, water-unacceptability has begun at level XV, the Jugī.

Many of the families and individuals in these *thar*s now make their living primarily from farming, small shops and business enterprises, and government jobs, but we will list the traditionally *thar*-ascribed occupations still practiced by some or many individuals in each group. Gāthā are performers of the major ritual dance cycle, the Nine Durgās cycle, during which they incarnate a particular set of deities (see chap. 15). They are also growers of flowers for religious use. Bhā perform actions in the course of upper-status death ceremonies to help assure a human form for the spirit of the dead person (chap. 10, app. 6). Kata: women cut umbilical cords and dispose of placentas following birth. Cāla(n) lead funeral processions to clear the route and prevent inauspicious cross traffic at crossroads. Kusa: are litter or palanquin bearers. Nau are barbers, who do both cosmetic shaving and haircuts and are essential for major "ritual" purification (chaps. 10 and 11). Kau are ironworkers and blacksmiths. Pu(n) are painters of religious objects and makers of masks used in religious ceremonies. Sa:mi are pressers of mustard seed for the production of a commonly used kind of oil.[24] Chipā are dyers of cloth. A few remaining families in a *thar* called "Pasi" are now considered to be at this level. Some members of the Pasi *thar* traditionally had the duty on the tenth day following a death to wash contaminated clothes worn during the ten-day mourning period by the chief mourner in upper-status *thar*s (app. 6). This *thar* probably once had a considerably lower status.[25]

We call this group (level XIII) "borderline unclean" in that there is now an optional response to them by higher-status people as water-unacceptable and they are not considered by middle-ranked groups to be unclean. Their marginality is reflected in their treatment in previous descriptions and records of Newar status levels.[26] In contrast to the groups still lower than they are, they participate along with the clean *thar*s in one of the most significantly Newar rites of passage, the mock-marriage, or *Ihī* (app. 6).

Starting with the next group, the Nāe, we enter the clearly contaminating segments of the status system.

XIV. Nāe. There is one *thar* at this level, the Nāe, who use various *thar* names. These are hereditary butchers who slaughter water buffaloes and sell their meat.[27]

Below this level there are some five or six (depending on whether the Hālāhulu are to be considered as a "macrostatus level") of the city's lowest ranks. Only two of these, Jugī and Po(n), now have more than a very few members, but those two are of major significance in the status system in both the services they perform and their use in giving intellectual representation and emotional significance to the low end of the status system (chaps. 10 and 11).

XV. Jugī. Members of this group use three *thar* names, Darśaṇdhārī, Kapālī, and Kusle. There is another *thar*, Danyā, which is ranked with the Jugīs by others, but that the Jugīs and the Danyās themselves consider an inferior *thar*, performing pollution-accumulating services for the Jugīs in the Jugīs' death ceremonies. The Jugīs are musicians, hereditary performers on the *mwāli*, a double-reed instrument, and also on certain kinds of drums (Hoerburger 1975, 71–74). They have important functions during the course of death ceremonies (chap. 10, app. 6).

XVI. Do(n). Members of this *thar* play a kind of trumpet, used during funeral processions of high-status people.[28]

XVII. Kulu. The members of this *thar* were traditionally drummakers, whose use of animal skins for drum heads accounted for their low status.

The next levels are the true "untouchables," whose functions and prescribed way of life follows traditional South Asian patterns. For Bhaktapur the focal and most clearly defined untouchables are the Po(n)s. The other two categories are ambiguous.

XVIII. Po(n) or Pore.[29] The members of this level are one *thar*, whose *thar* name is Mātaṅgī. These are sweepers, cleaners of latrines, fishermen, and makers of certain kinds of baskets. They have important "ritual" functions as accumulators of pollution (in relation to death and more generally) and of "bad luck" (chaps. 10, 11). They must live just outside the city boundaries, and thus help define those boundaries and the meaning of city space (chap. 7).

XIX. Cyāmākhala:. The Po(n)'s function as transporters of fecal material may have been one of the occupations ascribed in earlier periods to a still lower *thar*, the Cyāmākhala:. Nineteenth-century accounts give the traditional occupations of the Po(n)s such as fishermen, executioners, dog killers, and basket-makers (Oldfield [1880] 1974; Hamilton [1819] 1971; Earle 1901 [cited in Chattopadhyay 1923]; Hodgson n.d.), but specify that they will not remove "night soil" which is said to be the function of the still lower Cyāmākhala: (Chattopadhyay 1923, 546, 558). One account (Hamilton) described the Cyāmākhala: as "dressers of leather" and "shoemakers," which is what the Sanskrit origin of the name (Manandhar 1975, 123) means. There is one household in Bhaktapur that is still designated as Cyāmākhala:. Some of its members have subordinate "ritual" relations to the Po(n)s, accepting polluting offerings during death rituals.

XXI. Hālāhulu. This is a miscellaneous category of true outcastes—drifters and beggars, Newars, and others, who have been excluded from the status system for one reason or another, but are sometimes listed as a lowest social category. There were none in Bhaktapur at the time of this study, but they were said to exist in Kathmandu.[30] They are inferior to the Po(n)s (as well as the Cyāmākhalas:) and, it is said, sometimes perform polluting ritual functions for them.

THE MACROSTATUS SYSTEM: BUDDHIST *THARS* AND SOME NOTES ON NEWAR BUDDHISM

Buddhism may well have existed in the Kathmandu Valley from the time of the Buddha's own teachings. During the Licchavi period there is evidence for both Theravāda and Mahāyāna versions. By the seventh century A.D. Vajrayāna forms are attested (Slusser 1982, vol. 1, p. 39) that reached their "full flowering" 200 or 300 years later (ibid., 48) to become the dominant form of valley Buddhism. All three forms had been monastic, centering around monks and monasteries, *vihāras*. Starting at the end of the twelfth century, monastic life began the transformation that characterizes contemporary Newar Buddhism; the monks began to marry (various reasons for the transition have been offered) and, following the Brahmanic pattern, established hereditary lineages of priests.[31] As many observers have noted, the priestly Buddhism that developed among the Newars is much closer to Newar Hinduism in its social, philosophical, and ritual forms than it is to classical Indian Buddhism. As Oldfield wrote in his nineteenth-century report on Nepal, "Buddhism ought to be considered as it is in Nepal as a branch of Hinduism and not as a distinct faith" ([1802] 1974, vol. II, p. 286).[32]

The descendants of the married monks are called "Bāre" in Bhaktapur (in Kathmandu Newari, "Bare"), and are divided into two segments, a higher group who continued to act as temple and family priests, the Gubāju or Vajrācārya, and a lower segment that does not take the special initiation required to become a priest, the Śākyas. While only the Vajrācārya work as priests, both groups now work as gold and silversmiths, which previously, reportedly, was the *thar* profession only of the Śākyas (Locke 1976, 12). The two sections intermarry.

Traditionally associated with the Bāre, whose priests they were, were various *thar*s of traders and craftsmen, collectively known elsewhere in the Kathmandu Valley as "Urāe," a term not used for a social category in Bhaktapur.[33] It is difficult to know exactly which of the present *thar*s in Bhaktapur might have been designated as Urāe. Different authors (e.g., Lévi 1905; Rosser 1966, 86, Chattopadhyay 1923, 521) have given different lists of associated *thars*.[34] Their residue is found in some groups of merchants and craftsmen situated at the Jyāpu level, who use Vajrācāryā either exclusively, or in conjunction with Brahmans as family priests.

Fürer-Haimendorf, in an influential article on Newar social structure (1956), suggested that those "castes" whose members employed Brahmans as hereditary family priests for domestic rituals be considered Hindus, while those who employed Newar Buddhist priests be considered Buddhist. But, as Colin Rosser subsequently pointed out "on grounds of religious belief and practice . . . it is incredibly difficult if not impossible to identify the vast bulk of the Newar population as being either Hindu or Buddhist" (1966, 78). Once we go beyond the Bāre themselves and the one Urāe *thar*—the Tulādhar—which persists in Bhaktapur as an exclusive patron of the Bāre, the basis for any distinction becomes problematic. The Vajrācāryā priests also perform priestly services in different ways for various *thar*s, who are not, therefore, necessarily to be considered "Buddhists." There are some *thar*s who use *both* Vajrācāryās and Brahmans as priests, usually with the Vajrācāryā officiating at rites of passage and the Brahman at household *pūjā*s (worship) (app. 4). There are some *thar*s of marginally clean status—Sa:mi, Chipā, and some sections of Pu(n)—who exclusively use Vajrācāryās. For such marginally unclean *thar*s the Buddhist priests compete with other non-Brahman priests in an "opportunistic" offering of priestly services to groups that the Brahmans will not serve (chap. 10).

The 1971 census asked people in Bhaktapur to identify themselves and their family members as "Buddhist" or "Hindu." As we have noted, about 3,000 of Bhaktapur's total population were so identified as Buddhist. As the average household size in Bhaktapur is six members, this would represent approximately 500 households. There are about 260 households of Bāre (see table 1 [below, next section]). This would suggest that there are approximately 240 additional households among Bhaktapur's total of 6,484 households in 1971 that both use Vajrācāryā for some or all of their rituals and that identified themselves as Buddhists on the census. Which particular households these are within those various *thar*s which do use Vajrācāryās in one way or another would require further studies.

The Newar "Buddhists," whatever the nature of their Buddhism might be, as Sylvain Lévi put it "extend Hindu society beyond the 'Brahmanic church'" (1905, vol. I, p. 244f.). For Bhaktapur they are, with the exception of the Bāre (and perhaps the Tulādhars), an integral part of Bhaktapur's Hindu core system.

NON-NEWARS: BRAHMANS

There are two groups of Brahmans who have been in the Kathmandu Valley since Malla times, and who will be discussed in chapter 10. These are the Bhaṭṭa Brahmans and the Misrā or Jhā Brahmans. They say they are not Newars, and they are not considered Newars by others. They serve in Bhaktapur as temple priests and as family priests within their own groups. The Bhaṭṭas serve some families in one upper-status Newar *thar* as receivers of gifts in illness, and thus as surrogates for Newar Brahmans in a pollution-transferring service (chap. 10).

NON-NEWARS: *MAṬHA* PRIESTS

There are three groups whose principal hereditary function in Bhaktapur is as priests of the imposing *maṭha*s, centers for the reception of

Shaivite ascetics, usually wandering Indian renouncers, which were built by the Malla kings as acts of piety. They are still pilgrimage centers and hostels for renouncers and Shaivite pilgrims, still mostly from India. They have no connection with the internal symbolic ritual organization of Bhaktapur.

There are thirteen *maṭha*s in Bhaktapur (Korn 1976). Their priests belong to three groups of families, settled in Bhaktapur since the Malla period, which are derived from medieval Indian sects traditionally associated with such *maṭha*s. These are the Ja(n)gam of the Liṅgayat sect, and the Giri and Puri of the Gosāin sect.

NON-NEWARS: OTHERS

There is, in addition to these long-established groups, a miscellaneous residual of non-Newar Nepalis living and working in Bhaktapur:

1. Some families of officials and functionaries of the national government temporarily assigned to Bhaktapur.

2. A few Muslim households. These families have lived in Bhaktapur for generations and have a small mosque and burying ground within the city. They are shopkeepers specializing in bracelets, ornamental cords used for decorating women's hair, and plastic shoes. They also are knife sharpeners.[35]

3. Gāine. A few members of a non-Mongoloid "tribal" group who are traditionally performing musicians.[36] They perform for tourists in Bhaktapur.

4. Sārki. A low-status Indo-Nepalese "caste" of shoemakers. (There is no traditional Newar shoemaker *thar*.)

5. Dhobī, washers of clothes. For most (but not all) present informants they are non-Newars. They were included among Newar "castes" by the *Muluki Ain* of 1854 (Höfer 1979, 45) and by Lévi (1905, 235). They are not included among Newar "castes" by Rosser (1966, 86).

6. Tamang. These are members of a Tibeto-Burman-speaking hill tribe from the hills surrounding Bhaktapur. The few Tamang living in Bhaktapur are mostly painters of Tibetan-type *Thang-ka*s for the curio trade for tourists.

THAR, MACROSTATUS, AND THE ORGANIZATION OF OCCUPATIONAL AND RITUAL ROLES

The organization of *thar*s into macrolevels sorts out their members into the hierarchical system, and in so doing organizes by level (and by larger groupings of macrolevels) much of their members' economic activity and standard of living. The levels they belong to determine whether they can be served by Brahmans, or by other priests, or—if they are sufficiently low—only by *ad hoc* priests in their own *thar*s. It is the levels that entail the organizing implications of the Hindu hierarchical system—purity; patterns of association, commensality, and marriage; and relative public esteem—to which we will return later in this chapter and in chapter 11. The relationship between status level and occupation is obscured by those status levels that include only one *thar*. When there is more than one *thar* in a status level, it is evident that levels join together occupational *types*, not specific occupations. They sort such categories as court officials, shopkeepers, farmers, craftsmen, and providers of essential symbolic-ritual services that are demeaning to those who do them. Individual *thar*s may specify narrowly defined professions within these larger groupings. In those cases where there is only one *thar* at a particular level, this is simply a special case where occupation and status level coalesce so that the classical definition of a "caste" is approximated, but it is a special case of considerable interest. In some cases such as Tini and Tama: this exclusive convergence seems to be an historical residue of some problem in categorization. However, most of the examples of such "castes" are *thar*s that are essential not only for their specific vocation but also for the very definition, constitution, and maintenance of the symbolic component of the hierarchical system; Brahman, Nāe, Jugī, and Po(n) are evident examples. It is also of interest that the isolation of *thar*s into discrete status levels as "castes" is represented at the top of the system with the Brahmans only (the king is traditionally included with various Kṣatriya *thar*s) but pervasively throughout the "unclean" *thar*s from level XIV down, each of whom is ranked at its own discrete level. This is one of many suggestions that Brahmans and the unclean *thar*s are joined closely in the same enterprise.

In contrast to the effects of all *thar*s on occupation because of their placement in a particular status level, and the resulting assignment of its

Figure 3. A member of the Kumha: (potter) *thar* making pots on his wheel.

Figure 4. Awa:s (masons) and Ka:mis (carpenters) building a house.

Figure 5. Young wives chatting while collecting water at a communal tap.

members to some general class of activities (e.g., farming or shopkeeping), there are about forty-five *thar*s whose membership at present specifies for its members either a particular and exclusive hereditary trade and/or some hereditary "ritual" function, that is, a function in the marked symbolic realm of the city. There are various combinations of occupational and ritual functions. Some *thar*s have ritual functions that reflect their occupational functions (e.g., potters and carpenters). There are some groups whose hereditary occupational functions have disappeared but who may still have ritual responsibilities deriving from and faintly echoing those functions. There are groups with occupational specialties (e.g., Ayurvedic physicians) and no ritual functions. There are groups whose occupation is a ritual occupation, that is, entirely within the realm of marked symbolism (e.g., priests). Among these various groups there are some *thar*s whose ritual or occupational function accounts for most of the livelihood of most of the adult male members of the group (e.g., Brahmans, sweepers). In contrast, there are other *thar*s for whom the ascribed occupational or ritual function, while it is limited to the *thar* and tends to explain or justify its status in the overall system, may actually be performed by only a few of its members, selected in some way by the *thar*, and sometimes involving only a small segment of the selected member's time and economic activity. Such variety, which, furthermore, has shifted during the course of Bhaktapur's history, makes the question as to how *thar* membership determines differentiated ritual and occupational behaviors of its members very complex.

For the purposes of the city's organization, we may emphasize again that it is the output of the *thar* that is essential, not its internal affairs and organization—as long as those internal features guarantee that output. The important thing for the city as a whole is that sufficient numbers of the members perform their essential functions within the traditional system, and that their *other* economic functions and social behaviors do not appear dissonant with the status of the *thar*. The city is, in fact, differentially exigent and severe in its pressures on different *thar*s to maintain their traditional functions. This is for both material and "symbolic" motives. The city can now do without local drum makers if necessary, but for many reasons it cannot do without the economic and/or symbolic functions of, say, Brahmans, potters, and sweepers. The symbolic practitioners, in fact, *must* be locally in place. One can import pots from another town, but such actors as Brahmans and sweepers are essential constituting components of the city system, and must be in place for the traditional system of city action to work at all.

In order to sketch the relation of *thar*s to differentiated urban roles, we will use an *ad hoc* sorting that, however, reflects some important contrasts in the implications of *thar*-assigned roles. In listing these specialized *thar*s we will briefly gloss their special functions that have been given already above, many of which will be discussed elsewhere in the book. The roman numerals following the *thar* names indicate the status level. Recall that occasionally the same *thar* name may occur at more than one status level.

1. Priests, auxiliary priests and "para-priests" (see chap. 10). Rājopādhyāya Brahmans (level I), Lākhe Brahmans (level I, lower section) (priests), Jośi (level II) (astrologers), Ācāju (level III) (auxiliary priests, with Tantric specialties), Jośi (level III) (astrologers), Tini (level IV) (priests), and Ācāju (level IV) (auxiliary priests, with Tantric specialties).

2. *Thar*s who are allied to group 1, the priests, in that their traditional roles, services, products, and behaviors are expressive of and constituent of a special component of the city's symbolic order, which is associated with purity and impurity, "ordinary" deities, and "priestly morality." We will delineate this component in later chapters, and contrast it with other aspects of symbolic order and of power. In contrast to the priests, the functions of these *thar*s are overtly stigmatizing or at least associated with a depressed status:[37] Cyo (level XI) (purifying services during the cremation phase of the death ritual cycle of upper-level *thar*s), Gāthā (level XIII) (flower growers, deity-possessed performers as the "Nine Durgās"), Katā (level XIII) (cut umbilical cords and remove and dispose of placentas), Nau (level XIII) (barbers, purifyers), Pu(n) (level XIII) (painters of religious images and mask makers), Bhā (level XIII) (death ritual services for upper-status *thar*s); Cāla(n) (level XIII) (services in funeral processions of upper-status people), Khusā (level XIII) (esoteric services for one of the Tantric deities during the Mohanī festival cycle), Sa:mi (level XIII) (oil pressers, special functions in the Biska: festival cycle), Nāe (level XIV) (butchers, kill animals in some sacrifices in major temples), Jugī (level XVI) (tailors; performers on drums, trumpets, and shawms; important roles in the cycle of death ceremonies and other pollution-accumulating tasks), and Po(n)

(level XVIII) (sweepers, fishermen, basket makers; various important pollution representing and pollution accumulating functions).

3. Stigmatizing, occupational specialties with no marked symbolic functions. These are craftsmen whose craft has a traditional status-depressing implication, but who, in contrast to the other *thar*s listed in group 2, do not have (in the present at least) corresponding additional symbolic functions: Kau (level XIII) (blacksmiths, workers in iron), Chipa (level XIII) (dyers of cloth), and Do(n) (level XVI) (players of trumpets).

4. Nonstigmatizing occupational specialties: Baidhya (level II) (Ayurvedic physicians), Baidhya (level III) (Ayurvedic physicians), Tama: (level VI) (caster of metal pots, plates, and icons), Kumha: (level VII) (potters), Awa: (level VII) (house builders), Kami (level VIII) (wood carvers, carpenters), and Loha(n) kāmi (level VIII) (stone carvers). (In this group some families of Tama: and Kumha: have some ritual functions in some rites of passage.)

5. *Thar*s including members who have ritual or ceremonial functions in Bhaktapur's focal festivals (chaps. 12 to 16) and/or in association with the Taleju temple. This represents the "symbolic reconstruction" of the old society centering on the Malla court and the temple of its tutelary deity Taleju: from level II (above), Malla, Pradhānā(n)ga, Hādā, Bhau, Tācābhāri, Muna(n)karmi, Bhāri, and Go(n)ga; from level III, Mādikami and Bhāri; from level V, Suwāl; from level VIII, Kālu, Caguthi, Muguthi, Hāleyojosi, and Jatādhāri; and from level XII, Dwi(n). (Among *thar*s included in other lists, those with additional special Taleju ritual and/or ceremonial functions include Jośi [II], Ācāju [III], Tama:, Kumha:, Gāthā, Khusā, Pu(n), Jugī, Nāe, and Po[n].)

6. We can add to this list those groups outside the Newar Hindu core group who have essential occupational or ritual functions. We noted previously some of the occupational specialities of these groups (shoemakers, knife sharpeners, washermen, etc.). Only two groups outside of the core group have ritual-symbolic functions for the core system. The Bhaṭṭa Brahmans have a very limited (but theoretically interesting) function for one upper-status *thar* (chap. 10). The Bāre Buddhist *thar* provides the children who become the "living goddess" Kumārī and her attendant gods and goddesses during the major ceremonial cycle, Mohanī (chap. 15).

There are, thus, some forty-five *thar*s in the core system, about 13 percent of the city's approximately 340 *thars*, whose membership in itself (rather than through its status level) entails ritual and/or occupational specialties. For the city as a whole, seventeen of these *thars*, particularly the upper-status ones, whose ritual activities are confined to the Taleju temple, are of minor differentiated importance. So it is, finally, some twenty-eight *thars*, about 8 percent of the whole, whose members have *major* specializations—against the more diffuse background of farmers and merchants and craftsmen and specialists in being impure, which is organized by the larger macrostatus system. In addition to the total number of specialized *thars* we need to consider their relative size and the number of households and individuals that they contain. Their combined *size* is, as we shall see, a larger percentage of the city's population than their *numbers* alone would indicate.

THAR AND MACROSTATUS DEMOGRAPHY

In an attempt to get some rough idea of the numbers of families and individuals in the various *thars* and status units, we asked various informants for estimations of numbers of households in various *thars*. Subsequently Gutschow and Kölver (1975), using an early version of our macrostatus and *thar* lists, gathered survey data on the numbers of households in many of the units.[38] The total number of households located by Gutschow and Kölver was 5,216. Assuming that the 1971 census report of 6,484 households is accurate, this sample is incomplete, but not biased in any evident way. Certain *thars* are clumped in their report—for instance, some groups of Chathariyā and the large groups of Jyāpus. Their materials (with four additions from our informants' estimations), however, give a basis for estimating rather closely the number of households incorporated in various segments of the system. The previous section listed the number of *thars* that had various kinds of differential significance. As some *thars* contain only two or three households while others may contain hundreds, however, a composite listing of *thars* and the number of *thars* at each level gives us limited demographic information. The number of discrete specialized *thars* is of a different kind of significance for the structure and organization of the city than the quantitative extent of their various memberships.[39]

Table 1, modified from Gutschow and Kölver (1975), gives what is probably a close approximation of *thar* and status level demography.

Table 1 shows that out of a total of 6,450[40] households all but some

TABLE 1.

NUMBER OF HOUSEHOLDS IN BHAKTAPUR CLASSIFIED BY MACROSTATUS LEVEL

Level	Household	Number
I	Brahman	32
II	Chathar	677
III	Pa(n)cthar	247
IV	Tini	2
V	Jyāpu	1,867
VI	Tama:	19
VII	Kumha:	419
	Awa:	99
VIII, IX	Combined, Jyāpu *thars*	1,420 (total)
X	Chipi	466
XI	Cya	5
XII	Dwi(n)	1
XIII	"Borderline clean *thars*"	437 (total)
	Gāthā	56
	Bhā	19
	Kata:	2
	Cāla(n)	16
	Khusa	1
	Nau	46
	Kau	27
	Pu(n)	25
	Sa:mi	160
	Chipā	82
	Pasi	3
XIV	Nāe	177
XV	Jugī	57
XVI	Do(n)	4
XVII	Kulu	1
XVIII	Po(n)	90
XIX	Hālāhulu	1
	Non-Newar Hindu households	
1	Śākya Buddhists	260
2	Misra and Bhaṭṭa Brahmans	26
3	Maṭha priests	6
4	Gāine	7
5	Sarki	6
7	Muslim	3
8	Dhobi	2
9	Other ethnic groups (Tamang and Indo-Nepalese)	129

eighty are "Newar." Of the Newars, approximately 6,110 households are in the Hindu core system, while 260 households are Buddhist Bāre households, which are not directly involved in the core system. For the broader hierarchical and functional divisions of the core system, 32 households are Brahman; 924 households are at the "sāhu" levels; 4,389 households are in the several Jyāpu farming groups; and 765 households are engaged in services, crafts, and professions that are considered in some way to be polluting. Of these polluting households 435 have a borderline status, and 330 are unequivocally polluting.

By adding other available information on the number of households in particular *thar*s within the status levels amalgamated in Table 1, we can suggest the number of *households* within those *thar*s that have differentiated functions. Arranged in the grouping we used in the previous section, the number of households are as follows:

1. Priests, auxiliary priests, and para-priests. Total of 333 households: Rājopādhyāya Brahmans (32), Jośi level II (44), Ācāju level III (85), Jośi level III (120), Tini (2), Ācāju level IV (50).

2. *Thar*s engaging in stigmatized ritual-symbolic activities. Total of 649 households: Gātha (56), Kathā (2), Nau (46), Pu(n) (25), Bhā (19), Cāla(n) (16), Khusā (1), Sa:mi (160), Nāe (177), Jugī (57), Po(n) (90).

3. Stigmatizing, nonritual occupational specialties. Total of 113 households: Kau (27), Chipā (82), Do(n) (4).

4. Nonstigmatizing occupational specialities. Total of 844 households: Baidya level II (3), Baidya level III (8), Tama: (18), Kumha: (508), Awa: (99), Kami (194), Loha(n)kami (14).

5. *Thar*s, some of whose members have ritual or ceremonial functions in Bhaktapur's focal festivals and/or in association with the Taleju temple. The total number of households in the seventeen *thar*s with such functions is about 650.

The number of households in the forty-five specialized *thar*s, is on the average far more than those in the nonspecialized *thar*s. When we listed all the *thar*s in the city with a specialized function, they represented about 13 percent of all the city's *thar*s, among which twenty-eight, or 8 percent of all the city's *thar*s, had major differentiating importance. In terms of the number of households, however, there are some 2,589, or 40 percent of the city's households that are in *thar*s having some differentiated importance to the city, and about 29.5 percent of the households in *thar*s having major specializations.[41]

The numbers of households in a *thar* that follow its traditional speciality,[42] and the number of individuals in a household who do, vary greatly from *thar* to *thar*. Sometimes women are involved in the *thar* specialization (e.g., farmers, barbers, as purifiers); sometimes they are concerned with subsidiary aspects of the speciality (Brahman's wives for some rituals), or perhaps exclusively with the general running of the household and with other nonspecialized or subsidiary economic activities. Moreover, we do not know from such enumerations how those who do not participate in a *thar's* traditional activities, activities that define the *thar*, are affected by their membership.

These internal questions are not our present concern, however. It is the Kumha: as potter, not as farmer or bank clerk, who concerns us here, that is his defining and constituting role in the hierarchical urban system that becomes interwoven with deities, symbolic space, and symbolic performances in the mesocosmic segment of the city's order. For such purposes these demographic notes give a rough idea of the available numbers of role players in that mesocosmic system, numbers distorted by social change and by the loss of some of the controls that may once have more closely regulated the supply of labor in such immobile societies.

ENTAILMENTS AND MARKERS OF THE MACROSTATUS LEVELS

Membership in a *thar* in itself may determine many features of an individual's life—occupation, aspects of marriage, residence, details of religious practices, and the various effects of the *thar*'s special culture and internal organization. Much of this may derive from the special history and distant origins of the *thar* itself and much from the effects of the *thar*'s incorporation, its way of being fitted into the macrostatus system. The *thars* are, in a way, the given raw materials thrown up by history on which the city-wide hierarchical system, the system of macrostatus levels, opportunistically builds. The macrostatus system is a means of ordering and making sense of its multitude of component units by ordering them into much simpler systematized groupings. That system is a typical Hindu "caste system," sharing the ideologies, the central metaphors of purity and impurity, the entailments of rank, and the rules for interactions among ranks that are found throughout South Asia. Such systems have been described frequently and at length, and we will simply sketch some of the entailments of Bhaktapur's twenty macrostatus levels here to indicate what Bhaktapur has maintained and emphasized in its Hindu orthodoxy.

Our sketch is concerned with the central rules of status ordering and their insisted-upon, publicly controlled, and sanctioned expressions. Deviations are internally controlled by family and *thar* councils, motivated by fear of loss of public respect and of economic and physical sanctions, and externally by people at superior levels who, if necessary, apply such sanctions. The rules concern—characteristically of Hindu status systems—mostly physical contact in relation to eating, drinking, and touching, and regulation of proper marriage. They also include for the lowest *thar*s rules regarding place of residence, and, until recently, clothing, decoration, and house type. In addition to these centrally important and carefully regulated behaviors there are many other important *signs* of status level—such as proper language and other behaviors indicating deference, respect, and adherence—and a host of more or less secondary or covert *implications* of status level, such as economic and educational opportunities, nutrition, differential vulnerability to disease, and many aspects of standards of living.

The centrally controlled behaviors are questions of traditional proper behavior, aspects of the *dharma*. The implications are often otherwise explained—as misfortune or the results of bad *karma*. The central system of regulations is highly conscious, involves clear rules and regulations, is based on pervasive and deeply felt ways of viewing the world, and is continuously symbolized and reinforced in ritual and symbolic forms. To anticipate later discussions, we may note here that the separation and ranking of the macrostatus system is considered a positive, dynamic, and activity-requiring process, the result of constant effort. People talk of "sending people to, and keeping them at" their particular level. Separation and ranking is in tension with other ideologies and experiences of blending and equality, and is not based on any theory of fixed, essential, "biological" differences justifying the hierarchy. It must be actively and constantly maintained.

The violation of central regulations is sanctioned, ultimately by the threat of expulsion of an individual, a family, or an entire *thar* from its status level. These regulations are central in that they *constitute* the hierarchical system, as the rules for the moves of chess pieces constitute the game of chess. The primary formula, which in itself implies all the separations and hierarchical rankings that make up the hierarchy is, as everywhere in South Asia, that boiled rice and certain boiled legumes (or "pulses") can be eaten only if prepared by a member of one's own level or of a higher level. This rule is associated with ideas of impurity, which we will consider in chapter 11, and blends with other ideas about the status-derived purity of the provider of food, who must also be pure in other regards, not contaminated, for example, by contact with death or menstruation. From the point of view of any individual in the system there are two groups. There is an upper group including one's own level, from which one will accept boiled rice.[43] Below any individual and distinct from and in opposition to the upper segment in which he or she and his or her peers are included are those groups who will accept boiled rice from the members of that segment, but from whom they will not accept boiled rice. Boiled rice is the basic domestic staple grain of the Newars, and the regulation involves an unavoidable, salient issue. In relation to the acceptance of food, of "being fed," the group to which an individual belongs, except for Brahmans, is always at the bottom of an upper segment.

The process of being excluded by those above and excluding those below effectively slices the hierarchy into its levels.[44] The asymmetry has other implications, however. In the acceptance of rice, one is *open* to all above and to those at one's own level, and *closed* to all below. Thus, in terms of the acceptance of rice (which in the ideology of purity [chap. 11], implies the sharing of bodily substance), *every* individual is in the same "body" as all above (but always significantly at the lowest, most dependent position) and in opposition to all those below in rank. The refusal to take rice from those lower in status is one's own active (and conflicted) responsibility, supported by powerful ideas and feelings, many of which are related to dirt and disgust. But it is, in contrast, by the stigmatizing decision and action of others at superior levels, that *our* rice is rejected. Any given level gets carved out between its own strongly motivated restrictions toward those below it, on the bottom side, and something quite different, the rejecting behavior of other higher levels toward it on the top side. The solidarity of belonging to "one body" signaled to any individual by the downward flow of boiled rice is countered by an opposition, a radical breach in solidarity signaled by rejection of its upward flow. Looking down the system, one sees people who belong to, derive from, and depend on one, but whom one places on the other side of a barrier of disgust and pollution. Such complex asymmetries encourage in those given to reflection the kinds of intellectual complexity, the "sophistication," which, we have suggested in chapter 2, is an important distinguishing feature of Bhaktapur's people and the uses they make of its marked symbols.

While the differential acceptances and rejection of boiled rice carves out *each* successive step in the macrostatus system (as do the marriage regulations to which we will return), there are various other designations of differential purity that are arranged hierarchically and refer to particular status levels or groups of status levels, but which are not a regularly increasing and differentiating quality of each successive level. These mark hierarchy in a grosser way, and we may for convenience call them "classes of purity."

While (again typical of Hindu communities) a given group will not accept boiled rice from people in the levels below it, it will accept most other foods until a certain level is reached; at that level its members are considered so impure that no food, not even water, may be accepted from them. This group of people are called "*Ña calae ma ju phu(n),*" people from whom water may not be "moved," or "*Tiye nae ma tya phu(n),*" people who should not be touched while you or they are eating. In the first phrasing, it is understood that as water is not acceptable, then no other food and drink is acceptable.[45]

The first division, "water-unacceptability," produces a first large distinction among the levels in classes of purity. In the class of levels below the "water line" a second division is made to create a distinct lowest category, the "*Tiye ma tya phu(n),*" people who must not be touched—whether one is eating or not.[46]

In previous sections we noted which levels are considered in each of these categories. There is some variation in the placement of the level of water-unacceptability, depending on the status of the higher, "purer" person. This is reflected in our "borderline" level, level XIII. Middle and lower levels differ in their conceptions of water-unacceptability even in relation to *thar*s below level XIII, but every *thar* agrees on the position of at least two *thar*s—the Jugī as water-unacceptable and the Po(n) as untouchable, and these two *thar*s are the present-day inheritors and foci of these positions.

The Brahmans and the upper-status Chathar families who model themselves on them add another distinction. They further divide the group from which they will accept food and drink. Within this group there is an upper strata, those groups from which they will accept all foods except boiled rice and pulses, the groups—as they are sometimes categorized—from which they will accept "salt." These are the Pa(n)-cthar and above. Below this group is a second strata, people from whom they will accept all foods that are neither boiled (and therefore, of course, not boiled rice or pulses) nor salted. This group, named by contrast with the segment below it, is often called the "people from whom one accepts water." These are for the most part the farmers and "clean" craftsmen.

There were in the past many associated markers of sequential status relationships and classes of purity. One of the most enduring of these has been respect levels in language. In ordinary usage, there are three respect levels indicated in pronouns and in a very few nonpronominal lexical items (most saliently verbs for coming and going and for eating and drinking). People use a formal language in addressing or referring to others who are of higher status than themselves or in addressing or talking about equals in formal situations and a familiar language for people of lower status or for equals with whom they have intimate relations. The third level is a high-respect language used for addressing royalty, Brahmans (and, usually, Buddhist priests), and deities. There are also customs for proper greeting, for respect gestures, terms of respectful address, and more subtle behaviors of deference and authority, which respond to and mark relative hierarchy.

In the past a variety of associated regulations brought some, at least, other aspects of life into accord with purity rankings. Much of this was directed to the lowest most impure classes and facilitated their identification and separation. Thus, according to some of the chronicles, in Malla times members of the butcher *thar* had to wear sleeveless jackets; sweepers, butchers, and drum makers were not allowed to wear caps, shoes, or gold ornaments; and the sweepers had to live out of the city, and were not allowed to have the roofs of their houses tiled (D. R. Regmi, 1965, part I, p. 647). Many of these restrictions lasted through the Rana period and are remembered by older people but are not enforced now. But some such regulations, although not supported (and, in fact, illegal) under modern Nepalese law, persist. Thus Po(n) untouchables must, in fact, still live beyond the city's boundaries and in simple houses. Another very salient spatial marking of the major polluting *thar*s also has persisted. This is how far into the space of a house a person of a given polluting class can penetrate. Untouchables can enter only the *cheli*, the ground floor, which is conceptually considered outside of the house (chap. 7). Higher levels of unclean *thar*s can go further into the house, at least as far as the first floor above the ground level, the degree depending on the claims to purity of the individual household or its *thar*.

Foods eaten at different levels are frequently used to indicate status differences. Among the most salient are the foods that the Brahmans refrain from eating—certain vegetables and the meat of certain animals (water buffalo and [previously] fowl),[47] which are for others common Newar foods. At the other end of the scale is pork, which is eaten only by the lower segments of the unclean *thar*s, Po(n), Nāe, Jugī, and the unclean Indo-Nepalese groups. It may be noted that pigs, like dogs, which are not eaten, are scavenging animals in Bhaktapur, eating, among other things, refuse of all kinds, including remnants of food in human feces. The low Newar groups further distinguish themselves from the Indo-Nepalese shoemaker and leatherworker group (Sarki), whom they claim eat the carcasses of animals that have died of natural causes, which the low Newar groups consider to be much more polluting than eating butchered pigs.

The separation and hierarchy organized by the macrostatus system entail rules about marriage, which make up part of the regulations for proper marriage (see chap. 6). Macrostatus regulations for a proper marriage depend on whether the marriage is a "primary" marriage—one contracted for perpetuation of the lineage.[48] Primary marriages should be within the same status level.[49] In those secondary unions in which the wife may be of a lower level, she cannot legitimately prepare boiled rice for her hushand, and their children will belong to neither the husband's *thar* nor to his level. They will either take the wife's *thar* name and level, or in rare cases be given a new *thar* name and placed at some intermediate level within the system. In these cases the man still is a member in good standing of his *thar* and can involve himself in its ritual, associational, and economic life—but his descendants no longer belong to it. If he were to marry or form a liaison with someone of an impure *thar*, however, he would be ostracized from his own *thar* and level.[50] All primary marriages and the majority of secondary marriages are endogamous within any given status level. The controls here, somewhat like the controls on boiled rice-taking, are asymmetrical. People at any given level are concerned only that their women should not be given as wives to men at lower levels. Their active control is directed to the lower boundary. They have no ritual or social objection to taking wives from levels above them (and when such marriages do occur, they are vaunted), but those upper levels will not, if they can possibly prevent doing so, provide wives for them. It is through each level's concern with maintenance of its lower boundaries that a segmented system of status-level endogamy is created.

We should note that the actual regulations for accepting wives do not correspond exactly to the regulation for accepting boiled rice, and does not "map" the macrostatus levels as exactly. In Bhaktapur there are subgroups within some macrostatus levels who consider themselves as a higher subsection, and will accept wives only from the same subsection, even though they will accept boiled rice from all *thar*s at the same general macrostatus level. Other considerations affecting exogamy may also limit marriage to only one section of the general commensal group, or may force people to seek wives outside the city. Thus, while rice acceptance is always directly related to hierarchical relations of macrostatus units in the city, marriage choice is not. Food and contact regulations are constantly at issue and are enforced and reenacted in every act of eating and food preparation; arranging a proper marriage, in contrast, is hardly a daily issue for any given individual.

STATUS RANKING OF AND BY OUTSIDERS

People in Bhaktapur's core system rank all outsiders—both in and beyond Bhaktapur—into a hierarchical system of relative purity and impurity and, in turn, are ranked by at least some of those outsiders, most importantly by Nepal's dominant Indo-Nepalese. While the ranking of the internal components of the Bhaktapur core system is repeatedly represented and reinforced in symbols and concepts and in action and is very generally agreed upon, these external rankings are a different matter. The objects of Newar or Newar Hindu ranking may well be ranking the Newars in their turn by a different calculus, and do not accept (or sometimes care or know about) Newar decisions about their position. Some of the northern Mongoloid groups do not even accept the underlying assumptions which support the general notion of Hindu hierarchy.

We will list these external rankings in a summary fashion:

1. *Groups within Bhaktapur: Buddhist Bāre.* For Rājopādhyāya Brahmans, the Buddhist Bāre (including both sections—priests and precious metal craftsmen) were considered water-unacceptable. The justifications given by Brahmans for their low rank are miscellaneous, but not necessarily more *post hoc* than other such justifications for status. These include their metalworking, their traditional performances on "contaminating" musical instruments, and their short seven-day period of contamination after death—such short periods being characteristic of low-level groups. Furthermore, the Bāre do not, in con-

trast to Hindus, maintain a residual queue of hair in the course of the shaving of their heads at the time of (and in purification rituals subsequent to) boys' ritual initiation into their *thar*. This last, a reminder of their original status as monks (Buddhist monks' shaving of the entire head being a sign of renunciation of ordinary lineage and social ties), probably reflects one of the historical reasons for their ambiguous rank—recalling the ambiguous social ranking of all Hindu renouncers. For other members of upper-level *thar*s, Chathariyā and Pa(n)cthariyā, the Bāre were considered on the levels of the Jyāpus, and thus "water-acceptable."[51]

2. *Groups within Bhaktapur: non-Newar Brahmans and Maṭha priests.* Rājopādhyāya Brahmans traditionally considered the Jhā and Bhaṭṭa Brahmans and the Maṭha priests to be water-acceptable. The Newar Chathariyā and Pa(n)cthariyā treated them as they did the highest segments just below themselves; that is, they accepted all food except boiled rice and pulses from them. Middle-level and lower-level Newar groups accept rice from these priests. Conversely, the Jhā and Bhaṭṭa Brahmans accepted rice from neither Rājopādhyāya Brahmans nor the levels below them.

3. *Relations to other non-Newar Nepalis, both in and out of Bhaktapur.* Newars in general divide non-Newar Nepalis into two groups. Mongoloid peoples, thought generally to have Tibetan connections, are called "Sāe(n)." This term is said to derive from an old Newari term for a Tibetan[52] or, according to some, for Lhasa.

For the non-Mongoloid hill peoples, who are in large part the groups from western Nepal associated with the Gorkhāli invaders, the term "*partyā*," or "hill-dweller" is used in polite reference.[53] The ordinary term, considered pejorative, is "*khae(n)*," derived, apparently, from the tribal designation "*khas*."[54] This general term refers in some contexts to the upper-status divisions of the western Khas group, the Brahmans ("Khae[n] Brahmans") and the upper "Kṣatriya" divisions (the latter also referred to distinctively as "Chetri") but in other contexts also may include the very low status (generally untouchable) occupational Khas groups such as blacksmiths, tailors, shoemakers, and leatherworkers.[55] Furthermore, other non-Mongoloid hill groups who may be of dubious historical Khas connections, such as the Gāine, are included as Khae(n).

For Newar Brahmans, Partyā Brahmans and Chetris are only water-acceptable. The Chathariyā and Pa(n)cthariyā, in general, accept all foods and drink except boiled rice and pulses from the Partyā Brahmans and Chetri. Those Khas groups untouchable to the Partyā Brahmans and Chetri themselves are also untouchable for the Newars.

The Sāe(n) were generally treated as water-unacceptable by Brahmans. The Chathariyā and strict Pa(n)cthariyā accepted water (but not boiled and salted foods) from them. Most, but not all, Jyāpu accepted all food except boiled rice and pulses from them.

The residual group, neither Khae(n) nor Sāe(n), are Muslims, and these are generally treated as untouchable by the highest levels, and water-unacceptable by those below them.

4. *Partyās' conceptions of Newars.* As Lynn Bennett (1977, p. 30f.) puts it, for the Khas Brahmans and the Chetris,

> The higher twice-born Newari castes . . . exist in a kind of "separate but parallel" status with respect to the high caste Parbatiya. The remaining castes . . . all fall under the rubric of *matwāli* or "liquor-drinking." From the Brahman-Chetri point of view this large middle-ranking group includes most Newar and other Tibeto-Burman speaking peoples. . . . Members of this group . . . are touchable and water as well as . . . uncooked food or food cooked with ghee can be accepted by high caste individuals from them.

Newar untouchables and the clearly water-unacceptable groups (such as Nāe and Jugī) are also untouchable or water-unacceptable to the upper-ranking Chetris and to Partyā Brahmans. These rankings reflect the rankings and ambiguities of the *Muluki Ain*, the attempt to legislate a Nepalese national status system. Its attempts to integrate the entire Newar status system into a national system was very awkward for all parties, and "often deficient or ambiguous and at variance with the self-assessment of the Newar castes" (Höfer 1979, 140).

ENVOI

The order generated and represented by *thar* and macrostatus level relates to hierarchy and specialization, separation and interrelation, although it hardly sorts matters in the simple manner of Bouglé's definition of a "caste" that we quoted at the start of this chapter. In one way or another, however, *thar* and status level in various combinations assign and control most of the differentiated production of goods and services necessary for Bhaktapur's traditional and early modern urban life.

This order ensures that the many specialists such as masons and metalworkers—and above all, masses of farmers, will be replaced and maintained from generation to generation. It guarantees that "Kṣatriyas" will hold on to the places they have been able to capture, at least for the length of a dynasty. It also provides the priests and untouchables the exemplars and technicians of the system of marked symbolism which presently will concern us. The way that the precise roles and the more diffuse qualities that *thar* and level attribute and assign to the people who are born into them are—or are not—made use of by the symbolic order, and the ways that the symbolic order expresses and reinforces the status system will concern us in the following chapters.

CHAPTER SIX

Inside the *Thars*

INTRODUCTION: THE INTERNAL STRUCTURE OF THE *THAR*

In chapter 5 we considered the *thar*s and their arrangement into larger levels and groupings as the building blocks of Bhaktapur's urban society. We remarked that as long as they continued to produce the goods, services, and relational behaviors that were essential to urban organization, the internal organization of the *thar*, like that of many corporate units in Bhaktapur, was carefully and properly hidden from the scrutiny of outside observers. We have said that the internal forms were of no concern to the city. That must be qualified, for the internal forms generate many of the shared and contrasting experiences and meanings that the public urban system must express or work with or counter. These internal arrangements provide a background of private meanings and private problems which the integrative forms of the city must take account of.

We will sketch something of the internal structure of the *thar*s here. This is not our main concern in this study, and we must be superficial and general, collapsing differences among the *thars* insofar as they may exist and concerning which we have only limited information. Much is similar throughout the hundreds of units of the macrosystem; other aspects vary according to the local histories and traditions of the *thar*s, or in accordance with larger social and economic forces that variously affect them. Within the *thar*s we will consider aspects of the household, kinship structure, extended-family organization, and aspects of marriage. As we are here for the space of a chapter approaching the intimate lives of individuals we will, in contrast to our general procedure in this volume, make some limited use of transcribed accounts of interviews.

In passing from aspects of the macrosystem and its component units to the internal institutions of the *thar*s, we are crossing a threshold. On one side are the processes that belong directly to the organization of the city in itself; on the other are the sustaining smaller processes more systematically related to the person and the household, the extended family, and the neighborhood. The content and forms of organization of these two worlds are different.

HOUSEHOLD AND HOUSEHOLD SIZE

For most economic, organizational, moral, and ritual purposes, the smallest social unit of the *thar* is the household. It is an important economic unit, coordinated usually by the male head of the household, who decides, within the limits imposed by the macrostructure, what activities will be undertaken, and who collects and distributes the family income. The household is the setting for intimacy, for the education of the young, for preliminary (and usually effective) attempts at controlling deviant behavior, and for much family religion. Like the *thar* itself, the family has a clearly bounded corporate and spatial (chap. 7) inside and outside, and tries to protect the inside through privacy and secrecy. There is no specific name for the household in Newari, but its members sometimes refer to each other with the Nepali (and Hindi) term *jahān*, in this sense "household family," which is distinguished from other, larger family units. Sometimes the group is referred to by terms that refer to the sharing of boiled food, particularly rice, such as *chaga jāsi*, "one rice pot." If a household separates into separate units, it is conventionally phrased as "having stopped sharing a kitchen area," or "having stopped eating boiled rice together." The main metaphor for the household, as is generally true of household units in other parts of the world, is that its members share a common cooking and eating place.

When families separate, usually at a time when there are two or more sons with their own wives and children, they may, if the house is large enough, divide up the space in the house in which they were living, or add to it so that uncles, brothers, cousins, and so on, live in more or less close contact, but have separate cooking areas or cooking times, separate household heads, and separate household shrines. According to a survey by the Nepal Rāṣtra Bank (1974*a*), a majority of all Bhaktapur households shared larger housing structures with (at least) one other household.[1]

This same survey showed for Bhaktapur an average figure of six persons per household, the same figure as that given in the National Census of 1973. The survey also has figures on the distribution of size of households for the entire city population: 5.2 percent of the households included only one person; 33.2 percent, two to four persons; 37.2 percent, five to seven persons; 13.4 percent, eight to ten persons; and 10.9 percent, eleven or more persons.[2] The available surveys do not consider the distribution of household size in relation to the variables of macrostatus and *thar*. Tables on average monthly expenditure in relation to household size, however, show that the larger households are not only correlated, as one would expect, with larger total monthly expenditures but also in a direct and regular correlation with increasingly higher per capita monthly expenditures. For example, households averaging 4.2 members spend fifty-three rupees (Rs. 53) per member per month, households with 7.7 members spend Rs. 67 per member per month, while the largest households averaging 17.5 members spend Rs. 84 per member per month. These larger households are the wealthier households, the houses at the upper levels of the status system. These are also the people with the largest houses, which are more likely to contain two or more closely related households. People living in the upper, say, 25 percent of the Bhaktapur macrostatus and economic system, from well-to-do farmers and up, may sometimes live in large family units of twenty or more people in a house, because of the larger households and the multiple households in a house.

The Nepal Rāṣtra Bank Survey also gives a rough overall idea of the average number of component "families" or "subfamilies" in a household. They define additional family units as those consisting of a married couple (with or without children) other than the identified head of the household and his spouse, or of a widowed man or woman with children. They found that 30 percent of households had a least one such additional unit, almost 30 percent of the multiunit households having two additional units, and 9 percent having three or four. The sample survey suggests that there are about 2,920 such subfamily units, living in the 6,494 households of Bhaktapur, dependent on or subordinate in some way to the household head. In accordance with the distribution of numbers of people in households, we may also assume that the larger and more prosperous and generally the higher the household is in the macrostatus system, the more likely it is to have a membership made up of such separate nuclei.

Thus from the upper strata of farmers and above, people are more liable to live in larger houses, in larger households, with more complexly nucleated household structures, and in close contact with closely related households. Most middle farming families and the levels below them tend to separate quickly into smaller and physically separated units as brothers marry. It would seem this has various consequences for other aspects of social organization, and for the differential developmental and family experience of people of both high and low status.

HOUSEHOLD ROLES

Roles of the family members within households ideally—and under the constraints of the ideal, as far as we can tell, to a considerable degree in fact—exemplify very general South Asian Hindu patterns.[3] In the Newars' own perspective there is, however, one major difference: the status of Newar wives compared to that of wives in the non-Newar Indo-Nepalese Hindu society, the Brahmans and Chetris, the Newar's most salient comparative model of Hindu family and social structure.

A summary report on family ideals resembles, not surprisingly, the domestic pole of fairy tales, the state that other forces threaten to derange, or that, if already deranged, is the yearned-for absent safe harbor. We can summarize briefly the norms that are shared with other Hindus. The father, most particularly when he is head of the household, is to be offered maximum respect and deference. As household head (a position that he will keep until he reaches old age and is moved off in a series of rites of passage [app. 6] into a semidivine role where he prepares for death and heaven or a good rebirth), he settles internal family problems and ultimately makes decisions for the household that affect the relations between the household and the outside world, particularly economic relations. There is a certain restraint between him and his children (in an emphasized contrast with the mother's brother) because, it is said, he has the difficult responsibility for making sure that his children behave properly in relation to the larger society, and any sentimental affection might weaken his authority and resolve.

Often the father is even cooler toward his daughters than toward his sons, and often withdraws still further from his daughters after they marry and leave the house. His sons, or some of them—the elder or eldest, at least—tend to stay with the household to help "support the lineage" through their work and their progeny. The respect due to the father is also due from younger sons and daughters to older sons, particularly the first-born, and very often that oldest son acts as the surrogate father, particularly as the father ages and the oldest son may begin to "act in the father's name."

In comparison with an interrelated variety of ways in which the Newar woman is less disadvantaged than the "northern Hindu" and Indo-Nepalese woman (below) a daughter's situation in the household is "high." Michael Allen (1982, 200) has summed this up in an essay on Newar girls' prepuberty rites:

> The high status of Newar women, at least as compared with that found in more orthodox Hindu communities elsewhere in the Himalayas and north India, is evident not only in the context of marriage and divorce, but in a wide range of other areas of social and religious life. Sons, though perhaps slightly preferred to daughters, especially in the case of the first born child, are not accorded the exaggerated importance found in most Hindu communities. There is no evidence of female infanticide,[4] either now or in the past, and the birth of a daughter is not in any way regretted.

The senior women in the household, particularly the *naki(n)* or female leader of the household, has the responsibility of supervising the general housekeeping and, especially in lower-level families, for a great deal of important economic activities—farming, weaving, basket making, and many specialized *thar* occupations. She is assisted by her daughters, and in particular by the wives of her sons. The *naki(n)* of the household has many ritual responsibilities in household worship and in rites of passage for family members. As wife, she is supposed to defer to her husband, treating him with public respect, particularly in upper status families, where she may bow to his feet at the start of the day. As a mother she is ideally, and to a large extent it would seem in actuality, indulgent and affectionate to her children.

The relationship between brothers and sisters is supposed to be intimate and warm.[5] After the sister marries, her brothers, usually represented by the eldest, will represent her natal household to her new family. The brother becomes her children's maternal uncle, their *pāju*, and his warm relationship with them will complement their own father's relative austerity.

WIVES AND HOUSEHOLDS

As the story unfolds, the true drama of the household tale begins with the arrival of a bride. Who is the Witch and who the Princess depends on whether the bride or the groom's parents, particularly his mother, is put at the center of the story.

While elder sons remain in their parental household, and younger sons may remain (and ideally should remain, permanently if possible) at least for a while after marriage as long as circumstances of economy, space, and temperament permit, daughters must marry out into other households. They enter these households as young wives. This sharp transition from daughter in one's "own home" (*tha chen*[*n*]) to wife has both general South Asian features and some special Newar emphases. For it is in relation to a daughter's marriage that traditional Newar culture resisted, as it were, the imposition of Indian forms and conserved some Himalayan patterns. This is most evident in certain of the rites of passage of girls, particularly the *Ihī* or mock-marriage ceremony and in related modifications of menarche ceremonies (app. 6), in the nature of the close continuing relationship between a wife and her natal home, and in the lack of the hypergamous implications of marriage characteristic of Indo-Nepalese groups, which we will discuss in a later section of this chapter. These differences are significant in the contrast of the Newars to neighboring groups, but from a non-Hindu perspective the married woman's situation is quite characteristically Hindu.

When a young woman becomes a wife, one of the more dramatic discontinuities of situation and role that are so characteristic of Bhaktapur is produced. A Pa(n)cthariyā man describes in an interview how his seventeen-year-old bride changed in the early days of their marriage.

> Before marriage she was like a bird, natural, but once she got married her behavior changed, because the environment changed. She didn't talk freely any more, she *couldn't* talk freely and frankly with everyone [in the household] and her face seemed very serious and complicated. And she was shy. Before that she was never shy. But after marriage she became shy with everybody. And her work was difficult. During her girlhood she didn't have to work. Now she has to work. She didn't have any practice before but she has to practice [i.e., learn how to do things] in my house. It was always like an experiment for her, and she was always distressed when she was working. If her cooking [for example] was not good, there would be trouble. She always has doubt in her mind, her life was complicated. And she became nervous.

An unmarried young woman from the Kumha:, potter, *thar* describes the duties of a young wife in the household:

> She gets up early in the morning, sweeps everywhere throughout the house. Then she goes to bring water [from the well or public tap]. After that she bows down to her father-in-law and her mother-in-law, and then she bows to her husband. Then she prepares the meal, whatever it is that is going to be served, and serves the meal to her father-in-law, mother-in-law and husband. Only after that can she eat herself. Then she does whatever work is necessary, like the sewing of clothes, or whatever her mother-in-law gives for her to do. Later in the day she again has to fix the noonday meal and serve it to her father-in-law, husband, and mother-in-law. Then she cuts up the vegetables, cleans them and cooks them. Then she has to get water again for dinner. Then she cleans the kitchen and prepares the rice [the supper meal]. She feeds her mother-in-law, father-in-law and husband and only after that is finished can she eat. Then she cleans the dishes and the cooking pots. After she has finished the kitchen work, she massages her father-in-law, mother-in-law, and husband with oil. Then she goes to sleep.

This is, at least, what a "good" wife does. If she is lazy or ill and doesn't do her work it is hard, the informant says, for the mother-in-law.

As elsewhere in India in such households the young husband and wife are not supposed to show any special interest, let alone affection, for each other. They rarely have a conversation in front of other members of the household. Often, however, in the secrecy of their room the husband may give the bride a small secret present, often some sweets or rich foods that he bought in the bazaar. Some women recall this as their first stirring of love for their husbands, and of the knowledge that he cared about her. This must be hidden from the household. The new wife "belongs to the household"; she is a threat to its closed, self-protective secrecy, and she is potentially divisive. If her husband cares for her more than for the household, she can, through him, stir up trouble between brothers or between parents and the son, and lead to a division of the household. Any obvious affection or concern shown to her in public by her husband would be a sign that he is vulnerable to this threat of a shifting loyalty. And any material present that he gives her privately is a diversion of household income.

The young bride is expected to relate herself primarily to her mother-in-law, whose "support" she is. She acts toward her husband with the same respectful gestures she uses to other senior members of the household. In strict and upper-status houses she will walk behind him, some ten feet or more, on the town streets, when they are going somewhere together. She and her husband call each other by neither their given names nor relational terms of address; circumlocutions must be used. A husband, for example, may be reduced to such devices as calling to his wife on the floor above, "The person who is upstairs, come down." Jyāpus sometimes refer to their wives by the name of the neighborhood they came from. The young wife finds herself treated as a low-status, potentially polluting, and potentially trouble-causing outsider. She is, as we will see, at the bottom of the family's hierarchical food-giving system as the symbolically salient low *thar*s—Jugī and Po(n)—are in the macrostatus system. Like them, she is polluting.

If there are family disputes, and particularly if there are schisms within the household ending up with one or more of the brothers establishing their own homes, one or more of the new brides is often blamed. People say such things as the separation is caused by a *phunga ki*, a pillow insect, the wife's talking in bed at night, and that if a man listens to his bride's opinions, "everything will be over." This is often scapegoating; it is easier for the household to put blame on the outsider, but in fact a tactful and skillful young wife can be very helpful in *helping* the household deal with the problems stirred up by her addition to the family, and some husbands are grateful about this when they later think about the early stages of their marriage.

As elsewhere in South Asia, the shift comes with the birth of the new wife's first child, particularly her first son. Now she becomes, in a phrase that is used repeatedly, the "supporter of the lineage (*kul*)." She has now a new relationship to the household through the child. She may refer to her conjugal family now as "my child's father's house." She begins to develop, often, and especially in households where the daughters have already married out of the household, warm relationships with her mother-in-law and father-in-law. Now that her relationship to the household is fully legitimate, her sexual and personal relationship to her husband is much less suspect. The father-in-law's relationship to his daughter-in-law is often warmer than that to his own daughter, and apparently in the majority of households warm working and personal relationships develop between the mother-in-law and the daughter-in-law after the birth of children. Often the birth of a second child augments this relationship, for the mother-in-law would take over much of the care of the first child at this point. The birth of a child binds the young wife to the household in another way. The child "belongs to the household" and for the wife to break up the marriage entails the risk of losing her children. The young wife becomes related to the inner life of the household, that which goes on within the walls of the house. In farming families she helps out with the farmwork and with supplementary crafts such as weaving, and in lower *thar*s women may be involved with the specialized activities of the *thar* (although mostly with supplementary activities). In upper-status families she would not (this is changing in recent years) be involved in the family trade or shop. She does not shop in the bazaar; this is a male activity. Her main duties are the care of the household and its internal maintenance and economy.

For the young wife the main time out of the household in the course of a day is when she goes to the river, well, or public tap to gather water, a time when she can chat with other young wives (fig. 5). She (and the older women) will also leave the household in connection with religious activities—visits to temples, community festivals, and to the households of kin for feasts associated with calendrical festivals, special household events, and rites of passage of the extended patrilineal family. During such events she will meet with the wider circle of her husband's kin.

She will also go to feasts involving the kin of her natal home, and as frequently is the case in South Asia, she often returns to her natal home after the birth of a child, usually one month after, and she and the child may remain there one, two, or even more months.[6] A wife is also expected to return to her parental house for special feasts, *nakhātyā*, which are associated with many festivals[7] and all rites of passage, including, importantly, the end of mourning sequences immediately following deaths in her natal household.

And, finally, as her children grow and as her mother-in-law and father-in-law age, the wife's security, prestige, and authority in her husband's household gradually increase and now either in her husband's natal household, or if there has been fission, in her own new household, she becomes in her turn another daughter-in law's mother-in-law.

Much of this is the usual Hindu family pattern. The Newars share it. What is diffierent is the contrast in a wife's relations to her own home, as well as in aspects of the meaning of marriage in general, which contrast with the Hindu social patterns of the Newar's neighbors. Also peculiar to the Newars in this contrast is the nature of the way the family is related to the larger kin group. We will return to this after first saying something about the household hierarchy, in which, in fact, the young wife has a peculiar position.

HOUSEHOLD HIERARCHY, AUTHORITY, AND PURITY AND THE *CIPA* SYSTEM

We have discussed the city-wide assignment of roles and their arrangements into hierarchical levels in chapter 5, and we will discuss the complex of ideas and actions concerned with purity, impurity, and purification in chapter 11. Hierarchy and purity are also used within the household—and as in the larger system primarily in relation to eating and drinking—to define and order household status. The hierarchy, and some assent to it, is also indicated by the use of respect gestures and language.

The male head of the household is called the "leader," the *nāya*:. On his death, or absence from the household, the succession for the new *nāya:* proceeds among males by age within ranked generations. That is, the title and role would pass from the head of the household through his progressively younger brothers living in the household even if the younger brothers in the father's generation were younger than one of the previous *nāya*:'s sons in the succeeding generation. Generation here takes precedence over relative age.[8] The actual leadership of the household is informally taken by someone else when old age, youth, or incompetence make the nominal leader unable to lead the household. The nominal leader would, if possible, however, maintain the ritual roles of the *nāya*:. The female religious leader of the house, the *naki*(*n*), will ordinarily be the wife of the *nāya*:. She will retain this title and its ritual functions even after the death of her husband, however, so that the wife of the new *nāya*: will not necessarily become the *naki*(*n*) if a senior wife (as ranked by the order of the husbands) is still alive, active, and competent.

Hierarchy in the daily life of the household is indicated in the way orders are given and accepted, and in a rough way in usages of respect language and gestures. Hierarchically arranged relative purity, the central idiom of the macrostatus system, is constantly signaled and enacted in the family in regulations regarding *cipa* (chap. 11). The term "*cipa*" designates food or drink that has become polluted because it or the utensil in which it is prepared or served has come in contact directly or more likely through the medium of fingers with a bodily pollutant, particularly saliva. That is, while a woman of the proper status level (and who is not temporarily "ritually" impure) will not pollute food while she is cooking it (as would a man or woman of lower level simply through touch), she would pollute it if she touched it after tasting it or if she put it in a utensil from which she had previously eaten and that had not been properly and traditionally cleaned. Most generally in practice this becomes a question of the sequence in which people are served and eat at each freshly prepared meal.

If someone of higher status in regard to *cipa* takes *cipa* from someone of lower status he or she is polluted and must purify himself or herself, albeit in a perfunctory way (chap. 11). In parallel to the pollution ideology of the macrostatus system, it is not polluting for a lower-status household member to eat a higher person's *cipa*, but on the contrary it is desirable and proper, particularly in the case of wives who *should* eat some of their husbands' *cipa*. Less prescriptively, more "naturally" the junior members of the household eat and are fed the *cipa* of their superiors. This, as such intake generally does (chaps. 5 and 11) indicates the sharing by the inferior person of the superior person's substance and his or her dependence and incorporation in a larger and superior "body."

The family *cipa* customs have a strong form among the more "orthodox" families (that is, "strict" Brahman families, and families in other *thars* who emulate them), primarily among the upper two status levels, and a weaker form among less orthodox families in those levels and among all families at lower levels. The key restraint that persists through the very lowest levels is that a husband will not eat his wife's *cipa*, but she will eat his. In the more orthodox families the constraints are more extensive. We may summarize the stronger regulations as follows: (1) each "ritually adult" male of the family will accept the *cipa* of all those of either sex older than he is, but not that of any younger member of either sex; (2) women (and girls) generally in the family will eat anyone's *cipa*, except (a), some very strict upper-status women will try to avoid eating their sons' or daughters' *cipa* (but this is rare) and (b) very generally at all levels, all women in the household will not eat the *cipa* of the wives of their sons or younger brothers; and (3) boys, before receiving their initiation into their *thars*, can eat the *cipa* of still youner boys and girls, and thus such boys—like girls whose younger brothers are unmarried—in fact have no *cipa* restraints.

In the weaker form of the system the father still will not accept his wife's *cipa*, but he will accept his children's *cipa*,[9] and all other members of the family will accept *cipa* among themselves. As noted, however, even in such households when the sons begin to marry and bring brides into the family, now at all levels, older siblings of both sexes as well as members of the older generation will not accept the *cipa* of the brother's or son's wife.

It is clear that the *cipa* system insists throughout on marking women who are brought into the patrilineal family from "outside." They become insiders to the system only to their own children, and to their husband's younger siblings to whom they have a quasi-maternal role, as he has a paternal role. In upper-level families a further hierarchical ordering of family members is added.

When we go beyond the case of the introduced wife, in the weak form there is no further family *cipa* discrimination. In the strong form, and if we exclude the case of the introduced wives—except for the most strictly "Brahmanical"—there is an internal gender asymmetry. Men and women accept the *cipa* of elder *women* who, in turn, accept theirs. Men and women accept the *cipa* of elder *men*, who do *not* accept theirs. There is probably a different significance in these two cases. The acceptance of superior women's *cipa* in the family reflects the position and meaning of the mother—in part shared by all elder household women—who is due honor, respect, and deference, which takes some of its sentimental meaning from its contrast with paternal, patrilineal, and macrostatus systems of order and deference. It is only the men who do not take inferiors' *cipa*, and thus follow the conditions that carves out status in the larger urban social system. In this sense it is really only the men, and among them those who have been initiated into *thar*, whose status is differentially defined by the system in the course of their accepting *cipa* from both men and women above them and rejecting it from those below. While everyone, like lower *thar*s in the macrostatus system, must be careful to avoid the moral error of contaminating those above them and compromising their superiors' statuses, for the women this is within the family (introduced wives aside) their *only* status concern. Thus the familial *cipa* system can now be said to (1) mark outside wives during the long period of slow integration during which they maintain their alien aspects, (2) honor mothers and maternal roles, (3) teach everyone how to conform to status generating behaviors, and (4) teach men how to assume differential status.

THE COMPARATIVE FREEDOM OF THE NEWAR WOMAN IN THE NORTHERN HINDU CONTEXT

The Chetri anthropologist Dor Bahadur Bista wrote that "the Newar woman in her husband's house has much more authority and freedom than her [Indo-Nepalese] Brahman or Chetri counterpart. She is readily accepted into the extended family group and adapts quickly to her new role in relation to the family and in particular to her husband" (1972, 24). This relative freedom within the Nepalese Hindu context is obscured in the first descriptions of a wife's role, with its implicit comparison to modern Western ideal forms.

The Newar family is in most respects what Karve (1968) has called a North Indian type, and which she takes to be a continuation of ancient Hindu patterns. "The present northern family is a continuation of the family of the ancient times with slight modifications. It is patrilineal, patrilocal and patriarchal. The marriage is generally outside of the kin-group and the local group. It is a joint family in which the brides are all brought from the outside and the girls are all given away. The behavior is strictly regulated according to generations, according to whether one is born in the family or married into the family and finally according to whether one is a man or a woman" (1968, 136). All this holds for the Newars, with the important exception of marriage outside the "local group."

The Newar kinship system, like the Newar family, is essentially, as we shall see (app. 3), a "Northern system." Karve (1968, 251) sets this Northern system in contrast with a Southern "Dravidian" system, in which a man can marry his younger female cross-cousins or a daughter of one of his elder sisters, producing—among other consequences—a freer, more comfortable position for women in their husbands' households:

> A man does not bring a stranger as a bride to his home, a woman is not thrown among complete strangers on her marriage. Marriage strengthens existing bonds. The emphasis is on knitting families closer together and narrowing the circle of the kin-group, a policy exactly the opposite of the one followed in the north. The whole tone of the southern society is different. The distinction between the father's house and the father-in-law's house is not as sharp as in the north. The distinction between "daughters" and "brides or wives" is not as deep as in the north. A girl's behavior in her husband's family is much freer. After all, her husband is either her uncle or her cross-cousin and his mother is either her own grandmother or her aunt. Neither is she separated for long periods from her parents' house.

The Newars have within a northern marriage and kinship system, partially subverted it, as it were, with the result of modifying the condition of women into a somewhat less patriarchal and patrilineal Hindu form. The "Northern" characteristics of a wife's separation from her natal home, physically through separation in space,[10] and socially through the loss of status of the wife's family in relation to the husband's family through "metaphorical hypergamy" (discussed below), are not present. The Newar wife's relationship to her natal home is strong in comparison with the North Indian and the Indo-Nepalese situations.

The continuing strong relation to the wife's natal home is inversely related to aspects of Newar marriage that weaken (again when compared with the North Indian pattern) the dominance of the husband's household. This, in turn, derives its ritual justification ultimately from a peculiar Newar rite of passage, the *Ihī* or mock-marriage to the god Viṣṇu/Nārāyaṇa (app. 6) and to associated modifications in menarche rites. The legends associated with these rites and the rites themselves reveal certain anti-Brahmanical and antipatrilineal biases. Their legendary origin was in an innovation introduced into the Kathmandu Valley by the goddess Parvatī, whose natal home it was, in order to prevent the disabilites of widows, a severe problem in the traditional Hindu social system, through the device of a first ritual marriage to a god. A woman's subsequent marriage to a mortal becomes a secondary marriage, and as her primary, true husband cannot die, she will never become a widow. The mock-marriage also weakens the ideological support for child marriages, that is, that a girl should be married and living in her husband's household prior to the onset of menstruation. Now it is necessary only to marry her to the god Nārāyaṇa before menarche.

With its ritual expression in the *Ihī* rite, the modified Newar marriage contrasts in fact with Chetri and other northern Hindu marriages in *relatively* easy separation and remarriage under certain circumstances, relatively little stigmatization and disadvantaging of widows, a lack of hypergamic stigma for the wife's family, and a wife's close continuing relations with her natal household.

NEWAR MENSTRUAL DISABILITIES IN COMPARISON WITH THE INDO-NEPALESE

Differences in comparative disabilities during their monthly menstruation is another way in which the Newar women feel themselves to have a better situation than Indo-Nepalese Chetri and Brahman women. A discussion of menstruation belongs most centrally to an examination of the "private lives" of Newars, but it may be useful to say something about it here in relation to the question of the comparative position of Newar women in relation to other Nepalese Hindus. Lynn Bennett's report on a Kathmandu Valley community of Indo-Nepalese women based on a study made at the same time as this present one suggested the extent of their stigmatization (Bennett 1983, 215):

> In Brahman-Chetri culture menstrual blood is a strong source of pollution—particularly to initiated males. During the first three days of every menses, women become polluted and untouchable. As one woman explained, "We

> become like female Damai. . . . We become like female dogs." For these three days a woman must not enter the kitchen, touch food or water that others will eat or drink, or even worship the gods or the ancestor spirits. She may not comb her hair or oil it, and she sleeps separately in a downstairs room. Also she may not touch an adult man. . . . The segregation of women during their menstrual periods is strictly observed. . . . Older informants told me that in the time of their mothers-in-law . . . women were hidden in a dark room away from the sun[11] . . . and out of the sight of all males for the first three days of their periods.

Bennett also notes that Brahman-Chetri women of Jumla in western Nepal "may not enter the house at all for three days and so they must sleep in a cattle shed or outside with a fire. Linda Stone reports that this rule holds also for the Brahman-Chetri women of Nuwakot" (Bennett 1983, 215).

According to both male and female informants, Newar women's restrictions in Bhaktapur are, in comparison to these examples (insofar as they may be representative of Indo-Nepalese practices now or in the past), considerably less. Menstruating Newar women in Bhaktapur do comb their own hair, and may continue to sleep in their usual place, although they sometimes go to another household woman's sleeping area to sleep. Most upper-status families reportedly do not let women cook during menstruation, although according to Jyāpu informants, in most Jyāpu and middle-level (and probably lower-level) families, menstruating women can cook everything except rice to be used for ceremonial purposes. In many *thar*s, including Pa(n)cthariyā and Chathariyā (but not Newar Brahmans), menstruating women attend ceremonial family feasts. At all levels menstruating women are not supposed to carry water or touch god images, sacred utensils, or priests. They are not supposed to pluck flowers used for religious offerings. In the farming *thar*s, menstruating women work on the farms, but are not supposed to touch certain plants (e.g., ginger, chili peppers, turmeric), which would be harmed by their touch.

During menstruation Newar women may worship deities in the same way that a polluted man (say, during the course of death pollution) would. If initiated, she will perform the necessary worship of the Tantric lineage god (in upper-status families), but away from the actual shrine, using a dish and uncooked rice (app. 4), and worshiping a mental image of the god. She may also perform daily worship in the same way, imagining the steps of the *pūjā* (app. 4). She may also perform what would ordinarily be household shrine worship at the side of the river. Women are supposed to eat rich foods during menstruation to prevent ill effects (including dizziness) from loss of blood. Cloths are used to absorb the menstrual blood, which are washed by the menstruating woman and kept for repeated use.

The period of contamination is supposed to last four days, following which the woman must purify herself and her sleeping area by bathing and cleansing with specially pure water—(*Ga*[*n*]*gā jal* [app. 4]). For upper-status women, they may have a more formal purification with services of a woman of the barber *thar* (chap. 11). After purification women have no further menstruation-related disabilities, with the exception that they are not supposed, at least in upper level *thar*s, to participate in commemorative worship to deceased ancestors during the six days following purification.

Intercourse is supposed to be discontinued from the onset of menstruation until the fourth day after onset, that is, after the purification. Men believe that if they have intercourse during the wife's menstruation they will become seriously and perhaps chronically ill. They fear contact with the menstrual blood. (Menstrual blood is regarded, apparently, more as a dangerous[12] and powerful rather than a disgusting substance.[13] As we will see in chapter 9, chapter 11, and elsewhere, "disgusting" versus "dangerous" is a significant distinction in Bhaktapur's symbolic world.)

All this echoes G. S. Nepali's (1965, 115) earlier report on other Newar communities:

> Menstrual impurity other than the first one [i.e., menarche rites] is not observed by the Newars as strictly as by the Gorkhās [the Indo-Nepalese]. During menses, a Gorkhā woman lives practically in isolation. On the fourth day after her bath she is considered clean. But still she is not allowed to touch water and attend to religious duties until the fifth day. Among the Newars, on the other hand, a woman during her menses can even attend to the domestic duties including kitchen. The only restriction imposed on her is that she should have her bath before attending to her normal duties. At the most she is forbidden to come in physical contact with objects of religious worship.

The details of menstrual practices vary among *thar*s within this general characterization. It is of great interest that one extreme exception was among the untouchable Po(n)s, among whom women must leave the inside of the house and go to the *cheli* (the porch or lowest story of the house which is considered outside the house) during their period of contamination, which lasts for six days, two days longer than for most Newar women.

We hope to deal elsewhere with the local doctrines explaining the origins of menstruation. It is not associated by our informants with bad *karma* or with a woman's own "sin." The widespread Hindu legend that it is one result of a great sin by Indra, his killing of a Brahman, is known but told in a considerably less misogynistic form than the version given by Bennett (1982, 216). It is said that menstruation represents the periodic draining of impurities from a woman's body. The male anxieties represented in interpretations of menstruation are, in short, more subtly and much more mildly expressed in the Newar response than in those of their Hindu neighbors.

A WIFE'S NATAL HOUSEHOLD'S RELATION TO HER CHILDREN: THE MOTHER'S BROTHER

Not only does a woman frequently return to her natal home, which is most often within Bhaktapur (and if not, often in a relatively nearby Valley community) and thus maintain close ties with it, but some members of her natal family will, after she has children, have important ceremonial, and very often, emotional and educational responsibilities to those children.

The central representative of the mother's natal household is her brother, whose relationship to his sister's conjugal family comes into being when she gives birth to her first child[14] and he becomes, for that child and for subsequent children, "the mother's brother," the child's *pāju*. All of the mother's biological and classificatory brothers are nominally *pāju*s (app. 3). They decide informally among them who will participate in particular ceremonies for their sister, and often several of them will go as household representatives to those feasts at their brother-in-law's house which include affinal kin. The lack of insistence on a hierarchy based on age among the *pāju*s is, perhaps, a significant exception to the usual emphasis on hierarchy by age within a generation in aspects of family organization involving the male lineage, and is congruent with a cluster of "maternal" meaning and emotion associated with the *pāju*.

The wife's natal house is for her always her "own house," her *tha che(n)*, but for her children and for her, by extension, when she is talking to or thinking about those children it is "mother's brother's house," *pāju che(n)*.[15] The birth of the first sister's first child produces a generational change in her natal household. Her brothers now become *pājus* and representatives of their household in its relations with allied households. For a *pāju* his sister's children whether male or female are his *bhe(n)cā*s (*bhi[n]cā* in Kathmandu and Patan Newari). As elsewhere in South Asia, a *pāju* has important functions in the rites of passage of his *bhe(n)cā* (app. 6).

The *pāju-bhe(n)cā* relationship, symbolized and strengthened in formal ceremonial actions, is of great importance for Newars. While the father, as we have noted, often acts toward a child relatively sternly because of his responsibility to assure his children's proper social behavior in the face of the extended family and the larger city, and in his representation of the restrictions of economic and social constraints, the *pāju* is usually warm and relaxed and, perhaps, a bit subversive with them. People tend to talk about their relation to their *pāju* in terms of love, rather than the respect and fear they felt for their father. Many children, particularly boys, spend parts of their childhood in their *pāju*'s household. Boys and girls (the latter probably less commonly) go to their *pāju*s for advice, comfort, and sometimes for financial support.[16] The *pāju* may act as an intermediary for his sister or her children with the father (and the patrilineal kin) if there is a problem about, for example, marriage, a career choice, or some serious household conflict. The *pāju* represents the moral authority of the wife's household in the protection of her interests. He functions to weaken the patriarchal authority of the patriline over the household and its children and represents "maternal" support for his sister's children in contrast to the strict demands of the patriarchy. He has a comparatively greater force than Hindu mother's brothers elsewhere because of the whole pattern of rituals and marriage forms giving some comparative independence and high status to Newar women, the lack of a hypergamic stigmatization of the wife's family, and again from the fact that spatial patterns of marriage ensure that they are not, usually, too far away. Men are, of course, fathers to their own children and at the same time *pāju*s to their sisters' children, in one of the many complex multiple positions characteristic of the city.

MARRIAGE

Dumont has remarked on the importance for South Asia of separating a "true and complete marriage" from other kinds of "marriage." He makes some terminological distinctions that are useful for a discussion of marriage in Bhaktapur (1980, 114 [original italics]):

> The only true and complete marriage whereby one moves from the category of an unmarried person to that of a married person is the first. But the cere-

> mony which effects this transition is especially important for the woman, and one must distinguish the case of a male from that of a female. In the case of a woman we shall call the first marriage the *primary* marriage. Once this marriage has been contracted, either it is indissoluble even by the death of the spouse (superior castes) or else the woman may, after her husband's death or even after divorce, contract another union, legitimate, but infinitely less prestigious, involving much less ritual and expense, which we shall call *secondary* marriage. Secondary marriage, being of lower status, is freer, sometimes much freer, than primary marriage. In the case of a man his first marriage becomes the *principal* marriage only if it bears him children, preferably sons. But a man has the option, either in the case of the barrenness of the first marriage, or freely in other castes (royal, etc.) of taking other wives, either with *full rite* (necessary for the wife if she has not been married before) or with *secondary* rite (if the wife has already been married). Thus for a man there are supplementary or *subsidiary* marriages, with a corresponding hierarchy of wives.

Dumont further notes that, "in various groups, in order to secure for women great freedom of [secondary] marriage or of sexual unions in general, primary marriage is, or rather was, reduced to a mere ritual formality. Sometimes women are married in this way to a god, an object, a fruit, or a man who immediately disappears from their lives" (1980, 118). Dumont, in fact, cites the Newar *Ihī* as one of his examples, although he erroneously believes that the consequences of the mock-marriage is to allow Newar girls "probably to have unions with men of inferior status" (ibid., 119).

The Newar mock-marriage is not, in fact, fully equivalent to a "primary" marriage, for the first "real" or "social" marriage still retains in its ceremonial and social implications most of the implications of primary marriage in contrast to any possible further, fully, and "really" "secondary" marriages. The mock-marriage has at least *some* of the force of a primary marriage, however, in that it allows the "real" marriage to be a postmenarche one, and in that it is associated with a somewhat greater liberality of divorce and with a considerably less disadvantaged position for women.[17]

Until the late 1950s the Newar Brahmans followed orthodox Hindu marriage practices rather than the Newar modification. They did not have mock-marriages, and were married to premenarche child brides.[18] In the later 1950s the Rājopādhyāya Brahmans decided to follow Nepalese law banning child marriage and to ease their restrictions on divorce and remarriage.

For non-Brahman Newars in the past (and for Newar Brahmans now) the great majority of social marriages take place when the girl is postmenarche. Some few premenarche marriages exist among farmers, where the motivation is said to be economic, for in a small and often poor family the bride will help with the work of her conjugal home. Such marriages are illegal under Nepalese law and are frowned upon even among other Jyāpus. It is said by Jyāpu informants that the ideal age for a woman's marriage among them should be between sixteen and eighteen. Before sixteen she is too young to work and to be of much help in her husband's house,[19] and if she marries too much later than eighteen, it is said that her children will be still too young to help their father at the time in his life when he ages and will need help in his farming. The Jyāpu husband should be somewhat older, between the ages of, say, twenty and twenty-three, among other reasons because "it will be easier for them to manage a younger wife, who will fear them." The daughters of *sāhu*—Chathariyā, Pa(n)cthariyā, and those lower *thar*s who are in business and shopkeeping—are said to marry later, often at twenty-two or twenty-three.[20]

For his "principal" (to use Dumont's terminology) marriage, that is, for the vast majority of marriages, a man will marry a woman who has not been married before (with the exception of the *Ihī*), who is within the proper intermarrying macrostatus level, and who is at the proper exogamous distance. The marriage ceremony will be a "major marriage ceremony," modified somewhat from the orthodox Indian marriage ceremony to take the *Ihī* into account (app. 6).

People are forbidden to marry within an extended and active patrilineal group, the *phukī* (below), and more vaguely within larger groups thought to have a significant and close patrilineal connection, to be the same patrilineage or *kul*. Such larger exogamous units are distinguished within different *thar*s in different ways. Tracing degree of relationship and permissible and impermissible unions through female lines is more difficult, as it is not revealed in present organization, and has to be based on genealogical information. Ideally, any relationship derived from the out-marriage of any woman of the *kul* within less than six generations (the seventh generation being permitted) is forbidden. In practice, no objection is made after five generations if there is some "good reason" for that particular marriage.[21]

Almost all the *thar*s marry within Bhaktapur by preference, and often within the same part of the city.[22] Almost all marriages are still arranged. The availability and qualities of potential spouses are first discussed among informal networks of friends and relatives. Ideally, as elsewhere in South Asia, a wife should be modest and shy, respectful to elders, in good health, and willing and able to work as necessary in the particular *thar*. She should not have any disfigurements, particularly skin diseases, the facial scars of smallpox having been considered particularly disadvantageous. A prospective son-in-law should be able to support his wife through his own efforts or his household situation. He should be of good moral character, a support to his own family, and not a gambler or a heavy drinker. He should be good-natured, and not irritable and potentially abusive to his wife. The reputation and behavior of the other household members, and the extended-family group, the *phukī*, are also of great importance. Immorality, crime, insanity, scandal anywhere in this group will affect the desirability of all its members.

After an informal decision has been made, a representative of the man's household, a *lāmi*, is chosen from among family or friends, and begins a more formal investigation of the potential bride's nature and situation. Eventually, if she seems acceptable, the *lāmi* approaches her family to discuss the prospects, and later the arrangements, for the marriage. A symbolic sequence begins at this point which in a number of phases gives the marriage increasing social reality; we will discuss the sequence in relation to rites of passage (app. 6).

In the past the perspective spouses did not see each other before the marriage ceremony, although they usually had some idea about each other from networks of friends or relatives. They could refuse when the marriage was proposed, but this was reportedly quite rare. Now it is customary for the couple to see each other, often at a mutual friend's house, before the arrangement reaches a formal phase, a meeting that may provoke objections to the marriage.[23]

There were always "love marriages" in the past, as there are now. These are marriages that were in violation of the parents', or *phukī* members' wishes, and were motivated by romantic love or, sometimes, by pregnancy. As long as these were within the acceptable macrostatus marrying sections, they usually became acceptable to the couple's families. Only marriages violating these regulations caused a rupture of family and *thar* relationships. Incestuous marriages within the bounds of kin exogamy would be "a great sin" or crime, *mahā aparādha*, and would result in outcasting and banishment.

The bride's family will provide a dowry and will also bear the expenses of the first portion of the sequence of marriage ceremonies, which take place at her house. The groom's family will have the expenses of the subsequent major marriage ceremonies and feasts. They also provide presents to the bride, which include (particularly among farmers) substantial quantities of gold jewelry. If a husband divorces a young wife, or forces her to leave him, and if this is not considered to be through her fault, she has the right to take back her dowry and keep the jewelry she has been given. If she leaves the household because of her own dissatisfaction (an attribution that the wife's family may dispute, and that may require arbitration), she forfeits these. Among some Jyāpu groups some of the wife's dowry is withheld by her family until after she has borne a child, a guarantee that the marriage will probably be permanent. It is estimated that the total expenses of the bride's side and the groom's side at the time of marriage are about equal, or, in the case of Jyāpus, somewhat higher for the groom's family.

While the contribution from the bride's side is overtly said to be a dowry, a payment for taking the daughter, the expenses of the groom's side are interpreted as indicating the ability and commitment of the groom's family to the continuing support of the bride. The groom's side also gives gifts to the bride's family in the course of the ceremonial sequence preceding the marriage. Among some *thar*s these involve substantial cash gifts. G. S. Nepali, in a discussion of such gifts among the Newars, notes that when cash offerings are given in lieu of "symbolic" offerings of sweets by the groom's family, "though the payment of cash is looked down upon by the society, since it amounts to paying for a wife, it has not diminished at any rate; and it is a favoured practice among the poor. There is no social sanction against it, except the moral disapproval" (1965, 215). The moral disapproval comes from Brahmanical ideology of the wife as a free gift or offering, a *kanyā dāna.* In actual practice for all except the most Brahmanical families, there seems to be a balancing of both symbolic and material calculations of the value of the marriage transaction to both the giving and the receiving families. Among the middle and lower levels, where the economic value of the wife is most clear, there is an additional emphasis on the tentativeness of the contribution from the bride's side, as it protects her and will be returned if she is rejected by the groom's family. Dumont (in a comment on a claim of L. S. S. O'Malley for Bengal that "bridegroom price" characterized high hypergamous castes; and "bride price," low castes) remarks that it may be supposed for Bengal, as elsewhere, that "there is an *exchange* of prestations, in which the tangible prestations dominate in one or the other direction (Dumont 1980, 379). In the Newar case the general emphasis on equality of prestations corresponds to an emphasis on isogamy.

There exists, relatively rarely among upper levels and somewhat more frequently among farming *thars*, "barter" marriages, *hilābulā*, between two households, in which a son and daughter from one household respectively marry a daughter and son from another.[24] Much less wealth needs to be amassed by the participating families in these cases (cf. G. S. Nepali 1965, 215).

A couple will be married in an elaborate set of ceremonies for a principal marriage (app. 6) and a simpler set for subsidiary ones. The vast majority of marriages are monogamous and endure until one of the partners dies, the survivor living on as a widow or widower. However, the marriage may break up in one way or another for other reasons than death or may be altered by the husband taking a second, additional wife.

Hindu societies, while making it relatively easy for the husband or his family to dissolve a marriage, have severely limited or prohibited a wife's right to divorce. The Newar woman's relative freedom to dissolve her marriage compared to other, including neighboring Nepalese, Hindu groups have led, among those accustomed to standard Hindu practices, to exaggerated statements regarding her freedom and her "licentiousness." Kirkpatrick wrote in 1793 (comparing the Newars and the matrilineal Nayars of Kerala, as is still frequently done), that "It is remarkable enough that the Newar women, like those among the Nairs [Nayars], may, in fact, have as many husbands as they please, being at liberty to divorce them continually on the slightest pretenses" ([1811] 1969, 187). Francis Hamilton visited the Kathmandu Valley a few years later during a fourteen-month period in 1802/03. His remarks on the Newar women are also a mixture of realities, misunderstandings, and prejudice. We can identify the probable source of the prejudice in one Ramajai Batacharji, who accompanied Hamilton on his visit. Batacharji was "an intelligent Brahman from Calcutta, whom I employed to obtain information, so far as I prudently could, without alarming a jealous government, or giving offense to the Resident, under whose authority I was acting" (Hamilton [1819] 1971, 1). Newar manners, Hamilton/Batacharji remarks, are "chiefly remarkable for a most extraordinary carelessness about the conduct of their women" (ibid., 29); to wit:

> The Newar women are never confined. At eight years of age, they are carried to a temple and married with the ceremonies usual among Hindus to a fruit called Bel.[25] When a girl arrives at the age of puberty, her parents, with her consent, betroth her to some man of the same caste and give her a dower,

> which becomes the property of the husband, or rather paramour. After this, the nuptials are celebrated with feasting and some religious ceremonies. Among the higher casts [castes] it is required that girls should be chaste till they have been thus betrothed; but in the lower casts, a girl, without scandal, may previously indulge any Hindu with her favours, and this licentiousness is considered a thing of no consequence. Whenever a woman pleases, she may leave her husband; and if, during her absence she cohabits only with men of her own cast or of a higher one she may at any time return to her husband's house, and resume the command of the family. The only ceremony or intimation that is necessary before she goes away is her placing two betel nuts on her bed.[26]

Hamilton ([1819] 1971, 42f.) further writes:

> So long as a woman chooses to live with her husband he cannot take another wife until she becomes past child bearing; but a man may take a second wife when his first chooses to leave him or when she grows old, and at all times he may keep as many concubines as he pleases. A widow cannot marry again, but she is not expected to burn herself, and may cohabit with any Hindu as a concubine. The children, by the betrothed wife, have a preference in succession to those by concubines. The latter, however, are entitled to some share. A man can be betrothed to no woman except one of his own cast, but he may keep a concubine of any cast whose water he can drink.

This kind of view of Newar practices, which starts with a perception of relative differences, and then salaciously exaggerates them, still is held by some non-Newar Nepalis about the Newars, and, indeed, *mutatis mutandis*, suggests the way upper-status Newars regard the morals and nature of women in the lower Newar *thar*s—and the way all Newars seem to think about what they take to be the free behavior of women among northern hill peoples. We can find some basis for such reports in some persisting present practices. Other aspects may have referred to practices of particular *thar*s at the time, or may have been based on misunderstandings. What was fundamentally distorted, however, was the romantic picture of liberty or anarchy.

G. S. Nepali (1965, 247ff.) provides some indication of the amount of separation and remarriage among 734 Newar men and women in 1957/58. Among his 353 male informants, 13.3 percent of their marriages had ended in separation. Some 40 percent of those separations were by formal divorce and the remaining 60 percent, by informal separation. Among his women informants 14.4 percent of their marriages were reported as ending in separation. Of these, about 15 percent were reported as ending in formal divorce and 85 percent in informal separation. Among the men some 72 percent of the men whose marriages had ended in separation remarried, as did about 41 percent of the women.[27] Nepali's tables do not indicate to what degree divorce or separation was initiated by the husband or the wife, but his discussion implies that many of the nondivorce separations, at least, involve desertion by the wife. Nepali's survey of divorce and separation suggests, in fact, that marriage among the Newars, if not as fluid as reported by Hamilton, is relatively fragile. We do not have statistics on separation and divorce for contemporary Bhaktapur; it is very possibly similar to Nepali's rates, and almost certainly significantly higher than for non-Newar Hindu Nepal.

"Divorce" is usually referred to in phrases using the word "*pār*" or "*pā*," which in other phrases signifies the conclusion of a transaction by making a final payment. Simple separation is phrased in various ways, often simply as *totā beigu*, "to let go of." Until recently neither marriage nor divorce had a clear legal status under Nepalese national law, which followed the varieties of local customary law. Bennett, in a study of the relations of both traditional and national law to the situations of Nepalese women, writes "Under the present [National Civil] Code, the performance of any form of wedding ceremony or simply evidence of sexual relations (even as a single event) can amount to marriage" (1979, 46). A "divorce" implies the consent of both parties and their kin to the separation, initiated by some kind of formal discussion. The one who wishes to dissolve the marriage obtains permission, often in writtern form, from the spouse or the head of the spouse's household or patrilineal extended-family group, the *phukī*. The wife must agree to leave the household; if she objects to this and resists a separation, the husband may use various means to force her out. Previously, and still in some *thar*s, the simplest way for a man to separate from his wife was to leave her at her natal home when she returned there for a visit; she was not supposed to return to her conjugal home from these visits unless a member of the husband's household came to fetch her. Another device the husband or other members of his household can use to force a separation is to begin to mistreat the wife and provoke quarrels with her, thus attempting to make her decide to return to her natal home. If the wife wishes to initiate the separation, it is simpler: all she has to do is to leave her husband's house.

Separation is complicated for both husband and wife if there are children. They belong to the father's household, and will be raised by the women there. This is general in Hindu Nepal. "Nepalese law considers the right of child custody as well as the duty to maintenance of the child as the right and liability of the father. A mother has no right upon the issue she has given birth to. The law is based on the Hindu concept of woman as *jaya* or one who bears children for her husband. The mother simply gives birth to children for her husband" (Shilu Singh, quoted in Bennett [1979, 64]). The comparative special rights of Newar women do not include rights over the possession of their children.

There is less social stigma attached to an agreed-upon separation, a divorce, than to a unilateral separation. A "divorced" woman is free of the insults and interference that might come from her husband's home if she were only separated, and still in some sense belonged to the household. Divorced or separated, all parties can remarry, however, with a simplified ceremony of remarriage, which, as the figures cited from G.S. Nepali (above) indicate, is frequently done.

The most frequent reasons given for breakdown of marriages in Bhaktapur are, as everywhere in Hindu families, one or another of the difficulties of fitting a new wife into the husband's household, that is, her relations with various family members other than her husband, particularly her mother-in-law.[28] Such problems may arise and cause the marriage to break up even if (and sometimes to some degree because) the husband and wife may like each other and are close to each other. Modernization has produced a different kind of marital problem. In the course of higher education or professional careers young Bhaktapur men and (more rarely) women of the upper levels often meet potential lovers or spouses—sometimes from other communities and ethnic groups—who are attractive to them often because they share more modern values and interests. These men and women have often been previously married in an arranged marriage with a spouse who (again, this is the case particularly for the men) has a more limited, traditional, and conservative upbringing and experience. Although the families have approved and arranged such marriages, the spouse becomes a target of the husband's (or wife's) resentment. The wife and her children have close relations with others in the household, but the husband (who may have a "girlfriend" outside the household) will be cooly proper and more than conventionally distant from her. Occasionally such marriages also end in separation.

REMARRIAGE AND MULTIPLE MARRIAGE

Following separation, divorce, or the death of his wife, a man may, usually in the case where there are no children (or no surviving children), enter a new principal marriage, that is, a marriage for producing children for the support of the lineage and the household. In this case there would usually be, as in a first marriage, a major marriage ceremony. It would be a primary marriage for his new wife and the marriage would be as carefully arranged as was the first marriage.

A woman, following separation, divorce, or widowhood, can marry again, but this would be, for her, a (truly) secondary marriage, and she would have a minor marriage ceremony. In this respect it does not matter whether her previous marriage had been terminated formally, in divorce or death, or simply through an informal separation.[29] We may note again here that widows can remarry, and the younger ones, at least, often do. This is in the context of the relative lack of social or ritual stigma attached to Newar widowhood. It was, as we have noted, specifically to prevent the problems and stigmatization of widowhood characteristic of other Hindu communities that, in local legand, the *Ihī* ceremony was founded by Parvatī, whose natal home was the Himalayan area, and who had been given the Kathmandu Valley by her father for her dowry.

Whatever the form of marriage or of marriage ceremony the woman becomes a *misā*[30] or "wife." In the case where there are (at once or in sequence) more than one they are often designated as first wife, *ha:thu*, and later wife (or wives) *lithu*. One common explanation for a multiple marriage, that is, where the first wife is kept in the household and a *lithu* added, is a failure to have children, which is almost always ascribed to barrenness of the first wife and not the sterility of the husband. In most cases when a second wife is taken for this purpose, the first wife (who is otherwise likely to be a satisfactory wife and daughter-in-law) remains in the household.[31] Multiple marriage for this reason is relatively common in Chathariyā and Pa(n)ctharīyā households where the household can afford the expense of marrying and maintaining another wife. Farming households sometimes take second wives even if there are children by the first marriage, if the first wife is, for example, chronically ill and unable to help sufficiently with the household and farmwork. They may also do so sometimes even if the first wife is healthy if there are large farm holdings and a second wife could profitably help in the farmwork. Other additional marriages, which are considered permissible but by many as not really "decent," are those initiated by (and "for the sake of") the husband, not the household, and explained variously as owing to the first wife's lack of sexual attractiveness or the man's excessive sexual lust, or because of some dislike for his first wife in a situation where separation for one reason or another is difficult.

Polygamous marriages are generally considered to be stressful for everyone concerned, particularly if there are children from both wives. They are confined to wealthier households and compared to non-Newar Hindu Nepalis seem to be relatively rare. Lynn Bennett, in her study of an Indo-Nepalese Hindu community, reports that among eighty-eight married men, seventeen had more than one wife, several had three wives, and one man had five (1977, 327). In contrast, G. S. Nepali (1965, 237) found among 256 married Newar men only eight who had more than one wife.[32] The relative lack of polygamy among Newars in spite of their comparative wealth is another aspect of the Newar wife's relatively superior status in Hindu context.

THE LACK OF HYPERGAMIC IMPLICATIONS OF MARRIAGE

In marriages that are not "principal marriages" undertaken for purposes of having children "to support the household and lineage," a man *may* take a wife from a somewhat lower macrostatus level. Newar marriage is for the principal marriage rigidly (and for subsidiary marriages more often than not) isogamous. Lynn Bennett, in her study of Nepali Indo-Nepalese Brahmans and Chetris, notes that although they do not have formal hypergamy (and, in fact, cannot, in that neither the Brahmans nor the Chetri have ranked "clans"), they have a marked informal—what Bennett calls an "*ad hoc*"—hypergamy. She relates this to Dumont's statement about India that the "hypergamous stylization of wife-takers as superior and wife-givers as inferior pervades the whole culture" (Dumont 1964, 101).[33] Among the Indo-Nepalese Brahmans and Chetri "marriage itself creates a ritual superiority of the groom's people—and hence a hypergamous situation—where there was formerly equality" (1977, 264). Bennett discusses various ritual and social interactions that indicate the inferiority of a male "vis-à-vis groups to which his father had given a sister or to whom he has given a sister or a daughter. . . . On the other hand, he is superior to the groups from which his mother and his wife and his son's wife have come and they must respect him" (1977, 264).[34]

This status difference between giving and receiving families is denied in discussion and in action in the Newar system. Among any two fathers-in-law, for example, the eldest is the one given the highest status. There are ways of denying and reducing any possible covert implication of the superiority of the groom's family in the relation of a wife's father to his son-in-law. He may, for example, use his son-in-law for menial tasks. For example, if the father-in-law is involved in some important family ceremony, he will often ask a son-in-law to supervise the family shop. Among the farmers, when the father-in-law is planning a large family feast, it may be his son-in-law who is expected to travel throughout Bhaktapur giving oral invitations to the prospective guests. In middle-level *thar*s, after certain of the initiation ceremonies for boys, during which they are purified by having their heads shaved, it is often one of the husbands of a "daughter of the house" who is expected to take the hair cuttings to the river and dispose of them. Such use of a woman's father's sons-in-law and, in contrast to the Indo-Nepalese, the lack of any ritual or social indication of "*ad hoc*" hypergamy, indicate the absence among Newars of even informal overt hypergamic patterns.

ADOPTION AND MARRIAGE

The major cause for a multiple marriage, and one of the major reasons contributing to divorce or separation, is the wife's failure to produce children for the household and the lineage. When a childless marriage is otherwise satisfactory, the household sometimes considers adopting a son. The adopted son, called a *dharma putra* or *dharma kāe*, would most likely be taken from the patrilineal extended family, the *phukī*, but people can also, but less desirably, take a boy related through the out-marrying women of the patriline, a sister's son, or (in the case where a man has daughters, but no surviving son) a married daughter's son. The *dharma kāe* would often but not necessarily, live with and have his economic support from the adopting family. As a *phukī* member, he would not change his ritual relation to the lineage and lineage gods by being moved to another household—except that he would have a son's special ritual responsibilities in the case of death of his adopting parents. If the son is adopted from a daughter or sister, he will most frequently remain in his natal family, or if he does live in his adoptive home, will return there for important family ceremonies and for his own rites of passage. He belongs to his genitor's, his biological father's lineage, and is involved in the worship of his biological father's (and not his adoptive father's) lineage gods. However, he has the additional ritual function of being centrally involved in the death ceremonies for his adoptive parents. Adoptive sons are taken when very young, perhaps one to three years of age. They are always middle sons, as the eldest son is supposed to do death ceremonies for his father and (among some *thar*s) the youngest for his mother in their natal families.

Adoption is, in fact, extremely rare, and I could find no cases in the families of my informants. G. S. Nepali did not find any cases among 224 families he studied, nor was he able to identify any cases in a study of the village of Panga (1965, 97). Direct ties of biological descent are strongly emphasized,[35] and childlessness is dealt with whenever possible by remarriage.

MAJOR KIN GROUPINGS: (I) *KUL, PHUKĪ*, AND THEIR WOMEN

Terminology as well as ritual and social relations distinguish two large groups of kin for each individual. First are those most closely associated with the *phukī*, a group of men agnatically related through the paternal lineage plus those of their women who are married to them, or fathered by them and (for most purposes) still unmarried. The other group of kin are those who have become related through marriage of women into and out of the patrilineal group, the *tha:thiti*, discussed in the next section.

The household is embedded in these two groups. Individuals include as their intimate kin not only their nuclear segment of the household and the larger household itself but also another group that has members from both larger kin groupings. These are the "*syaphu*(*n*)" or "*syasyaphu*(*n*)," the people "one cares most about, to whom one is closest." The word "*sya*" (*phu*[*n*] means "people") is given various local etymologies and thought to be derived from *syā gu*, to hurt ("thus people whose pain one feels also") or from *sya*: (bone marrow, "as close to one as marrow to bone"). People, when asked to list *syāphu*(*n*), characteristically begin with nuclear family members, then add others in the household, and then mother's brother (*pāju*) and his household, father's sister (*nini*) and her household, their own married sisters and their children, and last (and in the case of men not always included) their own spouses. Special ties of affection or circumstance may enlarge, this list in various ways.

The largest patrilineal unit[36] is all those people who are thought to descend from a common male ancestor, whose men (and unmarried women) share the same surname, and who are forbidden to marry each other.[37] Such a unit has been called a patrilineal exogamous "clan" (e.g., Fürer-Haimendorf 1956). As we have remarked, this unit is not equivalent to a *thar*. A *thar may* be a "clan," in that its members believe they have the same name and constitute a social and occupational unit because they have descended from one man (this is most often the case among the Chathariyā and Pa(n)ctharīyā), but in many *thars* the shared name and group membership is believed by *thar* members to derive from a common origin in some profession or historical group. These latter *thars* will often have within them intermarrying sections. There is no unambiguous local term for a "clan," but it is often referred to as a *kul* (from the Sanskrit *kula*, meaning group, family, lineage).[38] "*Kul*" refers to either a patrilineage throughout time, or in other contexts, to the living members of that lineage, usually to the male members of that lineage, although, as is the usage with "*phukī*" (see below), it may include certain female members. Usually "*kul*" is used in a limited sense to refer to one segment of patrilineally related kin, the *phukī*, but in certain contexts refers to the maximal unit, a cluster of *phukī*s that had split into separate *phukī* units in the past, but whose historical connections are remembered and given some ritual representation in the worship of common lineage gods. The *kul* as a "clan" has the characteristics that have been noted for such units elsewhere in Hindu South Asia. "It is a grouping rather than a group, a taxonomic category rather than the basis for joint action. . . . [It] is mainly used to classify *jāti* fellows into eligible and ineligible spouses" (Mandlebaum 1970, 135).

G. S. Nepali (1965, 253) wrote that:

> The Newar joint family [the household unit] has specific characteristics which make it distinct from the normal Hindu joint family. Despite residential and property separation, several joint families act as a single unit among them for purposes of social and ceremonial functions, be it domestic or communal.

This unit is the *phukī*, for almost all purposes except exogamy the broadest patrilineal unit of social importance.[39] Each *phukī* is made up of groups of households, often living in close proximity, who are brothers and/or the male descendants of brothers who had split off from a single ancestral paternal household in a relatively recent period. Although, like all members of the same *kul*, they share *kul* marriage prohibitions, what characterizes them as a group is that they, or rather the leaders representing each household, meet to consider the affairs of their constituent households, particularly marriage, divorce, and economic or legal difficulties. They act together as a major moral and ritual unit. They worship the same lineage gods on the same day of the year in the same place (chaps. 8 and 9). They unite for the performance of major rites of passage for *phukī* members (and for the feasts associated with them) and share major pollution entailed by the death (and to a more limited degree by birth) of any of their members. The sharing of ritual duties, particularly the prolonged death pollution, is one of the limits to the number of households that can conveniently constitute a *phukī*. If it were too large, everyone would be continuously occupied in the rites of passage of members, and often in major, socially disabling pollutions. When a *phukī* is sensed to be too large, members begin to look for a confirming sign from the lineage gods or from the deified ancestors of the *kul* that it is a proper time to split the *phukī*.

In the upper level *thars*, at least, *phukīs* seem to split when they have more than twenty member families. People estimate the typical upper-level *phukī* group to consist of fifteen to twenty families. Lower level *thars* may have many less families in a *phukī*.[40] The split segments are called *bāphukīs*, or "split *phukīs*." They will use the same shrine for their annual lineage god worship, but will worship on different days now, and they will no longer be affected by pollution caused by birth and death in the other *bāphukī*. And now each will confine itself to discussion and regulation of the affairs only of its own member families.

The term "*phukī*" is used in some contexts to mean only the men (and in its most limited usage only those men who have had their initiation into their *thar* or lineage), and in this usage people speak of the women associated with the *phukī* as the (1) "daughters of the *phukī*" (the still unmarried women) and (2) the "women who have come into the *phukī*" (the wives of members). Sometimes, however, the word "*phukī*" is used to include these women. Daughters and sisters who marry "out" into other *phukīs* are no longer members of the *phukī* in strict definition, and as they are also not members of the other large category "feminal kin" are in an in-between category.

There is a decision-making *phukī* council made up of the male heads of the component households. Its members are ranked by the same principle that ranks male members of a household by age within successive generations. The senior member of the *phukī* council, the *phukī thakali* or *nāya:*, and his wife, the *phukī naki(n)*,[41] have ceremonial roles in all rites of passage, and other ceremonies involving *phukī* members. The organization and functions of the *phukī* council vary by *thar*, as does its integration into still larger organizations representing the *thar*.[42]

MAJOR KIN GROUPINGS: (II) FEMINAL KIN, *THA:THITI*

Those people who are related to an individual through all links of marriage with that person's *phukī* members form a large group with amorphous outer limits called the *tha:thiti*.[43] This is a heterogeneous group. At the center of it are the members of the mother's natal household and the husbands and children of one's own household's outmarrying daughters.[44] For a man, all *tha:thiti* are related through a woman at the proximal link, and this is also the case for a woman, with the important exception that she becomes related to her husband's *tha:thiti* through her marriage to him. In this case, however, it is a woman's movement out of her natal home that creates the link. All these links involve the medium of a woman who has married either into or out of the patrilineage. Mandlebaum (1970, 148) suggests the useful term "feminal kin" for this kind of cluster.

Each married individual has a unique constellation of *tha:thiti*, and the potential ramifications are enormous but are, in fact, generally limited to at least moderately close connections whose extent varies with the particular reason for using or gathering these kin. Newars say that the close contact with a large circle of *tha:thiti* for whom they feel familial "*love*" (*māyā*) is an important way in which they differ from the Chetris.

"*Tha:thiti*" is sometimes used as the only available term of reference for an affinal relative who has no other specific kin term of reference, or whose "proper" classificatory name is unclear to a particular individual. The central core members of the *tha:thiti* have ritual functions in rites of passage of household members; some segment of the wider group is invited to certain of the household feasts, *nakhatya*, those that are centrally characterized by the return of married-out daughters to their natal homes.

PHUKĪ AND *THAR*

The *phukī* is for almost all purposes the largest kin organization significant for the ceremonial and social organization of individual households. On some occasions, as we have noted, representatives of two or more *phukī*s will join to discuss some problem affecting a *kul* as a whole. For those *thar*s that consist of groups of *kuls*, it would be only an extremely unusual circumstance relating to some problem for the entire *thar* that would bring all *phukī* (or *kul*) leaders together. Most of those affairs within a *thar* that traditionally do require the cooperation of groups larger than *phukī* are the business of cooperative organizations called *guthi*, discussed later.

Each *thar* differs in size, internal composition, and organization. The study of the political organization and function of *phukī*s in relation to *thar* organization remains to be done.

RITUAL FRIENDSHIP AND FICTIVE KINSHIP

As elsewhere in South Asia, the patrilineal kin group can be extended through a ritual in which a man's close male friend becomes his "ritual brother," and, in a special Newar emphasis, a girl's female friend may become her "ritual sister." In becoming ritual siblings, they become subject to the same marriage restrictions, at least in relation to close kin, as a biological or classificatory "brother" or "sister." This ritual friend or fictive sibling is called a *twāe*. A man refers to or respectfully calls his *twāe* "*twāe ju*" (*ju* is a term of respect), while a woman calls hers "*twāe bhata*."[45] Women conventionally and usually form these relationships at the time of their mock-marriages, whereas men form them at any time during their lives. The formation of ritual friendship was very common for both sexes in the past, but it is now less common for men. It allowed men to further cement a friendship (friendships, in their contrast to the heavy moral pressures and emphases on correct behavior in kin relations, are of particular importance for people in Bhaktapur), or, for men in business, to put a business relationship on a kin-like basis.[46] *Twāe ju* and *twāe bhata* are invited to major *phukī* feasts, and may optionally be included in smaller *phukī* feasts or non-Tantric ceremonies.

Twāe relations have one interesting peculiarity. They do not have to be at the same macrostatus level and are often, in fact, outside of the level within which one can marry or share boiled rice and pulses—although they would not be made between clean and unclean levels. This means that like friendship itself and like the mock-marriage, they are part of a larger segment of Bhaktapur life and symbolism that is organized in contrast and sometimes in opposition to its otherwise orthodox Brahmanical hierarchical structure.

KINSHIP TERMINOLOGY

We have placed an extended presentation of Bhaktapur's kinship terminology and a discussion of its relation to other North Indian kinship terminologies in appendix 3, where it may be used for reference. We will restrict ourselves here to some remarks on the relation of that terminology to the categories of kin we have taken note of in the preceding sections.

Many of the terms in the Newar kinship system designate very large classes of kin; a whole generation of consanguineous and affinal male kin may be designated as "brothers," "grandfathers," "grandchildren," and so on. However, much smaller segments of these classes are usually at issue in the discussions and actions of ordinary life. The segment involved is, as always in such classificatory systems, indicated by the context in which the term is used, and/or by various verbal devices. Thus, by adding terms designating "one's own," (*tha:*) or "true/real" (*khās* or *sākhai*, terms derived from Nepali or Sanskrit), one can designate a "biological" nuclear mother, father, or sibling within the larger class and can designate a biological mother's biological brother or biological father's biological sister in the same way. For siblings these terms specify that the siblings share the same father. If it is necessary to distinguish a common mother of two siblings, terms indicating birth from the same maternal "abdomen," such as *chaga pwā*, are used. Such terms and various contexts of use discriminates "ego's" (the person in relation to whom a set of kinship terms have their meanings) core family.

The next larger grouping that is commonly distinguished is that segment of the various generations of kin who belong to ego's patriline, his *kul* and *phukī*. If the context leaves any room for ambiguity, the term "*phukī*" can be added. Thus those males of the same generation as "ego" (*dāju-kijā*) who belong to the patriline can be designated as *phukī dāju-kijā*. In most speech it is clear whether the kin reference is to (1) the core family group, (2) members of the *phukī* (including one of the women attached to it), or (3) the residual of classificatory kin related through affinal and feminal links. Members of this residual group can be further distinguished and grouped by additional terms if necessary. For descending generations beyond the first it is possible through the addition of *mhyāe* (daughter) as a preface to the generational term for a descendant of a given generation, to indicate that the descendant is being traced through a daughter at some point and does not, therefore, belong to the *phukī*, as would be implied by the use of the term in most contexts. As appendix 3 indicates, kin acquired through ego's own marriage are clearly discriminated as a group, although in a different fashion for men and for women.

The subclasses of the larger classificatory kinship terminological system, which are significant and must be understood and signaled in one way or another are, of course, the important social structural components of the kin-group. These are, in sum, the nuclear family, *phukī*, mother's brothers and their families and extensions, the group of *tha:thiti*, and ego's affines. The very large terminological classes of "brothers" and "sisters," "mothers" and "fathers," "grandchildren," and so forth are easily placed in the proper smaller category

GUTHIS, ORGANIZATIONS FOR SPECIAL PURPOSES

Newar society has from very early times included miscellaneous associations of people formed for various special purposes called *guthi*s. The word is derived from the Sanskrit term *goṣṭhī*, "assembly, company, fellowship." D. R. Regmi cites inscriptions from Licchavi times suggesting some of the early functions of these *goṣṭhī*, as the inscriptions then still called them. Some were for the purpose of providing drinking water to travelers, some for the maintenance of water conduits, and others were concerned with various aspects of the maintenance of temples and palaces. The early inscriptions also refer to donation of agricultural land by the state for material support through a portion of the land's yield for the purposes of the *guthi* (D. R. Regmi 1969, 289). Such land is called "*guthi* land," and is one of the fundamental kinds of land tenure in Nepal.[47]

A large variety of *guthi* groups persisted into the recent past. Older informants at the time of this study could list twenty or thirty named *guthi*s, but the list seems to be quickly diminishing as the central government takes over some of their functions, and others disappear with modernization. In addition to *guthi*s using the income from specially designated lands for the maintenance and repair of temples, shrines, *maṭhas* (chap. 8), and palaces and for the support of public ceremonies of various types,[48] there were (and are) groups dedicated to one or another god, or who came together for some special purpose during one or another calendrical festival, or who worshiped in some particular way (with torchlight processions or with one or another of the traditional forms of music, or who sacrificed unusual forms of sacrificial animals such as sheep, etc.). There were some groups representing a particular *thar* or profession,[49] such as palanquin carriers or Ayurvedic physicians, and others whose members included different *thar*s. *Guthi*s choose one of their members as a leader, have a tutelary god, meet for periodic feasts, and raise money in various ways, often from a tax on members—and by fines for violation of *guthi* rules.

In recent years various new kinds of organizations—scouts, women's organizations, and literary societies—which represent larger social units than Bhaktapur society (or, indeed, Newar society) are arising and are locally understood to be replacing or competing for people's commitment to some of the traditional *guthi*s. The most numerous enduring *guthi*s are "death *guthi*s" (those assisting with funerals; see app. 6) and those dealing with *phukī* and *thar* affairs.[50]

THE INSIDE OF THE *THARS* IN RELATION TO THE CITY'S MESOCOSM

This chapter has been a miscellaneous tour of some of the forms that are located within the *thar*s and their component units. Much of it is not directly relevant to our main questions in this volume, and the chapter is a sort of an appendix that has broken loose and drifted forward into the book. As we have remarked, however, these smaller structures are those that most intimately affect the learning and experience of individuals. These are the successively smaller and successively more private cells in which people have their intimate relations, and where they are most closely observed, punished, and rewarded. They provide forms that the public symbolic order expresses or uses or must struggle with. They are in the background for the concerns of the rest of this book, but will be of greater importance, along with those aspects of family and private religion and of rites of passage and the like which we have managed to keep in the appendixes at the back of the book when we elsewhere bring individual experience to the center of our concerns.

PART TWO

The Construction of the Mesocosm

CHAPTER SEVEN

The Symbolic Organization of Space

There is no world without Verona walls,
But purgatory, torture, hell itself.
Hence "banished" is banish'd from the world,
And world's exile is death.

Shakespeare, *Romeo and Juliet*

INTRODUCTION

Frank Kermode wrote of the London portrayed by Joseph Conrad in the *Secret Agent* that it "is the raw, dark, dirty middle of the world, where there is not structure in space or in time that enables men to know one another, or even to familiarize themselves with inanimate objects" (1983, 48). Bhaktapur is also at the middle of the world, but a polar world to Conrad's structureless turn-of-the-century London. In Bhaktapur space is created and made use of to enable the city's inhabitants to know one another and to know—in fact, to animate—objects.

In the 1850s Ambrose Oldfield ([1880] 1974, vol. I, p. 98) found some confusion in the spatial arrangements of Newar cities:

> The streets through the different cities are mostly narrow, crooked and dirty. . . . The streets do not appear to have been laid out on any particular system. Two or three of the principal streets radiate from some of the gateways on the circumference of the city towards the darbar [the royal palace], which is usually situated near its center, and in their course they pass through some of the small squares (or *toles*) with which each capital abounds. Other smaller streets connect the different squares and leading thoroughfares together, and these again are intersected by numerous narrow lanes, which ramify about the city in all directions.

But there was also order, (ibid., vol. I, p. 95f. [original parentheses]):

> During the time of the Niwar [sic] Rajas each city was surrounded by a high wall, in different parts of which were large gateways, which gener-

> ally remained open, but in times of danger or disturbance could be closed and defended. Since the Gorkha conquest of the valley the walls have been allowed to decay. . . . The limits of each city are, however, still strictly marked along the line where the ancient walls stood, and no Hindu but those of good caste are allowed to dwell within its precincts. . . . The number of gateways corresponded exactly with the number of squares (*toles*) within the city, each gateway being associated with a particular square, and placed under the municipal control of the same local authorities, who were as much responsible for the repairs and defense of the gateway as they were for the general management of the square. In each city the largest and most important building is the royal palace. . . . It is situated in a central part of the city, and opposite to its principal front there is an open irregular square . . . round which temples of various kinds are clustered together

Oldfield was glimpsing something of the spatial order of the later Malla cities after seventy years of decay. The construction of villages, towns, and cities as symbolic structures is ancient and ubiquitous in South Asia, and Bhaktapur, like the other Malla centers, had borrowed and developed for purposes of such an order a widespread and ancient areal vocabulary of significant spatial forms.

In this chapter we will present what we consider to be the most significant aspects of the organization of space for the organization of the life of Bhaktapur—"significant," that is, for the creation of order through the organization of symbolic form. Obviously, much of the city's urban order is significant in other ways, but such matters as the urban location of various kinds of craftsmen, the channels of transportation and communication in the city, and the spatial residues of (and potential clues for) earlier urban arrangements are of secondary interest for this study.[1]

One of our first approaches to the study of Bhaktapur was a mapping of various aspects of city life—residence areas of *thar*s, location of temples and shrines, and festival routes—onto maps derived from aerial photographs of the city. During the course of the field research we learned that the urbanologist Niels Gutschow had been doing similar mapping. Gutschow has freely shared with us his maps of Bhaktapur's "ordered space" as he has called it (Gutschow and Kölver 1975), and we have made use of his maps and published writings as a major supplement and extension to our own mappings.

We start, then, with those spatial divisions—areas, lines, and points, that are sources and receptacles for meaning in themselves, that provide meaningful locations for the placement of other symbolic forms and that set out the stage for what once seemed to be the city's endlessly repeated civic dance.

THE CITY AS AN ICON OF A GOD

Bhaktapur, as we have noted in our discussion of its history, grew through time in conformance with the limits of early settlements and of topographic constraints. As attempts were made to organize its space as a symbolic resource it was necessary to deal with hard and resistant forms and forces. The forms that resulted from the interactions of planning and what was—from the viewpoint of an ideal symbolic order—accident or constraint could be coerced into that order in various ways. An existent form might be discovered to have a direct, iconic resemblance to something of transcendent significance; approximate relationships could be abstracted and transformed imaginatively into ideal geometric forms or iconic representations.

The inhabitants of Bhaktapur were thus able to imagine its irregularly ovoid shape as a direct representation of something significant, while at the same time, as we shall see, for other and more important purposes they conceived that shape as a perfect circle. In the eighteenth century Kirkpatrick wrote that Newars described Bhaktapur as resembling "the Dumbroo, or guitar, of Mahadeo" ([1811] 1969, 163). The "dumbroo" was undoubtedly the *ḍamaru*, the hourglass-shaped drum of Śiva. Oldfield, writing of the Nepal Valley in the 1850s, said that Kathmandu, according to Buddhist Newars, was built to resemble the sword of its founder in Buddhist legend, Mañjuśrī, while according to Hindus it resembled the sword of Devī ([1880] 1974, vol. I, p. 101). Patan, a largely Buddhist city, was said to resemble the wheel of Buddha (vol. I, p. 117), while Bhaktapur (vol. I, p. 131) was said now to represent the conch of Viṣṇu, which is what many present inhabitants still say.

In the case of Bhaktapur (and as far as we know the same is true for the other Newar cities), such iconic images that connect the cities to gods have no ritual or doctrinal significance at all. In contrast to the geometrically regular idealized spaces of the city, they are not used in any way in the actions and elaborations of meanings that constitute the symbolic order of the city. The identification of Bhaktapur's shape with Viṣṇu has no present significance. The city is sometimes thought of as Śiva's, sometimes Pārvatī's, sometimes the Tantric Goddess's, but never Viṣṇu's city.

Figure 6. Ceremonial bathing in the Hanumante River.

A NOTE ON HILL AND RIVER

Bhaktapur, like very many cities, makes use of a hill—on which it is built—and a bordering river (see fig. 6), but characteristically elaborates and adds to their elementary "practical" significance—the hill as potential citadel, or as a residential center for the exploitation of the surrounding arable farmland, the river as a source of water (but not, in the Kathmandu Valley, for navigation). The hill, with its higher-status temples, palaces, and residential areas located toward its crest, adds to the more significant orientation of central-peripheral (discussed below) an additional dimension of higher-lower. Bhaktapur is situated in accordance with the traditional ideals of South Asian town planning on the right bank of its river (Dut [1925] 1977, 24), the Hanumante. As is the case for all Newar royal cities and for those secondary Newar towns situated on rivers, the direction of the flow of the river is one basis for the discrimination of an important division of the city or town into two halves, an upper half (upstream), and a lower half (downstream). The river, a locus for dying, cremation, and purification, is outside the traditional boundaries of the city and takes much of its meaning (which it shares with the ideal symbolic Indian river, the Ganges) from its transitional position at a boundary to another world and its flow toward still another, whose orders are other than that of the city.

THE IDEALIZATION OF SPACE: BHAKTAPUR AS A *YANTRA*

In map 1, a schematic illustration of the location of the shrines of the nine guardian goddesses of Bhaktapur (those who protect its boundaries and what we shall refer to as its "maṇḍalic sections"), one of the city's Rājopādhyāya Brahmans represented the goddesses' locations as points in a symmetrical diagrammatic city. The drawing is labeled "Yantrākāra khwapa dey'"—"Khwapa dey'," "the city of Bhaktapur," portrayed as a "*yantra*." The diagram shows Bhaktapur's boundary as a circle, a *maṇḍala*, a pervasive South Asian representation of a boundary and its contained area within which "ritual" power and order is held and concentrated.[2] The circumference of the *maṇḍala* separates two very different worlds, an inside order and an outside order, and suggests the possibility of various kinds of relations and transactions between them. Within the *maṇḍala* in the drawing is the *yantra*, "a mystical diagram believed to possess magical or occult powers" (Stutley

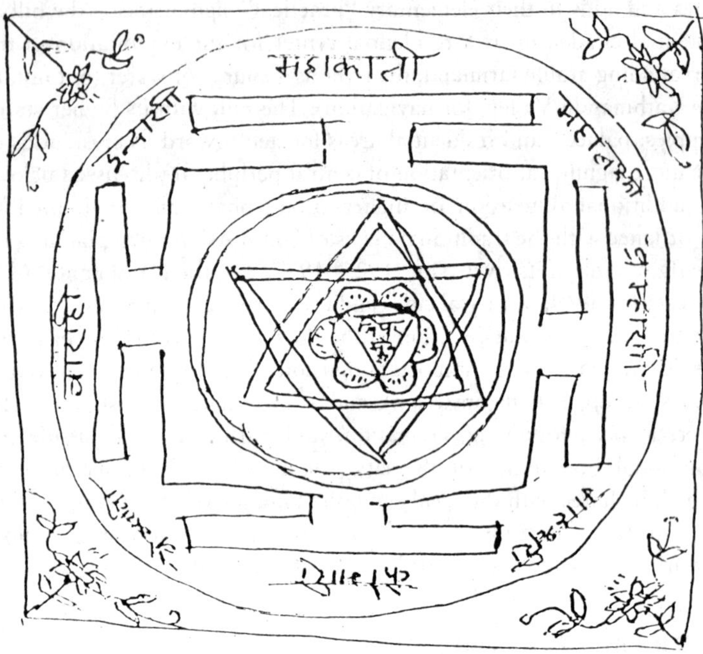

Map 1. Idealized symbolic form. A drawing by a Bhaktapur Brahman of Bhaktapur as a *yantra* with the nine Maṇḍalic Goddesses represented at the eight compass points and at the center. The actual spatial location of the nine goddesses is given in map 2.

and Stutley 1977, 347), typical of Bhaktapur's imagery (chap. 9), here made up of two overlapping triangles, representing the relation of opposites, of male and female principles, unified in a point at the center of the diagram. At that central point is written the name of one of Bhaktapur's nine protective goddesses, Tripurasundarī. Toward the periphery, at the circular boundary are the names of the eight other protective goddesses. They are exactly arranged at the eight points of the compass, with the top of the diagram conceived as representing the north.

These goddesses exist in the actual space of Bhaktapur (map 2), but

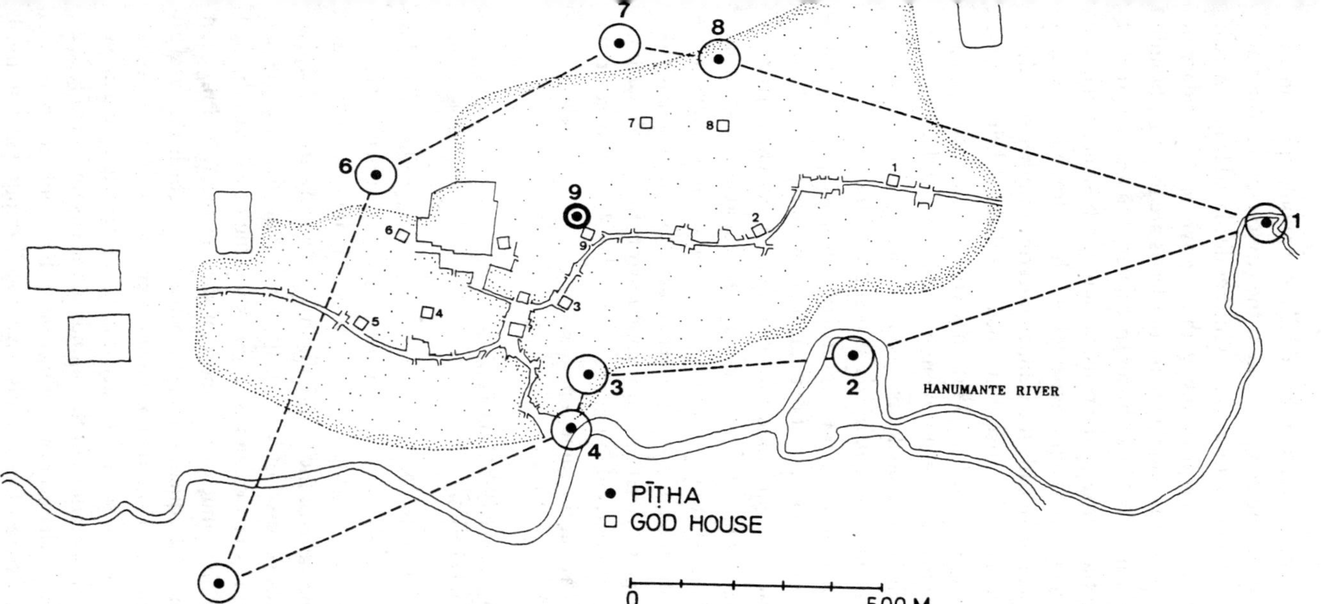

Map 2. The spatial positions of the *pīṭha*s of the nine Maṇḍalic Goddesses. These are the actual spatial locations of the idealized points of the symbolic *yantra* and *maṇḍala* in map 1. The numbers designate the deities in the sequence in which they are worshiped when treated as a united collection of deities: (1) Brāhmaṇī, (2) Maheśvarī, (3) Kumārī, (4)Vaiṣṇavī, (5) Vārāhī, (6) Indrāṇī, (7) Mahākālī, (8) Mahālakṣmī, and (9) Tripurasundarī. The dense band of dots in this map and the following maps indicating the extent of the city represents the edge of the presently built-up area of the city, the "physical city," and does not necessarily correspond to the city's symbolic boundaries. Map courtesy of Niels Gutschow.

the central shrine and the ones at the boundaries are only approximately at the eight points of the compass and at the city center (cf. Auer and Gutschow n.d., 22). One of them is even further displaced from where it is "supposed" to be, being physically within the symbolic boundary of the city instead of at or beyond its outer border as are the other boundary protecting shrines. As Mary Slusser speculates of that shrine, that of Mahālakṣmī, in the course of the construction of a boundary-marking city wall "the sanctity of the [preexisting] old shrine forbade moving it to an optimal location outside the wall; engineering or other considerations dictated the latter's course, thus enclosing the . . . [shrine] within the city walls" (1982, vol. I, p. 346). In accordance with the struggle and the dialogue between the given on the one hand and the ideal symbolic form on the other, Bhaktapur had to construct and imagine a *yantra* and its encompassing *maṇḍala* as best it could.

This imaginative process takes features of real space, many of them constructed under the impetus of that imagination, and perfects them—the city becomes a bounded circle instead of a flattened irregular oval. Simultaneously in a dialogue of imaginative and actual space city halves, "mandalic sections"—various axes and centers—have been constructed. Those imaginatively perfected forms exist in real space like a geometric image reflected in a distorting mirror. But people have no trouble finding their ways about in one or the other kind of space or, for that matter, in both at the same time.

THE CITY BOUNDARIES AND THE BORDERING OUTSIDE

Bhaktapur, like the other Newar royal cities, was, as we have noted in chapter 3, once more or less surrounded by a wall that was pierced by gates. The wall had a defensive use, as descriptions of Bhaktapur's resistance to the siege of the Gorkhālis in 1769 vividly attested. However, the defensive uses of city walls, Paul Wheatley has argued, "in both Nuclear America and Asia [he is writing of early traditional cities] . . . were often much less important than in the West European city. In fact, not infrequently those constructions which the modern mind is predisposed to interpret as fortifications, and which may indeed have been pressed into service as such during emergencies, were in reality symbolic representations of the bounds of the cosmos" (1971, 372). Bhaktapur's wall (whatever other functions it had) and the boundaries it once marked were of enormous "symbolic" importance, as those boundaries still are. Those boundaries may not represent the boundaries of *the* cosmos, for there is some sort of world beyond them, but they represent the boundaries of its central order, the order that is congenial to human beings and to what we will call (chap. 8) the "ordinary deities."

The various spatial features of importance of the city's symbolic organization, which we will be concerned with in the remainder of this chapter, are anchored in real city space by physical features—particular stones, shrines, temples, roads, and pathways. In the course of the "symbolic enactments" that take place in relation to these markers, significant points, boundaries, axes, and areas are clearly designated. In most cases these significant spatial features can be precisely mapped. When the city walls and their gates were still intact, the boundary of the city as a whole was, of course, clear. At that time it was, in fact, the only one of the spatial boundaries we are concerned with that was entirely represented in a physical, material form. Now in Bhaktapur the wall has disappeared except for a few gateways placed at the old ceremonial entrances into the city, and the problem for the people of Bhaktapur in knowing exactly where the city's boundaries are at all points is greater, often considerably greater, than it is for locating the boundaries of smaller units. Kathmandu still has a processional route, annually followed by members of families bereaved during the previous year that follows and thus traces and retains in civic memory the ancient and now leveled walls of that city (Slusser 1982, vol. 1, 93). Bhaktapur does not have any such ceremonial tracing of its boundaries (although there is something like it in orderly sequential visits to the shrines of the boundary-making goddesses during the autumnal harvest festival, Mohanī; see chap. 15), but rather marks and infers the boundary by the contrast of certain events and conditions held to take place properly outside of it but not inside. The city boundary is a dimensionless line producing an instant transformation between the inside of the city and the outside. The symbolic emphasis is on the *outside* of this line, what happens to citizens at home in Bhaktapur when they cross this line, and what kind of a contrasting world they find there. The inside and the outside help define each other. Not only is the emphasis on the outside of the line in its contrasts to the inside (and not on the line itself), but the emphasis is for the most part on a special aspect of the outside, the immediate outside, the *bordering* outside. The distant outside—where in Malla days one would eventually reach the other Newar cities, and beyond them Lhasa and India—is something else.

We will note some of the things and events that exist or take place just beyond the boundaries. This, like much of this chapter, will serve to introduce subjects dealt with in more detail and in different contexts later in the book.

CITY BOUNDARIES: THE BOUNDARY-PROTECTING GODDESSES

As we noted in the discussion of the drawing (map 1) of Bhaktapur as an ideal *maṇḍala* or *yantra*, there are the shrines of eight goddesses placed at the eight points of the compass at the boundary, and a ninth at the center.[3] The nine goddesses as a set are related to the internal division of the city's space into nine "maṇḍalic areas," and we will discuss this division below. The eight external goddesses preside each over her own area of the city, but together they protect the boundary itself. As a group of eight, they are the Aṣṭamātṛkās, the "Eight Mothers," whose positions, marked by open, aniconic shrines called *pīṭha*s, are conceived to be (although as we have noted, one of them is, "in fact," not) not only exactly at the eight points of the compass (which again they are not "in fact") but just outside the boundary of the city (see map 2). The Aṣṭamātṛkās are important members of a special class of deities, the "dangerous" deities, and represent a major component of that class, the manifestations of the "dangerous goddess," "*the* Goddess," Devī. We will return to Devī as a deity in chapter 8, in relation to the specific worship of the dangerous deities and Tantra (chap. 9), and again in that portion of the annual calendrical cycle devoted to her (chap. 15). The group of dangerous deities (who are ritually specified in that they—in contrast to the "benign deities"—receive blood sacrifices and offerings of alcoholic spirits) represent dangerous and at the same time vital forces that lie beyond the city's inner moral organization and also represent the defenses against those dangerous forces through a transformation in which those forces have been tenuously captured and controlled and placed at the service of the city. These particular goddesses ring the entire city and protect it from specific kinds of danger, such as earthquake, disease, and invasion. It is proper for them to be placed to the exterior of a boundary because they are the *kinds* of deities who are, as we will see, "semantically" proper for their particular job. Their position at the city's boundaries is not only a defense but a reminder of the kind of a world to be encountered there and of the contrast of that world with the interior where—within small protective perimeters of various kinds also defended by the dangerous deities—a quieter moral order can proceed under the tutelage of other kinds of deities.

As is the case with most of the significant symbolic markers of Bhaktapur's mesocosm, an encounter with the Eight Mothers and the boundary they represent, protect, and characterize is ineluctably brought about in the course of certain necessary symbolic enactments. The protective goddess of a person's particular residential area of the city must be worshiped during the course of certain major rites of passage by the male members of the extended patrilineal family unit, the *phukī*. Almost all of Bhaktapur's people also visit the boundary shrines (and their central focus), over the course of nine days of the major autumnal harvest festival, Mohanī (chap. 15). People visit each one on its particular designated day, proceeding in the course of the nine days in the auspicious clockwise direction from one shrine to the next, finally, in effect, circumambulating the city's borders.[4]

CITY BOUNDARIES: THE EXTERNAL SEAT OF THE LINEAGE GOD, THE DIGU GOD

The people of Bhaktapur must cross to the outside of the city's boundaries (see map 3) to worship their *phukī*'s lineage deity, represented usually by a "natural" stone and worshiped through the rituals proper to dangerous deities (chaps. 8 and 9). This god is the Digu God (or sometimes and popularly, the Dugu God), the lineage deity of a *phukī*. The Digu God worship is for the highest *thar*s, (Pa[n]cthariyā and above)—that is, those who have upper-class Tantric practices—only one of two major components of lineage god worship (chap. 9), but for the middle-level and lower-level *thar*s it is the only form. The location of shrines for the worship of lineage gods on the outside of a settlement or village is also the practice of Nepalese Chetri communities (K. B. Bista 1972, 66) and has been described in other Newar communities (e.g., Toffin 1977, 31). Informants in Bhaktapur cannot explain why the shrines of the Digu God are outside of the city; explanatory stories are vague, and it is unclear to what possible historical reality they might refer. One story is that in the days of the Malla kings all families of Newars went to the same town (Hadigaon)[5] for their lineage god worship, with each lineage presumably having its own shrine there. But, the story goes, as this was too far away the shrines were moved to the outskirts of each of the Valley cities. Some others say that the place

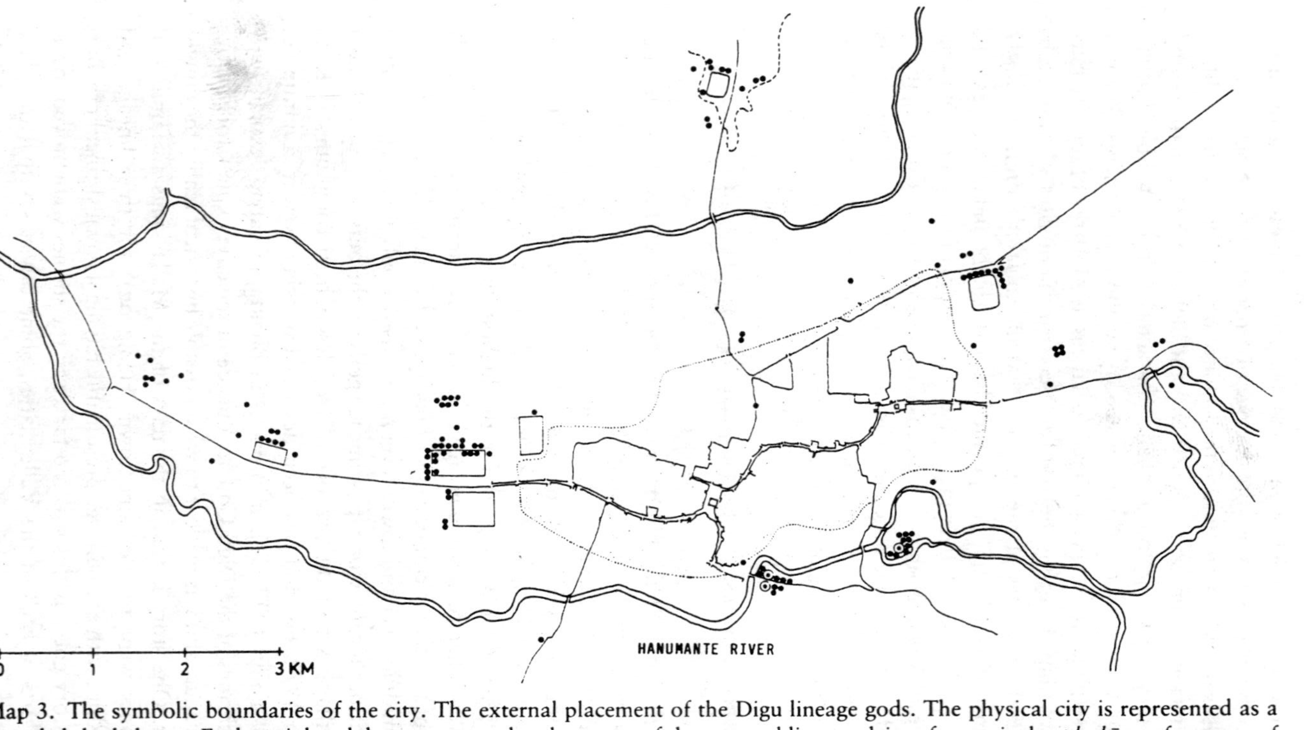

Map 3. The symbolic boundaries of the city. The external placement of the Digu lineage gods. The physical city is represented as a bounded shaded area. Each peripheral dot represents the placement of the external lineage deity of a particular *phukī* or of a group of split *phukīs*. Map courtesy of Niels Gutschow.

where the shrines are located is the place where the original founders of each family lineage entered the city. This comment on the exterior position of the Digu God shrines suggests an actual or fantasized connection of their locations in the past to the historical origins of the city's ancient patrilineages.[6] If this connection (if it ever really existed) is now mostly lost, the Digu Gods must nevertheless be worshiped just to the outside of the city's boundaries, and it is the kind of worship and they are the kinds of gods that point outward beyond the organized interior life of the city.

CITY BOUNDARIES: CREMATION, DYING, AND PURIFICATION

The river is considered to be outside of the city's boundaries to the south, as are the *ghāṭ*s (Bhaktapur Newari, *gā:*) or steps leading down to the river on its city side. At the river clothes are washed and people bathe as a phase of major purification procedures (chap. 11). People approaching death are sometimes brought to the river *ghāṭ*s so that their feet and legs may be immersed in the river at the actual moment of death (app. 6). The city's three cremation grounds (Newari *dip*, from Sanskrit *dīpa*, burning, blazing) are also outside the city, as they are in all South Asian Hindu communities. Two of the major cremation grounds are beyond the river and, as they should be ideally, to the south of the city. These two cremation grounds (Khware Dip and Mu ["main"] Dip) are each associated with one of the *ghāṭ*s on the city side of the river, and are connected to them by bridges spanning the river. There is a third major *dip*, Bramhāyani (Sanskrit Brāhmaṇī),[7] to the east of the city, named after the protective boundary goddess of the eastern pole of the city.

Although we are concerned here with city boundaries and inside/outside contrasts and relations, it is convenient at this point to introduce some other aspects of the cremation grounds in their relation to city space and to its status system. The three *dip*s are for the "clean" *thar*s, the "unclean" ones use various fields outside the city (although on the city side of the river) away from the three main *dip*s. Various Newar chronicles suggest that the cremation areas of most of the significant macrostatus groups were, or at least were held ideally to be, separated. Thus, according to Hasrat's chronicle, Jayasthiti Malla "distinguished and classified thirty-six tribes according to their trades and professions. . . [and] constituted for each of the thirty-six a separate masān [cremation ground] or place for burning their dead" (Hasrat

1970, 55ff.). There are now traditional places within the grounds for some *thar*s, but as a whole the cremation grounds are related to areas of the city, rather than to social status. People who have been brought to die at Hanumañ *gā:* are cremated at the Khware Dip. Those who had been brought to die at Cupi(n) *gā:* are cremated at the Mu Dip. It is a matter of family custom and choice which *gā:* they are brought to. Most people die at home, within the city, and these people are usually cremated at Brāhmaṇi Dip if they live in the upper half of the city, and Mu Dip if they live in the lower half.

Gutschow and Kölver (1975) called attention to the fact that funeral processions to the *dip*s were determined by residence in a particular *twa:* (a village-like division of the city; see below). "Now there are exact prescriptions regulating not only who has to use which [cremation ground], but also the way a corpse has to be borne to his proper place of burning. The decisive feature in this is geographical. The body of a man who belonged to a particular ward [*twa:*] has to be carried along the way prescribed to all the members of his ward" (Gutschow and Kölver 1975, 27). These differentiated routes, based on *twa:* residency, recall Oldfield's statement, previously quoted, that the number of gateways in the old city walls exactly corresponded to the number of toles (*twa:*s) in the city, and that the maintenance of the gates was the responsibility of the local *twa:* authorities (Oldfield [1880] 1974, vol. I, p. 95f.). Because of the mixed collection of *thar*s in many *twa:*s, this arrangement, as Gutschow and Kölver point out, tends to neutralize the distinctions of caste (1975, 27).

This "*communitas*," represented by a collapse of status distinctions in funeral procession and place of cremation, is typical of many activities that are outside and beyond the ordinary civic structuring of Bhaktapur; for example carnival and Tantric rituals. In all of these, however, there is always a residue that is excluded from the egalitarian community, in this case the lowest *thar*s, who are refused even the common cremation grounds.[8]

CITY BOUNDARIES: THE UNTOUCHABLES' PROPER PLACE

In all traditional South Asian cities the lowest segment of the social hierarchy had to live outside the city, and was thus designated as being in opposition to the pure inhabitants of the inside of the city.[9] The ancient classical Indian treatise on applied politics, the Arthaśāstra of Kauṭila, states that "heretics and candālas shall live beyond the burial grounds" (quoted in Dutt [1925, p. 151]), which themselves were to be outside the city.

Various chronicles or *vamśāvalī* presenting Jayasthiti Malla's formalization of Bhaktapur's religious, social, and economic organization, note that Poriyā (Bh. Po[n] or Pore), had to live outside the city (see map 4), and could not enter the city after sundown (Hodgson manuscripts, n.d., vol. 11, p. 114; Basnet [1878] 1981). Oldfield, in the sequel to some remarks that we have already quoted, wrote of the Newar old "capital cities" (in which he included the large secondary town of Kirtipur) that, "The limits of each city are . . . still strictly marked along the line where the ancient walls stood, and no Hindus but those of good caste are allowed to dwell within its precincts. This rule does not apply to Mussalmen, several of whom reside within the city of Kathmandu, but it is strictly enforced against Hindu outcasts, such as sweepers, butchers, executioners, etc., all of whom are obliged to live in the suburbs of the city" ([1880] 1974, vol. I, p. 95).

The sweepers and executioners are the Po(n)s, whose symbolic functions are, as we will see, of great persisting importance in Bhaktapur. The inclusion in this quotation of "butchers," the Nāe, introduces a problem, and almost surely an error into the literature on *thar* residence patterns.[10] Nāe at present live within the boundaries of the city, although they are located at its periphery, at the farthest from its high-status center (map 9, below). There are other low *thar*s, some of which are even lower and more impure than the Nāe who live within the city, and to all evidence always have, for example, the Jugī (map 10, below).

The question of the position of the Nāe in relation to Bhaktapur's boundaries is connected with another question, one concerning the position of the city's main city-wide processional route, the *pradakṣiṇāpatha*. In ideal ancient Indian tradition the *pradakṣiṇāpatha* surrounded the village or city (Dutt 1925, 33), and Mary Slusser has argued that this was the case in Kathmandu (1982, vol. 1, p. 93). The Bhaktapur *pradakṣiṇāpatha* (map 12, below) moves *within* the city as a flattened meandering oval, roughly paralleling the city's boundary, running through and thus tying together all except one outlying *twa:* (below) as well as the upper and lower cities. Bhaktapur's internal *pradakṣiṇāpatha* position within the city also is found in the Newar town of Panauti. Barré et al. argue that in the town of Panauti the processional route acts as a "boundary of purity," as the butchers and sweepers live in its exterior (1981, 40f.). Such a tempting distinction does not work for the distribution of *thar*s in Bhaktapur (and even in

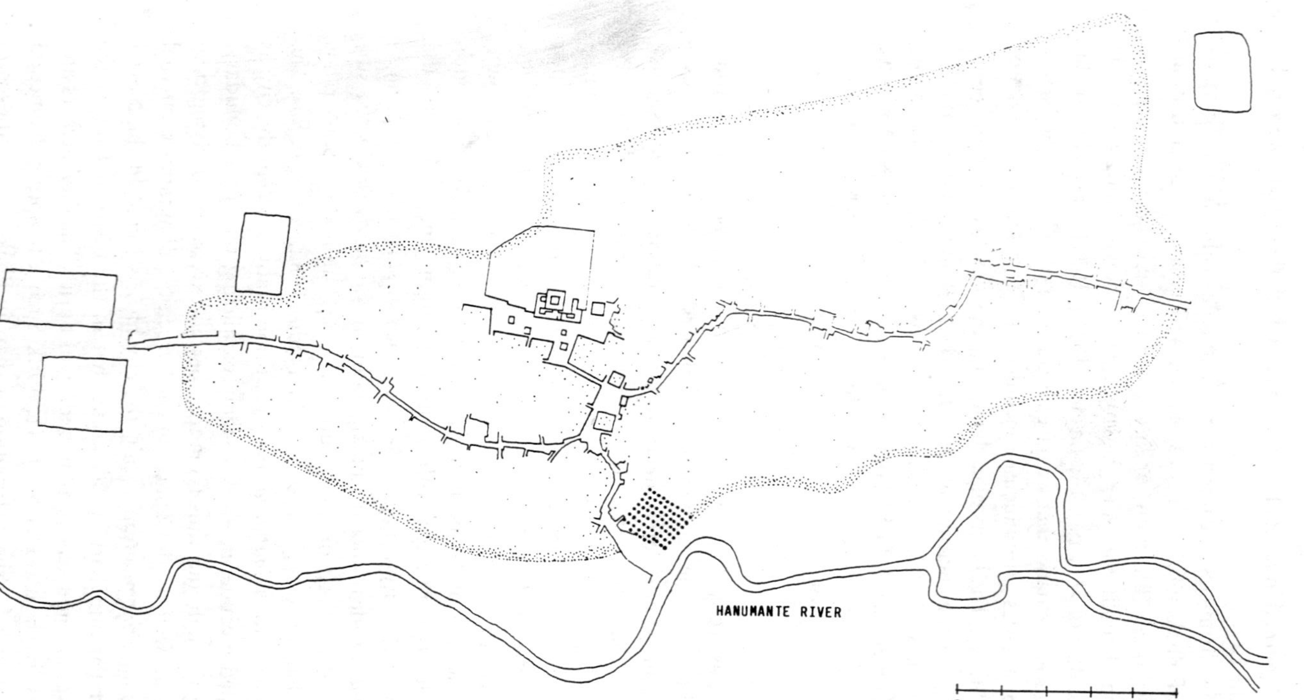

Map 4. Space, status, and the symbolic boundaries of the city. The settlement of the Po(n) untouchables at the southern edge of the city. The settlement is considered to be just beyond the symbolic boundaries of the city. Map courtesy of Niels Gutschow.

the cited account of Panauti there are admitted exceptions, like the dwellings of the very low Jugīs within the central area). As we have noted, the interior position of the *pradakṣiṇāpatha* in Bhaktapur, and the fact that both the sweepers and the butchers live peripheral to it, led Gutschow and Kölver (1975, p. 21) to speculate that it follows the external boundary of some earlier city of Bhaktapur, but there is no apparent collaboration for this in other historical, archaeological, or persisting social forms.

It is unequivocally the Po(n)s, the sweepers, however, who have the special symbolic function of being intimately joined to the city to represent its most salient and necessary outsiders—they are the ones who must live just beyond the boundaries, and who in their conditions of life and in their powerful embedded meanings represent the transforming significance of that boundary to those privileged to live within it.

ON BOUNDARIES

The city walls and most of its gateways are long gone, but everyone in Bhaktapur knows that they exist, that the city is a clearly bounded entity, surrounded by an outside of contrasting nature, and they know approximately where the boundaries must be. They cannot ignore the boundary as they must cross it to the outside for worship of lineage gods, for worship of the "Eight Mothers," often to die and always to cremate others and be cremated themselves, and they must be sure that the untouchables, with whom they are deeply concerned, are fixed in their right place. The outside with which they are necessarily engaged is not everything outside of Bhaktapur, but a highly symbolized zone of encirclement. The far outside, which may be contrasted with this encircling, bordering near outside, includes areas of very mixed meaning—other Newar cities, pilgrimage sites, non-Hindu countries, and so on. But the near outside represents the anticity. The relation of bordering outside to inside characterizes not only the city as a whole but also the relations of many of its nested units to their particular outsides, and is reflected in many ways, in kinds of gods, kinds of worship, and the interplay between power and morality, kings and Brahmans. We will be concerned with these relations throughout the following chapters.

The relations of outside and inside are not a simple opposition. The outside has its special values—it has something to do with fertility and useful power as well as danger. As the kinds of deities who character the two realms suggest (chap. 8), outside and inside have different logics, different relations to moral order. But all this is complementary. The major supernatural creatures at the outside are gods themselves, not antigods like Satan. The ordinary deities, like the ordinary people, need those outside gods, even if they are not comfortable with them.

In the symbolic representation and symbolic enactments concerning the city boundaries, it is the bordering outside and its nature that is emphasized. That outside is of such a nature that after a brief, lively, and instructive encounter with it, people are moved to reenter ordinary civic space with some relief. From the point of view of its impact on citizens for the purposes of social order the symbolization of the outside tends to push people back within the civic boundary.[11]

When the public space of the city as a whole is the focus of attention, as it is generally in this book, the external outside beyond the encircling borders is only one way out of the public city. Insofar as the behavior of an individual, a family, or whatever unit is out of the general public sight and of the direct influence of the city system, they are, from the point of view of that system also "outside," and thus households, *thar*s, *guthi*s, and so on, as well as the private "inside" part of a person's thoughts are outside the public moral world of the urban mesocosm. The inside of the city as a public moral civic space can be escaped in various directions, and the outside beyond the civic boundaries often joins in meaning with the small private realms hidden within the city.

BHAKTAPUR AS A *MAṆḌALA*: THE NINE MAṆḌALIC SECTIONS

When Bhaktapur is conceived of as a *yantra* placed within a bounding *maṇḍala*, the segmentation of its interior space is now at issue. Now the Eight Mothers, the Aṣṭamātṛkās, not only protect the external boundaries of the city at the eight points of the compass but also individually protect the particular octant of the city lying in their general direction and, thus, under their influence. The protective goddesses for the octants are Brāhmaṇī to the east; Maheśvarī to the southeast, Kumārī to the south; Bhadrakālī (sometimes represented as another goddess, Vaiṣṇavī) to the southwest; Vārāhī to the west; Indraṇi to the northwest, Mahākalī to the north, and Mahālakṣmī to the northeast (map 2).[12]

Each goddess has a "god-house" in her city segment, where her portable images is kept (map 2). During one of the year's major festivals, Biskā: (chap. 14), the images are brought from the interior of the city each to its boundary shrine, and the internal image and the external aniconic shrine are united. The emphasis has shifted from the protection of the boundary to an internal radiation of the power of the goddesses. That power not only plays over the eight peripheral octants into which the city is divided but is also focused and concentrated at the center of the *maṇḍala*, in the shrine or *pīṭha* of still another, a ninth goddess, Tripurasundarī. This Goddess protects the city's central area in a circle around her. The city is thus divided into nine areas—a circular center and eight peripheral sectors. We may call these nine segments "maṇḍalic sections." These nine divisions are also conceived by Bhaktapur theorists as a lotus, with a center and eight petals, a very common Hindu form, corresponding to one classical Indian ideal village form (Dutt 1925, 29).

Each maṇḍalic segment is designated by its protective goddess plus any term for area or place, for example, *Mahākālī ya ilākā*, signifying the territory under Mahākālī's protection. People are thought to belong to the maṇḍalic section in which their father's patriline had been "established." That is, if they move to another part of the city, their protective goddess and that of their descendants born in the new section is the goddess of the maṇḍalic section where they had previously, and presumably "always," lived. After marriage, a wife is considered to belong to her husband's maṇḍalic section and ordinarily prays to that section's goddess, although she is still related to her natal goddess in those rituals of her natal family in which she continues to be involved.

The maṇḍalic segment that one belongs to determines which specific Aṣṭamātṛkā shrine or *pīṭha* one must visit during certain important rituals, particularly during those associated with the *saṃskāra*s, or rites of passage. During the annual harvest festival, Mohanī, in which the whole city is supposed to visit each of the nine *pīṭha*s in daily turn over nine days, the people in each goddess's section are responsible for decorating her *pīṭha* and god-house on her particular day. In some Tantric initiations for higher-level *thar*s, the particular *mantra* used and the tutelary god assigned to the person being initiated is based on his particular maṇḍalic segment (chap. 9).

The central goddess Tripurasundarī is, as we will discuss in the next chapter, the proper kind of dangerous goddess to be at the center of the *maṇḍala*'s power. She is a "full" goddess, and the peripheral forms are partial and more specialized. She is represented at the center of the lotus or *maṇḍala* where power is concentrated and at its maximum, and sometimes to similar effect as a point sending out rays of power in each of the eight directions of the compass to each of the eight *pīṭhas* at the boundaries. In contradistinction to the way the city uses other "full," maximally powerful forms of the Goddess (such as Taleju and Bhagavatī), however, and in spite of this schematic superiority to the eight peripheral goddesses, there is no special emphasis of any kind now on Tripurasundarī's central shrine, nor on the central maṇḍalic section that she protects. In action and interpretation, Tripurasundarī (in her function as a central *pīṭha* goddess) is the exact equal of the other Maṇḍalic Goddesses. Some local diagrams of Bhaktapur as a *maṇḍala* have the Newari word for king, *juju*, written next to Tripurasundarī. Some Bhaktapur informants speculate that the shrine's centrality may have reflected a possible ancient relationship to the twelfth-century royal palace, Tripura, which they believe to have been near the present *pīṭha*, and they assume that the Tripurasundarī *pīṭha* may have then been the special shrine for the king and his court (cf. Slusser, 1982, vol. I, p. 345ff.). In the seventeenth century the court and its associated temple of Taleju was moved to its present western site.[13] Tripurasundarī lost her central political importance. This suggests that she remains as a striking example of a once powerful symbolic statement that later lost much of its social, ritual, and personal meaning in a transformed Bhaktapur, where now the curious thing about her is the absence of what she once was.

CITY HALVES: RITUALLY ORGANIZED ANTAGONISM

The bounded units we are considering are in part defined by their contrasts with their adjoining units, in a contrast where that adjoining unit is often an encompassing one (the city and its environment, the house in its *twa:* or neighborhood), although it may be, as in the case of adjoining maṇḍalic sements, a contrast of units at the same level. For the most part any antagonistic implications of these contrasts are mitigated by a pervasive Hindu metaphorical move, an emphasis on the organic unity and interdependence of the contrasting units to form some higher vital synthesis, the various units being metaphorically related (like the ancient four Varṇas) as being like the parts or organs of the body. Neither the high head nor the lowly feet, although different and of different status, can live without the other; they are joined into something superior on which they are dependent, on which their very lives depend.

However, there is one symbolically marked division of the city, its halves, where the major emphasis is precisely on conflict, albeit a conflict periodically and tenuously resolved in symbolic acts. This emphasis on the antagonism of the halves seems to deflect other more dangerous antagonisms within and among smaller city units.

Bhaktapur is divided into halves, an upper half (*cwe*, or up, or *tha:ne*, above, upward) and a lower half (*kwe*, down, or *kwane*, below, downward) (map 5). As D. R. Regmi wrote, the division may have been a general feature of all Newar settlements and "obtained in every case whether it was a town or townlet" (1965–1966, part I, p. 554). The division has been described for Kathmandu (Regmi 1965–1966, part I, p. 554; Slusser 1982, 90–91), for the Newar village of Theco (Toffin 1984, 186ff.), and for the large Newar town of Panauti (Barré et al. 1981, 46). As Barré writes, the division into upper and lower city is "a characteristic common to Newar settlements whether urban or rural."

It is often stated that the upper and lower segments are designated in relation to the flow of neighboring rivers (e.g., Toffin 1984, 200) with upstream locating the direction of *cwe*, downstream of *kwe*. Inhabitants of Bhaktapur attempt various explanations of the designations "up" and "down." Bhaktapur's "upper half" for some is upper because it is more northerly, for others because it is in the direction of the high Himalayas, in contrast to the progressively lower, that is, less elevated southern regions. This north-south interpretation of "upper" and "lower" is reflected in a use of "*kwane*" among Valley Newars, at least until the last generation, to indicate India. Other speculations are that the upper half, *cwe*, was the earliest part of the city settled (as was, in fact, true for Bhaktapur), followed by a later settlement, *kwe*. (Here the usage corresponds to the temporal terminology for ancestors [*cwe*, up] and descendants [*kwe*, down].) Still other people give the upstream/downstream, explanation. It is possible, at least, that the upper/lower contrast is basic to the social organization of all Newar settlements, and that a variety of relations to physical space and settlement history can be used to choose between the terms of the distinction or to justify them. Bhaktapur's upper and lower cities are divided by a line perpendicular to the long (the southwest-northeast) axis of the city, and thus consist of a somewhat northerly eastern portion, and a somewhat southerly western portion, which are respectively upstream and downstream in respect to the Hanumante River (see maps 5 and 11 [below]).[14] As D. R. Regmi writes, in contrast to Kathmandu, where the royal palace was at the central position in the city and provided a locus for the division of the city into upper and lower halves, "the [Bhaktapur] Royal palace was situated at the western extremity of the town and the center dividing the city was the courtyard surrounded by the Nyatapola [Ñātāpwa(n)la] and Bhairava temples" (1965–1966, part II, p. 554). This square, Ta:mārhī (also pronounced or written Tamāri, Taumaḍhī, Taumarhi, etc.), is conceived as at the center of the city division in one of its most important ritual expressions, the struggle between members of the two halves of the city to pull a huge chariot positioned there into their respective halves of the city during the Biskā: festival at the time of the solar New Year, a struggle sometimes marked with considerable violence (chap. 14). At that time the square is considered the neutral center between the halves, but ordinarily it is considered as belonging to the lower city and the people living around it consider themselves at all times to be members of the lower city. Gutschow and Kölver note that the Ta:mārhī Square has a "profuse endowment" of religious buildings and is the site of the highest temple (and building) in Bhaktapur, the Ñātāpwa(n)la temple (fig. 10). They argue that this profusion of monuments may be understood as a device for unifying the town by installing a mediating center and affirming the unity of the city (1975, 50). Although the old Malla Royal Palace, the square in front of it, and the adjacent residential area of the Rājopādhyāya Brahmans (maps 5 and 6) is, like Ta:mārhī, in the lower half of the city, during the struggles of the city halves in the course of the Biskā: festival that area is also said to belong to neither the upper nor lower city. It is often said that the Malla kings encouraged the division and conflict between the two city halves, which they transcended, to strengthen their power and divide any potential opposition. Thus, if Ta:mārhī Square acts as a neutral ritual center between the upper and lower cities, the royal central area, in spite of its peripheral western positions, is in its own way also a neutral point.

In recent years conflict between members of city halves has also sometimes broken out at certain other festivals, but these rare and recent struggles are considered to be accidental and unintended disorder and breakdown. The peculiarity of the Biskā: festival is that it includes as one element in its complex dramatic structure a prolonged struggle between the two city halves, a struggle that eventually comes to a resolution.

Ritualized struggles (that is, struggles induced and regulated by traditional forms and conventions—which does not prevent them from having, sometimes, serious consequences) between socially organized

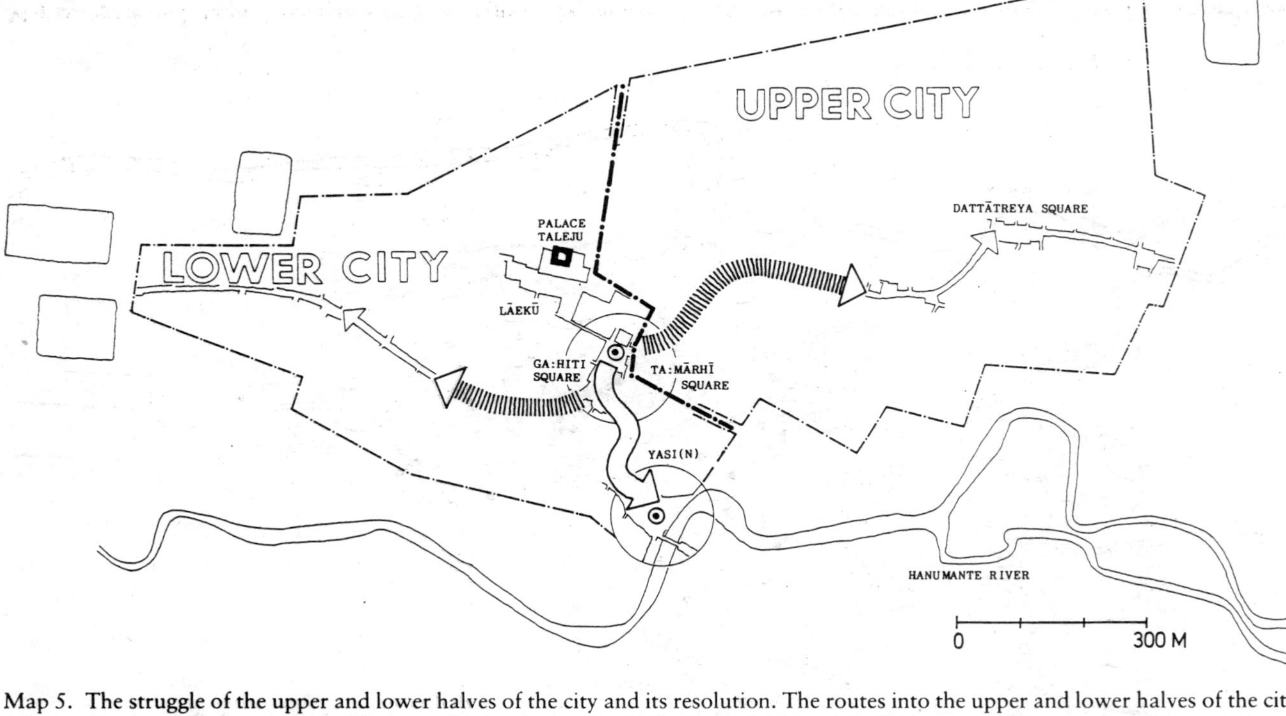

Map 5. The struggle of the upper and lower halves of the city and its resolution. The routes into the upper and lower halves of the city contested in the struggle to pull the Bhairava chariot during the Biskā: festival (chap. 14). The arrows in the upper and lower segment of the city show the ideal termini of the chariot and the acceptable shorter termini if there is not time to reach the ideal ones. The southerly arrow shows the chariot's ultimate "central" route into Yasi(n) Field, where it must witness the raising of the Yasi(n) God to mark the solar New Year. Map courtesy of Niels Gutschow.

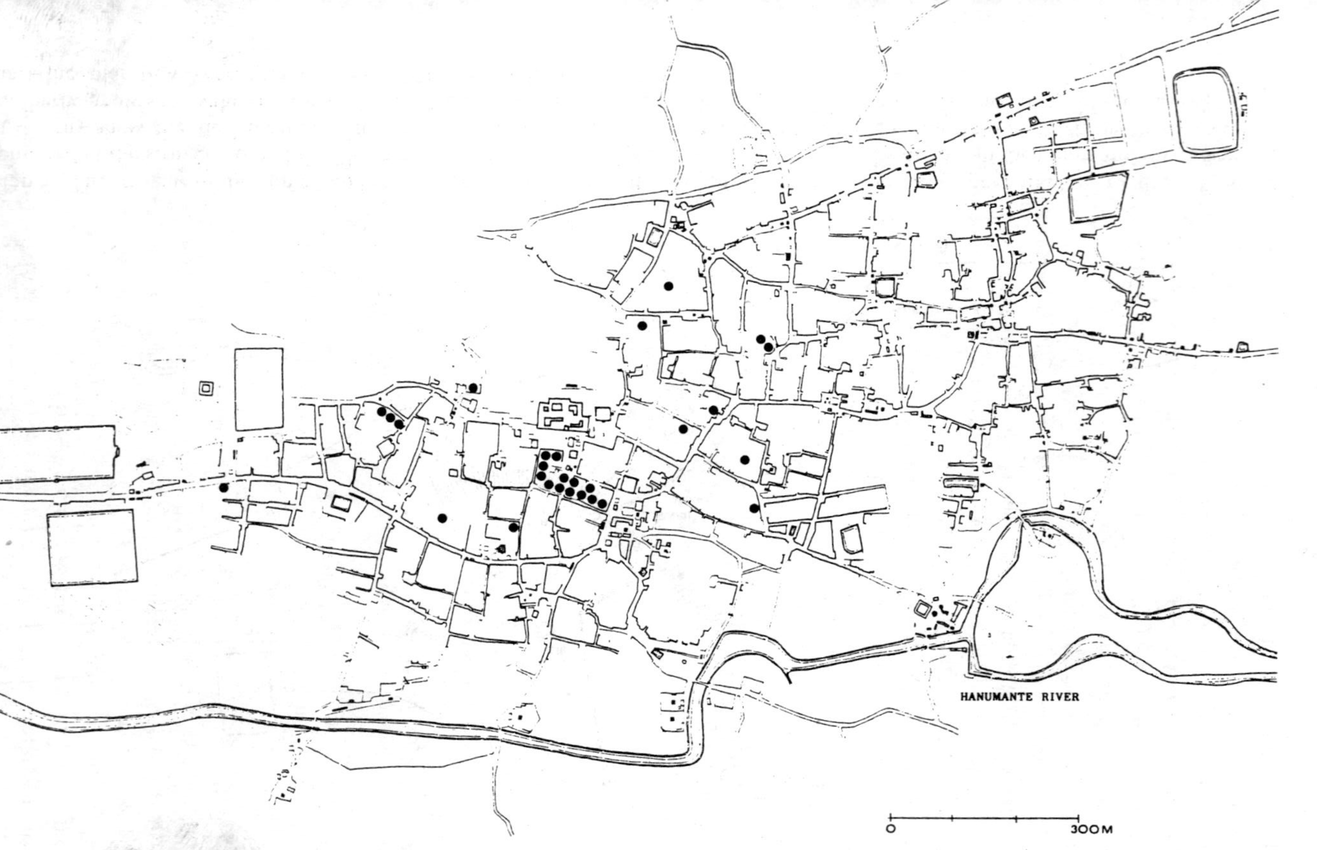

Map 6. Space and status. Households of Rājopādhyāya Brahmans. The greatest concentration is just south of the Taleju temple and the Royal Palace and represents a center of the city. Map courtesy of Niels Gutschow.

halves or moieties of a community—are reported for traditional South Asian communities as they are elsewhere in the world. Dubois, for example, remarked on the struggles between the "left-handed" and the "right-handed" factions in the Deccan and Madras areas in the early nineteenth century, factions to which "most castes" belong, which "proved a perpetual source of riots, and the cause of endless animosity amongst the natives" (1968, 24f.). He also remarks on something that has a bearing on the conflict in Bhaktapur, that "in the disputes and conflicts which so often take place between the two factions it is always the Pariahs [the untouchables] who make the most disturbance and do the most damage" (ibid., 25). And, he states, also in an echo of Malla Bhaktapur, "the Brahmans, [and] Rajahs . . . are content to remain neutral, and take no part in these quarrels. They are often chosen as arbiters in the differences which the two factions have to settle between themselves" (ibid., 25).

Hamilton cites a report for the turn of the nineteenth century by a Colonel Crawford, which describes a "vile custom" of the Newars of Kathmandu, who had previously been described by Hamilton as being an otherwise peaceable people ([1819] 1971, 43f.):

> About the end of May, and beginning of June, for fifteen days, a skirmish takes place between the young men and boys of the north and south ends of the city. During the first fourteen days it is chiefly confined to the boys or lads; but on the evening of the fifteenth day it becomes more serious. . . . [A fight then takes place which] begins about an hour before sunset, and continues until darkness separates the combatants. In the one which we saw, four people were carried off much wounded, and almost every other year one or two men are killed: yet the combat is not instigated by hatred, nor do the accidents that happen occasion any rancor. Formerly, however, a most cruel practice existed. If any unfortunate fellow was taken prisoner, he was immediately dragged to the top of a particular eminence in the rear of his conquerors, who put him to death with buffalo bones. . . . The prisoners are now kept until the end of the combat, are carried home in triumph by the victors, and confined until morning, when they are liberated.

There has been speculation, deriving from a further remark of Hamilton's (1971, 44) that some people alleged that the Kathmandu battle reflected some old division of the city into two towns under two Rājās and first arose as skirmishing among their respective followers, that the division in Kathmandu, at least, and perhaps in other Newar towns may have reflected some earlier antagonistic political segments later merged into the towns (Slusser 1982, vol. 1, p. 91;

Toffin 1984, 201f.). Yet, the ubiquitousness, persistence, and evident usefulness of the division in Newar communities would suggest that such historical explanations would only apply to some towns, and would only help explain the location of the halves, not their existence and persistence.

In some ways the upper and lower cities in Bhaktapur *are* two different cities. it is said that people usually marry within their own half of the city. In many contexts, they identify themselves as belonging to one or another half. Significantly, when there are crimes or disturbances in the city whose perpetrators are unknown, it is common to hear remarks by people from the lower city that it must have been someone from the upper city, and vice versa. Although the lower city has the main concentration of Brahmans and high-status Chathariyā, and the upper city the main concentration of upper-status Buddhists, for the most part each city half has a full representation of important social and occupational units.

For ordinary considerations of residence (where we can ignore the maṇḍalic sections), the city halves are the next largest segment after the village-like *twa:*s (see discussion below). It is our impression that the antagonism directed toward the relatively distant other city half, out of and away from one's own closely interdependent area, deflects intra-*twa:* resentments that would affect relations between families, *phukī*s, *thar*s, and macrostatus levels—relations whose disturbance would be disruptive to the basic integration of the social system—to the other city within the city where they can be expressed in comparatively very much less disruptive and dangerous ways. Members of lower *thar*s who are annoyed and resentful of their treatment by higher groups find it easier, like the pariahs in the quotation from Dubois, to help precipitate a fight against members of a disliked group in the *other* half of the city, where it would be interpreted as a spatial struggle rather than one within the social system.

STATUS AND SPACE: CONCENTRIC CIRCLES

It is convenient to introduce in this chapter aspects of the urban spatial distribution of some of the *thar*s and status levels (see fig. 7). Only a portion of this distribution is directly related to the urban symbolic order in our present sense, the greatest part being closely related to aspects of economic function, to communication and transportation, to

Figure 7. The Royal center. Statue of King Bhūpatīndra Malla in Lāekū Square.

relations of power, to the special needs of the old court, and to historical "accident," thus reflecting other kinds of meaning.

In his study of the classic Indian treatises on town planning, Dutt (1925) notes the planned "segregation of the classes following different pursuits. . . . Every ward was set apart for a caste or trade guild . . . which enjoyed an autonomy of its own" (1925, 147). In some classic texts, such as Kauṭilya's, detailed prescriptions are set out for the location of many occupational specialites and castes, as well as the location of royal kitchens, elephant stables, water reservoirs, camel stables, and so on (Dutt 1925, 149f.).[15] But, as Dutt points out, in cities, because of the larger scale and because "corporate life connotes manifold needs and responsibilities and consequently necessitates interdependence and inter-communication," various areas or sites were subdivided to have a representation of occupations, and became "a prototype of the whole city on a smaller scale." And, he adds, in a suggestion connected with our interpretation (above) of the city's halves, "This admixture and congregation of classes came as a remedial measure against possible accentuation of class differences" (1925, 148). We have argued that the city halves are such city prototypes in Bhaktapur, as are, to some degree, the *twa:*s, which we will discuss in the next section.

Although many of the *thars* are widely distributed through the city according to the kinds of functional principles suggested above, the arrangement of certain symbolically important groups has the kind of idealized mythic arrangement characteristic of marked symbolic space. When these *thars* are considered—the king and his associates, Brahmans, farmers as a group, butchers, and untouchables—a geometrically idealized Bhaktapur is organized in a series of concentric circles from a center out, and at the same time, as it is built on a hill, from top down. At the center of high status is the palace of the Malla kings, and the temple of the Malla kings' lineage deity, the supreme political goddess of Bhaktapur, Taleju. Just to the south of the palace, but also centrally located is a major concentration of Rājopādhyāya Brahmans (map 6), including those families who were the king's and his goddess' special priests. Intermingled in central residence with the Brahmans, but filling a still larger segment of the city are the Chathar and Pa(n)cthar groups of *thar*s (map 7), formerly royal officials and suppliers. Still more peripheral from the center are the various farming *thar*s, the Jyāpus (map 8), who fill most of the city's area except for the Brahmans' area and those portions of the Chathariyā and Pa(n)cthariyā area adjoining the east-west road, the city's bazaar, where the Chathariyā and Pa(n)c-

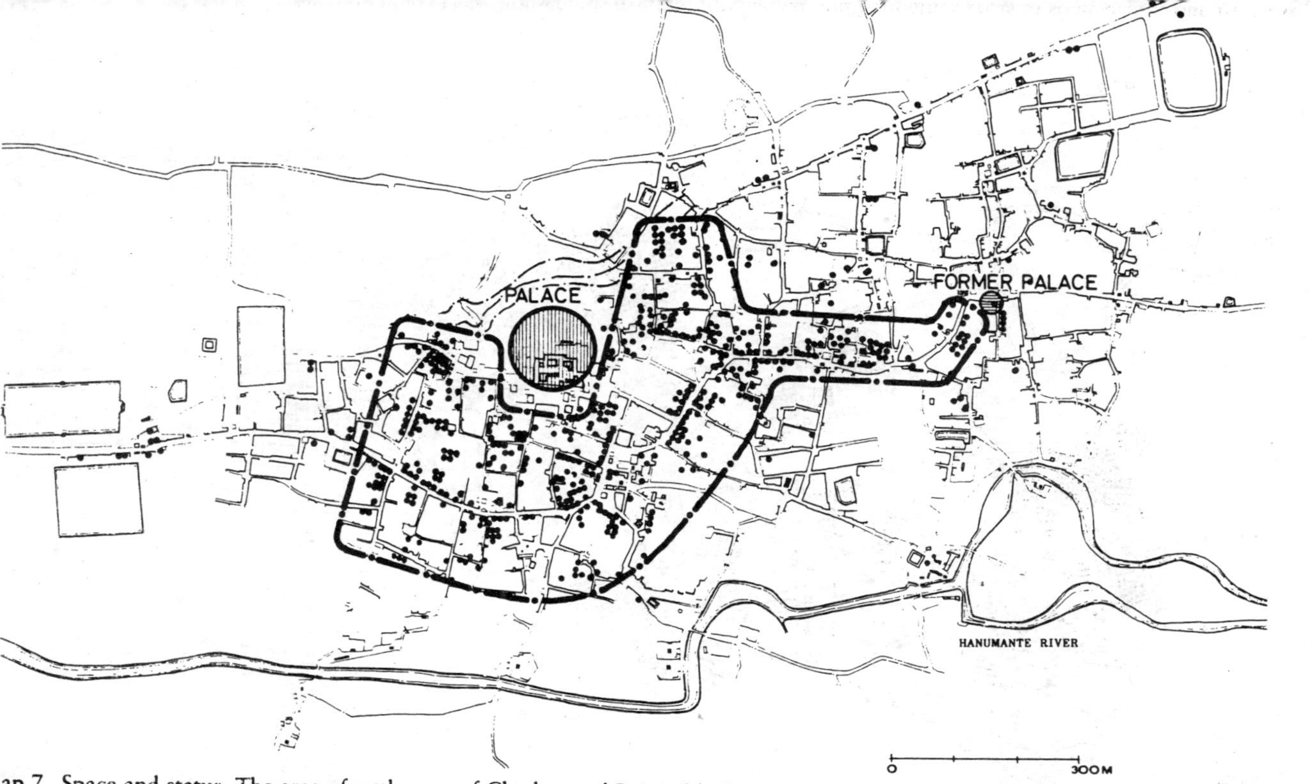

Map 7. Space and status. The area of settlement of Chathar and Pa(n)cthar households. They occupy the city's central sector. Compare the distribution of Jyāpus in map 8. Map courtesy of Niels Gutschow.

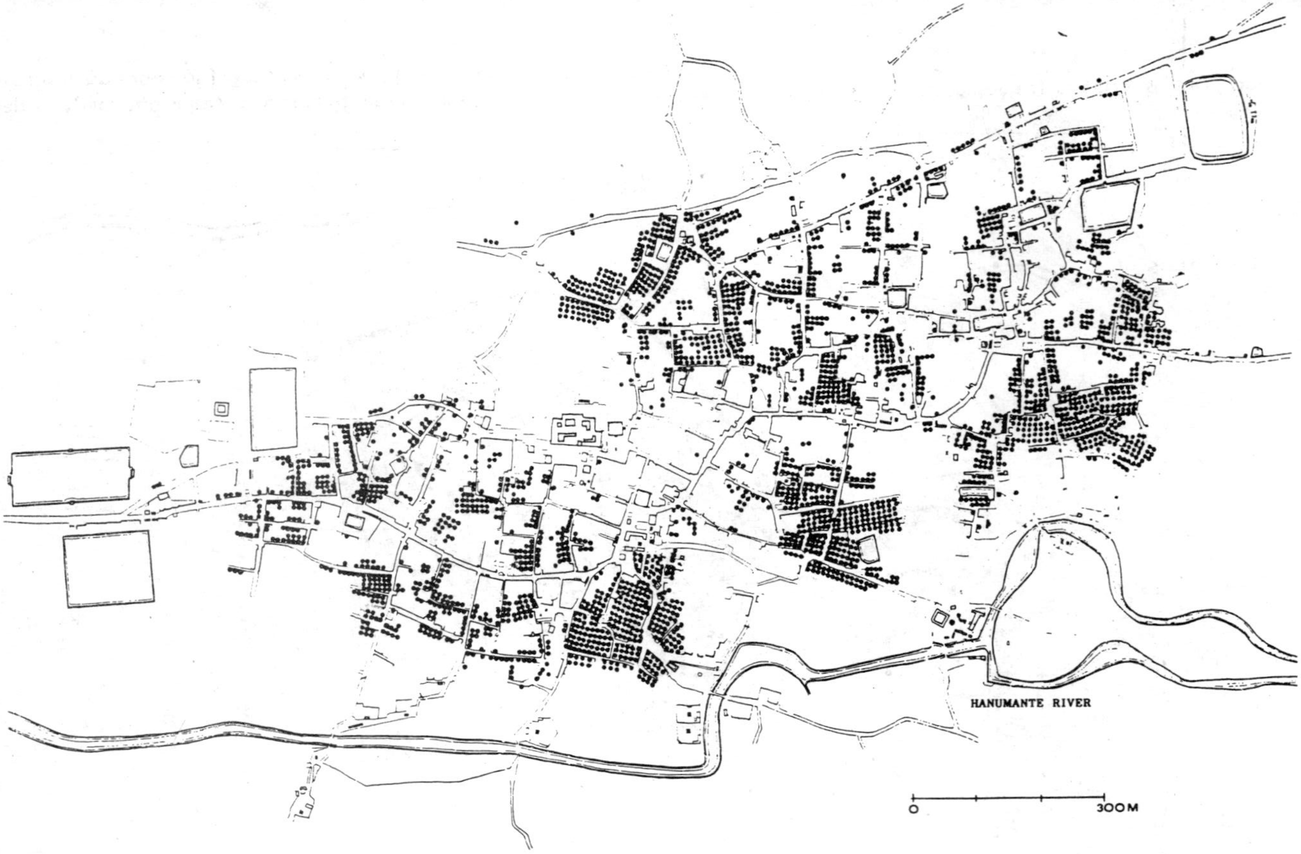

HANUMANTE RIVER

0 300M

Map 8. Space and status. Jyāpu household. These households overlap the Chathar and Pa(n)cthar areas to some degree but are most

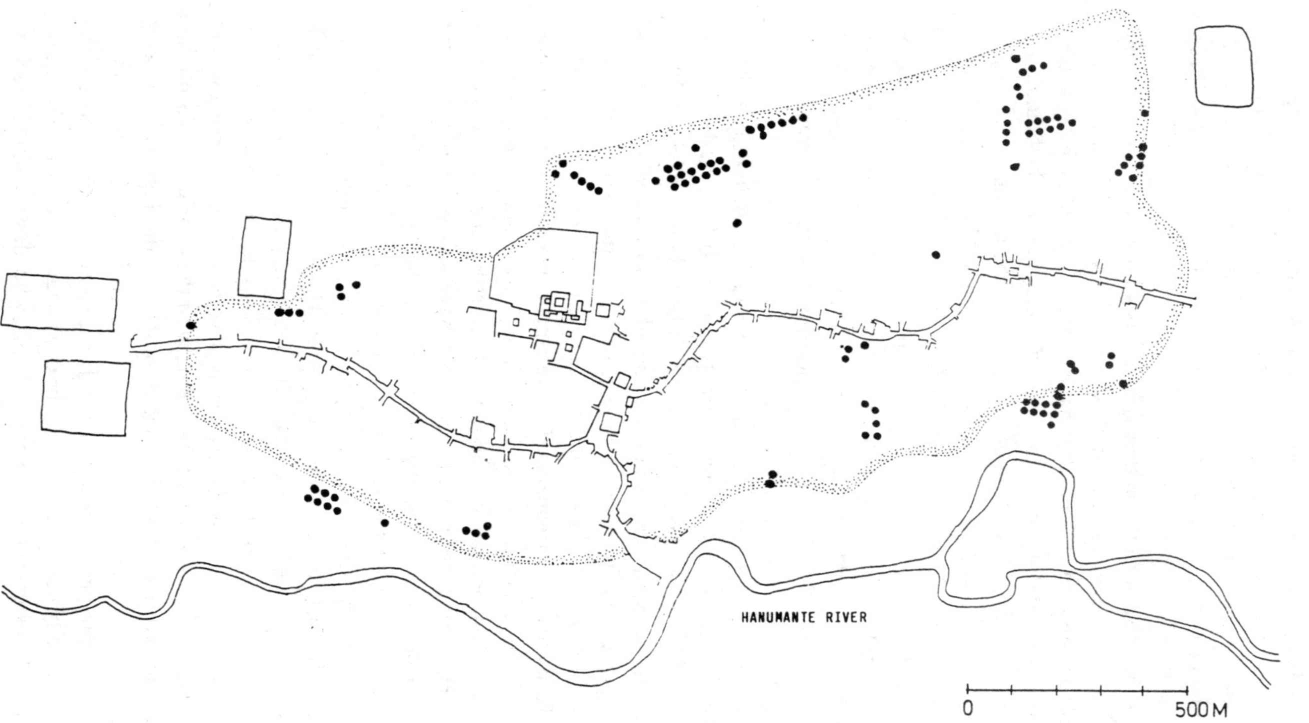

Map 9. Space and status. Butcher households. The households of the Nāes (butchers) are located along the edges of the built-up area of the city. They are conceived to be within the symbolic boundaries of the city. Map courtesy of Niels Gutschow.

thariyā have their shops and, often, adjoining houses. At the very periphery of the farmers' area, and forming a ring around the outer extremes of the city, are the houses of the butchers (map 9). Finally, outside the city to the inauspicious south, live the untouchable sweepers, the Po(n)s (map 4, above).

The hill on which Bhaktapur is built has a broad plateau at its summit with no visible distinctly highest spot. The Malla palace and Taleju temple are situated on a plateau that is bordered by slopes that gradually descend some twenty meters to meet the fields outside the boundaries. This slope adds a dimension of top–down to the imagery of central to peripheral. The highest spot of the plateau at 1,339.8 meters (slightly higher than the site of the palace at 1,335 meters) lies just to the west of the Tripurasundarī *pīṭha*, the central maṇḍalic shrine, and during the twelfth to sixteenth centuries was apparently part of the site of the large Newar Royal Palace compound of the day, Tripura (Slusser 1982, vol. I, p. 204). At that time the highest point in the city was, in fact, within the royal precincts.[16]

Detailed maps of the location of the various craft *thar*s, which are ranked in the lower segments of the Jyāpu and below, made by Gutschow and his associates (Gutschow 1975; Gutschow and Kölver 1975), show the occupational castes distributed in various ways, generally throughout the city, except for the central area, the area of the palace, the main Brahman cluster, and the central portion of the Chathariyā and Pa(n)cthariyā settlements. The craftsman areas are in the outer portions of the Chathariyā and Pa(n)cthariyā areas and throughout the area of Jyāpu settlement. The number of settlements of any one *thar* vary. The Chipās or dyers, for example, have only one settlement, but other professional *thar* groups have several. The Kumha:s, potters, for example, have one large settlement in the south, and two in the northeast of the city. The oil pressers, or Sa:mis, have four clusters, two toward the east, and two toward the west. The barbers, or Naus, live in six clusters throughout the city. The house masons, the Awa:s, have three settlements, one to the west, and two to the northeast. The Jugīs live (map 10) in an irregular pattern with some central clustering within the city, cutting into and intermingling with the Chathariyā, Pa(n)cthariyā, and farmers' areas. This inner location of the Jugīs is in striking contrast with what might have been expected in the status gradient from center to periphery signaled and created by the arrangement of the most centrally important *thar*s in the city hierarchy, and in marked contrast to the external position of the Po(n)s, who along with the Jugīs are

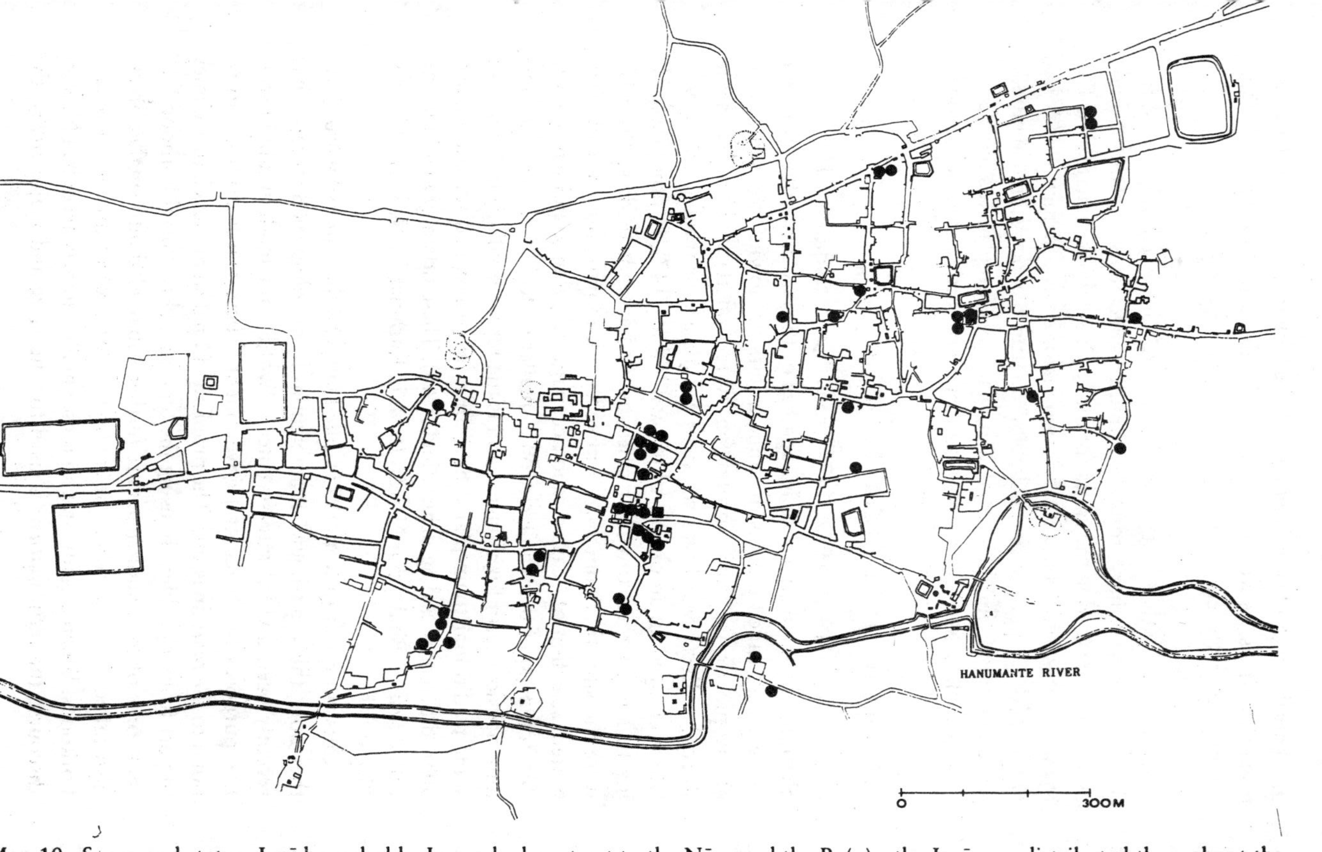

Map 10. Space and status. Jugī households. In marked contrast to the Nāes and the Po(n)s, the Jugīs are distributed throughout the

the central foci of ideas regarding pollution (chaps. 5 and 11). The position of the Jugīs, as we will see, seems closely related to aspects of their significance in the city order.

In contrast with the other spatial features discussed in this chapter, the center-to-periphery, top-to-bottom, arrangements of status are not used or emphasized in the course of the city's symbolic enactments. The royal center is a focus in the city's two major festival sequences (Mohanī and Biskā:) and the untouchables' quarter has occasional symbolic representations, but the overall spatial status arrangements, insofar as they do reflect a symbolic order, are not given further representation.

THE VILLAGE IN THE CITY, THE *TWA:*

Binode Dutt ([1925] 1977, 147) wrote that in traditional Hindu city planning the main streets or Rājapathas of the city divided it into a set of "wards," called *grāma*s. In some traditional towns "the same caste or people of the same profession were congregated in the same ward. . . . Every ward was set apart for a caste or trade guild of note which enjoyed an autonomy of its own" (ibid., 147). In other (according to Dutt, larger) towns or cities, as we have noted, these "wards" were the sites that contained a mixed, and, in part, functionally integrated, selection of "castes" and occupational groups, and which were "prototype[s] of the whole city on a smaller scale." "*Grāma*" is a common Sanskrit term for village[17] and is the term for village in Nepali. In some traditional town plans the *grāma*s were assigned to, and named after, different presiding deities (ibid., 143). These urban *grāma* units are called *twa:* in Bhaktapur Newari (*twā:* in Kathmandu Newari and *ṭol* in Nepali).[18]

Gutschow and Kölver (1975), like Dutt, call these units "wards." As they note, this is a somewhat ambiguous terminology as Bhaktapur has recently been divided into seventeen "wards" for modern administrative purposes by the central government. These wards do not correspond to the *twa:* divisions. The problem of English nomenclature comes in part from a problem in using the tempting gloss "neighborhood," in that some of the major *twa:s* are further subdivided into smaller areas, also called "*twa:s*" (when the context is clear) which *are* clearly neighborhoods. When a contrast with these smaller units is needed in Newari discourse the term *mātwa:* is used for the large and major *twa:*s, the prefix *mā* deriving from the trunk of a tree of which the smaller neighborhood *twa:*s are branches.

Bhaktapur is always said to have twenty-four major *twa:*s,[19] and these have various ritual representations. These have probably shifted somewhat over time through splitting and coalescing, but our map (map 11) is a close approximation to the traditional *mātwa:*s. Accepting the traditional number of twenty-four *mātwa:*s, an average *twa:* would consist of about 270 households and about 1,600 people. It is perhaps significant that these numbers are equal to the median population of Kathmandu Valley Newar towns or "compact settlements" (His Majesty's Government, Nepal 1969, 81). The average number of houses in a *twa:* also happens to fall within the range given in classical definitions of a *grāma*. Kauṭilya gave a range of between 100 and 500 houses as defining a *grāma* (Slusser 1982, vol. 1, p. 84). However, in comparison with classical *grāma*s, which were distributed over a large area, the Mauryan *grāma*, having an area of from two to four square miles,[20] the otherwise analogous *twa:*s of the Newar cities are compressed into densities more than ten times more compact.

As Auer and Gutschow have pointed out, if one asks a Bhaktapur Newar where he lives he often answers with the name of his *twa:*. This is one of the important loci of his identification. There is a well-known Newar saying: "If the household is in proper order, the *twa:* can be 'frightened off' (*khyāegu*); if the city is in proper order, the country can be 'frightened off.'" "*Khyāegu*," "frighten off," has the sense of chasing away a cow that enters a field, or an intruder into a courtyard. In these successively inclusive units, whose boundaries must be protected at each level, the *twa:* takes its important place between the household and the city.

Gutschow and Kölver (1975, 26) described some of the general characteristics of Bhaktapur's *twa:*s:

> As a rule, a . . . [*twa:*] will be centered around a spacious square. This is usually paved and serves various agricultural and commercial purposes: during and after harvest, it is a threshing floor, a space for winnowing grain, for drying rice and certain other vegetables. . . . In potters' wards, unbaked jars or pots are placed there for drying. Women will here prepare the warp before weaving. Almost all squares are hemmed in by arcades, where people will congregate in the evening for various social purposes. . . . In most wards, the central square has a well. A temple or shrine to Gaṇeśa [is] found in every ward.

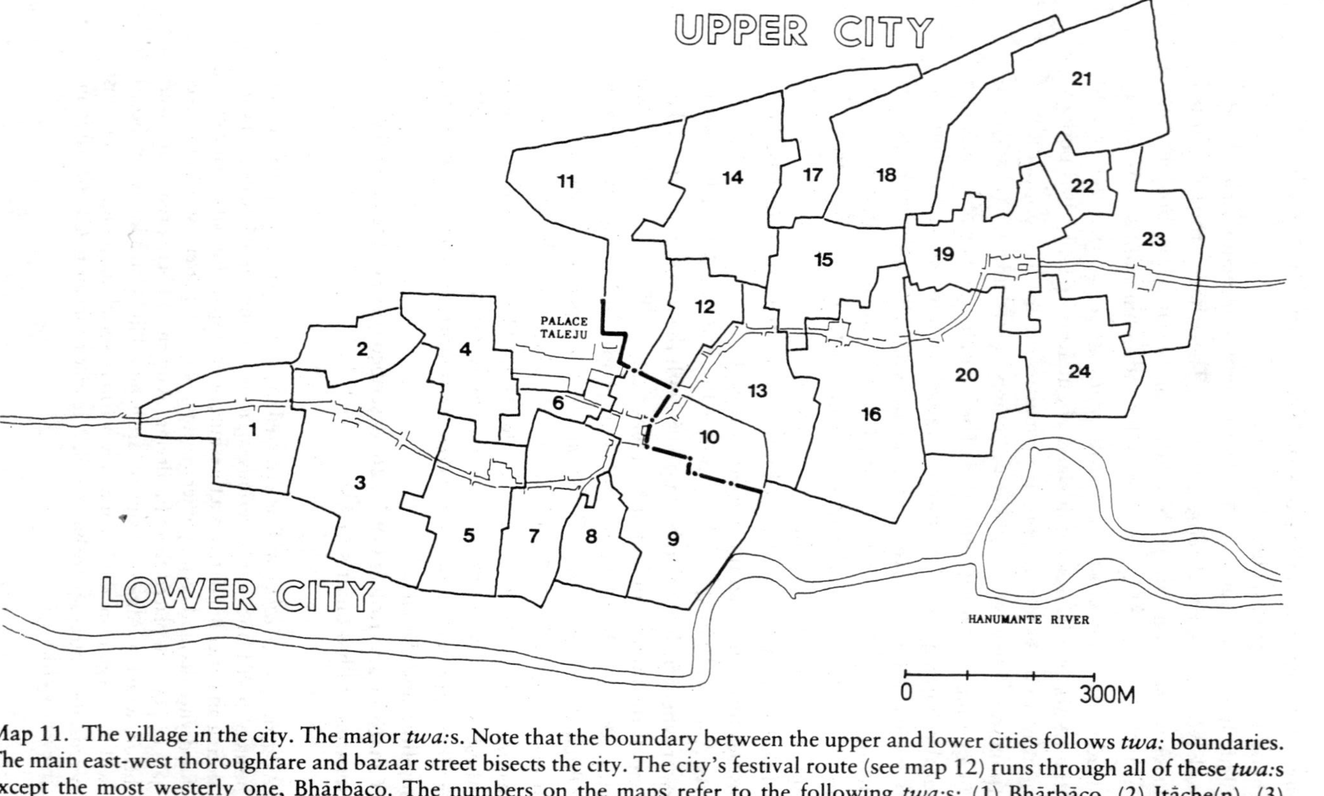

Map 11. The village in the city. The major *twa:*s. Note that the boundary between the upper and lower cities follows *twa:* boundaries. The main east-west thoroughfare and bazaar street bisects the city. The city's festival route (see map 12) runs through all of these *twa:*s except the most westerly one, Bhārbāco. The numbers on the maps refer to the following *twa:*s: (1) Bhārbāco, (2) Itāche(n), (3) Tekhāco, (4) Khaumā, (5) Ma(n)galāche(n), (6) Lāskuḍoka, (7) Bolāche(n), (8) Lākulāche(n), (9) Ta:mārhī, (10) Kwāche(n), (11) Yālāche(n), (12) Tulāche(n), (13) Tibukche(n), (14) Coche(n), (15) Yāche(n), (16) Gwa:mhārhi, (17) Bholāche(n), (18) Thālāche(n),

They note that the "wards" usually have their own shrine of the deity Nāsadya: (chap. 8) and often one of Viṣṇu, but these are secondary in their specific importance to the *twa:* to its Gaṇeśa shrine. Gutschow and Kölver's mention of the "potter's ward" reflects the fact that although all *twa:*s have at least some mixed occupational and status membership, one group may dominate the *twa:* numerically, and may sometimes give it a local flavor and identity.

*Twa:*s vary not only in the details of their membership, but sometimes in identifiable aspects of their spoken language, and, in popular conception at least, in the behavioral style of their members, their "manners" (cf. D. R. Regmi, 1965, part II, p. 554). *Twa:*s, or their major segments, are the face-to-face communities beyond the extended family where people know each other personally and where mutual observation and gossip are important sanctions. It is here that children's play with nonfamily children and adult associations with non-*phukī* members provide the ground for the considerations of mutuality and equality and for judgments on personal qualities that compete with or influence hierarchical orientations. The reason that the household must be organized to chase off the *twa:*, as the saying puts it, is that the *twa:*, or one of its neighborhood subdivisions, is the place where individual or family misbehaviors are likely to be first known and of considerable interest and where family reputation, or "face," *ijjat*, is at risk.

The *twa:* is continuously represented for its inhabitants in symbolic actions. Like most units in the city (as we will discuss in the chapters on calendrical events), the *twa:* is sometimes represented as a significant locus for action, as a maximal unit in itself, and sometimes in a kind of "parallel" representation as one of a set of similar units that are all doing the same thing at the same time or in sequence, and thus indicate their equivalence as categories and, at the same time, their significance as units constituting the city. The most salient inner representation is the *twa:*'s central shrine of Gaṇeśa. Gaṇeśa must be worshiped as a preliminary to all important household ceremonies and all rites of passage. Some *twa:*s also have a special protective deity in addition to their central Gaṇeśa. This may be Bhairava or a form of the Dangerous Goddess. In some *twa:*s the protective goddess is worshiped once a year, and carried on the processional route of the *twa:* (chap. 13).

*Twa:*s have some ordered relationships to the larger city. We may recall Oldfield's report that the number of gates in the old Newar city walls "corresponded exactly with the number of squares (toles) within the city, . . . each gateway being associated with a particular square, and placed under the municipal control of the same local authorities, who were as much responsible for the repairs and defense of the gateway as they were for the general management of the square" (Oldfield [1880] 1974, vol. 1, p. 95f., original parenthesis). We have also noted Gutschow and Kölver's observation that each *twa:* has its prescribed route for carrying corpses to the cremation ground (1975, p. 27).

The twenty-four *twa:*s are represented together as constituative elements of the city in one of the climactic events of the annual festival cycle—the sacrifice of twenty-four male buffaloes to the Goddess at the Taleju temple during the autumn harvest festival of Mohanī. Most of the central *twa:* squares are also in their proper annual turn the site for the ritual dance-drama of the Nine Durgās, the possessed dancers, whose movements during nine months through Bhaktapur each year are considered by many to be Bhaktapur's most important symbolic performances (chap. 15). These *twa:*-based dramas deliver, as we will argue, some of the city's most powerful messages about the proper moral integration of individuals into the ordered life of the city.

SOME NOTES ON THE SYMBOLIC CONSTRUCTION OF THE HOUSE

We have so far been moving into successively smaller spatial units. When we reach the house, we are at the boundary of one of the city's (here, literally) walled-off units, whose internal organization is hidden as far as possible from larger units, whose integrations and controls are largely internal, and whose concern to the larger city is in their public outputs. Although the symbolic organization of the house, like the life of the households within it, is, of course, elaborately influenced by Newar culture and tradition, it is for our purposes here, "below" or "outside" the level of public city life, and is part of the host of smaller private forms that are sometimes consonant with, sometimes antagonistic, sometimes irrelevant to the integrating forms of the public city. The interiors of these units—and above all the life within the house—reflect larger public institutions and arrangements, stand against them, prepare members for them, defend members and console them against them, and punish and reward members in their own ways and for their internal needs as well as the needs of the larger system.

This chapter is a convenient place for a summary description, making much use of others' studies,[21] of some spatial characteristics of the

Figure 8. Farmers' houses. Adjoining houses of families of one Jyāpu *phukī*.

Bhaktapur Newar house (see fig. 8), sharply bounded from outer city space by a precisely marked symbolic boundary. The ideal Newar urban house is built, repaired, and lived in by the middle and upper *thar*s, and those members of the lower *thar*s who can now find the money for it. The poor, notably the Po(n), live in much simpler ones, often single-story thatched houses. The ideal traditional Newar house consists of four, and occasionally five, stories. It is constructed by means of a wood frame and beams and thick supporting walls of fire baked bricks made of valley clay held together by a mud-based mortar.[22] The roofs, traditionally of tile and now sometimes of metal sheets or wheat straw thatching, slope from a peak towards the front and back, the peak, being at the long axis of the rectangular (as viewed from above) houses. The eves are supported by external struts that buttress the roof against the walls of the house; on a few houses these struts are elaborately carved. The upper story opens out into a porch, the *ka:si*, of occasional important ritual use, including the worship of the sun (chap. 8).

The house is internally divided longitudinally into two equal halves, front and back, by a division that runs parallel to the front of the house and consists of a wall in the lower stories and columns in the upper ones. The sections formed by this middle division are called *dyā*, and are designed as "outer" (*pine*) or "inner" (*dune*), with "outer" being the half on the street side. The inner half often faces on a central courtyard, which is ideally surrounded on all sides by houses of members of the *phukī*, or at least of the *thar*, although this pattern is often disrupted in recent building.

The house is symbolically set off at its boundary with the outer city, and its vertical space and horizontal space are used as resources for symbolic meanings. In its vertical dimension the house becomes progressively more sacred, differentiated, and vulnerable to pollution at progressively higher levels. The lowest floor of the house, the *cheli*, is, in fact, in some contexts "outside" of the house, a kind of bordering outside, like the zone just outside of the city's boundaries. The origin of the word "*cheli*" is uncertain. Manandhar (1976) proposes that it may come from "*che(n)*," "house," plus "*di*," support. Some Bhaktapur scholars surmise, in what is perhaps a folk etymology but is suggestive of their sense of the connotations of the term, that it may be derived from "*che(n)*," "house," plus "*li*," an "old term" said to mean the lower and impure part of the body below the umbilicus. Middle-status and lower-status families sometimes keep livestock on the *cheli*, but even upper-status families often keep animals such as goats who are being kept for sacrifice, and sometimes pet animals, such as rabbits and turtles in this out-of-the-house space. It is sometimes said that animals kept on the *cheli* will absorb diseases and the malevolent influence of dangerous spirits trying to enter the house and will thus protect people in the upper part of the house.[23]

The "outside" status of the *cheli* is further shown in that people from polluting *thar*s were—and for the Po(n) this is still true—allowed to enter the *cheli*, but were forbidden to go any higher into the house, which would have been polluted by them. Work areas for occupational castes and shops are often located on the *cheli* level of houses and are adapted in various ways. The *cheli* is also often used for the storage of materials that are said to be "not worth stealing," such as firewood, straw, hay, bricks, and old furniture.

The next floor (the second floor in the American system of designation, which will be used here), is the "floor of the *māta(n)* (or *mātā[n]*)," the *māta(n) talā*. This second story is the entrance to the first of the house's internal and progressively more inward areas. It is reached from the *cheli* by an interior stairway, which must be placed so that persons using it do not face the inauspicious direction south. On the *māta(n)* ordinary visitors (those who are not family members or of higher status than the family) and friends of junior members of the household are received. The *māta(n)* story is divided by a longitudinal partitioning wall, producing a large front room running the length of the house and facing on the street. This is the *māta(n)* proper, although in other contexts the entire floor may be referred to as the *māta(n)*. The back half is divided by perpendicular secondary walls or partitions into small rooms that serve as sleeping quarters and storerooms for valuable goods.

The next higher story is the "floor of the *cwata*." The longitudinal dividing wall is represented here by columns, so that the entire floor is open, and constitutes a large "hall," the *cwata*. Traditionally in high-status houses, and still remaining in many old houses, large carved ornate trellis windows (one of the representative forms of Newar art [S. P. Deo 1968–1969]) were located here, allowing people to look out on the streets without being seen. It is on this floor that the formal feasts associated with many family ceremonies, particularly for auspicious rites of passage, are held and high-status guests are received. In Brahman, Chathariyā, and some Pa(n)cthariyā houses this floor (or sometimes the floor above it) is the site of a shrine of the Tantric lineage goddess, the Āga(n) God (hidden in a room of its own), in accordance with the ideal that that shrine should be located toward the physical center of the house. The *cwata* is also the place where important Brahman-assisted family worship is usually held. Such worship is associated with rites of passage, and with some major festivals and other *ad hoc* special occasions (app. 4). Some members of the household, often the older ones, sleep here and there on bedding on the unpartitioned *cwata*.

The household shrine and images of household gods, in contrast to the Āga(n) God, are placed at one of the highest levels in the house. This is usually on the next highest floor, which is often the top floor, the "floor of the *baiga*." This is usully under the overhanging eaves of the house and is the location of the cooking and family eating area as well as the household shrine and its associated equipment. Daily household worship is held here and, occasionally, Brahman-assisted rituals if the group involved is small and does not include people from outside of the household or *phukī* group. Many houses have a fifth story. In this case the floor above the *cwata* is called a "fourth floor," and the top floor is still called the *baiga* (Korn 1976, 23).

Korn (1976, 3) provides a useful sketch of the typical furnishing of a Newar house:

> The interior furnishings and decorations are very simple in contrast to the often extravagant facades. After the clay and tile oven, the most important is the all-purpose straw-mat which serves as a carpet during the day and for sleeping on during night. Other carpets and blankets may decorate the floor, but these are reserved only for eating on special occasions. In the morning the bedding of blankets and cotton rugs is rolled up and stored away. Clothing and valuables are kept in wall recesses and wooden chests. A stove as a heating apparatus is unknown, and in its place portable clay bowls of various size are filled with burning charcoal. The kitchen is seldom used as a meeting place. Clay or metal oil lamps, available in many different shapes and sizes, stand in wall recesses to give light during the dark hours. Stocks of rice and other grain are stored in wooden chests or clay pots, while potatoes and vegetables are kept in bamboo baskets hanging below the overhanging roof. Clay and brass pitchers are used as water utensils. Wood, carried into the town from hills by porters, is the usual heating fuel although the poorer people burn dried cow dung. Foreign influences, however, have recently introduced Western-style furnishings. Electricity and kerosene have simplified the tasks of cooking and lighting.

In horizontal space the house's boundary with an exterior encircling space is indicated by a stone placed about two to three feet before the front door, under the forward edge of the front overhanging eaves. The stone, the *pikhā lakhu* (which is also the term for the area it covers), is considered to be the seat of a protective divinity (chap. 8). The *pikhā lakhu* is used in many rites of passage as the division between the inner world of the household and the outer world. It is here that a bride is greeted by the chief woman of the household to be purified of spirits and malevolent influences before being conducted into the house. It is at the *pikhā lakhu* that the corpse of a household member is left for a moment and then is picked up by the members of a funeral *guthi* to be carried to the cremation grounds. The *pikhā lakhu* is cleansed and purified each morning, as other god images in the house are, and it is also purified before major household worship.

Houses are ideally supposed to be oriented to one of the cardinal points of the compass other than the inauspicious south, with the most auspicious direction being east. In fact, the available spaces for city building, the meandering direction of many of the roads and alleys, the attempt by middle-level and upper-level families to build adjacent family houses in a rectangle around a central courtyard, all require violations of these orientations, which are largely ignored.[24] Within the horizontal space of the house, however, there are some arrangements following compass orientations. Thus the cooking area is generally toward the east, as is the household shrine.[25] As we have noted, stairways must be placed so that people using them do not face the inauspicious south. Similarly people avoid sleeping with their body in a north-south axis. They do not want to have their heads facing south. But if they were facing north, then their faces would face south when they sat up. Therefore, the entire north-south axis is inauspicious.

Because the front of the house faces on the street, and the back faces on the inner courtyard, the front/back contrast is equivalent to outer/inner. What are considered the private parts of the house—the bedrooms, the treasury, and the position of the Tantric shrine are at the back or inner section of the house.

At the time of the construction of a house, there are very elaborate additional symbolic spatial characterizations. The detailed symbolism of the construction of a Newar house would require a full study in itself. A significant beginning has been made by Vogt (1977) on which the following description is based. The choosing of the site for a new house, the setting of the proper date to commence construction, the construction itself (by masons and carpenters), the completion of the building of the house, and the purification of it after its physical completion, all entail a vast collection of symbolic references and practices. The new house and its foundations are being carved out of a "natural" area, disturbing the deified earth, Pṛthivī, and the supernatural serpents, *nāga*s, beneath its surface, as well as the spirits who may have clustered there. The disturbance of the natural space is dangerous, and powerful Tantric rites, including blood sacrifice, must be performed at key points. Sacrifices are made to the dangerous gods who protect civic space against external chaos and who—along with the dangerous god Bhairava who inhabits the wood block forming the base of the threshold of the main door of houses—exist protectively at the boundaries of these spaces. The house is considered, by the ritual experts responsible for its proper symbolic construction as a body and some of the successive rituals performed during its construction, as something like human rites of passage. The house, if improperly sited (in space and time), improperly constructed, or improperly purified, is dangerous. Without the proper ceremonies people may die, not only the construction workers (who have their own protective rituals, and rituals for effectiveness) but also members of the immediate or even the extended family. But, as we emphasize in many analogous situations (e.g., the symbolic procedures during the construction of masks or icons), most of this symbolism concerns the activities and special understandings of the experts involved in the physical and symbolic construction of the house—the carpenters, masons, astrologer, and Tantric priest. Most people live in houses that were constructed before their birth. They have to think about its setting or construction only if some family illness or disaster is attributed by some diagnostican of the supernatural to a disturbance in the house's relation to its environment, whereupon they must attempt the proper ritual readjustment or placation. Those who have a new house built or live in an old one need only to know that it is, or has been, properly done.

COLLAPSED STRUCTURE INSIDE THE CITY: CROSSROADS

The space beyond Bhaktapur's boundaries with its associated deities and symbolic enactments takes much of its meaning from its contrast with the moral and logical orders that are represented in the differentiated internal space of the public city. The outside represents a radically different kind of order. Some of this inside/outside contrast is, as we have noted, also found as part of the representation of the cellular components of city life in their contrast with their immediate outside environments, which are in weaker form something like the relation of the city as a whole to its outside. There are other kinds of locations where differentiated order is collapsed and transformed and that are loci for symbolic representations and actions with connection to the symbolic aspects of the encircling outside of the city. The city's central points—the royal center and the Taleju temple, the Tripurasundarī *pīṭha*, the central point between the two city halves, the point at which a pole, the Yasi(n), is erected to signify the start of the solar New Year (chap. 14)—all take some of their meanings from the transcendence of ordinary differentiated order. Another important example is the major crossroads in each *twa:*. At such crossings paths and roads radiate off to distant parts of the city. Each *twa:* has at least one of these crossings and more than one if it is a large *twa:* and divided into major neighborhoods. The major crossroads are the loci for uncarved stones (usually buried partly in the ground). The stone and the crossing point and the divinity thought to be located there are called the *chwāsa*.[26] (The general term for crossroad is *dwakā*.) The *chwāsa* is sometimes considered as a divinity in itself, sometimes among the more erudite as the seat of the Tantric goddess, Mātaṅgī.

The *chwāsa* is one of the places where polluting materials are deposited so that they will no longer be dangerous or problematic. It is there that the clothes a person has been wearing at the time of death are brought to be gathered up by a Jugī as part of his *thar* duty. Certain remains of formal feasts—particularly the portions of the head of a sacrificial animal that are distributed in a particular order to reflect the hierarchy of the leading men at the feast (chap. 9)—must be discarded there. The *chwāsa* not only can absorb the polluted materials placed on it, materials that would be strongly contaminating if placed in any ordinary space within the city,[27] but is also said to protect the area around it. The main *chwāsa*s are said to protect the entire *twa:*. This combination of the power to absorb problematic ("polluting") material and to "protect" through power is generally characteristic of a class of deities, the "dangerous" deities, of which the *chwāsa* (and Mātaṅgī) is a member (chap. 8).

In his study of a Newar village, Pyangaon, Toffin notes that it has only one *chwāsa*, which is at the northwest entrance to the village rather than inside it (1977, 33). That *chwāsa* lies at a crossroad (personal communication)[28] and is thought to be a gathering place for potentially harmful spirits. It is also the place where people discard cloths soiled by menstruation, the umbilical cords of newborn infants, clothes of the dead, and food as offerings to potentially harmful spirits.

The association of crossroads with the unpropitious, the uncanny, and the "liminal" is widespread in South Asia and elsewhere in the world.[29] Elsewhere in South Asia the inauspicious crossroads are sometimes associated with some form of the Tantric goddess. According to D. D. Kosambi, crossroads were "from the stone age, places where the Mothers were normally worshiped by savages whose nomad tracks met there" (1960, 144). He also quotes the classical writer Varāhamihira that crossroads bring evil repute upon any house near their junction, and are to be included among inauspicious places (1960, 18).

Asked why the seat of the *chwāsa* within the city is always a crossroads, a Newar Brahman said that perhaps it was because these crossroads are places where all sorts of people meet—clean and unclean, kings and humble people. The *chwāsa* reminds people, he continued, that they are approaching a crossroad and they should proceed carefully. His speculation suggests the significance of these crossroads as deriving from the collapse of ordinary spatial order.

Not all crossroads are *chwāsa* nor have uncanny significance. It is not clear which factors determine that a crossroads should become the seat of a *chwāsa*. They must represent the tying together of important outreaching routes for one thing. In an interesting variation of this theme, royal palaces are often in close approximation to major crossroads. In the town of Panauti, "The palace is placed so that all the routes coming from the exterior and all the main arteries of the city converge on it" (Barré, Berger, Feveile, and Toffin 1981, 43 [our translation]). Similarly, in both Kathmandu and Patan the Malla Palace was placed at major crossroads defining the axes of the old city. Mary Slusser, commenting on those cities, remarks that "given the traditional attitude in Hindu culture toward the inauspiciousness of crossroads, it seems surprising that such a site would have been conceived proper for the palace" (1982, 200). But the *chwāsa* has the power to protect the *twa:*, and the dangerous goddess it represents has the power to protect the city, and, indeed, the cosmos. The alliance of royalty and Tantric deities and ideas in a common concern with power and with the transcendence of the ordinary civic categories and restraints—here suggested by this double use of crossroads—is, as we will see, widely represented in Bhaktapur's symbolism and symbolic action.

THE UNDERCITY

The *chwāsa* is a stone embedded in the ground. In some places it is below the surface. It belongs to a class of "stone gods" to be considered in the next chapter which share among themselves a number of features. They require blood sacrifice, and many of them in one sense or another absorb polluting materials, often by "eating" them. In some cases the deity whose position is indicated by such stones is conceived as being beneath the surface of the ground. This subterranean realm is also the territory of the *nāga*s, the supernatural serpents that may be disturbed as we have noted, by excavations for buildings. We note these fragments here as a reminder that one of the boundaries of the city in its relation to what is outside itself is the boundary with the underneath, the earth. This realm for Bhaktapur does not have developed and clearly characterized chthonic gods (with the possible exception of Yamā, the king of the realm where the dead are judged, who is of negligible cultic significance for the city in itself), and is thus in strong contrast to the developed representations of other aspects of the "outside" and "beyond" of the city. It is outside of the city's circumferential boundaries—where the city's farmlands are—that the earth as a basis for fertility is assimilated to the symbolism of the Tantric goddess and to that sustaining and problematic outside beyond ordinary civic controls.

SYMBOLIZED SPACE BEYOND THE CITY

The symbolically marked spaces we have been considering have as their maximal area the bounded city, placed in contrast and relationship to a "dangerous" outside. The great majority of symbolic enactments during the course of the year concern the city and its bordering outside and its subunits. But the hinterland of Bhaktapur (once part of the kingdom of Bhaktapur), the Kathmandu Valley itself as the ancient seat of the Newars, the larger modern Nepal, and the Hindu homeland of India, are all full of significant shrines and sacred spots and mark out significant space beyong the boundaries of the city. Many of these have little contemporary use, but some of them still concern the people of Bhaktapur in visits, pilgrimages (see fig. 9), and attendance at great religious fairs or *melās*. In these encounters the Newars of Bhaktapur join with Newars of other cities, with non-Newar Nepalis, or with Indian Hindus

Figure 9. Outside the city. A group of Nepalis on a pilgrimage to a mountain shrine.

to celebrate solidarities beyond that of the city. We will return to these in our discussion of symbolic enactments in later chapters.

Gutschow (1979*a*, 27–65 passim), Slusser (1982), and others have argued that some of the shrines and temples in the Kathmandu Valley trace maṇḍalic patterns characterizing the larger Valley. Gutschow and his associates have also found what they believe to be evidence for a maṇḍalic structure extending beyond its boundaries within which Bhaktapur is centered, as suggested by certain schematic paintings of the city as a *maṇḍa* (Kölver 1976; Auer and Gutschow n.d., 38; Slusser 1982, 346). These structures may possibly have had general or much more likely esoteric speculative meaning in the past but have now lost contemporary popular or esoteric significance.

INTEGRATION OF SPACES

We have begun our survey of Bhaktapur's symbolic civic organization with a discussion of its space. The meaningful spaces we have been considering in this chapter are related to many ideas and actions in Bhaktapur's civic life that will be elaborated on in later chapters.

We have presented nested, bounded spaces, each representing some kind of "solidarity" in contrast to an outside. In all societies individuals find themselves belonging to different groups depending on the context, and thus in opposition to some contrasting group. Bhaktapur, however, not only organizes these oppositions, most generally, by successively inclusive levels—nuclear family, household, *phukī*, people of the *twa:* as neighborhood or village, people of the maṇḍalic section, people of the antagonistic mirror cities of the city halves, the citizens of the total city, and finally the people, creatures, and forces of the city plus its environment—but also gives most of these a spatial definition and anchoring. It is this anchoring that is one of Bhaktapur's significant "typological" characteristics.

There are two general ways that Bhaktapur's spatial units and levels are realized in symbolic action. First, they are the places where certain kinds of actions are typically and repeatedly performed during the course of the year (chap. 16), or of a lifetime (app. 6). The house, *twa:*, crossroads, and so on, emerge as meaningful areas in the course of these repeated actions. However, people are also aware that all or most other houses, or *twa:*s, or maṇḍalic sections, or whatever unit, are doing the same thing at the same time or in some fixed sequence. The spatial unit becomes significant in its identity and contrast with similar units; it

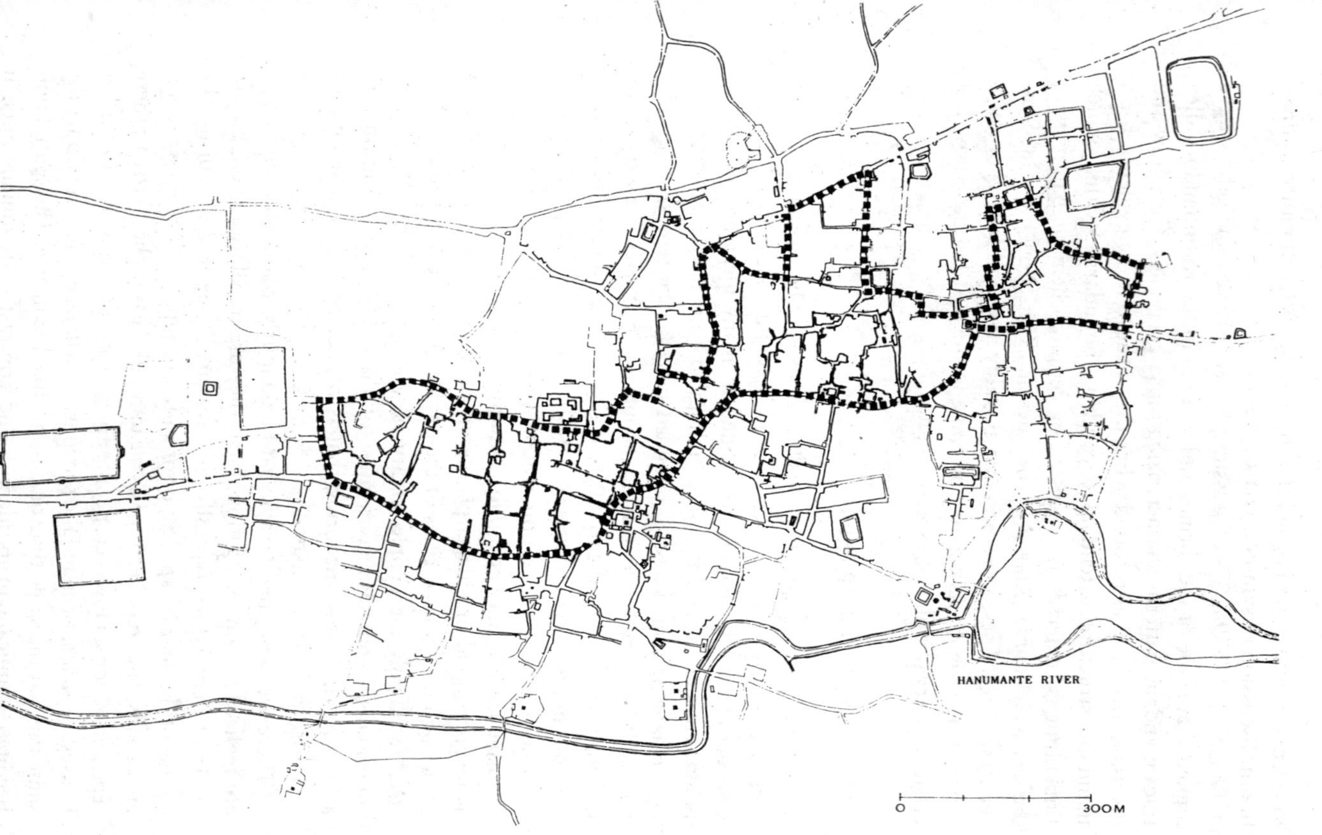

Map 12. The integration of space. The *pradakṣiṇāpatha*, the city's festival route, is marked by a dotted line. It ties together the upper

becomes a member of a class of like spaces. In the first kind of representation, *the same person* is, in various contexts, a member of different kinds of spaces, and there are systematic ways in which he or she moves or is moved from one kind to another. That movement tells some kind of a story. The second kind of representation, a static one, is that of *different persons doing the same thing*. These are two different ways of using and marking space. We will consider them again in the chapters on annual events.

One way of tieing together different units in space is through traditional processional routes. These exist in each *twa:*, each maṇḍalic section, and for the city as a whole. We have discussed the major city-wide processional route, the *pradakṣiṇāpatha*, in connection with the relation of low-status groups and the boundary of the city, and noted that in contrast to the situation in some other Hindu communities it is within the city (map 12) where it binds all but the most westerly and probably most recently settled of the city's twenty-four major *twa:*s together.[30]

Bhaktapur's spatial divisions both give meaning to and take meaning from their special divinities, symbolic enactments and their associated legends and myths. Some of the meaning they contribute to this dialogue of forms derives from some of the universal potentials of spatial meaning, widely exploited throughout the world. The meanings of the face-to-face neighborhood, the uncanny nature of thresholds, borders and crossroads, the danger of the beyond-the-borders, the antagonisms of balanced and opposing civic units, and the primacy of the center and the hilltop are all very general semantic possibilities for space, aspects that can be understood in a fairly direct way. Yet others of the meanings contributed by the spatial units are, of course, local matters, local histories, legends, and forms and require special knowledge to be grasped.

We will trace these dialogues of meaning throughout the following chapters.[31]

CHAPTER EIGHT

Bhaktapur's Pantheon

INTRODUCTION

The city of Bhaktapur contains many material representations of gods, a witness to its long history and to close contacts since its earliest days with India, that great incubator of forms of divinity. The multitude of gods whose representations have persisted in Bhaktapur and the Kathmandu Valley are of great importance to the historian of South Asian religion and of art,[1] but only some of them are alive at present, foci of action, meaning, and emotion. The others are dormant, perhaps to be revived for some future fashion or need.[2]

It is precisely because Hindu deities can be induced into material objects, the "idols" of the Judeo-Christian-Islamic iconoclasts, that they are able to serve the purposes they do in the construction of Bhaktapur's mesocosm. Those objects can be anchored in space or moved through it. They are constructed of meaningful elements and emerge as units of meaning in themselves. They have their own semantic import, their direct implications for meaning, but they are so constructed that their various similarities and contrasts can be used to build a structure of meaning within an overall civic pantheon, the coherent total domain of the gods. That structure helps map the city's symbolic space and its conceptual universe. The crafted gods, the "idols," are joined by more shadowy supernatural figures, some vaguely represented in astral bodies, some in natural stones, and some in the shifting and vague form of ghosts and spirits. These latter figures have their own uses—the various kinds of *embodiment* that the members of the large realm of divine and spooky beings have, considerably influencing their meanings and uses.

As usual, we are primarily interested in the level of civic order; hence we are concerned here in the way the deities are used by the public city. Many of Bhaktapur's component units have their own internal deities; most, but not all, of them (an exception, for example, is the deified figure Gorakhnāth, the tutelary deity of the Jugīs) are versions of the same deities used as the city's public deities. We will comment on some of these component units, on the interior deities of the household and the *phukī*, and have included some remarks on the special deities of the Brahmans and of the "royal center" and on the ghosts and spirits of importance to individuals.

We will begin by presenting the city's urban divinities in considerable detail. This will give us a basis for considering exactly what it is they contribute to Bhaktapur's mesocosmic organization and how they are able to do it.

APPROACHES

In the course of the field study we began our investigation of Bhaktapur's divinities with attempts to locate and list as many of the city's active shrines and temples as we could. By "active" we mean those locations that are regularly used by some group of people in Bhaktapur, and that may have some attendant priest. (Some shrines with a priestly attendant have no significant public use or meaning.) Any of the many "inactive" shrines and temples, relics of some past period, may be loci of casual or private devotion by passersby, but they are not important to the city in the same way as the active ones that concern us. The active shrines and temples were mapped on detailed aerial maps of Bhaktapur, which gave us a first basis for approaching the spatial location and implications of groups or categories of divinities. Subsequently, Niels Gutschow put at our disposal maps that he and his associates prepared of temples and shrines, and we have used them, when noted, to amplify, supplement, and correct our own materials. These surveys were supplemented by discussions with religious experts on various aspects of the divinities and by materials on their use (presented in later chapters and appendixes) and on their personal meanings to various individuals.

In this chapter, and throughout the book, we have chosen to give divinities their Sanskrit names, rather than either the Newari approximation of that name or the popular Western equivalents. We use the Newari form in a few special cases where it has only an attenuated connection or no connection with a Sanskrit form.

DIVINITIES: HOUSING AND SETTING

We have used "temples and shrines" as a covering phrase for the various settings in which the divinities are found, but those settings are more complex. Local usage differentiates "temples" (*dega:*, from Sanskrit, *devāgṛhā*); "god-houses" (*dya: che[n]*); *pīth* (Sanskrit, *pīṭha*) "hypaethral shrines"; and an otherwise nonspecified residual of "gods' places"—stones, fountains, trees, and so on. There is also a class of supernatural beings, ghosts, and spirits who have no anchored setting, airy nothings lacking a local habitation, if not a name. This lack of a home, like the vagueness of their form, is an essential aspect of this latter group's meaning and use.

1. *Temples, dega:s.* These are buildings of various degrees of elaborateness (see fig. 10), acting as foci for the worship and the spatial influence of the particular god (or gods) they contain. They add to the meaning of their contained god their own symbolic meanings (Kramrish 1946). The historical connections and stylistic and structural features of Newar (and Nepalese) temples have been treated in monographs by Weisner (1978) and Bernier (1970) and as part of larger studies by Korn (1976) and Slusser (1982). Bhaktapur has two kinds of temple buildings with very different external appearances: the traditional Indian form and the tiered-roof "Nepalese" temple, which somewhat resembles the "pagoda" temples of China and Japan. These two local styles are not differentially named, and they do not differ in function.[3]

Mary Slusser (1982, 128) writes of the Newar temple (her remarks applying to Hindu temples in general):

> The dwellings of the gods of Nepal are quite unlike those in many other parts of the world that are designed to house both the divinity and a congregation assembled to worship. Despite many collective sacred rituals, Nepali worship is fundamentally an individual matter. The temple, therefore needs to make no provision for a congregation. With notable exceptions, the worshiper ordinarily does not penetrate the temple at all. He tenders his offerings

Figure 10. A Newar-style temple. The Ñātāpwa(n)la temple in Ta:mārhi Square.

> through a priestly intermediary from whom, in return, he receives the physical sign of the god's blessings (*prasāda*). Further, not only is the god within the temple an object of worship so is the temple itself.

The "notable exception" for Bhaktapur includes some of the events at the royal temple complex, Taleju, where large numbers of people are involved as actors and congregation. But Slusser's remarks generally characterize Bhaktapur's other *dega:*s. In Bhaktapur, as we shall see, the proper loci for "congregations" are in other spaces.

2. *God-houses, dya: che(n)s.* Although *dega:*, "temple," is ultimately also derived from a Sanskrit phrase for "god's house," the *dya: che(n)* (literally in Newari "God's house," *dya:*, god, plus *che[n]*, house) is where portable images of divinities are kept. These images are carried outside for various rituals, processions, or festivals, and then returned to the house. Some of these buildings are quite elaborate in themselves. Although many important portable gods have their own god-house, many portable images are kept within a temple, where they are separate and distinguished from the fixed temple image of the divinity.

3. *Shrines.* There are many figures representing divinities in Bhaktapur that are not enclosed by buildings. These may be free standing statues or simply carved or natural stones. The latter shrines are "aniconic." Often arches or canopies are placed behind or over these representations. Included here are the "hypaethral" or open-to-the-skies shrines of the nine Maṇḍalic Goddesses. These shrines are *pīth* (Sanskrit *pīṭha*), a class of shrines of certain Tantric goddesses in the classic Hindu tradition marking places where pieces of the goddess *Satī's* dismembered body fell from the sky (see below). Slusser (1982, 325) claims that some temples of the Newar Tantric goddesses reflect such hypaethral origins:

> Many [goddesses] have only hypaethral shrines. Still others have had temples built over what were obviously once typical hypaethral shrines. Characteristically, the sanctums of such later-day enclosures are very open, the temple's multiple doorways or colonnades permitting an unobstructed view, and the sanctum itself often sunken well below the present ground level. These sunken and airy sanctums have much to say about the antiquity of many of these goddesses and their ultimate chthonic origins. Symbols of such divinities should be open to the skies and woe to the misguided votary who closes them in.

4. *Non-Newar-Hindu structures.* Bhaktapur has many Buddhist religious structures—stupas, *vihāras* (religious centers derived from monastic precursors), and god-houses, as well as non-Newar Hindu centers (*maṭhas*) for holy men, which are peripheral to our present concerns.

GODS WITH TEMPLES AND SHRINES—SOME NUMBERS

Shrines and temples are the seats of one segment of Bhaktapur's supernaturals, the "Purāṇic deities" of classical, post-Vedic Hinduism. By our count and criteria there are about 120 active shrines and temples within or just outside the boundaries of Bhaktapur. They are one of the two sets of spatially fixed representations in the public city; the other is a numerous and heterogenous class of "deified stones." The shrines and temples are distributed among these deities as follows, with the number of shrines and temples given in parentheses: Viṣṇu (29), Śiva (28), Gaṇeśa (24), Sarasvatī (3), Bhīmasena (3), Naṭarāja (2), Hanumān (2), Kṛṣṇa (2), Rāma with his consort Sītā (3), Bhairava (1), Jagannātha (2), Dattātreya (now regarded primarily as a combination of Śiva and Viṣṇu) (1), and the group of dangerous or Tantric goddesses that includes some fourteen major named forms (26). We thus have some twenty-six classical Hindu divinities represented in public urban space. Eighty-two of these shrines and temples have various kinds of temple priests, *pūjārī* (see chap. 10). The other structures do not have *pūjārī*s. We will discuss the spatial locations and the uses of the various temples and shrines later in this chapter and elsewhere in this book, but we may note here that about one-quarter of the temples and shrines are primarily related to the city as a whole, while the rest are related to one or another of the city's major constitutive spatial divisions.

SORTING SUPERNATURALS—SOME PRELIMINARY REMARKS

To consider a particular divinity as a member of a pantheon or of some larger domain of supernaturals in a certain community during a certain segment of that community's history is radically different from considering that divinity throughout its long history and its South Asian (and beyond) areal variations. Śiva as a member of Bhaktapur's pantheon is not the same as the Śiva considered in a general and unrooted sense, through, say, a compendium of his various mythological accounts and his historical usages and forms throughout South Asia.

When Hindu divinities are considered from an historical or South Asian areal viewpoint, they have a very great number of accumulated forms, names, meanings, myths, aspects, philosophical implications, and contradictions. Several attempts have been made at encyclopedic approaches to the whole Hindu pantheon (e.g., Banerjea 1956; Mani 1975; Rao 1971; Daniélou 1964) and to individual divinities or to some of their aspects (such as O'Flaherty's exhaustive survey of materials on asceticism and eroticism in the mythology of Śiva [1973]). Bhaktapur has selected only certain deities from the Hindu tradition for emphasis. For the particular deities it has selected, it further selects and emphasizes only certain aspects of their potential—variously realized elsewhere—for meaning, form, and use. For some of them Bhaktapur sometimes even adds its own attributes, perhaps borrowed from other deities, sometimes ancient local ones.

It is possible for some purposes to consider Bhaktapur's pantheon as a sort of museum, a collection of divine South Asian flotsam that has drifted into the Valley. We cannot avoid our general knowledge of important aspects of the meaning of the divinities in space and time beyond the city, a knowledge shared by the people in Bhaktapur who introduced these figures and who continue to use them, but what is important for us is what is done with the deities in Bhaktapur, their local uses and relations.

The sorting of Bhaktapur's divinities and other assorted "supernatural" figures that follow in this chapter is a sorting, then, for that purpose. We will sort the supernatural beings into several large groups that have morphological and functional contrasts. The groups are:

1. "Major city gods." These are familiar major gods of Purāṇic, post-Vedic, Hinduism. They have, at least in some of their important city forms, anthropomorphic or creatural forms, and are located in named temples and shrines known to the city as a whole. These "major city gods" are divided into two contrasting groups, "ordinary gods" and "dangerous gods." The latter require blood sacrifice, are attended by a special class of priests, and are the foci of a special set of ideas and procedures (chap. 9).

2. "Stone gods." This is a group of deities represented by natural stones. They are related to other natural objects (as opposed to objects created through human craft, like statues) that have divine properties

(springs, lakes, ponds, trees, etc.) but, in contrast to such other natural divinities, have systematic placements and usages.

3. "Astral divinities." These are associated with the sun, moon, and various heavenly objects and events; are associated mostly with astrological ideas and practices; and have their own special priests.

4. "Ghosts and spirits." These are a miscellaneous group of vague entities that may be usefully introduced here, and that have some significant contrasts with the other supernaturals.

MAJOR GODS: THE "ORDINARY" DEITIES

We have characterized the "major gods" of Bhaktapur as being derived from the most salient and important gods of the early Hindu Purāṇic tradition, of being situated in temples and shrines of city-wide importance, and of having anthropomorphic forms (some having a mixture of anthropomorphic and animal features). These gods are foci of ideas and symbolic enactments concerning the representation and integration of the city as a whole and of its larger constituent units.

Within this group of "major gods" there is an essential and sharp contrast of two subgroups. One of these is a group of gods who are (when necessary) attended by Brahmans or "Brahman-like" priests (chap. 10). These gods are never offered blood sacrifice or alcoholic spirits. Their icons are in the form of idealized human types, or humanized animal forms. The central divinities in this group are male. The other group of major gods are (when necessary) publicly attended by a special class of priests, the Ācāriya. These gods are offered blood sacrifice, meat, and alcoholic offerings. Their icons are often in the form of demonic, bestialized human forms, marked by bulging eyes, fangs, and sometimes extreme emaciation. They are sometimes represented garlanded with necklaces of human heads or skulls, and carrying a human skull cup for drinking blood in one of their many hands. Sometimes these gods are represented as exaggeratedly erotic forms with the faces of beautiful young women and with full breasts. These kinds of gods are predominantly female. When it is necessary to distinguish these two groups in speech, the first are sometimes called "ordinary" gods, and by some Brahmans (mistakenly in historical perspective) "Vedic" gods. The second group are sometimes called "dangerous" gods (in contrast to "ordinary") or "Tantric" gods (in contrast to "Vedic"). There are other significant contrasts in the nature, internal relations, uses, and significance of these two groups of major divinities, but these remarks will serve to introduce them.

Within the two groups of major gods (as within the other groups of divinities) each particular divinity has his (or her) own personality and significance derived in part from his history, from his present relations with others of Bhaktapur's divinities, and from the uses to which Bhaktapur puts them.

ŚIVA

When people in Bhaktapur are asked which of the Newars' two "religions" they adhere to, a question that is usually phrased as which path, or *mārgā* they follow, those whom we have been designating as "Hindus" in contrast to Newar "Buddhists," answer by saying they are Śivamārgi, followers of the path of Śiva ("Siba" in local pronunciation). Śiva (see fig. 11) is most commonly referred to in Bhaktapur as *Mahādya:*, the Newari version of the Sanskrit *Mahādeva*, the great god. He is represented in a variety of anthropomorphic images, and as the abstract phallic *liṅga*. Śiva's status in Bhaktapur is considerably more complex than that of the other benign gods in that he has several levels of meaning. His most striking aspect is that while he is pervasively present as an "idea," as one of the central references helping to locate and explain in various ways the other city gods, he is in comparison to them distant, relatively absent from the concrete arrangements and actions of city religion. Śiva's meanings may be distinguished approximately as follows.

1. *Śiva as the creative principle.* For some more theoretically inclined people in Bhaktapur Śiva is the creator god, out of which all the forms of gods (including a particular concrete divinity also called "Śiva") are generated. This is a theoretical and philosophical position. In other contexts, as we will see, Devī, the "Goddess," is thought of and praised (by the same people) as the supreme creative force. For the most part the basic, divine, creative principle, called the *brahman* or *paramātman* in sophisticated theological discussion, is amalgamated to a general featureless deity, neither male nor female, neither Śiva nor Goddess, vaguely conceived as a combination of all gods. This condensed divinity is what some, at least, people have in mind when they think of "god" in some general way, often in such thoughts or phrases as "god help me," in the face of some problem. This generalized deity is called

Figure 11. Śiva as a fertility god.

simply *dyā:*, or sometimes addressed with some honorific Sanskrit appellation, as Paramesvara, Isvara, Bhagavān, and the like. This generalized deity—unlike the traditional idea of the *brahman*—is aware of the individuals who call on it, and may help. It is not represented in civic symbols or ritual enactments, and represents a "monotheistic" potentiality that must in all likelihood wait for the breakdown of Bhaktapur's present religious system and its eventual "modernization" to realize its social potential.

2. *Śiva, first among the gods.* A more common phrasing of Śiva's greatness is that he is the most important of the gods, the one whom the others respect. This importance is not based on his power, however, nor on his concrete uses in Bhaktapur. He is not like Indra had been in an earlier stage of Hindu belief, the "king" of the gods. His importance, like that of the central, "full" form of the Tantric goddess seems to have something to do with his centrality as a generator of or container of the contrasting meanings of the lesser divinities.

3. *Śiva as the generator of the dangerous gods.* Śiva is, in ways that we will note below, one of the "ordinary" gods. However, he is the agent by which in one context and conception the "dangerous" gods are generated. Many prominent symbolic forms in Bhaktapur concern this generation. They include the idea of Śiva's emanation Śakti (below) as well as other types of transformation. Much, but not all, of the symbolism of the *liṅga* is related to this transformation, as is much of the symbolism of Tantra. We will return to this in our consideration of Śakti, the dangerous divinities and Tantra (chap. 9). In other contexts, as we shall see, the "dangerous gods," particularly the central, generating forms of the goddess, are conceived as existing independently of Śiva. In such contexts Śiva becomes quite peripheral, the goddess becomes the central creative force, and Śiva's importance or presence becomes greatly attenuated.

4. *Śiva as one of the group of ordinary gods.* At this level Śiva is one of a community of divinities related by the ordinary social ties of family and friendship. The central group of ordinary gods are Pārvatī, Gaṇeśa, Viṣṇu, Lakṣmī, Sarasvatī, and some secondary divinities associated with Viṣṇu. Pārvatī is Śiva's wife or consort, Gaṇeśa is his son, Viṣṇu is Śiva's essential friend, and Lakṣmī is Viṣṇu's wife. Sarasvatī

stands outside these relations. Śiva is sometimes represented as a young man with a moustache (see color illustrations). In this form he is thought of as an unattached and dreamy young bachelor. Sometimes he is shown with his consort Pārvatī to his left, his arm tenderly around her shoulder. He is absent-minded, a dreamer, stumbling in his abstraction into socially dangerous errors from which his friend Viṣṇu must extricate him. He dresses improperly, like a jungle dweller, and sometimes goes naked. He moves at whim from place to place. He is usually gentle and benign in his abstracted way unless roused to fury, and that fury is elemental and potentially randomly destructive. Sometimes he incarnates his vehicle, the bull Nandi. Sometimes he is found in deep meditation on Mount Kailash in the mountains to the north of Bhaktapur. Sometimes he is found in the cremation grounds, or even in the refuse dump in the inner courtyard of the house. His destructive power can be focused and put to use against impersonal and external dangers to the city, but in this transformation we are soon no longer dealing with Śiva, something new arises.

Śiva represents the human tension between self-absorption and asocial sexuality on the one hand and social involvement taming such problematic states and passions on the other. As Pārvatī's consort and Viṣṇu's friend, he is under the socializing restraint of those social relations, he needs them. Śiva alone—adolescent, yogi-like, alternating between sexual passion and ascetic self absorption—is recognizable both as forest dweller who has escaped from the city and as one important aspect of the man of the city. As the Mahābhārata says of this Śiva (quoted in Atkinson 1974, 721) [from the *Mahābhārata*, Anuśāsana Parva, chap. 14]; cf. Mani 1974, 808).

> He assumes many forms of gods, men, goblins, demons, barbarians, tame and wild beasts, birds, reptiles, and fishes. He carries a discus, trident, club, sword and axe. He has a girdle of serpents, earrings of serpents, a sacrificial cord of serpents and an outer garment of serpents' skins. He laughs, sings, dances and plays various musical instruments. He leaps, gapes, weeps, causes others to weep, speaks like a madman or a drunkard as well as in sweet tones. With an erect penis he dallies with the wives and daughters of the Rishis.

Śiva's essence is in his transformations, which make him both elusively shifting and generative. As O'Flaherty (1973, 36) notes, he is both a *yogi* and its antithesis, the lover of Pārvatī. She adds, however, in regard to this and other apparent oppositions in his mythology:

> The mediating principle that tends to resolve the oppositions is in most cases Śiva himself. Among ascetics he is a libertine and among libertines an ascetic; conflicts which they cannot resolve, or can attempt to resolve only by compromise, he simply absorbs into himself and expresses in terms of other conflicts. . . . He emphasizes that aspect of himself which is unexpected, inappropriate, shattering any attempt to achieve a superficial reconciliation of the conflict through mere logical compromise. . . . Śiva is particularly able to mediate in this way because of his protean character; he is all things to all men.

But this protean character in itself limits the semantic possibilities of Śiva in Bhaktapur. There is one thing he cannot be to all men, that is a fixed character, and that provides his major contrast to Viṣṇu, who is fixed in his purposes and his conventional forms.

Yogi, bachelor, friend, and husband are all Śiva, but Śiva disappears in his supernatural transformations. When he has been transformed into his dangerous form, Bhairava, when he emits his *śakti* ("power"; see chap. 9) or the goddess Devī, these dangerous forms are immediately thought of as independent actors. They have their own myths, legends, and histories. In thought and action they are for the most part disconnected from Śiva, except for vestigial traces and markings—a Śiva mask carried but not worn, Śiva's vertically rotated third eye sometimes, but not always, placed on their foreheads (see color illustrations). And in a further limiting and bounding of the protean Śiva to his proper human-like area, it is the "goddess" herself—although in some contexts thought of as generated by Śiva—who becomes the shifting, generative force. While Śiva's generative activities, the center from which he moves are in the *social* world, and are related to recognizably human activities and modes of a certain sort—the lover, the adolescent, and ascetic, intoxicated or ecstatic states—it is another figure, the "goddess," who is the center of generation in a much more radically *extrasocial* world, the world outside the city and its order. Thus, although Śiva represents a bridge to the world beyond the city, and beyond all cities, those bridges become burnt for the most part once crossed, and as his transformations come to life, Śiva, overtly in Tantric imagery, becomes a corpse. His ongoing and continuing life in Bhaktapur is as a representative of that dimension of the social person which is valued, although in tension with social and moral order. In his transformations to representations of the extrasocial world, Śiva becomes almost forgotten. Similarly, when thought of as a creator God, this cosmic Śiva is also lost from view when his creation is being considered. In his own anthropomorphic right, however, he represents a complex of traits which are unified in being thoroughly human, but in one way or another problematic for social order. This Śiva provides problems which must be dealt with by his friend Viṣṇu at the service of the moral community. It is important to emphasize that from the point of view of the corpus of South Asian myths about the relations of Śiva and Viṣṇu this is a local choice of emphasis. There are, for example, South Asian stories where it is Śiva who must free Viṣṇu from some passionate bondage (e.g., O'Flaherty 1973, 41). Bhaktapur, in fact, develops selected meanings suggested by the major persisting myths and representations of the two gods. Their relation is epitomized in one of the local interpretations of the complex symbol of Śiva's power, the *liṅga*, whose more central meanings are related to the idea of Śakti (below here, and chap. 9). The *liṅga* consists of a column at whose base is an encircling band. In this interpretation of Śiva as a component of civic order (rather than as the generator of cosmic forces), the upright column represents Śiva and his explosive and expanding energies and the encircling band at the base represents a restraint placed by Viṣṇu around that column of energy to protect, control, and channel it.

There are about thirty active Śiva shrines and temples in Bhaktapur. Of these, fourteen are found in four clusters outside the traditional boundaries of the city to the south near each of the bridges to which the city's southern and southeastern roads and paths lead. Another nine are grouped in the two central squares of the town, the Lāekū Square in front of the palace and the Ta:mārhī Square, both of which, it may be recalled, are (in different contexts) centers of the city. These central shrines and temples were built by the Malla kings and by wealthy families and *thar*s (such as one group of shrines built by the Kumha:, the potters) as variously motivated acts of private devotion to Śiva. Many of the structures outside of the city are of relatively recent post-Malla origin, and it is said they were built there because there was more available space on which to build. Some of these shrines and temples have attendant priests whose stipend is funded by grants of land that were set aside for this purpose at the time of the building of the structure, but may have no other worshipers. Others are the object of worship of descendants of the founding group, or sometimes by people who have made a pledge to worship Śiva, perhaps at that particular shrine, in exchange for the fulfillment of some wish. One of the largest and most visually impressive temples in the northern half of the city is devoted to the divinity Dattātreya (Newari, Dattātri), who is thought of as a combined incarnation of Viṣṇu, Brahma,[4] and Śiva. In the Dattātreya temple Viṣṇu is iconographically dominant, but Śiva is thought of as the main power embodied in the temple. The temple priests are non-Newars (Jhā Brahmans), and the inner sanctum is closed to Newar Brahmans. The temple's main function is as a pilgrimage center for non-Newar Shaivite devotees from India and other parts of Nepal.

For the Newars of Bhaktapur, the Śiva shrines and temples, in marked contrast to those of certain other major divinities, are not used to designate any of the internal structural features of city organization. Correlated with this is that there is only one minor annual festival (Mādya: Jātrā; see chap. 13), specifically devoted to Śiva. The great Śiva festival for the Newars of Bhaktapur and elsewhere, as well as for Nepalis and for many Indians, has its center out of Bhaktapur (and of the other major Newar cities) at the great Valley shrine complex of Paśupatinātha devoted to Śiva as the "Lord of the Beasts," during the major South Asian Shaivite festival, Śivarātrī, in the late winter. Bhaktapur itself on that day is a secondary focus for some Shaivite pilgrims, and some of the city's men perform an unusual—in contrast to other forms of local worship—type of devotion to Śiva spending the night by fires along the city's public streets, sometimes smoking cannabis, in an enactment that, with its associated legends (see chap. 13, "Silā Ca:re" and our discussion there) illuminate Śiva's meaning as a bridge to a transcendent realm.

In Bhaktapur there are several divinities with limited functions, and with names and attributes of their own sometimes said to be "forms" of Śiva. There are some statues in stone of a figure with an erect penis locally identified as Śiva which are worshiped by families who wish children or specifically a son (fig. 11). Śiva is worshiped in the rite of passage of people in their seventy-seventh year as Mṛtyum Jaya, the god who conquers time and prolongs life. He is sometimes said to be Naṭarāja, the god of the dance, who is worshiped by musicians and actors. (Naṭarāja as the Newar god Nāsa Dya: has accumulated, as we will note, other meanings and uses.) Śiva is the god buried in the inner courtyard of houses who destroys the wastes thrown there. He is Viśvakarmā (Newari, Biswarkarma), the god of crafts and trades, who gives power to the tools and implements of the various traditional and modern crafts: the barber's razor, the driver's truck, the farmer's tools.

Śiva's meaning in Bhaktapur's supernatural domain is deeply affected by his position in the larger system. We have introduced some of this, but we must turn to the other members of the domain, each of whom provides context for the others.

VIṢṆU-NĀRĀYAṆA AND HIS AVATARS

Viṣṇu is usually referred to in Bhaktapur by one of the names historically associated with Viṣṇu, Nārāyaṇa (Newari, Nārāyan). Viṣṇu (as we will here refer to this divinity for comparative convenience) belongs centrally to what we will call the "moral interior" of Bhaktapur. Although other gods may be addressed on their special days or for particular unusual problems, Viṣṇu and Lakṣmī, his consort, are at the foci of ordinary household prayer. Viṣṇu is that fragment of divinity that dwells in individuals as their soul or *ātmā*, in the Newar version of the ancient South Asian correspondence of soul and cosmic divinity.

Although there are several and conflicting ideas about the possible fates of the soul after death and about various heavens, and a number of theories as to what determines a person's postdeath state, the focus of most belief and action in regard to personal fate after death centers on Viṣṇu. In the ceremonies devoted to dying, attention is focused on Viṣṇu, and the dying person must pray to Viṣṇu, meditate on him, and address his or her last words to him. In the kingdom of the Lord of the Dead, Yama Rāj, it is Viṣṇu's representative who argues the case for the deceased in front of King Yama. This case is based on the individual's merits and sins, virtues and vices, in relation to his following or violating the moral law, the Dharma. Those who follow the Dharma can expect to go to Viṣṇu's heaven. To get to Śiva's heaven one must make Śiva a focus of meditation, another and radically different path to salvation from the moral path of following the social Dharma. In Viṣṇu's heaven one keeps one's social identity and is joined with one's family in reward for one's social virtue. The salvation associated with Śiva and the Tantric gods, *mokṣa*, has, in contrast, a problematic and uncanny relation to the social self.

Viṣṇu is represented in Bhaktapur by idealized, princely human forms. Occasionally he is represented in the forms of one of his incarnations, or *avatars*. He is also represented occasionally by small, rounded stones, locally called *śālagrāms*.[5] In contrast to other places in South Asia, Viṣṇu's *avatars* (Sanskrit, *avatāra*) in Bhaktapur have minimal cultic significance in themselves and are of major importance only as aspects of Viṣṇu.[6] In contrast to Viṣṇu's twenty-nine active temples and shrines in Bhaktapur, only two temples are actively devoted to Kṛṣṇa and three to Rāma and his consort Sītā (see fig. 12). One of the two Kṛṣṇa temples is in Lāekū Square, and was one of the temples built by the Malla kings for their personal merit. It is attended by a Rājopādhyāya Brahman and contains a portable god image, which is carried around the city once a year. The other temple, in the northern part of the city, has no priest and is used in a casual way by some local people or passersby. Both of the active Rāma temples are outside the city boundaries at places where roads meet the river. One of them is part of a complex of temples built by the potter *thar*, the Kumha:s, living in the southern half of the city, and is attended by Kumha:s and people living in nearby areas. The other, to the southwest, is of some general importance once a year, in connection with the worship of one of the Eight Aṣṭamātṛkās, Vārāhī.[7] There are two Hanūmān temples associated with the southwestern Rāma temple that are visited by many people on the same day of the annual festival calendar as that temple. Hanumān, a divinity in monkey form associated with Rāma in the Hindu epics, is also represented in other Viṣṇu temples. Newari art represents still other of Viṣṇu's avatars (particularly Vāmana, and Narasiṃha), as it also represents Viṣṇu in relation to his cosmogenic aspect,[8] but these representations have no contemporary uses.

The conception of Viṣṇu's *avatars* is closely related to the idea of Viṣṇu as the divine portion, the *ātma*, of each individual. The *avatars* represent the incarnation of a portion of Viṣṇu into the ordinary world, as part of a mixture that is in part human (or animal) and part divine.[9] Viṣṇu's *avatars* are not only incarnated in human or animal forms, but by and large they lead recognizable social lives, albeit with legendary heroic powers.[10] The lives of the incarnations were furthermore located in real space and historical time. These lives were lived for the purpose of reestablishing some desirable social order for humans or for the gods after that order's derangement through some antisocial force usually personified as a "demon" or antigod, an *Asura*. This is in marked contrast to the case of Śiva, whose transformations, such as Bhairava and the Goddess, are emanations in which Śiva's identity is transformed and lost, and which are themselves "demonic" forms of the same sort as *Asuras*. Rather than exist through a unique lifetime, as Viṣṇu's *avatars* do, Śiva's transformations appear and are "reabsorbed" in some contexts or, in others, are as eternal as Śiva himself. Although they can defeat the Asuras and other forces of disorder, they are, in themselves, dangerous and problematic to the orderly social world, and must be controlled in turn. In another significant contrast, while Śiva's emana-

Figure 12. Rāma and his consort Sītā. Note the difference in size.

tions (or in some versions the emanations of Pārvatī herself) defeat other demons through brute magical force, Viṣṇu's *avatars* characteristically restore order through cunning and other social skills allied to their divine power.

In Bhaktapur's stories it is Śiva in his wanderings and absent-mindedness who is either sometimes dangerous himself, or who allows some devotee to accumulate through meditation and austerities some god-like power, which he then uses in defiance of the gods' order for his own selfish purposes. Viṣṇu must undo the damage, calm Śiva, overcome the magic power of Śiva's devotee, and restore order. In this contrast Śiva is the passionate, romantic dreamer for whom social propriety is a burden. Viṣṇu represents sobriety, decency, and order. The pair represent a familiar universal tension within societies and within individuals.

The twenty-nine Viṣṇu temples and shrines are distributed around the city in close proximity, for the most part, to the city's main processional route. Of these, two are large temple complexes—one immediately south of the upper-lower city axis, and the other in the eastern part of the upper city. Although these two largest temples are located in the lower city and upper city, respectively, they are not considered representative of these city halves in the way that other space-marking deities represent spatial units, and there is no special religious activities that tie them to the halves as such. All these temples are attended optionally by people in their vicinities, sometimes for casual prayer, sometimes in quest of support in some undertaking. Usually Viṣṇu is worshiped not in a temple or shrine but at home. Viṣṇu, along with his consort Lakṣmī, is, as we have noted, the usual focal god of the household, the focus of most of the ordinary household *pūjā*s. They represent the ordinary relations, the moral life of the household, in its inner life. As we will see, for the family Viṣṇu contrasts with another quite different kind of deity, the lineage deity, most often a form of the Dangerous Goddess, which binds the households of the *phukī* group into a unity and protects them against the dangers of the outside (chap. 9).

Viṣṇu resembles Śiva in not being used, in contrast to certain other gods, to mark off the city's important spatial units. He is, as we shall argue, not the proper kind of a divinity for this for Bhaktapur's purposes. Viṣṇu has no major festival in the public city space. He is a major focus of household worship throughout the year, and of special household and temple worship and of out-of-the-city pilgrimages on some annual occasions, particularly during the lunar month of Kārtika (Newari, Kachalā, October/November) as he is elsewhere in South Asia at this time.

In recent decades the worship of Viṣṇu-Nārāyaṇa at the two major temples with music and dancing and without the mediation of a priest in expression of an individual direct devotion to the god free from the spatial, temporal, and social orderings of Bhaktapur as a city, has been growing. Viṣṇu and his avatars have become the object of *bhakti*, loving devotion, a focus for private salvation and private emotion. Here he is not functioning as a component in a complex system of urban order, but as the kind of personal god who arises when such a city-based system begins to break down. This is no longer the Viṣṇu who is Śiva's complement. This is, to recall our conceits of chapter 2, a transcendent "postaxial" Viṣṇu.

GAṆEŚA

Śiva in Bhaktapur is a bridge joining different forms of divinity. Gaṇeśa (Newari, Gandya:), an elephant-headed god, is a bridging and transitional figure of a different kind; he provides in several ways for human entrance into the area of the divine. As such, we may contrast him with other divinities, dangerous and uncanny, who are at the threshold of the human moral world and the orderly divine world into areas of chaos and danger. Properly for such uses, he is as attractive in his person as they are horrifying.

Let us consider some aspects of Gaṇeśa as an entrance. As is generally the case in South Asia, one prays first to Gaṇeśa before praying to any other god or before undertaking any important religious activity. The worship of Gaṇeśa is necessary for effectiveness, *siddhi*, in the worship and manipulation of other divinities. This is an aspect of a more general attribute of Gaṇeśa as "the overcomer of obstacles" (Mani 1975, 273):

> Gaṇapati [Gaṇeśa] has the power to get anything done without any obstructions [and has] also the power to put obstacles in the path of anything being done. Therefore, the custom came into vogue of worshiping Gaṇapati at the very commencement of any action for its completion . . . without any hindrance. Actions begun with such worship would be duly completed.

It is necessary to worship Gaṇeśa before both ordinary and Tantric *pūjās*. This is connected with one of his unique features in Bhaktapur, specifically, that he can be either a dangerous or an ordinary god.[11] Any image of Gaṇeśa[12] may receive either the worship and offerings that are proper for the ordinary divinities (e.g., grain, yogurt, cakes) or the blood sacrifices and alcoholic offerings that are proper for the dangerous divinities. (He has, however, a particular animal that is uniquely proper for sacrifice to him: the *khasi*, or castrated male goat, another image, perhaps, of his marginality.) He is the entrance to these two different realms, otherwise often placed in opposition.

In some settings his image[13] may indicate, represent, or suggest a Tantric emphasis. It may show Gaṇeśa with many arms, and he may be seated next to his Śakti, variously identified as Siddhi (the personification of his power for effectiveness) or Ṛddhi, "prosperity, wealth, good fortune." In his dangerous form he is sometimes called "Heramba," and thought of as a guru who instructs and therefore introduces students in Tantric knowledge.

There is still another sense in which Gaṇeśa is the entrance into the religious realm. As a benign, humanized animal, a sweets-loving child, the child of Śiva and Pārvatī in their domestic imagery, he is a favorite of children, and in the memory of some respondents was the first god form to whom they became attached—in contrast to others whom they feared as children—and it is Gaṇeśa who (at certain specific temples) is prayed to for help to children who are slow in learning to walk or talk.

As he is elsewhere in South Asia,[14] Gaṇeśa is the divinity of entrances in space as well as in temporal sequences. He is conceived to reside on one side of gates and arches (usually on the right side) while his "brother," Kumāra (who has little other significance in Bhaktapur, except in connection with the *Ihī*, the mock-marriage ceremony) is imagined to be on the other.

Gaṇeśa's shrines and temples are the main fixed divine markers of the *twa:s*, the village-like units in the city and of some of their component neighborboods (map 13). This local areal Gaṇeśa, or *sthān* Gaṇeśa (from sanskrit *sthāna*, place, locality), is considered common to the *twa:*. Although, as we have noted, a particular *twa: may* have one or more other divinities that in some sense "belong" to it and are its particular responsibility and that may be celebrated in some annual *twa:* festival, every *twa:* has its *sthān* Gaṇeśa. Everyone in the *twa:* worships here before important out-of-the-house ceremonies and during all rites of passage for members of the household. Thus Gaṇeśa is one of those divinities who have an important relationship to a significant component of urban space, as Viṣṇu and Śiva do not. The great majority of

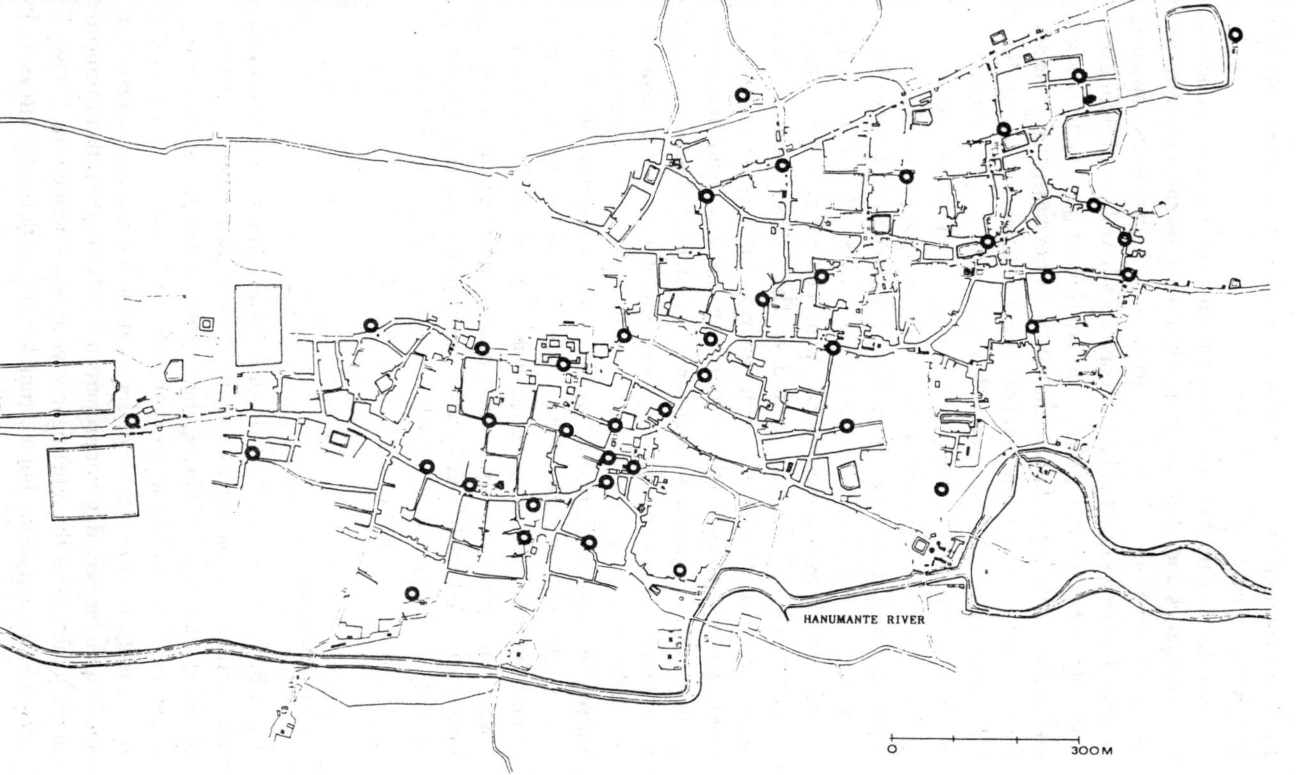

Map 13. The distribution of Gaṇeśa shrines in the city. The shrines are distributed throughout the city, with most of them on or near the *pradakṣiṇāpatha*. Map courtesy of Niels Gutschow.

these *twa:* shrines are located on the city processional route (see map 12) which connects the *twa:*s, and thus these individual centers are tied into the larger city.

There are a number of Gaṇeśa temples and shrines, some within the city boundaries and some without, which have specific purposes that can be accomplished only at that particular location with its particular Gaṇeśa. People go to Bālākhu Gaṇeśa if they have lost something and wish help in finding it. Children who are slow in learning to talk are taken to a temple just outside of the city to the northeast, Yatu (Nepali, Kamala) Gaṇeśa. One shrine, that of Chuma(n) Ganadya:, is worshiped by the entire city during the solar New Year festival, Biskā: (chap 14). All these shrines are also worshiped by local neighborhood people.

The most important Gaṇeśa shrine outside of the city for the people of Bhaktapur is Inara Dya: (Inara God),[15] known in Nepali as "Sūrya Vināyaka." This shrine, set on a forested hillside south of Bhaktapur, is visited regularly once a week by many people on one of Gaṇeśa's special days of the week, Tuesdays or Saturdays. These trips are considered as both a religious undertaking and an outing. Family members or a group of young friends will go to the shrine taking food with them. In addition to his general function as an overcomer of obstacles ("Vināyaka"), and a first object of worship before approaches to other gods, Inar Dya: can also help children who are slow in learning to walk. According to Slusser, Sūrya Vināyaka is also "widely consulted as a curing god by the deaf and dumb" (1982, 263). This shrine is not only attended by people of Bhaktapur but also is an important shrine for the Kathmandu Valley both for Newars of other places and for non-Newar Hindus. It is sometimes considered one of four Gaṇeśa temples forming a kind of *maṇḍala* in the Kathmandu Valley, and which are sometimes visited in sequence (Auer and Gutschow n.d., 17; Slusser 1982, 263).[16]

A NOTE ON YAMA

Yama Rāja, the ruler of the "kingdom" where in some versions of the adventures of people after death they go to await the fate that the results of their moral behavior, their *karma*, and/or the proper performance of death rituals secures for them, and who presides over the hell where the perpetrators of some enormous sin must remain for some equitable period, is not properly a member of the urban pantheon in the same way as the other figures we are considering here. He is the personification of death, but a certain kind of death or of death viewed in a certain way. As such, he belongs among the "ordinary" deities, is in contrast to the dangerous deities, and should be noted here. The dangerous deities can kill, but that is not associated with the sort of dying that Yama is concerned with. Yama, or his messengers, come to collect people in "ordinary" dying. He is a moral agent, part of the ordinary religion of Bhaktapur and is related to the worship and meanings of the ordinary deities (some of whom preside over the heavens where Yama will most likely send the dead individual if he or she is not to be reincarnated back into this world). In either one of the various heavens or the usually foreseen rebirth, the individual will live a pleasant social life, in consort with his or her loved ones (if in heaven) or perhaps with their transformations (in a rebirth). There are other "religious" representations of death—or, more precisely, of being killed—in Bhaktapur that are not within the moral realm. These are within the realm of the dangerous deities or the malignant spirits, within realms where accident and power, not moral behavior, prevail. Against them only avoidance or powerful "magical" devices (chap. 9) might prevail. Yama's judgment and the timing of his visit can, however, be affected not only by good behavior, but also by affection and solidarity in the family, and various kinds of distractions and social deceits can be used to confuse or distract him or his messengers and deflect him.

Yama is variously represented in the annual calendrical sequence, most centrally in the course of the lunar New Year's sequence (chap. 13). He is there representative of what we will call the "moral beyond" of the household, not the "amoral outside," which is vividly represented in other annual symbolic enactments in relation to other deities.

THE ORDINARY FEMALE DIVINITIES: LAKṢMĪ, SARASVATĪ, AND PĀRVATĪ

In a later section we will be concerned with a cluster of ideas about "the goddess," a form sometimes conceived of as an emanation of Śiva, as his "Śakti," and sometimes as an independent divinity having many names and forms. The word "Śakti" is often also used in Bhaktapur to refer to the consort, the female companion, of a male god. In this sense it means little more than wife, constant companion, or lover. There is a sharp distinction in cultural definition, personal meaning, and associated religious action between those ordinary goddesses who are the consorts of ordinary gods and important foci of ordinary religion, and those other goddesses, emanations of Śiva or aspects of some form of the Tantric goddess, the Śaktis *par excellence*, the objects of Tantric worship.

The three ordinary goddesses are Lakṣmī, Sarasvatī, and Pārvatī. Of these, only Sarasvatī has her own temples. Lakṣmī and Pārvatī are respectively represented in the temples of Viṣṇu and his *avatar*s (with the consort of the particular *avatar* being sometimes considered an incarnation of Lakṣmī) and of Śiva in his anthropomorphic forms. In contradistinction to Sarasvatī and to the Tantric goddesses, they are secondary figures in the external city religion. Their abode and realm is in the household.

Sarasvatī (Sasu Dya: Sasu God, in Newari) has four major shrines in Bhaktapur. These shrines may be worshiped as a personal act of devotion by local people and passersby, but her main special meaning is as the goddess of learning, to whom all people who are engaged in studies of one kind or another (in recent times particularly modern school studies) come to pray. Sarasvatī can grant them effectiveness or *siddhi* in learning, as Gaṇeśa does to children for walking or talking. Her main temple is just to the south of the city across the river. All school children go to this shrine, the Nīla (Blue) Sarasvatī on the same day, or Śrī Pa(n)camī, once a year (chap. 14). Sarasvatī is usually represented in an ordinary, if idealized, human form, like the other ordinary goddesses (identifiable by her swan vehicle and her "lute," the *vīṇā*). She was formerly embodied in all books, and now still in those that are not specifically modern and secular. In a major Purāṇic tradition Sarasvatī is considered as the daughter and sometimes the consort of the god Brahmā. In Bhaktapur she is conceived of as an independent goddess.[17]

Lakṣmī (Newari, Lachimi) is a major household divinity, but she has no public shrine or temple, although she is understood to be present in Viṣṇu's temples as his consort, or as incarnated as Rādhā or Sītā, the consorts of his major *avatar*s. She is understood to be nevertheless a goddess in herself, although she has in Tantrism some theoretical and cultic connections with goddesses such as Vaiṣṇavī and Vārāhī through shared associations with Viṣṇu. As everywhere in South Asia, as a household goddess, Lakṣmī is the promoter of the proper ends of the household—fertility, success in the household's economic activities, accumulation of food and wealth. She is the object of daily prayer and must never be neglected. She, like Viṣṇu, is a protector of ordinary life. She has one annual festival in Bhaktapur, which is during one day in the course of the five-day lunar New Year festival (chap. 13).

With Pārvatī (Newari, Pārvatī or Pārbatī) we approach the complex web of ideas joining Śiva, Śakti, and Newar Tantrism. Although Pārvatī is, as we shall see, one bridge to these ideas, she is for the most part an independent Goddess in her own right, one who belongs firmly to the ordinary realm. Pārvatī as a household figure is Śiva's loving bride—the ideal wife—and the daughter of Himālaya, the personified mountain range. As Himālaya's daughter, the Kathmandu Valley, that is, the traditional Nepal of the Newars, is her paternal homeland, and she has special concerns with it, particularly with its Newar women. Like Lakṣmī, Pārvatī has no independent external representation in her own shrine, nor any external ritual significance for the public city.[18] She is a focus of some romantic fantasy (as is Kṛṣṇa's consort Rādhā in other parts of South Asia), represents married romantic love for the household, and is prayed to by women for the welfare of the household (with perhaps a less material emphasis than Lakṣmī) and for the birth of sons. Although she may change into dangerous forms in the legends of the Goddess she, like Śiva when he emits his Śakti, is lost in the form, and (as we shall see below, as the *Devī Māhātmya*, one of the main sources of Bhaktapur's ideas and imagery about the Goddess suggests) is unaware that she has an alternate wild and demonic state.

THE TRANSITION TO THE DANGEROUS DIVINITIES

The dangerous deities, which we are now ready to discuss, are in many contexts and for many purposes considered as independent deities. The "Goddess" who in some contexts is thought to derive from Śiva, in others is not only independent and self-created but also usurps his role as the creator deity. For certain purposes in Shaivite and Tantric Bhaktapur, however, Śiva is considered as their source. One aspect of this idea is related to the conception of Śiva/Śakti, which is of basic importance in Tantric theory (chap. 9). Sometimes Śiva is thought to transform himself into another god, such as Bhīmasena. Sometimes Śiva is thought to be first transformed into his dangerous form Bhairava, who may then, in turn, generate other dangerous gods. Śiva's transformation into Bhairava is described as not a transformation of himself, but rather as a sending out of a force or power from within himself, an emanation, a *ni:saran*. Emanation is also the way in which the dangerous goddesses are said to be generated, as Śiva is conceived as generating a powerful form of the goddess, who then, in turn, generates or is transformed into subsidiary forms.

We are now concerned with relations of a different kind than those that obtain between the "ordinary" gods. Those were familiar and relatively fixed social relations: spouse, child , friend. These relations are relations of metamorphosis and emanation and are often shadowy and uncanny. Their proper worship, uses, and meanings differ from those of the ordinary deities. They belong to a different realm of the world and of the mind.

MAJOR GODS: THE "DANGEROUS" DEITIES

The major divinities that we are categorizing as "dangerous" have many features of representation, conception, and usage, that separate them from the residue of "ordinary" gods. We have borrowed a salient Newari verbal distinction where when it is necessary to refer to the set as a whole they are refered to as *gyā(n)pugu*, "dangerous." When such distinctions are necessary, the "nondangerous" divinities are often distinguished from the *gyā(n)pugu* ones by one or another term for "ordinary," such as the Sanskritic term *sādhāran*.[19] The contrast between the two sets, "ordinary" and "dangerous," responds to, reflects, and helps create important distinctions and complementarities. As we will see throughout this study, the two sets of deities are related to distinctions of inside and outside, of morality and power, of Brahmans and kings, of civil logic and dream logic, and of realms in which purity and pollution create distinctions and those within which they are irrelevant—in short, to some of the fundamental distinctions in Bhaktapur's conceptual world. The two sets not only represent these tensions and contrasts, they can be used to show relations of various sorts among them.

There are many more or less concrete markers of the contrast between the two sets of deities, their appearance, positions in the city, associated myths and legends. Some of these markers might (extremely rarely) be ambiguous; a benign deity may, for example, have a horrible form (such as Viṣṇu's *avatar* Narasiṃha). But there is one differentiating sign that people are forced to pay attention to, and that ensures the proper classification of any of these deities that they may have to encounter. This is what they are to be offered in proper worship. The dangerous gods should be given animal flesh and alcoholic spirits,[20] the ordinary gods, (including Gaṇeśa in his non-Tantric aspect) must never be given such foods. In ordinary speech the emphasis is on the "deities who drink alcoholic spirits," rather than on their acceptance of meat

Alcoholic spirits in this context are specially named, *nyā(n)* rather than the usual term *aelā.*

We will begin our discussion with the dangerous female divinities. Among the ordinary gods, the male gods are central and predominant and the female goddesses are peripheral to them; among the dangerous gods, the female divinities are predominant in quantity, complexity, and centrality in symbolic action.

THE DANGEROUS GODDESS AND HER TRANSFORMATIONS

Among the community of ordinary divinities are female divinities, various "ordinary goddesses" including Śiva's consort Pārvatī. However, South Asia has had goddesses of a different sort who separate and coalesce in the course of history, in the course of individual mythic accounts, and in the conception and action of Bhaktapur. The coalesced figure is *the* Goddess, whose names, aspects, forms, and allies in Bhaktapur we will sketch in the following sections. In her most powerful and dangerous form as depicted in the *Mārkaṇḍeya Purāṇa*, a scripture that contains one of the major sources of Bhaktapur's imagery of the Goddess (P. K. Sharma 1974, 46 [emphasis added]):

> She is a goddess warrior, incarnating herself on earth by using various devices at various crucial moments in order to destory the demons who were formidable challenges to the denizens of heaven. Indeed, in her perfect nature, she has been described as the most beneficent; but her fierceness as a martial goddess, equipped with the sharpest weapons and reveling in her terror-striking war-cries, *is definitely a different tradition from that of Pārvatī-Umā, whom we always find in an altogether different setting.*

The goddesses whom this goddess spawns or is ready to absorb are often represented as similar to the "formidable" demonic forms that they oppose, a similarity that helps explain their effectiveness in combating them. In some conceptions, such as the legends associated with the Nine Durgās (chap. 15), it is clear that the dangerous deities are sometimes, in fact, demonic entities that have been captured by "magical" power, often by some expert in Tantric spells, and then eventually forced into the service of the human community. As such, they may have fangs, cadaverous sunken cheeks and bodies, garlands of skulls or decapitated human heads around their necks, or cloaks of flayed animal or human skins over their shoulders. They have multiple arms, bearing weapons and carrying a human calvarium as a drinking cup, understood to be full of blood. Sometimes they are represented as beautiful, full-breasted figures of an almost hallucinatory sexual desirability, but the many arms of these representations bear the same murderous weapons as the frankly horrible forms, and like those forms, they, too, demand blood sacrifice. The beautiful forms are simply another manifestation of the same dangerous kind of goddess.

There are at least twenty-five major temples and shrines devoted to these goddesses, who have eleven major forms and a number of minor ones, all systematically related in a number of conceptual schemes activated in various contexts. Classification is complicated in that the same manifest goddess may have different names (as do most important Hindu gods), and conversely by the fact that the same name (Mahākālī, for example) may represent different aspects of the Goddess in different contexts. The goddesses' main usages in Bhaktapur's civic religion may be divided into four interrelated emphases, each with its centers, members, and ritual forms and each with its particular major implications for Bhaktapur's civic organization. We will designate them as (1) the goddesses of the maṇḍalic system, (2) the goddesses of the Nine Durgās' annual dance cycle, (3) the generalized protective goddess usually referred to as Bhagavatī, and (4) the political goddess Taleju and her related goddesses. Some individual goddesses, or at least some individual names of goddesses, may belong to more than one set, but much of their significance is largely determined by their membership in the particular set under consideration.

Each group of goddesses has a central member who represents a maximum concentration of what we may term "potential power." This goddess form is most general, full, and abstract. When there are other goddesses around her, they are more limited. Their manifestations, functions, and power are more shaped to the concrete needs of a particular event, a subsection of space, a particular set of ritual and symbolic functions. They are less omnipotential; they do some specific work in the world.

THE MAṆḌALIC GODDESSES

In the previous chapter we introduced the eight goddesses who protect the boundaries of Bhaktapur while also each one having a special segment of the city under her protection—the city being divided for this purpose into eight peripheral octants and a central circle with its own, a ninth, protective goddess (see maps 1 and 2 above). These goddesses protect the city, in the words of one humble citizen, from "ghosts, evil spirits and diseases like cholera." Others add earthquakes, invasions, destructive weather, and other disasters. As do all the dangerous gods, these goddesses protect the city against those external disorders that threaten the ongoing life of the city. That ongoing life has within itself its own protective resources, resources that may most generally be thought of as "moral." We have discussed these goddesses in relation to space, here we will, with some overlap, consider them as members of the pantheon.

The eight peripheral goddesses are often referred to in Bhaktapur as the Aṣṭamātṛkās, the "Eight Mothers."[21] In less elegant Newari they are sometimes called the *pigandya:*,[22] the group (*gaṇa*) of gods (*dya:*) living in the *pīṭha*, a special sort of open shrine. The ninth goddess at the center of the city when it is conceived as a *maṇḍala*, is included or not in the set, depending on whether the emphais is on the outer protective boundary or on the internal space that is being protected.

The eight goddesses at the periphery have each the same basic function in her proper space, although some have additional specialized functions. They are, to introduce an important classificatory principle for the dangerous gods, all at the same level. The goddess at the center has the same protective function as the peripheral goddesses for her central maṇḍalic section, but in addition, as we have noted in chapter 7, she concentrates their individual powers in an eightfold increase at the center of the *maṇḍala*. She is thus, in this way, something more than any of them separately, she is at a higher level. This contrast is reflected in the traditional characteristics of the particular goddesses chosen for placement at the center and at the periphery. The central goddess, Tripurasundarī, is (in contrast to the peripheral goddesses) not one of those goddesses designated as "mothers," *matṛkās*, in the Hindu Purāṇic tradition. As we will see (below here and chap. 15), the legends and scriptural accounts of the Matṛkās that are significant in Bhaktapur (and elsewhere in South Asia) treat the Matṛkās as components or limited or lesser aspects of some complete, full, maximal form of the goddess, often called "Devī." Tripurasundarī is a version of that complete, omnipotential goddess, characterized in some of the Upaniṣads (the Tripurā Upaniṣad and the Tripurā Tāpini Upaniṣad) as the "primeval embodiment of Śakti that gives birth to the world" (P. K. Sharma 1974, 21).

We will introduce the Maṇḍalic Goddesses in the order in which they are worshiped during the succeeding days of the autumn harvest festival of the Goddess, Mohanī, an order that begins with the eastern goddess (map 2), follows the boundary of the city in the auspicious clockwise processional direction, and proceeds on the ninth day to the central summating central shrine of Tripurasundarī.[23] The goddess to the east, the first in the sequence, is Brāhmaṇī (Newari, Brahmāyani); to the southeast, Maheśvarī (Newari, Māhesvari); to the south, Kumārī; [24] and to the southwest, Vaiṣṇavī (Newari Vaisnavī, often written and pronounced "Baisnabī"). The goddess of this particular location is on one occasion during the year—the complex spring solar New Year festival, Biskā:—taken to be a quite different goddess, Bhadrakālī. To the west is Vārāhī (Newari, Bārāhi:), to the northwest is Indrāṇī (Newari Indrāyani:), to the north is Mahākālī, and to the northeast is Mahālakṣmī (Newari Mahālachimi).

These peripheral goddesses are, with one only apparent substitution, familiar representatives of the various Purāṇic sets of "mothers" (P. K. Sharma 1974, 234), but are for the most part connected in their membership and in the exact order in which they are arranged to a particular traditional Hindu text, which is the basis for much of Bhaktapur's imagery of the Goddess, the *Devī Māhātmya*. In the account of the *Devī Māhātmya* the Śaktis, goddesses emitted from the various gods of the pantheon, either fight as assistants to the goddess Caṇḍikā, considered a transformation of Pārvatī, or become absorbed into her to augment her power.

In one passage of the *Devī Māhātmya* (VIII, 12–20), which we will discuss at some length below, the Śaktis of various gods who come to join the full goddess, Devī, are listed in sequence. The first five goddesses in the protective ring formed by Bhaktapur's Aṣṭamātṛkās (starting with Brāhmaṇī to the east and proceeding in a clockwise direction), are arranged in the same sequence: Brāhmaṇī, Maheśvarī, Kumārī, Vaiṣṇavī, and Vārāhī. Bhaktapur leaves out the *Devī Māhātmya*'s sixth goddess (Nārasiṃhī) and proceeds to its seventh, Indrāṇī. The *Devī Māhātmya*, like many of the Hindu sources, lists only seven mothers. Bhaktapur uses six of them and adds at the end two more, Mahākālī and Mahālakṣmī, commonly listed members of the Matṛkās as given in other Purānas. Mahākālī is also known in Bhaktapur as Cāmuṇḍā, a form of the goddess in her most terrifying aspect who also appears in the *Devī Māhātmya* as an honorific title given to the goddess form Kālī as the slayer of two powerful Asuras Chaṇḍa and Muṇḍa (*Devī Māhātmya*, VII, 25; Agrawala 1963, 101). Mahākālī and Mahālakṣmī, among the Maṇḍalic Goddesses, are just two ordinary Matṛkā, although in other uses of the Goddesses in Bhaktapur, Mahākālī's association with Kālī-Cāmuṇḍā and some of the legendary attributes of Mahālakṣmī are given some special significance.[25]

Like several other divinities in Bhaktapur, the nine Maṇḍalic Goddesses have "houses," literally, *dyā che(n)* or "god-houses" situated within the city (map 2). Portable images of the goddess are kept at these buildings, and daily *pūjā*s are held there, conducted by a Tantric temple priest, an *ācāju*. These *dyā che(n)* images are carried in various processions during the year, particularly during the course of the solar New Year festival, Biskā: (see chap. 14). Sometimes there is worship by a group of worshipers in the god-house rather than the *pīṭha* shrine, if the participants wish to keep the ceremonies secret, as is often the case in Tantric worship.

However, the proper and usual seats of the worship of the Maṇḍalic Goddesses are their *pīṭha*s, open, roofless, imageless shrines, which are the maṇḍalic markers. The nine maṇḍalic *pīṭha*s are very vaguely associated with the idea of the Devī *pīṭha*s, the 108 places in South Asia where pieces of Śiva's wife Satī fell to earth (cf. Banerjea 1956, 495n.; Mani 1975, 219). These places became sacred to the Goddess. While the maṇḍalic *pīṭha*s are associated only by some metaphorical extension with the Devī *pīṭha*s, for the Newars the important "true" Devī *pīṭha* is that of Guhyeśvarī[26] in the major Valley cult center Paśupatinātha, where in esoteric doctrine Satī's vagina fell to earth.[27] There is no esoteric connection between the Guhyeśvsarī Devī *pīṭha* and the maṇḍalic *pīṭha*s.

The maṇḍalic *pīṭha*s, as we have noted, are the required foci of attention and worship for families during important rites of passage, and for the city as a whole during the course of the Mohanī festival sequence.

THE NINE DURGĀS

Historically in South Asia, various groups of dangerous goddesses have been grouped together as the Navadurgā, the Nine Durgās (Banerjea 1974, 500n.; P. K. Sharma 1974, 231–233). Slusser has written that, "in practice . . . the Nepalese Naudurgā [Navadurgā] are synonymous with the Aṣṭamātṛkās, to which a variable ninth manifestation is joined to complete the set. Thus, when the Nepalese speak of the Naudurgā, they in fact refer to the Aṣṭamātṛkās" (Slusser 1982, vol. 1, p. 322). This is not true for Bhaktapur, where the distinction is essential. There the Nine Durgās refer to a group of divinities, represented primarily as masks (see color illustrations) who possess the bodies of a group of dancers during an annual sequence that each year begins at the harvest festival of Mohanī and lasts for the following nine months. We will be concerned with this sequence at length in chapter 15. The Nine Durgās have close relations with the Maṇḍalic Goddesses, as they do with the other major forms of the goddess in Bhaktapur, but they have, as we will see, their own legends, meanings, membership, and iconography. Although they share some of the same names with the Aṣṭamātṛkās and some of their reference to the *Devī Māhātmya* they differ in the meanings of the deities common to both sets, in other of their members, in their legends, and in their uses.

The Nine Durgās group share seven members with the Aṣṭamātṛkās: Mahākālī, Kumārī, Vārāhī, Brāhmaṇī, Vaiṣṇavī, Indrāṇī, and Maheśvarī.[28] Of these the last five have very subsidiary roles, and are peripheral to the main actions of the cycle. The group also includes the male divinities Gaṇeśa, Bhairava, and Seto Bhairava and the goddesses (often thought of, however, as a male and a female) Simā and Dumā.[29]

These twelve deities are represented as masks, and are worn by the dancers who through possession become the gods they represent. There are also two other gods associated with the group of the Nine Durgās. One is Śiva, who is represented as a small mask without eyeholes that is carried by one of the dancers. He is not present as a possessed dancer nor as a performing god. Finally the entire group of gods have their own god, whose portable image they worship. She is generally known as the Sipha goddess, after the red leaves of oleander (*sipha*) placed as a garland around her metal image. She is known to religious specialists as Mahālakṣmī. Mahālakṣmī is one of the equally ranked peripheral goddesses of the Aṣṭtamātṛkās—although, as we have noted, she is not one of the *Devī Māhātmya*'s "seven mothers"—and is placed in the eighth and last peripheral position. As the Nine Durgās' own goddess she is in a superior position to them, as Tripurasundarī is to the Aṣṭamātṛkās. She represents the "full goddess"; the other performing members of the group are special manifestations. There is another important hierarchical distinction within the Nine Durgās. As we will see when we discuss them in detail, the predominant form in the group of mask-gods is Mahākālī, the "Goddess" in her most frightening form. We will return to these hierarchical relations later.

The Nine Durgās, in contrast to the Maṇḍalic Goddesses, are characterized by movement (map 14 [below, chap. 15]). Their original home (chap. 15) was, in legend, a forest outside Bhaktapur. They have now, however, an elaborate temple-like god-house in the city. During

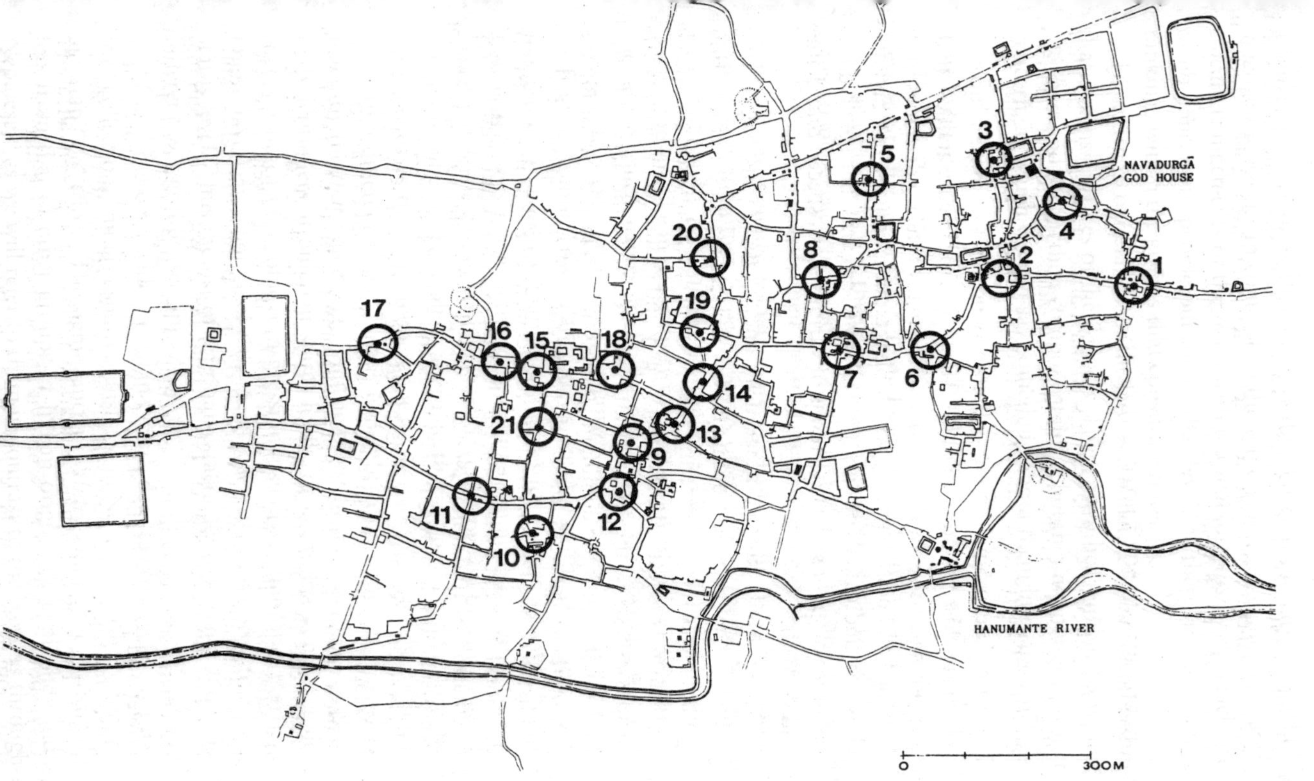

Map 14. The sites for the sequential Nine Durgās dances dramas or *pyākha(n)*s within Bhaktapur throughout the year. The numbers show the sequence in which the dances take place. Map courtesy of Niels Gutschow.

the nine months of their annual existence, the masks of the dancers and other ritual equipment are kept there when not in use in their sequential visits to the city's neighborhoods.

TALEJU, BHAKTAPUR'S POLITICAL GODDESS

An integral part of Bhaktapur's Malla palace complex of buildings and courtyards[30] is the temple of the goddess Taleju. The temple is approached through an elaborately decorated outer "golden gate" leading from Lāeku Square, and is built around a set of inner courtyards which are closed to non-Hindus.[31] Taleju was the lineage goddess of the Malla kings. As such, she was one of the many tutelary divinities of the bounded and nested units of which Bhaktapur is constructed, divinities chosen by individuals or "given them" by their *gurus*, lineage divinities, divinities of *guthi* and associations of various sorts, special *thar* deities, and so forth.

As the Malla king's lineage deity and located in his palace compound, Taleju became a dominant city deity as manifest in the various symbolic enactments centering on her temple, reaching a dramatic climax during the festival that most clearly and dramatically portrays the various aspects of the Goddess and their relations, the harvest festival Mohanī. Taleju is the dominant goddess and, in fact, deity, of Bhaktapur in those contexts where the centrality of royal power is being emphasized. She has survived the replacement of the Malla dynasty by the Gorkhāli Śāha dynasty as, for Bhaktapur, a powerful symbolic representation of traditional Newar political forms and forces, one that persists alongside of the new symbols and realities of modern politics.

There are extensive legends about the introduction of Taleju into Bhaktapur combining aspects of history, myth, and explanatory speculation about local topography and about aspects of the symbolic enactments that are associated with Taleju. The sketch of a version of the story that follows is derived from a lengthy written version provided by a Bhaktapur Brahman who works as a public storyteller, and is based on his public stories. His account begins with a short summary statement situated within the secular realm, and having to do with power and politics. "The Sultan Gayasudin Tugalak," the account begins, "having gained power in Bengal, attacked the town of Simraun Gaḍh. The king of Karṇātaka, Harisiṃhadeva, having been defeated by Gayasudin, ran away to Nepal with his soldiers and captured Bhaktapur from King Ānanda Malla, who had been its ruler. Then Harisiṃhadeva established the goddess Taleju in her [supernaturally determined] proper place in Bhaktapur. The place where the Goddess was ritually established is called the Mu Cuka [the main courtyard of the Taleju temple]. The goddess Taleju was brought by King Harisiṃhadeva from Simraun Gaḍh."

Now the account abruptly shifts from legendary history to the mythic and epic realm of Hindu tradition. "Once the Yantra of Taleju had been kept in Indra's heaven. [The *Yantra* is the powerful mystic diagram that embodies the goddess in this account, and is the only way she is represented in this account aside from her appearance as an anthropomorphic form in dreams]. There the god Indra worshiped her properly [her proper worship is an issue in the account]." Now (to continue in a paraphrase of the account) Taleju was stolen from Indra by Meghanāda, the son of Rāvaṇa, the demon king of Lanka, in the course of Rāvaṇa's attack on heaven. Taleju was taken to Lanka and worshiped there. When Rāvaṇa was defeated in Lanka by Rāma, the hero of the *Rāmayaṇa*, Rāma took Taleju, in the form of her *yantra*, to Ayodhyā, his capital in India. In time the goddess Taleju appeared to Rāma in a dream and told him that he must throw the *yantra* in the river Sarayū, which flowed past Ayodhyā because no one would worship and sacrifice properly to her after his approaching death. After five or six generations a descendant of Rāma, King Nala, found Taleju's *yantra* in the water, and brought it to his palace, but he did not worship her properly (which would have been with blood sacrifice), and had to return her to the river. Subsequent kings of Ayodhyā, Nala, Pururāva, and Alarka, had the same experience, each finally returning her to the river. The kings of this dynasty, the Solar Dynasty, were finally defeated by the Mlechhas (non-Indo-Aryan barbarians).

Now the story's mode shifts into a sort of fairy tale, as it is recounted how through wondrous signs the goddess comes into Harisiṃhadeva's possession, in a turn of events that will lead to Bhaktapur. Now, according to the story, King Nānyadeva, a king of the Solar Dynasty, had "lost his country" and become a servant of the Mlechhas. One day wandering restlessly here and there he happened to stop to rest at the bank of the Sarayū river. He dreamt there of a beautiful girl who said to him, "Oh, King Nānyadeva, your lineage god is in the Sarayū river. You must find her in order to worship her. I am she, your lineage goddess. Black insects will be flying around the surface of the river where I am hidden." The king awoke immediately and went to search for the goddess in the early morning. He found her by means of the black insects.

He found a copper casket. Inside it was a smaller box of gold. On the golden box was an inscription saying that it contained a hidden treasure that had been Rāma's and Nala's and was to be Nānyadeva's. The treasure, contained in the box, was Taleju's *yantra*, that is, Taleju herself. The story then continues in its wondrous mode to recount how with Taleju's council given in a dream, Nānyadeva has encounters with wondrous serpents, hidden treasure, twelve architects, a host of workers, and a female demon (rākṣasī), resulting in the magical construction in one night of a city that came to be called "Simraun Gaḍh". The legend begins to correspond to history here.[32]

The story goes on to recount that Nānyadeva worshiped Taleju properly, that is, with Tantric worship and with flesh-and-blood offerings, and that after his death she was so worshiped for another five or six generations. During the time of Nānyadeva's descendant Harisiṃhadeva, however, the Muslims were expanding their territories and thus came to Simraun Gaḍh. Then, following the orders of the goddess Taleju, King Harisiṃhadeva, having fled Simraun Gaḍh, entered Nepal through the forest carrying Taleju.

Now the story begins an attempt to explain certain aspects of Taleju's cult in Bhaktapur and to record and to account for her historical displacements within and near Bhaktapur. On their trip through the forest, Taleju informs Harisiṃhadeva that if no proper sacrificial animal can be found, such as a goat, then it would be permissible to sacrifice a water buffalo, an animal that had previously not been acceptable to her—and that is now the main sacrifice, along with goats, offered to her during Mohanī.[33] The king, having found a buffalo, then noticed a man defecating facing east (a sign that he was not of twice-born status) and selected him to kill the buffalo.[34]

Then, the story continues, Harisiṃhadeva came to Bhaktapur and became king. He established the goddess Taleju in the "Agnihotra Brahman's" house in Bhaktapur. (This is her present site. "Agnihotra Brahman" refers to a particular Rājopādhyāya Brahman; see below here and chap. 9.) The story now moves backward a little in time to tell of the prior search for the proper location. Taleju has told the king that the proper place for the installation will be known when a hole is dug and the soil removed from it will, upon being returned to the hole, fill it exactly to the surface. The story tells of the various places where Harisiṃhadeva tested the ground unsuccessfully. First he tried in the village of Panauti (just outside the Kathmandu Valley, to the southwest of Bhaktapur). "He dug there in the Dumangala Twa:." The soil did not fill the hole. Nevertheless he established a temple to her there (from the point of view of Bhaktapur and this story, a secondary temple). "The people of Panauti still say that the goddess Taleju came to Dumangala from Simangala, which is Simraun Gaḍh." Next he began to dig in Bhaktapur, first at the Dattātreya temple area in northeastern Bhaktapur. This time the soil overflowed the hole. He then went to dig in a "garden," called "Megejin," but the replaced soil overflowed the hole. He went on to the Kwāche(n) Twa: in eastern Bhaktapur (where there is now an important Bhagavatī temple associated with Taleju), but this also proved not to be the proper place. Finally he went on to the home of the Agnihotra Brahman, in the area of the present Lāeku Square. Here he dug, and the soil exactly refilled the hole. "Therefore the king established the goddess Taleju in that place."

The story now introduces another theme, which seems to echo some now obscure past events, perhaps the establishment of a new group of Royal Brahmans (see chap. 10). The Rājopādhyāya Brahmans who had lived in the place did not want to leave their homes. King Harisiṃhadeva gave them money and a substitute house. This substitute house still exists; it is still called the *paliśā che(n)* or *palsā che(n)*, literally "substitute house." The Agnihotra Brahman (whose name in the story is "Agnihotra") was a Tantric practitioner. He did not want to leave his family land, even if he were given money and a substitute home, he was not a greedy man. He always sat on Chetrapal Bhairava's stone (an area-protecting "stone god" in the Taleju main courtyard) which was then bordered by four stone pillars, each with an image of Gaṇeśa and Durgā. The Brahman wanted to kill himself rather than leave his own ancestral home. King Harisiṃhadeva finally chased Agnihotra away from his ancestral home by force. Agnihotra committed suicide in his temple there, a temple of Śiva (Mahādeva), because he had lost his public prestige. Agnihotra became a ghost (*preta*) because he had killed himself. The ghost gave Harisiṃhadeva trouble every day. Thus, Harisiṃhadeva had the Śiva temple entirely destroyed. He then did the necessary pacifying rituals.

Then, the story concludes, the four pillars with the Gaṇeśa images were sent to various places. One, a dangerous form of Gaṇeśa, was placed at the left side of the Golden Gate (the entrance to the Taleju temple complex). Another is at Bidya *pīṭha* (Tripurasundarī's *pīṭha*). Another was brought to the Indrāṇī *pīṭha*.[35] (Our story doesn't mention the fourth pillar.) Then, the story concludes, "In the Beko courtyard (the courtyard just outside the inner gate and compound of the Taleju complex) the Bhairava Chetrapal stone where that Brahman used to sit exists, still, until now."

It seems likely that Taleju had, in fact, been introduced to the Kathmandu Valley from Mithilā, although not by Harisiṃhadeva, who never reached it (chap. 3), and that the pressures of the Turkish Muslims on Mithilā with the consequent movement of Maithilī Tantric Hindus into Nepal contributed to the subsequent importance of the goddess and of Tantrism to the valley. Slusser summarizes the historical evidence as follows (Slusser 1982, vol. 1, p. 318):

> That Taleju's cult in the Kathmandu Valley antedated Harisiṃhadeva is documented history . . . but Taleju appears to have been held in high regard in that country [Mithilā], and it is not improbable that she was the tutelary of Nānyadeva's dynasty. She was almost certainly well-known to Harishiṃha's queen, the omnipotent Bhaktapur refugee, Devaladevī. It is abundantly clear that Taleju was favored by Sthitirājamalla [Jayasthiti Malla] and with his subsequent eruption into the affairs of Nepal Maṇḍala, the goddess was apparently raised to an eminence she had previously not enjoyed in Nepal. As we know, on Sthitimalla's visit to Patan, the fractious nobles made haste to please the new Valley strong man by restoring the run-down temple of Taleju. . . . That many of the Newars associated with Taleju's cult claim Maithilī descent [as do the Rājopādhyāya Brahmans of Bhaktapur] is also suggestive of the deity's ties with Mithilā.

Whatever its historical relevance, the story as it is still told in Bhaktapur also suggests some special aspects and qualities of this particular goddess in the domain of Bhaktapur's goddesses. She is located first in a traditional Hindu heaven, in contrast, say, to the members of the Nine Durgās troupe whose legends identify them first as forest-dwelling demonic figures (chap. 15). She is the favorite goddess of a particular god; as a divinity's divinity, this places her in a hierarchy—her devotee is a figure remembered as the "king" of the gods. Her subsequent history is associated with invasions, thefts, and dynasties, and with politics and power struggles. From the start she is embedded, available for use by humans and quasi-humans, in a concrete form, a diagrammatic representation on a piece of metal. The form when properly worshiped is protective. The proper worship is Tantric with blood sacrifice. This captured divinity, with its history and functions relating it to power, belongs to a political dynasty, a legitimate form of power. The legend associates it not only with Indra, but with Rāma, an *avatāra* of Viṣṇu, a divinity closely associated with Newar (and Hindu) royalty and with civic moral order. When Taleju was established in Bhaktapur, she necessarily took precedence over other deities with similar political claims, which may perhaps be part of the significance of the displacement of the Agnihotra Brahman, the destruction of his Śiva temple, and his suicide.[36] We may note that in contrast to other forms of the Goddess, Taleju is not conceptually related to and in a sense dependent on Śiva, but is the Tantric goddess as independent and self existing and fully powerful.

Taleju is kept in a secret inner part of the Taleju temple. The nature of her image is also secret. Only a very few Rājopādhyāya Brahman priests from households traditionally providing Taleju Brahmans, and who have special initiation are allowed to see the image. Outsiders generally follow the description in the legend and assume that it is a *yantra*. Hamilton was also told at the beginning of the nineteenth century that "there is no image of this deity which is represented by a *yantra*" ([1819] 1971, 210f.).[37] In worship in the Taleju temple, Taleju is represented by various forms—*yantra*, the metal vase-like container called the Thāpi(n)cā (or alternatively Ku(n)bha, a vessel that also represents the true Devī *pīṭha* goddess, Guhyeśvarī), sometimes by a metal vessel with a pouring spout (a Kalas), and sometimes by an anthropoid image.

Like most of Bhaktapur's component organizations the Taleju temple has its esoteric internal ceremonies and public external ones related to the larger city organization. The internal functions center around the worship of Taleju by her attendant priests[38] during the course of the year. Many of these take place during city-wide calendrical festivals, but there are some thirty-five important annual internal worship ceremonies unconnected to external urban events. Many of these commemorate Taleju's functions as the Malla kings' lineage goddess. These acts of worship or *pūjā*s are called *thā* (Kathmandu Newari *tha*) *pūjā*, or *thā taegu*, "elevation worship," or "elevation producing and maintaining" acts. *Thā taegu* is thought of as a kind of initiation, *dekhā* (chap. 9). It lacks some features of a full Tantric initiation, and is sometimes thought of by those who have such full initiation as a *bāga dekhā*, a "half-full" initiation. Those *thā pūjā*s that commemorate the Malla king and, in fact, treat him as if he were still present, take the Malla king (represented by a priest) through three successive levels of initiation, during each of which he is presented new *mantra*s, new secrets, and new instruction on ritual procedures. There are other *thā pūjā*s as well as full initiations given at Taleju, all necessary for Taleju temple's internal functions. These are necessary not only for the staff and for the "king" but also for all those for whom Taleju is in one way or another a special deity. Descendants of the Malla kings, that is, members of the present Malla and Pradhānāṅga *thar*s, have Taleju as their lineage goddess, and male *thar* members have some of their initiations at the Taleju temple, although they do not receive the highest levels of initiation in Taleju's mysteries. Those are reserved to the chief Taleju Brahman. He is considered to be the surrogate for the Malla king in many rituals, and the king was entitled to higher levels of initiation than his male kin and descendants (who are furthermore now considered by the priests to be no longer "pure Mallas"). The Taleju principal priests who were the king's *guru*s, had even higher levels of initiation than the king himself, a fourth level, one beyond the Malla king's three. Taleju is also the object of special devotional rituals of the other temple priests. She is considered a sort of lineage goddess for them, in the limited sense that the temple priesthood is inherited in their families' lineage. All these priests also have in all other contexts another Tantric lineage divinity, for ordinary family rituals and rites of passage (see below and chap. 9).

In addition to the two *thars* of Malla descendants and three priestly *thar*s attendant at the temple, there are about twenty *thar*s throughout the macrostatus system, some of whose members (as we have noted in chap. 5) have some special assigned ritual function at some time or other during the year at the Taleju temple. Many of these people must be given *thā taegu* initiations, in which they must swear secrecy about their duties and about what they see in the temple.[39]

Taleju's external function is uniquely important to the Tantric component of Bhaktapur's symbolic system. Through her priests and by means of her *mantras*, she is understood by initiated practitioners to empower all city-level legitimate Tantric procedures in Bhaktapur.[40] The Brahman Taleju priest is in this context considered the ultimate *guru* of all who have Tantric power. Some of this power must be transmitted annually. For the rest, the great majority, such as the special knowledge and efficacy of various Tantric priests (chap. 9), or the effective ritual knowledge of the people who make religious paraphernalia, it is said that the special knowledge, initiation, and mantras were *originally* given to ancestors by a Taleju priest, but then passed down within the family or the *thar* from father to son or *guru* to student in repeated internal initiations.

Taleju's external relation to the city is manifested and enacted at length in the course of the harvest festival, Mohanī. In the course of this festival Taleju, as we shall see (chap. 15), is brought into relation with several forms of the Goddess—with all the Maṇḍalic Goddesses, with Kumārī (as another deity than the similarly named Kumārī of the Maṇḍalic group of goddesses), with the Nine Durgās group of deities, and with the Goddess Devī herself in her form as Bhagavatī. In this festival Taleju is seen as participating in the basic myth of the Dangerous Goddess and, in fact, temporarily becoming Mahiṣāsuramardinī herself (chap. 15). During Mohanī, Bhagavatī/Taleju represents the maximally powerful and full form of the Goddess. This maximal Taleju then becomes manifest in certain ways, controlled and mediated by her temple priests. She possesses a maiden to become manifest in the form of Kumārī, in which form she can give oracular advice to kings. She provides the *mantra* that empowers the partial forms of the Nine Durgās troupe to begin their annual nine-month cycle of manifestations of the Goddess throughout the city. Taleju is a central focus in the interrelated set of symbols and symbolic enactments associated with the dangerous deities of Bhaktapur.[41]

BHAGAVATĪ

In her anthropomorphic representations Taleju is usually represented as a form of the goddess that people in Bhaktapur in other contexts identify as "Bhagavatī." This is a female form with many arms, clearly a dangerous goddess, but lacking any further identification (through location or specific iconographic features) as one of the "partial" goddesses.[42] The representation identified as Bhagavatī is also very often (in both temple and household images) that of the Devī of the *Devī Māhātmya* account in the form of the slayer of the buffalo Asura, that is, as Mahiṣāsuramardinī.

Bhagavatī is a traditional title for what we have been calling the full goddess. She is equivalent to "Devī," to "Śakti," to "Prakṛti" (Mani 1974, 113). For people in Bhaktapur, however, Bhagavatī is a separate goddess, a divinity in her own right. She has three temples. All of them have Taleju staff priests as temple priests, and are closely connected with Taleju's internal rituals. One of these is housed at the Ñātāpwa(n)la ("Nyatapola") Temple (fig. 10), a large five-tiered temple, one of the most striking traditional buildings in Nepal. The Ñātāpwa(n)la goddess is in the same square as the main temple of the city's major male dangerous divinity, Bhairava, with whom she has an esoteric connection for the purpose of "controlling him." The story of the temple is presented in one of the chronicles (Wright [1877] 1972, 194f.):

> Bhūpatīndra Malla built [in Bhaktapur] a three-storied temple, the length of which ran north and south, and placed in it, facing west, a Bhairava for the protection of the country, and the removal of sin and distress from the people. This Bhairava gave much trouble, and the Raja in consequence consulted many clever men, who told him that if the Īswarī [goddess] of the Tantra Shastra [texts], whom the Bhairava respected, were placed near him, he would be appeased. He therefore, at an auspicious moment, laid the foundation of a five-storied temple. . . . The pillars were of carved *agrās* wood, and there were five stories of roofs. This temple is the most beautiful, as well as the highest in the whole city. In building it the Raja set an example to his subjects by himself carrying three bricks, and the people brought together the whole of the materials in five days. When the temple was finished he secretly placed in it a deity of the Tantra Shastra, who rides on Yama-raj whom no one is permitted to see, and who is therefore kept concealed.

This goddess has a secret name and form, and is supposed by some experts to be "Siddhi Lakṣmī." However, she is known publicly as "Bhagavatī." The two other Bhagavatī shrines in addition to their use by Taleju Brahmans have some local worshipers.

Bhagavatī has only one minor processional festival, which had been inaugurated in Bhaktapur only some ten or fifteen years before this study. In spite of this sparse representation in public space, however, Bhagavatī is one of the principle divinities of Bhaktapur. She is the most common local name for the goddess in her full power, in the form where she has incorporated the power of all lesser forms of the goddess. She is thought of as a warrior goddess, as most clearly portrayed in her Mahiṣāsuramardinī representation and legend (see section on principles of classification of dangerous goddesses, below). Her main concrete presence is in the household. Bhagavatī is the name and form of the household image in which the Dangerous Goddess is worshiped in home *pūjā*s as one of the group of household gods. She is at the focus of home worship during the important household ritual components of the Mohanī festival. Bhagavatī is also the main deity worshiped in many Tantric *pūjā*s. She is also the secret Tantric family goddess, *āga(n) dya:*, of the majority of upper-status households (chap. 9). For Bhaktapur's people Bhagavatī is the city's main protective goddess when they are thinking of the city as a whole, rather than the protection of its boundaries. For the Taleju priests she is sometimes conceived of as "Taleju's older sister," because they believe she long preceded Taleju in Bhaktapur's history and in legendary status. But she is also alternatively conceived of by them as Taleju's "assistant," for she protects the city at Taleju's wish and direction.

MISCELLANEOUS DANGEROUS GODDESSES

There are some dangerous goddesses in Bhaktapur of circumscribed present importance. Some of these are auxiliary forms associated with Taleju in the Taleju temple, and others are goddesses located elsewhere in the city, where they have some specific and limited functions.

Taleju temple contains a number of Tantric images of various degrees of secrecy. These include Maheśvarī (whom we have mentioned above) represented by a stone, Guheśvarī considered as secondary to the major Guhyeśvarī Devī *pīṭha* goddess at the Paśupatinātha shrine, and Dui Māju. Dui Māju is said to be the goddess of an internal *pīṭha* in Taleju temple, and to be "Taleju's own *pīṭha* goddess." In the Padmagiri chronicle Dui Māju is said to be the lineage deity of a "caste" of Maithilī invaders, and to have helped King Nānyadeva take possession of Bhaktapur. In time, the account says, when Harisiṃhadeva in turn captured Bhaktapur as "he had received immense wealth from Dwimaju Deva whom he regarded as his Penate [lineage god] [he] established a Devāli Pūjā [lineage *pūjā*] to her" (Hasrat 1970, 50, 52). The dim reflection of some historical reality distorted in the chronicle, and the special esoteric position of Dui Māju now in Taleju temple suggest something of her possible historical identity.[43]

Another important esoteric form associated with the Taleju temple is Ugracaṇḍī, who is represented in some of the events there during Mohanī, and who is thought by some to have an esoteric relation to the Nine Durgās.

There are some goddesses represented in the collection of shrines and temples built by the Malla kings in proximity to their palace, which we will discuss below as "gods of the Royal Center." The two goddesses in this group, who have no relevance to the rest of the city, are Baccalā[44] and Annapūrṇā.

Of the few miscellaneous goddesses scattered throughout the wider city, some have special functions, and others had some past function and meaning and are now dimly remembered as a shrine or image that has some residual power. Kulachimi (or Ku Lakṣmī) (located in the Tulá *che(n) twa:*), identified as Lakṣmī's "older sister," is considered to be a "bad god."[45] She is worshiped daily by an assigned temple priest, probably, in a pervasive idea about such deities, to keep her from doing harm.

The Pālu(n)pālu(n) goddess, identified with Kumārī and represented by a stone, is located in the Ināco Twa:. It was popularly used in the past as part of a curing ritual for children—rice held first to a sick child's head, was then brought to this shrine and offered to the goddess.

Śītalā (Newari Si:talā), a goddess of frightening mien whose vehicle is a donkey, is found at the river at Hanmān Ghāṭ. She is the goddess thought to have been efficacious for curing or preventing smallpox. On the twelfth day[46] after the first signs of infection people went there to pray for cure and for protection from disfigurement. She is a well-known goddess in South Asia and can produce smallpox as well as cure it (Stutley and Stutley, 1977, 278; Slusser 1982, vol. 1, p. 328). Bhaktapur's Śītalā has a broken nose, reportedly broken by a father whose son died in spite of his prayers.

Another goddess with curative functions is represented by a hole with a stone at its bottom in the Ināco Twa:, which is identified as Bālkumāri. People go here to pray for the cure of someone with a bleeding nose or who is coughing up blood.

In the Sukhu Dhwākhā neighborhood there is a goddess called the "Durupo" or "Durupwa:" goddess, literally the "breast" goddess. She is also considered to represent Draupadī, the wife of the five Pāṇḍava brothers of the Mahābhārata epic, and to be at the same time one of the ten Tantric goddesses of the Mahāvidyā. These varied attributions attest to her historical interest, but she now has no function or worship. Another such historical remnant is the Tantric goddess, Chinnamastā, also one of the Mahāvidyā, but of no present significance.

DANGEROUS GODDESSES: SOME PRINCIPLES OF CLASSIFICATION

After we have introduced the remaining classes of divinities, we will attempt to distinguish some of the important contrasts among the classes that are made use of in Bhaktapur to build a symbolic order. In this section we will introduce some of the "ordering potentialities" of the dangerous goddesses. They share most of these with the dangerous male divinities, but as the goddesses are a much more numerous and salient set and as they have some distinctive features of their own, they warrant discussion at this point.

Although Bhaktapur selects aspects of the goddesses as they are portrayed in South Asian tradition for its special purposes, it follows closely the ideas and specific forms (as we have seen in the placement of the Aṣṭamātṛkās, for example) presented in the *Devī Māhātmya*.[47] We can therefore begin with some passage from that text that convey these ideas. The *Devī Māhātmya* describes in various ways what we may call a maximal or full form of the goddess (see fig. 13) whose power is in the

Figure 13. The Goddess in her supreme manifest aspect.

concentration of other divine principles, principles that are partial in relation to the full form. (*Devī Māhātmya*, II, 9–17; Agrawala 1963, 45f.):[48]

> From the face of Viṣṇu filled with intense indignation as well as from that of Brahmā and Śiva sprang forth fierce heat. From the bodies of other Devas also headed by Indra issued forth a resplendent luster. All this light became unified into one. The Devas saw in front of them a Pile of Light blazing like a mountain whose flames filled the whole space. Then that matchless light born from the bodies of all gods gathered into a single corpus and turned into a Woman enveloping the three worlds by her luster. Her face was produced from the light of Śiva, her hair from that of Yama, her arms from the luster of Viṣṇu, her breasts from that of the Moon; her bust from that of Indra; her thighs and legs from that of Varuna.

The *Devī Māhātmya* goes on to list the derivation of other parts of her cosmically inclusive body. In this particular description she is being generated to fight a demon who has also, significantly, concentrated power of other more limited divinities into himself, and is thus beyond the control of any of the ordinary gods. Mahisha, the king of the Asuras, had "taken over the authority of Sūrya, Indra, Agni, Vāyu, Chandra, Yama, and Varuṇa as well as other gods. The wicked Mahisha has turned out all the gods from heaven who are now stalking their life like mortals" (*Devī Māhātmya*, II, 5, 6; Agrawala 1963, 45).

For another battle against the Asuras, the Goddess absorbs into herself the other dangerous goddesses, themselves the emanations or Śaktis of gods, who had fought together in an earlier battle. The Asura Śumbha taunts the Goddess for winning a battle with the help of these other goddesses (*Devī Māhātmya*, X, 2–5; Agrawala 1963, 123):

> O Durgā, you are puffed up with the pride of strength. Do not be haughty, you are exceedingly proud but fighting with the strength of others. The Devī said: "I am all alone in the world here. What other is there besides me, O you wild one. See that these goddesses are my own powers entering into myself." The Rishi said: "Then all those Matṛkā, Brāhmaṇī and others, became absorbed in the body of the Goddess. Thereupon Ambikā alone remained." The Devī said: "Through my power I stood here in many forms; all that has been withdrawn by me [into myself] and now I stand alone."

In still another passage the full Goddess is represented as springing directly from the body of Śiva's consort, the benign goddess Pārvatī (*Devī Māhātmya*, V, 38–40; Agrawala 1963, 85):

> O Prince, while the gods were thus engaged in invoking the Goddess through praises and in other ways, Pārvatī came there to bathe in the waters of the

> Gaṅgā. She of the lovely brows said to the gods, "Who is being praised by you here?" Then sprang forth from her physical sheath Śiva Kauśikī [an appellation of the goddess] who replied, "This hymn is being addressed to me by the assembled gods vanquished by the Asura Śumbha and routed in battle by Niśumbha." Because that Goddess came out of Pārvatī's bodily sheath, she is sung as Kauśikī amongst all men.

It is important to note here that the benign goddess Pārvatī seems, as Lynn Bennett puts it in a comment on this passage, "unaware of her powerful war-like ego"—and that after the Dangerous Goddess appears "Pārvatī withdraws and has no part in the ensuing battle scenes" (1983, 268). The Dangerous Goddess seems, however, to be aware of Pārvatī. The Goddess as portrayed here can absorb other subsidiary goddesses into herself, can emit subsidiary goddess forms, and is capable of taking different forms at her own full level.

The *Devī Māhātmya* also deals with the Goddess in another and very different way as the ultimate creative force. Here she is no longer produced by Śiva or the other gods, or through a transformation of Śiva's consort. The Goddess as creative force is the subject of some of the *stotras*, the hymns of praise, to the Goddess, which introduce and intersperse the accounts of the heroic cosmic battles of the *Devī Māhātmya*. Here she is called simply Devī, Goddess, or sometimes Mahāmāyā, the generator of the concrete and illusionary forms of what is taken to be reality, who "forcibly seizes the minds of even those who have knowledge and leads them to delusion. . . . This animate and inanimate world is created by her. . . . She is supreme eternal knowledge being the cause of *mokṣa* [escape from delusion]. . . . She is eternal having the universe as her form . . . the supreme knowledge, the supreme power, the supreme mind, the supreme memory and the great delusion . . . the giver of manifest form to the gods Brahmā, Viṣṇu and Śiva . . . the supporter of the world, the cause of its maintenance and dissolution" (*Devī Māhātmya*, I passim; Agarawala 1963, 37–43). Devī in this aspect has various titles or equivalences besides Mahāmāyā, such as Śrī, Īśvarī, and Prakṛti. These titles and names are different than those given to the "manifest" goddesses, either full or partial. This cosmic creator Goddess is referred to in Bhaktapur; for example, she is represented in the central point of the city as a *maṇḍala* under her name of Tripurasundarī. But much more salient to Bhaktapur is what we have called the "full goddess," the manifest form of Goddess, who is different from the creator Devī of the *stotras*.

This form, the central protagonist in the drama of the *Devī Māhāt-*

Figure 14. The Dangerous Goddess in her horrible form.

mya, is manifest at a position in space and a moment in time, albeit mythic space and time. This is the goddess who combines the forces of all the other and separate divinities, who freely yield them to her for their defense. As she fights for the defense of the divine order, she is described as a warrior, "filling the three worlds with her splendor, bending low the earth with the force of her strides, scratching the sky with her pointed diadem, shaking the nether worlds with the twang of her bowstring and standing there filling the ten directions of space with her thousand arms" (*Devī Māhātmya*, II, 37–38; Agrawala 1963, 51). In the *Devī Māhātmya* this full form of Devī is most commonly called "Chaṇḍikā." However, she is given various other names and titles, such as Ambikā, Bhadrakālī, Mahādevī, and Durgā. She also shares some appellations with the creator Goddess such as Śrī and Prakṛti. The full form has as her vehicle a lion. In some battles Chaṇḍikā fights as herself, but in others she emits another form, Kālī, who has a terrifying aspect and who does the fighting. This special terrifying form has a description which is repeatedly represented in Bhaktapur's art, icons and masks, and which is of great ritual importance (*Devī Māhātmya*, VIII, 5–8; Agrawala 1963, 98):

> Kālī of terrible countenance [see fig. 14], armed with a sword and a noose, carrying a . . . skull-topped staff decorated with a garland of human heads, clad in a tiger's skin, looking terrible . . . [with] emaciated flesh, with a widely gaping mouth, . . . with lolling tongue, . . . deep sunk reddish eyes, and filling the quarters of space with roaring voice, she impetuously fell upon the great Asuras, killing them and devoured the army of those enemies of Devas.

In some passages Chaṇḍikā fights alongside of Kālī (e.g., VIII, 52–62). Yet, repeatedly in the *Devī Māhātmya* Chaṇḍikā gives orders to Kālī, and confers praise and titles on her. Kālī in this account is not just an aspect of Chaṇḍikā; she is a subordinate, a more limited, more specialized being.

A rank still lower than Kālī, still more limited and discrete in their forms are the Matṛkās, the gods' Śaktis, who fight in one episode alongside the Goddess as Chaṇḍikā. Kumārī fights with her spear, Brāhmaṇī by throwing water that is given power through her *mantras*, Maheśvarī with a trident, the boar-goddess Vārāhī with her tusks, and so on (*Devī Māhātmya*, IX). However, as the *stotra* that follows this account (which we have quoted above) insists, these various Matṛkās are all *aspects* of the one Goddess, Devī.

These relations of whole to part allow for the two dimensions of classification that we have suggested in relation to spatial units, and, following the approaches of others, in relation to social hierarchy. The whole includes the part, but may emit it in some way so that the part can be considered as a unit in itself. In this case the part and the whole are in a vertical relationship, share some of the same qualities, and are hierarchically arranged, with the whole superior to the part. Furthermore, the whole tends to be more abstract and less specified, whereas the part is more concrete and more specialized in its function and meaning. This arrangement also allows for horizontal relations because entities at the same level of inclusiveness are equal to each other. We have noted a distinction in the *Devī Māhātmya* of the full goddess Chaṇḍikā from a cosmic creative Goddess of a still higher order, the absolute divinity prior to all manifestation. The manifest form of the Goddess in her full power was differentiated from the cosmic form in name, and sometimes was described as a form created by the male gods in concert. Bhaktapur's city religion puts four goddesses in different contexts at the same highest level (and makes no use of a distinction between the rank of a cosmic and a full manifest goddess). Two are related in tradition to names of the creator Goddess, Tripurasundarī and Mahālakṣmī (who is a supreme goddess in her context as the Nine Durgās' own deity). One refers to the full manifest form of the Goddess—Bhagavatī in Bhaktapur's usage. The fourth, Taleju, is both in her legend a god's god (and thus in a rank above "ordinary" gods) and also, through her participation in the symbolic dramas of the harvest festival, a version of the fully manifest warrior goddess.

Three of these goddesses, Tripurasundarī, Mahālakṣmī, and Bhagavatī, show their equivalence by having as their identifying Vāhana or "vehicle" the lion, as does the manifest Devī in the *Devī Māhātmya*. So do, significantly, the two goddesses within the Taleju temple who are thought to be royal or warrior deities absorbed by Taleju, namely, Dui Māju and Māneśvarī. Taleju is, however, popularly said to have a horse vehicle. This probably refers to the white stallion that is used during the procession of Taleju during the Mohanī festival. Slusser suggests plausibly that this white horse derives from the "sanctified horse required in ancient Indian coronation ritual, as it was in ancient Nepal, and is in the coronation of the kings of Nepal today" (1982, vol. I, p. 317). Whether the horse is considered the vehicle of the goddess in her *Yantra* representation is dubious, but that vehicle is an esoteric secret.[49] The other dangerous goddesses, like the other ordinary goddesses, have each their own particular vehicle. Vaiṣṇavī has (like Viṣṇu) the half-bird Garuḍa,

Vārāhī, a water buffalo; Indrāṇī, an elephant; Brāhmaṇī, a goose; and Maheśvarī, a tiger. The ordinary goddess Sarasvatī, like Brāhmaṇī (because of her traditional associations with the god Brahmā, whose vehicle it also is) has a goose vehicle.

There is one figure whom we encountered in the *Devī Māhātmya* as the special agent of the full manifest goddess Chaṇḍikā. This goddess, Kālī in the *Devī Māhātmya*, is in Bhaktapur called "Mahākālī." She represents the most frightening form of the Goddess and is used as such in the powerful symbolic enactments of the Nine Durgās group. Here she is below the full Goddess (as the Nine Durgās' supreme goddess Mahālakṣmī), but in a superior position to the remainder of the goddesses in the group. This Mahākālī is a flesh-devouring, blood-drinking, intoxicated, cadaverous form. She has a male equivalent, whose consort she is, the god Bhairava, whom we shall discuss below. Mahākālī does not have the full goddess' lion vehicle. Her vehicle is an anthropomorphic male form, supine at or under her foot, which is locally identified as a Kālī *preta*, a kind of dangerous spirit.

The lesser goddesses are thus distinguished from the full manifest form, the Devī, in several ways. They are sometimes literally described as *a(n)sa* (Sanskrit, *a[n]śa*) Devī, as "partial Devīs." "Partial," we must emphasize, has a particular meaning here. It does not mean imperfect, but more concrete and more specialized, and in being more specialized, therefore limited. The lesser goddesses as a group are generally of equal status, although in some domains, such as the Nine Durgās, some of them may have special salience. In a few contexts a form that is a full goddess in another context may be conceived of as a partial goddess. This is the case of Mahālakṣmī as one of the peripheral Maṇḍalic Goddesses, and of Tripurasundarī when she is thought of as only the central maṇḍalic area's protective local goddess, and not the concentrating center of the *maṇḍala*. However, in these two particular contexts, while goddesses may be treated in more limited ways, the reverse, the treatment of a limited goddess as a full goddess, does not occur. Each of the full goddesses is located in a different context, within which are clustered her own dependant partial goddesses, in the cases where these exist. Relations and equivalences among the full goddesses in the various sets, horizontal relations, are signaled in various ritual actions. All of the relations between the full goddesses are enacted during Mohanī, which is one of the reasons that the festival will be of special interest to us (chap. 15). Finally we have noted the barrier between Pārvatī and the forms of the Goddess we have been considering here. The same barrier separates the other "ordinary" goddesses from the Goddess. They belong to a civic, although heroic, sunlit world, she to a peripheral world of shadows.

The dangerous goddesses are used in differentiated ways to create a structure to represent and create order in Bhaktapur. This must be emphasized in the face of a tendency within the Tantric segment of Newar religion to absorb and blend all divinities, particularly the goddesses, and such resulting claims as David Snellgrove's that "there is no need for us to follow the development of these different goddesses, for they all tended eventually to accord with one basic form, that of the Great Mother Goddess, in whom they all more or less lost their separate identities" (1957, 81).

DANGEROUS MALE GODS

There are a few male divinities in Bhaktapur who must be offered meat and alcoholic spirits, and who have frightening representations. Compared to the female dangerous divinities, they are fewer in kind, much less systematically related, and of more limited civic function. In another contrast with both the dangerous female divinities and with the ordinary gods, the male dangerous divinities seem to be further from the classical traditions of South Asia, comparatively more locally adapted and transformed. For that reason we prefer to use their local names, rather than the names of their distant classical ancestors. We have already mentioned that Gaṇeśa may be a dangerous divinity when he is used to "enter" and give *siddhi* to the worship of a dangerous divinity, usually in Tantric ritual. In addition there are three exclusively dangerous male divinities who are prominent in Bhaktapur's urban religion—Bhisi(n), Nāsa Dya: and a somewhat complex category, Bhaila Dya:.

BHISI(N) (BHĪMA)

Bhisi(n), or Bhisi(n) Dya:, "Bhisi(n) God (see fig. 15)," as he is usually referred to, is related tenuously to the Mahābhārata's epic hero, Bhīma or Bhīmasena, one of the five Pāṇḍava brothers. He is included in most households' sets of gods (discussed below), but he is in Bhaktapur the special divinity of shopkeepers.[50] He has three major city shrines, two of which are significantly located along that portion of the city festival route that follows the bazaar. The third one is just to the south of the

Figure 15. The merchants' special deity, the Bhisi(n) God.

city. Shopkeepers worship him at home and in his temples for good fortune in their commercial affairs. He is also the focus of one annual festival, centering on the temple of Suku Bhisi(n) Dya: in Dattātreya Square in the northeastern part of the city. Representations of Bhisi(n) show him as a powerful man with a full moustache, usually subduing a kneeling vanquished figure, said to be the epic's Kaurava King, Duśśāsana.

Slusser notes D. R. Regmi's claim (1965–1966, part II, p. 612) that the earliest reference to Bhisi(n) in the Kathmandu Valley is 1540 A.D., and remarks that all of his images are works of the late Malla period, suggesting a relatively recent (in terms of Newar history), introduction of the figure as a separate god, independent of his position as one of the five Pāṇḍava brothers. How he became a god of commerce is unclear. Slusser surmises that he may have been "first associated with the fields as a heroic guardian figure, and later, by extension, guardian of the granary and of trade" (1982, 258f.). It is not clear whether any of the special characteristics of Bhīma as portrayed in the Mahābhārata, where he is a kind of marginally socialized figure of great strength, facilitate his semantic appropriateness for the merchants. One may, perhaps not entirely frivolously, note the following. When Bhīma fought and killed the Kaurava King Duryodhana "the two were well matched, but when Bhīma was losing he struck an unfair blow with his mace, thus disregarding an ancient rule that a blow should never be dealt below the navel. This blow broke his adversary's thigh, and hence his epithet Jihmayodhin, the 'unfair fighter'" (Stutley and Stutley 1977, 45). Whatever his specific appropriateness to commerce may be, there are considerations that make a dangerous god more appropriate to the sphere of commerce than an ordinary god, as we shall argue in the summary section of this chapter.

NĀSA DYA: (NṚTYA NĀTHA)

Throughout Bhaktapur are a large number of shrines associated with a divinity locally called Nāsa God, Nāsa Dya:. Niels Gutschow mapped twenty-one of these shrines in a 1975/76 survey (personal communication). Of these, one in the southwestern part of the main festival route is considered the main one, and is a center for sacrifice and worship to him. Nāsa Dya: gives skill and effectiveness to public performers; thus people who are to take part in dance or drama or musical performances pray and offer flesh and alcoholic offerings to Nāsa Dya: before the performance. Similarly people who are learning one of the performing arts, including those whose traditional *thar* profession is music of one kind or another, worship Nāsa Dya: in the course of their training. Jugīs, for example, on the completion of their formal study of their special musical instrument, a double-reed woodwind, make a flesh and alcohol sacrifice to Nāsa Dya: "*Nāsa*" means grace and skill in social as well as "artistic" performances. Someone who has *nāsa* is "cultivated, delightful in social intercourse,. . . entertaining, the life of the party" (Manandhar 1976, 253). Thus people also worship Nāsa Dya: for such social skill. Nāsa Dya: is represented by holes in the wall of a shrine (or often in private homes). These may be single or in sets of three, and of various shapes, sometimes as triangles with the apices pointing downward. Brahmans identify Nāsa Dya: with the South Asian Śiva in his aspect as Nṛtya Nātha Rāja, the "Lord of the Dance," but there are probably no shrine images of him in this form in Bhaktapur. Mary Slusser had identified one such image, of "exceptional interest" precisely because of its unusualness, in the Paśupatinātha shrine complex (1982, vol. 1, p. 233, n.76; vol. 2, pl. 356). She notes that most Nāsa Dya:s "are inconsequential images. . . or they decorate the *toraṇas* [decorated arches placed above major shrine icons] of Śiva temples" (1982, vol. 1, p. 233, n.76). Like Bhisi(n) Dya:'s relation to Bhīma, Nāsa Dya:'s to Nata Rajā is very distant.[51]

BHAILA DYA: (BHAIRAVA)

Bhaila Dya:, "Bhaila God," the Newar version of the Hindu deity Bhairava (see fig. 16), is a divinity, or group of divinities, whose images, supremely dramatic in some of their anthropomorphic representations, are widely represented in Newar communities. In the Purāṇas Bhairava is sometimes a son of Śiva and Pārvatī, sometimes an emanation emitted by Śiva when infuriated. The Newar's Bhairava is associated with this emanation. In his anthropomorphic form he is represented with fangs, bulging eyes, dark blue or black coloring, carrying destructive weapons in his many arms, and wearing garlands of shrunken decapitated heads or skulls. He is thus an iconographic male equivalent of the Kālī or, for Bhaktapur, Mahākālī aspect of Devī. Bhaila Dya: is also present in a vague nonanthropomorphic form. Here he is a spirit-like creature who is located at or below the surface of the ground—in the cremation grounds or within the city in association with certain powerful natural stones. Finally he is theoretically related to the genesis and classification

Figure 16. An image of the dangerous deity Bhairava in front of the city's main Bhairava temple.

of the other dangerous male deities who are in certain contexts considered as "kinds" of Bhaila Dya:s.

The anthropomorphic Bhairava has two main presences in Bhaktapur, Ākāśa (Sanskrit *ākāśa*) "Sky," Bhaila Dya: and as the Bhairava of the Nine Durgās cycle. The Ākāśa Bhaila Dya: is housed in one of Bhaktapur's major temple structures located in Ta:mārhī Square, a square located on the axis that divides the upper half of the city from the lower half, and which is one of the ritual centers of the city. This is the center that becomes the pivot of the drama of the division and reunification of the city during the spring solar New Year festival, Biskā: (chap. 14). Ākāśa Bhairava and his consort, the dangerous goddess Bhadrakālī, are one of the symbolic foci of the dramatic sequence of the festival that dramatizes in their separation and coupling—in concert with a variety of other vivid symbolic enactments—the conflict and unification of the divisions of the city. The Ākāśa Bhaila Dya: temple has several representations of Bhairava. In front of the temple, in a recess on its front wall, is a small frightening figure (see fig. 16), sometimes given the name of Kāla Bhairava or Kāla Bhaila Dya: (because, in one explanation, "even Kāla, the Lord of Death trembles before him" [Sahai 1975, 119]). Within the temple are images used in the festival procession, and the major fixed temple image, which is a head without a body. This image is related through various legends (chap. 14) to a headless image of the god in Benares (Varanasi) in India.[52]

Ākāśa Bhaila Dya:'s vehicle is Betā Dya: (from the Sanskrit Vetāla). In those Purāṇic accounts where Bhairava is the son of Śiva and Pārvatī, Vetāla is Bhairava's brother (O'Flaherty 1973, 69, 106), but in Bhaktapur he approximates more the South Asian idea of Vetāla as "a class of demons, ghouls or vampires who frequent burial grounds, and are said to re-animate the dead" (Stutley and Stutley 1977, 331), a conception that is related to Bhairava's attributes as a stone god (below). Betā Dya: himself is conceived as a sort of agent for Bhaila Dya: in the exercise of his powers. Like many other deities in Bhaktapur, Ākāśa Bhairava is balanced by another deity. In this case it is the goddess "Bhagavatī" in the nearby N̄yātāpwa(n)la temple as we have discussed above. In the account of the building of the temple and the installation of "a Bhairava for the protection of the country, and the removal of sin and distress from the people" it was the Bhairava itself that gave people trouble (which is a general potential of the dangerous gods), and it was necessary to balance him with a complementary dangerous goddess. This conception of the goddess of the N̄yātāpwa(n)la temple as calming the dangerous Bhairava is still the popular explanation in Bhaktapur for the juxtaposition of the two temples.

The anthropomorphic Bhaila Dya: has a second dramatic presence in Bhaktapur's civic symbolism and ritual in the Nine Durgās sequence (chap. 15). Here he is represented in his fully powerful and frightening form, as a mask that is the symmetrical complement of the mask of the sequence's most frightening goddess, Mahākālī (see color illustrations). Among the group of divinities who make up the Nine Durgās group, Bhairava and Mahākālī have the predominant roles. In some of their performances he is the most prominent character, particularly in his presiding over certain animal sacrifices. In the most important of their performances, however, the calendrically determined sequential *twa:* performances, Bhairava is peripheral to Mahākālī. There is also in the Nine Durgās troupe of divinities a god form called "Seto Bhaila Dya:," the white Bhairava, who is in his relation to the female deities of the group a clown-like, ineffectual figure. In his iconographic representation the mask of this Seto Bhaila Dya: is a transformation of Śiva, who is also represented as a mask in the performance (see color illustrations). He reflects Śiva's ineffectiveness in relation to the Śaktis, who have become independent dangerous goddesses.

Bhairava as a vague demonic spirit inhabits the cremation grounds. He is found sometimes located in buried stones under the cremation pyres and is the focus of some Tantric *pūjā*s, and in popular assumption, at least, of *pūjā*s by spirit doctors, Tantric magicians, and witches. This sort of Bhairava is also thought to be the power in certain stones that "protect" the areas in which they are located. He is related both to ghosts and spirits and to the divinities of such stones, and we will return to him and some of the details of his cremation ground and stone habitations in a later section. Gutschow and his associates have reported eight Bhairava shrines in the city that appear on some paintings as part of a set of maṇḍalic circles in Bhaktapur's city space (Kölver 1976, 69–71; Gutshow and Kölver 1975, 21f.; Auer and Gutschow n.d., 38). These are all natural stones. The same set is represented by anthropomorphic statues within the Taleju temple complex. These Bhairavas are considered as consorts of a corresponding set of goddesses.[53] They have no meaning for public urban symbolic enactment, and little for contemporary Tantric esoteric religion.

The other dangerous male gods of Bhaktapur are vaguely related to Bhaila Dya:. Nāsa Dya: is said by some to be an emanation of Bhaila Dya:, and Bhisi(n) Dya:, with his human attributes, to be a sort of avatar of Bhaila Dya:. In spite of such ideas, however, they are treated for the most part as independent divinities.[54]

Bhairava/Bhaila Dya: encompasses a fairly diffuse class of beings in comparison with the elaborately formulated relations among the dangerous goddesses. There are fewer forms, and many of them are quite vague, which, as we will argue, give those aspects of Bhairava some of their semantic force. While the frightening form of the Goddess, most clearly exemplified by Mahākālī, is only one of the forms of the Dangerous Goddess, Bhairava exists only in his frightening form and is in many ways a lesser figure than the Dangerous Goddess. She may be the supreme deity, whereas he never is. Furthermore, his theoretical relation to Śiva is even more vague than the relation of the Dangerous Goddess to Śiva, for even if in many contexts she has separated herself from Śiva, in Tantric theory and practice the relation of Śiva and the Goddess as Śakti are obsessively investigated and enacted. And, finally, while the Goddess as Bhagavatī is a usual member of collections of household gods, Bhairava is only very rarely included, and that only by upper-status households who have special Tantric initiations and, therefore, powers. These asymmetries are significant.

NATURAL STONES AS DIVINITIES

The figures that we have been calling "major gods" in the previous sections are so referred to because of the overlapping of two qualities: (1) they are major and widely shared figures in South Asian Hindu oral and scriptural traditions, particularly that of the Purāṇas, and (2) they are made use of in the integrations of the city as a whole. In addition to such "major gods," however, there are other classes of supernatural figures, with special characteristics and special urban uses. We will discuss them here and in the following sections.

In the previous sections we have been concerned with divinities whose anthropomorphic (or on occasion diagrammatic) forms can be indifferently represented in "man-made" forms in carved wood, cast metal, painting on cloth, paper or wood, masks, or possessed human bodies, or in the case of some Tantric worship (chap. 9), clear mental images. We have noted in this and previous chapters that some divinities were represented and embodied by unworked "natural" stones. Some of these stones may be marked with some kind of symbol carved on them, but it is their "naturalness" that mostly seems to characterize them and give them some special possibilities of use and meaning.

PĪṬHAS

In his book on Hindu iconography, J. N. Banerjea notes that from very early periods in India "aniconism" existed along with iconic forms, anthropomorphic and, more rarely, theriomorphic images. Among these aniconic objects were, and are, sacred stones "scattered over different parts of India, which are taken to stand for one or [an]other of the cult divinities. . . . The well-known Śākta tradition about the severed limbs of Satī falling in different parts of India and about the latter being regarded as so many *pīṭhasthāna*s, particularly sacred to the Śakti-worshipers, should be noted in this connection. In modern times, the most important objects of worship in many of these shrines are usually stone blocks covered over with red cloth" (1956, 83). At the core of Bhaktapur's *pīṭha*s are such unworked stones, and the *pīṭha* goddesses we have discussed are located in them. Almost all *pīṭha*s are marked by stones, but an apparent exception is Guyeśvarī, the true Devī *pīṭha* located in the Paśupatinātha shrine complex, which is "a water-filled pothole surrounded with the carved stone petals of a lotus" (Slusser 1982, vol. 1, p. 327). In such apparent exceptions there is often a popular or an esoteric understanding that somewhere beneath the surface there is, in fact, a stone that is the seat of the divinity. There are various groups of deities associated with *pīṭha*s. These are manifestations of the Tantric Goddess and groups of gods associated with her in Tantric theory and imagery among the Newars. Several of these are present as esoteric or lost historical residues in Bhaktapur (Slusser 1982, vol. 1, p. 326; Kölver 1976), but the important persisting ones in Bhaktapur are the *pīṭha*s of the Maṇḍalic Goddesses, and, for the internal religion of Taleju, those of superseded royal lineage goddesses, as we have discussed above.

THE DIGU GOD, LINEAGE GODS

Outside the city boundaries in several directions (chap. 7) are natural stones,[55] which are the divinities that various extended family groups (*phukī*) worship once a year as their lineage god. These stones are called "Digu Gods," or, popularly, "Dugu Gods," after the goats, *dugu*, which are often sacrificed there. *Phukī*s also have shrines and icons of their lineage gods within the city. In those groups in the upper levels of the macrostatus system, those that are entitled to Tantric initiation, the images, called the "Āga(n) God," are elaborately housed and worshiped. The Āga(n) Gods are usually anthropomorphic forms of the Tantric Goddess. The pairing of an external open shrine with its aniconic stone divinity and an internal anthropomorphic or sometimes *yantra* god-form housed within the city, is parallel in both structure and certain aspects of worship to that of an Aṣṭamātṛkā's external *pīṭha* Goddess and her iconic image in her god-house within the city. The Digu God's shrine is sometimes referred to as a "kind of *pīṭha*." The Digu Dya: stone is usually backed by a carved arch or *toraṇa*.[56] Rarely there is no stone visible in front of the *toraṇa*, and the ground is considered the sacred spot, with the stone often assumed to be beneath it. The Digu God is sometimes considered as the lineage god in itself, but for upper-status families it is generally considered as the seat of the particular form of Devī which is their lineage divinity. Whatever the conception of the Digu divinity, it is necessary to offer it blood offerings and alcoholic spirits. We will return to the uses and worship of the Digu God and the Āga(n) God in chapter 9.

PROTECTORS OF LOCAL SPACE, *CHETRAPĀL* AND *PIKHĀ LĀKHU*

Everywhere in Bhaktapur are natural stones, some lying flat, some protruding from the ground, which are identified as "area protectors," *chetrapāls*, from the Sanskrit *kṣetra pāla*, a guardian of a field or place, or, within the realm of divinities, a "tutelary deity of the fields" (Macdonnell 1974, 79). These are popularly called *chelpa* gods. They are found near all *dya: che(n)* (god-houses), all Āga(n) *che(n)* (the special houses for upper-status *thar*s' Tantric lineage deities), near many private houses, and near or within the grounds of many temples. Each *twa:* or important sub-*twa:* has its own central *twa: chetrapāl*. The various *chetrapāl*s are regarded as distinct individual divinities, and may have local names. Some of the *chetrapāl*s in public city spaces are identified with Bhairava or Kumārī. In theoretical discussion all *chetrapāl*s are said to be a "kind of Bhairava," following a general South Asian association of such area protectors with Bhairava, or with a "portion of Śiva" (cf. Stutley and Stutley 1977, 153; Mani 1974, 434). Some *chetrapāl*s have a *yantra*, or "mystic diagram" engraved on them—a lotus, a triangle, a six-pointed double triangle, or a more elaborate *Śrī yantra*—but others are left uncarved. *Chetrapāl*s protect the nearby structure or the area around themselves from thieves, from illness, and from misfortune caused by evil spirits. They are the kind of divinity (typical of the dangerous divinities) that can cause trouble if inadvertently neglected or mistreated, and can thus in themselves cause illness or misfortune. Tantric physicians will sometimes ascribe illness to the inadvertent stepping on, spitting on, or otherwise offending some *chetrapāl*. The major *chetrapāls* in each *twa:* must be given offerings of food by each household at the finish of major household feasts. Some households make an optional additional offering before the beginning of the feast. *Chetrapāls* protecting god-houses and Āga(n) houses may also be offered food offerings in conjunction with feasts in honor of the particular deity whose house they protect. Sometimes people worship local *chetrapāls* in hopes of propitiating an offended *chetrapāl* or curing or preventing some misfortune. The major areal and neighborhood *chetrapāls* are sometimes covered with a decorative honorific canopy and smeared with colored pigments.

Several of the *chetrapāl* have particular legends associated with them. Two are of general city importance. One is associated with the Bhairava who inhabits the cremation grounds. Another, called "Swatuña Bhairava," is of importance as the spot where the power of the goddess Taleju is transferred to the Nine Durgās performers at the beginning of their annual cycle (chap. 15). We will discuss these two figures further in the next section.

There is a kind of aniconic stone divinity that is sometimes regarded as a kind of *chetrapāl* and sometimes as an independent and different form that is of considerable importance for symbolic action. This is a stone placed in front of the main door of every house, between that door and the road (chap. 7). This is called the *pikhā lākhu* ("*pikhā*" has the sense of moving or depositing something "outside"; "*lākhu*" [*lakhu* in Kathmandu Newari] is an old Newari word for path or road). This stone, embedded in the ground, may have been found there, but usually is brought from somewhere else during the construction of the house. It is usually engraved with the same kinds of figures sometimes carved on *chetrapāls*. It is sometimes theoretically identified as Kumāra, thought of as Gaṇeśa's brother, a god who has little significance in Bhaktapur. In its use, the *pikhā lākhu*, popularly called the *pilā lāki* god, is in each of its locations an individual god in itself. This stone marks the point in front of the main entrance, which locates an imaginary line at some distance from its actual external walls, separating its symbolic interior from the exterior public space. We have noted in chapter 7 something of the uses of that boundary.

Finally, the *chwāsas*, the stones marking major crossroads whose principal functions ally them to the group of pollution-disposing stone divinities that we shall consider in the next section, are also sometimes secondarily considered as area protectors, and thus as *chetrapāls*.

MEDIATORS TO THE UNDERGROUND—DISPOSERS OF POLLUTION

An important use of stones as deities is in the marking and protection of boundaries. The forces of the boundary protectors are directed to the outside of the boundary. They keep things out, rather than in. As we have noted in the last chapter, Bhaktapur has another boundary, that with whatever it is that lies beneath the city. While the space above the city is open to the sphere of the astrologically important "astral deities" and to the vaguely conceived heavens of the various gods, it is not conceived as separated from the city by a boundary. What is below is somewhat more problematic. It joins with the outside of the city beyond its encircling boundaries as a realm of somewhat nebulous forces, such as the *nāga*s, which may be dangerous if disturbed or inadvertently encountered.[57] The underground, like the area outside the city is a realm into which waste and pollution can pass. Stones that are the loci for the passage act as a kind of valve, which consume the dangerous pollution and/or prevent its return. Like all deities of similar function, the stone deities involved are dangerous in themselves. In the last chapter we discussed the *chwāsa*, stones placed at the major crossroads in each neighborhood. Portions of the head of a sacrificial animal which were used ceremonially at feasts must be brought there by the senior woman of the house. Clothes worn by a person at the time of or just before death are also brought to the *chwāsa*. It is the traditional responsibility of designated members of the Jugī *thar* to remove these clothes from the *chwāsa*. We have noted in the last chapter other polluting materials deposited at the *chwāsa* in Bhaktapur and other Newar communities. For some religious theorists the god of the *chwāsa* is the dangerous goddess, Mātaṅgī. Mātaṅgī (or more popularly the "*Chwāsa* god," or the "Kāla god") consumes the dangerous pollution of the materials left on it.[58]

Food left over from a feast and thus polluted may be given to a Po(n), as a human pollution remover, or it may be thrown into a garbage pit in the courtyard at the rear of the house. The courtyard is the seat of a form of Śiva,[59] Luku Mahādya:, the "hiding Śiva." This is a stone buried in the courtyard and worshiped once a year on Sithi Nakhā, the day that ceremonially marks the end of the dry season and the anticipation of the annual rainy season (chap. 15). According to Vogt, Śiva as

Luku Mahādya; "feeds upon the waste of the houses and transmutes it into creative power. To do this he takes the form of a ghoul. Otherwise the *pisaca* [a dangerous spirit, see below] . . . would come and feast on it. They [*pisacas*] are evil ghouls with only skeleton frames who are associated with decay and madness" (1977, 103).

A third set of disposers of symbolic waste or pollution are found outside the city in the cremation grounds, and are also natural stones. These are the Masān (cremation ground) Bhairavas. In the main *dīpa* or *masān* (Nepali, from Sanskit *smasāna*), the Cupi(n)ga:, the Masān Bhairava or Masān Bhaila Dya: is represented and focused in a stone believed to be under the ground at the place where the cremations are done. In the other two *dīpas* there are visible stones at the surface of the earth, representing and embodying the divinity. During cremations Masān Bhairava is conceived as being below the burning body. The body must be consumed before the spirit is free to leave the locality. The fire does this, but Masān Bhairava also is associated with the destruction of the body and the liberation of the spirit. In his main location at the Cupi(n)ga: *dip*, Masān Bhairava is worshiped or at least thought to be worshiped by various peoples whose powers are independent of the ordinary priestly system of the city. These include non-Newar Shaivite pilgrims and sadhus, shaman-like spirit doctors, members of the Jugī *thar*, and witches. Some Tantric *pūjās* are rumored to be offered to him there. These are all quests for religious/magical power or *siddhi* beyond the ordinary interior moral controls and institutional arrangements of the city.

The taming of Masān Bhairava is reflected in a legend. The Bhairava of Cupi(n)ga:, whose stone is supposed to have a *yantra* engraved on it, is associated with an anthropomorphic form of the deity that roamed the city in the past and was the cause of much trouble, including the death of many young people in Bhaktapur. A Tantric priest of great power, understanding the cause of Bhaktapur's troubles, seized Masān Bhairava and pulled out his tongue and cut it into three parts. The three pieces of the tongue are now three contiguous stones, named "Swatuña Bhairava," which function as a *chetrapāl* in the Ināco Twa: in the eastern part of the city, and as important markers for certain important festival actions during the Mohanī and Biskā: festival sequences.[60] The remainder of the Bhairava remains now usefully fixed in the cremation ground.

Masān Bhairava is a clear example of the theme common to many stories and ideas about the dangerous deities—that they are destructive forces captured (more or less tentatively) through power for some special purpose, and put to the use of the city as a city divinity (compare the Nine Durgās legend, chap. 15).

ASTRAL DEITIES

Bhaktapur, like all South Asia, has a body of astrological theory centered on the Navagraha, nine heavenly bodies and events,[61] which are also thought of as divinities of benign or malignant influence. In the course of Hindu and Newar iconography these Navagraha have been given iconic representations, sometimes, particularly for Sūrya the sun god, elegant ones (Pal and Bhattacharyya 1969). The Navagraha are studied by astrologers (chap. 10)—with the help of detailed printed annual astrological charts and calendars—in their relation to the time of an individual's birth for the purpose of guiding decisions about important undertakings of many kinds and to diagnose and recommend treatment for certain illnesses and misfortunes.[62] Astral considerations are also used in some *pūjā*s and festivals to determine their exact proper timing. In general, astrological procedures are used, particularly in the anticipation of risky undertakings or in problems arising out of errors in previous undertakings, to adjust individual action to impersonal cosmic order. The action at issue must be, of course, one where choices are free in some sense—aspects of a journey, a marriage, a business undertaking, or the timing of a ceremony, which are not specified by some other aspect of urban order. Astrology fills a gap, where the more common kinds of ordering of action, that determined by role, city area, annual calendar, or phase of the life cycle, do not operate.

Astrological considerations are important throughout the life cycle starting with the astrologically orienting time of birth. Worship of the sun, sometimes taken as the representative of all the Navagraha, is part of each of the life-cycle ceremonies. In one set of ceremonies, those associated with a girl's first menses (app. 6), the sun has particular importance, as the girl is "presented" to it and worships it after a prolonged period of seclusion in darkness.

The sun, and to a much lesser extent the moon, have other symbolic usages drawn from other aspects of the Hindu tradition, particularly those remnants of early Vedic religion that are parts of Brahmans' internal *thar* religion, and the Vedic component of their service to high-status clients such as the *Homa* ceremony. Ordinary people pray to the sun in a perfunctory manner on Sundays from the open roof porches of their houses. Finally, many collections of household gods also include an image representing the sun.

The Navagraha have no special shrines and are not used to mark city space. As we have noted above in the discussion of the peripheral Maṇḍalic Goddesses, the Pūjāvidhi section of the Agni Purāṇa contains a diagram associating the Navagraha each with a specific Matṛkā (Pal and Bhattacharyya 1969, 39f.) in a sequence that has some correspondence to the sequence of those goddesses at Bhaktapur's perimeter. The circle of peripheral Maṇḍalic Goddesses in Bhaktapur, which are thought of and dealt with as arranged starting at the east and moving clockwise in almost exactly the same order as the listing of the Śaktis of the gods in the *Devī Māhātmya*, corresponds at the same time—with one problematic position interposed—to the order of the planets as days of the week when the Matṛkā–planetary correspondence noted in the Pūjāvidhi is taken account of. This dim possible echo of astrological associations has no contemporary meaning.

THE BRAHMANS' VEDIC GODS

The term "Vedic" is sometimes used in Bhaktapur to separate the "ordinary" gods and religious practices from the dangerous gods and their associated worship, which are then sometimes called "Tantric." In this usage "Vedic gods" are for the most part the Purāṇic gods of later Hinduism. However, there are many ancient truly Vedic gods, who are invoked in the litanies, mantras, and practices of some ceremonies of the Rājopādhyāya Brahmans for their own internal *thar* and family uses, and for aspects of ceremonies performed for their clients. As Michael Witzel writes in an article entitled "On the History and the Present State of Vedic Tradition in Nepal," "the Vedic religion, which preceded both Buddhism and medieval Hinduism, had already in Licchavi time largely been superseded by Purāṇic and Tantric elements, yet this oldest form of Aryan worship and learning has come down to the present age" (1976, 17). Witzel traces the history of Vedic practices and texts in Nepal, and (for our present purposes) notes the continuing performance of some ancient rituals such as the Agnihotra through the centuries. He also reports the persistence into the present of an annual Vedic Soma sacrifice. Bhaktapur Brahmans still learn and chant the *Yajurveda*, although (as Witzel notes) the knowledge of the other Vedas is dying out and there has been a diminution in Vedic studies among the Brahmans in recent generations.

The persistence of these rituals and their associated gods is of considerable historical interest, but from the point of view of Bhaktapur's city religion, these Vedic gods are the internal gods of the Brahmans and a canonical reference in some phases of Brahman conducted worship for others. These Vedic gods are the gods that add special supernatural effectiveness to the Brahmans' practices. Many other *thar*s also have special internal divinities of diverse origin, who are of importance to the life of the city insofar as they guarantee the effectiveness of the *thar*'s output into the city system, although for these other *thar*s they have later historical origins. Thus, for city religion the true Vedic gods have become the internally validating *thar* deities of the Brahmans as one cell in Bhaktapur's complex religious system.

PILGRIMAGE GODS OF THE ROYAL CENTER

There are a number of shrines and temples that are found for the most part in the large square in front of the Malla palace and within the Taleju temple complex which represent gods that are not important to the public ritual or symbolic life of the city. These include such forms and appellations as Paśupatinātha, Guhyeśvarī, Annapūṇa, Jagannātha, Rāmaśvara, Kedarnātha, and Badrinātha. These shrines were erected by the Malla kings to represent gods found at famous pilgrimage centers in India[63] and in other parts of Nepal, particularly the Valley shrine complex, Paśupatinātha. These shrines are now maintained and worshiped in a perfunctory way by Rājopādhyāya Brahmans in their continuing function as the Malla kings' priests. They were conceived of as places where worship could be a substitute for pilgrimages for the convenience of the court. The Malla kings, local Brahmans say now, could get as much merit from erecting them and in subsequent generations praying at them as by going on a pilgrimage. It is also said that such shrines were especially important when war or other external conditions made such pilgrimages impossible. These sites are now sometimes worshiped by passersby or local residents, and sometimes the local Paśupatinātha and Guhyeśvarī may still be worshiped as a substitute for a visit to their main shrines at the Paśupatinātha temple complex.

The structures are of interest to our present study in that in contrast to most of the temples and shrines and associated gods of Bhaktapur, they have a reference to real space and location elsewhere than Bhaktapur and its immediate environment. The placement of these sites at

Bhaktapur's Royal center, their Royal use, and their identification with "foreign" shrines, echoes, perhaps, a symbolic device for relating a city as a "cosmo-magical" symbol, as Paul Wheatley phrases it, to an "empire." Wheatley illustrates this with a summary of Paul Mus's (1936, 1937) study of twelfth-century Bayon in Cambodia, a city that contained statues of provincial gods, "so that Bayon as a whole constituted a pantheon of the personal and regional cults practiced in the various parts of the kingdom. By thus assembling them at the sacred axis of Kambujadeśa, the point where it was possible to effect an ontological passage between the worlds so that the royal power was continually replenished by divine grace from on high, Jayarvarmin, the King, brought these potentially competitive forces under his own control" (Wheatley 1971, 432).

Traditional Bhaktapur's "imperial" impulses began to fade rapidly beyond the boundaries of the Valley, but they were, in however attenuated form, an aspect of royalty and its symbolism, as we will see in other contexts. The loss of Bhaktapur's Malla kings, that is, of its "own kings," exaggerated and distorted the balance toward Bhaktapur's inner orientations. The "Gods of the Royal Center" are, perhaps, a wistful sign of past Royal conceits.

HOUSEHOLD GODS

One of the cellular units in Bhaktapur is the household. Like other such units, households have their own internal gods. Daily household worship, *pūjā*, in households are offered to "all the gods" (usually, as we have noted, with Viṣṇu as the central figure), but these gods are really a limited group, as represented by the images that may be present in households. On special occasions, however, one or another of these household gods is the focus of worship. Upper-status households (in the past only the groups higher than the farming *thar*s, but now including also most of the economically comfortable farming families) have in the *pūjā kuthi*, or *pūjā* collection, not only a variety of equipment for *pūjā*s but also collections of images of gods usually as bronze or brass statues. There are, according to Brahman family priests, some god images that are virtually always included in these collections, and others that are only occasionally found there, at the whim of the household.

All *pūjā* collections in households able to afford a collection of metal god images will include images of Gaṇeśa, Viṣṇu-Nārāyaṇa, Śiva, Bhagavatī, and among shopkeepers and those engaged in commercial enterprises, Bhisi(n) Dya:. Viṣṇu may be represented by an anthropomorphic image either alone or with his consort Lakṣmī, or by a stone or fossil *śālagrāma*. Śiva is represented by an anthropomorphic figure, by himself or with his consort. In these combined figures of Śiva and his consort as household deities, Śiva is generally called "Maheśvara" and his consort, "Umā." Śiva is also represented commonly by some form of the *liṅga*. Other deities commonly represented are Sarasvatī, the Sun and Moon (usually in a combined image), and certain of Viṣṇu's more popular *avatar*s and their associates—Rāma and Kṛṣṇa, with or without consorts, and Hanumān. Upper-status families with Tantric initiation may also have a metal plate with an engraved *yantra* representing Śiva and Śakti and an image of Bhairava in their ordinary household collection. (They will also have special Tantric lineage images kept in a separate room with restricted access.)

Among the less common images found in some collections are images of the gods' consorts by themselves—Lakṣmī, Pārvatī (often in this form called "Annapūrṇā"),[64] and Rāma's consort Sītā. Among the rare images are vehicles associated with gods, such as Śiva's bull and Indra's elephant. These latter seem to be of aesthetic or novelty interest as much as for their connection with a god. There are also rare images of major gods in unusual forms such as the cosmic Viṣṇu reclining on a serpent, and images of the minor *avatar*s of Viṣṇu, such as the dwarf, turtle, fish, or boar *avatar*s. There may be images of Ṛṣis, Vedic "seers," and of the minor god (for Bhaktapur) Kumāra. The collection may also include other kinds of divinized objects—images of *nāga*s, river stones representing various gods, books divinized as Saravatī, and so forth.

The common household pantheons consist for the most part of the major ordinary gods, the gods that represent, as we will argue, ideal and representative images of civic persons. To this group an image of the goddess in her protective warrior form is added. Then there are the various idiosyncratic household choices, which are generally representatives of the benign, ordinary deities. In these collections some images can represent any subsidiary gods that they "contain"—Viṣṇu's image can represent his consort and his avatars and their consorts; Bhagavatī can represent all the forms of the Tantric Goddess.

GHOSTS AND SPIRITS

The various supernatural beings we have been discussing are all called "*dya:*" in Newari, a term that we have variously glossed by the historically cognate terms "divinity" and "deity," as well as by "gods." In addition, Bhaktapur also has a diverse assortment of beings that are not *dya:*, nor in Western conception "gods." These beings are heterogeneous nebulous forms having wills, understanding, motivations, and some sort of corporal identity. They are usually, but not always, malignant, and of various degrees of potency. All of them are uncanny, the subjects of thrilling accounts and horror tales. In comparison to the divinities with their canonical representation and traditions, these forms, "ghosts" and "spirits," are more vaguely defined and there is much less agreement on their nature and proper names. The social and psychological implications and uses of these creatures differ in important ways from those of the *dya:*s. Our purpose for introducing them in this chapter is a limited one—to see what light they may throw on the nature of Bhaktapur's aggregate of supernatural actors. These beings may be roughly sorted into those that are somehow derived from some spiritual substance left by humans after their deaths, and those that are independent beings in their own right—as are other living creatures in general, including gods. There is not always agreement if a particular kind of uncanny creature belongs in one or the other category. Most of these beings are familiar South Asian forms, some few are perhaps of Northern origin.

The ghost-like creatures, associated with spirits of the dead, are often called *preta* or *bhūt-pret* (from the Sanskrit *preta*, locally pronounced "*pret*"). "*Preta*" refers to the particular spiritual principle or entity that represents the continuation of a person after death, and that undergoes various transformations. For the first twelve days after death the spirit is conceived to be in a *preta* form, after which it is variously conceived as becoming an ancestor spirit or *pitṛ*, or of being safely on its way to some place of judgment, or state of reincarnation (app. 6). The corpse itself is also referred to as a *preta*. There are various mishaps that can prevent the proper passage through and beyond the *preta* stage, and the *preta* then will become a troublesome earth-bound ghost. A person who was not "ready" to die or did not want to may become a permanent *preta*. Someone who dies in such a way that the proper rituals cannot be done—such as in an accident away from home or whose death is considered "unnatural"—can also become such a *preta* (cf. G. S. Nepali 1965, 124f.). The presence of these ghosts is often harmlessly manifested in such events as a window or door moving by itself or a chair shifting position. They stay around their former homes usually, and will not harm family members if as many as possible of the proper postdeath rituals have been performed. There are, however, more malevolent varieties that may enter a person and consume them from the inside,[65] causing them to lose weight and become ill, and which require the services of a special spirit exorcist.

Bhūtas (from the Sanskrit *bhūta*, in Bhaktapur pronounced "*bhut*") are differentiated from *pretas* (by more theoretically inclined Newars at least) as being uncanny forms that are not derived from human spirits and that are independent beings.[66] They are responsible for the same kinds of phenomena as *pretas*—unexplained movements of inanimate objects, illness, apparitions, and sleep disturbances. There are still other beings that for some people are kinds of *bhūta*s, for others kinds of *preta*s, and for still others neither *preta*s nor *bhūta*s but independent beings. Among these is the Khyā,[67] which exists in two forms, white and black. The white is benign and guards the house from other spirits. It sometimes may snuggle up to a person, and produces a tickling feeling. Black ones may produce frightening nightmares. They may press on people's chests during sleep, making it difficult to breath or to move. While for some people Khyās are independent spirits, but not *bhūta*s, for others they are a kind of *bhūta*; for still others they arise from a body that has not been thoroughly cremated so that some flesh remains. Another group of spirits are Twa(n)s, which shriek at the moment of the death of someone in the area, and whose shriek may cause the death of people who hear it. Another is the Kini or Kikini, which has the form of a beautiful woman who tries to seduce young men. If they yield they will sicken and die. The only clue to her spirit nature is that her feet are placed backwards on her legs. There is also the Kawā(n), a particularly dangerous spirit, which looks like a skeleton and makes a rattling sound when it moves. If you run into one, it will kill you. Kawā(n)s help guard the goddess Mahākālī and are represented by boys in the Nine Durgās dance dramas. People talk of actual encounters, their own and others, with such spirits. Legends and "literary" tales told in the city tell of still other demonic forms—such as the giant Rākṣasas and goulish Piśācas who are not, however, thought to be encountered in the ordinary life of Bhaktapur as the other spirits and ghosts may be.

The ghosts and spirits cluster at crossroads, inhabit the woods and fields outside of the city, lurk in the dark, and are driven away by bright lights. Sometimes they may invade a home but usually lurk in outside shadowy areas. An encounter with them is usually a matter of some accident or inadvertent mistake. There is a period lasting about one month in the spring of every year when rice planting is under way in the fields around Bhaktapur when the "*bhut-prets*" are free to enter the city (chap. 15). This freedom is explained in that the protective Nine Durgās have completed their annual cycle, and have left the city. The spirits must be chased out of the city during the subsequent Gāthā Muga: Ca:re festival. Usually, however, ghosts and spirits are the private concerns of individuals or families. This, we shall argue in the context of the other supernatural beings in this chapter, is reflected in the attributes that are ascribed to them.

NĀGAS

There is one creature that is difficult to classify. It is spirit-like but also is like a powerful "natural" serpent. It usually dwells beneath the earth, but may shake the foundations of people's houses, or leave its underground domain and enter them. These are the *nāga*s, "supernatural snakes." They are most important in considerations of new building on previously undisturbed ground, and astrologers must determine how to avoid disturbing them and how to placate them (chap. 7). The shaking or collapse of houses may be ascribed to them, as are some episodes of disease among household members. Sometimes people glimpse a *nāga* moving in snake-like form within the house. When the *nāga* of the foundations is in harmony with the house, it serves to protect it from harmful influences. As we have noted, holes are placed in the walls of houses so that the *nāga*s can easily get out.

BHAKTAPUR'S PANTHEON AS A SYSTEM OF SIGNS

Underlying our presentation of Bhaktapur's deities and supernatural figures is the assumption that the many individual deities, objects, and creatures we have discussed are imagined, created, and arraged in such a way that they can be comprehended by people in Bhaktapur and that they are able to make, each in its own way, their special contribution to the representation, creation, and maintenance of the city's mesocosm. We have noted that the active members of the pantheon are, for the most part, selected from the great South Asian historical and areal lending library of god forms. There are both economic and semantic reasons for the selection.

In a study of the *meaningful* (as opposed to "known about") deities in the "personal pantheons" of a Chinese and a Hindu informant,

Roberts, Chiao, and Pandey (1975) found that although the Chinese informant knew in some detail about some sixty deities and the Hindu informant about more than one hundred, their "meaningful god sets" —the ones that had "personal significance and salience" for them—was, for each, fifteen deities. After examining some of the aspects of meaning by which each informant compared, contrasted, and sorted the members of his pantheon, they concluded that "Meaningful god sets appear to be symbolic small-group networks, with believers ordering their thoughts about their gods in terms of a relatively small number of major dimensions. Since they seem to have few members, it is probably the case that every god within this limited number must carry his full religious and psycho-cultural weight" (Roberts, Chiao, and Pandey 1975, 145f.). The number of active gods in Bhaktapur's urban pantheon that are of general urban importance are also limited in number, although there are more of them than the fifteen in those two sample private meaningful pantheons.[68] There are somewhat more than forty if the ghosts and spirits are included, and less than forty without them. That quantity is probably small enough so that each deity may carry a "full religious and cultural weight" for city dwellers. This is to argue, following Roberts et al., that the civic pantheon is a "meaningful god set" to the city's *individuals*, for the numerical constraint has something to do with individual cognitive capacities. However, the gods' identification, meaning, and use are made easier by their location in a few more general meaningful *classes*. Those classes, in fact, contribute importantly to the deities' differential "religious and psycho-cultural weight" in the public urban order.

In his summary work on ancient Greek polytheistic religion, Walter Burkert writes of Greek ritual that "the same repertoire of signs is employed by various groups in various situations" (1985, 55). The Greek pantheon, in contrast to, say, the vast Hittite and Babylonian pantheons, is distinguished by its "compactness and clarity of organization . . . the Greek gods make up a highly differentiated and richly contrasted group." And, he adds, "The primary differentiations are taken from the elementary family groupings: parents and children, male and female, indoors and outdoors" (1985, 218).[69] If a common "repertoire of signs" is to be put to concrete uses in a community and thus to be understandable and learnable, it must, as the paper of Roberts and colleagues suggests, be sufficiently compact and differentiated for such uses.

There have been some anthropological approaches to Hindu pantheons as "repertoires of signs" (Babb 1975; Wadley 1975; Harper 1959) in comparatively simpler Hindu communities which will later provide some useful comparisons with Bhaktapur. As Babb put it for the area of Madhya Pradesh that he studied, "The pantheon is not a haphazard congeries of gods and goddesses but a system of symbols that formulate a view of reality. The pantheon symbolizes a world, the world in which ritual action takes place" (1975, 215). When we consider a deity (or any other type of cultural object or event) as a "sign" and as a member of a domain of signs, we are interested in its meanings and uses to a particular community of sign interpreters and its meaning for certain purposes—here, as throughout this book, for the most part for the purposes of urban integration. The deity's history is of interest in such an analysis only as it is "living" and informs present meaning and use. In a sense "extra" history clings to it, however, and makes it something more than present systematic community usage may require[70] and gives it a creative potential for some emerging future conditions.

But to what do those meanings cling?

BHAKTAPUR'S PANTHEON AS A SYSTEM OF SIGNS: SOME NOTES ON IDOLS

At the turn of the nineteenth century, the Abbé Jean-Antoine Dubois, carefully considering the question of "idolatry," wrote that Hindu idolatry was "grosser" than pagan idolatry, in that while the pagans worshiped fauns and naiads, the beings who presided over the forests and the rivers, Hindus worshiped the "material substance itself, . . . water, fire, the most common household implements" (1968, 548). "Idolatry" here means the violation of the Judeo-Christian-Islamic profoundly transforming program and dictate to pagan and "primitive" religions to worship the distant creator rather than the environing creation.[71] But, Dubois continues, "It is true that they admit another kind of idolatry which is a little more refined. There are images of deities of the first rank which are exposed to public veneration only after a Brahman has invoked and incorporated in them these actual divinities. In these cases, it is really the divinity that resides in the idol, and not the idol itself, that is worshiped" (1968, 548). This is what sophisticated—and probably most—people in Bhaktapur still hold. This does not allow us to dismiss the "idols" themselves, however, the "idols" that, as Dubois reminds us, embody specifically "deities of the first rank."

The "idols" are, that is, only one of several kinds or classes of forms of deities. Those classes of forms are centrally important for carrying, each in its way, an important category of significance. *Within* the class of "idols" their members' differentiated identities are constituted by their own iconographic components—the gestures, postures, paraphernalia, associated "vehicles," crowns, arrangement of hair, and so on, which are the subject of iconography, and which serve to identify the particular divinity. These components, which turn, for example, a carved piece of stone into an adequate representation of Śiva, are for the most part neither our concern nor the concern of the people of Bhaktapur once the minimal adequacy of the image to represent what it is supposed to represent has been assured. The central problem in the urban uses of the pantheon is to know that an image is or is not Śiva. The constituting parts of the image are of concern only where they may have some direct semantic import and thus contribute to the meaning as well as the identification of the image, and in the rare cases where the iconographic details of a particular version of a divinity may give the image one rather than another of its possible significances and uses.

BHAKTAPUR'S PANTHEON AS A SYSTEM OF SIGNS: CLASSES OF MEANINGFUL FORMS

Each of Bhaktapur's urban supernaturals is from one point of view a somewhat fuzzy clump of ideas and feelings and urges to action in peoples' minds. These are usually manifest in or focused on concrete material objects or, in the case of spirits and ghosts, an imagined object. Whatever the ideas, emotions, and calls to action understood to be associated with these objects, it is the concrete objects that exist in some sort of external space, make an impact on the senses, and have perceivable boundaries. Many of these objects can be manipulated, placed and fixed in space or moved through it and used as central references for action. The object is a *part* of the meaningful deity considered as a "sign," but it is important for our purposes to distinguish it from other meaningful aspects. It is something like what Charles Morris (1938) called a "sign vehicle." The sign vehicle, in concert with the other sorts of meanings that it focuses makes up a sort of "god sign," which, following the semiotic analogy somewhat further, can be combined and contrasted with other such signs in various ways making possible an infinite variety of symbolic statements.

The meaning of a city god, like all "natural" sign systems (in contrast to logically constructed ones) is a multilayered, context-dependent, and sometimes ambiguous fabric. The god-bearing objects and man-made images not only carry great quantities of history, myth, and legend but also absorb the implications of their uses, their relation to status, space, time, and specific symbolic enactments, and that absorbed meaning, in turn, makes them fit for new relations from which they again absorb meaning in a continuing process. However, the objects and images are not just sponge-like units absorbing any meaning of placement and use, Humpty Dumptyish terms that can mean anything one chooses to make them mean. Certain aspects of their meaning are more central, less fluid than others, and give to the gods as signs their adequacy to be used or located in certain ways. This can be called, for want of a better term, their "primary contribution" to the field of meaning. These "primary" aspects include the major legendary characteristics ascribed to the god in Hindu tradition. Much of their "primary contribution" comes from very general aspects of their form, however, and that form is at the same time—and in specific relation to its context-resistant contribution to their meaning—an important aspect of their classification.

The formal aspects that may be used to sort the pantheon into *classes* of deities are different from those that differentiate the *members* of the various typological groups. The members are usually differentiated by *conventional* iconographic features. Hierarchical relations among members, where they obtain, may be indicated by *relative* features—comparative size or position (right vs. left, center vs. periphery). The *classes* of gods are distingusihed by neither conventional iconographic signs nor relation, but by discontinuous and "directly meaningful" (rather than "conventional") contrasts.

The *classes* of deity differentiated by "directly meaningful," easily understandable, contrasts of form are those fundamental contrasting sets we have discussed throughout the chapter, the sets that are put to extensive symbolic use in the city. Let us recall those classes, rearranged for present purposes in an order different from that in which we presented them above. These classes are: astral deities, ghosts and spirits, stone deities, and major civic deities (of which there were two subclasses, benign and dangerous). The other deities we discussed (e.g., royal pilgrimage gods, household gods) belong in their form to one or another of these groups.

The contrasts that serve to sort the types of supernaturals and bear on their meaning and use are in the following dimensions:

1. *Proximity.* *Proximate* forms are present in city space (including its bordering outside where they may be directly encountered, and are in contrast to the *distant* impersonal forces represented by the astral deities, who *are* for the most part, the distant heavenly bodies.

2. *Materiality.* Among the *proximate* beings are those having a fixed *material* form, which may be contrasted with those whose forms are *immaterial*, the ghosts and spirits.

3. *Artifice.* Among the beings with *material* forms, there are those whose forms are *humanly worked* in contrast to those whose forms are aniconic "*natural*" forms.

4. *Ordinary versus uncanny humanly worked forms.* Among forms that are *humanly worked* there are the *ordinary forms*, whose imagery is closely derived from the forms, logic, and relations of the social world of objects and persons, in contrast to the *dangerous forms*, whose imagery is derived from dream-like or hallucinatory forms, logic, and relations. A diagram of these contrasts indicates certain aspects of this branching typological schema:

Proximate versus Distant (astral deities)
↓
Material form versus Immaterial form (ghosts, spirits)
↓
Humanly worked versus Natural stones (stone gods)
↓
Ordinary forms (benign deities) versus Dangerous forms (anthropomorphic dangerous and Tantric deities)

The main movement of this classification as the contrasts at each level are isolated—the right-hand terms above—is a progressive movement toward the everyday moral life of the city, ending with the ordinary deities, those deities that are thought of and dealt with as "persons," and who represent community ideals and norms. They are proximate, material, shaped through culture, and not demonic. Let us recall some of the aspects of the formal sets distinguished by these contrasts to suggest their contributions to meaning.

1. *Proximate versus distant.* This first distinction separates the astral deities from all the rest. The astral group are essentially impersonal cosmic forces. Their movements are regular and they provide the external rhythm and tempo that must be understood and *adjusted* to, as opposed to the manipulations and avoidances possible within other realms. This is true of both the calendar-determining phases of the moon and movements of the sun and the influences on "luck" of the whole astral set. The function of the astrological expert, the Jośi, is to map the exact state of the astral realm and help individuals and priests adjust to it. Most ritual activities addressed to other kinds of deities are fitted in various ways to one or another indication of cosmic rhythms given by the astral bodies. Although they may have some iconic representations, the astral deities are embodied in their existent forms as distant astronomical forms and events in the skies. In contrast to the astral deities, all the other divinities and ghosts and spirits are immediately present and closely encountered in and around the city, and in contrast to the regular clockwork movements of the distant deities, the proximate beings have minds and passions and whims and thus have some freedom of action, make decisions, and can be influenced by individuals in one way or another.

2. *Material versus immaterial.* The proximate beings can be divided into those that are embodied in some concrete form for most city purposes, and those that are not so embodied, which remain "immaterial." The nonembodied forms are the spirits and ghosts. The identification and classification of the nonembodied forms are, as we have noted, comparatively vague. These beings have relatively little cultural construction, local tradition providing only vague identifying sketches. They are not objects of any cult or community religion, and are the only beings we have listed here who are not in one or another context referred to as *dya*: or "gods." They are of personal and immediate local concern only. They are only rarely, fleetingly, and haphazardly encountered, although they provide the basis for many exciting accounts. The work they do for the community is to give some shared name and vague form to a range of vague private encounters, perceptions, and psychological states. The embodied beings, in contrast, constitute the working civic gods. Because of their embodiment in material objects they can be perceived in common, and can be related to significant space, either as fixed in a particular spot or carried through some particular area. The embodied deities are public objects, and as they are objects that affect

the senses in a discrete and controllable way, they serve perfectly as civic "sign vehicles."

3. *Worked versus natural.* The embodied material beings can, in their turn, be sorted into two groups, "worked"—those that are given some conventional form through the efforts of artists and craftsmen following the traditional canon for the production of valid images—and "unworked"—naturally occurring objects that are credited with embodying a divinity. The unworked objects of importance in the public city religion are, for the most part, stones, almost always embedded in the ground. These unworked stones represent in local conception as they do in their form something intermediate between the formless spirits and the crafted deities, having both spirit-like features and god-like features. The gods they represent are vague in their conception and classification when compared to the gods of the worked images. The stone gods are never portable, and thus never used to mark out an area through their movements; they mark or protect fixed boundaries between some socially differentiated interior unit and its less social or nonsocial outside. They belong mostly to that vague outside, and mark the outer, the relatively nonsocial face of the boundaries at which they are fixed. They share some features with one division of the worked divinities to form a crosscutting group of "dangerous" divinities.

4. *Benign versus dangerous.* When we turn to the divinities who are represented by humanly worked and formed images, icons, we enter the realm of the major gods of Hinduism, those that are usually considered as constituting a pantheon. These gods all have anthropomorphic images, although some part of the image, usually the head, may have an animal form. We are now encountering figures that not only are sentient beings but also have at least external human characteristics. They represent a movement away from uncanny beings, toward something more understandable—understandable, that is, in a particular way, the way we understand humans as "persons." It is this group that is the focus of most calendrical festivals, whose myths, legends, and relationships order most ritual action. These divinities have houses and temples, and may be fixed in a position in space or be carried in festival processions or embodied in human agents. They are present in the city at rest or in movement as anthropomorphic, embodied beings, very much as the citizens of Bhaktapur are so present.

This final division of classes of divinity is within the set of culturally worked anthropomorphic gods. Here the distinguishing formal contrast is the appearance of the images themselves. One set has various features that suggest emotionally driven dream-like images, features that escape from the constraints of ordinary everyday reality. They include fangs, cadaverous bodies, bulging eyes, garlands of decapitated heads or skulls, mantles of flayed human skin, and multiple arms. The arms carry human calvarias (understood to be drinking cups full of human blood) and various destructive weapons. The female forms of this type (and not the male ones, which, when shown as being sexually aroused, maintain their demonic forms [fig. 17, chap. 9]) include images of exaggerated seductive sexuality, with exaggeratedly rounded, youthful faces, hips, and breasts. Their hands, however, bear the same objects as those of the frightening figures. Both versions—beautiful and horrible—may be conceived of as dream-like and hallucinatory images. This group represents the "dangerous anthropomorphic gods"—"dangerous *anthropomorphic* gods" because the group of "dangerous gods" also includes the stone gods, with whom these deities share some characteristics. These anthropomorphic dangerous gods are the foci of many city festivals. They and the associated stone gods are the major symbolic resources for the marking of significant city space. The anthropomorphic dangerous gods have potentialities beyond the stone gods. They, like the benign set, may be arranged in differentiated sets; they can move through space, and they thus allow for differentiated and specialized statements in their use in the various symbolic enactments that mark, relate, and protect various units of the city.

With the group of culturally crafted anthropomorphic gods, we begin to have identified individuals who are embedded in characterizing relations with similar beings. We have something like a socially created, morally controlled *person*. The dangerous deities, however, as we have noted in earlier sections, are uncanny persons; they are too dream-like, shifting and flowing in their forms and in their logical relations with each other. When we have followed our main axis from distant to proximate, to materiality, to anthropomorphic form, and finally to *ordinariness*, however, we are at the end very close to full "persons," as defined by the roles, needs, and possibilities of a social community. These residual "ordinary" anthropomorphic gods are heroic persons, with extraordinary—albeit not unlimited—powers and with graspable minds. This is manifest in their prevalent imagery as idealized human types. Even if they are partially animal in form, such as Gaṇeśa, Hanumān, or Viṣṇu's vehicle Garuḍa, they are humanized animals, in con-

Figure 17. An esoteric image of a Bhairava.

trast to the frequently bestialized humanoid forms of the dangerous anthropomorphic gods. They represent the moral interior of the city and both represent and are models for the moral dimensions of human relations (above all, those of the household and other intimate relations) and of the self.

Walter Burkert argues that the Greek Homeric gods move beyond the anthropomorphic gods of the Near Eastern and Agean neighborhoods of Greece. *Those* gods "speak and interact with one another in a human way, . . . love, feel anger, and suffer, and . . . are mutually related as husbands and wives, parents and children." But the Greeks, he says, add something to this. "The Greek gods are *persons*, not abstractions, ideas or concepts. . . . The modern historian of religion may speak of 'archetypical figures of reality,' but in the Greek, locution and ideation is structured in such a way that an individual personality appears that has its own plastic being. This cannot be defined, but it can be known, and such knowledge can bring joy, help, and salvation. These persons as the poets introduce them are human almost to the last detail" (1985, 182–183 [emphasis added]). Jean-Pierre Vernant, on the contrary, asserts that "the Greek gods are powers, not persons" (1983, 328). He argues this on the basis of their difference from what he takes to be the essence of social persons—namely their being as "autonomous focuses of existence and action, ontological units." Claiming that "a single person cannot be several," he calls attention to the various states and conditions referable by term such as "Zeus." However, this does not affect the argument that in particular temporal and spatial contexts and uses these gods are "persons" in a way that the members of some other pantheons are not, and that this quality as manifest in these contexts is of considerable importance for understanding the ancient Greeks and their religion. It is their person-like aspects that most clearly locate the forms, meanings, and uses of the ordinary gods as members of a particular class in Bhaktapur's civic pantheon. When, in contrast, a member of this set is considered in historical perspective, and its uses in other settings and conditions and in differently arranged pantheons are all added to the identity of the divinity, another type of figure, of great mythic complexity, emerges. As we have noted, such histories surround all the gods of the pantheon but are distant background to the choices and simplifications that must be made for the god's synchronic civic uses.

"Person" refers to a universal social invention, "someone" as the legal definition has it, "who is capable of having rights, and being subject to duties and responsibilities," that is, a relatively fixed actor in the give and take of a moral system. Not all individuals in a community are "persons" in this sense; infants and often the mentally ill and defective are not. The benign gods have many of the characteristics of persons in this sense. They look like humans, and their special differentiating aspects are all social. They are embedded in and defined by social relations, out of which a larger community of related divine individuals is built. Their relations to each other are in part moral, matters of understood obligations and limits, and in part passionate. But their passions and motives—annoyance, rage, lust, compassion, respect, and fear—are ordinary social ones. The benign gods are in large part fixed in their forms and in their relations, and usually work things out within the constraints of logic and ordinary reality to which is added a superhuman (but limited) power that they use in times of special need. Like ordinary persons, they are subject to pollution (compare the discussion of the Nine Durgās in chap. 15), which indicates that they must, like all mature citizens of Bhaktapur, take care in order to maintain their social definition as persons (chap. 11). The dangerous gods have no such concern.

The benign gods as persons represent, as Babb has proposed, "certain key values of Indian civilization" (1975, 224). But they represent not only ideal values but also aspects of "normal" behavior, that which is tolerable for humans. What they do not represent (except transiently in the history of that generative and bridging form, Śiva) is "insanity" and other modes of operation and understanding of the mind peripheral to the "person." This is done by the dangerous deities in various ways. As representations of the ideal and "the human," the benign deities become foci of identification and guides for proper behavior and moral standards, and also for tolerant understanding. Their soteriological functions have to do with reward or punishment of the *ātma*, the particular spiritual entity that is for most people closely connected with the idea of the self and its persistence after death. This reward or punishment is based on moral performance within everyday life and with the proper devotion or "service" to the god and, in marked contrast to the effects of encounters with the dangerous gods, with inner intentions as well as external behavior. The benign gods, like all the gods, are subject to ritual manipulation. But their proper devotion and ritual manipulation consists primarily of a mimesis of honorific and respectful behavior, in the course of which they are offered the same honor, hospitality, gifts, and services that would please any honored guest or person of high status. Such rituals reinforce and reaffirm the worshiper's social relation to the benign deity. All this does and can go on only within a rational, dependable world. These gods are "ordinary" and not "dangerous" precisely because they respond dependably to anyone with adequate social and moral skills, anyone who has, in part with their help, become a competent person by Bhaktapur's standards.

For other tasks and meanings Bhaktapur employs other types of divinities, divinities who are much more peripheral to the moral world of persons than the ordinary gods, and who thus represent other realms and ideas and who must be dealt with in other ways. The dangerous anthropomorphic gods vividly represent this nonmoral realm precisely because they have *some* characteristics of persons—names, forms, and anthropomorphic embodiments. They are radically peculiar and unacceptable persons, however, persons in flux—to recall Vernant, they are not *quite* "ontological units." They are outside the constraints of both logic and morality that are the essence of true persons. They represent the bordering outside of the ordinary world in a variety of ways—they are related to the forces and forms of "nature" beyond the city, wild and dangerous but at the same time vital, and also to certain psychological modes—dream, insanity, and those passions and impulses (e.g., cannibalism) that are beyond what are acceptable even to a tolerant view of what a person is or should be. As they do not operate through moral interactions and manipulations, they operate in the only other available mode, through power, and that is the way they, in turn, must be dealt with. This constellation of characteristics used to portray the hinterlands of any moral community has many familiar echoes throughout the world,[72] but the uses of the dangerous gods have a particular development, force, and legitimacy in Bhaktapur. In contrast to many other Hindu communities (below), the dangerous gods have a special status in Bhaktapur as legitimate and high-ranking members of the pantheon, and as Tantric gods they are (as we will see in the next chapter) in many ways the foci of aristocratic and royal worship.

The dangerous deities represent not only the nonmoral exterior of the city but also the *relatively* nonmoral aspects of the exteriors of various of the city's component units. In some contexts, they are associated with individual's bodies and, particularly, with danger to those bodies in contrast to people's selves, souls, or "personhood," all associated with the benign moral deities. Most generally the dangerous gods protect the perimeters of the community, of its components, and of its members, within which the ordinary moral life, represented by the ordinary gods, can go on, while at the same time repesenting aspects of the external dangerous forces. In protecting the boundaries of moral units and civic spaces, however, they also represent and protect such units *as a whole*. It is in this way that they can be made to represent the city as a whole, a lineage, *guthi*, or a neighborhood.

The use of dangerous deities as the representatives of a moral maximal unit warrants more comment. Let us recall the emergence of Devī in the *Devī Māhātmya*. When the world of the gods is threatened by danger from the Asuras—that is, when that world emerges as an entity precisely and only because it is set against a dangerous, contrary world—the Devī arises. She uniquely represents the world of the gods, even though she is not a "normal" member of that world. If she were, she could not protect them. She can protect them only by sharing in the nonmoral power of the external forces she has to defeat. In analogous ways Bhaktapur uses nonmoral deities to represent, as well as protect, moral units.

There is another important aspect of the use of nonmoral dangerous deities to represent a moral unit. They protect that unit in a very real way (as we will discuss in later chapters, particularly in relation to the Nine Durgās in chap. 15) by helping to ensure the adherence of its members to its moral system. The dangerous deity, usually a goddess, in concert with the meanings of blood sacrifice offered to her, represents the destruction that will overtake members of a group if they violate their adherence to the moral system and moral solidarity of the group. She binds members into the group as well as defending the group's boundaries and representing it as a whole.

Insofar as the dangerous deities themselves represent the kinds of external dangers they protect against, they must first be captured in order to be put to work for the community. As we will see in later chapters, this is done in local legend through the Tantric power of exceptional individuals. For ordinary individuals the dangerous deities can be controlled, albeit somewhat tenuously, not through social deference and good behavior as are the ordinary gods but through an individual's initiation into secrets of power, and the use of spells (*mantras*) and, above all, through the use of one of the most important ritual resources in Bhaktapur, blood sacrifice, whose meaning in relation to the dangerous gods we will discuss in later chapters. Most of the time one deals with these powerful and erratic deities by trying to avoid them, or not to anger them or—if one has reason to assume that they are angry—asking forgiveness and making restitutive offerings, even if (in contrast to the moral deities) they may have become angry "without cause." As the dangerous deities do not represent moral values, they cannot be, as the ordinary deities are, models for ideal or tolerable behavior. Their psychological functions for individuals, like their uses for th city, are quite different from those of the benign deities with whom they contrast within the formal supernatural class of humanly worked deities.

A few *classes* of deities differentiated among themselves by a few structural features do, as classes, much of the work of organizing realms of meaning in Bhaktapur. Their contrasts use kinds of meanings—near versus far, vague versus clearly formed—which are easily apprehended, and require minimal special cultural knowledge. The situation changes radically in relation to the organization and uses of the differentiated supernaturals *within* the classes of deities.

BHAKTAPUR'S PANTHEON AS A SYSTEM OF SIGNS: DISTINCTIONS WITHIN THE TYPES OF GODS

The differences among the sets of gods, essentially the differences in their mode of representation, are, we have argued, based on certain contrasting structural features and are the basis for much of their meaning. *Within* the sets the distinctions are not the distinctions of classes or types, but, for the most part, distinctions among *individuals*. These distinctions are generally made on the basis of the clusters of iconic signs that identify each individual, usually redundantly—any one of several features will sufficiently identify the deity—as long as the other features are not too anomalous. These differentiating features are the usual ones emphasized in treatises on the iconography of the Hindu god images[73]—crowns, vehicles, markings on foreheads, objects held in the hands, vehicles, aspects of dress, color, and the like. Without considerable interpretation based on knowledge of their myths and histories, the meanings of many of these features—beyond their identifying uses—may (with exceptions to be noted below) seem more or less arbitrary as direct indications of the paricular individual's present meaning or use. The individual stone deities (helped by some associated markings) and most of the astral deities are identified by their positions.

In most sets of deities the different deities—Indrāṇī, say, in her contrast to Brāhmaṇī—do not contrast in their *general* meaning and use, in which they are often identical, but in the portion or component of some larger whole made up of equivalent or near-equivalent parts—such as the maṇḍalic segments of the city, the aspect of the full Goddess emphasized for some special purpose, the days of the week of astrological concern, or the set of all tutelary *phukī* deities—which they stand for. Each of these member deities in a set must be identified as an individual, but an individual whose particular individuality has little differentiating significance beyond their relevance to some specific sector of space or time or society. Often people who are not specially concerned with one of these individual member deities may not be entirely certain as to which member of the group they are, and may misidentify them or identify them with some lumping collective term.

The relation of deities within groups insofar as they mark equivalent divisions of space, time, or status is generally "horizontal" and more or less equal, but there are also some hierarchical relations within groups. These are sometimes indicated by size—anthropomorphic statues of an ordinary god and his consort usually depict him as larger (see fig. 12); the masks of Mahākālī and Bhairava are larger than the less powerful figures in the Nine Durgās group (see color illustrations), and so on—or by central versus peripheral positions—Tripurasundarī is at the center of the city *maṇḍala*, the vehicles of Śiva and Viṣṇu may be placed at the periphery of a temple, they at its central axis.) Above and below may also be used to indicate relative status, with a god's vehicle sometimes shown as kneeling at his feet, or placed below them. Among the benign gods the relation of the male gods and their consorts is shown by the consort being placed to the male god's left. Such *relative* features are not used in contrast between the different classes of gods who do not have hierarchical or consort relations across types.

Against these general features of the differentiation of the members of sets there is a very significant exception within one particular set, the benign deities. Within the set of the ordinary gods directly understandable implications in the images become, as they were in the case of classes of deities, once again salient for a differentiation of the meanings represented by each deity. Here the distinguishing features are the clusters—among the background of presently otherwise meaningless identifying iconographic features—which identify social behaviors and qualities. The tiger skin and yogic costume of Śiva in some of his moods, the modest beauty of Pārvatī, the cuteness of the benign Gaṇeśa, and so on, are such easily apprehensible meaningful features.

The benign deities in contrast to all the others *are* persons, and their forms help remind people of the kinds of persons they are. There local uses are rooted in these meaningful personal differences.

BHAKTAPUR'S PANTHEON AS A SYSTEM OF SIGNS: SOME CONTRASTS WITH OTHER HINDU SYSTEMS

A comparison of the organization of Bhaktapur's pantheon with reports from other Hindu communities highlights some of Bhaktapur's special features. Edward Harper, in a study (1959) of Totagadde, a village in Mysore State, found a local hierarchy of three levels of supernatural beings. The highest level were the familiar "vegetarian" gods of the major Hindu tradition ("Sanskritic gods"). These gods, locally called "Dēvarua," are "generally iconographically represented." They are most frequently worshiped so that the devotee will obtain *puṇya* ("merit"). This may be in the hope of good fortune in this life, or a good fate after death (1959, 228f.). We recognize in this group some of the characteristics and uses of the "ordinary" segment of Bhaktapur's pantheon. Harper's second class of deities, second in a hierarchy of purity, are locally called "*dēvate*s." These gods demand and accept blood sacrifices. They protect the village in various ways. They patrol the village boundary or guard designated parts of the village. They also protect various social segments, families, and lineages in the village. Some are attached to houses, where they "protect adults, children and livestock from spirits . . . who cause minor illness" (1959, 231). The same class of deities can possess individuals, and cause illness. While the first group of deities are responsible for trouble only in the sense that they withhold aid that might have been granted, this class may actively cause harm, and part of their worship is intended to prevent this. These deities resemble in nature and use Bhaktapur's dangerous deities, but there are important differences. For the Mysore village these "local gods" do not derive their names and legends from the high Hindu tradition. They "almost never" have iconographic representations. They are less pure, and thus lower than the "Sanskritic gods." Finally, within their ranks are some of the forms and functions (illness-causing possession) that are proper to some of the members of Bhaktapur's "ghosts and spirits."[74] Harper's village has a residual third group of supernatural beings "*devva*s," "free floating marauding spirits . . . malicious and destructive [which] perform no protective functions" (1959, 232). The main contrast with Bhaktapur suggested by Harper's sketch of Totagadde's religion is that there the dangerous deities are much closer to the realm of the immaterial ghosts and spirits than they are in Bhaktapur. The Tantric tradition has facilitated the capturing, embodiment, control, and legitimate civic use of a large segment of supernaturals of this kind in Bhaktapur, and does not place them in an inferior hierarchical relation to the "Sanskritic," that is, the benign Purāṇic deities.

In Susan Wadley's study (1975) of Karimpur in Uttar Pradesh, the supernatural beings in the "village experience" (that is, in contrast to the unknowable divine principle, the *brahman*) were the category of gods, "*deva*s" and a set of spirits and ghosts that, as in Bhaktapur and like Totagadde's "*devva*s," were considered outside the class of "gods." The class of *devas* includes, according to Wadley, both "normally" benevolent and always malevolent deities. The normally benevolent deities (which would include Bhaktapur's dangerous gods) she calls the *devatā*, the remainder "demons." Wadley's main concern is with the differentiations within the class of "normally benevolent *deva*s," where she suggests (as does Babb, whom we will consider presently) that a central distinction for functional differentiation within the group is the gender and gender relations of the various members. The male *deva*s are referred to as "*bhagavān*"; the female, as "*devī*."[75] The male *bhagavān* and his concrete manifestations such as Viṣṇu, Śiva, and Gaṇeśa, can help people if they are devoted to them. Devotion sets up a social relation, "a relationship based on hierarchical exchange because the gods and men have a commitment to each other" (1975, 117). This set of gods, male gods, can be helpful in gaining "relief from existence and the troubles of existence." These gods can help in getting through the problems of life, but they do not hurt, except presumably by failing to help. These are, thus, similar to Bhaktapur's benign gods, and to Harper's "Sanskritic gods." According to Wadley, the female *devatā*s, the Devī and the component *devī*s, "to a much greater extent than the male gods categorized as *bhagavān* are potentially malevolent." She cites Babb (1970) and Beck (1969), agreeing that "there is an ever present awareness that female power may become uncontrolled. And when male authority (usually a consort) is absent, the malevolent use of female power is almost assured" (Wadley, 1975, 121). She claims for Karimpur that male deities can always dominate the female deities while female deities have a "potential for malevolent action [that] makes them more suspect than male deities" (ibid., 121). Among the *devīs* there are "some who are almost totally malevolent and act positively only to remedy their own actions" (ibid., 121f.).

Before discussing these observations in relation to Bhaktapur's use of divine gender, we may note Lawrence Babb's extended consideration of the pantheon of various communities in the Chhattisgarh region of Madhya Pradesh. He begins with the familiar distinction about the "philosophical" status of the undifferentiated "world-soul" of Hindu tradition, which he calls the *paramatma.* This is "an object of contemplation not of worship. Divinity becomes active in the affairs of the universe and men only when it is differentiated into particular divine entities. With this differentiation we move into the world of everyday religious practice. Of all the different kinds of differentiation found within the pantheon, one seems to be particularly stable, that of sex" (Babb 1975, 216). Gender, he argues, sorts two basic qualities of the pantheon. The male "*devta*s" are "essentially protective and benevolent." The female *devī*s are "the very embodiment of malevolence when unrestrained or unappeased" (ibid.). Babb, starting with suggestions from the *Devī Māhātmya*, recalls the association of the female goddess as Śakti with "energy" or "force." He notes that in the male–female polarity as conceived in Hindu Tantrism, "the 'female principle' is conceived as the active, dynamic component of reality, while the male principle is regarded as static and passive" (ibid., 220). Taking the angry, destructive, embattled Devī of the *Devī Māhātmya* in her Kālī form as emblematic of that force whose "only discernible emotion is anger—black, implacable and bloodthirsty," he finds female deities in such benign and non-Tantric manifestations as Lakṣmī problematic, that is, as secondary, and asks, "what is the context in which the Goddess becomes Lakṣmī?" He suggests that when the male and female deities are related in the ordinary social relation of marriage, with the god dominant—as husbands are—and the Goddess dutifully subordinate, this "imposition of social order" yields deities embodying key values of Indian civilization. He also notes that these social relations allow for "the elaboration of divine attributes in accordance with basic order-producing values—hence the great variety in this sector of the pantheon." In contrast, where the goddess is either alone or dominant, and "if the god appears at all, it is not in the role of husband but of henchman and servant, [then] . . . the pairing as a unit takes on the sinister attributes of the goddess herself. The goddess in this form is not conceived primarily as an exemplar of values and principles, but as the embodiment of an impersonal force—one that can be used, but that may be dangerous to the user, as indeed it endangers the gods themselves until it is contained" (ibid., 225). In a summary he argues, "Within the pantheon a very dangerous force is symbolized, but this is a force that seems to undergo a basic transformation into something almost anti-sinister, the loving wife, the source of wealth and progeny, when placed within the context of a restraining social relationship, that of marriage. An appetite for conflict and destruction is thus transformed into the most fundamental of social virtues, that of wifely submission which, on the premises given in Hindu culture, makes the continuation of society possible" (ibid., 226).

These suggestions of Wadley and Babb illuminate a powerful component of the pantheon's semantic force, and are congruent with other meanings of male and female persons and their relations in many societies and as particularly emphasized in Hindu social systems. But these suggestions are not fully applicable, at least in Bhaktapur's version of things. The creative Goddess in her absolute, full form is not malevolent or sinister, and no more uncanny than concepts of Viṣṇu or Śiva as creative gods, and certainly no more destructive. She seems to represent a component of a maternal image that is prior to the submissive role of a wife, one worthy of trust and adoration. There are also male forms of considerable malignity, Bhairava, and to a lesser extent the minor dangerous male gods, who are not "henchmen or servants" of a goddess. In some cases the relation to a goddess (as in the case of the Ākās Bhairava) helps to make the male dangerous god, *less* dangerous—in some reversal of the argument. Furthermore, there is at least one female goddess of complete benignity who has in Bhaktapur no present reference to a male controlling and socializing consort, namely, Sarasvatī. Furthermore, Śiva, when not controlled by social relations, either as a husband or by his friendship to Viṣṇu, is a potentially wild and dangerous being. Finally, the dangerous ghosts and spirits of Bhaktapur are not predominantly female. Granting such qualifications, however, the predominance of the male deities in the domain of moral and social order, on the one hand, and the predominance of independent female ones at the boundaries of that order on the other, is, of course, also characteristic of Bhaktapur. Bhaktapur's imagery and symbolic action treats these independent goddesses as not only dangerous but also as necessary, vital, and protective.

Insofar as Bhaktapur's use of divine gender is less categorical and oppositional than the forms proposed in the studies we have cited, this is congruent with the way Bhaktapur's social system and culture has allowed for the comparatively independent position of women in the family within a Hindu perspective and the resulting modification of the role and meaning of wife and mother in that perspective. Some of that different emphasis may also be related to the movement of the dangerous female deities from a "non-Brahmanical" social and spatial periphery, as the "folk goddesses" characteristic of Indian villages, to the high-status central position in a socially integrated Tantra (chap. 9), which they have in Bhaktapur.

A FINAL REMARK

We have added the supernaturals to our static collection of elements of Bhaktapur's mesocosmic ballet. Status, space, and deities are variously combined in action in progressively more complex structures of meaning. We will in the following three chapters consider some aspects of action, concept, and role bearing on the manipulation of aspects of the symbolic order before, finally, adding time and tempo and considering the ballet in its full action.

CHAPTER NINE

Tantrism and the Worship of the Dangerous Deities

INTRODUCTION

In our discussion of Bhaktapur's pantheon we have emphasized the division of the deities most centrally concerned with the organization of the public city into "ordinary" and "dangerous." These two categories of deities are related to two general modes of religious activity in Bhaktapur and in the Hindu tradition. The mode focusing on the ordinary deities takes special definition in Bhaktapur from its contrast with the worship of the dangerous deities. The worship of the dangerous deities has roots in popular and folk tradition in South Asia but has within it a differentiated aspect that has had a literate development of its own in South Asian high culture. This is "Tantrism," which Bhaktapur differentiates in a traditional South Asian distinction from the "Vedic" practices of the ordinary religion.

Esoteric Tantrism must be distinguished in Bhaktapur on the one hand from the worship of the ordinary deities (which has in itself, as we will note, "Tantric" references) and on the other from the exoteric worship of the dangerous deities by noninitiates. It is Tantrism in itself that will be central to our discussion of the worship of those dangerous deities. For Tantrism not only is the developed mode of relation to the city's dangerous deities in the esoteric practices of the upper social levels of the city but also lies behind much of the public urban symbolism and symbolic enactments centering on those deities which are experienced by all of Bhaktapur's citizens. And it is Tantrism that gives Bhaktapur and the Newars (as it does neighboring Tibet) much of their special qualities in South Asian religious perspective.

TANTRISM AS A RELIGIOUS MODE

There is a substantial literature discussing aspects of the Tantric tradition in Buddhism and Hinduism (see, particularly, the synthesis by Gupta, Hoens, and Goudriaan [1979]). Tantrism has been characterized as an "historical current" within the larger South Asian tradition, a current that is relatively easy to recognize in its manifestations and notoriously difficult to define. "The extremely varied and complicated nature of Tantrism, one of the main currents in the Indian religious tradition of the last fifteen hundred years, renders the manipulation of a single definition almost impossible. There is, accordingly, a general uncertainty about the exact scope of the word" (ibid., 5). These authors attempt, however, a definition, which will serve as a useful introduction to Bhaktapur's Tantrism (ibid., 6 [emphasis added]):

> In our opinion, it is mainly used in two meanings. In a wider sense, Tantrism or Tantric stands for a collection of practices and symbols of a ritualistic, sometimes magical character (e.g., *mantra*, *yantra*, *cakra*, *mudrā*, *nyāsa*...). They differ from what is taught in the Veda and its exegetical literature but they are all the same applied as means of reaching spiritual emancipation (*mukti*) or the realization of mundane aims, chiefly domination (*bhukti*) in various sects of Hinduism and Buddhism. In a more restricted sense, it denotes a system, existing in many variations, of rituals full of symbolism, predominantly—but by no means exclusively—Śakti, promulgated among "schools"... and lines of succession... by spiritual adepts or *gurus*. What they teach is subsumed under the term *sādhanā*, i.e. the road to spiritual emancipation or to dominance by means of Kuṇḍalinīyoga and other psychosomatic experiences.... *It is important to remark at this point that the true Tantric sādhanā is a purely individual way to release accessible to all people, women as well as men (at least in theory), householders as well as ascetics.* At present the practicers (*sādhaka*) of the Tantric system are mainly people who live an ordinary life within family and society. But beside this ordinary reality, they try to come into touch with a higher stratum of divine reality by a course of identification with their chosen deity who is usually the Goddess.

Elsewhere in South Asia the individualistic, anti-Brahmanical, anti-social-structural aspects of Tantrism, although they influenced renouncers of Hindu society (see, for example, fig. 18) and those who tried to manipulate the world through magical power, became for most

Figure 18. Outside the city. A wandering Indian *sādhu* doing *yoga* on a public porch in a mountain village.

practitioners—for those who "live an ordinary life within family and society," that is, within the Brahmanical order—comfortably bracketed into safe and nondisruptive contexts (ibid., 32):

> The Kulārṇavatantra states that anything which is despised in the world is honorable in the Kula [a particular school of Tantrism] path. On certain occasions, the texts even express a preference for anything which is associated with low social standing or with the breaking of taboos. . . . Of course, this was an important factor in creating for Tantrism its bad repute with the orthodox. But anti-caste statements should never be read outside their ritual context. Returned into ordinary life, no high caste Tantric would think of breaking the social taboos. One might even argue that the predilection for contact with low-caste people, especially women, in a ritual environment served to render the high-caste practicer still more conscious of the violent breakthrough of his ordinary situation which he had to make in order to proceed on the way to spiritual emancipation. Seen in this light, the ritual egalitarianism of Tantrism in practice acted as a caste-confirming and class-confirming force. One can compare the confirmatory and stabilizing role of festivals like Holi or Śabarotsava, during which caste or class relations are temporarily eliminated.

Bhaktapur has gone further in the use and transformation of Tantrism than as an exciting and cathartic antistructural fantasy for upper status men—although that is still one of its important uses. It has transformed the Tantrism of transcendence of Brahmanical order for the purposes of individual salvation and individual power and put it to the use of the civic order, in so doing complexifying that order. Legendary accounts of the capture of Bhaktapur's protective deities, the Nine Durgās (chap. 15), vividly portray this double movement. The stories tell how the demon-like deities who make up the group once lived in a jungle outside of Bhaktapur where they killed and ate the innocent passers-by whom they happened to encounter. Eventually the gods were captured by the spells and wiles of a powerful Tantric practitioner. He took them into the city, put them in a secret room in his house, and, using them for his own private amusement, "played with them" and made them dance for him. But then through the interference of his wife—representing one of the central symbolic mediators from private masculine pleasure to social order—the demon deities escaped his private control and fled the house. The Tantric practitioner was able to recapture them, but by now they had taken measures to prevent his taking them back into his house. Now unable to use them for his own purposes, he, in a compromise, forces them to pledge to protect the public city, to use their power against those external forces of disruption that they originally represented in themselves. The Tantric expert who presided over this transition (who in some versions is different from the magician who originally captured them) was, significantly, a Rājopādhyāya Brahman. However, once the secret was out, once the dangerous, blood and alcoholic spirit-swilling, order-destroying, and polluting[1] gods were out in the visible public space of the city, special kinds of priests, *Ācājus* (chap. 10) had to replace the Brahman to deal with them in public—although the Brahman's descendants would continue to be engaged with them in more esoteric arenas.

For Bhaktapur's "Newar Brahmans" (chap. 10) and Kṣatriya-like Chathariyā and Pa(n)cthariyā groups, Tantrism is not only, as it was for the Tantric master who captured the Nine Durgās in the self-indulgent time before his wife's interference, a source of private fascination but also central to the worship of their partilineal lineage deities. Their exclusive right to Tantric initiation is, in fact, one of the most important markers setting them off from middle-status and low-status groups in the city. This "gentrification" of Tantrism existed in other parts of South Asia. "The study of later Tantric literature seems to reveal an ever tightening grasp of Brahmans and other intellectuals on the movement—or, as one could as well say, an ever greater hold of Tantrism upon the traditional bearers of Indian literary culture" (Gupta, Hoens, and Goudriaan 1979, 27). This elite domestication existed and exists in a somewhat uneasy relation with Tantrism's asocial and, in fact, antisocial central thrust, as well as with the low origins and family connections of its central deities.

The problem is clarified by the situation of the dangerous deities in non-Tantric communities. In a consideration of ritual in the Indian village of Konduru in Andhra Pradesh, Paul Hiebert made a distinction between the "high religion" of the village and its "low religion." The "high religion" centers around the benevolent Hindu gods of the "great tradition." Its priests are Brahmans (for the higher castes), the offerings to the gods are vegetarian. The "low religion" centers around "regional Hindu gods and local gods linked to Hinduism" (1971, 133). Hiebert further notes (pp. 135–136):

> Chief among these [supernatural beings] are the local and regional goddesses who reside in trees, rocks, streams and whirlwinds and are enshrined in crude rock shelters in the fields, beside the roads, and in the home. Capricious and bloodthirsty, they demand the sacrifice of animals to satisfy their desires; therefore, the Brahmans refuse to serve them. Their priests are Washermen, Potters, and Leatherworkers. . . . All villagers fear their anger

> which can bring disease and death to those who neglect them, blight to crops, fires to houses, barrenness to wives, and plague and drought to the village. Even the local Brahmans who deny their existence take no chance and send their offerings by the hand of a family servant to be sacrificed to the goddesses of their fields.

This village arrangement reflects the hierarchical predominance of "Sanskritic" over the other deities in Indian village pantheons that we noted in the last chapter, but it also emphasizes the social peripherality of such "local and regional" deities whose worship and characteristics are those of Bhaktapur's dangerous deities. Even as the status of the dangerous deities—who have been, like the Nine Durgās, captured and taken into the city, albeit in an ambiguous incorporation—has changed in Bhaktapur, so has the social status of their cult and their priests. Yet, the Indian village situation clearly suggests the contradictions and tensions in the apparent urban respectability of these deities in Bhaktapur. The Newar Brahman, the Rājopādhyāya Brahman, has, as we will see below and in chapter 10, important Tantric functions, but these are hidden within private, esoteric arenas of the city's worship. Public Tantric worship is usually done by other priests, the Ācājus (which has sometimes led to the erroneous statement in descriptions of the Newars that they are somehow the "Tantric priests" in some sharp opposition to the Brahmans as "Sanskritic priests"). As we will see in chapter 10, the interlocking roles and relations of Brahmans and Ācājus in relation to Tantrism and ordinary Hinduism in Bhaktapur are complex. As he is in Hindu communities everywhere the Brahman is a central priestly figure in the "ordinary" Hinduism of Bhaktapur. In relation to the Tantric component of the city religion, however, he has special functions—as *guru*, giver of *mantras*, officiant at some Tantric ceremonies for clients, performer of his own private and family Tantric ceremonies, and as priest at the Royal temples of the dangerous deities (particularly Taleju)—which make him, the priestly master of Bhaktapur's urban, civilized Tantrism, a much more complex figure than the ideal Sanskritic Brahman.

TANTRISM IN POPULAR FANTASY

People in Bhaktapur without Tantric initiation have various interpretations and fantasies regarding Tantrism. Such fantasies are encouraged by the Tantric strategy of protecting esoteric doctrines through multiple veilings and obfuscations of its doctrinal and symbolic implications (cf. Bharati, 1965, chap. 6). Those veilings and obfuscations are, as we will discuss below, often associated with some sort of an "advertisement" that there *is*, in fact, a secret that is being hidden. For the noninitiate, Tantrism means primarily "magic" practices, sometimes referred to as *tantra-mantra*, that is, to practices that are capable of direct manipulation of supernatural power for worldly ends. Noninitiates, particularly —although not exclusively—lower-status ones, assume that this magic power is used for legitimate, albeit usually private, ends, such as curing disease, chasing off evil spirits, and keeping wandering bulls out of cultivated fields.[2] Occasionally, it is assumed, the power may be used for love magic or for harming an enemy. It is also popularly believed that particularly powerful Tantric experts can (and could more frequently in the past) levitate themselves or objects, travel through the air to distant places, and control and dominate powerful supernatural beings. From the viewpoint of the legitimate practitioner, such *direct* personal uses of "power" are possible but illegitimate and peripheral to their goals. However, even sophisticated initiates believe that outside the civic esoteric system, out of Brahmanical and civic moral control, there are such figures as sādhus (wandering "renouncers") witches, sorcerers, and healers who use a degree of Tantric power sometimes for good (in a struggle against a contrary harmful supernatural power), sometimes for evil.

Noninitiates often believe that Tantric *pūjā*s are associated with major violations of ordinary moral and religious regulations such as the eating of forbidden foods and overt sexual intercourse—including (according to one informant) even the incestuous intercourse between brothers and sisters. In general, however, noninitiates seem to believe that legitimate Tantric practice is, albeit strange, good behavior and in the pursuit of socially acceptable goals. These same people also seem to believe that most Brahmans, at least, do not know much Tantrism, their fantasies about the *dharma*-violating procedures of Tantrism are directed to the secular upper *thar*s. This interpretation is, in fact, consonant with another essential aspect of Bhaktapur's Tantrism, its alliance with the realm of power of the king in opposition to the realm of moral order of the Brahman, in his role (for Bhaktapur only one of his roles) as a priest of the benign deities.

UPPER-STATUS TANTRISM

As we have noted in chapter 5, there is an upper segment of Bhaktapur's macrostatus system whose male members, after completing initiation as full members of their *thar* (and whose female members under certain conditions and restrictions), have the right to Tantric initiation. These are the Rājopādhyāya Brahmans, all the *thars* at the Chathariyā and Pa(n)cthariyā levels, the Tini, and one Jyāpu *thar* with some priestly functions, the Jyāpu Ācāju.[3] All of these *thars* share certain rights and customs in contrast to other, lower, *thars*. Their male members have the exclusive right to wear the sacred thread, the *jonā*; they alone have a special kind of lineage deity, the *Āga(n)* God; they alone have the right to have Tantric *gurus* (who are Rājopādhyāya Brahmans), initiation, and practice. The worship of the dangerous deities by people of the middle and lower *thars* is not considered Tantrism by upper-level initiates, nor by members of the lower-level *thars* themselves.

We will follow this distinction and consider Tantrism *per se* as the practices of initiates. We will begin with Tantric worship, that is, Tantric *pūjā*, in Bhaktapur. We can then consider the uses of that worship. These are of two general kinds for upper-status initiates, worship directed to the *phukī*'s lineage god and practices directed to *mukti* or "individual salvation." We will then turn to forms that span both esoteric initiate religion and the symbolism and religion of the larger city.

UPPER-STATUS TANTRISM: *PŪJĀ*

In part three of Gupta, Hoens, and Goudriaan's book *Hindu Tantrism* (1979), a section entitled "Modes of Worship and Meditation," Sanjukta Gupta presents the "fully developed" Tantric *pūjā* in detail. The "fully developed" Tantric *pūjā*s performed in Bhaktapur by priests and their upper-status clients are minor variations on the sequence Gupta describes and interprets.[4] Descriptions such as Gupta's relieve us to some degree both of our ethnographic responsibility to record Bhaktapur's esoteric practices here and of our conflcting moral responsibility to keep them secret.

Tantric worship has many of the features and sequences of ordinary worship (app. 4), but there are additions, emphases, and occasional reversals, which take their force from their contrasts with those ordinary procedures. Ācājus and Brahmans have manuals of instructions, *paddhatis*, often in the form of palm-leaf manuscripts, which outline the steps of all complex priest-conducted worship sequences used in Bhaktapur. For basic Tantric *pūjā*s, such as those held in conjunction with important family or *phukī* worship to the Tantric lineage deity (see below), *paddhatis* include about a dozen major phases. We will follow one of these *paddhatis* in order to give a rough and superficial paraphrase of an illustrative sequence for our present limited purposes, namely to suggest the Tantric *pūjā's* special features.[5]

Prior to the *pūjā* there must be worship and offerings to the local areal Gaṇeśa and at the proper maṇḍalic *pīṭha*. The participants must purify themselves in preparation for performing *pūjā*, as they must for all important worship (chap. 11). The area in which the worship is to be done has also to be purified and marked out in colored powder with diagrams, *maṇḍalas* and *yantras*, and the proper utensils and materials for the worship are assembled.

The first preparatory phase of the worship is done by the principal worshiper, the *jajamān*, and will be done subsequently by the officiating priest. This is called a *nyāsa*, a Sanskrit word that apparently originally included the meaning of "laying aside" and "renunciation" (Macdonell 1974, 148). The *nyāsa* is a mimesis of *yogic* practices; the sorts of things that *yogis* do at length to produce altered states of awareness in conjunction with meditation and a quest for "escape" or *mukti* are done here as ritual gestures. "*Nyāsa*" in Bhaktapur's usage seems to refer to a less specified range of *yogic* activities than the term does elsewhere (cf. Gupta, Hoens, and Goudriaan 1979, 143f.). "*Nyāsa*" varies in the details of the procedure depending on the particular kind of *pūjā* in which it is used. It includes various gestures, movements, and hand signs, *mudrās*, and meditative acts, which among other purposes, are said to be for the purpose of establishing the worshipers' bodies as the *maṇḍalas*, or sacred circles, in which the deity will be realized. It also includes rudimentary breath control procedures (*prāṇāyāma*), essentially the alternate closing of the right and left nostril during the inhalation and exhalation of air and the holding of the inhaled breath, with the various phases being accompanied and timed by the mental recitation of a *mantra*. The *nyāsa* prepares the *jajamān* for the *pūjā*.

On the completion of the *nyāsa* the *jajamān* dedicates the *pūjā*, identifying its central deity and its conventional purpose, for example, as part of a marriage, a death memorial ceremony, or as some focal worship of the Āga(n) lineage deity. After the dedication, the *sa(n)kalpa*, the *jajamān* touches and makes an offering to a ritual waterpot and to a container of various ritual items that will be used in the later worship and hands them to the priest.

The priest, in a purification and preparation for his part of the ceremony, washes his mouth and performs a *nyāsa*. He now becomes the central performer in the remainder of the *pūjā*, instructing the *jajamān* when the latter has to participate. The next step is *snana*, offerings of various kinds made to the primary and attendant deities of the *pūjā*. The attendant deities include an oil lamp (representing Gaṇeśa, Śiva, and Śakti), "the deity dwelling in one's own heart," and the worshipers' quasi-deified *gurus*. Offerings to these deities include flowers, vegetarian foods, grain, and light, the same offerings that are given at all *pūjā*s. In a departure from ordinary *pūjā*s, some aspects of the *snana* sequence precede the worship of Gaṇeśa within the *pūjā*. (He has been worshiped at his neighborhood shrine prior to the *pūjā*.) This violation of the usual preliminary worship of Gaṇeśa as the *siddhi*-giving god is explained locally as showing that the Tantric goddess (the usual focus of the *pūjā* in one or another of her forms) "comes before all." The *snana* is followed by a *pūjā* to the officiating priest's own *guru*, and at this point he performs *nyāsa* for the second time.

The next step begins a sequence in which there is worship by all assembled to, first, the secondary gods and goddesses and, then, to the main goddess through offerings of flowers, grains, colored powder, and the like. This sequence is concluded with an offering by the worshipers to themselves—to the internal representation of the deity in their body. In the course of these offerings uncooked polished rice, known in ritual contexts as *kiga:*, which is of central importance as an offering in all *pūjā*s (app. 4), is presented in a flicking motion to the deity by the left hand rather than with, as would be done in ordinary *pūjā*s, the right hand.

After an interlude in which the client performs *japa* meditation (see below) comes a sequence called "giving *bali*." "*Bali*"—Sanskrit for a food offering—is used in the context of worship of the dangerous deities to designate an animal sacrifice. At this point there is no actual animal sacrifice; that will come later. What is offered now is *samhae* (a mixture of fish, meat, ginger, and grains; see section entitled "Symbolic Complexes: Sacrifices") and alcoholic spirits, either fermented rice beer, *tho(n)* or, more commonly, a clear distilled alcoholic spirit, *ailā* (Kathmandu dialect, *aelā*).[6] These offerings are a further reversal and violation of what would be the proper worship of an ordinary deity.

In the next episode oil-lamp wicks and incense are first worshiped to give them power, *śakti*, and then lit and presented to the gods by the priest as he rings a bell. The flaming wick and burning incense, used in all *pūjā*s, have here special meaning in relation to the Tantric use of the imagery of Śakti and Śiva (below).

Now the priest, as the *jajamān* had previously, performs *japa* meditation. He covers his left hand, in which he holds flowers and *kiga*:, with a cloth and counts off a number of *mantras*, usually 108, which he mutters or says silently to himself. He then offers some of the *kiga*: and flowers he held during the *japa* meditation to the goddess. Next he puts some on his own head, as an offering to the internal goddess who dwells within him.

A *stotra*, a hymn of praise, is now read by the priest from one of the Tantric texts. He rings a bell in the course of this, and then worships the goddess with *kiga*:, throwing it three times, again from his left hand. As in all *pūjā*s, this presentation of *kiga*: accompanied by sound announces one of the major climaxes of the *pūjā*. The climax here is a blood sacrifice. This is usually a goat or a drake in upper-status *phukī pūjās*. On some occasions, however (often for economic reasons), an egg or *samhae* may be substituted at this step. We will return to the procedures and interpretations of animal sacrifice in a later section.

Now the priest and the *jajamān* (and the other participants) take and eat some of the fish and meat-containing *samhae* that had previously been offered to the Goddess—which will now also have some of the sacrificial animal's blood splattered on it—and they also take some of the *ailā*, the alcoholic spirits presented to the god and drink it. This is here not only *prasāda*—the taking back of materials that have been offered to the gods and "contaminated" by the gods, and then by eating them putting oneself in a dependent but inferior hierarchical relation to that god (compare "*cipa*," chap. 6)—but something more. The eating of the substances represent, in part, an offering to the participant's body and its internally dwelling Goddess, whose Tantric, nonordinary status, and contrast to the moral entity of the "self" (represented by another internal god, Viṣṇu, who dwells in the "soul" or "heart" [chap. 8]) is repeatedly emphasized.

If the Ācāju were performing a Tantric *pūjā* for a client at a *pīṭha*, he would not himself eat part of the offering, for the *pīṭha* is a relatively public setting. In this case some of the offering, *samhae*, with blood and *ailā* sprinkled on it would be sent to the client households. This mixture would be eaten by members of these upper *thar*s who sponsor *pīṭha pūjā*s, including Brahmans, in the same way as they would eat the blood-spattered *prasāda* in worship within their homes.

Now flowers are taken back from the Goddess as *prasāda*. *Dakṣiṇā*, a gift of money, is given by the *jajamān* to the *Ācāju*, and finally a farewell ceremony to the gods is performed, thus ending the *pūjā*.

This basic *pūjā* varies somewhat as it is used in different settings and for different purposes. However, variations are within this general pattern. The offering and sharing of meat and drink make this "left-handed," or Vāmācāra Tantrism.[7] These are two of the five "forbidden substances," the five *makāras*, whose use as witnesses of the true Tantric adept's supposed ability to be spiritually impervious to practices and substances that would represent dangerous and profound violations of the moral order for an ordinary person characterize the *kaula* school or tradition within Tantrism, a school that "is without doubt the most important—and certainly the most characteristic—movement within Tantrism" (Gupta, Hoens, and Goudriaan 1979, 45). Bhaktapur's upper-status Tantrism includes (in at least gestural form) these five *makāras*. The other three forbidden substances or actions (besides meat and alcohol) are fish, "*mudrā*" (probably originally thought of as an aphrodisiac), and sexual intercourse. One of the substances presented to the gods, and tasted during the course of the *pūjā*, *samhae*, contains fish. "*Mudrā*" is identified with some of the grain offered and eaten during the *pūjā*.[8] Although there is speculation among noninitiates (which is characteristically not discouraged by initiates) that there is sexual intercourse during Tantric *pūjā*s, this does not normatively exist. The sexual act, like whatever sexual reference *mudrā* may have, is a matter of symbolic reference. In many Tantric *pūjā*s that are performed for householders or *phukī* groups, one or more women who have the proper "half-*dekhā*" or "half-initiation" may take part, as they do in ordinary *pūjā*s, but most Tantric *pūjā*s have only men participants. In all these *pūjā*s, the parts of the prayers and *stotra*s that refer to sexual intercourse are read only in Sanskrit and, in contrast to some other Sanskrit passages, are not translated into Newari. References to the performance of sexual intercourse that occur in some of the *pūjā* sequences are represented by hand positions (also called *mudrā*s) and are, it is said, not thought of as directed to a particular woman participant. Some initiate informants believe that sexual *pūjā*s were performed in the past, but this was privately by husband and wife "for the purpose of procuring a son." This is in contrast to the fantasies of noninitiates about sex between nonspouses, including men with women of lower social levels, a fantasy that is closer to some reported actual practices of the *kaula* school, to which Bhaktapur's symbolic Tantric forms and a considerable portion of Tantric practice are related.[9] Whether these sexual practices existed among Newar Tantric initiates in the past and constituted an acceptable aspect of aristocratic Tantric practice seems unknowable now.[10]

The upper-status Tantric *pūjā* represents a struggle and a compromise between proper social behavior as defined in the ordinary civic *dharma*, the behavior that is necessary for the maintenance of social respectability, *ijjat*, and, in fact, for the maintenance of social status (for there is, or was, the threat of outcasting for serious violations of the *dharma*), and the anti-*dharmic*, antinomian behavior, which in the context of Tantric ideology and practice, represents the transcendence of that *dharma*. The transcendence is suggested in the mimesis of Yoga, that attempted escape from the illusion of phenomenal reality. However, it is clearest in the transgressions of what would be fundamental violations of *pūjā*s to the moral deities. In Bhaktapur's moral system where reputation, rectitude, and proper behavior is closely monitored in what is for the middle and upper social levels, at least, a rather puritanical system, the violations inherent in the Tantric *pūjā*s, even if some of them are, in the case of sexual acts, "symbolic" (or more precisely a much weaker symbolic act than actual Tantric intercourse), are still presumably potentially moving and meaningful to the participants, as the rumors of these acts are to outsiders.

In comparison with Tantric rituals that take place in vegetarian Hindu communities, the eating of fish and meat and the drinking of alcoholic spirits is perhaps less powerful in that Newars do these things in other settings—although the offering of these products of slaughtered animals to gods in the context of the radical inappropriateness of this to the benign moral gods is still a clear antinomial reversal. As "slaughtered animals" suggest, however, the most significant aspect of meat eating is the taking of life, and this is quite overt in the animal sacrifice—which is at the climax of major Tantric *pūjā*s—whose blood splatters the *prasāda* and whose flesh will be consumed by household members or the *phukī* group or some larger group of kin in the ceremonial feasts, *bhwae*, which follow many major Tantric *pūjā*s and are held in connection with auspicious rites of passage and some major calendrical occasions. The sacrifice is ideally done by the *jajamān* himself on behalf of his family group; he should himself cut the animal's throat. We will return to this central antinomial act, sacrifice, later in this chapter and in connection with urban symbolic enactments centering on Devī in chapter 15. For Bhaktapur, however, *the* violation of the ordinary *dhar-*

ma in the worship of the dangerous deities, which most resists becoming routine and trivialized during ritual repetition, is the sacrifice itself.

The participation of Brahmans in some of the most esoteric and "powerful" Tantric *pūjās* is another profound violation of the implications of the city's ordinary religion. Newar Brahmans can eat certain meats, but are never supposed to drink alcohol, which would be a violation of their basic status regulations. In the course of the Tantric *pūjās* in which their participation is essential, the worship of Taleju as the Malla lineage deity and as a central civic deity—which is witnessed by the auxiliary priests of Taleju, and in worship held for and witnessed by high-status clients in the most elaborate Āga(n) House *pūjās*, and in their own *phukī* Āga(n) God worship, the tasting of alcoholic spirits by the Brahman priest as part of the five *makāras* is necessary. These spirits are specially prepared and purified, both physically and ritually. They are not called "*ailā*," "alcoholic spirits," but "*Ga(n)gā jala*" (app. 4), the purest of the various pure waters used in rituals, and considered in some contexts as *amṛta* or nectar, and in others as Śakti herself. Furthermore, in some Taleju ceremonies and in their own Āga(n) God *pūjās*, Brahmans must perform animal sacrifice. All this involves a genuine risk for the Brahman, not only in the usual Tantric sense that what is clearly a violation and a sin in an ordinary context must somehow become transmuted into a proper religious act but also because their behavior (like all Tantric behavior, but the Brahman has the most to risk) can be used as an attack against the status of participants by those who discount the validity of the Tantric ritual.[11]

UPPER-STATUS TANTRISM: FAMILY AND *PHUKĪ* WORSHIP—WORSHIP OF THE LINEAGE GODS, THE ĀGA(N) GODS, AND THE DIGU GODS

We have remarked that the consideration of upper-status Tantrism may be divided into group worship and individually centered worship. Group worship is primarily that of the family—household or *phukī*—and centers on the lineage deity. The various kinds of internal esoteric worship at Taleju temple are closely related to such family worship, for Taleju is worshiped as the lineage deity of the Malla kings. Tantric worship of the lineage deity is amalgamated with and added to a worship of the lineage deity as the "Digu God" which is shared by all Newars.

We have introduced the basic Tantric group *pūjā* in the previous section. Such *pūjā*s are required for the rites of passage of family members, and in the course of certain annual events. They may be performed at the maṇḍalic *pīṭha,* rarely in the god-house of the Maṇḍalic Goddess, sometimes in a special room of a family's house—the Āga(n) Room, and most commonly in a special house for the *phukī*'s lineage deity, the Āga(n) House. Although a householder may perform or lead a perfunctory ritual by himself, most important Tantric family rituals are performed under the direction of, and in part by, an Ācāju. On very important occasions a (sometimes more than one) Brahman may preside, and the Ācāju will assist him. In the case of those upper-status families without initiates, or without an available one, an Ācāju must perform the *pūjā* alone in the name of the family.

In addition to required Tantric *pūjā*s there are optional ones, and in these cases the household may be free to choose between a Tantric and an ordinary *pūjā*, the latter usually directed to Viṣṇu. The optional Tantric *pūjā*s are performed in relation to some "serious problem." Examples are a major disease of a family member; an outbreak of disease in the city from which the family wishes to be protected; a prolonged inability to have children for which lesser remedies have not worked; a period of bad luck thought to be due to astrological forces; or the wish for success in some major, risky undertaking. Tantric *pūjā*s are considered more powerful than *pūjā*s to a non-Tantric god. It is said that optional Tantric *pūjā*s are more directed toward the granting of a wish, while non-Tantric ones have to do with maintaining relationships with the gods. As a Brahman put it, the ideal attitude in an ordinary *pūjā* to the benign gods is, "We are here to serve and honor you. When you are here we have no problems." The distinction is important and emphasizes contrasts in the general meaning and uses of the two kinds of deities, although, in practice, favors are often hoped for from the ordinary gods and conversely one does not overtly confront the Tantric gods with the concrete goal of the Tantric *pūjā*, which is rather "kept in the mind."

An optional Tantric *pūjā* may have been given at the time of seeking help with a problem. More often a promise or pledge, a *bācā* is given mentally to the Āga(n) God, to the effect that *if* the wish is granted, a *pūjā* will be performed. In these cases, in fact, even if the wish is not granted, a perfunctory *pūjā* is often given to the god; people may worry that perhaps the Āga(n) God was angry at them and that was why the favor was not granted, and that if they then neglect the proposed *pūjā*, they will have even worse luck. Misfortune is sometimes explained by some such neglected promise to a dangerous god, which may have just passed rapidly, even unconsciously, through someone's mind and which might even have resulted in the granting of the desire.

Once a decision to have a *pūjā* to solve some problem has been made, there is often (although not always)[12] some choice, as we have noted, as whether to have a Tantric *pūjā*, or a Brahman-assisted non-Tantric *pūjā*. While a Tantric *pūjā* is said to be more powerful than a non-Tantric one, it is also liable to be more elaborate, time consuming, and expensive.[13] Furthermore, the participants, in contrast to the participants who can be gathered in a major Brahman-assisted *pūjā* to the ordinary gods, must have the proper initiation. In recent decades non-Tantric *pūjā*s have become increasingly common as the upper-level groups have less money (and are less likely to devote it to religious activities), and less time, and are less liable to have received initiation. The Tantric *pūjā*, centering as it does on the lineage deity, is essentially a *phukī* activity. Thus the shift to the non-Tantric *pūjā* (a *dhala[n] dạnegu*; app. 4) has the additional characteristic that it is less exclusive and is sometimes attended by non-initiates, friends, and invited neighbors.[14]

Most of the Tantric *pūjā*s performed now (as was probably the case in the past) are not optional but required ones. They were dedicated primarily to the Tantric lineage deity, with an associated emphasis on the areal Maṇḍalic Goddess.[15] The Āga(n) God in the Āga(n) House is supposed to be given daily *pūjā*s by an initiated family member or an Ācāju, and a more elaborate *pūjā* once a month (on the fourteenth day or "*ca:re*" of the dark half of the lunar month; see chap. 12). There is also special worship on the first, eighth, ninth, and tenth days of the autumn Mohanī festival (chap. 15) and during the course of the lunar and solar New Year festivals. During all of a *phukī*'s rites of passage there is special worship by the Ācāju and initiated males. Previously many *phukīs* had also dedicated themselves to one or two large annual feasts—often in commemoration of the death of some important *phukī* ancestor—which must be preceded by elaborate Āga(n) House worship, and need the assistance of one or more Brahmans as well as an Ācāju.

We have in the chapters on space and on deities discussed the Digu Gods, the stones placed outside of the city limits, which represent the lineage gods of various *phukī* groups. These deities are dangerous deities, variously identified, and require offerings of meats and alcohol.

The Digu Gods are, in turn, related to representations of the lineage gods within the city, which are for *thar*s with Tantric initiation, the "secret gods," the Āga(n) Gods.[16] The Āga(n) Gods, in turn, are closely related to the Maṇḍalic Goddesses who preside over the sector in which the *phukī* members live or, rarely, in the case of movement of a family within the city, where they had their origin in the city. The relation of the stone lineage deity outside the city and the housed image within reflects the relationship of the Maṇḍalic Goddesses' external *pīṭhas* and internal god-houses. The Digu God's stone is, as we have noted, sometimes referred to as a *pīṭha*, and its form and placement resembles the *pīṭha*s of the Maṇḍalic Goddesses. The pairing of the two locations also recalls a characteristic theme in the arrangements, legends, and symbolic enactments of the dangerous deities, that is, the description of a form related to and representative of the dangerous but generative forces surrounding the city and its society, on the one hand and, on the other, the introduction of that form into the city—for the city's protection—under the careful control of powerful Tantric ritual safeguards.[17]

From the point of view of sophisticated upper-status people, both the Digu God outside of the city and the Āga(n) God within it are representatives of the same deity, the lineage god, the *Kula* (or *Kul*) *devatā*. Families below the level of those that have elaborated Tantric secret gods and worship, often have a god image that they keep hidden somewhere in the house and which they often call their "Āga(n) God." That lower-status image is thought of as the family's secret lineage god and is often a *yantra* worked onto a metal plate, an image of Bhagavatī, or a small stone. This image is hidden in cloth wrappings and kept in a safe place in the house, usually, of the leader of the *phukī* group. This house image is brought in a procession to the family's Digu God location outside the city on the proper day during Dewālī, the annual occasion for the worship of the lineage god. Household members in these middle-status and lower-status families are allowed to see and know about the hidden god for the first time for boys after the *Kaetā Pūjā* ceremony, during which they are initiated into membership into their *thar* and for girls after their *Ihī* or mock-marriage ceremony (see app. 6).

The upper *thar*s, in fact, have similar portable deities, which they use during the external annual worship of their Digu Gods, but these are different from the main image of their Āga(n) God, the form that is thought of as *the* Āga(n) God. Ideally, that main Āga(n) God image is kept in a "secret (god-) house" an *Āga(n) che(n)*, of its own, often an elaborate four-story structure[18] belonging to the *phukī*.[19] Sometimes, the Āga(n) God is kept and worshiped in a special room, the *āga(n) kothā*, "secret room," on the *cwata* floor (chap. 7) of the house of the leader of the *phukī*. Each household in the *phukī* group will have a secondary image of the Āga(n) God in their Āga(n) Room, which will serve as the locus of some of the individually centered worship of household members (below). The main image of the Āga(n) God requires daily worship, which is now usually done by an Ācāju, who may have several such shrines to attend to each day. It is worshiped by male family members with proper initiation during major Tantric *pūjā*s, but in many families in recent years there are no members with the proper initiation, and only the Ācāju attends the god in the Āga(n) House.[20]

In spite of the understanding by religious experts that the Digu God and the Āga(n) God are both "the same god," the lineage god, the two foci are, in general, regarded differently and have some important contrasts. The Digu God is often regarded as a specific deity, called "Digu God," and the Āga(n) God is sometimes also thought of as a separate deity, "the Āga(n) God," in its own right. The true identification of these gods is something that is revealed to members of the family during the course of various initiations. men (women have only perfunctory and limited initiations) learn during their initiation the name of their particular lineage god and the mantras appropriate to its worship. All lineage gods for the *thar*s with rights to Tantric initiation in Bhaktapur are, in fact, most probably forms of the Goddess, and the majority of them the form locally known as "Bhagavatī," the goddess in the form of the slayer of the buffalo demon, that is, as Mahiṣāsuramardinī. The remainder of the lineage deities are probably the same as the Maṇḍalic Goddess of the area in which the family group is established or from which it moved in the city. Most families, however, not knowing what Āga(n) deities other *phukī* groups have, are able to think of their own Āga(n) God as uniquely special to their own lineage.

The Digu God is represented in and in a sense is the stone itself. However, there may be several images and representations of a *phukī*'s Āga(n) God. The central one, the focus of the *phukī* worship is, like Taleju is supposed to be, a *yantra*. There may be secondary images kept at the Āga(n) House. They include anthropomorphic figures, often elaborate images, which are the sorts of images usually carried to the Digu God location at the time of the annual Dewālī lineage worship there. The image brought to the external shrine at Dewālī may not necessarily be kept in the central Āga(n) House, it may be kept in the house of the *phukī*'s senior leader, or of the particular senior *phukī* member whose turn it is to be principally responsible for the Āga(n) God worship. Other secondary images are kept in the Āga(n) Rooms in the houses of the individual *phukī* households. As we will see later, most individual Tantric worship among these upper-status families takes place not in the Āga(n) House, but in these household Āga(n) Rooms.

An important aspect of the meaning of—and the contrast between—the Āga(n) God and the Digu God is their relation to the lineage groups, which they and their symbolic enactments centrally define. Both define the *phukī* group, but there is a certain difference in emphasis, the Digu God serving to hold together a larger grouping. The core *phukī* group consists of those households who during the Dewālī period go to the same Digu God shrine at the same time. This ceremony, a procession carrying an image of the Āga(n) God to the Digu God shrine, is an integration of the internal and external representations of the lineage deity. It must take place during the period of some seven weeks, beginning during the waning lunar fortnight of Caulāgā in late April (chaps. 12 and 13), finishing seven weeks later prior to the day of Sithi Nakhā (chaps. 13 and 15), which signals the ceremonial end of the dry season and the anticipation of the annual rains. The ceremony at the Digu God shrines is called either "Digu God *pūjā*" or "Dewālī *pūjā*."[21] The core *phukī* group, those households who go to the same Digu God shrine together, is the *phukī* group (chap. 6) which is united in the rites of passage of all its members. Particularly salient for members of this group is their sharing of ritual pollution at the birth or death of members, the latter entailing the necessity of prolonged purifying rites. This group shares in ritual feasts and may act (albeit rarely) as a council to discuss problems concerning the group of related families. Its member households tend to live in close proximity to each other, sometimes around a common courtyard. This is also the same group which will have a common Āga(n) House, the house and its god belonging to the *phukī* groups as a whole. As we noted in chapter 6, these groups must always split when they become too large. What happens now in the case of the Āga(n) House and Digu God is not quite the same.

As the *phukī* becomes too large and splits, the members of the two newly formed groups still have the same Digu God, but they now go at different times. They have become two bā-*phukī*s, or "split-*phukī*s," who, although sharing common male patrilineal ancestors, are now no longer a ritual unit, and do not share the birth and death pollution of the other split-off group. They are no longer, in this sense, one body.

Through repeated splittings there may be a large number of *phukī* groups that worship the same Digu God at *different* times. As all these *phukī* groups worshiping one Digu God are assumed to have a common male ancestry, they are not supposed to intermarry.[22] Thus the Digu God acts as a sign of the group that is subject to exogamy. The different *phukī* groups represented by the same Digu shrine have, through long periods of time, often become scattered throughout various areas of the city. It is thus believed that the Digu God protects the maximally extended patrilineal group within and throughout the city, and by extension in concert with other Digu God shrines (and in analogy with the protective ring of maṇḍalic *piṭhas*), protects the entire city.

The Āga(n) House, with its central image of the lineage deity, is the center for each upper-status *phukī* group within the city. When a *phukī* group splits, ideally a new Āga(n) House will be built and a new representation of the Āga(n) God made, which is ritually "established" or consecrated (*pratiṣṭhā*) in the new house so as to partake of the power and nature of the original deity.[23] While in one sense the Āga(n) Gods which have become duplicated and established in various different Āga(n) Houses are the "same" god, the duplicated deity begins to lose its unifying identity. Once it is in different Āga(n) Houses, there are no longer any ritual enactments tying those houses and the various split-*phukī* segments together. The different Digu God ceremonies at the same shrine are tied together through the visible identity of the shrine; it is understood that the Digu deity is the same, and the proper *mantras* used in its worship are also understood to be the same for each of the split-*phukī* groups. The Āga(n) Gods disappear from the view of other *phukī* sections, however, and each comes to be regarded as the protector of a special corporate group in a circumscribed area of space within the city.

UPPER-STATUS TANTRISM: INDIVIDUALLY CENTERED PRACTICES AND INITIATION

The aims of the Tantric tradition for the achievement of *mukti*, "spiritual emancipation," or *bhukti*, "domination," as the quotation from Gupta, Hoens, and Goudriaan (1979) at the beginning of the chapter epitomizes it, are aims to be achieved by individuals, not by groups of Tantric followers, and certainly not by traditional Hindu social units. This is the aspect of Tantrism that is emphasized in popular books directed toward the West and toward modern South Asians. Tantrism, so conceived, is a practice that is supposed to alter the relation of the individual practitioner of Tantrism to the ordinary social, religious, and logical reality in which he or she lives. Able through Tantric practice to see that reality as *māyā*, illusion, an individual achieves liberation from it.

Thus, as put in a passage typical of such books (L. P. Singh 1967, 2):

> In an esoteric sense Tantra means "the spiritual cult by which divine knowledge is unfolded." . . . The mystic definition of Tantra is that it is the spiritual cult which liberates from the bondages of crudeness and ignorance. . . . Tantra is a process . . . which relieves one from the fetters of crudeness. Thus Tantra is an intuitional science which stands for the progressive realization of the divine. It liberates one from the cimmerian darkness and leads unto the divine effulgence. It is a path of salvation. It is a science of the soul. The authoritative definition of Tantra is, that which brings liberation, emancipation from the bondage of Maya.

This particular path to salvation among the several offered by Hinduism, a salvation centered on the nature of the individual, his or her personal and private effort and transcendence of *māyā*, links Tantrism to those South Asian practices such as yoga, meditation, and social renunciation, which are based on temporary or permanent withdrawal from social relationships and modes. Such practices, like *bhakti*, devotion to a personal god, are antithetical to Hinduism's and Bhaktapur's dominant emphasis on submission to—and salvation by means of—the sacralized forms of social life, a submission phrased as adherence to the *dharma*. It is the very density of the familial and larger social world regulated by *dharma* that gives renunciation its special oppositional force and motivation in South Asia. In Bhaktapur the "reality" that is being seen through includes in large part the symbolically constructed mesocosm itself and the self that is to be dissolved is the socially constructed self. The salvation produced by escape from moral reality, the salvation of *mukti* or *mokṣa*, is, on the face of it, quite different from and subversive of the idea of salvation produced by adherence to the moral and religious system of the city.

The technique for achieving *mukti* and its consequences is, like the goals of Tantric practice, typically described in effulgent terms even in the scholarly literature. Thus Gupta, in a discussion of *nyāsa* and the associated practices of *bhūtaśuddhi* in Tantric *pūjā*s, describes the sequence in terms that are typical of Tantric commentary (Gupta, Hoens and Goudriaan 1979,136):

> Using his yogic technique and his highly developed powers of imagination and concentration, the Tantric practicer envisages all the ontological realities that go to make up his personality. He then proceeds to envisage within himself the process of cosmic creation . . . in reverse order. . . . He follows every single step, imagining the dissolution of each element into its preceding cause, until in the end he is ultimately dissolved or immersed in his cosmic source. He then envisages his own resurrection, retracing each step of cosmic creation. Only now, having burned away with cosmic fire and blown away with cosmic air all his human imperfections and limitations, he experiences bliss and, permeated with it, remains immersed in the cosmic source. . . . He now has a body made of pure substance . . . identical with that of the deity's and he is free to invite her to descend into it—to invoke the divine ego to descend on to his ego.

What is the relation of such ideal transcending procedures—these techniques for a blissful escape from self, family, and city in Bhaktapur—to the actual individual uses of individual Tantrism there? As we did in the yogic references in familial Tantric *pūjā*s, we will find echoes of these antistructural, reality-transcending, and self-altering programs in the goals and forms of individual practice and symbolism, transformed and tamed, as all Bhaktapur's Tantrism is, by a careful fitting into in the civic system.

Individually centered Tantrism is presented to upper-status males in conjuction with a sequence of initiations, *dekhā* (sometimes *dikhā*, both deriving from *dīkṣā* in Sanskrit), which are conducted by the family's Brahman *guru*, the same Brahman who is also the family's *purohita*, or family priest. In the course of each initiation certain information is passed on by the *guru* to the pupil or initiate (*śiṣya* in Sanskrit). There are three significant levels or stages in relation to Tantric knowledge for the upper-status *thar*s: (1) the initiation to "caste," the *Kaetā* ("loincloth") *Pūjā* (app. 6); (2) the initiation into the worship of the Āga(n) God; and (3), an initiation in preparation for dying, death, and "salvation," the *mokṣa* or *mukti* initiation.

There are many kinds of initiation in Bhaktapur. They all entail the transmission of some esoteric knowledge by the *guru*, or his equivalent, and a solemn and sacred pledge of secrecy by the initiate. When, for example, a new wife comes to a household, or a new Ācāju is employed, they are told the names and some of the *mantras* of the particular form or forms of the household lineage gods they must deal with, in a ceremony in which they pledge secrecy. Such initiations are sometimes called *bā dekhā* (or "*bāga dekhā*") or "half-initiations" by those familiar with more advanced Tantric initiations. There are also many special initiations within those *thar*s that have a craft profession, such as the playing of some particular musical instrument, the making of masks, or the making of metal images. These initiations initiate and make sacred the teaching relation between *guru* and initiate, introduce the appropriate *mantras* and procedures of worship to the deity who will give effectiveness to the studies, and may introduce technical instructions or esoteric knowledge.

At all levels and in all *thar*s, now including the Po(n)s, there is an initiation of boys into their *thar*, the *Kaetā Pūjā*. All *thar*s have *Kaetā Pūjā* ceremonies that are associated with the idea of a radical change of status for a boy, his entry into his *thar*'s secrets, and his becoming fully morally responsible for following the *dharma*. The *Kaetā Pūjā* is a *saṃskāra*, one of Bhaktapur's rites of passgage (app. 6) derived mostly from the Hindu tradition. In the upper *thar*s, the boy receives not only a loin cloth symbolizing his maturity but also the *jonā* or sacred thread. For these upper-status boys this is the first in a potential series of initiations. For boys of other *thar*s it is the last (with the exception of craft initiation, which is sometimes given in conjunction with the *Kaetā Pūjā*). During the *Kaetā Pūjā* boys are told something about their lineage god and are given some *mantra*s to use in worship. These *mantra*s, given by the *guru* (who in lower-status households may be a family member), like the *mantra*s given in more advanced initiation, are those shared by the larger *phukī* group and are thought by the *phukī* members to be their particular and special *mantra*, although they may, in fact, like the name of the *phukī* Āga(n) God, be common, not only to other groups that have split off from the lineage, but also to much larger groupings.

The next level of initiation, possible only to the upper *thar*s, is the one that is usually designated by the unqualified term "*dekhā*," the initiation to the *phukī*'s Āga(n) God practices. In previous times almost all men in the upper *thar*s took this initiation as young adults. Now, except for those Brahmans and Ācāju priests who need this and other initiations for their priestly duties, many upper-status men delay taking this initiation until after the active years of their education and professional life—and some may never take it. Once having taken the Āga(n) *dekhā*, one has time-consuming obligations in the ceremonies for worship of the Āga(n) God. In this second *dekhā* the initiate enters into the secret Āga(n) religion of the *phukī*, is told the name of the god and its proper *mantra*, and can see it—or in those *thar*s where noninitiate family members are able to see the Āga(n) God wrapped and hidden in cloths on some occasions, see it uncovered—for the first time. The initiate is now also told the proper procedures necessary in the worship of the Āga(n) God. He is introduced to *japa* meditation, where he repeats the same *mantra* for some given number of times, while counting off the repetitions by means of the beads of a special necklace. The new knowledge and practice is taught to the initiate over several days (depending on the student's quickness and ability) by the family *guru*, who has now become *his guru*. In the context of this initiation the *phukī*'s Āga(n) God is referred to as the student's *iṣṭadevatā*, the student's own tutelary god.[24] The initiate is also told something about *cakra* meditation, the idea that the Goddess can be brought into his body, or resides in his body, and can be moved through a series of internal *cakra*s or centers. The meditative practices he is introduced to are not for his private purposes—for either power or for penetrating illusion in a quest for salvation—but as instruments in the worship of his lineage deity. These introductions to yogic procedures in conjunction with the remainder of the esoteric information he is given moves him into the group of initiates which constitutes his *phukī* in their focal shared relation to their secret lineage deity.

The third possible initiation is often called Nirbān (Sanskrit, Nirvāṇa) initiation. This is available to men in the upper *thar*s who had the previous initiations and who would typically take it in their forties or fifties. For Rājopādhyāya Brahmans, the techniques learned at this level of initiation are considered necessary for the really powerful forms of Tantric worship, particularly those associated with the Taleju temple,[25] for conducting Brahman-assisted Āga(n) God worship of upper-status families, and for undertaking the role of *guru* to members of these families in their middle- and upper-level *dekhā*s. Brahmans, like other upper-status men, also may undergo this stage of initiation for their own "salvation," for *nirbān,* or *mukti.* Not all practicing Brahmans have this level of *dekhā*; some will undergo it later in life, while others—those with middle-level clients or temple *pujārī* work—may never have it. Even fewer of the non-Brahman upper-status men now undergo it. Many of them do not even undergo the Āga(n) initiation, which is a necessary prerequisite to this one. However, for those men who are especially interested in continuing Tantric studies—either from interest in Tantrism in itself, or for the specific salvation promised by the initiation—this aristocratic option is available.

During the third-level initiation and studies, the initiate learns more about his Āga(n) Goddess and her secret connections with the other Tantric deities in the city. He is instructed further in meditation technique, particularly *cakra* meditation. This is often in a limited form in comparison with the way this kind of meditation is known and used by Tantric practitioners and *yogis* elsewhere, but is more elaborate than the initiate's previous meditation. It is considered to be a kind of Kuṇḍalinī Yoga for the purpose of moving the Goddess into the *cakra* located in the "heart," for meditation and worship. The instruction at this level requires daily study with a *guru* during a period of about one month. Following Nirbān initiation, the initiate may now also read esoteric books, often in the possession of families, which deal with meditation, with Kuṇḍalinī Yoga, and with the secret connections and relations of Tantric deities in the city. It is said that the unauthorized reading of such books without initiation leads to insanity or blindness.

What has this to do with *mukti*, or *nirbān*, that is, with "salvation"? The cosmic fire and cosmic air that the initiate experiences are considerably less freeing and transforming than our introductory quotations promised. He must await his death for their full effect, and even then his self, he hopes, will be only modestly transformed. People in Bhaktapur, like many South Asians, have various elaborate and inconsistent ideas about their fate after death. They believe, in one or another context, that it depends on their moral behavior during life (this life and previous ones), on their ritual activities and general actions at the time of dying, and on the proper ceremonies being performed by their family (particularly by their oldest son) after their death—especially during the first several days. Personal fate after death is also variously conceived. One joins the "fathers," the *pitṛs*. One wanders around somewhere for a period forming a spiritual body, and then goes to be judged by Yama, the King of the Dead, in his kingdom, whereupon one may be reincarnated or one may go to one of several heavens. Whatever *mukti* or *nirbān* means to the people of Bhaktapur and to the Nirbān initiate practicing meditation for "salvation," it does not mean that "highest [stage] . . . when the soul is absorbed in the Paramātman [the supreme soul] as the river is lost in the sea . . . [and where] there is no persistence of personality . . . and there is nothing left to do, or to attain to, or to gain" (Stevenson 1920, 187f.).[26] Whatever the highest theological speculations about the dissolving of the self as salvation, *mukti*, for those people with whom we have discussed this (and in their understanding of what others believe), this is neither what they believe nor what they want *mukti* to entail. It seems to mean, rather, the avoidance of painful new lives, and the chance to remain in some heavenly place, usually the particular heaven of the most unproblematic of the city's moral deities, Viṣṇu-Nārāyaṇa. This implies, for many, being surrounded by their family and remembering their present life. The main focus of Nirbān studies is the preparation for the time of dying, the *marān kāl* (Sanskrit, *maraṇa kāla*) the appointed time for "destruction." Tantric discipline leads to a control of mind which can be helpful at the *marān kāl* in two ways. At the time of death, the spirit resists leaving the body easily, the dying person will suffer for a long time. If he uses the proper *mantra*s and meditates on the god Nārāyaṇa (never on a Tantric deity), however, the soul leaves the body more easily and the adept has a quicker and less painful death. Tantric education, *sādhanā*, helps in this meditation. The other problematic aspect of dying is that bad thoughts during the *marān kāl*—worries about money, angry or vengeful thoughts, a wish for alcoholic spirits, and the like, will cause a punitive distressing reincarnation. Tantric discipline allows the maintenance of a peaceful mind and thus prevents a bad rebirth, and ideally any rebirth less comfortable than in "Nārāyaṇa's heaven."

However trivialized these practices and goals may seem from the point of view of Tantrism's highest philosophical ideals, and however woven into larger social practices, the underlying direction is familiar—a detachment from the realities, concerns, and passions of social interrelatedness, a detachment that will allow the practitioner to avoid, if only at the moment of death, becoming entangled in Bhaktapur's enveloping world.

Techniques learned during the Tantric *dekhā*s are used in the *phukī* worship we discussed above. These include special *mantra*s, hand gestures, and meditative practices. An important technique taught in these initiations is the visualization as a clear image—following some canonical description—of the deity to be worshiped and, eventually, the ability to mentally place this image within the body or within a *maṇḍala* drawn on a purified area on the floor. The ability to perform a *pūjā* to a mental image, to be able to dispense with a material external image, is considered to be one of the essential achievements of advanced Tantric practice in Bhaktapur, and one of the factors separating Tantrism from the externally somewhat similar worshiping of the dangerous deities through the sacrificial offerings of noninitiates.

In the remainder of his life after his initiation, the Nirbān initiate practices his *cakra* meditation during daily worship, which usually takes place in the morning during, roughly, one hour in the Āga(n) Room on the back half of the *cwata* floor of the house. This daily worship is to the Āga(n) God—(whose, most often, subsidiary image is in the Āga(n) Room)—and to the household gods, who will be represented there by secondary images.[27] In the course of his worship through one or another meditative procedure, he is supposed to put himself in the state of concentration and ability to create an image called (both in Bhaktapur and in Tantric theory) *dhyāna*. The imagined image has a specified form, color, number of arms, objects in its hands, significant gestures of some of its hands, a special vehicle, and so forth. *Dhyāna*, here, is not a dissolution of consciousness, but a kind of control or concentration of it.[28] The initiate may also come to the Āga(n) Room for silent meditation when he wishes to. He may now use *japa* meditation or some form of *cakra* meditation. Here the meditation in itself, the practice of *sādhanā* in itself, is his goal.

TANTRISM AND THE PUBLIC CITY

We have discussed Tantrism as the esoteric individual and familial practices of upper-status families.[29] Tantrism and the experience of and worship of the dangerous deities by noninitiates are intimately and reciprocally related, influencing each other. In the top–down perspective, Tantrism affects the larger city in many ways. The complex of activities in and centering on the Taleju temple represents the expansion of Taleju as the Malla king's Āga(n) God into the tutelary deity of the king's city. The Tantric *pūjā*s performed in Taleju, above all those done at the climax of the autumnal Mohanī festival, are, in part, for the "good of the city," as well as for the king himself. There are also other Tantric *pūjā*s performed under certain threatening circumstances for the protection of the city as a whole. These are called *chemā pūjā*, *pūjā*s done for "forgiveness" (*chemā* derives from the Sanskrit "*Kṣamā*" in its sense as "pardon"), or more adequately, as Manandhar notes, "to restore the worshiper to a proper relationship to deity" (1976, p. 135). *Chemā pūjās* have been performed in the past, for example, because of epidemics of smallpox or cholera, prolonged droughts during the rice planting season, fires, and earth tremors with threatening earthquakes. The *chemā pūjā* is addressed to the dangerous gods as a group. As we have noted, asking "forgiveness" of such gods is often associated with the idea that they may have been inadvertently offended, and therefore an act of redress may possibly placate them. Ācājus, Jośīs, and Brahmans take part in these *pūjās*, and offerings of prayer, music, meat, and alcohol are presented to the dangerous gods at their temples and shrines throughout the city. The food offerings are then distributed as *prasāda* among the city's people to restore their relations with the gods and to protect them.[30]

Many of the images of the public city, above all many of the images and actions of the annual cycle,[31] are the outward expression of Tantric forms whose inner meaning is supposedly known only to initiates. The public images, ideas, and practices surrounding the dangerous deities have their own qualities, however, and have some uses that are in marked contrast to Tantrism. Tantrism uses those images in a quest for control and transcendence; the exoteric religion uses them (as does Tantrism) to symbolize aspects of Newar experience, but, in contrast to Tantrism, it uses them entirely *for the purposes of* social integration and control, not to escape it. We will deal with much of this in later chapters on the annual cycles, but we may here consider two central clusters of ideas in relation to the dangerous deities, ideas that are related to both the esoteric and exoteric aspects of the worship of the dangerous deities. These are the conceptions of the relations of Śiva and Śakti, and the ideas about and practices of animal sacrifice.

SYMBOLIC COMPLEXES: ŚIVA/ŚAKTI

In our account of the mythology of the dangerous goddesses we discussed how the goddesses were emitted as a kind of force, *śakti*, by Śiva and by the other male benign divinities. These *śaktis* operated sometimes independently, sometimes coalesced into one supreme Goddess. This supreme Goddess is quite independent of the gods who in some accounts emit her or her component goddesses; in other accounts she is, in fact, prior to them as the ultimate supreme creative deity. The tradition that emphasizes the worship of the Goddess as the supreme deity is Śaktism. Both historically and in the way they are made use of in Bhaktapur Śaktism and Tantrism are "two intersecting but not coinciding circles" (Gupta, Hoens, and Goudriaan 1979, 6). Within Bhaktapur's Tantrism there is an important difference between the images, conceptions, and uses of the Goddess in herself, and the images, conception, and use of "Śakti." Śakti's use both in Bhaktapur's esoteric and exoteric doctrine is based on her relation to Śiva—here once again the supreme deity, albeit at a problematic moment in his supremacy—at the time of her emission from him, and the precursors and consequences of that act.

In Bhaktapur's imagery, *Śakti* has two implications that are quite different when seen in ordinary common-sense contexts, but which are related in the theory of Śiva/Śakti. These conflicting implications and their resolutions generate shifting ways of viewing certain forms and events that contribute greatly to the aesthetics and mystery of Tantric conceptions and symbols. These two implications derive from ideas about *śakti* as power, on the one hand, and *śakti* as passive, receptive female sexuality, on the other.

Local characterizations of *śakti* often begin with nonesoteric statements about the nature and interdependence of form and function. Any living and vital or potentially effective entity has both a containing form and a potential or ongoing function. The function is the object's *śakti* or "power." The *śakti* of an eye is seeing; of a bell, ringing.[32] When the object has lost its *śakti*, it is dead or powerless, it cannot function, and the eye becomes blind. In contrast, a function, *śakti*, that becomes disconnected from its form becomes diffuse and transformed in some peculiar way, in some cases uncanny, such as the sound of a bell that is not there. Śiva/Śakti conceptions are a divinized version of this idea. Śiva represents, at one point in a cyclical process, a living entity, a container with contained vitality; that is, he has his *śakti* within him. He is full of *potential* power. But in order to exercise power in the world (and not just social influence—we are at the edge of the non-moral arena of the dangerous deities here) he must emit his *śakti*, who now becomes Śakti, a divinity in herself. This emitted Śakti, often portrayed as a ray or an impersonal force, does actual "work" in the world, work that changes affairs through force, not by means of moral and social influence. Śakti is the power that is one of the goals of Tantric practice. But having emitted the power, Śiva is now empty and dead. Śiva without Śakti, the saying (based on a play on Sanskrit orthography) goes, is Śava, a corpse. The living Śiva is male, but he contains a female principle within him. The dead (or weakened or exhausted) Śiva is male, but now the female principle is external to him. He is incomplete. For his own sake and for that of society, it is essential to recapture the Śakti.[33] Now a second step and a partial transformation of the imagery occurs here. Śiva, the male principle, and Śakti, the female principle, can become reintegrated through the act of union of sexual intercourse—as well as through other and variously represented unifications, which never lose their coital implications. For this purpose Śiva may be represented as a phallus, a *liṅga*, and Śakti as a vagina, a *yoni*. But the phallus is active; the vagina is a passive receptacle, a container, in something like the way the form is the container for the force that gives it life. There has been a reversal in the signification of Śiva and Śakti.

The Sukundā, an elaborately formed combined oil container and oil lamp used in major Hindu Newar rituals, consists of a semispherical container for oil to which is attached an oval or triangularly shaped shallow container, which is the oil lamp itself, and at whose apex a wick is placed. The oil container is the living Śiva with his potential force, and both the burning wick and the triangular dish are Śakti, but in different ways. The burning wick is Śakti as energy; the triangular dish is Śakti as the sexual complement to the male, ready to restore his potential power. The oil from the container is put into the lamp dish as an act of union, and now the flame-Śakti can spring forth. Tantrism adds an emphasis on this vaginal and receptive Śakti as a consort in a sexualized act of union that is restitutive and which prepares the now enriched male for a new generation of power to the more general idea of the Śakti as Goddess and as an active and unrestrained (by civic order and morality) force in the world. Bhaktapur's religious, ritual, and festival imagery is replete with references to these ideas. Any pair of objects or events can be related to Śiva and Śakti through one or the other of their interrelational meanings. Meat and alcohol presented to the dangerous deities are respectively Śiva and Śakti: the flesh representing the embodied form and the alcoholic spirits, the vitalizing principle. A ritually presented grain of unhusked rice has Śakti as its potentially germinating kernel, Śiva, as its husk. Dualisms of right and left, double lines (commonly used in marking out *maṇḍala*s on the ground for Tantric *pūjā*s), overlapping pairs (or sets) of triangles, are used to represent the splitting and complementarity of form and function, male and female. Such opposities are symbolically brought together in festival and ritual enactments. The joining and collapsing of these oppositions is shown in visual imagery as a dot or point, a *bindu*, often placed in the center of the pairs or in a central position in a complex image (such as a dangerous god's face, where it may be placed at the bridge of the nose). The *bindu* represents unity in contrast to dualism—the beginning of phenomenological diversity—and it represents, among other things, the union of the separated Śiva and Śakti into a revitalized and rebalanced albeit now problematically self-contained, Śiva.

The oscillating meanings of the polarities of Śiva and Śakti and their necessary eternal couplings, condensations, and separations are very powerful symbolic resources for representing personal and social dilemmas. At the personal level these are resonances of vital, self-contained, self-sufficient, omnipotential fullness on the one hand—so well represented in the classical imagery of Śiva—versus the divisions that initiate a society and social identity on the other. These personal meanings also echo problems about the sexual other and the sexual act, problems that have special South Asian forms and emphases. On the social level, however, which is our present concern, the complex of Śiva/Śakti ideas and practices represents a tension between moral order, the heavenly order of the gods, with its static eternal balance, and the periodic need to mobilize an amoral power, a socially unrestrained force that becomes problematic once its job is done (even while it is doing it) as it is socially unrestrained and dangerous. The question then becomes how to get that power back under control, back into the heavenly quietude again. The Tantric interpretations and enactments of Śiva and Śakti represent and mimic all this.

SYMBOLIC COMPLEXES: SACRIFICE

The dangerous deities are usually distinguished from the ordinary ones in that their proper worship (as the legend of Taleju, for example, emphasized) requires that they be offered alcoholic spirits and animal flesh, (see, for example, fig. 19) which would be forbidden and sinful as offerings to the ordinary gods. The use of animal sacrifice in contrast to vegetarian offerings to mark a division and contrast among gods and types of ritual did not apparently exist in Vedic religion, where (contrary to what most nonscholarly Newar Hindus seem now to believe) there were both animal and vegetable offerings. "Ultimately," as Madeleine Biardeau put it, "the 'putting to death' of cereals or plants was scarcely less violent than the murder of animal victims" (Biardeau and Malamoud 1976, 139 [our translation]). The *Laws of Manu* (V, 40 [i.e., section V, verse 40]) includes plants in its attempt to justify the "murder" of various creatures. "Herbs, trees, cattle, birds, and (other) animals that have been destroyed for sacrifices, receive [in rebirth] higher existences" (Bühler 1969, 175). Biardeau points out that the Smṛti texts illustrate, however, a particular "embarrassment" in relation to the animal sacrifices, for animals were not to be eaten in non-sacrificial

Figure 19. Sacrifice of a young male goat to the goddess Bhagavatī.

forms. Thus, according to *Manu*, (parentheses are Bühler's; Bühler 1969, p. 174; *Manu* V, 31, 32, 33):

> "The consumption of meat (is befitting) for sacrifices," that is declared to be a rule made by the gods; but to persist (in using it) on other (occasions) is said to be a proceeding worthy of Rakshasas [malevolent demons].
> He who eats meat when he honors the gods and . . . [ancestral spirits], commits no sin, whether he has bought it, or himself has killed (the animal). . . .
> A twice-born man who knows the law, must not eat meat except in conformity with the law; for if he has eaten it unlawfully, he will, unable to save himself, be eaten after death by his (victims).

Significantly, Brahmans are included among the meat eaters. "A Brahman must never eat animals unhallowed by Mantras; but obedient to the primeval law, he may eat it consecrated with Vedic text." Yet, with all these (and various other) attempts to distinguish sacrifice from murder duly made, the Laws state, "a man who, being duly engaged (to officiate or to dine at a sacred rite), *refuses* to eat meat, becomes after death an animal during twenty-one existences" (*Manu* V, 35, 36; Bühler 1969, 174f. [emphasis added]). Sanctions were sometimes needed to *force* people to participate in the animal sacrifice. These ancient issues have persisted in full force in Bhaktapur.

Biardeau notes that the division between animal and vegetarian sacrifice has in recent millennia become associated with a hierarchy of lower and higher practices, deities, and priests. As we noted in descriptions of other South Asian communities (chap. 8 and above) the vegetarian gods there are higher than the meat eating ones, and their priests, Brahmans, are, in turn, vegetarian and superior to the priests of the flesh-eating gods, whose priests typically belong to lower and nonvegetarian castes (Biardeau and Malamoud 1976, 140). Bhaktapur, of course, has suppressed the hierarchy of the dangerous and benign gods, and hesitates, in fact, to decide which might be higher.[34] The suppression is an uneasy one. Newar Brahmans, as they did in the times reflected in Manu's laws, participate in blood sacrifice and eat sacrificially prepared meat. For them and for all the upper *thar*s, however, sacrifice and meat eating takes its meaning from the various violations of the ordinary *dharma* that they represent.

Animal sacrifice or an equivalent meat offering is the proper offering to dangerous gods—which in most cases means a goddess—and is required in upper-status Tantric worship to the Āga(n) God and to other Tantric deities. Sacrificial worship of the dangerous gods is optional for those without Tantric initiation, with one essential exception. Every household in the city *must* offer a yearly animal sacrifice or meat offering to Bhagavatī during the course of the household ceremonies during the harvest festival, Mohanī. Most households, if they can afford to at all, perform sacrifices several times during the course of the year. This is done during important rites of passage, during the *ad hoc* occasions when a worship of a dangerous deity may seem advisable, and during certain of the annual festivals that are occasions for large, semiritualized family feasts.

The kind of animal sacrificed is optional. An egg is considered a minimal but proper sacrifice to a dangerous deity, and it is offered often by very poor families, using the same terminology for the offering as is applied to other animal sacrifice. The offering of the egg is in fact sometimes called *khe(n) syāegu*, "killing the egg." A poor family may restrict itself to using a mixture, *samhae*, which is also used by upper-status families in the course of Tantric *pūjās* in addition to the actual climactic killing of an animal. *Samhae* is a mixture of black soybeans, ginger, beaten and fried rice, "puffed" or "popped" roasted rice, dried fish, and pieces of water buffalo meat. The dried fish are purchased in shops that also sell grain; the buffalo meat is obtained from the Nāe butchers whose *thar* profession is the ritual killing of water buffaloes. The water buffalo was traditionally the only animal that the butcher killed and sold as the only alternative kind of meat to an animal sacrificed in a family *pūjā*. These buffaloes are always killed by the butcher in the course of a perfunctory ritual sacrifice, and this makes the eating of their meat by others the taking of what is gesturally at least a consecrated *prasāda*.

Samhae or eggs may also be used by families at any social and economic level for perfunctory worship of one or another dangerous deity. However, the animal most commonly sacrificed in important household or Āga(n) House *pūjās* by people who can possibly afford one is the male goat. Poorer people may use a rooster on the occasion when a goat would otherwise be sacrificed. Other animals are sacrificed in special occasions and settings. Water buffalo are the focus of sacrifice at the Taleju temple and by the Nine Durgās group, where they symbolize the buffalo demon vanquished by Devī in the *Devī Māhātmya*. At certain sacrificial ceremonies, *pa(n)ca bali*, five kinds of animals are sacrificed: water buffaloes, goats, roosters, drakes, and rams. A sixth kind of animal, the pig, is sacrificed in special and limited contexts by the men who incarnate the Nine Durgā deities. A castrated male goat, called a *khasi*, sometimes regarded as a unique type of animal, is considered the ideal animal for sacrifice to Gaṇeśa. Sacrificial animals are almost always male animals.[35] There are some astrologically caused problems when the sacrifice of a female animal is required upon the advice of a Jośi (astrologer), and there are Newar festivals in other communities in which female animals are reportedly sometimes sacrificed, but almost all sacrifice in Bhaktapur is of male animals.

The most generally used term for an animal sacrifice is *bali*, (from Sanskrit, meaning tax, tribute, offering) and in some contexts, *bau*, which is said to be a Newari derivation of *bali*. ("*Bali*" and "*bau*" are also used for nonmeat offerings in one restricted context, death ceremonies, where rice offerings to ancestors and to crows and dogs as representatives of Yama are so named. Daily offerings of rice to the deceased ancestors of a household are also called *bali* offerings.) The sacrificial animal is also sometimes referred to as a *bāha(n)* (from Sanskrit *vāhana*, the—most usually—animal vehicle of a god), and thus a sacrifice may be called a *bāha(n) pūjā*.

As part of the attempt to distinguish sacrifice from murder ("Slaughtering for sacrifices is not slaughtering" [*Manu* V, 39]), the animal must indicate his assent to the sacrifice, so that he may (again echoing Manu) "receive a higher existence," and be freed of the bad *karma* that has caused him to be born as an animal.[36] The sign is the shaking of the animal's head or body in certain ways.[37] During the course of the dedication of the animal to the deity ritually pure water is sprinkled on it, often getting into the ear, which helps ensure the proper movement. Extremely rarely there are animals who are thought not to have assented and they are turned free to wander in the city, and must not be harmed. Throat cutting and death through the resulting exsanguination is considered the specifically Newar way of sacrificing. Rājopādhyāya Brahmans explain that the animal should have life in him to witness the sacrifice he is making as his gift to the deity, and this is not possible in sacrifice through decapitation. Non-Newar Nepalis who perform sacrifices do so by decapitating animals, and this is often referred to as one of the salient contrasts between Newars and others.[38] Fowl are decapitated by the Newars, but in keeping with the way mammals are decapitated, with the cut starting at the throat rather than at the back of the neck. The stream of blood from the severed carotid arteries of the sacrificial animal is sprayed on the image of the deity.

The sacrifice of the animal, most typically a male goat, comes (as we have seen in the description of the Tantric *pūjā*) in the course of a *pūjā* sequence, and at one of the major climaxes of the sequence. The animal itself is worshiped. Colored pigments and flowers are put on its head; people make gestures of respect to it; a special *pasu* mantra, a "beast" *mantra*, is said for it. The goat is told by the presiding priest or family worshiper that if it agrees it will be able to go to heaven. Sacred water, uncooked rice, and flowers are thrown on its body and head. People then wait for the sign of assent from the animal. A chicken, duck, or water buffalo (when killed by a butcher) must shake its head; a goat must shake its entire body as a sign of acceptance. A buffalo of special ritual importance (that is, all except those routinely but sacrificially killed to be sold as meat by butchers) must, like the goat, shake its body as a sign of acceptance. Although, as we have noted, the animal almost always eventually gives the assent sign, people must sometimes wait a while for it. Once the sign of assent is given, the animal may now be killed. After the throat is slit and the blood allowed to spray over the god image "to give drink to the deity," the head of the animal is cut off and placed on a metal plate, a *pūjā bha:*, which is placed in front of the deity as a food offering. Flowers and colored pigment are taken from the deity and placed on the *pūjā bha:* which will, bearing the head, be brought to the feast that always follows the animal sacrifice. Parts of this head will be distributed to the senior members of the *phukī* in a formal hierarchical pattern as we will recount below. At the time of the sacrifice the various offerings made to the god image previously, flowers, colored pigment, and food offerings become splattered with blood. Some of them are taken and distributed among the worshipers as *prasāda*, and among these the food offerings taken back as *prasāda* are eaten by the worshipers. In a goat sacrifice the abdomen may be opened and a length of intestine taken out, then knotted at one end and blown into to inflate it. The other end is tied, and the image of the deity is now garlanded with this intestinal balloon.

The body of the animal is now prepared for butchering. Its hair may be singed. This is considered necessary in some contexts, in *pīṭha pūjā*s, for example, but optional in others where instead the skin may be treated with boiling water to facilitate the removal of hair. The animal is now to be butchered, usually at or near the place of its sacrifice in preparation for a feast.

Who does the actual killing? This question illustrates the tension between slaughter as a sin and sacrifice as a religious duty. The two *thar*s whose traditional responsibilities include the killing of animals for food—(and, traditionally, in the case of untouchable *Po(n)* also the execution of criminals)—are among the very lowest in Bhaktapur.[39]

Fishing, the traditional source of the dried fish used in the *samhae* offerings, is one of the duties exclusively assigned to the Po(n)s, the untouchables. The Nāe who kill the water buffaloes are also close to the bottom of the status system.

The ideal is for the chief worshiper to kill the sacrificial animal himself. For Āga(n) God *pūjā*s in the household or Āga(n) House the acting head of the household or representative of the *phukī*, whether he is king—or his contemporary Brahman surrogate in Taleju, the king's Āga(n) House—Brahman, or Jośi, or any member of the upper *thar*s, must cut the throat of the sacrificial animals himself. In these cases it is not proper to delegate the sacrificial act to the Ācāju, although that is done, as we have noted, in cases where no one in a group has the initiation, or is available to perform the sacrifice. In public settings, however, attended by people beyond the circle of initiates, the Ācāju or one of the lowest *thar*s[40] may do the killing, protecting the highest groups in the public arena from the possible stigma of slaughter. Middle and lower groups also do their own killing in family *pūjā*s, although the middle groups may use a member of the Jyāpu Ācāju, or "farmer Ācāju" *thar*s on important or public occasions.

Sacrifice: The Hierarchical Division of the Head The deities who receive sacrifice are for the most part those who are the tutelary deities of one or another of Bhaktapur's nested components—*phukī*, *guthi*, maṇḍalic segment, city as a whole—and thus the sacrifice represents the members of the unit. The sacrifice, above all those done in the course of Tantric worship, are done in contexts emphasizing the "equality"—which for Bhaktapur means the collapsing of hierarchical distinctions—of the participating group. In the feast that follows *phukī* sacrifices large family groups are assembled. At the core is the patrilineal *phukī* group, but *hātānātā*—the out-married daughters and their spouses and children and more distantly related kin, as well as family friends—may also be invited. They all share in the sacrifical meal as guests of the *phukī* or household. However, within this communal egalitarian feast there is an important ceremonial fragment that recalls the male hierarchy of the *phukī*. This is the orderly distribution of segments of the head of the sacrificial animal.

The distribution of parts of the head is one of the customs that people in Bhaktapur consider to be specifically Newar, or at least specially important to the Newars.[41] The parts of the head of the sacrificed animal are presented just before the fruit course (the arrangement of courses in such feasts is always conventionally organized in detail), that is, toward the end of the feast. They are given and received in a non-solemn, informal, often joking manner, characteristic of the feast itself.

These hierarchically arranged portions are called *siu* (in Kathmandu Newari, *sī*). The particular parts of the head made use of and their hierarchical value varies in various communities and groups. For Bhaktapur, for most upper-level groups at least, the sequence of distribution from highest to lowest is as follows: right eye, left eye, right ear, left ear, nose, tongue, right mandible, and left mandible. Toffin gives for the predominantly Jyāpu Newar village of Pyangaon the following sequence: right "muzzle," left "muzzle," right eye, left eye, right ear, left ear, right mandible, left mandible (1976, pp. 329–338; 1984, p. 104). Manandhar in his dictionary of Kathmandu Newari (1976) gives the sequence: right eye, left eye, right ear, left ear, nose (or muzzle), tongue (1976, p. 593). Reportedly, this sequence is not used in Bhaktapur. There are variations in the lowest parts of the status system in Bhaktapur. The Po(n)s, who usually eat pigs during their *phukī* feasts divide the pig up in the sequence snout, right eye, left eye, right ear, left ear, right mandible, left mandible—to which they add the tail, which in contrast to upper-level restriction of *siu* to males, is given to a woman, the ranking woman in the family.[42] In some circumstances, particularly among lower levels, a chicken or a duck is used for a feast. Thus at the initiation of a member of the Jugī *thar*s in the learning of the *thar*'s traditional musical instrument, a chicken is divided. On this occasion the head is given to the *guru*, the right wing to the student's father, and the left wing to the student. Manandhar (1976, 593) gives the sequential order of distribution for a duck or a chicken as head, right wing, left wing, right leg, and left leg. All these sequences have some tendency to go from top down, or front to back, and always from right to left in the ranking of symmetrical parts. Upper-status Bhaktapur and Pyangaon, at least, divide their mammals into eight parts.

In the middle and upper levels in Bhaktapur the *siu* is presented in order to the eight highest members of the *phukī* group that is holding the feast. For upper-level and middle-level *thar*s, at least, the system of ranking among the *phukī* as symbolized by the *siu* division is arranged by age within a generation, rather than only by relative age. In other words, even if a member of an older generation is younger than a male in a descending generation, he has more status in the *siu* distribution system. If there has been an Ācāju assisting the *phukī* at the sacrifice, he may be presented the fifth-ranked piece, the nose. The recipients of the *siu* eat a mouthful of their portion. Sometimes one small piece of any of the portions of *siu* is taken and presented to a representation of the main deity to whom the sacrifice was presented. The remnants of the *siu* as well as other residues of the feast are brought, as we have noted, to the *chwāsa* at the *twa:* crossroads after the feast by one of the household women.

Sacrifice: Human Sacrifice People in Bhaktapur believe that human sacrifice was performed in Bhaktapur in the past and that it may still take place on certian occasions in remote Newar towns in the Kathmandu Valley. The chronicles contain scattered references to what seem to be actual, as well as rumored human sacrifices, in the past. Mary Slusser reviews some of these reports, remarking that "the late chronicles take . . . [human sacrifice] for granted in the Malla Period, and consider it an accepted Licchavi custom" (1982, vol. 1, p. 337), and adds that "the late chronicles offer several descriptions of human sacrifices that seem too specific and too graphic to be mere fantasy" (ibid., 338). As she sums it up, reflecting with her phrase "almost certainty" the kinds of rumors that persist in Bhaktapur about the distant reaches of the Valley, "Human sacrifice, a feature of blood sacrifice up to the very recent past, is almost certainly no longer practiced in Nepal" (ibid., 1, 217).

In Bhaktapur's civic symbolic enactments the idea of human sacrifice is associated predominantly with the legends and dramatic performances of the Nine Durgās (chap. 15). There are some historical accounts, as we will see in that chapter, indicating that their performances in the past in Bhaktapur once included real human sacrifices. The details of their contemporary performances clearly show that the blood sacrifice of an animal deflects the rage of the Goddess in her most terrifying form from those humans or ineffectual minor deities who have offended her. The idea of the animal sacrifice as surrogate for human sacrifice is overt in still other contexts. In discussion of spirits and dangerous gods it is sometimes said that the dangerous force wants a human death (perhaps manifested in the illness of an individual) and that some substitution, often an animal sacrifice, must be made to save the individual. It is said that an animal sacrifice must be made to a newly constructed house; otherwise it may take a sacrifice itself and someone in the house will die. Similarly, if a truck owned by some Newar family is not given a sacrifice during the Mohanī festival, it may cause an accident, again taking the sacrifice for itself. The close relation of animal sacrifice and threats to humans is experienced by some, at the least, individuals in their late childhood in a deeply felt way. We will return to such personal interpretations and responses in the excursion that follows on the significance of sacrifice in Bhaktapur.

Sacrifice: Aspects of Its Significance in Bhaktapur Sacrifice in Bhaktapur, as the foregoing sections suggest, has the characteristics that have made one or another variation of sacrifice a powerful and useful social resource, one that "has been found in the earliest known forms of worship and in all parts of the world" (R. Faherty 1974, 128). There is an offering of animals and once, probably, humans to a divine being; that offering is equivocal, as it risks being interpreted as murder; the sacrificial animal is in part a representative of and surrogate for humans, as a human sacrifice would have been a surrogate for other humans; and the life—or death—offered to the gods is in part taken back in a transformed state and shared in a communal meal by the sacrificer and the members of the social group he represents.

It is not our purpose here to attempt to relate these forms to the large literature attempting to explain the social, psychological, and historical functions and "origins" of sacrifice, much of it originating in late nineteenth-century and early twentieth-century social and psychological theory. We will here emphasize certain aspects of it that are highlighted in Bhaktapur's uses and in the responses and interpretations of some, at least, of its people. These considerations are in anticipation of later discussions of how some of the central symbolic forms and symbolic enactments of the annual festival cycle build on the implications of sacrifice to help bind individuals into the city's symbolically constituted mesocosm.

Blood sacrifice in Bhaktapur might be regarded as an extremely immoral act transformed by a powerful context, a "religious" one of a special kind. The immorality and, therefore, the power represented in transformation is greatly enhanced by the Hindu doctrine of reincarnation, which renders animals in this and other contexts of understanding morally continuous with humans. Not only the killing of animals, which is relegated to the lowest-status *thar*s, but even the eating of meat from animals unless they are sacrificial offerings is contrary to the ordinary *dharma*. Against the background of such understanding sacrifice in Bhaktapur is *the* antinomial act in which all levels of society participate, in distinction to those acts that exclusively characterize upper-status Tantric *pūjās*. The transformation produced by the context is equivocal; there is a conflict with not only "common sense" but also the tenets of "ordinary religion," a conflict within the realm of faith itself. The possibility of a characterization of sacrifice as murder is always there. Much of the significance of blood sacrifice derives from this. Peripheral people in Bhaktapur's society, adolescents, and members of lower *thars*, as well as Nepalese outsiders—including vocal Buddhist reformers—are skeptically aware that the apparent transformation of murder into sacrifice may be only self-serving hypocrisy, motivated in such skeptical interpretations by "superstition" in the quest for a good meal.

The location in Bhaktapur of some, at least, of the skepticism in the minds of older children or younger adolescents is particularly significant. As one informant, a member of a shopkeeper family, put it: "at first when we were young we used to feel afraid." (Why?)[43] "Killing is not good. Killing causes something to happen in your mind." (What?) "It is a kind of cruelty. Someone is doing something cruel to the animal and he may do something cruel to me. Every man is also like an animal. A man can kill with a knife. That's why I used to feel troubled. But afterward I got used to the religion and to all kinds of sacrifice. " He was about twelve years old when he began to "get used to" sacrifice. I [R. L.] then ask him what other feelings he had about sacrifice before that time. "The religious books were about peace and about not killing anything, not harming anything. But they [the adults] break all the customs of religion, or the reality of religion, and they kill the animals, they sacrifice the animals for their own satisfaction only, in order to eat the animal, that is why they sacrifice. I used to say that it is not really for the god, the god never told us to kill anybody. I used to say so at that time."

But then he grew up and he came to realize the "religious truth" about sacrifice. That is he had to make, as Kierkegaard ([1843] 1954) put it, a "leap into faith," a commitment to counterintuitive propositions, to the "absurdities" that mark membership in a "community of faith."[44]

The conflicts of meanings of sacrifice within the ordinary *dharmic* ethical system with the system of meanings and values of the worship of the dangerous deities means that the issues will be overt and conscious, that alternatives will be visible (i.e., to kill or not to kill), and that a choice is possible. The possibility of rejecting an adherence, on one or another level, to the symbolic forms is essential for the meaning of sacrifice, especially when the thing to be chosen or rejected involves a risk. *Choice* implies that for symbols of social importance (1) adherence must be motivated and (2) the act or state of adherence, being in some sense optional, means something in itself.

The acceptance of the religious interpretation that converts murder into sacrifice is not only a significant commitment to a system of doctrine; it is in part motivated by the powerful personal significance of animal sacrifice. The man we have just quoted has said, "someone is doing something cruel to the animal, and he may do something cruel to me. Every man is also like an animal." This overt association of not only "men" and "animals" but of one's self and the sacrificial animal is common in people's reflections on their thoughts and feelings about sacrifice when they were young. Another informant, a member of a high Chathar *thar*, said that when he was a child "I had pity for the goat, and I felt some sort of uneasiness which came into my mind. What if I were killed and given as sacrifice in that way, what would happen to me? That was the kind of feeling that came to my mind. If I were, you know, given as a sacrifice, you know, with my head turned up like that and a knife blade being put on my throat [he laughs] what would happen? That was the kind of feeling I had you know, a kind of gooseflesh, you know what that is, I can't express it. I used to have that kind of feeling, but these days I don't." Echoes of early understandings persist, although usually less clearly articulated in other adults. Thus, according to a man from the very low Jugī *thar* "we love the sacrificial animals like our own sons and daughters, because we brought them up and fed them and gave them drink."

These remarks show empathy for and identification with the animal as sacrificial victim. They also suggest a double psychological movement as individuals mature and fully enter the society, a movement that for boys roughly corresponds to their *Kaetā Pūjā*s, their initiation into their respective *thars*. The "leap into faith," the coming to "understand," the acceptance of the system of marked symbols as having its own legitimate reality, is motivated in part by a solidarity with adults, and hence the community, and that solidarity is aided, urged, by a sort of forced choice between an identification with the community of sacrificers and an identification with its sacrificial victims. One must not only accept the community's "ideology" but must also participate in sacrificial acts, and thus by implication in the whole mesocosmic symbolic system that they represent and protect. People are tempted by all kinds of oppositions to the full moral life of the city—memories of their own childhood, the life of the lower *thars*, and the freedom of the hill people. But these are also dirty, chaotic, animal-like. Sacrifice acts as a kind of continuing rite of passage, which emphasizes commitment to the costly order of household, *phukī*, and city. As we will see in chapter 15, the ritual performances of the Nine Durgās make the social implications of sacrifice quite clear—the wrath of the Goddess in her most destructive representation as Mahākālī is aroused by violations of respect due to her by an inferior, that is, by a violation of the fundamental hierarchical social order. She threatens the hapless violator, and can be appeased only by the substitution of an animal, a cock, whose head she tears off and whose blood she drinks.

After their leading male member kills the animal, the corporate group eats it. This common and much discussed aspect of sacrifice has evoked various explanations—such as shared guilt and the absorption of the substance of the representative "totemic" animal—to explain the solidarity that presumably results from this. The Newar feast is a joyful event, usually associated with drinking as well as meat eating in a further participation in the Goddess's realm. The atmosphere of the feast is joyous and communal, a mild sociable softening of the proprieties of hierarchical order and of ordinary dietary restraints. The communal feast humanizes and socializes further the sorts of procedures which Tantrism performs as esoteric rituals. The act of sacrifice is modulated down into a dinner party. The ritual murder (which in some societies might be in the realm of mysteries, of black magic, of evil, of Satan) is conveniently and typically captured by the city and transformed and given a paradoxical propriety in the realm of the dangerous deities and their worship.

SECRECY AND MYSTERY

Secrecy is a pervasive and fundamental aspect of Bhaktapur's life. Its major symbolic representation is in the worship of the dangerous deities—above all in the Tantric mode with its emphasis on esoteric secrets, swearing of oaths to keep those secrets, and levels of initiation into progressively deeper ones.

Secrecy is clearly associated with the cellular units of Bhaktapur and is, in fact, a condition of their cellularity.[45] What separates their affairs from outsiders is, in large part, the confidentiality of those affairs. In large part this confidentiality is to protect each unit from the moral scrutiny of larger units, to allow the unit to regulate its own affairs as far as possible. The moral scrutiny of a larger unit is liable to be censorious and carries a serious and consequential risk of the loss of the public prestige, the *ijjat*, of the unit.

On the religious level the secrecy is focused on the name, form, nature, and proper worship of the unit's tutelary deity, and on the special craft and professional knowledge of a *thar*. The revealing of any of a group's secrets by one of its members, usually implying a violation of an oath taken during an initiation, would be a very serious breach of an individual's relation to the group and, more generally, of his or her general status as an adequate "person." Secrecy makes the unit equivalent to a *maṇḍala*, a circle in which some sort of religious potency can be bound, collected, and isolated to some purpose. The boundary, which can be represented in space by a line, can in the life of a group be represented by a boundary of secrecy. In analogy to the *maṇḍala*, secrecy is similarly associated in the affairs of the units that have it with the concentration, boundedness and possession of some kind of "power" within the unit itself.

Many component units contribute elements to larger ritual or symbolic performances. Mask makers, ritual dancers, potters, image markers, astrologers, Brahmans, Ācājus, and so forth may all contribute objects and/or actions. As we have repeatedly emphasized, it is essential that their outputs into the ritual or festival be effective. These outputs are public. However, the way that the mask maker gathers the proper clay, forms the mask in traditional ways, and brings the preliminary stages of *siddhi* into the mask are secret. It is essential that the cell perform properly, but the details hidden by secrecy are not the concern of the larger group.[46] But the fact of the secrecy in itself, the knowledge that a group has its required initiations and hidden rituals, gives outsiders a conviction and a confidence that proper, effective, and powerful actions are being done within a unit to produce the efficacy of their contribution to the public city. This means that it is essential to know that there *are* secrets. A completely hidden secret, hidden so well that no one knew that a group had any would not convey this sign of corporate *siddhi* to outsiders. *In Bhaktapur, knowledge by others that a group has secrets, or more precisely has the secrets it is supposed to have, is a sign that it is an effective and necessary component of the larger system.*[47]

The secrecy of a group becomes a *mystery* for those who know there is a secret, but do not know what it is. To turn a secret into a mystery means that there often have to be ways of signaling, of advertising the presence of secrets. While it is common knowledge that corporate groups have special *mantras*, deities, and hidden rites, and that there are parts of temples and houses where no one but the initiate can enter, there are other ways of advertising secrets. One is to warn people to avoid stumbling on them, for they may, it is typically said, be dangerous to an outsider.[48] People know, for example, that the Nine Durgās perform important secret dances in various parts of the city late at night during certain phases of their annual cycle and, knowing where they will dance, avoid these areas. For, it is said, if they are seen, the person who saw them would then have extremely bad luck or might die. We have noted the related idea in Tantrism that if improperly initiated and qualified people try to learn Tantric secrets and procedures, they would become blind or insane or would die.

Thus secrecy has to be advertised in order to be effective in the larger system and, sometimes, to prevent outsiders from stumbling on it. The advertisement sometimes takes flamboyant forms. During Biskā:, the solar New Year festival (chap. 13), for example, where an image of a secret dangerous deity is to be brought out of its temple to some other part of the city, there is also a false secret image. While people are watching a procession carrying the portable public image of the deity, a priest will run through the crowd carrying something wrapped in cloths. People will say, with an air of special knowledge, that what is being carried is the "real" and secret image. The bundle that the priest is carrying is, in fact, just a decoy; the "real" image is being carried in true secrecy. This device of a false secret has the virtue of advertising the presence of a secret and at the same time protecting it.

The symbolically constituted dimension of Bhaktapur's life, its mesocosm, is in part structured through bounded information. These areas are the property of various corporate groups, and are organized into the larger hierarchical system of statuses. Secrecy is the means by which these bounded areas are maintained; and the possession of secrets is equivalent to the possession of economic and political force in the "material" realm. To tell the secrets is to destroy them as secrets essential to the special functions of differentiated, interrelated units, and thus is to destroy much of the effective structure of the city.[49]

The system of secrecy has one unintended consequence. It makes loss of traditional knowledge through time, knowledge located in a multitude of bounded groups, very much more likely than the loss of a widely shared knowledge would be, and at the same time it may prevent an awareness that some aspects of cultural knowledge have, in fact, disappeared. People assume that the esoteric meaning of various symbolic forms is known by "someone" within some one of the city's units. Experts, not knowing the meaning of some form or the details of some ritual technique, will assume that it is known to someone elsewhere. Thus, for example, the nature and meaning of certain faces placed in the headband of some of the masks of the Nine Durgās dancers are thought by Brahmans, mask makers, and the Gāthā dancers (see color illustrations) themselves to be known to one of the *other* of these three concerned groups, but the knowledge is apparently lost.

IN SUM

The presence of Tantrism as a legitimate, socially integrated component of Bhaktapur's marked symbolic life, like the legitimate and integrated presence of the dangerous deities, has transformed both Tantrism and Bhaktapur. Esoteric Tantrism and the exoteric religion of the dangerous deities allow for the representation of emotions and ideas that are not represented in—and are often in opposition to—the ordinary moral order of the city. Because of this legitimate and central representation, the ideas and emotions are not totally relegated to such peripheral forms as ghost beliefs, witches and shamans, or to the "imaginary" world of fairy tales and wonder stories, or to private fantasy. All these modes exist in Bhaktapur, although some of them seemed played down in comparison with some other Nepalese groups. (Bhaktapur, for example, uses mostly hill tribe shamans for spirit healers; it treats *sādhu* renouncers as a "non-Newar" tradition.) The dominant alternative supernatural mode is not only legitimate but also, in some contexts, at the apex of the social system.

Tantrism is intimately connected with the meanings of the dangerous deities who are the objects of its worship, and it shares their implications and uses. Those implications are apparently contradictory to ordinary social order, but they are related to that order in an elaborate, mysterious higher unification. Tantrism and the dangerous deities represent amoral forces and the force that controls such forces, and thus the possibility of using this force to protect the moral system itself; they represent the possibility of escape from the civic system in both its dangers and its attractions and yet, at the same time, a tool for binding the members of a corporate group to the group under the shared protection and threat of a dangerous deity; they represent danger and chaos, but also fertility and creativity, a realm that can destroy but that is necessary to the life of a community.

Tantric practice and the exoteric worship of the dangerous deities—although some of their symbolic forms may become routine and probably mostly empty of meaning for some or many of its practitioners—are nevertheless able to bring many of these meanings to repeated life, in ways that we have tried to suggest. Tantric practices, albeit somewhat timidly, violate some of the moral laws that are central markers of reputation and status in the public society. Blood sacrifice (less timidly) does this not only in Tantrism but also in the worship of the dangerous deities throughout the city.

Blood sacrifice and Tantrism's other antinomial moves have, among other meanings, a potential epistemological implication for people in Bhaktapur. The violations of the ordinary *dharma* which must necessarily be done in the worship of the dangerous deities are at the same time violations and not violations. They are "not violations" because they are done in the special transcendent contexts of Tantrism and sacrifice. The city's moral laws are thus valid only in a certain context. This is an important addition to Bhaktapur's large assortment of socially defined paradox-generating contexts, and of different kinds of realities which individuals experience. Tantra, however, in its doctrinal alliance with mysticism, carries the implications of shifting rules and definitions toward the implication that *all* contexts may be arbitrary and illusory. This is another way—alongside the direct category dissolving possibilities of the experience of meditation—that may lead to a sense of things in which an enlightened or "liberated" individual may come to see through (or, at any rate, peek through) the veil of illusion, *māyā*, in which the moral world and ordinary logic exist.[50] That is, the results of experience will support philosophical doctrine. The purposes of Tantric *pūjā* are conceived as either powerful action for the sake of the corporate group involved, which may in some cases be the whole city or, alternatively, personal "escape" as a transcendence of *saṃsara*, the ordinary moral world. Power and escape may look to an outsider as different matters, but in the context of Bhaktapur (and Hinduism) they are strongly unified, for they *both* represent an escape from and a transcendence of the ordinary moral system, the network of pressures, limitations, and relations of ordinary life.

It is this transcendence of the ordinary moral and social world that makes Tantrism significant both for the renouncer (the *sādhu* or *yogi*) and the upper nonpriestly strata[51] (the Kṣatriya kings, court officials, and warriors). For this latter group, their power consists, or consisted, precisely in that they have, on proper occasions, to rise above and violate the ordinary *dharma* in the performance of their necessary protective functions (chap. 10). The alliance of aristocracy, royalty, power, mystic renunciation, and the social legitimacy of Tantrism and the dangerous deities is characteristic of Bhaktapur.

CHAPTER TEN

Priests

PRELIMINARIES: PRIESTS AND KINGS— THE RELATIONS OF THE SYMBOLIC ORDER AND POWER

Bhaktapur—with its hallucinatory memories of its Newar king, its persisting Kṣatriya-like social segments, its continuing relation to the "new" centralized Śāha royal dynasty, its elaborate collection of priests and quasi-priests, and of the other "nonpriestly" traditional social role players who may be contrasted with them, all placed within or in relationship to a traditional dharmic moral order—throws some light on the Hindu peculiarities, variously described and emphasized in the scholarly literature, of the relations of the conventional moral order and "power," of religious and political realms, of priest and king.

In this chapter we will be concerned mostly with details of the types and functions of Bhaktapur's priests and their auxiliary helpers, as well as with those *thar*-based social roles and functions that are priest-like in one or another more or less covert way. The priestly realm has not only its significant internal divisions but also external contrasts with nonpriests which are essential for understanding how Bhaktapur's community life is organized. Those external contrasts are epitomized in the relation of Brahman and king.

It has long been evident to Western scholars that the realms and relations of king and Brahman in South Asian society were different from those of similar functionaries in most other societies. As Kolenda (1978, 31) put it in a summary review:

> As early as the eighth century B.C., Hindu thought had separated worldly power from other-worldly power. Since then, the two realms have been in the hands of different specialists—worldly power in the hands of the king, other-worldly power in the hands of the priest. In the Hindu ideology, the ritual power of the Brahman priest was more important than the secular power of the king, who was expected to protect and depend upon the priest. . . . Indeed, it was the duty of the king . . . to protect the populace, to ensure conformity to the class system of the time, and to wage war—always under the guidance of his Brahman . . . preceptor. The king was carrying out the religious law (dharma) that was in the keeping of the Brahman priest.

The Hindu king and his fellow Kṣatriya allies, counselors, and warriors protect and enforce the *dharma*, but their relation to that customary law was, and is, ambiguous. In Robert Lingat's (1973, 210–211) epitome:

> The kingship . . . belonged to him who possessed *kṣatra* ["warlike force," plus "sovereignty"] de facto, . . . i.e. the power to command, whatever might have been his birth and whatever might have been the circumstances which brought him to the throne. *Kṣatra* confers on the king independence, the right to act to suit himself without depending upon anyone else. The king is independent of his subjects, as is the spiritual preceptor of his pupils and the head of the family of the members of his household. . . . By contrast, *Dharma* is essentialy a rule of *interdependence*, founded on a hierarchy corresponding to the nature of things and necessary for the maintenance of the social order. To break away from it is to violate one's destiny and to expose onself to the loss of one's salvation. The peculiar *dharma* of the king is the protection of his subjects. If he is free to act as he pleases without having to account to anyone for his acts, he acquires merit only when acting in conformity with his *dharma*. . . . So finally the destiny of the king depends on the way in which he has been able to protect his subjects.

Although it is recognized that some kind of moral responsibility, some kind of "meta-dharma," must guide the king's freedom, his activities *as king* must, if they are to be successful, violate and transcend, and escape from that "ordinary" Hindu community *dharma* that is, it is worth repeating, "essentially a rule of interdependence, founded on a hierarchy corresponding to the nature of things and necessary for the maintenance of the social order." In his warrior's relation to the city's external enemies, his manipulative relations to the city's allies, and in his use of violence and power to enforce those *internal* violations of the civic *dharma* which that *dharma*'s sanctions of moral disapproval and karmic retribution cannot in themselves fully control, he must ignore the morality of interdependence and must perform acts which within the ordinary civic order would be sins.[1] In contrast, the king *as citizen and as person* operates within the ordinary *dharma* and, importantly for our present purposes, within the ordinary civic religion.

In Louis Dumont's statement contrasting the Indian king with kings in other ancient traditional societies where the king was either at the same time the supreme religious functionary or else superior in his status to "his" priests, the Indian king (1970, 68 [emphasis added]):

> loses . . . hierarchical preeminence in favor of the priests, retaining for himself *power* only. . . . Through this dissociation, the function of the king in India has been *secularized.* It is from this point that a differentiation has occurred, the separation within the religious universe of a sphere or realm opposed to the religious, and roughly corresponding to what we call the political. As opposed to the realm of values and norms it is the realm of force. As opposed to the *dharma* or universal order of the Brahman, it is the realm of interest or advantage, *artha*. . . . All [the implications that follow from this] can, in my view be traced back to this initial step. In other words, they would have been impossible if the king had not from the beginning left the highest religious functions to the priest.

These classic discussions of king and Brahman and the "realms" epitomized by their functions illuminate and yet at the same time tend to obscure the relations and functions of king and priest, and the actual internal divisions and interrelations of realms of "religion" on the one hand and "force" on the other. They obscure the different *kinds* of religion and priestly functions that in Bhaktapur and many places historically like it in South Asia were differentially related to "values and norms" and to "force," and they do not take account of the wider implications of "force" for characterizing a vertical social segment of Bhaktapur's society, within which the king and his paradoxical *dharma* is a special case.

The hierarchical system of *thar*s in Bhaktapur assigns roles and functions of two sorts. The roles are sorted into two hierarchical segments of the macrostatus system. One segment—ranging from Brahman to untouchable—is concerned with the manipulation and maintenance of the *dharma*-supporting symbolically constituted civic social system, whose central organizing metaphor is purity and impurity. This is the nexus of the interdependent life of the civic community. Its proper religion is the religion of the ordinary deities. Its functionaries, grouped as priests in an extended usage suggested by Hocart ([1950] 1960), are the subject of this chapter. The other segment, ranging from king down via farmers through the lowest-status craftsmen, have their representative functions within another realm that may be disentangled from the symbolically constructed, hierarchical, civic *dharma*. They deal, in comparison, with a more material world, and with symbolic forms other than those characteristic forms that organize the *dharmic* community—purity and impurity, *karma*, and the moral imperatives of the *dharma* itself. These are the potters, farmers, traders, wood carvers, dyers, and so on, as well as the king and other political and military functionaries. The cultural forms and symbols that shape and give meaning to their *functions* (in distinction to their status as citizens) have some qualities and relations different from those of the primary symbol technicians. The relation of their roles to hierarchy, and their work to the *dharma*, is a secondary addition. As citizens, their religion (like the king's) is the ordinary dharmic religion. However, as operatives in a world that has its own independent realities, forces, and forms, and which is necessary for the support, maintenance, and protection of the city's realm of values and norms, they share, in part, the classic situation of the king. Insofar, then, as they deal in "power," in one sense, and not in "norms and values," their realm is complexly related to the larger "religious universe." In relation to the dharmic religion of the ordinary deities, they perform "secular" functions. However, their relation to the religion of the dangerous deities is different. Those deities have the same sort of relation to the civic *dharma* as do the activities of the king, farmers, and craftsmen. They, and their special worship and meanings, express the realm of value-transcendent power in which the king and others like him operate, and they can be and are used in attempts to augment and protect that power. We have discussed the function of the dangerous deities and of their worship in earlier chapters; the chapters on symbolic enactments that follow will further indicate what they do, and how they do it. But for now we must note that these deities are precisely *not* "in the realm of values and norms" but, like the city's segment of "material technicians," are within the "realm of force," a force put to the service of those values and norms.

Bhaktapur's priests, including its Brahmans, operate in *both* these realms, both as the exemplary pure (and, in fact, exemplary impure) priests of the ordinary moral realm, the world of the *dharmic*, hierarchical, civic order and also as priests of the realm of power, where purity and impurity and the civic values of interdependency are irrelevant. In these two worlds the relations of Brahman to king, of priest to client, are basically different—and, thus, so is the meaning of the priest and his function.

PRELIMINARIES: KINDS OF PRIESTS AND PRIESTLY FUNCTIONS

The priests of Bhaktapur's civic moral realm have a central concern with correct moral behavior and the structuring efficacy of purity and pollution; the priests of the extramoral realm deal with a more direct power, a power that transcends morality as well as purity and pollution. The extramoral religion dealing with powers which transcend that civic moral realm, while at the same time ensuring its protection, is the special religion of Bhaktapur's version of the Kṣatriya as Kṣatriya, but has its echoes and uses throughout the city.

The Newar Brahman, the Rājopādhyāya Brahman, is at the summit of both these religious realms. Within the realm of civic ordering he is allied with a whole set of manipulators of purity, and thus of social order and of salvation-producing *dharmic* order. These allies are auxiliary priests and what we will call "para-priests," as well as various pollution-manipulating priest-like functionaries—purifiers such as barbers and collectors of impurity such as, above all, the untouchables.

In his role as Tantric guru and priest the Rājopādhyāya Brahman presides over that other world in which purity is not an issue, where the priests and practitioners of the world of the dangerous deities manipulate through those deities the extramoral world of physical events—a world of rain and drought, disease and cure, earthquake and war. Such priests manipulate the deities through devices of power, and the deities, in turn, manipulate the nonmoral world. The Rājopādhyāya Brahman's essential priestly ally in this realm is the Ācāju, the priest who performs in public those actions that the Brahman can do only in secret.

The two sorts of religion—the socially constructive *dharmic* religion and the religion of power—converge once again, as they had in the Rājopāhyāya Brahmans, on the untouchable Po(n), and the near-untouchable Jugī. These are the ultimate collectors of impurity, facilitating the purity of all above them. Yet, their ability to do this, whatever the enormous stigma to their social status may be, is a sign of a power to transcend some, at least, of the implications of that impurity. This is clearest in the ascription of Tantric knowledge to the Jugī, but is also a latent aspect of the meaning of the Po(n).

We have been proceeding as if the term "priest" in itself were unproblematic. It was not problematic in the discussion of the priest's contrasts with the king insofar as the "priest" has been the idealized figure of the Brahman. The Brahman in such discussions is subsumed comfortably under summary characterizations of "priests"—where the problem in characterization is usually to delineate the "priest" in contrast to other mediators with the "supernatural"—shamans, diviners, magicians, and prophets. Among these the "priest" is someone who "has a special and sometimes secret knowledge of the techniques of worship, including incantations, prayers, sacrificial acts, songs, and other acts that are believed to bridge the separation between the divine or sacred and the profane realms. . . . Because the priest gains his special knowledge from a school for priests, he is differentiated from other religious and cultic leaders . . . who obtain their positions by means of individual efforts. . . . As a member of the institution [the priesthood] that regulates the relationship between the divine or sacred and the profane realms through ritual, the priest is the accepted religious and spiritual leader in his society" (E. O. James 1974, 1007). Such an account emphasizes the social centrality and "routinization" of the institutionalized priesthood in making the priest the accepted "spiritual leader" of the community. In the terms of such a definition, we can discriminate among the functionaries who mediate between the sacred and profane and who belong to the central institutionalized civic order, certain "priests" who help the Brahman in conducting rituals or who act in lieu of Brahmans in rituals or who work for clients where Brahmans can or will not officiate. These are *auxiliary priests*. We are now left with one further distinction. In chapter 11 we will discuss activities, most particularly purification, that are "at the margins of the sacred." These activities are for the purpose of putting individuals in a proper state to enter into the sacred realm, the realm where priests operate, and do not in themselves entail "techniques of worship." The experts who perform these activities are not properly priests themselves. This is clear in the case of the vitally important purificatory work of the Nau, the "barber." The same claim may be made regarding the astrologers, the Jośis. We will call those whose functions are to prepare people for their encounters with the sacred *para-priests*.

BHAKTAPUR'S BRAHMANS

THE RĀJOPĀDHYĀYA BRAHMANS

In the general perspective of modern Nepal the "Newar" Brahmans of Bhaktapur are a problematic group of Brahmans, in some sense secondary to those Brahmans associated with the ruling Gorkhāli dynasty. In Bhaktapur, as in other Newar communities, the dominant Brahmans, who share the surname "Rājopādhyāya," must differentiate themselves not only from the Partyā: or Khae(n), that is, the Indo-Nepalese Brahman, but also from two other kinds of "non-Newar" Brahmans—the Bhaṭṭa and the Jhā Brahmans—who live and work in Bhaktapur. For the most part they identify themselves in contrast to other Brahmans by their *thar* name, Rājopādhyāya,[2] which identifies their connection with the Malla dynasty as the "king's counselor" (see fig. 20).

In their own legendary history the Rājopādhyāya Brahmans came from the great ancient Indian political, religious, and cultural center, Kanauj (also called Kānyakubja), in North India, the same city that they believe to have been the earlier seat of what became the Malla dynasty. Kanauj was in the area of India from which successive Muslim invasions in the eleventh and twelfth centuries drove many Hindus into nearby Nepal.

The Rājopādhyāya's historical legend tells how in the distant past two Brahman brothers came to Nepal from Kānyakubja. Their names were "Allas Raj" and "Ullas Raj." Ullas Raj settled in the mountains, while Allas Raj settled in the Kathmandu Valley. Ullas Raj became a Partyā: (literally, a "hill dweller") because he settled in the mountains. Allas Raj became a Newar because he settled in the Valley. Ullas Raj mixed with the Partyā: people. As he had done farming in Kānyakubja he remained in the hills, where his descendants continue to be farmers.[3] His children spoke the Partyā: language (Nepali). Allas Raj mixed with the Newar people, and thus his children spoke Nepal Bhāṣā (Newari). Allas Raj and Ullas Raj had no more relations with each other because they now had different languages and customs. They did not keep up their family relations. After a few generations their descendants did not even know each other. When Harisiṃhadeva came to Bhaktapur he brought new Kānyakubja Brahmans with him. Harisiṃhadeva gave those Kānyakubja Brahmans who had been in Bhaktapur prior to his arrival a "substitute house,"[4] which is now still used by the Rājopādhyāyas. As the Rājopādhyāya Brahmans who came with Harisiṃhadeva from Kānyakubja and the Rājopādhyāya descendants of Allas Raj were the "same kinds" of Brahmans, they mixed very easily with each other. They both became Rājopādhyāya Brahmans.

However, the account continues, Harisiṃhadeva also brought *other* Brahmans with him, these were Maithili Brahmans from the nearby area of Mithilā whose descendants are the Jhā Brahmans (one group

Figure 20. Rājopādhyāya Brahmans in a purification ceremony at the river.

of Bhaktapur's "non-Newar" Brahmans). He brought them "because they came from a place close to his town of Simraun Gaḍh," but his own royal priests were the Rājopādhyāya Brahmans from Kānyakubja. As the Kānyakubja Brahmans did not have enough Kānyakubja Brahman families to marry with in "Nepal" (that is, the Kathmandu Valley),[5] Harisiṃhadeva repeatedly brought in new Brahmans from Kānyakubja. Even now, this particular account concludes, the Rājopādhyāya Brahmans have a barely adequately sized group for marriages.

The legend that we have paraphrased reflects some historical reality. It seems generally accepted by historians that the Rājopādhyāya are of Kānyakubja origin, that they were associated with the Malla court, that they were dominant in that court among other Brahmans, and that they were centrally associated with the worship of the royal tutelary goddess Taleju. As a result of the integration of the new Malla dynasty with the preexisting society of the city into the historical synthesis that Bhaktapur looks back on as "Newar," this group of Brahmans were to become *the* Newar Brahmans, the only one of the various kinds of Valley Brahmans to become the focal Brahmans of the integrated Newar caste system.[6]

From the earliest records of the Kathmandu Valley communities who were to become the Newars, there have been reports of Brahmans. Thus in the seventh century A.D., the Chinese traveler Hiuen Tsang wrote that the Licchavi Valley society was ruled by a Kṣatriya dynasty, and that it had so many Brahman priests that he was unable to ascertain their exact number (D. R. Regmi 1969, 271). Inscriptions from Licchavi times refer to the "leadership" or eminent position of Brahmans (ibid., 272). What happened to these earlier Brahmans on the advent of the Kānyakubja Rājopādhyāya Brahmans? It is tempting to think of them as having become some of the lower-status auxiliary priests of Malla Nepal, but our own materials are silent on this.

Bhaktapur's Rājopādhyāya Brahmans consider themselves to belong to one exogamous lineage.[7] There are two major groupings of this lineage within Bhaktapur, named in accordance with the areas in and close to which they live or, in the case of now scattered households, once lived. These are the Ipache(n) and the Cucāche(n) branches. The Ipache(n) group are those who live in proximity to the Lāekū or Durbar Square, and thus to the Taleju temple (map 6; above). Both of these sections contain certain families who have the hereditary rights to be Taleju priests. These "Taleju families" also are the ones whose *jajamān*s include those upper-level Chathariyā families traditionally associated with the royal administration.[8]

The city's two geographically based groups of Rājopādhyāya Brahmans are partially separated lineage groups. They worship at the same Digu god shrine but at a different time. They have two different Āga(n) Houses for many purposes (but on some occasions make use of the same one). Their separation implies that they are not affected by each others *phukī* birth and death pollution, but the degree of relations they do have means that they cannot intermarry. Because there are no local Rājopādhyāya families into which they can marry, all Bhaktapur Rājopādhyāya men have to find their wives elsewhere, usually among the Rājopādhyāya women of Patan or Kathmandu. Similarly, all the Bhaktapur Rājopādhyāya girls have to leave Bhaktapur for marriages in Patan or Kathmandu.

At the time of this study almost all of the adult male Rājopādhyāya Brahmans of Bhaktapur did traditional Brahmanical work, in contrast to Brahmans elsewhere, whom they characterized as often being "only Brahmans through their descent."[9] The Brahmans' internal religion is a variant of orthodox Brahmanical practices. In contrast to "Sanskritized" Brahmans elsewhere, the Rājopādhyāya Brahmans do eat certain meat, that of the goat and duck, but other kinds of meat and certain foods (such as garlic or mushrooms) are improper for them. They deviate from such Sanskritized Brahmans most markedly because of their participation in the Tantric aspects of Bhaktapur's religion, as we have described in chapter 9. Within their own group the Brahmans must provide their own priests, a situation they share with the lowest *thar*s in Bhaktapur, those below the level that one or another kind of external priest will serve. A Rājopādhyāya Brahman's family priest or *purohita* must be someone who is not a patrilineally linked member of the family, and thus he must be linked through marriage to one of the family's men, with the important exception that the *pāju*, the mother's brothers, or their sons are also not acceptable.

Rājopādhyāya Brahman boys learn Sanskrit, the reading and chanting of the Vedas, traditional philosophical and scriptural aspects of Hinduism, and how to conduct ceremonies and the like from their fathers and uncles, beginning with a three-month orientation instruction at the time of their *Upanayana* initiation to full Brahman status. Until about fifteen years before this study, there was also a special school in Bhaktapur where the Brahman students received extra training in Sanskrit and the Vedas from scholarly teachers. Much of their training came more informally from observations, instructions, and discussion—first on the practice and meaning of the worship that took place in their own houses, and later, after their *Upanayana* initiation, while accompanying and helping their fathers and uncles as they performed ceremonies for others.

The Rājopādhyāya Brahmans have various functions as priests in Bhaktapur. Some are narrowly related to specific client families; others to the religious and symbolic life of the larger civic system. They act as domestic priests, *purohitas*, to a wide span of unequivocally "clean" *thars*; one definition of being fully "clean" is precisely that a Brahman will serve as the *thar*'s family priest. Those *thars* whom the Brahmans will serve as *purohita* are generally those at and above the status level X, in our listing of social levels in chapter 5, that is, from the lowest levels of the Jyāpu *thars* and above. In another socially circumscibed function, they serve the Chathariyā and Pa(n)cthariyā *thars*, as well as other families within the Brahman group, as *gurus* in the transmission of Tantric knowledge and in the conducting of some kinds of Tantric worship.

In addition to these services for client families, the Rājopādhyāya Brahmans have public functions. These include their essential representative position in the city at the summit of the purity-ranked aspect of the status system. In the terms of this system they represent the exemplary highest position. They help define, by means of contrast, king, aristocrats, and technicians of the ordinary, physical world in one kind of opposition, and the maximally impure, the untouchables, in another.

In the course of the public symbolic enactments of the annual festival calendar two major "focal" festivals (as we will call them) have as one central reference the royal palace in association with its temple complex, the king's tutelary goddess Taleju, the Malla king himself (represented by Taleju's chief Brahman), and the king's Rājopādhyāya "*Guru-Purhohita*." The Taleju Brahmans are focal actors in these two major festival sequences Mohanī and Biskā:. In Mohanī Taleju's chief Brahman presides over the sacrifices and the rites that bring the Goddess to her full power at the time of the agricultural harvest for "the protection of the city." In the Brahman's association here with king, palace, and Taleju, he is a focus of attention for the whole city. This royal context of power in a sense protects and isolates him as he represents publicly his role as a priest of the dangerous deities, a role that, as we saw in chapter 9, he usually performs in private arenas.

Some Rājopādhyāya Brahmans work as temple priests, *pūjārīs*, a function that, as we will note below, they share with other kinds of priests. Some also earn part of their living as public storytellers, recounting the stories of the Hindu tradition that form an important interpretive background for many of the city's ritual and festival activities.

In his central roles the Rājopādhyāya Brahman is a complex priest. On the one hand he is the exemplary pure figure of a "Brahmanical religion"; on the other he is the powerful priest of an extramoral religion of power.

LĀKHAE BRAHMANS

There are three or four families in Bhaktapur who have the *thar* name "Rājopādhyāya," but are considered to be of a separate and somewhat lower category. They are referred to as "Lākhae Brahmans," and do not seem to exist in other Newar communities (see chap. 5). They are interpreted in the way that intermediate-level *thar*s are usually interpreted as being the descendants of improper marriages, in this case of a Rājopādhyāya Brahman man to a Rājopādhyāya widow (these widows are not supposed to remarry) or to a previously married but separated Rājopādhyāya woman. The Lākhae cannot marry with the Rājopādhyāya proper and must find wives, with some difficulty, among village Brahman families. Their own priests are the ordinary high-status Rājopādhyāyas. They themselves are family priests for certain of the *thar*s at and just above marginally clean status—the Dwi(n), Nau, Gāthā, and Kau.

BHAKTAPUR'S NON-NEWAR BRAHMANS

As we have noted the Malla kings were said to have brought other Brahmans from India in addition to the Rājopādhyāyas. Since the Malla period there have been two such groups of Brahmans in Bhaktapur, who have lived there in separation from both the Newar Hindu and Buddhist community life. In this they resemble other such cultural isolates in Bhaktapur—the Muslims and the Maṭha priests (chap. 5). These two groups of Brahmans do not consider themselves to be either Newars or Newar priests. They are the Jhā Brahmans (whose family name is "Misra") and the Bhaṭṭa Brahmans. Some Jhā Brahmans work as temple *pūjārī*s and public storytellers in Bhaktapur, but most of them are professional workers in the modern political and economic sector of Bhaktapur and Kathmandu.

The Bhaṭṭa Brahmans, whose origins were in Mahārāṣṭra, are found in many Newar towns and villages. In Bhaktapur most of them are teachers and professionals, while members of some families are temple priests. Some work as *purohita*s for other Bhaṭṭa families. Members of two Bhaṭṭa Brahman families, however, have a closer, and in some respects curious, relation to Bhaktapur's Newar Hindu community life. They act as auxiliary priests to one group of families, a section of the Chathariyā Kāyasṭa *thar* called "Nākanda." In certain Brahman-conducted *pūjā*s held to cure illness or misfortune thought to be due to bad planetary influences, a mixture of different kinds of grain are held to the head of the sufferer. The families in this group then have the option of sending the grain to a Po(n) untouchable so that he may absorb the misfortune (which is what families other than those in this particular group would do) or else to send it along with valuable gifts to a Bhaṭṭa Brahman as an offering, a *dāna*. Although the transaction may be phrased as a gift, a *dāna*, it resembles in nature and function the offerings to lowest-status *thar*s, offerings that signal the inferiority and dependence of those *thar*s, and which serve to transfer pollution, as is suggested in the option of choosing either a Bhaṭṭa or Po(n) here.[10]

This equivalence of Po(n) and Bhaṭṭa Brahman here suggests the polluting implications of many priestly services, and is typical of the situation of the "auxiliary priests," to whom we will now turn.

OVERT AUXILIARY PRIESTS AND PARA-PRIESTS

Rājopādhyāya Brahmans in Bhaktapur in discussions of "religious work" identify a group of "Karmacārī," that is, "workers" or in this context "religious workers," whom we will group as "overt auxiliary priests and para-priests." These make up an important segment of traditional Newar society. Their services as a group are to all the clean or marginally clean segments of that society. They perform services necessary in the performance of various religious rites, and usually do these services for hereditary patrons, *jajamān*s, as the Brahmans themselves do. The various types of Karmacārī listed are all members of *thar*s whose distinguishing traditional and hereditary function are these services even though many of their members now do other things. They perform either priestly functions during the course of rituals, or in the case of the Nau and the Jośi (in their major functions), activities that are preparatory and prerequisite to participation in rituals. The Rājopādhyāya Brahmans often describe those auxiliary priests who perform ritual work (as opposed to the preparatory functions of the "para-priests") as "kinds of Brahmans," and often claim that their powers are, or were originally, passed on to them through Rājopādhyāya Brahmans as the *gurus* who provided esoteric teaching and *mantras*. This group of workers assist the Rājopādhyāya Brahmans in three ways: (1) the preparation for rituals, (2) assistance in doing rituals, and (3) the performance of rituals or aspects of rituals that would be polluting to the Rājopādhyāya Brahmans, and which would compromise their ideal status. We will call this group of religious workers *overt* auxiliary priests, in distinction to the very low polluting *thars*, whose essential priestly function is relatively *covert* and submerged and obscured by the more salient symbolic meanings and actualities of their traditional roles. We also find it useful to distinguish "para-priests" whose functions, in the terminology of the next chapter, are at the margins of the sacred.

JOŚI

There are presently in Bhaktapur two *thars* whose name indicates that their members' traditional professions were astrology. The *thars* and thus their members' surnames are "Jośi" (often written in Newari as "Josi"), a name derived from "astrology," *jyotiṣa* in Sanskrit. One of these *thars* is in the highest segment of the Chathariyā group. The other is at the Pa(n)cthariyā level. As is true of most upper-level *thars*, with the exception of the Brahmans, most members no longer follow traditional occupations. There are, however, a few families at each level, some of whose members perform astrological work for individuals, and who transmit professional knowledge about *jyotiṣa* to new generations within their family. Some families in the Chathariyā group have members who traditionally serve the Taleju temple, working there not specifically as astrologers, but for the most part as assistant priests.[11] As astrologers, the Jośis serve middle-status and upper-status people.[12] They prepare a written record (*jāta:*) of the time of the birth of children, an indication of their relation to the Nine *grāha*, or "Planets," at their birth. The *jāta:* in later life will be used by Jośis in the determination of the proper *sāit*, or astrologically proper time span, within which important activities should be initiated or avoided. The Jośi's advice based on his interpretation of an individual's *jāta:* is of particular importance in the determination of *sāits* for rites of passage and also contributes to judgments regarding proper marriage partners. The Jośi can also advise on procedures for mitigating the ill effects of astrological conditions, and can help supervise the proper ameliorative worship. Finally, Jośis help in determining the proper positioning and timing in propitiating the disturbed local forces when a home, temple, or other building is to be constructed.

Bhaktapur's Jośis make their predictions and decisions for individual clients by comparing the information on an individual's *jāta:* with a *pātra*, an annually published astrological calendar. This generalized calendar, used throughout Nepal, is a reminder, in fact, that the Jośi is concerned with worlds that are beyond Bhaktapur's civic mesocosmic system. He is concerned with the macrocosm represented by the *grāha*s and with the individual microcosm. His function is to adjust those two realms so that the individual starting from his idiosyncratic position is able to periodically realign himself with the macrocosmic forces. In so doing he can then successfully fit into the ongoing moral, social, and religious patterns of Bhaktapur, the middle world properly presided over by the Brahman. The Brahman explains unfortunate events in terms of improper relations to the city's deities, or to bad *karma* caused by some moral error in this life or a previous one. The Jośi ascribes unfortunate events most characteristically to a *dasā*, an astrological condition that can produce good or bad "luck," usually the latter.[13] This luck, being astrologically produced, does not derive *immediately* from moral sources as *bad karma* usually does,[14] nor does it derive from relations to the civic deities.

In his function as an astrologer the Jośi is not, properly speaking, a priest. He puts individuals into a proper relation with a macrocosmic world whose divine representatives, the "astral deities" (chap. 8), have the most minimal meaning as "gods," being rather impersonal forces, and he characteristically does this through advice on timing and choices, which is not "worship" in any sense, not an attempt to influence the divine. He advises corrections and adjustments that allow people to get on with their ordinary lives, one aspect of which is the timing of *pūjā*s and ceremonies, the realm of the true priests. In his rectifying and enabling activities, he is like another "para-priest," the barber, who "mechanically" purifies people in a nonsacred procedure and prepares them for worship. As astrologers, the Jośis do have *secondary* priestly functions. When bad fortune, or the possibility of bad fortune, is produced by a violation of order of certain types—those having to do with some reference to an astral deity, or, in the construction of a house, with the preexisting order of the space around and under the house (symbolized as a disturbance of the supernatural serpents, *nāgas*), the Jośis advise on and often lead special restituting worship. They also act as auxiliary priests in some elaborate Brahman-led ceremonies, such as ceremonies for the cure of illness of high-status clients, and they participate as auxiliary priests to the Brahmans in the major Taleju ceremonies. In such helping roles they are not astrologers, but simply *assistant* priests.

Rājopādhyāya Brahmans claim that Brahmans *could* do astrological work (as they do in many parts of South Asia), but that they "have given this right to the Jośis." Jośis are considered by Rājopādhyāya Brahmans to have been derived by some sort of downfall from the Rājopādhyāya Brahmans.[15] It is pointed out that they belong to the same *gotra* as the Rājopādhyāyas, the Bharadvāja *gotra*. This puts them into a more intimate relation with the Brahmans than some of the other priests who are distinguished as "a kind of Brahman" in terms of their function but not in terms of their descent. The theme of fall in status, for the Jośis from Brahmanical status, recurs in a variety of ways, as we will see, in regard to other auxiliary priests.

ĀCĀJUS

There are in Bhaktapur two *thar*s with the *thar* name Karmācārya, one among the Pa(n)cthar[16] and the other among the Jyāpu. The traditional profession of the men of these *thar*s is as a kind of priest called "Ācāju" in Newari (from the Sanskrit *Ācārya*, "spiritual guide or teacher," plus the Newari honorific particle *ju*). D. R. Regmi, in a discussion of the Jośis and Ācājus in Malla Nepal, gives a useful orienting account of their still persisting functions (1965–1966, part II, p. 715):

> The Ācāju functioned as an inferior priest in all Brahman led households. They accepted *dakṣiṇā* (gifts in money) as well as food in their host's house. . . . But they could not chant the Vedic mantras and also could not conduct the [Vedic] rituals. These were done by the Brahmans alone. The Ācājus and Jośi, however, were indispensable for any ritual. The Jośi was concerned with the task of finding out an auspicious time for any kind of rites to be performed. The Ācāju helped to arrange methodically the requirements of the ritual performance. He prepared the ground work for the actual rite. It was left for the Brahman priest to use them.

As the Jośis, in addition to being assistants to the Brahmans, have their independent function as astrologers, the Ācājus also have an independent function. The Ācāju are Tantric priests in *public* settings. This has lead to an impression in certain accounts of the Newars that only the Ācājus work as Tantric priests and that the Rājopādhyāya Brahmans never do. Like many of the auxiliary priestly performers, they undertake tasks that would be improper for the Brahmans, at some cost in status for themselves. However, in this case it is not the function itself from which the Brahmans are protected, but, as we have discussed in chapter 9 in the Tantric context, its *public* performance. The Ācājus also serve as surrogates for members of upper-status households in Tantric rituals in those cases where household members do not have the proper initiation or, sometimes in recent years, the available time to perform them. They also conduct ordinary Tantric *pūjā*s for their clients. In elaborate rituals with Tantric and sacrificial components (for example, the major rites of passage and rituals for the establishment of a new house), the Ācāju is required, for well-to-do upper-status and middle-status families, at least, as one of the priests in the ceremony. Here he is not only an assistant to the Brahman priest but also (in keeping with the public nature of the sacrifice) the performer of the sacrificial part of the ritual.

Among the Pa(n)cthariyā Karmācāryas there are approximately eight groups, who are differentiated in part according to where in the city they live and according to the particular kind of traditional work that they do. The Jyāpu Karmācāryas are unique in the Jyāpu group in that they, alone, have the right both to wear the sacred thread and to have Tantric initiations and practices. In spite of this they are not ranked in the upper levels of the Jyāpus, and the *thar*s that are in those levels (and cannot wear the sacred thread) will not marry them. When people in the lower levels of the status system were asked to rank Bhaktapur's *thar*s, they usually placed Brahmans, Jośi, and Karmācārya, in that order, at the top, because of their priestly status. In fact, among their peers the Pa(n)cthariyā and Jyāpu Karmācārya both have what would seem to be a more depressed status than their priestly status accords them in the point of view of those well below them.

Like many other kinds of priests, including the Rājopādhyāya Brahmans, members of the Karmācārya families also work as temple priests at many of the city's temples and shrines.

TINI

In Bhaktapur's status hierarchy there is one *thar* placed below the Pa(n)cthariyā level and above the great mass of Jyāpu or farming *thar*s.

This is the Śivācārya ("Ācāriya of Śiva") *thar*, whose members are priests, in Brahmanical phrasing, "a kind of lower Brahman." The priests of these families (and their members in general) are called "Tini."[17] It is said that the Tini exist only in Bhaktapur and in some surrounding villages. In the other Newar cities their special functions are performed by Karmācāryas.[18] In Bhaktapur a Tini priest is required during two important rites of passage. He is necessary for the performance of a purificatory fire ceremony, the *gha:su: jagye* ceremony, among middle and upper *thar*s, performed (depending on the particular *thar*'s customs) on the eleventh or twelfth day after a death (app. 6). The Tini priest makes a fire on the *cheli* of the house. Offerings to the fire are considered as offerings to Śiva (which is sometimes given in partial explanation of the *thar* name of the Tini, "Śivācārya"). In the course of this fire ceremony the Tini makes a meat-containing offering of *samhae* to the fire. It is believed that the smoke of the fire will penetrate the house and drive out the evil influences of illness and death.[19] Members of the family and at least one representative from each household of the extended *phukī* (who have shared in the death pollution) hold their hands over this fire to purify themselves and the members of the households whom they represent. In the course of the *gha:su: jagye* ceremony the Tinis have (in contrast to Karmācārya priests) the right to read verses from the Veda, which they possess in a simplified version in manuscripts passed on in their families. They also have the right to transmit, know, and use Vedic *mantra*s. The other important general community use of the Tini is as one of the necessary assistant priests to the Brahman (the others being Ācājus and Jośis) during the mock-marriage ceremony, the *Ihī* ceremony (app. 6).

The Tinis are the *purohita*s, the family priests, of the families of the Bhā *thar*, a *thar* of borderline clean status, whose members have, as we will see below, their own contaminating priest-like function. In terms of their right to know Vedic *mantra*s and read the Veda, their status, by traditional criteria, would approximate the Brahmans. Tinis are explained as being a "kind of Brahman" probably "fallen" because of some irregular marriage, although in contrast to the Jośis with their Taleju functions, the connection to the Rājopādhyāya Brahmans themselves seems much vaguer. In contrast to the work of the Jośis as astrologers, which Brahmans say that they *could* do but delegate to others, Brahmans say that they themselves could not perform the *gha:su: jagye* ceremony without losing their Brahman status. This is because that ceremony has to do with the removing of pollution, a procedure that always depresses the status of those who do it. This illuminates both the anomalously low status of the Tinis—they are lower than any of the other upper-status sections—Brahmans, Chathariyā, and Pa(n)cthariyā—and their protective or surrogate function for the high-status Rājopādhyāya Brahmans.

PURITY TECHNICIANS WITH LIMITED FUNCTIONS

The four Newar *thar*s we have considered so far—Brahmans, Jośis (in the priestly component of their traditional functions), Ācājus, and Tinis—are "priests" in the sense that they have the legitimate right and proper traditional knowledge to perform services for their clients that mediate for these clients in their relations with deities. Although, as we have argued, their statuses are depressed in their relation to the highest segments of the social hierarchy, their statuses are still high in the larger system and their polluting force and meaning for others is overtly simply the usual relations of higher and lower in the macrostatus system.

There are a number of other *thar*s whose traditional activities are necessary for the religious life of the city—both for that led by priests and for individual or household worship. Some of these are craftsmen, producers of objects necessary in worship. These include the Pu(n), painters of religious images and mask makers; the makers of images in metal (Tama: and the "Buddhist" Śākya), stone (Loha[n]ka:mi) or wood (Ka:mi); the growers of flowers for religious use (Gāthā); and the potters (Kumha:). There are also shopkeepers whose shops sell supplies and equipment necessary for performing *pūjā*s. These craftsmen and suppliers occupy a span of statuses, and are not apparently differentiated from other craftsmen or suppliers—either elevated or depressed in status—because they happen to make or deal with religious objects as one of their services.

There is another group of *thar*s whose status is what we have called "marginally pure"; that is, they are all polluting to the highest *thar*s who will not accept water from them, although the middle groups will. They are in the same level in the macrostatus system (level XIII; see chap. 5), a level that is intermediate between the clearly clean *thar*s above them and the clearly polluting ones below them. There are miscellaneous justifications given for the low status of the various *thar*s in this level. Three of them, however, Bhā, Nau, and Kata:, perform necessary services for higher *thar*s that allow for the restoration of purity or in the case of the Bhā a human form for the soul after death, and in so doing acquire pollution themselves. A fourth, Cālā(n), carrying a torch and a pair of cymbals, walks at the head of funeral procession to warn people because of the danger of crossing in front of it.[20] These four groups are included by Brahman informants as Karmacāri, religious workers in contrast to the craftsmen and suppliers on the one hand, and the lowest *thar*s whose "priestly" functions are covert, on the other. Insofar as they may be defined as *enabling*, through their actions, the ritual states and behaviors presided over by priests, we may call them, as we did the Jośi, "para-priests." In addition to the Bhā, Nau, Kata:, and Cāla(n), there was in the recent past an additional such group in Bhaktapur, the Pasi, whose function was to wash and thus purify the clothes of a family's "chief mourner" on the day of his purification after ten days of ritual mourning (app. 6).[21]

THE BHĀ

The Bhā, or Bhā(n), have the *thar* name "Kārañjit." In the course of death rituals for upper-status *thar*s, during the first ten days following death a Bhā acts as an instructor and assistant to the chief mourner (the *kriyā putra*, usually the oldest son) in a bereaved client household, and constructs some of the objects used during this period (app. 6).[22]

On the tenth day, the final day of the mourning period, the family makes a presentation of substantial gifts to the attending Bhā for the special work he must now do on that day. During the ten days after death the spirit of the dead person, which has been in the dangerous and marginal form of a *preta*, has been forming its "spiritual body" piece by piece in a definite sequence, and by the tenth day that body is completely formed (app. 6). The relation of the Bhā to this formation, and one of the reasons he is given substantial gifts on this day is not discussed publicly, in part to protect the public reputation of contemporary members of the *thar* and thus to ensure that the custom will continue.[23] Chattopadhyay (1923, 468) quotes from Brian Hodgson's early nineteenth-century descriptions of the functions of the various Newar *thar*s that

> The Bhāt [Bha:] are also connected with funerals; they accept the death gifts made on the eleventh [now, for Bhaktapur's upper *thar*s, at least, the tenth] day after the funeral of Newars of any caste (excluding outcastes) [now in Bhaktapur only for Pa(n)cthariyā and above]. In the case of the Kṣatriyas

> [Pa(n)cthariyā and Chathariyā] it is mentioned that a piece of the brain of the deceased is kept covered with sweetmeats, the rest of the body being burnt, and this is eaten by the Bhāt on the eleventh day as he accepts the death gifts.

The death gifts that the Bhā is now given include such substantial items as clothes, shoes, hats, mattresses, kitchen pots, drinking vessels, and substantial quantities of food. The Bhā, it is said, is now often given a bit of ordinary food to eat, rather than a part of the dead body, but this "ordinary food" may, in at least some, perhaps in most, high-status cases, be boiled rice previously touched to a fragment of one of the corpse's bones. This ingestion by the Bhā is said to ensure the *preta*'s eventual reincarnation in a human rather than an animal form. Another possible function (and alternate explanation for the Bhā's action) may be to ensure that the spirit itself has completed its change from *preta* to human-like form (app. 6).[24]

Brahmans say that if a Brahman were to go to the house of a mourner on the tenth day and were to eat anything, or to accept any offering, he would lose his status as a Brahman. In other parts of South Asia, similar ingestion is or was done by a Brahman himself on the death of people of very high status. The Brahman was then very highly compensated, but had then to live in exile outside of the community.[25] The Bhās relieve the Rājopādhyāya Brahmans of such unpleasant responsibilities. The Bhās are said by Rājopādhyāyas to be a fallen Brahman group, and they are, in fact, referred to in some texts as Mahābrāhmaṇa, "Great Brahmans."[26]

THE CĀLA(N)

Members of the Cāla(n) *thar* are placed second in upper-status funeral processions where—carrying a torch in one hand and small cymbals, which they clang together, in the other—they warn people that a funeral procession is coming, and thus prevent them from crossing in front of it at a crossroads, which would produce misfortune for all concerned.

THE KATA:

The traditional function of the Kata: for upper-status families, performed by women of this *thar*, is to cut and tie the umbilical cord after birth, and to remove the polluting placenta and bury it outside of the city boundaries.

THE NAU

The Nau are the barber *thar*. The men of this *thar* work as ordinary barbers, but both the men and women of the *thar* are necessary for the major purification procedures required by the middle-level and upper-level *thar*s following periods of pollution (usually the result of death or births within the *phukī*) or in preparation for some major *pūjā* or rite of passage. The Nau's functions, as we will argue in the next chapter, are outside of the realm of priestly ritual as such. However, they, like those of the other para-priests, belong to the larger symbolic context of purity and impurity within which those rituals exist. The Nau remove impurity as an essential precursor to ritual action.

HINDU USE OF BUDDHIST PRIESTS

The Newar Buddhist Vajrācārya priests have sometimes been referred to as "Buddhist Brahmans" (e.g., Greenwold 1974), but this is misleading. The roles they play within the Newar Buddhist community itself differs from that of the Rājopādhyāya Brahmans for the Hindu community in important respects. The Vajrācāryas perform many of the functions (astrology, Tantric sacrifice, aspects of death ritual, etc.) that the non-Brahman priests and para-priests do in the Newar Hindu system, and they also perform healing procedures done in Hindu Bhaktapur by special *thar*s of healers. The fact that the Vajrācāryas can perform these functions without compromising their status indicates an important difference between the Hindu Newar system and the "Hinduized" Buddhist Newar system. The Hindu Newar opposition and interplay between the traditional system of purity, headed and symbolized by the Brahman in his protected public image on the one hand and the "nonmoral" supernatural transactions, particularly those of the Tantric system, on the other, is blurred in the Newar Buddhist system, altering, among other things, the comparative significance of Newar Buddhist Tantra and of the Newar Buddhist high priests.[27]

There are various ways in which the Vajrācārya participate in the Hindu-centered system. People in the middle and lower *thar*s may use Vajrācāryas as astrologers or healers. Toffin (1984, 230) has reported of Newar communities elsewhere in the Kathmandu Valley that some *thar*s use Vajrācārya priests in the purifying (and contaminating) *gha:su jagye* ceremony to remove the contamination of a death from a house, a ceremony that is performed by Tinis in Bhaktapur. Some *thar*s in Bhaktapur (chap. 5) use Vajrācāryas as family priests, either exclusively, or, in the case of middle-level *thar*s, in some combination with a Brahman *purohita*. These clients include both the more properly "Buddhist" *thar*s and marginally clean *thar*s. Some marginally clean *thar*s are served by the Vajrācāyas as family priests, as others are by Tini and Lākhae Brahmans. This service is, perhaps, in large part, an opportunistic profiting from an economic opportunity left open to Vajrācāryas and these other priestly *thar*s by the purity constraints preventing the Rājopādhyāya Brahmans from working with families below the Jyāpu level.

We must include one residual service of Buddhist priests to Hindu Bhaktapur. An important segment of one of Bhaktapur's major Hindu festivals, the climactic festival of Mohanī, centers around the "living goddess" Kumārī, incarnated in an upper-status Buddhist girl (chap. 15). Certain Vajrācārya priests play a part in the selection and maintenance of that child deity.

COVERT PARA-PRIESTS: THE POLLUTION-ACCUMULATING *THARS*—PO(N) AND JUGĪ

The sector of Bhaktapur's symbolic civic order in which the Brahman has a supreme and ideal position is ordered through the idiom of purity and pollution. The auxiliary priests and para-priests in this system protect the Brahmans' position by performing the polluting and other unseemly actions that the civic ritual system requires. The ritual and enabling functions of these "religious workers" are clear, and centrally define their differentiated traditional *thar* duties. In contrast to this group are those lowest *thar*s in the city, whose polluting power is centrally and obsessively emphasized (see fig. 21). These groups, locally conceived in some contexts as the antithesis of the Brahman, can hardly be conceived of in Bhaktapur as "kinds of Brahmans" and in contrast to the other figures we have been discussing, including the Buddhist Vajrācārya, are not included on Brahmans' lists of "religious workers." Their functions as "religious workers" are ideologically hidden. In an analytic view, however, they are clearly para-priests, essential enablers of ritual action.

It is now widely recognized, following Hocart ([1950] 1960), that an important function of the lower castes is to absorb pollution from the higher ones, and thus to maintain their relative purity and the hierarchical system dependent on it. Hocart notes the remark of a Tamil in-

Figure 21.

formant about the barbers' traditional function in cremations that the barber is "like a priest on the cremation ground." Giving other examples of such funeral functionaries, Hocart concludes, "The barber and the washerman, like the drummers, are not so much technicians as priests of a low grade, performing rites which the high-caste priest will not touch" (ibid., 11). Gould has called the whole class of low-status Śūdra *jātis* "contra-priests." These were the groups "at the bottom of Hindu society who practiced such defiling occupations as washing clothes, barbering, sweeping, removing dead animals, midwifery, and cremating the dead. As it were, they absorbed the defilement in dealing with blood, death, and dirt so that the rest of Hindu society could be free of it and partake of the rituals that prepared the ground for rebirth into ever purer occupational categories" (Gould 1971, 11; see also Gould 1958). Gould notes Dumont and Pocock's remark that what is specifically Indian in the attempt to control defilement is "the employment of specialists who take upon themselves a part of the impurity, and to whom it remains permanently attached" (Dumont and Pocock 1959, 18; quoted in Gould 1971, 12).[28] Such "contra-priests," "by virtue of their specialized ritual functions, live permanently in that state of impurity which they help others to abandon as rapidly as possible" (Dumont and Pocock 1959, 18).

Many of the auxiliary priests and para-priests perform polluting tasks, and this is related to their relatively depressed statuses. The polluting entailments of their tasks are secondary to the importance of those tasks, however, and seldom are salient; they are, in fact, usually muted in public discussions. If their statuses are *relatively* depressed, they are still found in all the clean ranks of the status system. The "impurity" of these people is simply the relative impurity that distinguishes each stratum of the macrostatus system from those above it. But there are some low thars whose "permanent state of impurity" is their major defining characteristic, their most salient meaning to others, and whose priestly functions are secondary or covert.

For all people in Bhaktapur the dramatically polluting *thar*s are represented by two, the Po(n) and the Jugī. There are other low *thar*s that are near them in status. The Nāe, the butchers, are just above the Jugī in status, and in principle almost as polluting, and the remnants of some very low *thar*s—the Do(n), and Kulu—intermediate in status between the Jugī and the Po(n)—are also found in the city. However, these other *thar*s are almost never discussed in talk about the impure. That talk, often full of feeling, focuses on the Jugīs and most emphatically on the

Po(n)s. People are deeply concerned (in ways that will be presented elsewhere) with the conditions of life and the nature of these two groups in an orienting and defining contrast with their own way of life and their own nature.

The Nāes (like the borderline clean *thar*) are unclean because of what they do, the necessary service they perform, namely, killing water buffaloes as the main source of meat not derived from family sacrifices. However, the central service that the Po(n)s (and, secondarily, the Jugīs) perform is to accumulate pollution in particularly dramatic and—for the Po(n)—multiple ways, in short, *to be unclean*. The various polluting services that are assigned to them are in part justifications and attempts at objectification of their theoretical uncleanliness.

The Po(n)s in Bhaktapur have many of the functions that were classically associated with untouchables throughout much of South Asian history. They are fishermen; as the Nāes kill water buffaloes, they kill fish, the fish being (traditionally) bartered and now often sold to other *thar*s for food. The Po(n)s, in Malla times, were executioners, and thus also takers of human as well as animal life.[29] Most saliently now the Po(n) are "sweepers." They clean the streets, which entails the cleaning of much human and animal feces, and they remove excrement from house latrines and from the special fields used in the city for defecation by people without access to latrines. Traditional Indian untouchables, the Caṇḍāla, in addition to being executioners, had "as their main task . . . the carrying and cremation of corpses" (Basham 1967, 146). Bhaktapur's Po(n)s have a narrower funerary function. They must remove the mats and cloths with which bodies are covered during funeral processions from the cremation grounds, after which it is generally believed they use them as ordinary cloths and mats in their houses. As elsewhere in South Asia (e.g., Stevenson, 1920, 352) the Po(n)s are prominent after eclipses, when they go throughout the city receiving alms from anxious householders, thus drawing on themselves the bad influences associated with eclipses. Similarly, as we have noted in conjunction with the Bhaṭṭa Brahman, an offering may be made to a Po(n)—equivalently to the offer to the Bhaṭṭa Brahman—in order to remove astrologically produced misfortune.

The Po(n) have the vital function of making the city's organizing pollution system *real*, in the sense that they bring it into contact at its lowest point with a sensorially accessible world of real pollutants, and with the most dramatic of these, feces. In their degraded conditions of life they also make real the penalties of bad *karma*, and they thus validate the whole system of community *dharma* and help motivate people's adherence to it. Uniquely among the accumulators of pollution the Po(n)s must, as untouchables had to in South Asia since very early times (e.g., Basham 1967, 146), live outside the city, the city boundaries being in part defined by their external residence. In Malla and Rana Nepal they were not supposed to enter the cities after sundown, and there were strict limits on the kinds of houses they could build and clothes they could wear.

The Po(n)s were clearly marked and distinguished as those beyond the community who helped to define that community. However, in contrast to other images of the outside and beyond—other kingdoms, non-Newars, wild beasts—the Po(n)s are integrated into and controlled by the city, they are part of the city system, essential for its symbolic ordering. They belong to the defining, bordering outside. When people variously placed in Bhaktapur's social system talk about the Po(n)s, it is evident that the Po(n)s represent in a fantasy augmented even beyond the unpleasant reality of their condition what would happen if one ceased to follow the sometimes onerous duties and restrictions of the ordinary daily religious and moral code. Life would be disgusting, impoverished, without decency. People sometimes say, "Without the protection of the *dharma* we would all be like Po(n)s." The Po(n)s, in their maximal accumulation of poverty and social disability, represent the realization of the important sanction of the bad rebirth resulting from violations of *dharma*, as well as the "state of nature" resulting from the rejection of social order. While people tolerate and understand and feel helpless to prevent other groups rejecting their traditional stigmatizing *thar* duties, there is widespread and passsionate agreement that the Po(n)s must continue their work, and stay in their proper place. They are (as reflective citizens of the city articulate) as essential to the organized city order as are the Brahmans. Their function in this order is, then, not only in their particular necessary cleaning (and, traditionally, murderous) activities but also in the general meaning, value, and emotion, which accrues to them, which is strongly supported by the realities of their life, and which helps maintain and make sense of the city system. The Po(n)s not only are the "contra-priests" par excellence to the Brahman but also are joined with him in a special segment of Bhaktapur's symbolic order, the realm of the priests and the ordinary civic *dharma*.

"Po(n)," the ordinary term used to refer to this group, has a pejorative quality. The members of the group use the relatively neutral term

"Pore" (in Kathmandu Newari, "Poriyā"; in Nepali, "Poḍe") to refer to themselves. This term is also often used by others alternatively to Po(n). There is, as there is for almost all low *thar*s, an "honorable" and polite term that can be used in reference or in addressing them, namely, Dya:lā. This refers to their activities at the Aṣṭamātṛkā *pīṭha*s outside the city. "*Dya:*" means "deity," and "*lā*" is of uncertain reference for our informants.[30] Members of the Po(n) *thar* are assigned by their *thar* council in rotation to attend the *pīṭha*s, where they gather remnants of food offerings made to the deity and bring them to their households for food. The Po(n)s here, as the Jugīs do for some food offerings within the city (see below), join the other protective absorbers of food offerings to deities that must be discarded—crows, dogs, the goddess of the crossroads or *chwāsa*, and the river. They also have a responsibility for caring for some of the maṇḍalic *pīṭha*s and cleaning them.[31] This has sometimes been interpreted as a duty in which the Po(n) is a guard or a "keeper" (e.g., Manandhar 1976, 222), or even a "priest" (D. R. Regmi 1965–1966, part II, p. 576), but now, at the least, it resembles the Po(n)'s other functions, the cleaning up and absorption of polluted materials.

The Po(n) is a para-priest in that he performs functions that permit the priest's activities, functions that are defined in the religious theory of the city. However, there is a final implication to his role, suggested, for example, by his alliance with the crows, dogs, the goddess of the crossroads, the river, and the Jugī in the absorption and rendering harmless of food offerings. In these functions the dogs and crows are often thought of as quasi-deified agents of Yama, the ruler of the underworld, and the river as the goddess Gaṅga. As some Po(n)s as well as others are aware, the Po(n) is very much like that class of deities who operate outside of the realm of *dharma* and pollution, who operate through power. While degraded in the moral world, there is present in the ideas and emotions about the Po(n) the uneasy sense that he has the power to transcend it.[32]

Inscriptions from the Malla period already indicate the presence of the "Jugīs" in the Kathmandu Valley society. The Jugīs (Kathmandu Newari, Jogi), also known as "Darśaṇdhārī," their *thar* name, and as "Kapālī" and "Kusle,"[33] are believed (by themselves and others) to be descendants of followers of the Nātha *yogi* Gorakhnāth who may have been members of the Kāṇphaṭa *yogic* order (cf. Briggs 1938; Das Gupta 1969, part III).[34] Bhaktapur's Jugīs now consider Gorakhnāth to be their main deity, and their traditions and legends of their ancestry reflect something of these origins. Uniquely among Bhaktapur's Hindus they are not cremated but, in the ideal practice for Hindu renouncers, both men and women are buried in a sitting meditating position. Whatever dim remnants of their traditional practices still remain, they are an important part of Bhaktapur's craft and symbolic organization, and in the latter rank with the Po(n) as obsessively considered examples of pollution. One of their special *thar* professions within Newar society is that of tailors, work generally assigned to groups of very low status in traditional South Asia. They are also the traditional players of a musical instrument of special ritual and festival importance, the *mwāli*, a double-reed instrument closely resembling the medieval shawm.[35]

The Jugī's main traditional function for the city is in connection with the ceremonies that take place at the time of a death and also (depending on the customs and status of the particular *thar*) on the fifth or the seventh day after it.[36] Immediately after death while the body is being prepared in the family house for cremation, clothing is removed from the corpse and is brought, often by a daughter-in-law or a member of the funeral *guthi*, to the neighborhood crossroads, the *chwāsa*. If a person is wearing only a small amount of clothing at the time of death, sometimes another article of his or her clothing is touched to the corpse and then discarded on the *chwāsa*. A man of the Jugī *thar*[37] must go to the *chwāsa* and gather the clothes, presumably for his own family's use. On the fifth or seventh day after death a daughter of the bereaved household who has married out of the household returns. She boils rice on the *cheli* of the house. The rice is divided into three portions and worshiped by the household's chief mourner. One portion is placed under the eaves of the house and is later taken and thrown into the river, a second portion is offered to crows (messengers of the god of death) at the riverside, and a third portion is given to a Jugī, the same one who took the dead person's clothes earlier (see app. 6).

The Jugī's function here is clearly to receive and absorb death pollution and to dispose of problematic materials. As we have emphasized, in contrast to the "enablers of ritual purity" above him, he is, along with the Po(n), a focus for ideas and emotions about polluting *thar*s, whose person and conditions of life are disgusting. Upper-status discourse about pollution discriminates (or did discriminate in the years preceding this study) fine distinctions in the conditions in which Po(n) and Jugī could cause pollution, and the differences in purification procedures required.

The purifying workers above the Jugī and the Po(n) become polluted in the course of other activities. The barber, for example, in his cutting of hair and paring of finger and toe nails, helps separate those parts of the body, leaving the trimmed individual more "pure." The barber's low status is related to this work, but when he has finished, he discards the residues of hair and nails. The Jugīs and Po(n), in distinction, must eat the polluted food that they collect and wear the death clothes. The pollution literally enters their being, accruing directly to their persons in a much more direct way than those above them.[38] They are terminals for pollution.

The contrast between the Jugīs and the Po(n)s, the classical untouchable, is, in part, quantitative—the Po(n) not only absorbs a part of the death pollution in taking the funeral clothes but also executes a wide range of polluting and sinful actions of use to the community. However, there are significant differences other than quantity. The Po(n) must live outside of the city (see map 4), which is an important part of his meaning. The Jugī not only lives within the city, but in contrast to many other groups who live in one or more enclaves in the city, the Jugīs are widely scattered and distributed throughout the city (see map 10). Their contact with the clothes of a corpse is throughout the city at the *chwāsa*s found in all the city's neighborhoods. In their outside/inside contrast the Po(n) and the Jugī reflect a difference we have seen in the placement and uses of the dangerous deities and, most particularly, the stone deities (chaps. 7 and 8). Some of those deities are located close to the outer borders of the city and represent the environing contrasts of the immediate exterior to the internal city as a whole. The *pīṭha*s of the Aṣṭamātṛkās—where the Po(n) are, in fact, Dya:lā—are the main physical representation of these outer deities. The other placement of dangerous deities is within the city as markers and protectors of many of the significant nested spatial units within which moral communities of various kinds—neighborhood, *phukī*, and household—carry on their dharmic moral relations. One of these is the neighborhood *chwāsa*, the site of a goddess who moves pollution out of the area into some other realm, the place where the Jugī collects the death clothes.

The Jugī and the Po(n) also represent the ambiguous similarities and contrasts of the historical renouncer, as the Kānphaṭa Yogis once were, and the outcaste. Both were beyond the civic *dharma*, beyond the differentiating system of pollution and hierarchy. It is not clear to ordinary folks at least (and that includes Bhaktapuṛ's Brahmans in their attitude to visiting Sādhus from India, for example) whether the renouncer, although he "transcended" pollution, might not be polluting to others. At the very least, people say in discussion of this issue, they are—as a result of their way of life—disgusting.

Pō(n) and Jugī draw some of their meaning from groups that were "outside" the dharmic system but in different ways: the Po(n) from the untouchable groups beyond the moral pale of the traditional caste system, who became drawn into intimate and essential relations of service and meaning to it; the Jugīs from the renouncers, who, rooted in the system, went beyond it, becoming ambiguous to those who remained "behind." The echos of these two contrasts to the city's ordinary citizens may be found in their contemporary similarities and contrasts.

The Jugīs' main sources of income are as tailors and as musicians, playing instruments and music that are their *thar* specialties. Some families specialize in one or the other activity. Within the civic religious sphere the Jugīs have *thar* rights and duties that are in contrast to their role as collectors and exemplars of pollution. The Jugīs are thought to have their own Tantric tradition, knowledge, and initiation,[39] and each year during a certain period (chap. 13) one Jugī dons a bone apron associated with Tantric "magicians" (both among the Newars and in Tibet) and walks around Bhaktapur accepting offerings and prayers as an incarnation of Śiva as Mahādeva. Like the stone deities who accumulate and destroy pollution (among whom is the *chwāsa* itself), the Jugī has the power to transcend the effect of pollution, and thus the system of ordinary *dharma*. At its lowest point, untouchable and renouncer become joined with king and Kṣatriyas in opposition to those trapped in the interdependencies of the city.

TEMPLE AND SHRINE PRIESTS

At the time of this study there were approximately 119 temples and shrines in active use in the Newar Hindu system throughout the city.[40] Thirty-five of these had no attending priests. The others had priestly attendants, *pūjārīs*, whose duty, for the most part, is to worship the deity twice a day, in the morning and the evening. Those temples whose deity may be the focus of an annual festival (chaps. 12–16) will have an additional image, a *jātrā* image, which may be carried in a festival procession or otherwise shown to the public by the *pūjārī*. In the larger temples, above all in the Taleju temple, there may be a staff of priests with more elaborate responsibilities.

At the time of the study the *pūjārīs* included twenty-four Rājopādhyāya Brahmans, one Lākhae Brahman, twenty-one Jhā Brahmans, two Bhaṭṭa Brahmans, thirty-six Karmācāryas, and one Shaivite ascetic.[41] The Karmācāryas are *pūjārī*s at those temples where blood sacrifice is required—the temples of Gaṇeśa, and the temples and god-houses of the dangerous deities. The other *pūjārī*s serve the temples and shrines of the various benign deities in a seemingly random way as far as their relations to particular deities are concerned. The relations of particular priests to particular temples is a matter of the history of each temple—who built it, and for what purposes, and what happened subsequently. Shrines and temples built by the Mallas or Chathariyā often have Rājopādhyāya *pūjārī*s, even if they are now of minor use. Some temples reportedly had Rājopādhyāya *pūjārī*s in the past, but as relations with patrons and the economic desirability of the position changed, were given over to one of the other groups. Some other temples were built by farming-level *thar*s, notably the Kumha:, the potters, and had Jhā *pūjārī*s from the time of their establishment. Most of the temples with Jhā *pūjārī*s are minor ones whose deities do not have *jātrā*s. The most important temple they officiate at is the Dattātreya Temple, whose major importance is as a pilgrimage site for non-Newar Hindu pilgrims. The Rājopādhyāya Brahmans, although they serve many presently unimportant temples of the benign deities, still also serve most of the important ones—important in terms of either the status of their builders or their ongoing city-wide importance.

SOME REMARKS ON THE STATUS OF THE RĀJOPĀDHYĀYA BRAHMAN IN BHAKTAPUR

For Newar Hindu Bhaktapur, the Rājopādhyāya Brahman is *the* Brahman. Other priests, including other kinds of Brahmans, serve to enable his functions in one way or another, and to protect his status. Most of these other priests and priest-like figures protect the Brahman's status by performing necessary services for the management of pollution and thus the restoration or protection of "ritual purity" (chap. 11). One priest, the Tantric Ācāju, also protects the Brahman's status, but in this case not directly from pollution itself, but rather from the publicly visible performance of the morally equivocal act of blood sacrifice, an act that is permissible in esoteric Tantric contexts but not in public contexts where the Brahman must be the exemplary priest of the ordinary, purity-based dharmic civic system.

The civic elaboration of auxiliary and para-priests, both overt and covert ones, is derived in part from the Brahman's vulnerability to impurity. This vulnerability is reflected in an ambiguity and ambivalence regarding the Brahman's status both in his own view and the views of others, particularly upper-status people.

Lynn Bennett makes an observation about Indo-Nepalese Brahmans, which describes what is also a widespread South Asian pattern. When Indo-Nepalese Brahmans become economically and politically powerful, they "tend to give up their priestly work. They expressed the view that accepting *dāna* and *dakṣiṇā* [as *purohitas*] was somehow demeaning, like accepting charity" (1983, 251n.). It has been argued (and debated) that the acceptance of *dāna*, a gift, is more demeaning or problematic than the acceptance of the ritually prescribed routine "offering" of *dakṣiṇā* (see discussion and references in Fuller [1984, chap. 3]). Whatever the problems of the *purohita*, the salaried temple priest had, in other parts of South Asia, even lower status among Brahmans themselves. As Stevenson wrote of Kāṭhiāwār, although a temple priest in a big temple might become a wealthy man, "because he takes pay, he is not held in high esteem by other Brahmans" (1920, 377).

The reason why the *dāna* or *dakṣiṇā* may somehow compromise the Brahman is variously explained. Receiving payment for a service implies servitude. And what the Brahman may be paid for may be thought of as including the removal from the client of some substance-like sin and impurity, as well as simply guiding the client in that removal. This implication is clear in similar gifts elsewhere within the Brahman's realm. Why the Brahman is, or should be, somehow impervious to this is the subject of much Hindu apologetics.

All this has been taken to be problematic for statements that associate the Brahmans, "supreme rank" with their priestly function.[42] "For Brahmans themselves, as well as in the Brahmanical tradition as elaborated in the classical texts, the general notion is that priestly Brahman subcastes rank below non-priestly Brahman subcastes, and that Brahman individuals or families engaged in the priesthood are considered demeaned or degraded by their caste-fellows who are not" (Fuller 1984, 49). The argument (summarized in Fuller [1984, 62ff.]) is that Brahmans represent an *ideal* of purity that is, in fact, compromised by their priesthood, that the Brahman as priest is in a paradoxical position.

In Bhaktapur the Brahman cannot escape his priestly functions. The Rājopādhyāya Brahman, proud of his aristocratic historical alliance with royal power, boasts of his commitment and restriction to priestly work in contrast to non-Newar Brahmans. In a traditional community such as Bhaktapur the Brahman *must* fulfill his priestly responsibilities, although when conditions change, motivated by the contradictions in his role he may try to escape them. But within that traditional context, in Bhaktapur's version of a climax Hindu community, the ambiguities and paradoxes in the Brahman's role help generate an elaborate system of social roles and of complex actions, ideas, evaluations, and symbols that are the very stuff of traditional Hinduism.

CHAPTER ELEVEN

Purity and Impurity: On the Borders of the Sacred

INTRODUCTION

In our discussion of space, deities, Tantrism, and priests we have been concerned with elements of civic symbolic action in what we may as well call the "religious sphere" of Bhaktapur's life. In later chapters, adding time to these other elements, we will examine the city's integrated "symbolic enactments." The symbolic elements and enactments we are concerned with are for the most part, as we have asserted in chapter 1, "marked" in Bhaktapur as being extraordinary, somehow different from the banal, the "natural," the everyday. The dangerous and benign deities are creatures of that marked realm. In their proper homelands they inhabit mythic and transcendent space and time. Occasionally—and this is a major motif of many legends associated with annual festivals—they appear and wander in this world as ambiguous and uncanny violations of the ordinary, in historic encounters with kings and heroic citizens that have enduring significance for the city. In the ongoing civic actions in which the deities are encouraged to become immanent, and where they are repeatedly encountered by all of Bhaktapur's people, however, a separated arena is constructed for them, the arena of the "sacred." That arena's proper spaces are the temple or shrine, the purified, bounded, and isolated *pūjā* areas in houses, the ideal spaces of the city carved out through the positions and festival movements of the deities; its expert workers are the priests; its time is the calendrically determined eternally recurring times of festival or that of rites of passage or of crisis-generated or prophylactic *ad hoc* worship; and its proper action is in ritual and the traditionally specified actions of the festivals.

But there is much activity at the margins of this sacred arena. There are things that must be done to prepare sacred objects and officiants and to prepare the worshipers themselves. Thus, icons of the deities must be properly made; sacred force or "life," as it is often phrased, must be put into them, the deity himself or herself must periodically be brought into them, ritually pure areas must be prepared for their worship, new temples must be consecrated, and so on.

We have differentiated "priestly" from "para-priestly" activities by differentiating the performance of a "religious" activity in itself from the necessary preparations for such an activity. Among the para-priests, so defined, we included the Naus, the members of the barber *thar*, one of whose traditional duties was to aid in what is sometimes (and we will argue misleadingly) called "ritual purification"—for the act of purification, in which for middle and upper *thar*s the Naus are of major importance, is not within the sacred realm but within the realm of the ordinary. The ordinary has its own symbolic construction, its "embedded symbolism," but that symbolism, in contrast to the marked realms, is naturalized as part of the locally constructed common sense everyday world.

In this chapter we will discuss purity, impurity, contamination, and purification as aspects of Bhaktapur's "natural" world in their relation to the expression, ordering, and motivation of that city's mesocosmic symbolic order. Essentially, their meaning and use among the Newars in Bhaktapur is no different from those in traditional Hindu societies elsewhere in space and time. Relative purity is related to hierarchical social ordering; some impurity is or is made to seem unalterable, and some may be rectified through purification, thereby supporting the order associated with purity and/or preparing individuals for ritual action. Various attempts have been made to define the central or "essential" import of purity, impurity, and purification in their South Asian elaborations, and the result is a tangle of interpretations. But we may use Bhaktapur's "climax community" and our particular approach to it to encounter some of these and to make some discriminations regarding the power, uses, and limitations of the "purity complex" in Bhaktapur's public and private worlds.

A TANGLE OF INTERPRETATIONS

Bhaktapur has inherited in one form or another most of the concerns and ideas about purity set forth in the Hindu codes for proper behavior, the *Dharmaśāstras*. The subject is, on the surface at least, diverse. "*Śuddhi* (purification) is a very comprehensive topic including within it purification after *āśauca* (impurity on birth and death), purification of a person after contact with an impure object or on account of certain occurrences, purification of pots, wells, food, etc., after they are polluted" (Kane 1968–1977, vol. IV, p. 267). Because among these, birth and death pollution make their carriers unfit for most worship and were traditionally "the most important subject under *śuddhi* . . . therefore the Śuddhi-kaumudī defines *śuddhi* as the state of being fit for or capable of performing the rites that are understood from the Veda" (vol. IV, p. 267). The *Śastras* also refer to the impurities accrued by contact with the lowest social classes (included along with a multitude of other pollutants) and differentiate the required actions and tempos of purification by hierarchical social status, thus taking account of a "caste-differentiating pollution."

Anthropologists concerned with social structure and organization have selectively treated the complex of purity, impurity, and purification (which we may term the "purity complex") in its external relation to caste segmentation and hierarchy. Dumont, in an influential statement, argued that the opposition between "pure" and "impure" gives the caste system its "intellectual coherence." The opposition is the "single true principle" that underlies those features, which Bouglé's classic formulation (1908) proposed as the "essence" of caste, but which for Dumont are "analytic distinctions introduced by the observer" (Dumont 1980, 43). "It is by implicit reference to this opposition that the society of castes *appears consistent and rational to those who live in it*. The opposition underlies hierarchy, which is the superiority of the pure to the impure, underlies separation because the pure and the impure must be kept separate, and underlies the division of labor because pure and impure occupations must likewise be kept separate" (ibid., 43 [emphasis added]). Dumont's phrasing—"intellectual coherence," "consistant and rational" appearance, and the like—allows him to avoid giving any precise explanatory force to this intellectually satisfying opposition of pure and impure in the origin or, more relevant to our purposes, maintenance of caste.

Other writers, still centrally concerned on the one hand with Hinduism's exotic social order and on the other with an intellectualistic and cognitive approach to purity and impurity, emphasize the semantic or metaphorical force of purity and impurity: "Physiological pollutions become important as symbolic expressions of other undesirable contacts which would have repercussions on the structure of social or cosmological ideas" (Douglas 1968, 340). "Caste pollution," which is a special case, "is a symbolic system, based on the image of the body, whose primary concern is the ordering of a social hierarchy" (Douglas 1966, 125). For Douglas "pollution is the symbolic expression of an intellectual problem." She suggests that "we treat *all* pollution behavior as the reaction to *any* event likely to confuse or contradict cherished classifications" (1968, 338 [emphasis added]). Purity keeps categories separated; in the Hindu case, hierarchically ordered categories. Impurity is the blurring and the threatened collapse of categories.

One problem for Douglas's formulation is that although the blurring of any category is by definition problematic for order, "pollution" in its restricted sense of "dirtiness," as suggested by "physiological pollutions," applies only to *some* cases of the confusion of "cherished classifications." The problems, metaphors, uses, and rectifications of some other categories of confusion are quite different. Veena Das, following Douglas in asserting that "the symbolism of impurity serves basically as a metaphor for liminality" (1977, 115), makes one necessary (and fundamental) distinction. "Liminality" in Hindu social organization is not only the blurred, unpleasant, and polluting mess of contaminated social differentiation; it also represents the "creative transcendence" of the given categories of the social system, as in the religious life of Hindu ascetics. Here liminality and the destruction of "cherished classifications" results in a "transcendence" in which the purity complex is no longer an issue.[1]

Transcendence aside, "liminality," the state of being out of ordinary social categories, is not sufficient in itself to characterize (or explain) impurity. In certain liminal states, such as the early stages of rites of passages, individuals are in heightened states of purity, not in impurity. More problematically, as we have argued, only some *kinds* of confusion or collapse of categories are "polluting." If "pollution" is not to be endlessly extended in metaphor, many states of confusion, liminality, or mixture are neither pure, impure, nor "transcendent." The question of what *kinds* of confusion, of *what* kinds of "cherished classifications" is still open.

The escape from or blurring of social categories has another powerful metaphoric implication. "To have been in the margins is to have been in contact with danger, to have been at a source of power" (Douglas 1966, 97).[2] Bhaktapur uses the different implications of the delineation and blurring of categories—purity and safety, impurity and danger, membership in the ordinary system of social categories or transcendence of it—in a differentiated way, isolating various implications of categorization for complex differentiated meanings and uses. The purity complex has its meaningful position in this larger context.

Various positions have been taken about the relations of the purity complex to the religious and sacred spheres of South Asian and other societies. Here much depends on the definition of "religious" and "sacred," but we are again in a tangle of assumptions and pronouncements. Thus Dumont proclaims flatly that "in reality, even though the notion [impurity] may be found to contain hygienic associations, these cannot account for it, as it is a *religious* notion" (1980, 47 [emphasis added]). Srinivas (1952) similarly ascribes impurity to the realm of the "sacred," albeit the "bad sacred" in opposition to the "good sacred." Such statements reflect the attempts made by such earlier social theorists as William Robertson Smith ([1889] 1927) and James Frazer ([1890] 1955) to include ideas regarding pollution and ideas about the sacred together within some larger encompassing "supernatural" realm to which the two sets of ideas were thought to belong.[3] The claim that pollution and purity—that is, the aspects of pollution and purity that were of interest to these theorists—are within a "religious" or a "sacred" or a "supernatural" sphere encourages the implication that their manipulation through purification is a ritual act. Thus Sherry Ortner writes in an article summarizing the literature on the sociocultural aspects of pollution beliefs and practices in various cultures, "Because lost purity can be re-established *only by ritual* and also because purity is often a precondition for the performance of rituals of many kinds, anthropologists refer to this general field of cultural phenomena as 'ritual purity' and 'ritual pollution'" (1974, 299 [emphasis added]). The procedures used to "reestablish lost purity" in Bhaktapur are conventional but hardly rituals. Furthermore, although purification procedures are in a *general* sense "preconditions for rituals" in that a person has to be pure to participate in some (but by no means all) religious action,[4] in some cases purification is a direct and immediate preparation for important rituals, while in other cases the *immediate* motivation is to free people from the general social restrictions of birth and death impurity, or to remove the contamination produced by contact with a member of a low *thar*. Such purification is necessary for the eventual later performance of rituals, but is not directed toward a particular one. Later ritual performances will, in fact, require, in addition, the specific purification that always proceeds such rituals.

WHAT IS POLLUTED, AND WHAT IS POLLUTING?

The Śāstras traditionally treated polluted human bodies and polluted inanimate objects separately.[5] There were proper cleansing procedures of various types for purifying objects; the proper procedure depended on the object or material that was to be purified. Ashes, soil of various kinds and water were the main purifying materials. Various other materials (mustard-seed paste, ground-up fruit, cows' urine and dung, whitewash, etc.) were also used for cleaning certain polluted materials (*Manu* V, 110–126; Bühler 1969, 188–191). The materials and objects whose purification are discussed in the Śāstras are the materials and objects of everyday life—worked metal, stone and clay, cloth of various kinds, foodstuffs, houses, land, vessels for holding food and liquids, spoons, cups and so on. These are the materials and objects that are the unavoidable context of life, which must be touched, which envelop the body, which are foods, or which hold the foods that must enter the body through the mouth. Their purification is prophylactic, at the service of a central concern—the protection of the condition of the individuals that these objects and materials surround and with whom they may come in contact. The cleaning procedures are technically specified. "A man who knows (the law) must purify conch-shells, horn, bone and ivory like linen cloth (i.e., with mustard-seed paste) or with a mixture of cow's urine and water." This is all technical, mechanical, and mundane, whatever its distal religious justification might be. These materials and objects are in that segment of a person's world that the concerned person can control; they are extensions of his or her self, his or her body, and can be purified like the body itself. The impurities that threaten from outside this easily controllable circle of possessions can be produced by animals, by events (above all, birth and death of family members), or by other persons (above all, by those of lower and low status). These agents of pollution cannot be purified by scrubbing with an appropriate cleansing agent. Sources of pollution must be avoided if possible, but in those cases where avoidance fails or where they cannot be avoided, then procedures for purfication of the *self* become essential.

For objects and materials impurity is something that adheres to them, like the physical "dirt" that is one of the sources of the idea, and can be scrubbed off or (in the case of liquids) removed by filtration. The nature of the impurity produced by birth and death is more problematic; we will return to this. But what about the person who is concerned about the problem of pollution? *What* becomes polluted? *Where* does his or her pollution exist?

According to Kane, many Śāstras differentiated "body" impurity into "external" and "inner" kinds (1968–1977, vol. IV, p. 310). The "inner purity" refers to the "mental attitude." For some commentators the inner "mental attitude" was more significant than "external purity." Kane states: "The Padma emphasizes that it is the mental attitude that is the highest thing and illustrates it by saying that a woman embraces her son and her husband with different mental states" (ibid., 310). *Manu's Laws* include references to this mental or spiritual purity. "Among all modes of purification, purity in the acquisition of wealth is declared to be the best; for he is pure who gains wealth with clean hands, not he who purifies himself with earth and water." "The body is cleansed by water, the internal organ is purified by truthfulness, the individual soul by sacred learning and austerities, the intellect by knowledge" (*Manu* V, 106, 109; Bühler 1969, 187f.).

The reference to "inner impurity" seems to be a "philosophical" extension. The major traditional emphasis, and the present emphasis in Bhaktapur is on the "external impurity." In relation to the organization of a community such as Bhaktapur, a primary emphasis on internal purity and impurity would, in fact, have a revolutionary implication. Like Bhakti religion, it represents the possibility of a detachment from and transcendence of the network of the interrelational controls of the civic *dharma*, a kind of movement to a direct, individual, "Protestant," encounter with an altered view of the divine, an escape from the control of the Brahmanical mesocosm.[6] A Newar Brahman, queried, for example, as to what is affected when an individual is impure (*aśuddha*) replies that it is the *mhā*, the physical body. The *ātma*, the soul, he says, cannot be affected, it is always pure. Asked about the *manas*, the "mind," he says that mind is not affected directly when a person is *aśuddha*—although it is affected indirectly insofar as a person is concerned about his state.

The body and its "physical impurities" is also an important reference in the traditional explanation of the sequence of rites of passage, *saṃskāras*, which entail, among much else, the progressive transformation of individuals to higher and purer states throughout their life. "Manu says, 'By performing the Saṃskāras [those dealing with] conception, birth-rites, tonsure, and Upanayana [full initiation into his caste group for a male], seminal and uterine impurities are washed away, . . . Yājña-valkya also endorses the same view. Some kind of impurity was attached to the physical side of procreation and lying in the womb. Therefore, it was thought necessary to remove that impurity from the body by performing various Saṃskāras" (Pandey 1969, 29f.).

Bodily pollution is usually thought of as "external," in part because of its contrast with "internal mental pollution," and also because of the emphasis on the surfaces of bodies and of objects to which impurity adheres and that can be purified by washing, scrubbing, and so forth. But bodily pollution itself can be "external" or "internal." The implications of external or surface and internal bodily pollution for any given individual differ. The external surface pollution has to do with an individual's presentation of self, his or her social meaning, as mediated by the elaborate uses the city makes of pollution as a condition for proper relations and social position. The internal aspect of pollution relates in part to the meanings of one's status and the threats to it, but here something else is added; namely, the meanings of the oral incorporation, the ingestion of pollution. These meanings, associated with feelings of abhorrence and disgust, not only help motivate adherence to the public system of relations ordered by purity but also add important aspects of "intellectual coherence" to it.

POLLUTION, INGESTION, AND DISGUST

In an attempt to differentiate the meaning of pollution to Hindus from other kinds of "dangerous contact" as conceived elsewhere, Louis Dumont argues for an "essential difference between the Indian and the tribal case. Elsewhere, the dangerous contact acts directly on the person involved, affecting his health for example, whereas with the Hindus it is a matter of impurity, that is, of fall in social status or risk of such a fall. This is quite different, although traces of the other conception can be found in India" (1980, 49). This assertion, tacitly based on and restricted to surface pollution, is misleading in its claim that impurity "does not act directly on the person involved." It is also misleading insofar as it treats the implications of Hindu impurity of interest to Dumont, the risk of fall in status, as the predominant personal motivation for behavior in relation to purity and impurity. Although Hindu pollution may differ from "tribal" forms (such as the Polynesian fear of contact with a superior's *mana*, which is dangerous to one's physical state but not "polluting" in the Hindu sense) it acts very powerfully and directly on the "person involved," and does so in ways independent of and prior to the risk to status.

Pollution takes its meaning from the kind of contamination involved, a distinction blurred by structuralist attempts to put all contaminations in the same class. There is a difference in the personal meanings of swallowing, say, ground glass and swallowing feces, or contemplating food "contaminated" by one or the other. Both are "contaminating"; both are "matter out of place" (Mary Douglas's definition of "dirt"). However, glass is dangerous and is a "clean contaminant," while feces are disgusting and a "dirty contaminant." Similarly, someone whose body, self, or mind is disturbed by the adherence or entrance of such "contaminants" as a spirit, or disease, or "sin" is affected by something that we may designate by the oxymoron "clean contaminant."[7] Clean contaminations in Bhaktapur have explanations, induce emotional responses, and call for techniques of rectification, all of which differ from those associated with pollution in its usual sense. The usual designation for someone who is polluted through "dirty contaminants" and who needs one of the sorts of purification used in such cases is that he or she is "not *pure*," *asudha* (Sanskrit *aśuddha*). This term rarely is used for the other, the "clean contaminations," except occasionally in a rare metaphorical extension. The emphasis on being touched by "dirt," and above all by ingesting it, is precisely what gives the socially elaborated pollution beliefs their compelling special personal force, a force that is both emotional and conceptual.

According to some Newar Brahmans from the point of view of traditional law, the *dharma*, it is permissible for a high-caste person to accept water from wandering ascetics. It is, they say, nevertheless, a disgusting prospect. Private feelings and dharmic revelations usually converge, however; the case of the ascetic is an interesting and illuminating exception.

The impurity that may derive from birth and death, and from contaminated things, animals, or other people, and which then can affect one's body (and, secondarily and in varying ways, one's status) in an unpleasant way, is conceived and dealt with as if it were a transferable substance of some kind, which can adhere to the body or some intermediate object, which can be often conducted through or flow through some intermediary object, and which can be removed through physical cleansing procedures. Pigs, nondomesticated carrion and feces-eating dogs, feces, clothes that have been in contact with a sick or dead body, and food that has been in contact with the saliva of others, are salient examples of sources of pollution that are both dharmically impure and *sensed* as repulsive. Other ideas about pollution, such as birth and death pollution, whose polluting substance is puzzling to contemporary informants, are intellectually associated (with more or less conviction) with ideas and feelings aroused by such directly disgusting and repulsive substances.

The "elementary" experience of dirtiness is vividly conveyed in traditional writings on pollution and its removal. "Food which has been pecked at by birds, smelt at by cows, touched with the foot, sneezed on, or defiled by hair or insects, becomes pure by scattering earth over it." "As long as the foul smell does not leave an object defiled by impure substances, and the stain caused by them does not disappear, so long must earth and water be applied in cleansing inanimate things" (*Manu* V, 125, 126; Bühler 1969, 190f.). Much of classical and contemporary discussions of pollution centers around foodstuff, and the possibility of ingesting polluted substances in contaminated food or drink. Here the powerful emotion of *disgust* in its core sense of "strong distaste for food or drink, nausea, loathing," becomes centrally salient.

The status-regulating aspects of purity and pollution are clearly related to eating, to food, and thus to the possibility of ingestion of pollution. To be touched by a polluting person *while eating* requires a higher degree of purification (for an upper-status person) than simply being touched, and prohibitions about contact with inferiors are connected with an elaborate doctrine about the various kinds of food (which have different vulnerabilities and resistances to pollution) that may or may not be accepted from them. Thus, foods, particularly boiled rice, are central markers of hierarchy, of social exclusion, and inclusion. If a high-status person is polluted through contacts with a low-status person or a contaminated object, purification must be accomplished before the ingestion of any further food. Even without special contamination, the failure to wash before a meal (on the assumption that one has inevitably incurred some kind of impurity) is a *pāpa* or "sin." An insistence that they must now wash before eating is one of the relatively few abrupt changes required of boys who have undergone their *Kaetā Pūjā*, their movement into full ritual membership in their *thar*s.

The idea of disgusting substances that would be repellent to the body if ingested has an inverse, palatability, which implies and depends on the absence or the overcoming of disgust. Bhaktapur's entire status system—that of both the city and the family hierarchy (chaps. 5 and 6)—is, typically of South Asia, conceptualized and acted out in the rules and practices related to *cipa*, food that has been touched by someone else. It is considered proper to take *cipa* from superiors, but if taken from someone of lower status, the idea of ingestion of dirt becomes salient. Ideally this ingestion of *cipa* signals the acceptance of a protected incorporation and dependency in the organic system of hierarchy. The inferior takes of the substance of superiors as a baby takes its mother's milk. However, the ideologically suppressed contaminating and status-depressing implications of the acceptance and ingestion of the superior's substance, represented by vulnerable food such as boiled rice touched by him in the act of eating is perfectly clear to the lowest *thar*s, at least, who are frequently aware of such usually covert aspects of the hierarchical system. As an untouchable Po(n) put it, "*Cipa* is dirtier than feces. . . . When we hear that the *sahu* [merchants] have a feast we *Po(n)*, we poor people who have nothing to eat, go to the houses of our own patrons, and take their *cipa*, the food that has come out of their mouths, their leftover food. They collect the leftover food after they have eaten and give it to us. While they ate they mixed everything by hand, and when they chew the food they drop some of the food from their mouth. They mix and gather that kind of food for us, and we have to eat it. It may even have been on the floor. Their thrown away things are our meal, in which we get dust and hair, and everything. The main point is that we eat dirty food."

The Po(n) is expressing an implication of the flow of *cipa* down the system, which is usually muted. But he is consciously or unconsciously satirizing the conception that is associated with the prohibitions about the flow of foodstuffs, of *cipa*, in the reverse, the upward direction. What he describes as the disgusting characteristics of the food he takes from his superiors is, albeit here in broad overtness, what everyone fears—including, by the way, the Po(n) himself in relation to his inferiors, the Cyāmākhala:—may characterize vulnerable food touched by inferiors.

The lowest *thar*s stand for pollution, and are its concrete manifestation. The pollution of low *jāti*s is sometimes described in the literature as being a "kind of inherited defilement" (e.g., Kolenda 1978, 65), often thought to be the result of some ancestral member's sinful behavior in the legendary past. This produces a kind of permanent pollution in contrast to the temporary pollution acquired, for example, following the death of a *phukī* member or the contamination due to encounters with an impure person or object. Yet, whatever karmic theory—made use of in Bhaktapur for certain important but delimited purposes—may argue, in most discussions of the lowest levels both by members of higher *thar*s and by members of the unclean *thar*s themselves, their lower status is explained not in terms of their history or *karmic* state, but of their various *ongoing* pollution-accumulating behaviors.[8] Pollution-accumulating activities—such as by the Po(n) and Jugī in relation to death, by the Po(n) in relation to human and animal feces, by the Nāe butcher in relation to killing animals for meat, by the Nau barber in cleaning bodies, and so on—not only keep higher *thar*s clean (and as such are "para-priestly" services) but also ensure, in conjunction with other regulations that once controlled their living places, dress, their possible accumulation of capital, their access to other kinds of work and so on, that their dirtiness, disgusting qualities, and pollution will be continually maintained and thus *real in the natural world*, as that world is understood in Bhaktapur. "Inherited substance," an idea that suggests racial theories of status insofar as the resulting social position is thought to be based on some permanent inherited substance, is misleading insofar as it does not take into account the overwhelming importance of continuing action in generating and maintaining the impurity of the unclean *thar*s. The continued performance of degrading action is ensured by the vigilance and application of sanctions by the middle and upper *thar*s.

BODIES AND CORPORATE BODIES AND THEIR EXUVIAE

Erudite Hindus in Bhaktapur, like other such Hindus elsewhere, frequently use the classically rooted metaphor of a human body and its component organs and members for the interrelated, interdependent, and hierarchically arranged elements of the social system. Another, more covert and less idyllic model of the body may be discerned, one that has both social and private symbolic force. The *cipa* system, with its unidirectional flow, suggests this. In this model one belongs to the group whose food can be unproblematically shared. In some cases these are groups of relative equals, but as a member of the larger city social hierarchy, one can share the food of all above oneself, and belongs to an upper segment of the hierarchy, while one is at the lowest position within the segment. The food of the upper segment, so to speak, flows into, and succors the individual. One accepts not only succorance, but in respecting these upper groups, accepts their authority. One is a member of such a group in an intimate way, a way having some metaphorical resonance with the idea of palatability of food and the sense of one's own body boundaries.

Vulnerable food from people below an individual is forbidden, and becomes more and more clearly disgusting as the social distance increases and the bottom of the system is approached. The separation between an individual and these lower-status people is not mutual, however. They accept the upper-status person's *cipa*, or leavings—and are theoretically sustained by them (if covertly degraded)—but he or she would not take theirs. There is a *valve* in the system, sustenance, and—when things are working properly—pollution only flow downward.

If the incorporation of food into the body represents and enacts solidarity with the upper segment to which one belongs, the casting off of exuviae from the body represents not only a social opposition but a rejection of aspects of one's own self represented in the meanings given to the lower segments of the status system. Exuviae are "caste-off" bodily materials that are unproblematic while they are parts of the body but that are thought and felt to be more or less polluting and disgusting (as well as dangerous objects for the performance of "contagious magic" in some cultures) once they separate from the body. Newar Brahmans provide lists of polluting exuviae (including materials such as "dirt" on the teeth and the umbilicus, which seem closely related to the idea of exuviae) for which they use the Sanskrit word "*mala*," "dirt, bodily excretion." These include spittle, nasal mucus, feces, urine, dirt on the teeth, ear wax, dirt in the umbilicus, and in some contexts finger and toe nails and hair. Nails may be considered polluting where they separate from the underlying skin at the ends of the fingers. A similar list in *Manu* (V, 135; Bühler 1969, 193) of the "twelve impurities of the body" does not include hair or finger nails, materials that can, in fact, be considered peripheral but integral parts of the body, and which are important foci of major purification procedures in the course of which they are trimmed.[9] Hair and fingernails are detachable, rather than detached, and are not offensive in their attached state (unless they harbor dirt and are allowed to grow beyond a certain length, as in the case of ascetics).

Exuviae are not problematic or disgusting while they are parts of one's own body. They become problematic when they appear at the surface, characteristically at the exit of bodily orifices. Cleanliness consists of separating such materials from the surface, and once separated, they are alien and usually become disgusting; that is, there is a deeply felt disinclination to bring them into new contact with the body, and above all to ingest them.

WHAT IS POLLUTED AND POLLUTING IN BIRTH AND DEATH?

The emphasis on dirt and cleanliness, on disgust and palatability, and on the boundaries of bodies—an emphasis that is central to hierarchy and solidarity and to procedures for removing pollution—is problematic in discussion of an important class of acquired pollutions, *āśauca*, impurity caused by birth or death and in some *thar*s by menarche[10] to the household and to the patrilineal extended family, the *phukī*.[11] A Newar Brahman attempting to explain why family members become impure after births and deaths says (of death) "After a death and during the period of mourning the condition of the body is not right. People feel heavy and sad." It is, he says, this bodily condition which must be remedied by purification.[12] As to birth pollution (which starts for the *phukī* members at the moment that the umbilical cord is cut and the infant has been separated from the mother), he says, "who knows who it [the infant] is, or where it comes from." Dirt and disgust is not the central issue here, and the reason for pollution is not intuitively obvious and requires philosophical speculation. As Kane writes in his review of birth and death pollution in the *Dharmaśāstras*, "A question arises why birth and death should cause impurity to the members of the family or to relatives. Only a few [of the texts] have anything [to say] on this question. Hārīta says: 'The family incurs death impurity because by death the family feels overwhelmed (or frustrated), while when a new life appears the family increases (and there is gratification of joy)'" (Kane 1968–1977, vol. IV, p. 269f.). This echoes the uncertainty of the Newar Brahman's explanation, and its seeking for a naturalistic, physical, mechanical, and nonmoral explanation. Kane writes, as we have quoted, that the *Mitākṣarā* defines "*āśauca*," birth and death pollution, "as an emergent attribute attaching to a person, which is got rid of by lapse of time or a bath and the like..." (ibid., 268.) The "pollution" is dealt with in part as if it were dirty pollution, but it is only amalgamated to dirt by a kind of vague metaphorical extension.[13]

THE MANAGEMENT OF POLLUTION IN BHAKTAPUR: AVOIDANCE, SURROGATION, AND CLEANING

The large complex of ideas and feelings, of public doctrines and personal responses, of contradictions and rationalizations associated with the purity complex are very diffusely embodied in action in various aspects of the city's life. The area in which they are, perhaps, most focused, represented, and standardized in public action in Bhaktapur is that of purification and the management of pollution in general.

Pollution is managed by various combinations of avoidance, of absorption by surrogates, and of cleaning procedures. Food taboos, rules regarding what is unclean, and the status-structuring rules about what kinds of social contacts are permissible and impermissible in various contexts to people of various social statuses are made clear in traditional texts and in Bhaktapur's ongoing social *dharma*. A clear set of proscriptions for avoidance and for ways of life facilitating that avoidance become elaborated on the basis of these clearly defined and more or less avoidable class of contaminants.

SURROGATE ABSORPTION OF CONTAMINANTS—BOTH DIRTY AND CLEAN

We have discussed the idea of the surrogate accumulation of pollution as a service to others as a priestly function in chapter 10. Surrogation has two distinct aspects. First, there is the performance of an essential act—the purification of a house after death, the execution of a criminal, the moving of feces from latrines out of the city—which would be uncongenial or status-threatening in one way or another to the higher-status people who use their status to avoid and delegate the action. However, lower-status people not only are delegated status-depressing actions, which then maintain their own lowered statuses, but in some services are clearly doing something else; they absorb into themselves a contaminant, freeing others from it. The idea of helpful surrogate absorption is widespread in Bhaktapur. What is absorbed is often a dangerous but not necessarily impure (in the sense of dirty) substance.

Thus animals placed "under" the house (on the *cheli*) in Bhaktapur are said (according to Vogt [1977, 94]) to help protect the inhabitants of a house by contracting diseases that otherwise would affect the human inhabitants of the house. A piece of iron is sometimes used to draw dangerous spirits to it—for example, from the body of a bride who is to be newly introduced into a household. The special uses of the lowest *thar*s to absorb and draw to themselves the portentous dangers signaled by an eclipse or those inherent in the clothes and funeral objects of the dead involves the accumulation of more than "impurity." When the untouchable Po(n) begs, as he is traditionally required to do, for gifts from others following an eclipse, and, as he does on some other occasions of astrological trouble, he takes on not their status-threatening dirty impurity but their health or economically threatening astrologically produced "bad luck." In this and the other examples of the surrogate absorption of a *dangerous* substance, there is the implication of a *limited quantity* which can be moved from one locus to another.[14] The idea of flow of quantitatively limited powerful substances is found in the idea of *śakti* in Bhaktapur's religion of the dangerous deities. Thus when Śiva's power or *śakti* flows into his Goddess consort, he is emptied of it, and left as a corpse.

The idea of pollution—in the sense of dirty pollution—as a substance that flows, that has quantitative aspects, that can often be avoided, and that can be deflected and absorbed into others is thus a subcase of a larger category. The inverse idea of partaking of the substance of superiors through eating the *prasāda* of deities and the *cipa* of superiors is in this larger group. So is the complex of ideas and feelings centering on dangerous and unpleasant substances other than dirty, status-affecting pollutants. Many of the ideas, feelings, and experiential resonances connected with this nondirty dangerous class are associated with another set of moral issues—danger, punishment, evil, sin, guilt, and fear—rather than those centrally germane to the purity complex. These nondirty transferable substances are also closely related to the world of power and magic, which in a sense lies under and at the edges of the ordinary world expressed and stabilized through purity.

PURIFICATION

The third aspect of the management of pollution is its removal once it has accumulated. Here the major emphasis is not on the management of the flow or ingestion of some sort of substance but on mechanical procedures for the removal of dirt from *surfaces* and, in more extensive personal purifying procedures, the trimming of hair and/or nails. These procedures are extensions of the ordinary cleaning of foodstuffs, cooking utensils, living and dining quarters, clothes, and the body. For inanimate objects, water collected to ensure its purity, ashes, mixtures of cow dung and soil, and so on may be used following traditional prescriptions.[15] Such ordinary cleaning and scrubbing becomes loosely formalized into sets of procedures of various potency. The proper procedures are generally understood by ordinary people for most occasions, with the occasional advice of a Brahman. They depend on status, the kind of pollution undergone, and the goal of the purification (e.g., primarily for the removal of a pollution to restore ordinary purity, or for the removal of ordinary purity to prepare for a ritual, or the removal of *āśauca* impurity). Thus such purifications must be done in particular ways, and their neglect, like the neglect of any aspect of the *dharma* of ordinary life, is a moral violation, a *pāpa*.[16]

Formalized procedures for purification of the body are called *bya(n)kegu*—alternatively written *be(n)kegu*—meaning literally "to cause to become untied" and thus to become loosened or freed. The term is not used for the purification of objects nor of ritual equipment or areas, where the ordinary Newari term for "to clean or to arrange neatly," "*saphā yāgu,*" is used. "*Bya(n)kegu*" is generally divided into two kinds, which Brahmans sometimes distinguish as "ordinary" (*sādhāran*) or "special, important" (*viśeṣya*). For the latter group of *bya(n)kegu*, the unequivocally clean *thar*s, that is, those above level XIII, require the services of a man (*nau*) and woman (*naunī*) from the Nau, or "barber" *thar*.[17]

In the usual course of events the main motivation for a major purification is after death in the *phukī* in all *thar*s, and after birth within the *phukī* for high-status groups—low-status groups performing only an ordinary *bya(n)kegu*. Major purification was traditionally required by the highest status *thar*s in preparation for all major *pūjā*s and for all rites of passage for family members, but in recent decades minor *bya(n)kegu* procedures have been used for most of these. In addition, Brahmans and devout upper-status Chathariyās purified themselves with major purifications following contaminating contacts with low *thar*s. For lower-status *thar*s such purifications were perfunctory.

For an ordinary or minor *bya(n)kegu* there are three common procedures used in Bhaktapur. One is bathing in or at the edge of the river with river water, in the course of which a person first washes his or her feet, and then hands, then rinses the mouth and spits out the water, then washes the face, and finally washes the whole body or submerges it into the water. Another procedure is to use *khau*, mustard seed from which the oil has first been pressed. *Khau* can be used with nonriver water taken from wells or taps. Water is first used to clean sequentially the feet, hands, mouth, and face. Then *khau* is rubbed on the feet, the hands, the face, and then the rest of the body. Finally the body is rinsed with water again. A third procedure is to take *tulsicā*, the earth (*cā*) from around a basil plant (*Ocimum sanctum*), *tulsi*,[18] and use it in the same way as *khau* is used.

In a major *bya(n)kegu* extra procedures are added to the basic washing and scrubbing activities that characterize all purifications from dirty pollution. For such procedures a *nau* and a *naunī* come to the house of the person or (as is usually the case) persons who are to undergo the purification. Occasionally people may go to the workplace or house of the *nau*. In a client's house the purification procedure is done on the *cwata* or *māta(n)* floor. In the case of a man, "new water," *na:nā*,[19] is used to wet his head, which is then shaved.[20] The *nauni* pares his toe and finger nails, and colors the tips of his toes with a red pigment, *ala:*. For women there is no hair cutting; the major *bya(n)kegu* consists only of having their nails pared by the *naunī*, and the ends of their toes painted with *ala:*, which is applied more extensively than for men. Unmarried women may have a wider area of the tops of their feet adjacent to their toes painted, a procedure that is interpreted as cosmetic as well as purificatory. The cut-off hair and nails are supposed to be thrown into the river,[21] but they are often disposed of as ordinary waste. Following these pocedures by the *nau* and the *naunī*, the person must wash in the river or clean himself or herself with *khau* or *tulsicā* in the manner of an ordinary *bya(n)kegu*.[22] The entire procedure—the services of the *nau* and *nauni*, followed by the prescribed washing and cleaning—constitutes the major *bya(n)kegu*. These simple procedures are sufficient to remove dirty pollution.[23]

THE PURITY COMPLEX: PSYCHOLOGICAL RESONANCES AND SOCIAL ORDER

The purity complex weaves together complex sociocultural and personal meanings. It helps anchor Bhaktapur's realm of extraordinary religious symbols in a reality sensed both as natural and compelling.

We have noted that certain features of the purity complex place it in a larger field of "contaminations" where socially and experientially defined objects are compromised. The ideas of contagion, of flow, of transformation, of ineffectual bounding conditions that characterize or are implied by all contaminations contrast with conceptions of "uncontaminated" or unblurred or cleanly presented and represented bounded persons and objects, fixed order, and the kinds of meanings derived from the existence and relationships of such fixed persons and objects. The first set of conceptions is closer to reverie, dream, magic, child-like understandings; the second, to the more fixed and bounded categories of everyday logic, a logic in which social definition and categorization play a large part, the realm of ordinary events. Considerations of impurity are, so to speak, at one, but only one, boundary between order and disorder. The approach of that boundary results in psychological discomfort that serves to keep people within those social boundaries. On the other side is an altogether different kind of world. At the margins of Bhaktapur the untouchables serve to keep the clean citizens within the city. Yet, just beyond them is not the disgusting mess that the ordinary *dharma* and its associated benign moral deities threaten, but a world for whose ordering, uses, and relationships, impurity is no longer relevant.

There are various procedures for trying to keep oneself and others in the ordinary social and mental universe. Procedures for the management of purity are among them. The purity complex helps to ensure the definition of individuals as socially defined *persons*, and emphasizes the body as the sign and locus of that person. It makes use of the idea of the clean body as a sign of that individual's perceptible, sensible, acceptable adequacy to others, and thus that person's acceptability as a *unit* in the hierarchical system of human and divine relationships. Purity as a marker of personhood is associated for any individual with a complex of ideas and feelings about his or her social definition—reputation and face, embarrassment, and shame. The purity complex is related to only one segment of moral emotions and ideas. People who have become contaminated have committed no moral error, no *pāpa*, unless they became contaminated through some mistake on their part.[24] They have no cause to feel guilt. Guilt and repentance, their social sources, their personal meanings, and the procedures for rectifying them, in spite of their occasional labeling as inner impurities, have significantly different relations to social and personal order.

The uses of the delineation of body surfaces through purity and purification to define persons within the hierarchical system, echo a traditional system of sumptuary laws and other external markers of status. They are in contrast to systems of defining status and person by differences in inner essence, such as racism. Such efforts at fixing categories through surface delineation and marking take much of their significance from and contribute to local doctrines and experiences of a shifting, context-dependent selfhood.[25]

The purity complex makes use not only of the imagery of the surface of the body but also of the flow of foods into it to be incorporated in it, and of exuviae—above all, feces—flowing out of it, to be separated and rejected. This imagery of flow is not related to the exterior surface of the body—the body as a sign of a person—but to its interior composition and to the acceptance, incorporation, excretion, and rejection of substances into and out of that interior. This imagery is not related to the static bounded category of the person as *represented* by that person's surface presentability, but rather to the dynamics of the construction of a socially defined individual in systematic relation to the larger hierarchically inclusive and exclusive social "bodies" to which he or she belongs. In this field of the purity complex, ideas and feelings associated with palatability, thirst, hunger, and thus desire on the one hand, are opposed to disgust on the other. Things that do not belong to one's extended body, particularly if they have been cast off by it, flowed through it—as so many of the substances that are passed down through the status system seem to do—risk being marked as repulsive. Palatable versus disgusting substances, desire versus disgust, add to the concerns about proper surface appearance (and thus conformity) a dynamic of flow, and encourage the maintenance of structure by countering the anarchic desires (and available cultural doctrines, which are potentially subversive to the social order) of being equal to all[26] or else unrelated to all.

Interpretation of body symbolism and its cultural extensions is a particularly dangerous enterprise unless it is carefully related to its expression in particular peoples' personal discourse and experience—which we cannot do here. We can, however, offer a preliminary improvisation. The formula that determines the direction of flow, "palatable from equals and superiors, impalatable from inferiors," has a metaphorical implication that the body is in part constituted of substances flowing from above. Exuviae pollution is based on an opposition of inside and outside the body in which substances that are within body boundaries are unproblematic but once outside those boundaries become disgusting, that is, not to be reincorporated through eating. A corporate group such as *phukī* or *thar*—extensions of the basic household group defined by sharing one cooking area—is a group most of whose food can be shared without concern about pollution. They are in that sense one body.[27] However, the hierarchical *cipa* system adds further psychological resonance and social order to the more static group-defining shared commensality. It is during their infancy and childhood that people first encounter in the household *cipa* system the idea that all food is acceptable from all people higher in status. Feeding by others in the family begins, of course, in nursing, with its presumed experience of the infant's unbounded union with its mother whose milk and later feedings it shares, the two belonging in some sense to a single body. The model of the group within which *cipa*, "contaminated" by their substance, becomes sustaining food echoes not only the sustenance and support and dependence of such early experience with the mother but also, perhaps, a perception of one body within which all is acceptable, nothing disgusting.

This is the view looking up the system; looking down however something changes. You have a "maternal" relation to all below you because you feed them, and they are dependent on you. However, as such dependence moves out of the household, and to successively lower depths of the status system, an implication of the system that is muted elsewhere in it becomes more and more clear. The flow of substance and sustenance throughout the system is not only sustaining, it is progressively degrading and polluting. The excretion metaphor now gains an ever-increasing strength over the feeding metaphor. We may speculate that another of the many vital functions served by the lowest *thar*s is to isolate the stigmatizing implications of the *cipa* system, and to deflect them from the relationships in the upper reaches of the system onto themselves.

The pollution that affects surfaces, and the pollution that may enter into the body by ingestion have each their own specific clusters of personal meanings and public uses.

The purification procedures that restore the purity compromised by birth and death pollution and (for upper-status people particularly) contact with low status people,[28] and which prepare people to remove "everyday" pollution in preparation for religious acts, are all *bya(n)-kegus*—that is, purification is directed to "dirty contaminants," and, among these, to dirty contaminants on the body surface.

The rectifications of surfaces relates people to one aspect of the social order—that segment symbolized by the polarity of Brahman and untouchable, the specific segment ordered by the symbolic resources of the dharmic order. Purification relates people in the realm of the deities to the moral gods, the representatives of that civic order. The moral gods are themselves subject to impurity—purification prior to worship, and the purification and care of the images of the deities and of the "sacred" area in which *pūjās* are held protect the definition of the moral gods as well as the worshipers.[29] One important legend in Bhaktapur (chap. 15) tells how that city's major group of dangerous deities, the Nine Durgās, are impervious to the impurities of feces and pig flesh, which would pollute a god such as Viṣṇu. Similarly, during worship the dangerous deities are offered foods (meat and alcoholic spirits) that if not "dirty," are nevertheless forbidden to Brahmans and would threaten their status.[30]

In the case of the dangerous deities power overcomes the importance of purity. The dangerous deities escape from the constraints ordering the civic moral *dharma*; that is why they are dangerous, and that is why they are useful. This transcendence is allied to creativity and fecundity (as the agricultural meanings of the dangerous deities witness), to the protection of the perimeters of the civic system, and to danger. Even within the hierarchical order of separated and ranked units of Bhaktapur's city system, however, purity is of differentiated importance. Although the entire system of *thar*s is arranged in a hierarchy of purity with the Brahman and Po(n) at its extreme ends, it is possible, as we have argued in chapter 10, to discern two vertical divisions of that hierarchy. One segment—characterized by the Brahman, the untouchables, and the set of priestly functionaries, is central to that system. Not only are their functions related to the manipulation and uses of purity and impurity, but in their lives and status they *are* the representation of the socially constructive effects of the purity complex. A Brahman who becomes impure would no longer effectively be a Brahman, and were an untouchable to become pure he would no longer be an untouchable. But a farmer is a farmer and a king is a king no matter what their state of purity. The other vertical segment of the status system deals with realities beyond the construction of the mesocosmic symbolic order. Sometimes their effectiveness requires, as was clear in the case of the king, going beyond that order and contradicting it. Not only the king, but also the craftsmen, farmers, merchants, and others are fitted into the system by a kind of unstable tinkering. Their hierarchical position, rationalized into the purity system, is based in part on other often more obscure factors, deriving from history and power and class. In this perspective the king is closer to the farmer than to the Brahman, and the Brahman is closer to the untouchable than to the king.

Placing the purity complex in the realm of the sacred is misleading in various ways. On the one hand, there are essential components of the religious sphere, the realm of the dangerous deities and that of the ascetic, for example, where purity is not at issue, although its transcendence helps define that realm. On the other hand, where purity *is* related to religious conception and action (and to social order), it is in itself within the realm of the ordinary. It is precisely this seemingly natural aspect with its powerful intellectual and emotional implications which is made use of to anchor, motivate, and preserve the constructions built of it.

The idea of impurity as a natural substance, not a natural essence, is associated with complex ideas about the nature and management of that substance, how to avoid it, and how to get rid of it. Because it is not an essence, because the status implications of the purity complex are not biological and racist, the conditions of life of individuals at various social levels must be constantly arranged to ensure that they have the proper amounts of impurity. It is precisely this open interactive aspect between pollution and social structure that does more than rationalize and justify the social order; it *motivates* action in that order insofar as it must constantly struggle actively to maintain the congruences between the ways of life and the order-constructing states of pollution of its members.

PART THREE

The Dance of Symbols

CHAPTER TWELVE

The Civic Ballet: Annual Time and the Festival Cycles

INTRODUCTION

To bring Bhaktapur's symbolic order to coordinated life, a temporal system and a patterning of events within the tempos of that system are necessary. There are in Bhaktapur two large classes of symbolic enactments that tie together public space, individuals, social units, deities, and time into a larger assemblage. In these enactments, the various matters that we have dealt with in earlier chapters become elements in a *civic performance*. Social roles, significant space, the complexes of meaning represented by deities, priests, and modes of worship emerge and become realized in these performances, which, like their constituent aspects, follow traditional patterns. The first class of these civically significant enactments are the rites of passage, the *saṃskāras* (app. 6), whose sequence is determined—often with considerable leeway in their exact timing—by the stages of the life cycle, fine-tuned through astrological considerations. In Bhaktapur these rites entail references beyond the individual and household to the patrilineal extended family, the *phukī*, and beyond that to some larger civic units (primarily the *twa:* and the maṇḍalic area *pīṭha*). But the *saṃskāras*' central importance is in defining the individual in relation to household, extended family, and, with marriage, to an allied kin group within his or her status level. Their relation to the larger city is secondary, and for the most part simply emphasizes the *phukī*'s relation to neighborhood and Maṇḍalic Segment, as all *phukī* worship does. It is the second class of temporally coordinated ritual enactments that are the true civic enactments. That group is primarily constituted by those activities that take place in the city following the dictates of the calendar. These include practices that are appropriate—in many cases necessary—for particular days of the week, of the lunar fortnights or of the solar month. However, at the center of our concern in this study are those events whose occurrence depends on the annual cycle itself. This particular temporal set, the yearly events, has special urban emphases and uses in contrast to the smaller and larger cycles.[1]

Many of these annual events are associated with feasts encompassing one or another social unit, and are designated as *nakhā cakhā* (Kathmandu Newari, *nakha: cakha:*), literally "to feed and associated activities."[2] "*Nakhā cakhā*" may be glossed with appropriateness by "festival," with that word's connections to "feast" and "festive." The term "festival" also works well for some of the other major and public events of the year, particularly if "festival" is extended to include some restrained, minor, or routine "celebrations." However, there are other significant annual events—a day for the protective rubbing of bodies with oil, a day on which the moon should not be viewed, and so on—for which the term is inappropriate. Hindu calendrically determined events include two sorts of events that, although distinguished by classical terminology, are blurred in actual usage. These are *vrata* events and *utsava* events. "*Vrata*" implies a "religious duty," and is used often in Bhaktapur in the strong sense of "religious or ascetic observance taken upon oneself, austerity, vow, rule, holy work such as fasting and continence" (Macdonell 1974, 304). The other term, "*utsava*," indicates, traditionally, "festival or holiday." Gnanambal, in a report on surveys of Indian "festivals," notes that the term "*vrata*" has a wider usage in many parts of India to include "festivals," especially where fasting is a necessary element (Gnanambal 1967). There is, nevertheless, in usage, he adds, a "faint distinction" of *vrata* and *utsava* as evidenced by the presence of the two terms in many parts of India. Kane (1968–1977, vol. V, p. 57) also remarks on the difficulty of using the terminological distinction for discriminating actual events.

The annual events we will consider contain among them elements of *vrata* and *utsava* and sometimes of neither, and we will use various glosses for them, all meaning no more than "calendrically determined event of general civic importance." During the course of the year in Bhaktapur there are some seventy-nine of these, and as on some days there are more than one and as, in contrast, a few last for two days, there are a total of seventy-four *days* each year during which some part or all of the city is involved in one or another such event. This is in addition to weekly and monthly activities during the course of the year, as well as the pilgrimages and *melā*s or "fairs," taking place elsewhere in the Valley (or beyond) every year or every few years in which people in Bhaktapur may participate.[3] These gross enumerations are, however, misleading as our discussions in later chapters and a more refined enumeration in chapter 16 will indicate. Later chapters will provide a clearer view of the types and density of calendrical events in Bhaktapur.

The calendrical events, derived from South Asian tradition and the Kathmandu Valley's long history, are, like the supernatural members of the city's pantheon, of interest to us primarily not as a collection of witnesses to that history but as aspects of an ongoing, meaningful contemporary urban life. We will say something, if only in passing, about each calendrical event, but we will treat certain events at much greater length, and among these we will be most particularly concerned with what we call the "Devī cycle" and its climaxes in Mohanī, the Autumn Harvest festival sequence, and in the related performances throughout nine months of the year of the Nine Durgās troupe. The events we emphasize are, evidently, those we take to be of particular integrative importance.

THE CALENDAR

Bhaktapur, typically of South Asia, has both a solar annual calendar and a lunar one.[4] While the great majority of festivals are determined by the lunar calendar, there is one major festival sequence (Biskā:, the solar New Year sequence) and one other annual event which are determined by the solar cycle. The lunar year is normally divided into twelve lunar months. The lunar month begins on the day following the new or dark moon, which ends the previous month.[5] The Newar lunar month is divided into a first "bright" half, corresponding to the waxing of the moon, and ending with the full moon; and a second "dark" half, corresponding to the waning phase of the moon and ending with the new moon. The bright fortnight is called *tumlā*; the dark fortnight, *khimlā*.[6] To designate individual lunar fortnights, terms for the dark half and light half of the lunar month—*gā* and *thwa*, respectively—are added to the name for the particular month. The name of the month is itself a compound including the morpheme *lā*, meaning lunar month. Thus the

TABLE 2

LUNAR FORTNIGHTS

Month	Newari	Sanskrit
October/November	Kachalāthwa	Kārtika
November	Kachalāgā	
November/December	Thi(n)lāthwa	Mārga
December	Thi(n)lāgā	
December/January	Pohelāthwa	Pauṣa
January	Pohelāgā	
January/February	Sillāthwa	Māgha
February	Sillāgā	
February/March	Cillāthwa	Phālguna
March	Cillāgā	
March/April	Caulāthwa	Caitra
April	Caulāgā	
April/May	Bachalāthwa	Vaiśākha
May	Bachalāgā	
May/June	Tachalāthwa	Jyeṣṭha
June	Tachalāgā	
June/July	Dillāthwa	Āṣāḍha
July	Dillāgā	
July/August	Gu(n)lāthwa	Śrāvaṇa
August	Gu(n)lāgā	
August/September	Ya(n)lāthwa	Bhādra
September	Ya(n)lāgā	
September/October	Kaulāthwa	Āśvina
October	Kaulāgā	

"*Thwa*" is the waxing fortnight, ending with the full moon. "*Gā*" designates the waning fortnight, ending with the new moon.

first lunar fortnight of the lunar year, Kachalāthwa, means the bright or waxing fortnight (*thwa*) of the lunar month (*lā*) of Kacha, which is followed by Kachalālāgā, the dark fortnight (*gā*) of the month of Kacha. Table 2 lists Bhaktapur's lunar fortnights, the Sanskritic equivalent months, and the approximate correspondences of the fortnights to the Western year. The table does not include the intercalary period, which has to be added every third year to adjust the lunar to the solar year, and which does not usually affect the ritual calendar.

The full-moon day, which ends the bright lunar fortnight (the first half of the month), is called *punhi*, and the dark or new-moon day, which ends the dark fortnight is called *āmāi*.[7] The other days of each lunar fortnight are given ordinal numeric Sanskritic names, with the exception of the fourteenth day of the dark fortnight, whose Sanskrit name, *caturdaśi*, is usually replaced by the Newari term "*ca:re*". The lunar days are called *tithi.* Although they vary in length (from about 21.5 to 26 hours), they are, for most purposes, made to correspond to ordinary solar days.

The solar year, which is of very much lesser importance for the ritual cycle, contains twelve months. The names of these months are the same as for the Lunar months,[8] although there is, perhaps, a tendency to use the Sanskritic forms more for them. The days of the solar year, *gate*, begin at sunrise. They are arranged in a seven-day week deriving, as the solar calendar in general does, from the same sources thus sharing some of the same astral references as the Western days of the week. The occasional necessity of relating the solar and lunar years requires a complicated set of rectifying conventions that are not relevant here.

APPROACHES TO MEANING

In the next three chapters (chaps. 13 to 15) we will describe the annual calendrical events. We will look for aspects of form and thematic content, and for similarities and contrasts that contribute to the meaningfulness of clusters of and subcycles of calendrical events, as well as of the entire annual collection. We will introduce here some of the issues and approaches that will concern us in our detailed presentation of the festival year.

CYCLES

There are many ways of sorting Bhaktapur's calendrical events. Our first rough sorting has been into events of the solar year and of the lunar year, and then a further division of the lunar year into one set that constitutes a clearly interrelated and extremely important group, the "Devī cycle," and another, residual, lunar group. The solar calendar has only one important festival sequence, Biskā:. The lunar cycle as a whole (as opposed to the clearly integrated Devī cycle) seems on the surface at least to be a mixture of miscellaneous events. We will, however, be concerned with its deeper patterns insofar as they may—or may not—exist.

Marc Gaborieau (1982) has proposed a "structure" for the Indo-Nepalese calendar that, although problematic for the Newars at least, provides a useful point of departure for a discussion of the meaning of the overall lunar cycle. He notes that some writings on Hindu time (he cites Mus [1932–1934] and Zimmer [1951]) represent it as having the following properties: (1) each of the different divisions of time (days, years, cosmic periods, etc.) is arranged in a cycle; (2) these cycles are formally similar; (3) each cycle has a beginning and an end; (4) each cycle has a movement from order toward disorder and culminates in a state of chaos that precedes the regeneration, which will mark the beginning of a new cycle; and (5) the stages of chaos and regeneration are not considered parts of the temporal cycle, but temporary escapes from time. They represent the "axis which communicates with eternity."

Gaborieau argues that this schema is reflected in the Indo-Nepalese festival cycle. For the Indo-Nepalis, he writes, the four-month period beginning with the summer solstice—the period of the monsoon and the major work prior to the rice harvest—are considered inauspicious months, but it is also the period for the majority of the year's festivals. The period begins with the festival of Hari Śayanī, the time when Viṣṇu goes to sleep for a period of four months "leaving the earth to the demons." In Gaborieau's speculation, those months are out of ordinary secular time. The first two months correspond to the period of disorder, the second to the period of "regeneration." The festivals during this period "manifest radical disorders and reversals followed by profound restorations of order" (1982, 16). In contrast, he argues, the eight-month period beginning with the first winter month (Mārga in November/December) is an auspicious period where life follows its normal course, and household ceremonies for good luck, and prosperity, and the like, take place as do lineage ceremonies. He further argues that those inauspicious events, the disorders and reversals, that do take place during this period primarily concern the lower castes. The "cyclical mystery" of the year as expressed in its festivals is the privileged experience of the upper, twice born castes.

How far this schema is adequate for the sorting of the Indo-Nepalese festival calendar is for others to judge; the involution of festival practices, the relative secularization of most of the Indo-Nepalese groups, will make an anthropological critique difficult. In its details, this schema does not work for Bhaktapur's calendar, but for certain aspects of that calendar and with different timings, it will provide (in chap. 16) a useful point of departure for an analysis of the possible implications of the arrangement of all the components of the annual cycle within that cycle.

Whatever the internal structure of the overall annual calendar of events may be, there is the partially related question of how the meanings of the events might be affected by external cyclical events of a different order. Is there any relation of the meanings of festival events to the phases of the moon and to the sun's course and seasons beyond their clock-like uses in coordinating the cycle? The kinds of data we deal with show only scanty echoes of these cosmic events. But when we consider still another external cycle (in turn, dependent on the seasons), the rice agricultural cycle, particularly in its relation to the Devī cycle, the connections are of central importance.

SELECTION FROM THE HINDU SET OF FESTIVALS

Although most of the elements of Newar symbolic life are taken from the inventions and developments of South Asian history—supplemented by some significant but quantitatively minor Newar and Himalayan forms—there is, as we have seen in relation to the urban pantheon, a necessary selection among these elements. There are quantitative considerations—only a certain number of elements can be understood and put to use in the civic system. There are also considerations of propriety; some forms do not fit in, or are redundant, have their places filled, as it were, by other symbolic elements. As is the case with all inventories of South Asian possibilities, the list of calendrically anchored events noted in the classical literature and religious texts is very large. Kane has what is presumably an almost exhaustive list of calendrical *vrata*s and *utsava* containing well over one thousand events throughout India's vast history and extent (1968–1977, vol. V, pp. 253–462). These vary in their general importance and occurrence throughout historic time, space, or class of devotees.[9]

Bhaktapur's calendar selects and rejects from this group, and invents—or often pieces together from existing fragments—its own festivals. The most salient contrast of the Bhaktapur calendar for Bhaktapur's citizens is with other Newar calendars and with Indo-Nepalese calendars. Not only does the presence or absence of calendrical events in Bhaktapur reflect an active selective in relation to other calendars, but so, and often more significantly, does their local importance. Thus a festival of general South Asian importance may be present in Bhaktapur, but only in some residual and unimportant manifestation. We will consider the questions of selection and emphasis in the following chapters.

ASPECTS OF THE ANALYSIS OF CALENDRICAL EVENTS

When we narrow our horizon to look at Bhaktapur's various calendrical events in themselves and in their similarities and contrasts to each other, we must seek appropriate and relevant aspects for analysis and contrast. We must attend to the social and spatial units involved. What are the static and dynamic uses of those units? Which deities are made use of? Is the deity or deities moved; do people move? Where? To what purpose? Who are the human actors and audiences? What are the different sorts of actions? What are the themes and narratives portrayed and recounted? Are there narrative "plots," with conflicts, tensions, climaxes, resolutions? What kinds of symbolic forms and rhetoric are used to contribute to meaning? What kinds of themes are there in various events? What problems seem to be dealt with? How do participants seem not only to act in but also to respond to particular calendrical events? How are various city units tied together— through "parallel" devices (with various units doing the same sorts of things at the same time) or through "serial" or "interactive" devices, with some sort of meaningful movements and encounters systematically interrelating different kinds of actors and social units in the course of the event?

Such questions are in the background of our considerations of calendrical events, but we have not dealt with these issues explicitly in relation to all the calendrical events noted in the following chapters, for many minor festivals many of them are irrelevant. These various elements of festival meaning become fully relevant only in the more developed festivals, those that are more important to Bhaktapur by various criteria which we will present in the following chapters.

A catalogue of their *potential* resources for generating and expressing order and meaning, in fact, is liable to make the annual events seem more exhaustively integrative and constitutive of the city's symbolic system than they really are. That task falls on selected ones. The question of which potential resources are, in fact, used or neglected by particular individual events and throughout the course of the annual cycle is an empirical one.

We will see that the events vary in importance from "trivial" to what we call "focal" events, events of central importance to the city,[10] and we will make an estimate of the relative importance of the various calendrical events as being of minor, moderate, or major importance. In the next three chapters we will lose ourselves among the trees of the annual cycle. In chapter 16 we will return to the view of the forest, and the consideration of its differential contributions to urban order. What do these annual events do for Bhaktapur and its people? How do they do whatever it is that they do?

THE INCLUSION AND SEQUENTIAL NUMBERING OF CALENDRICALLY DETERMINED EVENTS

Some arbitrary decisions regarding two issues were necessary. First, when is a day of the year that is given a particular name really to be considered an event of some civic importance and thus to be listed? In some cases, for example, a particular full-moon day, the day may be given a special differentiating name, but the activities characterizing it are no different than for other such days, the day being an unexceptional member of the, for the most part, internally undifferentiated set of twelve full-moon days. A particular day may have some special differentiating feature of very minor present importance, or be of interest in only a personal and optional way to some few individuals or households, or to some particular *thar*. It has been optional in some few cases whether to include or exclude an event; we have usually (but not consistently) excluded it unless there is some clear suggestion of civic importance according to our criteria. The minor processions of certain deities that we include and list among the "minor" festivals are also of very marginal importance, in this case because they have little or no present following or attendance—but they are clearly public urban events dictated by the calendar, echoes sometimes of events of some past importance and possible nuclei, in some interesting cases, for some future efflorescence.

A second problem is how to distinguish separate events for enumeration within some larger festival sequential complex, such as the autumn Mohanī festival or the solar Biskā:. We have dealt with this in somewhat different ways in those two cases, in large part following local conventions.

In should be noted that the sequential numbers that we use to designate festivals in the following chapters are derived from the sequence of the *entire* group of annual festivals starting with the lunar New Year's Day. Thus the numbering of the events in the three individual cycles indicate their position in the overall annual collection of events. (The annual festival calendar is given in summary form in app. 5.)

CHAPTER THIRTEEN

The Events of the Lunar Year

INTRODUCTION

The great majority of the annual events in Bhaktapur's yearly collection of calendrically determined events are determined by the lunar calendar. The sequence of these events constitutes a cycle in the dictionary sense of "a period in which a certain round of events or phenomena is completed, recurring in the same order in equal succeeding periods." So defined, the solar events form a cycle of their own, as their position within the lunar sequence varies from year to year. Do the events of the lunar year form a cycle in the literary sense of a group of poems, myths, tales, and the like with a common theme and, perhaps, some integrated structure? Quests for an overall structure of the events of the lunar year—such as Gaborieau's (1982), which we discussed in the previous chapter—suppose that they do form a cycle in this latter sense. One group of lunar events—which we call the "Devī cycle"—is of major and central importance to Bhaktapur precisely as a clearly integrated annual thematic cycle, taking much of its meaning and tempo from the cycle of rice agriculture, and carrying some of the most powerful "messages" in support (as we shall argue) of the symbolic integration of the city, and we have isolated it for extensive treatment in a later chapter. In the present chapter we will note when the events of the Devī cycle take place, but will defer their discussion. We may expect that some of the residual events of the lunar cycle with their historically determined calendrical position may have relatively isolated significance. Others are related to each other and the larger cycle as smaller thematic groupings or, more significantly, in terms of formal similarities and contrasts, expressing some kind of structure or rhythm within the year.

In the chapters on calendrical events we face the problem of what to present about particular events. Any major calendrical event would in itself require special studies and a volume to describe and interpret it in something like full detail. We will present in this and the following two chapters the details necessary for the purposes of our arguments about Bhaktapur's civic religion, swollen by occasional additional ethnographic description, particularly in those events that are either unique to Bhaktapur or of special importance there.

The numbers given in brackets following the names of individual events in the next three chapters indicate the sequence of the events in the *entire* annual calendar. The solar events are numbered according to their position within the lunar calendar of 1975/76. Although this chapter discusses only those events of the lunar year aside from the Devī cycle, all lunar and solar events are noted in this chapter to take account of the overall collection of events (see also app. 5).

SWANTI AND THE LUNAR NEW YEAR [77, 78, 79, 1, 2]

It is the lunar New Year's Day[1] that begins the fundamental year—the sequence of lunar months, the basic calendar within which the solar events are variously located from year to year. As P. V. Kane writes, the lunar New Year "in ancient times . . . began in different months in different countries [in South Asia] and for different purposes" (1968–1977, vol. V, p. 569). At present the lunar year begins in India, for the most part, in Caitra (March/April) or Kārtika (October/November). The Indo-Nepalese year begins in Caitra. The Newar lunar year begins in Kārtika, a time which, in its contrast to the Indo-Nepalese New Year, is considered in Bhaktapur to be a distinctively Newar practice, and with an event, Mhā Pūjā [1], which is considered to be a uniquely Newar event. The New Year's Day falls on the fourth day of a five-day set of events called "Swanti."

Although "Swanti" refers to the five-day sequence, it is said to be derived from *swanhi*, "three days," that is, the last three days of the sequence—the day before the new year, the New Year's Day and the succeeding day.[2] Alternative scholarly names, such as Pa(n)carāta, referring to the entire five days, are much less used. The festival is related to and derived from the South Asian Lakṣmī festival, Divāli or Dīpāvalī (the "Festival of lights"), a festival that is also associated with the lunar New Year in some other parts of South Asia such as Gujarat, where the lunar New Year is "inseparable from and part of the Divāli celebrations" (Gnanambal 1967, 6).

The five days of Swanti are characterized by a unity of themes and significant forms. They emphasize in both form and in theme the existence and importance of relations within the household. The core reference is to the feminine—sisterly, wifely, maternal—centrality in the emotional and physical life and the economic management of the household. The supportive role of women is related to the benign goddess Lakṣmī, and placed in opposition to a destruction represented by the personification of death as Yama and his messengers. The Newars begin their month, and thus their new lunar year, with the bright, waxing lunar fortnight. Therefore, Swanti's first three days are at the end of the dark fortnight, ending in the dark, new moon, and the New Year's Day events of Mhā Pūjā come at the first day of the waxing lunar fortnight of Kachalāthwa.

During the weeks preceding and following Swanti there are activities in most households which set some of the context for the Swanti ceremonies. Oil lamps are placed on the *ka:si*, the open porch on an upper floor, which is also the principal site of the worship on the first two days of the Swanti sequence. In some households the *pikhā lākhu*, the deified stone marking the boundary of the house, has also been worshiped during the preceding weeks as it will be in the course of the Swanti ceremonies. Family members go to the *ka:si* to worship *swarga*, "heaven." Children are expected to take important parts in this worship. In some houses during this period the individual rooms of the house are worshiped and offerings are made. Oil lamps are placed, often by children, on the *pikhā lākhu*, in the various rooms of the house, and on the *ka:si*. Children, house, household, and the boundaries of the household with an encircling world are emphasized. The world encircling the household—in contrast, as we will see later, to the Devī cycle's world encircling the city—is a moral world.

These preliminary activities are echoed in the events of Swanti itself. The first two days of the sequence, which are the last two days of the lunar year, are respectively, Kwa (sometimes alternatively spelled *Ko*) Pūjā [77] and Khicā Pūjā [78], namely, "Crow Pūjā" and "Dog Pūjā."

Both of these creatures are understood here as "messengers" or agents of Yama, the ruler of the realm of death, as they are similarly conceived in the course of rituals following death. On the day of Crow Pūjā an offering is made on the *ka:si.* Flowers, oil-lamp wicks, incense, uncooked unhusked rice, ceremonial threads, and bits of cooked vegetarian food are placed within a *maṇḍala* that is drawn on the floor of the *ka:si.* Crows frequently come to carry off some of the food. There are no worship activities outside of the house. Kwa Pūjā, like all the events of Swanti, is related to the city in parallel fashion; similar units, households, are doing very much the same things everywhere throughout the city at about the same time.

On this first day of Swanti gambling begins, traditionally by casting cowrie shells and now also with card games.[3] During this period the whole city gambles. Men gamble among groups of friends[4] and fellow *phukī* members, and men, women, and children gamble in the household. In religious interpretation the gambling of this period is a sort of *pūjā* directed to Lakṣmī, the goddess of household wealth. If a gambler loses money it is an offering to Lakṣmī, which she will later return. If the gambler wins it is a kind of *prasāda*, an offering to the deity that has been received and returned, a sharing in the deity's substance that affirms a dependent relationship—and a consequent protective responsibility for the now parental deity. This theme is repeated in the offering of money to Lakṣmī during household worship on the third day of Swanti. The festive gambling is also said to be distracting and pleasing to the messengers of Yama Raja, so that they forbear to carry off any victims, a theme that will surface again during a later day of Swanti. Gambling as a reversal of household economic order is also an "antistructural" element of a kind that we find in several other annual events.

Khicā Pūjā, "Dog Pūjā," on the second day of Swanti, is observed like the Crow Pūjā, except that the *maṇḍala* and offering are placed in front of the ground or *cheli* level of the house, and usually eaten by stray dogs.

On the following day, the last, the new-moon day of the waning fortnight of Kaulāgā, the old lunar year ends with Lakṣmī Pūjā [79].[5] Dīpāvalī elsewhere in South Asia is (as indicated in its name), a festival of lights. Oil lamps and wicks have been important offerings on the earlier days. On this day in Bhaktapur householders place oil lamps at each window (at least two to each side of the window) two at the main door of the house, two lamps at the door of every room, two lamps on the *ka:si*, and one at the *pikhā lākhu*. In addition, lamps are put at the door to the *dukhu:*, the storeroom for valuable items, which will be the site for the household *pūjā* that is performed on this day, during which offerings of light will be made to Lakṣmī.

The *pūjā* on Lakṣmī Pūjā Day is a kind of *apāsa(n) cwanegu*, a relatively simple non-Brahman-assisted household *pūjā* (app. 4). Among the offerings made to Lakṣmī there is a prominent offering of money. This is related to the idea of gambling as an offering. The worship of Lakṣmī in the *dukhu:* is associated with the hope of wealth and good fortune for the household in the coming year.

On the day of Lakṣmī Pūjā some members of the household will first go, as they do preceding all important household *pūjā*s, to the local neighborhood Gaṇeśa temple, to ensure effectiveness for the later worship. Upper-status families send a portion of the offerings of the household *pūjā* to their Āga(n) God, and, for those who have Taleju as an auxiliary lineage deity, to Taleju.[6] Aside from these minimal procedures, which are followed in all important household ceremonies, there is not—on this nor the other days of Swanti—any activities outside the boundaries of the household. There may be a special household dinner on this evening; it does not include the women who have married out of the household. They will return for a feast on the fifth day of the Swanti sequence.

Lakṣmī Pūjā is the first of the three main days of Swanti. On these three days the area between the *pikhā lākhu* and the main doorway to the house is purified with cow dung. This represents a pathway for benevolent and protective deities to enter the house.

The fourth day of the five-day sequence, and the middle day of the focal final three days, is the lunar New Year's Day itself, the first day of the waxing fortnight Kachalāthwa. This is Mhā Pūjā [1], the one unit in the Swanti sequence that the Newars consider to be specific and special to themselves, not shared with other Nepalis. The term "*Mhā*" (Kathmandu Newari, *mha*), means "body," here representing the physical "seat" of each of the individuals living in the household. Essentially Mhā Pūjā is the worshiping of each member of the household by the *naki(n)*, the senior active woman of the household.[7] In preparation for this ceremony, a *maṇḍala* is first drawn on a purified surface of the floor for each of the attending members of the household, as well as for any temporarily absent members who will be worshiped *in absentia*. Some households make *maṇḍala*s for pets living in the house, such as turtles and pet dogs. The *maṇḍalas* represent the human or animal body. Five piles of unhusked rice are placed on each *maṇḍala*. They represent the five *mahābhūta*, "great (or major) elements." This refers to the Hindu conception of "the gross elements, earth, water, fire, air, ether; of which the body is supposed to be composed and into which it is dissolved" (Macdonnell 1974, 208). A covering of leaves is placed over these piles, and various offerings are placed on it, such as beaten rice, water, ceremonial threads, flowers, incense, and lamp wicks.[8] The *naki(n)* worships each member of the household, first males, then females, in order of descending age, in the same way in which the benign deities are worshiped. She repeats the same sequence for each household member. She begins by putting some *swaga(n)* (a mixture of husked rice, curds, and pigment; see app. 4) on his or her forehead, and then presents offerings of threads, flowers, garlands, sweets, and fruits. Next the *naki(n)* pours the contents of a rice measuring pot, in which have been placed husked rice, popped rice, flowers, and pieces of fruit, spilling it in three successive portions over the person's head. Next the *naki(n)* offers the meat and fish containing mixture, *samhae*. This is striking as a small sacrificial gesture to the body as deity, which is at this phase treated (albeit in a minimal fashion) as a dangerous deity. The *maṇḍala*, which had been drawn in colored rice powder, is swept up, sometimes before, sometimes after the *samhae* is given, depending on the family custom. After the *pūjā* there is a feast for members of the household. The Mhā Pūjā is interpreted as helping to ensure long life and good fortune for the household members.

The final day of the Swanti sequence is Kijā Pūjā [2], literally "younger brother *pūjā*." Once again the sequence follows a general Nepalese and South Asian pattern. It is on this day in Swanti that the women who have been married out of the patrilineal household return to their natal homes. The *pūjā* is, as in many places, related to a tale about a sister who was able to protect her younger brother from death. She asked death's messenger if he would delay taking her brother until she had finished worshiping him, and until the flowers and fruits that she would present as offerings to her brother had wilted, faded, and spoiled. The messenger accepted her pious request. Through her prolonged *pūjā*, and through the presentation of special kinds of flowers and fruits that did not wilt, fade, or spoil, the sister was able to prevent Yama from taking her brother's life. Although the story and the name of the *pūjā* specify a sister's relation to a younger brother, and emphasizes her protective, "maternal" behavior, all the sisters in or related to a household worship both their elder and younger brothers.[9] During the

Kijā Pūjā all men in the household are worshiped by their sisters, if necessary by classificatory "sisters" from the mother's brother's (*pāju*) family. A *maṇḍala* is made in front of each man, and on it are placed a number of foods and flowers that resist decay and fading. These are presented to the men by the women present, who worship them in the *apāsa(n) cwanegu* fashion (app. 4). After the *pūjā*, brothers give sisters presents of *sāris* and money. There is a movement of married women throughout the city, as they try to return to their natal home during this day. Sometimes, for example, for those women whose husbands live in the Terai, long journeys are necessary. For the majority of women, however, their natal homes are elsewhere in Bhaktapur, and the older women will try to return again from their natal homes to their husbands' homes at some time during the day to intercept and see their own visiting daughters. The day, and thus Swanti as a whole, ends with a feast at each house, with the returned married-out daughters participating.

The old lunar year comes to an end, and the new lunar year and its festival cycle begins with a set of calendrically specified events that center about Bhaktapur's smallest corporate unit, the household. In contrast to the extended patrilineal *phukī* unit with its dangerous lineage deity worshiped by Tantric and sacrificial rites, the household worship of Swanti, reflecting the focus of almost all household *pūjā*s on benign deities, becomes focused on the benign deity Lakṣmī, the ideal figure of the good housekeeper, and the deified members of the household, who are worshiped as benign deities—with the minor, but interesting exception of a minimal meat offering to the bodies of the household individuals. The unit emphasized throughout is the household and its members. The space is the house. The boundaries of the house and its component units are repeatedly marked during the course of Swanti. Exterior *pūjās* are minimal—worship at the neighborhood Gaṇeśa shrine, necessary before all major household worship, and a gesture to the Āga(n) Deity in upper-status households.

The realm that is emphasized is the moral realm, the ordinary civic world of social relations. The rewards in this world and the ideal conditions for its activities are physical well-being, wealth, and security. The ultimate opposition that is emphasized to this world is here not the outside world of the demonic forces and dangerous deities beyond the borders who are the symbols of the outside in many other events (above all, those of the Devī cycle), but death as personified by Yama and his messengers and agents. Yama, the king of the realm of death, is a moral agent. Souls of the dead go first to his realm, where the reckoning is made as to whether they will proceed to heaven, a rebirth, or hell. The emphasis in relation to death here is on the movement of soul, not as it is in the dangers of the Devī cycle on the destruction of the body—quite a different kind of problem and threat. There are other symbols of destruction in Bhaktapur's festivals—they have to do with impersonal forces external to the human moral realm. However, Yama as death is an important part of that realm. He can be resisted by affection and solidarity; he and his agents have human characteristics—they can be fooled, and distracted by gambling. When he does prevail in time, the dead individual must leave the household but continues in his identity in a way that has been determined by his moral and dharmic activities. The temporary overcoming of Yama is through the emotional solidarity of the household, and this solidarity is represented by sororal emotional support and by the exchange of gifts. This is in contrast to the ideas, symbols, and emotions relating to the solidarity of the *phukī* group, *guthi*s, and larger corporate units where impersonal power in relation to dangerous deities is most central to their representation and protection.

Swanti also illustrates a symbolic movement. There is a flowing into the household of the protective power of the benign deity, and a return of the women the household had generated and who had left it. While the elementary unit of solidarity is the household there is the secondary solidarity of a parallelism of similar units. *All* households in Bhaktapur are going through the same sequences, and while most of this sequence is known to be Hindu, and more saliently Nepalese, one segment, Mhā Pūjā, the day of the new year, is thought to be uniquely Newar, an event that, typically of Newar specialties, has Tantric and Yogic references added to the interpersonal emphases of Swanti, albeit in very attenuated form.

The Swanti sequence is of major importance in Bhaktapur as a "focal" household festival.

MISCELLANEOUS EVENTS [3–7]

The lunar year contains many individual events of varying importance that are thematically independent units, in contrast, for example, to the thematic integration of Swanti. Their patterning and relations with other events in the cycle, if any, involves more abstractly structured relations, which we will consider in the appropriate places.

JUGĀRI NA:MI [3]

The ninth day of the bright fortnight Kachalāthwa is in October/ November. This is an event in commemoration of Viṣṇu-Nārāyaṇa's victory—in the form of his *avatar* Vāmana—over an Asura king. It is a time for a pilgrimage to shrines of Viṣṇu, ideally to the four major shrines of Viṣṇu in the Kathmandu Valley, although this is now limited to a visit to one of them and often, even more conveniently, to one of the two major Viṣṇu temples within Bhaktapur. The visits may be made by a group of family members or by one person representing the family. This special day is in the context of two fortnights (Kachalāgā and Kachalāthwa) specially dedicated to Viṣṇu. During this period, people who wish to may worship him daily at one of the Viṣṇu temples.

People who go to the valley shrines of Viṣṇu do this along with non-Newar Nepalese, joining them in a *melā*. In keeping with the theme of Vāmana's outwitting of the Asura, people may pray at the shrine for protection against demons, evil spirits, earthquakes, destructive rains, and the like—the nonmoral dangers that are, in the system most properly centered on and localized to Bhaktapur, the concern of the dangerous deities. From the perspective of Bhaktapur's civic religion this is an event of moderate importance.

HARI BODHINĪ [4]

This, like Jugāri Na:mi, which it follows by two days, is a valley-wide festival dedicated to Viṣṇu, celebrated in visits to his four Kathmandu Valley shrines. This day commemorates Viṣṇu's awakening after his four-month cosmic sleep, and is celebrated throughout South Asia. It is the last day of the four-month Caturmāsa Vrata (see section entitled "Ya Mārhi Punhi [9]"). The Valley's activities are described in some detail by Mary Anderson (1971, chap. 20). Thousands of people from Bhaktapur usually participate in these pilgrimages, as they participate in *melā*s in general, for the fair-like excitement of the event. The visit is given a less frivolous justification as a fulfillment of some pledge to Viṣṇu, or in order to gain some religious merit.

Gaborieau (1982) has, as we have noted, argued that for the Indo-Nepalese, Hari Bodhinī and the waking of Viṣṇu marks the end of the four-month inauspicious period in which ordinary time is mythically held in abeyance. We will return to this suggestion in chapter 16, but may note here that, in contrast with other events, it is of no internal significance to Bhaktapur, and does not mark any immediate shift in festival events. (Moderate.)[10]

SAKI MANĀ PUNHI [5]

The day and night of all full-moon days or *punhi*s, that is, the last day of the bright fortnight, is the regular monthly occasion for special activities in Bhaktapur. Some individual full-moon days are differentiated in some way, as are some other monthly occasions—such as the new-moon day, the fourteenth day of the dark fortnight, and the first day of the solar month.[11] Only some of these specially named *punhi*s are listed in the written annual calendars; some are specially noted only because they precede an important calendrical event in the following fortnight. It is often arbitrary as to whether such relatively insignificant differentiated days should be considered as a special annual event. We have listed only those specially named full-moon days that seem associated with some activity or symbolism of more than routine differentiated importance. One of these is Saki Manā Punhi. "Saki manā" refers to the edible boiled root of a certain flower. Participation in the associated events of the day is optional. There are groups of men who go on the evening of all *punhi*s to various temples to play music as a religious offering. On this particular *punhi* evening they bring mixed grain and uncooked beans to the particular temple where they customarily play and construct an elaborate picture of the temple out of the grain and beans. This is the last day of the two fortnights dedicated to Viṣṇu/Nārāyaṇa. Many people go from one shrine and temple to another, listening to music and inspecting the pictures, but the two major Nārāyaṇa temples are particular foci for visits and offerings. As this is a *punhi* evening, people also worship the moon at home, as they do on all *punhi*s. After the Viṣṇu and moon *pūjā*s many households eat special foods—as they do on many calendrical occasions. On this day it is *saki manā*, the boiled root that gives the *punhi* its name, and sweet potatoes. On this day, in which the household is emphasized as well as the benign deity Viṣṇu and the astral deity, the moon, there is a parallel participation of households, not only in similar *pūjās*, but in the eating of the same food. The movement out of the household is in a stroll to various nearby temples, which individuals, household groups, and close friends may decide to visit. There is no larger interactional civic form given to the day's events. (Moderate.)

GOPĪNĀTHA JĀTRĀ [6]

This event is the first in the bright fortnight Kachalāgā in November. While many calendrical events are associated with movement of people to one or another temple or pilgrimage site in a more or less haphazard manner some calendrical events are characterized by systematic and formalized movements through some unit of space. Sometimes a deity is moved through space, sometimes and more rarely devotees move to a temple or shrine, or to a series of them, in some prescribed order. Both the carrying of the deity and the more formalized movements of worshipers through the city is called, as it is elsewhere in South Asia, a *jātrā* (from the Sanskrit, *yātrā*, "journey, festive train, procession, pilgrimage"). These processions—most typically lead by special *jātrā* images[12] of the focal deity carried in the arms of a priest or in a palanquin, or sometimes in an enormous chariot—move over prescribed routes. The route is often the main festival route of the city, the *pradakṣiṇāpatha*, but for many festivals it is one of the less extensive routes within some other significant unit of the city (chap. 7). The paths by which the image and the major participants move from a temple to join the festival route are themselves conventionally prescribed. It should be noted that the extensiveness of the *jātrā* route is no necessary indication of the importance of the festival. Minor *jātrās* may follow the main *pradakṣiṇāpatha*, while important ones that become foci of interest for the entire city may occasionally move only through a local area.

Gopīnātha Jātrā is an example of a minor *jātrā* that follows the main city route. "Gopīnātha" is an appellation of Kṛṣṇa. The organization of the procession is the responsibility of the temple priest, the *pūjārī*, of the Kṛṣṇa temple in Lāekū Square. Some men of the Jyāpu Rājcal (also called "Kāla") *thar*, members of families that had been granted tenancy of land in exchange for this service, accompany the image playing flutes, drums, and cymbals. Observers are usually casual bypassers who often must ask who the deity being carried is. Bypassers often give coins as offerings to the deity, and the members of the procession give them flowers as *prasāda* in return. (Minor.)

BĀLĀ CA:RE [7]

Ca:re, the fourteenth day of the dark lunar fortnight, is always special to the Dangerous Goddess. On this particular *ca:re* members of families who have lost someone through death during the year join other Nepalese at the great Valley shrine and temple complex of Paśupatinātha (Anderson 1971, chap. 24). The various procedures on the day—bathing, visits to temples of Śiva, Bhairava, and the goddess (at her Devī *pīṭha* as Guhyeśvarī), all associated with various traditional and local tales—are interpreted as protecting the dead person from trouble in the afterlife of the first year, and as aiding his or her entrance into heaven.[13] Most people in Bhaktapur who have had a bereavement during the previous year try to join in this pilgrimage, which is a kind of *melā*. Those people who are unable to go to Paśupatinātha on that day may go to the equivalent temples and shrines of the "royal center" (see chap. 8, section entitled "Pilgrimage Gods of the Royal Center") on Bhaktapur's Lāekū Square. This is one of the days within the lunar year with a central or secondary reference to "normal" death.

On Bālā Ca:re a member of the Jugī *thar* begins to perform in Bhaktapur as Mahādeva, Śiva as the "great god," performances that will continue until the beginning of the solar New Year sequence [20].

The day's major event concerns only some of Bhaktapur's people in any given year, but through their lifetimes as they become bereaved most people will take part in it. (Moderate.)

SUKHU(N) BHISI(N)DYA: JĀTRĀ [8]

This *jātrā* begins on the fourteenth day of the waning lunar fortnight Kaulāgā and ends on the last day, the fifteenth, the day of the new moon. It is special to Bhaktapur, and honors Bhīmasena (in Newari, Bhisi[n] God), the special protective deity of Bhaktapur's tradesmen and shopkeepers. An image of the deity taken from the main Bhīmasena temple in Dattātreya Square is carried part way around the city on the main festival route, the *pradakṣiṇāpatha*. During the *jātrā* procession straw mats—*sukhu(n)*—and piles of straw are burned along the route "to keep Bhisi(n)dya: warm." There are various legends about Bhīmasena, one of the heroes of the Mahābhārata epic, which are used to explain this and other details of the festival. The image is left in a protected shrine along the side of the festival route during the first night, and the procession proceeds around the remainder of the route the following morning. Shopkeepers and tradesmen perform sacrifices (most often of a male goat) to Bhīmasena on these days and have *bhwae*, formal feasts, at their homes. These are *nakhā cakhā*, which include *phukī* members in addition to the household members, and the *phukī*'s married-out women are invited. This *jātrā*, then, is special to Bhaktapur, uses the main festival route, and involves all of Bhaktapur as a spatial unit, but concerns only one of its social components, the "*sāhu*," tradesmen and shopkeepers. It is the first of the year's important annual festivals taking place within the city to focus on a dangerous deity, and to entail blood sacrifice. It is the first important festival of the year to make use of—in its *jātrā* aspect—the public civic space. (Moderate.)

YA: MĀRHI PUNHI [9]

Calendrical events are distributed throughout the year in clumps. The first two fortnights of the lunar year has a relatively high density of festivals. Now commencing with Thi(n)lāthwa in November/December Bhaktapur has four lunar fortnights with only two very slightly differentiated full-moon days and a minor solar festival—a specially differentiated first day of a solar month. With the third fortnight of this period a month-long *vrata*, a period of special devotion important to all the Valley women, begins.

Ya: Mārhi Punhi [9] is one of the differentiated *punhi*, or full-moon days. This particular one is related to the agricultural cycle, and is the first of a number of such festivals. Most of the other festivals connected with the agricultural cycle (this one being a significant exception) are tied together in the stories and actions of the "Devī cycle," which we will consider as a unit below. Ya: Mārhi Punhi takes place at the end of the rice harvest (whose beginning was signaled in the major autumnal festival of Mohanī [67–77]). At this time the rice harvest is usually entirely completed. During this day in most households a mixture of husked and unhusked rice is worshiped in the room used for storing grain. The purpose of the prayer is said to be that as the grain is used up the worshipers hope that the storeroom will be filled up again. The rice mixture is taken to represent Lakṣmī. A specially kind of sweetcake, *ya: mārhi*, is presented as an offering to the deified rice, and after being left in the store room for four days, is eaten as *prasāda* from Lakṣmī. Three of the cakes had been formed into images of Gaṇeśa, Lakṣmī, and Kubera, a quasi-deity who has little other reference in Bhaktapur and is never worshiped at any other time, and who has as one of his legends the custodianship of wealth (Mani 1975, 435).[14] This is the traditional day for the giving by a tenant farmer of a share of the rice harvest to the owner of the land—although the share may now, in fact, be paid before or after this time. In the evening of this festival there is a *nakhātyā*, and married-out women are invited to their natal homes for a feast in which various kinds of food special to the occasion are added to the ordinary feast menu. This is a household centered feast, and the household is reconstructed in the invitation to the married-out daughters. The deities are benign ones. The emphasis here—in contrast to the agricultural meanings of the Devī cycle—is not on the growth of the grain but in its location in the household as part of the household's prosperity. This is a significant illustration of the difference between the relations of the Dangerous Goddess (and her Devī cycle) to fertility and the benign one, Lakṣmī, to household management and well-being. Ya: Mārhi Punhi is considered to be an exclusively Newar festival. (Moderate.)

MISCELLANEOUS EVENTS [10–11]

Ghya: Cāku Sa(n)lhu [10] is a festival in the solar cycle that fell on the thirteenth day of Pohelāthwa—late December in 1974/75. It always falls within a few days of this lunar date, and is noteworthy in that it is associated with the winter solstice and the beginning of the "ascending half" of the solar year, the six-month period during which the days progressively lengthen. It will be discussed in the next chapter. (Moderate.)

Chyālā Punhi [11] is an ordinary *punhi*, with the addition that it is customary on this day to discard clay kitchen pots that are unusable on the neighborhood *chwāsa*. Chyālā is "a curry made from bamboo shoots, potatoes, peas and other vegetables" (Manandhar 1976, 136) which it was presumably customary to prepare on this *punhi*. It is an arbitrary decision as to whether to include such minimally differentiated monthly occasions in a list of annual events. (Minor.)

THE MONTH OF THE SWASTHĀNĪ VRATA

As we have noted in the last chapter, the term "*vrata*" is often used in South Asia for any calendrically prescribed religious activity, but it has a stronger sense of "religious or ascetic observance taken upon oneself, austerity, vow, rule, holy work, such as fasting and continence" (Macdonnell 1974, 304). Noting that Nepalese calendrical events can be sorted into *jātrās*, *melās*, and *vratas* in this stronger sense, Bouillier (1982) has noted that among upper-caste Indo-Nepalese while participation in *jātrās* and *melās* is "collective," *vratas* may be individual, and done at home. She notes that those calendrical events special to women are *vratas* "performed for the most part discretely within the family group" (1982, 91). Traditionally in South Asia *vratas*, in contrast to many other forms of worship, were proper to persons of all caste levels as well as to women (Kane 1968–1977, vol. V, p. 51), but Kane notes that the Purāṇas and digests of ritual procedures prescribe several *vratas* that were specifically to be performed by women. Although there are differences in the participation of Newar and Indo-Nepalese women in festivals, Bouillier's remarks have some relevance for Bhaktapur. Thus, while men do participate in *vratas* in Bhaktapur, the city's major special annual event special to women is a *vrata*, the Swasthānī (Sanskrit, *svasthānī*) Vrata.

Pohelāgā and Sillāthwa, the two lunar fortnights in January and February that begin on the day following Chyālā Punhi, constitute one of a number of two-fortnight periods in Bhaktapur's annual calendar devoted as a whole to some special theme and activities. Within such periods some specific calendrical events may be connected to the theme, but others that occur may be independent of it. These four weeks are the period of the Swasthānī Vrata. This is an important festival month for the women of the Kathmandu Valley of various ethnic groups. It has been studied at length by Linda Iltis with a focus on participation by Newar women (1985) and by Lynn Bennett as an aspect of her study of Chetri women in the Valley (1977, 1983). The *vrata* is based on a group of legends (*Swasthānī Vrata Kathā*: See B. M. P. Sharma [1955]),[15] which combines various traditional stories about Śiva, Satī, and Pārvatī. The oldest known manuscript of this collection is in Newari (Iltis 1985, 8):

> The *Śrī Swasthānī Vrata Kathā* text is a compilation of 29–33 stories, some of which are unique versions of Purāṇic stories popular in Hindu communities throughout South Asia, as well as others which are unique local legends which concern people and places in the Kathmandu Valley of Nepal, and explain the origins and benefits in rituals honoring the Goddess Swasthānī.
>
> Rooted in Newar language and culture, the worship of Swasthānī has spread to other ethnic groups and cultures in Nepal via the trade networks of the Newars, and primarily through Newar scribes. . . . The *Śrī Swasthānī*

Vrata Kathā text has been translated into Nepali, Hindi and perhaps Maithili.

The text is read aloud in successive portions, one each evening, in households in Bhaktapur in its Newari version. It is read traditionally by men, but its message, as Lynn Bennett emphasizes for the Chetris, is directed to women. Before turning to the actions of the Swasthānī Vrata, something should be said of the text which is summarized in Bennett (1983, 274–306). The text deals with themes and especially conflicts of romantic love and arranged marriage; of sexuality and marriage; of sexual passion, jealousy, faithfulness, and duty; and of the transformation of a man, in this case Śiva, from self-absorption to social usefulness through marriage. In the course of the stories, Pārvatī, the central human-like protagonist, must deal with these conflicts. She is able to get Śiva, the man she loves, as husband through devotion and works (*vrata*) dedicated to Swasthānī (an appellation of the transcendent form of the Goddess), but it is her proper social behaviour, "her attention to the details of the ritual, her distribution of alms, and above all, her religious devotion [which are] stressed along with her asceticism" (Bennett 1983, 224). Bennett sums up the significance of Pārvatī in the Swasthānī stories and their associated rituals (and in general) (ibid., 272f.):

> The many contradictory elements which go into the Devī's role as perfect wife and mother are [now] apparent: she must be both sensual and ascetic; flirtatious and faithful; fertile and yet utterly pure. In the myths about her gentle aspects—most notably as Pārvatī—the goddess is all these things. She represents an ideal, a blending of opposing qualities which actual village women can never fully achieve. . . . In Hindu mythology [Pārvatī] . . . is the impossibly perfect model, embodying the contradictory values of Hinduism particularly as they affect women in Hindu patrilineal social structure. This, I maintain, is why the gentle side of the goddess is especially important to village women.
>
> Like Durga, of course, Pārvatī is worshiped and greatly revered by both men and women. But, just as men are largely responsible for the worship of Durga and more conversant than women with the texts about her, women are more involved with the rituals and texts concerning Pārvatī and the other gentle forms of the goddess.

Although Swasthānī is the Goddess as full creative deity, in accordance with the emphasis on Pārvatī as the ideal woman centrally located in the social and moral world the festival is devoted to the ordinary deities, and in the stories and in the symbolic enactments, it is Pārvatī's conventional relations to the benign male deities Śiva and Viṣṇu that are emphasized. The events of this month are not part of the Devī cycle. We may note here that among other valley Hindu groups there is another very important women's festival connected with the Swāsthanī stories, Tij, which is *not* observed by the women of Bhaktapur (see section on miscellaneous minor events [52–58], below).

During this month the general Valley pattern is followed. Successive sections of the *Swasthānī Vrata Kathā* are read in the household each evening during the month. Girls and women past the Ihī ceremony, and, for those who had had a "social marriage" whose husbands are still living,[16] will take part in the other ceremonies, the *vrata*s themselves. These "married" girls and women (in some, but not all *thar*s) may wear red *sāri*s, the color of marriage *sāri*s, during this period. Some of them fast by not eating meat. They worship Śiva, usually as a *liṅga*,[17] both at home and at various designated *tīrthas* at the riverside. While a majority, perhaps, of women remain in Bhaktapur and do not participate in the major valley pilgrimages of the period, many women do participate in the valley-wide *melā* (described in detail in Iltis [1985]). The motives for womens' religious activities during the period are said to be ones similar to those Bennett (1983, 276) has noted for valley Chetri women—for example, for married women, to protect their households and their husbands; for unmarried girls, to help ensure a good husband in the future.[18]

Men in Bhaktapur also participate in the festival, but what was reported as having previously been daily participation had diminished greatly by the time of this study. The foci of the men's worship were Viṣṇu and Śiva, important actors in the Swasthānī story. On each day of the month men would go in groups, following a leader, to bathe in the river and then on to the city's main Viṣṇu and Śiva temples to do *pūjā*. The leader of the group would call out the names of Viṣṇu and his *avatar*s and the various names of Śiva, and the men in the group, carrying banners, would chant "Hari Mādya:." ("Hari" is one of the appellations of Viṣṇu/Nārāyaṇa and "Mādya:," that is, Māhadya:, the Great God, a major appellation of Śiva.) The activities of the Swastānī month end on the full-moon day, with the Mādya: Jātrā [14], which we will discuss below.

SARASVATĪ FESTIVALS [12, 13]

Sarasvatī Jātrā [12] takes place on the night of the fourth day of the fortnight, and is part of a unit or sequence that includes the events of the following day ([13], below). On the day of Sarasvatī Jātrā students, for whom Sarasvatī is a patron deity, go to her main temple, and massage the legs of her *jātrā* image. It is said that she has just returned from a long journey from Lhasa in Tibet, and her legs are tired.[19] In the course of the day the image, on this day referred to as "Sarasvatī who has returned from Lhasa" is carried around the main festival route, in a small procession, or *jātrā*. (Minor.)

Śrī Pa(n)chamī [13], which occurs the next day, continues the special worship of Sarasvatī or (an alternate appellation) Śrī, in common with other Nepalese Hindus. This is again primarily a festival for students and their households. The students fast by not eating meat on this day. They go to the main Sarasvatī temple to pray for success in their studies. *Prasāda* from the deity is brought back to the household to be shared. Men and women Jyāpus also go on this day to the temple and pray to Sarasvatī for aid in the weaving of cloth and in farmwork. People from other groups may worship her at her temple on that day, particularly those who, like the students, have or wish to have skills that require study and memory.

Jyāpu *bhajana* groups play music at the Sarasvatī temple on this day. They play special music called "Basanta" or "spring music"—although Basanta, starting in Caitra (Caulāthwa), is still two months away, for this day is the traditional lunar event associated with the early part of the "ascending half" of the year, which had begun some three weeks earlier.

Śrī Pa(n)chamī is important to essential members of the city's society and is thus in our scale of "moderate" importance for the city.

MĀDYA: JĀTRĀ [14], END OF SWASTHĀNĪ VRATA

This *jātrā* comes on the final day, the full-moon day, of Sillāthwa. This day is also the last day of the four weeks of the Swasthānī Vrata. This full-moon day is called "Swasthānī Punhi" or "Si Punhi." The day is said to be an important event—but many of the activities previously associated with it have been discontinued. A procession honoring Śiva begins at the riverside at the Khware *ghāṭ* and proceeds to the nearby Gā:hitī Square, where it joins the main festival route, and then proceeds around it. The procession stops temporarily at the two main Nārāyaṇa temples, one in the upper half of the city and the other in the lower half, then continuing its circumambulation of the festival route returns to

Gā:hitī Square, and then to the river, where it disbands.[20] This *jātrā* takes place during the day. Previously in the evening children and adults dressed as Śiva and Pārvatī were carried around the city in palanquins, accompanied by torches and music. Still now on this day people often perform special *pūjās* to Śiva as "Mādya:" (Mahādya:, the "Great God") in their homes and to his representations as *liṅgas* at the riverside. These activities are an extension of the worship of Śiva *liṅgas* during the course of the Svāsthanī month. In the evening there are household suppers in which various sweets, including special forms of sweetcakes dedicated to Mahādya:, are eaten. Traditionally 108 of these tiny cakes were presented to wives, who would then eat one hundred of them, and present the remaining eight to her husband.[21]

The themes of the previous month are summed up with this act of wifely household devotion in the context of worship of the benign deities. What is added here is a *jātrā* that emphasizes the integration of the city through its visits to the two Viṣṇu temples, and the circumambulation of the main festival route.

The procession is a relatively small one now. Most people do not join it but go about their ordinary activities during the day. (Moderate.)

SILĀ CA:RE (ŚIVARĀTRĪ) [15]

The following waning fortnight, Sillāgā (in February) has only one festival event, of moderate importance for Bhaktapur as a city—although of major importance for all Shaivite Hindus.

This *ca:re*, the fourteenth day of the dark fortnight, is—like all *ca:re*—special to the Goddess, and there are as on other *ca:res* special ceremonies for the Āga(n) Gods and at the temples of the Tantric deities. This particular *ca:re* is also devoted to Śiva.[22] On this day the major valley shrine complex of Paśupatinātha becomes a center for Shaivite pilgrims from India and Nepal. Bhaktapur's Dattātreya temple is a secondary pilgrimage center at this time. Many Shaivite pilgrims from India and elsewhere in Nepal—both "householders" and *sādhus* —come to Bhaktapur at this time. Some of the *sādhus* are housed at one or another of the city's *maṭhas*, "monasteries," for wandering Hindu renouncers, built as acts of piety by Malla kings. As we have noted, neither Dattātreya temple nor the *maṭhas* have "Newar" priests. These pilgrims (and others during the course of the year) come to Bhaktapur in a sort of benign invasion of interest to its citizens, but they are not, as such, part of the Newars' own city-centered symbolic life.

People in Bhaktapur may go themselves to the Dattātreya temple, and, as pilgrims themselves, to the fair-like *melā* at Paśupatinātha. Within Bhaktapur in the evening fires are made along the roadside and in the main neighborhood squares. Many men—from *thar*s throughout Bhaktapur's social structure (except the untouchables)—sit by the fires all night chanting the name of Śiva, some of them smoking cannabis, which is commonly smoked by Shaivite pilgrims during the festival, and which was, at the time of this study, sold by stall keepers at Paśupatinātha during the *melā*. The legends told to explain the fires are variants of a widespread Hindu tale associated with the day (cf. Kane 1968–1977, vol. V, p. 255). In summary, the legends recount that once upon a time a hunter caught in the woods at night sat shivering under the particular kind of tree whose wood is supposed to be burnt for the fires made that night. Śiva, hearing the sounds "sh, sh" made by the shivering man, thought that the man was calling his name, and manifested himself to offer the hunter a boon. The hunter requested that he be able to stay forever with Śiva in his heaven, and Śiva granted his wish. The salvation of the shivering hunter under his tree, is said by some to be associated with the approach of spring when trees are beginning to bud again and that Śiva who periodically destroys and recreates the world is bringing it to life again in its annual cycle of death and rebirth. There are no feasts or special household activities on this day.

This is one of the calendrical events in which the borders of the domestic moral realm is represented by means of the ideas and images associated with the benign deities. Śiva responds, in his absentminded but recognizably human way, to the needs of the hunter. That response is produced by a misunderstanding, a kind of trickery, for the hunter[23] has done nothing in the *dharmic* moral realm to earn it. The legend, the fires in the public spaces in whose warmth some men spend the night, the smoking of cannabis, the references to and mimicking of the absentminded and yogic Śiva, probe at the human outer boundaries of the moral realm.

In the day's explorations of the "benign margins" of the moral realm, neither the household nor the integrated city are directly referred to but are present as that which is being, for the moment, escaped. (Moderate.)

THE MINOR FESTIVALS OF KṚṢṆA (HOLI) [16, 17]

Cillāthwa, the bright fortnight of the following month (February/ March) includes a period—from the eighth day until the full-moon day—which in the other Newar cities of the Valley as in South Asia in general is a time for major activities devoted to Kṛṣṇa. In Bhaktapur the activities of the period are comparatively quite minor. The first day, the eighth, is called "Cīr Swāegu" [16], which means "to erect a *cīr*," that is, a bamboo pole to which a banner of varicolored cloths has been attached. The practice, which gives its name to the day is, significantly, *not* done in Bhaktapur now (although it was, on the evidence of the name, probably done sometime in the past), although it is still done in Kathmandu (Anderson 1971, 250). In Bhaktapur the day simply introduces the week, but has no special activities of its own. In both Kathmandu and, even more so, in Patan Kṛṣṇa is associated with major festivals. In Bhaktapur some of these are ignored, others given only minor importance. This is an example of the selection of deities and emphases that are open to each community.

In the period between the Cīr Swāegu day and the full-moon day, called "Holi Punhi," some people go in processions around the city, and throw *abhir*, a red powder (app. 4). The men in these processions, few in number compared to the numbers participating in the city's major *jātrās*, are mostly from the Jyāpu *thar*s. Their throwing of the powder is restrained in that they are, it is said, "afraid" to throw the *abhir* at men of superior *thar* status. This is in contrast to Anderson's account for elsewhere in the Valley that "the erection of the *cīr* pole gives eight-day license to one and all to drench almost anyone he meets, including cows and dogs, with powder of the most brilliant vermilion" (1971, 251). She reports that the traditional license of the period was being brought under control in Kathmandu because it was becoming a public nuisance.

As we have argued previously in our discussion of Kṛṣṇa and Rāma as objects of *bhakti*, personal devotion, *bhakti* religion is antithetical to the traditional community organization that Bhaktapur's Hinduism helps constitute and support. Gopal Singh Nepali found some evidence in the phrasing of a folk song about it, that Holi (as the week-long period is called elsewhere) is a "culture trait introduced from outside [Nepal]" (1965, 338). Its popularity in Kathmandu and Patan, along with that of other Kṛṣṇa festivals, may attest to a relative breaking away from traditional priestly Hindu civic organization at the time of its introduction in contrast to the more conservative and traditional Bhaktapur.

On the last day of the period, Holi Punhi [17], or, as it is also called, Kṛṣṇa Jātrā, in Bhaktapur an image of Kṛṣṇa that is kept in the Taleju temple[24] is carried around the city's main festival route. Not many people go out of their way to watch the procession. There are no other special activities on that day. (Both [16] and [17] are comparatively minor events in Bhaktapur.)

THE APPROACH OF THE SEASON OF ANXIETY [18, 19]

The waning fortnight Sillāgā (March) has no special events, with the exception of Pāsā Ca:re [18], the fourteenth day, one of the *ca:re*s with special features. "*Pāsā*" means "friend." In Bhaktapur the day is also called Piśāc Ca:re, a *piśāca* being a ghoul-like evil spirit. In Kathmandu, where the day was traditionally the occasion for more elaborate celebrations than in Bhaktapur, the day is called "Pāhā(n) Ca:re," that is, "Guest Ca:re." In Bhaktapur there are special emphases on the day in the Tantric worship of tutelary goddesses required on all *ca:re*. Thus, in the Taleju temple it is necessary to offer an animal sacrifice to Taleju, while on most other *ca:re* the meat-containing mixture, *samhae*, is sufficient. In Āga(n) *pūjā*s people add references to the *piśāca* and ask for protection. Many farmers' *guthis* perform blood sacrifices to dangerous deities. Those people who have protective pollution-consuming deified stones, "Luku Mahādya:," in their courtyards (chap. 8), clean them on this day. The main idea on this day, is protection from vague evil forces. Anderson remarks that this *ca:re* comes at a time "when typhoid, dysentery, cholera and smallpox flourish with the advent of hot weather, prior to cleansing monsoon rains. It is a time of uneasiness" (1971, 264). The anxieties symbolized by spirits and the special worship of the dangerous tutelary gods, are thematically balanced by feasts in households, to which married-out women and friends are invited—hence the names "Pāsā" and "Pāhā(n)." As Anderson puts it, "traditionally on this day homes and courtyards are thoroughly cleaned and decorated to welcome relatives and acquaintances in the hope that such a display of goodwill, generosity and mutual love will dispel evil thoughts and harmful spirits. Especially it is important to invite married daughters back to paternal homes for family feasts, that sisters may meet in good fellowship" (1971, 265).[25] (Moderate.)

Two days later, on the first day of the following fortnight, the bright fortnight Caulāthwa (March/April), is the day of Cika(n) Buyegu [19], the "oil-rubbing" day. For the upper *thar*s, the Chathariyā and above, there are no special activities on this day, but the farming *thar*s and some *thar*s below them in Bhaktapur and in other Newar communities rub mustard-seed oil, *cika(n)*, on their own and their children's bodies. It is thought that this will protect them from sickness during the following year.[26] This is followed by a special household supper. (Minor.)

The themes of dangerous spirits and illness and of protection against them, which are introduced here, are the first anticipatory references in the lunar cycle to a time of the year in which a long season of disease and the critical early stages of the main agricultural cycle, the rice cycle, bringing major risks for individual and civic well-being, are approaching. These anxious themes become represented in later calendrical events (mostly within the Devī cycle) with increasing density and interrelation.

BISKĀ:, THE SOLAR NEW YEAR [20–29]

In 1975/76 the solar New Year sequence began on the eleventh day of the waxing lunar fortnight Caulāthwa, during April. This sequence lasts for nine days, and includes several component events. We will present these in the following chapter in conjunction with the other events of the solar calendar. The sequence as a whole is of focal importance for Bhaktapur, in ways that we will specify. It centers around the dangerous deities, and is concerned with the integration of city units in the face of the passions that can destroy that unity.

THE DEWĀLĪ PERIOD, THE WORSHIP OF THE DIGU LINEAGE DEITIES [30]

The period starting on the first day of the dark fortnight, Caulāgā (April) and ending some fifty days later on the day before Sithi Nakhā [36], is the span during which the worship of each *phukī*'s externally situated lineage deity, the Digu Dya:, must take place. Each *phukī* has a particular day within the Dewālī period when it customarily does its Dewālī *pūjā*. We have discussed the events of this period in chapter 9. The Dewālī worship is to a dangerous deity through meat and alcoholic offerings. It is the most important ritual marker of the *phukī*. (Major.)

THE MINOR DASAI(N) OF RĀMA [31, 32]

In our consideration of the Kṛṣṇa ceremonies of Holi we had examples of ceremonial days in Bhaktapur's calendar which are of interest because they are *unimportant* in comparison with the way they are treated in other South Asian or Nepalese communities. While such comparative emphases may be due to factors that are tangential to the concerns of our study, certain examples of relative neglect or emphasis may be related to Bhaktapur's particular kind of symbolic organization. This seems to be the case in celebrations of Viṣṇu's *avatar*s, whose cult elsewhere in South Asia is a response to special needs and conditions that have not characterized traditional Bhaktapur. This is true not only of Kṛṣṇa but also of Rāma, whose cult is important elsewhere throughout South Asia. Two calendrical events in the fortnight of Caulāgā associated with Rāma are of considerable importance elsewhere but of relatively minor importance in Bhaktapur's calendar of festivals.

The eighth day of the fortnight is called "Cait Dasai(n)" [31]. The name refers to a nine-day period observed elsewhere in South Asia, beginning on the first day of the fortnight and ending the following day, Rāma Navamī, a period during which portions of the *Rāmāyaṇa* epic are read. The worship of this spring festival lasts in Bhaktapur for only one day. In Bhaktapur's Devī-centered interpretation, the importance of this day is said to be that on it Rāma worshiped the Goddess for help in his battle against Rāvaṇa. This gives it a thematic connection with Bhaktapur's major Dasai(n), Mohanī [67–77], the autumn harvest festival. In accord with its reference to the Dangerous Goddess, many households sacrifice animals and have feasts, and there are sacrifices to the Āga(n) deities, to Taleju, and to other Tantric deities at temples. In contrast to the autumnal Mohanī, animal sacrifice is optional. Although the Dangerous Goddess is a focus of worship, this festival is not integrated into the Devī cycle. (Moderate.)

The following day, the ninth day of the fortnight, is Rāma Navamī [32]. This, the birthday of Rāma, was traditionally a very minor day in Bhaktapur, only commemorated by the temple priests of the Rāma temples in their own worship at the temples. In recent years some followers of a new *bhakti* cult of Rāma go in groups to pray at his temples on this day. (Minor.)

HONORING MOTHERS [33]

The last day of the dark fortnight, the new-moon day, is called Mā(n) yā khwa: swāegu [33], literally "looking at mother's face." This, like a later parallel day for fathers [51], involves all Kathmandu Valley Hindus and Buddhists. People whose mother has died more than one year previously and who are thus beyond the first year's period of mourning and commemorative ceremonies go, if at all possible, to join other Nepalese at a pilgrimage site, Mātā Tīrtha, which is two adjoining ponds about six miles to the southwest of Kathmandu.[27] They do a commemorative ceremony, a *sora śrāddha*, with, for well-to-do farming and upper-level *thars*, assistance from their family priest. An offering of food is given to their family Brahman as a special offering, a *dāna*, for the mother. If unable to go to Mātā Tīrtha, people will bathe and make their offerings at a *tīrtha* at the river in Bhaktapur itself.

Those whose mothers are living return to their mother's home,[28] to "see their mother's face." The mother is worshiped as a deity. Men and women, boys and girls, bow their heads to their mother's feet, then wash them, and place offerings of small coins on them. In some *thars* the worshipers take some of the water that has been used to wash the feet and drink it as *prasāda*, which, as we have noted in our discussion of *cipa*, polluted food (chap. 11), dramatically symbolizes the worshiper's dependent and incorporated relationship to the mother and thus her continuing responsibility to them. Children who have left home try to return on this day, bringing with them offerings of sweetcakes, curds, eggs, and *swaga(n)*. The mother returns some of these offerings to her children as *prasāda*. If their mother is not living people on this day may offer beaten rice and sweetcakes to the wife of their family *purohita*. After a series of festivals devoted to dangerous deities this day returns to the household, with its benign deity—here the deified mother. The emphasis again is on the inside of the household, and the reaffirmation of its internal relations against an opposing theme of loss and death. (Moderate.)

AKṢAYA TṚTĪYĀ [34]

The third day, the Tṛtīyā of the waxing fortnight Bachalāthwa (April/May), is a very minor holiday in Bhaktapur, but is of interest in at least one other Newar community. In Hindu tradition it is an ancient *vrata*, "one of the 3 and 1/2 days popularly believed to be most auspicious in the year" (Kane 1968–1977, vol. V, p. 89). In Bhaktapur on this day Śiva is worshiped in many homes with a special offering of a sugar and water syrup. The day has the peculiarity—a residual of its traditional auspiciousness—that marriages and other rites of passages can be done on it without the necessity of determining astrologically the proper *sāit*, the exact propitious day and time for the ceremony, which would otherwise be necessary.

According to Toffin, in the Newar town of Panauti, Akṣaya Tṛtīyā is the day on which the *Ihī*, the mock-marriage of young girls, is annually performed (1984, 403). (Minor.)

CAṆḌEŚVARĪ JĀTRĀ [35]

On the last day of the fortnight there occurs one of the year's several local *twa: jātrā*s. Although they center in one particular neighborhood or *twa:*, they are listed in the annual calendar and are often of general city-wide interest. This one takes place in the Tibukche(n) *twa:* and is devoted to Caṇḍeśvarī, a form of the Goddess, who has no other civic significance in Bhaktapur. The *jātrā* image is carried around the *twa*: on that day, and there are, characteristically of such *twa: jātrā*s, feasts, *nakhātyā*, in many houses in the festival area in which not only relations but friends from other parts of the city are invited. (In comparison with certain other of the *twa: jātrā*s, it is a minor event.)

BUDDHA JAYA(N)TĪ AND A NOTE ON "BUDDHIST" FESTIVALS IN BHAKTAPUR

In previous chapters we discussed the relations between the Hindu and Buddhist aspects of the Newar society and religion of Bhaktapur. For some purposes, as we emphasized, they can be considered separate components, while for others they blend or overlap. The case is similar with festivals. There are some that can be said to be Hindu, some Buddhist,[30] some (the great majority) common to both, although in the latter case the interpretations may vary. These differentiations are, in any detail, beyond the scope of this study. There are a few festivals in Bhaktapur that are mostly of concern to the city's "Buddhists" (as we have defined them in chap. 5). In other festivals the same festival image will be defined differently by Buddhists and Hindus so that the *jātrā* is relevant to both groups. An example is the predominantly Buddhist festival centering on images of the Five Dhyāni Buddhas, which are identified by Hindus as the Five Pandava Brothers (see section on Gunhi Punhi, below).

This day, Buddha Jaya(n)tī, takes place on the full-moon day of Bachalāthwa, the same day as the Caṇḍeśvarī Jātrā. It commemorates the day that the historic Buddha was born, received enlightenment, and died—all having occurred on the same day of the year. An image of the Buddha is carried around the city's main festival route. While high-status Hindus say that this *jātrā* has no significance for them, other Bhaktapur Hindus may view the *jātrā*, make small offerings to the deity, and receive *prasāda*.[31] This is typical of all such "Buddhist" festivals in Bhaktapur.

SITHI NAKHĀ [36]

The festival calendar has no events in the waning fortnight of Bachalāgā in May. However, the following fortnight, the bright fortnight Tachalāthwa, includes on its sixth day an event, Sithi Nakhā, which signals the preparation for the ending of the year's relatively uneventful phase and introduces an anticipatory period of about one month until Bhagasti [40], when with the annual death of Bhaktapur's major protective goddesses, the Nine Durgās, a new phase of Bhaktapur's festival year will begin.

The seven-week Dewālī period, the period within which the *phukī* lineage gods, the Digu Gods, are worshiped, is terminated on the evening of the day before Sithi Nakhā.

Sithi Nakhā [36] is the first occurrence within the lunar year of the Devī cycle, a set of closely interrelated annual events ([36], [40], [45], [67–76] and the Nine Durgās' performances) during a nine-month period, which reflect important stages of the rice agricultural cycle and whose imagery centers on the forms and activities of the dangerous goddess. We will devote a chapter to that cycle, but in this chapter will simply list and briefly characterize those events to indicate their position in the overall cycle. Sithi Nakhā is the day by which the annual performances of the Nine Durgās must be completed. It is the day on which wells and ponds are traditionally to be cleaned in anticipation of the coming rains which will make that annual activity impossible. It is the day which anticipates the last weeks of the dry season and the time at which the planting of seed rice must begin. (Moderate.)

CAṆḌI BHAGAVATĪ JĀTRĀ [37]

On the same day as Sithi Nakhā Day, a local *twa: jātrā*, that of Caṇḍi Bhagavatī, an appellation of Bhagavatī, is held in the Kwāche(n) *twa:*. A locally housed image of the goddesses is carried around the *twa:* festival route. This is a typical local *twa: jātrā* of minor civic importance (compare Caṇḍeśvarī Jātrā [35]).

DASA HARĀ [38]

This calendrical event of minor importance for Bhaktapur is common to all Hindus. It is on the tenth day, *dasa* (Sanskrit *daśa*), of the month. In its traditional Indian version it was a day for removing "sins," through bathing in the Ganges, and later in other large rivers (Kane 1968–1977, vol. V, p. 90f.). In Bhaktapur the custom persists with, it would seem, an emphasis rather on protection from external misfortunes. People in Bhaktapur go to bathe in the river at the Kware *ghāṭ*, considering their ritual bath as worship to the river Ganges, and present certain vegetables—cucumber, red pepper, and an edible root, *phākha(n)*, to the river. This bathing and presentation is supposed to remove "bad luck" from the bathers. On this day there may be small family dinners in special commemoration of the day. Otherwise there are no special activities. (Minor.)

PANAUTI JĀTRĀ [39]

This annual event on the last, the full-moon day of Tachalāthwa, is listed in Bhaktapur's annual lunar calendar. This is an occasion for a *melā*, starting with a pilgrimage out of the city to Panauti, a town to the east of Bhaktapur, which had been part of the hinterland state of Bhaktapur in the Malla period. Thousands of people from Bhaktapur join throngs of people from elsewhere in the valley to bathe in the river at Panauti and to worship at a hill-top shrine there.[32] There are no ritual events in Bhaktapur on this day (apart from the regular full-moon worship). (Moderate.)

BHAGASTI [40], THE DEATH OF THE NINE DURGĀS (DEVĪ CYCLE)

The eighth day, the *aṣṭamī*, of the following month, the waning month Tachalāgā (June), is Bhagavatī's *aṣṭamī*, or Bhagasti. In the weeks following this day as the rains start the young rice plants are transplanted into the muddy paddy fields. On this day the masks of the Nine Durgās are "cremated" and those deities die, to be reborn in the course of the Mohanī festival, some three-and-one-half months later. (Moderate.)

MINOR FESTIVALS OF VIṢṆU [41–43] AND THE BEGINNING OF THE CĀTURMĀSA VRATA

The bright fortnight Dillāthwa (June/July) includes three events related to Viṣṇu. On the second day of the month is the Jaganā God Jātrā [41]. Jaganā (Jagannātha) is an avatar of Viṣṇu, usually thought of as a form of Kṛṣṇa. For Bhaktapur this is a very minor city *jātrā*. The *jātrā* image of Jaganā God from the temple of Jagannātha near the Durbar Square is carried around the city by a small group of people, and the *pūjārī* of the temple must perform special worship on that day. (Minor.)

The eleventh day of Dillāthwa, the *ekādaśī*—which is in all fortnights special to Viṣṇu—is of differentiated importance in this fortnight. It is called, as everywhere in South Asia, "Hari Śayanī [42]," Viṣṇu's sleeping." It is on this day that Viṣṇu begins his four-month cosmic sleep, from which he will awaken on the *ekādaśī* of Kachalāthwa four months later, on the day of Hari Bodhinī [4], "Viṣṇu's awakening," in the following lunar year. This *ekādaśī* marks the beginning of a four-month *vrata* called "Caturmāsa," the "four months." Gaborieau (1982), who gives this period critical importance in his account of the structure of the Indo-Nepalese calendar, remarks that for Hindus the Caturmāsa is considered an inauspicious period within which, for example, initiation and marriages, and worship for the protection of the village and lineage cannot take place.

For Bhaktapur the special status of this period of Viṣṇu's sleep is not salient in the annual festival cycle. Other major deities in Hindu tradition leave the world to sleep at various times, also typically for four months. For Bhaktapur the annual departure of the Nine Durgās at Bhagasti seems to be a more critical marker of transition, as are the events in the autumnal harvest festival that lead to their rebirth. The Caturmāsa period is, however, of Sanskritic importance to people of the upper *thar*s. Individuals may decide to perform a *vrata* during the period, as is the case in all *vrata*s in fulfillment of a vow or in hope of some good result. Typically people may alter their diets—renouncing meat or salt, eating once a day, or eating from special leaves rather than dishes for the period of the *vrata*. They may do special worship, including elaborate *pūjā*s, to Viṣṇu during the period. During Caturmāsa Brahman storytellers tell stories about Viṣṇu in the public squares.[33]

The twelfth day of the fortnight, also devoted to Viṣṇu/Nārāyaṇa, is Tulasī Piye Day [43], the day of the planting (*piyegu*) of the *tulasī* plant. *Tulasī*, a variety of basil, is a plant that has various mythic meanings in Hindu tradition, but which here has its major meaning as representing

Viṣṇu. On this day people everywhere in the city plant *tulasī* seedlings in small clay pots, using one pot for each person in the household. If the plant dies during the next month, that is a sign that the individual whom it represents may experience some misfortune. During this period people pray to the plant as Viṣṇu/Nārāyaṇa, and after watering it take back a bit of water from one of the leaves and drink it as *prasāda*. Some upper-status people put a bit of gold in the holes in which the seedlings are placed as part of the offering. Although it is only the duration of the first month that is significant as an omen, the plants are kept alive as long as possible. After they die, the leaves are kept for use in death ceremonies, where the leaves represent Viṣṇu as "Tulasī Nārāyaṇa." They are joined with *piṇḍa*s, representations of deceased ancestors, during the ceremonies. The day in itself is a minor event.

GURU PŪJĀ [44]

The last day in this fortnight, the full-moon day, is the day of Guru Pūjā, when people are supposed to worship their *guru*s. Although the day is included in local calendrical lists, it is observed—otherwise than as an ordinary full-moon day—by only a relatively few families in Bhaktapur. It is considered to be generally a Partyā, a non-Newar Nepalese Hindu tradition. (Minor.)

GĀTHĀ MUGA: CA:RE [45] (DEVĪ CYCLE)

This is the only festival in the waning fortnight of Dillāgā, in July. It takes place on the fourteenth, the *ca:re*, and it is a major event in the phase of the Devī cycle characterized by the absence from Bhaktapur of the protective Nine Durgās. Gāthā Muga: Ca:re takes place when the rice plants have, ideally, been transplanted into the paddy fields. It is the culmination of a period of conventional shouting of obscenities, culminating in the chasing of effigies of demons out of the city where they are cremated. It is the last event in the Devī cycle before the focal Mohanī harvest festival [67–76]. (Major.)

NĀGA PA(N)CAMĪ [46]

The entire duration of the tenth lunar month, Gu(n)lā (July/August), is of special importance to Newar Buddhists throughout the valley (Lewis 1984, 349ff.; Anderson 1971, chap. 7), and there are daily processions and other special events involving the Buddhist population of the city.

But in Bhaktapur's Hindu calendar the first half of the month, the bright fortnight Gu(n)lāthwa, contains only two annual events: Nāga Pa(n)camī, of moderate importance; and Gunhi Punhi [47], on the last day of the fortnight, introducting a sequence of focal importance. The fifth day, the *pa(n)camī* of the waxing fortnight Gu(n)lāthwa, is Nāga Pa(n)camī [46]. On this day the supernatural serpent, the *nāga*, is worshiped, as it is in various ways on this day throughout South Asia. In Bhaktapur, drawings on paper of *nāga*s are placed at the main doorway of each house, and at the entrance of each room of the house. The paintings are worshiped and offered a special mixture of grasses, rice, beans, and cow dung. This is said to help protect people from poisonous snakes, which have become more numerous at this season, and from the equivocally malevolent *nāga* itself, who is often asked to refrain from troubling the house. (Moderate.)

GUNHI PUNHI [47], BEGINNING OF THE DENSEST FESTIVAL SEASON

The four lunar fortnights starting with the last day of Gu(n)lāthwa in August and ending with the last day of the elaborate autumn harvest festival, Mohanī, on the tenth day of Kachalāthwa (September/October) contain thirty-one of the year's seventy-nine annual calendrical events, and thus constitute the year's densest season of such events. This is the quiet segment of the agricultural rice cycle. The rice planting has been completed at its beginning, and major harvesting will begin only at its end. The great farming segment of Bhaktapur's community has only routine maintenance work to do during this season, and is not fully engaged in the fields.

The full-moon day of Gu(n)lāthwa, Gunhi (or, sometimes Guni)[34] Punhi [47], is the time for a group of events in Bhaktapur. Two among them are of special interest. One of these is a variation of a pan-Hindu set of procedures customary on the day (Kane 1968–1977, vol. V, p. 127) that in Bhaktapur emphasizes the purification and rededication of Rājopādhyāya Brahmans. The other is the introduction of an annual carnival and festival of the dead, a festival that is specially elaborated in Bhaktapur. On the day before the full-moon day, that is, on the fourteenth day of the fortnight, Brahmans and some "orthodox" Chathariyā shave their heads (as always, with the exception of the queue),[35] and supervise the purification of their houses with cow dung. On the morning of the full-moon day the Chathariyās go to the river at Kware to bathe and change their *jonā*s, or sacred threads. Then, at a later time, all the Rājopādhyāya Brahman males who had their initiations as Brahmans go to the river at the same spot for a ritual bath. No one else is supposed to enter or cross the river when the Brahmans are in it. After bathing the Brahmans replace their *jonā*s, while passages from the Vedas are being recited. They mark their foreheads with vertical and then horizontal triple parallel lines, and put small pieces of cow dung above their eyes, all of which is said to represent the Trisul and other symbols of Śiva, and marks their vocation as Shaivite priests. The seven eldest Brahmans present represent the seven Ṛṣis, and the other Brahmans pray to them and to their *pitṛ*s, their patrilineal ancestors, and make offerings. These proceedings are considered by the Brahmans as a reestablishment of their sacred authority through purification and rededication to the seven Ṛṣis from one or another of whom all Brahmans claim descent.

There are also symbolic actions of exchange and solidarity at this time. Each Brahman brings with him many yellow threads and small cloth bags containing a mixture of dried white flowers and two kinds of seeds. These represent the household from which the Brahman, or most often a group of Brahmans, come. The threads and bags are put in the purified area in which the Ṛṣi *pūjā* is to take place. Then, at the end of the *pūjā*, one of the Brahman leaders, fastens bags from all households on each of the Brahmans, tying them to their left wrists by means of the yellow threads. Then each Brahman takes threads and bags from his household, and ties one in turn onto the wrists of each of the other Brahmans.[36]

There are a miscellany of other customary activities during the day of Gunhi Punhi. Many people from Bhaktapur, including Hindus, go to the important valley Buddhist religious center, the great stupa Svayambhūnātha, on this day. There are special ceremonies among farmers in Bhaktapur, including the worship of frogs (whom farmers inadvertently kill while working in the fields), who help protect those fields from malevolent spirits. On this day people traditionally eat a kind of soup prepared from nine varieties of beans, which is said to protect them from intestinal ailments.

On the late afternoon of the day there is an event that acts as a preamble to the focal festival, which will begin the following day. On the night of Gunhi Punhi there is a minor procession that is supported by funds from the Guthi Saṃsthān, the Central Government Committee which now provides the centralized and bureaucratically controlled support of many cultural events. The participants, who receive funds from the committee for their costume and incidental expenses, are members of one of the Jyāpu *thars*, from a group of families living near Lāekū Square. Some six or eight men from these families, wearing traditional Jyāpu costumes and taking the roles of both men and women, perform traditional farmers' dances accompanied by *thar* musicians. This small group dances around the *pradakṣiṇāpatha* in the late afternoon. Masses of people go to watch them. The procession is a preamble to the events of the next day, when similar but greatly more elaborate dances are elements in that day's festival. (Moderate.)

SĀPĀRU [48], THE COW FESTIVAL OF THE DEAD OF THE PREVIOUS YEAR, AND THE ANNUAL CARNIVAL

The first day of the waning fortnight Gu(n)lāgā (August) is the time for a major festival (see fig. 22) commemorating those who have died in Bhaktapur during the previous year. The festival includes two elements in an intimate mixture, commemorations of death and carnival. The day's events and the inaugural procession of the previous afternoon introduce a period of related activities lasting until the eighth day of the fortnight. The day is called "Sāpāru" (sometimes "Sāpārū") or "Sāyā" in Newari, and Gāi Jātrā in Nepali. "*Sā*" means cow, and *pāru* (according to Manandhar [1975, 577]) may derive from *parewā*, the name of the first day of the lunar fortnight. In local speculation the word derives from *sāpā*, "cow mask," with the *yā* of Sāyā supposedly deriving from *jātrā* or *yātrā*, "procession." All these terms refer more specifically to one of the day's elements (which gives the day its name) a procession of real and symbolic cows. The carnival that is mixed with this procession, but which is a distinguishable aspect, will be discussed below.

There are various stories that relate the cow, death and this particular day (Anderson 1971, chap. 10; Nepali 1965, 353ff.).[37] The consensus is vague and the details vary but it is on this day that the "Cow Goddess" can help the wandering spirits of the dead who had died during the previous year to cross the river Vaitaraṇī into death's realm.[38] Once the spirit enters death's kingdom, Yama's realm, it can, in traditional doctrine, be "judged" and then transformed into its proper next stage. Much more usual in Bhaktapur seems to be the idea that it is on this day with the help of the Cow Goddess that the wandering spirits will enter "heaven," the idea of judgment in Yama's realm being ignored or suppressed.

Figure 22. The Sāpāru festival. An image in the form of the Cow Goddess Vaitaraṇī representing someone who has died during the previous year.

Some of the other annual calendrical commemorative ceremonies for the dead, namely, those devoted to mothers [33] and fathers [51] apply only to those who have been dead for *more* than one year, that is, after the first year's period of mourning has been completed. However, the Sāpāru festival, as its legend indicates, concerns those who have died within the past year, with the exception of the period just prior to the festivals, in which case the first sequence of death rites is still being performed and the members of the household and the *phukī* are still impure. Members of all *thar*s except the untouchables take part.

Although the cow *jātrā*, thought to be a specifically Newar festival, exists in other Newar communities, in Bhaktapur it is highly elaborated, and many Newars and other Nepalese come to Bhaktapur from other places to watch it.

The procession is made up of constructions in the form of the Cow Goddess and, rarely, actual cows representing her, each of which represents a particular dead person. Each cow figure is preceded by a carnival group made up of friends or *phukī* of the household to which the dead person belonged.[39] The groups vary in number, but in the case of important or particularly popular people they may include hundreds of participants. The symbolic cows may be either "long" or "short" ones, the long ones representing adults, the short ones children.[40] Other aspects of their decoration indicate whether they were male or female. It is commonly said that in the Malla period officials standing at the palace—which the procession must pass on the festival route—could, by counting the figures, tell how many men, women, boys, and girls had died in Bhaktapur during the previous year. In the few cases now where living cows are used, they are not differentially marked. The long images have a mask of a cow mounted toward the top end of an elaborately decorated long pole. The pole, which requires four men to carry it, is carried in the procession by representatives of the family. The short cow is simply a basket with a mask on it, which is worn over the head of the family representative. Traditionally for the upper *thar*s these representations were carried or worn by farmers who farmed portions of the deceased person's family's land and performed various services for the family. Those of the middle and lower *thar*s were carried by *phukī* members.

Each family supervises the production of the figure that will represent them in the *jātrā*. They are assisted by *phukī* members, friends, and neighbors. The day before the *jātrā* the household members undergo a major purification. On the day of the festival the cow figure is worshiped by all family members, male and female, as the Cow Goddess, in a *pūjā* that is referred to as *tarae yagu*, literally "crossing a bridge or river," in keeping with the legend explaining the day's events. The cow figure is asked to help the dead person get into Vaikuṇṭa, Viṣṇu/Nārāyaṇa's special heaven. Participation in the Sāpāru procession and the related worship is considered a necessary part of the long sequence of rituals done after the death of any individual (app. 6). In keeping with the legend associated with the festival, it is believed that the dead person will remain as a *preta* if this participation is neglected, as would also be the case if the various other essential death rituals were neglected.[41] Most upper-status participating households have also on this day and prior to the procession, a *gau dān*, a special memorial ritual requiring a Brahman *purohita*'s assistance, with the main ritual mourner, the *kriyā putra* (ideally the eldest son) as the central worshiper. The Brahmans themselves, will—in contrast—have their *gau dān* following the termination of the procession.

The cow *jātrā* procession moves around the city's main festival route. Each symbolic cow, preceded by revelers, enters the festival procession at a point on the *pradakṣiṇāpatha jātrā* route near each family's home. The group makes a circuit of the route, which takes roughly two hours, and then leaves the procession when they are back at the same point at which they entered it. Family members, consisting of the chief mourner, his brothers, and some *phuki* members, close affinal relatives and friends, will walk as mourners behind the cow. This group consists of men and children of both sexes. Women watch from the sidelines of the procession. Each group enters the procession at its end as it passes their entrance point, but the result, because of the mixed social constitution of most *twa:*s, is that the various *twa:*s are represented in the line of the procession in more or less random social order.

When people from all other neighborhoods have entered the procession the people from the large Lākulāche(n) sub-*twa:* in the Ta:mārhī main *twa:* enter it. They then arrange themselves differently than the participants of the previous *twa:*s, in a way that makes an impressive visual climax to the procession. For this group all the carnival dancers and maskers representing *all* the participating households in that neighborhood enter the procession as one group. This group of carnival dancers is joined by anyone in Bhaktapur who wishes to join in the carnival whether or not they are connected to any bereaved household. The dancers are followed, in turn, by a large group of musicians playing the special dance and processional music associated with the *jātrā*.

Behind the musicians men carry a tall image constructed of bamboo and rice straw in shape resembling the long cow images but painted and dressed to represent Bhairava rather than the Cow Goddess. Behind the Bhairava image all the cow images from the Lākulāche(n) Twa: households are carried one after the other in a dense mass of images and followed by the household mourners. This large group constitutes the end of the procession. When it gets to Lāekū Square, it circumambulates the statue of the Newar King Bhūpatīndra Malla, which is located there, three times and then disbands.

Except for the Brahmans, who still have to do their *gau dān pūjā*, the day's religious activities are finished. People return to their houses, and the cow images are taken to the river and thrown into it. Household feasts are held in the bereaved households for all who have worked with the household on the image and/or accompanied it in the procession. The married-out household women are expected to return to the household for this feast.

Although the aspect of the Sāpāru jātrā to which we have referred as "carnival" is, as we have seen, an integral part of the day's events, it is convenient to discuss it separately. It is often terminologically distinguished from the remainder of the *jātrā* by referring to it as "Ghe(n)tā(n) Ghesi(n)[42] Mhetegu." The term "Ghe(n)tā(n) Ghesi(n)" is said to refer onomatopoeically to the sound of a particular kind of drum beat. *Mhetegu* means to play, as to play at a game. The activities referred to by the term take place only at this time, beginning with the preliminary performances on Gunhi Punhi evening, which we have noted above. Traditionally only farmer *thar*s and above (including, it may be noted, young Brahmans) participated, but now people from lower groups, with the exception of the untouchables, do. Traditionally, and still, only men take part. This is an "antistructural" festival, but as always in Bhaktapur within strict limits.

On the Sāpāru day people are free to choose their costumes and their dance performances. Sometimes a subgroup of those preceding a cow image may work together as a thematic unit, but often individuals have their own individual theme. The "free choices," however, usually are among a conventional set of forms, which can be illustrated from the examples we have seen:

1. A popular group of costumes and performances portrays Jyāpu activities, and is done both by Jyāpus themselves and by upper-level

participants. Many of these are derived from traditional Jyāpu dances. People may mimic breaking the soil with a hoe, or cutting grain stalks. Frequently the dance represents a Jyāpu couple, with one man taking the man's part, and another the woman's.[43] It is important to remark that these dances are not lampoons but serious and graceful dance forms.

2. A variant portrayal of Jyāpu life shows a Jyāpu and Jyāpuni, represented by either dancers or puppets carried on the tops of poles by masked dancers. The farmer and his wife often carry sticks, and the couple performs a burlesque fight something like a Western Punch and Judy performance.

3. In addition to dancing Jyāpunis, men may sometimes dress and dance as pretty girls of undetermined social status (see fig. 23). Sometimes they perform as a mother, cradling a doll baby (see fig. 24). Such dances, like the Jyāpu-Jyāpuni dances, are not done satirically but, often, with considerable grace, beauty, and seriousness.

4. There are gross and obscene sexual references in some portrayals, of a kind that would be publicly unacceptable otherwise except during the Devī cycle's Gāthā Muga: Ca:re [45] celebrations. In these dances, for example, two men will dance as a heterosexual couple, embracing and moving their hips in coital movements. Others may construct a large model penis and vagina, banging them together in mimicry of sexual intercourse in time to the music of the festival musicians who accompany each group of mourner-revelers. Other men may add mock genitalia, such as a banana and two globular fruits or vegetables to their costumes.[44]

5. Some dances mimic drunkenness, the performer pretending to drink from a container, and staggering.

6. Another popular group is animals and supernatural forest creatures—bears, tigers, monkeys, Yetis, demons of various types, and so forth.

7. Participants frequently dress as *sādhus* and other types of holy "renouncers."

8. Men dress as various deities, both male and female. These include most prominently Śiva (who is perhaps the most frequent deity chosen) and Pārvatī, Kṛṣṇa and Rādhā, and Rāma and Sītā.

9. Performers often dress as Moghul Rajas, with turbans and robes.

Figure 23. Sāpāru carnival. Man dancing as a woman.

Figure 24. Sāpāru carnival. Young man dancing as a mother and carrying a doll child.

10. Sometimes the costumes and decorations are purely abstract and decorative, such as a face painted half black and half white.

There is another category of role-taking that we have saved until last because it has been emphasized in some of the literature on this festival[45] but seems, at least in Bhaktapur in the period of this study and the years preceding it, to be a minor and muted one. This is the category of *satire* with some possible political implication. There are some examples of this. People may carry a placard with a caricature of some unpopular figure in the government, sometimes as part of a mock-funeral procession. Most often the satire is more veiled. In one procession, for example, a man danced as a particular rhesus monkey that lived near (and often on) the Bhaktapur royal palace, which now houses some central government administrative offices. It was clear to the onlookers with a little coaching that this represented the chief administrative officer of the district at the time. But the political satire is carefully guarded, and really important figures would be represented, if at all, in most veiled, ambiguous, and—it is hoped—safe forms. Other upper-status figures are represented, but gently—Brahmans dressed in *dhōtis*, public storytellers (who are traditionally Brahmans) represented as telling obscene stories, tourists complete with Western garb (or a reasonable facsimile thereof) and mock cameras hung over their shoulders. Although these representations are both muted and rare at present, one can imagine conditions in which they might become dominant.

The carnival performances of Sāpāru play with the constraints of Bhaktapur's social structure. Satire is only one small component of this. On this day the participants can express things that are usually difficult to express in ordinary civic life. Constraints of gender, role, decent behavior, and (more carefully) respect for hierarchy are overcome, within the usual limits that Bhaktapur imposes on such Dionysian behavior. It is said by older people that on Sāpāru anyone can be king; anyone can be anything he wants. In fact, however, social criticism and political criticism, is limited; women and the lowest-level *thar*s cannot take part; among those who do take part, upper *thar*s usually represent lower ones, and the reverse is less frequent. This latter constraint, however, indicates perhaps something more than some limit on lower-status people escaping the system even in fantasy. The lower-level *thar*s represent for the upper *thar*s not only the negative aspects of lower status but also a greater freedom from constraints, including the sexual constraints whose fantasized overcoming is represented in many of the carnival performances. Upper *thar*s in Bhaktapur, conversely, represent greater constraints of propriety and self-control for people in the lower *thar*s looking up. Motives of satire and resentment aside, it would be contrary to the spirit of escape symbolized by the carnival to change ones role for what is, in a certain sense, a still more socially constrained one.

In its involvement of the entire city in public space, the procession on the *pradakṣiṇāpatha*; in its concern with the deaths that took place in the city during the preceding year; in its differentiated representation of those deaths by age, sex, and area; and in its carnival expression of the kind of fantasy that reveals something of the structure of the city's life through the freedom and constraints of its "antistructural" play, Sāpāru is a major festival of *focal* importance for Bhaktapur. However, its concern with ritual assistance for the *preta*s of its recently dead to enter heaven—based essentially on the *individual* work of each bereaved household and reflecting no social differentiation of any significance to the city beyond maturity and gender—as well as the antistructural play of its carnival, puts Sāpāru in marked contrast to the greatly more elaborate focal festivals of *structure*, Biskā: and Mohanī, that we will consider in later chapters. Sāpāru may be labeled as an "antistructural focal festival."

The week following Sāpāru, coming to an end on the eighth day of the fortnight, is a period in which many *pyākha(n)*s, or "dance dramas," are presented throughout the city. These are of different kinds. One group is of particular interest in that the unmarried girls in a household may join in it, this being the only time in which women in Bhaktapur dance publicly now, although, as we have noted above, women and girls in some *thar*s must have danced at some time in the past. These particular dances, often called for some reason "Rāmāyaṇa," usually danced to the music of the Indian instruments, *tabla* (small drums) and harmonium, accompany songs written by family members to commemorate a person in their family who has died during the year. Family groups, with their singers, dancers, and musicians, walk around the city festival route. Friends and relatives intercept them at various points and invite them to their houses where the group performs their *pyākha(n)* in the public space in front of the friend or relative's house watched by neighborhoods and bypassers.

Other *pyākha(n)*s are performed by various groups during this week.

Some of these are traditional stories, some newly created ones, some serious and sentimental, others comic, satirical, or farcical. This is one of the two periods during the year when such *pyākha(n)*s are presented. The other is during the eight days of the Indra Jātrā sequence [59–65] in the following lunar fortnight. Many of the *pyākha(n)*s done during the Indra Jātrā period are the same or similar to those done following Sāpāru, but comic dances are done only in the Sāpāru period, extending the carnival emphasis as the "Rāmāyaṇa" *pyākha(n)*s extend the commemoration of the year's deaths.

MISCELLANEOUS EVENTS: KṚṢṆA JANMĀSTAMĪ [49] AND ŚĪTALĀ PŪJĀ [50]

On the eighth day of the month there is a small festival of Kṛṣṇa. A Kṛṣṇa image is taken from its god-house and carried around the festival route, and there is worship of Kṛṣṇa in some homes and by some devotees at the city's Kṛṣṇa shrines, which the devotees visit in turn in a procession. This *jātrā* had, reportedly, been introduced into Bhaktapur only some eight to ten years before the study. The devotees were said to be the same people who had become *bhakti* devotees of Rāma (compare Rāma Navamī [32] above). As is always the case with Bhaktapur's festivals for these *avatar*s of Viṣṇu, the contrast with other parts of India is striking. Thus Janmāstamī is "probably the most important *vrata* and *utsava* celebrated throughout the whole of India" (Kane 1968–1977, vol. V, p. 128). (Minor.)

On the ninth day of the fortnight, the day of Śītalā Pūjā [50], people, women for the most part, used to go to the statue at Hanumān Ghāṭ of Śītalā, the goddess who represents and protects against smallpox, to ask for protection for the family. This calendrical event is thought to be specific to Bhaktapur. In recent years with the disappearance of smallpox these visits are rare. (Minor.)

On the fourteenth day of the fortnight, Pa(n)carā(n) Ca:re, there is an important Buddhist festival, that of the five Dīpankara Buddhas. Five giant and dramatic images of these Buddhas (supported by and enclosing the body of a dancer) march through the city, each coming from a different direction to a central point. These images are associated by local Newar Hindus with the Five Pāṇḍava brothers of the Mahābhārata epic. Hindus make respect gestures to the images as they are moved through the streets and take *prasāda* from their attendants.

GOKARṆA AU(N)SĪ [51], HONORING FATHERS

Exactly four months after the new-moon day on which mothers are honored and commemorated [33], on the new-moon day[46] closing the waning fortnight of Gu(n)lāgā there is an equivalent symmetrical event honoring and commemorating fathers. People whose fathers have died more than one year previously try to join other Nepalis in a *melā* at the village of Gokarṇa about five miles northeast of Kathmandu, at a spot on the Gokarṇa River adjacent to a Śiva *liṅga* shrine.[47] The pilgrims bathe in the river and perform a commemorative *pūjā* for their fathers and all their male deceased ancestors. People who cannot go to Gokarṇa nevertheless bathe and make the offerings at one of the *tīrtha*ś at the river in Bhaktapur.

Those people whose father is living worship him at home, married-out daughters and sons separated from the household returning for this purpose if possible. In the evening there is a feast in the house. (Moderate.)

MISCELLANEOUS MINOR EVENTS [52–58]: A NOTE ON TIJ, A FESTIVAL WHICH THE NEWARS DO NOT HAVE

The waxing fortnight of Ya(n)lāthwa (August/September) contains eleven festival events, in some cases two different festivals taking place in the same day. In the latter part of the fortnight the complex festival set of events, Indra Jātrā [59–65] begins. We will note here first those miscellaneous festivals that precede the beginning of the Indra Jātrā. On the second day of the fortnight is the Sūrya Vināyaka Jātrā [52]. The *jātrā* image of the Sūrya Vināyaka Gaṇeśa (chap. 8) is carried around the city's main processional route, followed by its devotees. Most of these participants are people from the village, just outside of the city, where the god's shrine is located, but others, as is the case in all minor *jātrā*s, but particularly for those of Nārāyaṇa and Gaṇeśa, are people who have taken the god as a "private god" for some period of time. The festival is held only in Bhaktapur. (Minor.)

On the same day is the Vārāhī Jātrā [53], commemorating Vārāhī as the maṇḍalic goddess of her particular section of the city. Local people take the *jātrā* image from the god-house and, accompanied by musicians, carry it around the city's main festival route. This is one of the few *jātrā*s in which both married and unmarried women, dressed in their better clothes, traditionally join men in their *phukī* group in following the deity. This festival is only held in Bhaktapur.

The third day of the fortnight also has two festivals. The first of these is the Dattātreya Jātrā [54]. This is primarily a local *twa: jātrā*, but in the course of the day an image of Dattātreya, whose temple is located in the Tachapāl *twa:*, is carried around the city's main festival route. The other festival of the day is a Bhairava Jātrā [55]. An image of Bhairava from the main Bhairava temple[48] is, in its turn, carried around the main festival route. These are minor *jātrās*, as are the others of this period.

The people of Bhaktapur define themselves differentially in part not only by the customs and festivals they emphasize, but by those followed by others, particularly those that are of great importance to others, which they do *not* observe. One such festival is Tij, which the Indo-Nepalese (and Hindus in general; see Kane [1968–1977, vol. V, p. 144f.) celebrate on the third day of the fortnight, and which the Newars ignore.[49] The Tij events contribute to a ritual complex that is thematically completed on the fifth day of the fortnight, Ṛṣi Pa(n)camī, according to Lynn Bennett's analysis (1983, 222f.). Some of the themes of Tij are present in attenuated form in Bhaktapur's Ṛṣi Pa(n)camī [58]; for example, women pray to be spared painful difficulties with menstruation, but other of the themes are not represented.

According to Bennett for the Chetri villagers she studied, "Tij is meant to ensure the long life of one's husband, while Ṛṣi Pa(n)camī is meant to purify women from the possible sin of having touched a man during their menstrual period. . . . In my view . . . the two are conceptually related" (1983, 222). Bennett (ibid., 225) emphasizes women's erotic activity during Tij, characterized by behavior that is a "virtual seduction of Śiva" (the legendary reference is to the relations of Pārvatī and Śiva, as set forth in the *Swasthānī Vrata Kathā*):

> The laughing, singing, and dancing at Tij . . . represents a complete reversal of the Hindu ideal of womanly behavior. To say that a girl is shy, embarrassed . . . is to prasise her highly. On Tij the high spirits, the flirtatiousness, the sexuality which women must ordinarily suppress are released *en masse* at Śiva's temple. However, this display of the erotic side of female nature is only permissible because, on Tij, it is held in check by the strict purifying fast which the women are undergoing for the welfare of their husbands. On the morning after Tij, women must perform a *pūjā* and make offerings to a Brahman priest dedicating the merit of their fast to their husband (present, future, or in the next life) before they can break the fast. The dangers of

female sexuality are thus firmly bracketed by the mutually reinforcing ascetic and patrilineal ideals.

The Chetri women go as a group to the riverside on Ṛṣi Pa(n)camī for an elaborate purification ceremony that removes the impurities associated with menstrual blood so that they "may be pure enough to touch men" (Bennett 1983, 225). The bathing is followed by a ceremony (which has a reference to the Ṛṣi, who give the day its name) in which in Bennett's interpretation "women are purifying their own sexuality. They are channeling it in the only direction acceptable to Hindu patrilineal ideology—toward their own husbands" (ibid., 230). In the light of this discussion, the Newar nonadoption of Tij and the very minor echo of the Chetri women's procedures of Ṛṣi Pa(n)camī (below) is consonant with one of the main contrasts between the Newar Hindus and the non-Newar Hindus, the social position of their women. The relative freedom of the Newar women, centrally represented in the mock-marriage and their relations to their natal homes, makes for a context in which the carefully bounded ritual expression of women's sexuality and its subsequent restoration to patriarchal control, which is (following Bennett) the meaning of Tij, is much less significant. As a remnant, perhaps, of their northern Himalayan heritage, these tensions are structured, expressed and controlled among the Newars in, comparatively more diffuse and less oppressive ways.

The fourth day of the fortnight is the pan-Hindu Cathā Gaṇeśa day [56]. "Cathā" derives from the Sanskrit, Caturthī, the fourth day of the lunar month. This is the occasion in most households for a special *pūjā* to Gaṇeśa, and offerings of the foods that are supposed to be his favorites. The day is associated with stories associating Gaṇeśa and this fortnight's waxing crescent moon which is supposed to be dangerous if seen on this day. It is said that there are at least some people, at all social levels in Bhaktapur, who try to avoid seeing it. They reportedly go to less length than do those noted in Anderson (1971, 124) and Nepali (1965, 404) who seal the windows of their house and remain inside on this day in order to avoid seeing the moon. (Minor.)

The last event in this miscellaneous group is on the fifth day, the *pa(n)camī*, of the fortnight, Ṛṣi Pa(n)camī [57]. The Ṛṣis are worshiped in some households, particularly in upper-status ones, with a *dhala(n) danegu pūjā* (app. 4). On this day some women worship the Ṛṣis for, it is said, good health, including protection against menstrual difficulties and for protection of the house and children in what is, apparently, an echo of the theme of the Chetri practice described by Bennett (1983), in that they are both derived from traditional Hindu *vrata*s of the day.[50] However, the Newar practices are individually performed in the household not in groups of women; they are minor *pūjā*s and not elaborate purification ceremonies, and they are not in the dramatic context of the Tij ceremonies, as are the Chetri women's practices of the day. (Minor.)

On the seventh day of the fortnight, the day of Umā/Maheśvara [58], in many households, but especially in Jyāpu houses, there is special worship of Pārvatī and Śiva in their manifestation as Umā/Maheśvara represented as an affectionate conjugal couple. Women present ceremonial threads to the idealized couple, and then take one back as *prasāda* and tie it around their husband's wrist. (Minor.)

EVENTS DURING THE PERIOD OF INDRA JĀTRĀ [59–65]: THE TRANSFORMATION OF FESTIVAL THEMES AND EVENTS IN DIFFERENT NEWAR CITIES AND TOWNS

From the twelfth day of Ya(n)lāthwa to the fourth day of the following waning fortnight of Ya(n)lāgā is the eight-day period of Indra Jātrā, which in some other Newar communities, most notably in Kathmandu, maintains aspects of an ancient Indian calendrical festival (V. S. Agrawala 1970, 55). In Kathmandu Indra Jātrā is a thematically integrated sequence that is one of the focal festival events of that city's annual calendar. Each of the Newar cities and towns have one or more such festival events or sequences that are specially developed in the community and which attract people from other communities as spectators. Conversely, a festival cycle that is highly developed in one community appears, by contrast, to be relatively (and sometimes completely) ignored in another. Indra Jātrā is an example of a festival that is comparatively ignored in Bhaktapur. The group of calendrical events that we are including together here as taking place during the span of Indra Jātrā contain some events [59, 61, 65], which are clearly represented in Kathmandu as integrated by certain local legends about Indra, and are understood to be related to these stories by some people in Bhaktapur. For many or perhaps most people in Bhaktapur, however, they are simply independent events, of the same disconnected kind as the other miscellaneous calendrical events that happen to fall within these eight days.

The equivocally component days of the Indra Jātrā (i.e., days that have thematic connections with the integrated sequence as it has been described for Kathmandu) are Yama Dya: Thānigu [59], Indraṇī Jātrā [61], Yau Dya: Punhi [62], and Pulu Kisi Haigu [65].

In Kathmandu Indra Jātrā is a major eight-day festival consisting of a number of dramatic and climactic events. Some of these events in Kathmandu are related to a legend of Indra's personal relation to that city. Others center on the dangerous deity Ākāś Bhairava (represented by huge dramatic masks), on Bhagavatī, on the living goddess Kumārī, and on other comparatively minor supernatural figures (Nepali 1965, 358–369; Anderson 1971, chap. 15).

We have suggested that some of the similar events of this period in Bhaktapur are transformed in meaning because they are not put in the context of a major integrative festival. Furthermore, it is noteworthy that some of the elements in Kathmandu's focal Indra Jātrā are moved in Bhaktapur to *other* times of the year and, for the most part, amalgamated into Bhaktapur's own major and focal festivals. Thus, for example, the Kathmandu Indra Jātrā festival is inaugurated and ends with the raising and then, eight days later, lowering of a forty-foot pole, the trunk of a particular kind of tree. The same kind of tree, gathered in the same place by members of Bhaktapur's branch of the same *thar* (the Sa:mi), is erected and lowered as one of the central symbolic foci in Bhaktapur's Biskā: festival. During Kathmandu's Indra Jātrā a procession (associated there with a group of legends about Indra and "Indra's mother") for the salvation of those who had died during the previous years is in some ways a transformation of Bhaktapur's Sāpāru procession. Indra Jātrā in Kathmandu is the period in which the living goddess, Kumārī, makes her main public appearance, and establishes her relationship to the Gorkhā king. In Bhaktapur this happens, with Bhaktapur's own Kumārī, during Mohanī. Kathmandu's Indra Jātrā period is the major time for the appearance of masked dancers representing demon-like gods who fight on the side of *dharma* against the *Asura*s and other antagonistic supernatual beings. One representation of this is the killing by the Kathmandu dancers of a buffalo representing an Asura king. All this is represented in Bhaktapur during the Mohanī festival and in the subsequent nine-month cycle of the Nine Durgās dancers.

Many people in Bhaktapur seem to know some local version of the

Indra story. Here is a brief sketch of one of Bhaktapur's versions: Indra's mother sent him to get some white flowers of a special kind from a particular garden on earth. A demon caught Indra taking the flowers, accused him of stealing them, and captured him. "Indra's mother," who is not otherwise named in the tale, not knowing where Indra was, sent Indra's vehicle, an elephant, to earth to find him. The elephant found Indra and reported his whereabouts to Indra's mother, who came to earth to rescue him. The demon released Indra when his mother came, and she gave the demon clouds and fog as a reward, the clouds and fog necessary for protecting the rice, which is still growing at this period of the year. When Indra and his Mother returned to heaven, people on earth wanted to follow them and so some of them left a trail of grain on the gods' path so that the humans could later find their way there.

The twelfth day of the fortnight, the beginning of the Indra Jātrā period in Kathmandu, is called in Bhaktapur the "Yama Dya: Thānigu" day [59], the day of the erecting of the Yama God. In Kathmandu the raising of a pole made from a tall tree trunk in a central square signals the beginning of the festival there and marks a focal spatial point. In many of Bhaktapur's *twa:*s, tree poles are erected.[51] They are said to represent the ruler of the kingdom of death, Yama. These local poles are left up, as is the Kathmandu central one, for the entire eight-day period. Flowers are placed at the top of the pole, and *twa:* people do daily *pūjā*s to it during the eight days. It is thought that this will help protect the local *twa:* people from death. (Moderate.)

On the fourteenth day of the fortnight—and with no reference to the Indra cycle—is the Ananta Nārāyaṇa Pūjā [60]. This is a local representation of a traditional South Asian Hindu event in honor of Viṣṇu/Nārāyaṇa. Many people go to one of the Viṣṇu temples on this day, as they did on the other city-wide Viṣṇu festival, Tulasī Piye [43]. Some Chathariyā families follow the traditional Hindu custom of pledging to do a Brahman-assisted household *pūjā* to Viṣṇu each year on this day for a period of fourteen years. (Minor.)

On the fourteenth day (the same day as Nārāyaṇa Pūjā) and continuing on the fifteenth and final day, the full-moon day, of the fortnight is Indrāṇī Jātrā [61]. Additional events of the fifteenth day are designated as the festival of that full-moon day, Yau Dya: Punhi [62], but they also represent the completion of the two-day Indrāṇī Jātrā. The Indrāṇī *jātrā* image is taken from her local god-house and carried in a procession around the entire city, followed by people from the local maṇḍalic area. Indraṇī is thought of, by some at least, on this occasion not as, or only as, the Indrāṇī of the Aṣṭamātṛkās group, but as Indra's consort. The image is carried to one of the artificial ponds in the city, the Ta Pukhū, and left there in an open building, a *phalcā*, overnight. (Moderate.)

The next day is the full-moon day, called "Yau Dya: Punhi" [62]. The name "Yau Dya:," the Yau God, seems to come from a set of three torches called *Yā matta* (or *Swarga* ["heaven"] *Yā matta*), which are carried around the city on a long stick by a member of the Sa:mi *thar* on the three days following this *punhi*. They are considered to be a manifestation of a god, and people try to see the lights, a view that is said to enable them to enter *Swarga*, heaven, at some time during the period. This reflects the Indra Jātrā's legend's theme of the following of Indra and his mother into their heaven. On this day people come from surrounding villages and towns (particularly from the large town of Thimi) and from other parts of Bhaktapur for ritual baths in the Ta Pukhū and to worship the image of Indrāṇī. The day is, thus, a *melā*. In the afternoon the image is carried around the city festival route and then returned to its god-house. (Moderate.)

The span of Indra Jātrā continues into the next fortnight, the waning fortnight Ya(n)lāgā (September). On the second day of the fortnight a man from a nearby village, paid by the central government's Guthi Saṃsthān, comes to Bhaktapur to begin three days of performance. He represents a demon called "Mu Patra," wears a metal crown (which is at other times kept in the Taleju temple), and dresses in the old Malla-period Moghul-style royal costume. He is accompanied by two demon attendants, called "Dhicās." He visits during these three days the poles that had been set up in the different *twa:*s on the Yama Dya: Thānigu day [59] representing Yama. He circumambulates each pole three times, hitting it with a traditional Malla period sword. People now are uncertain about the meaning of all this, although it seems to have been related both to the period's Indra legend and to another supernatural creature, the Pulu Kisi, who appears on the last day [65] of the period's set of events. G. S. Nepali wrote (of Bhaktapur) that the Mu Patra represented the demon enemy of Indra, and that the poles that he strikes thus represent Indra. According to Nepali, care is taken that Mu Patra does not encounter the Pulu Kisi, which "is the riding animal of Indra . . . [which] has come in search of its master. . . . In the event of their facing each other, there ensues a fight between the two, involving their respective supporters" (1965, 364). In fact, in recent memory they have not met, and the significance and possibility of their encounter seems no longer an issue. The violence that, as we shall see, does sometimes occur in relation to the Pulu Kisi—whose relation to Indra is now vague—is not related to the Mu Patra, who is a symbolic form that has now lost much of its meaning and power.

On the third day of the fortnight there is a small local *jātrā*, Chuma(n) Gandya: Jātrā [63], in one of the city's main *twa:*s, Coche(n) *twa:*. It is noteworthy and peculiar in that it is a minor version of a more important event with the same name, the same associated legend, and in the same location that takes place on the eighth day of the solar New Year festival, Biskā:. That event will be described in the next chapter. The one listed here is minor.

On the fourth day of the fortnight, the last day of the Indra Jātrā span, there are two festivals. The first, Śmaśāna Bhailadya: Jātrā, is not associated with the themes of the Indra story, although it reflects references to King Yama and to death. The second, Pulu Kisi Haigu, which ends this set of events, contains some reflections of the Indra story and some correspondences to its closing sequences in Kathmandu.

Śmaśāna Bhailadya: Jātrā [64], refers to the Bhairava who inhabits the Mu Dip cremation grounds (see chap. 8). "Śmaśāna" means cremation grounds in Sanskrit and Nepali. An image representing this Bhairava is painted on a *pulu*, a reed mat, by a properly initiated member of the Pu(n) *thar*, the mask makers, and painters of religious images. *Pulu*s are the mats used for covering dead bodies while they are being carried in funeral processions to cremation grounds. If the head priest of the Taleju temple has died during the previous year, his *pulu* is taken from his corpse, saved, and used in this procession; otherwise, it is a new and unused one. It is said that during the time of the Malla kings their *pulu*s were kept after their death. The *pulu* of a deceased king would be used every year in this annual procession until replaced by the next king's *pulu* following the death of that king. On this day now the *pulu* is hung in front of the main Bhairava temple. People either passing by or coming to the temple for the purpose, make respectful gestures to the *pulu*. People who encounter it fear it and, as is the case generally for dangerous deities, fear that if they neglect to worship it or show it formal respect they will be harmed in some way. At a designated time during the day a goat is sacrificed in the square adjoining the temple. The *pulu* is then taken and carried by a member of the Dwi(n) *thar* (level XII; see chap. 5) in a procession around the main city festival route until the

Bhairava temple is once again reached and the *pulu* is once again hung on the wall for the remainder of the day. (Moderate.)

On the same day as the Śmaśāna Bhailadya: Jātrā there is another event that makes for a kind of climax to the loosely grouped set of events of the eight-day period. This event is called "Pulu Kisi Haigu" [65]. (*Pulu* is the funeral mat, *kisi* means elephant, and *haigu* means to bring, thus the name means the bringing of the "Pulu Kisi.") The Pulu Kisi is an image of an elephant constructed of reed mats. The image is carried around the city, starting in the Lākulāche(n) neighborhood, and is carried and attended by local people. The elephant has a bell around its neck, which is rung by the attendants during the procession. During this time other bells in the city are not to be rung. When the image passes by, bystanders, both men and women, must uncover their heads as a gesture of respect. If they do not the attendants of the elephant, often carrying the elephant with them, may charge into the crowd, and forcibly uncover the offender's head, removing the hat or shawl. The elephant also is occasionally made to charge into the crowd of bystanders even if there is no show of disrespect. This is frequently the occasion for a general fight between attendants and crowd, sometimes extending to and dividing groups or individuals within the crowd. This day is one of the times when people traditionally drink, and the attendants of the elephant and many in the crowd are drunk. When the elephant, in its movement around the city's festival route, now followed by crowds of people, approaches Dattātreya Square in the northern part of the city, it leaves the route to "drink at a well" where Indra's elephant once drank. This is often the occasion for fairly serious fights, characteristically between members of the upper and lower halves of the city. These are sometimes precipitated by someone from the upper city ringing a temple bell in the square in contravention of the custom of the day.

The Pulu Kisi refers now secondarily to Indra,[52] but more clearly to death (the funeral mats, and its association with the Śmaśāna Bhailadya: Jātrā of the same day), to danger, and to threat. Its attacks on the crowd randomly or for not showing respect have parallels in the Nine Durga *pyākha(n)*s during the Devī cycle. Its connection to intracity fighting is an echo of the events of the Biskā: sequence. However, the similar themes in those two focal festival groups are coherently related to themes not only of ritual conflict but also the symbolic resolution of that conflict. In contrast with such festival events, and as we have noted, in contrast with the simultaneous events in Kathmandu, the events of the Indra Jātrā period in Bhaktapur are not integrated. They seem in a sense to be fragments of what may have been once in Bhaktapur—and that is now elsewhere—a coherent set. In spite of its drama, its significance and the size of its audience probably are "moderate" in comparison to other more important events.

During these eight days *pyākha(n)*s, resembling some of those performed after Sāpāru, are given in some parts of the city. The period closes after the Pulu Kisi Haigu procession with the removal of the Indra/Yama poles in the *twa:*s

THE REMAINDER OF THE YEARLY CALENDRICAL CYCLE [66–79]

There is one more calendrical event during this fortnight. This is Dhala(n) Salā(n) [66], which may optionally be observed on either the ninth day of the fortnight or the fifteenth, the new-moon day. This is a day for one of the ceremonies in the long sequence following death (app. 6). The ceremony is for the "*pitṛ*s," in this case all deceased ancestors of a *phukī* group who have been dead for more than two years, and the ceremonies are performed ideally at the riverside by large groups of associated *phukī* members. Occasionally *phukī* members conduct a continuous series of *śrāddha* procedures on sixteen consecutive days, starting with the day on which they do the Dhala(n) Salā(n) ceremony. (Moderate.)

The first ten days of the next fortnight, the waxing fortnight of Kaulāthwa (September/October), is the period of the focal autumnal rice harvest festival Mohanī [67–76], which will be discussed in the presentation of the Devī cycle in chapter 16. During the last three days of the final fortnight of the lunar year, Kaulāgā, three events take place which are the three introductory days of the Swanti sequence [77, 78, 79], which culminate and begin anew the lunar year, and which were described at the beginning of this chapter.

CHAPTER FOURTEEN

The Events of the Solar Cycle

INTRODUCTION

The vast majority of the annual events in Bhaktapur, as elsewhere in Hindu South Asia, are organized by the lunar calendrical cycle. Bhaktapur has a very few fortnightly and annual events whose timing is determined by the solar calendar. One set of these events, Biskā:, however, is one of Bhaktapur's focal festivals, rivaled in its sheer quantity of activities, complexity, integration, and urban importance by only the Mohanī festival [67–77].

GHYA: CĀKU SA(N)LHU [10]

"*Sa(n)lhu*" is the old Newari for the first day of a solar month. The Nepali Sanskritic term *saṅkrānti*[1] is used in ordinary references to this day. This *saṅkrānti*, Ghya: Cāku Sa(n)lhu [10],[2] comes in the second week of January (in 1974/75 on the thirteenth day of Pohelāthwa, in the Nepali month of Pauṣa). It was of special importance in traditional South Asia as Makara-Saṅkrānti (Kane 1968–1977, vol. V, p. 211ff.) in that it marked the winter solstice, and the beginning of the *udagayana*, the "ascending," brightening half of the year. Like other *saṅkrānti* in Bhaktapur, the day is special to Viṣṇu, but on this day there are some extra activities related to the story of Viṣṇu's dwarf avatar Vāmana, in which form Viṣṇu recaptures heaven and the earth from the Asura Mahābali. On this day an offering is given by every middle-status and upper-status household to its Brahman *purohita*, or family priest.[3] The offering consists of *jāki* (unhusked, uncooked rice), vegetables, uncooked pulses, and *ghya: cāku*, a mixture of clarified butter (*ghya:*, or ghee) and molasses (*cāku*), for which the day is named. The offering, at least according to Brahman and Chathariyā informants, signifies that the Brahmans as heirs to Viṣṇu/Nārāyaṇa were once the owners of all the land, an ownership that in some versions of the Vāmana story, (e.g., Stutley and Stutley 1977, 321) was contested by the Asura, Mahābali, and restored through Viṣṇu's *avatar*. In the morning of this day there are offerings of *ghya: cāku* to the household deities. People eat *ghya: cāku* during the day, and it is served at the household feasts that take place during the evening. Friends and affinal family, as well as *phukī*, are invited to these feasts, called *nakhātyā*. A peculiarity of these feasts is that on this occasion alone boiled rice is served rather than the beaten rice that is always otherwise served at feasts. *Ghya: cāku* is poured over the boiled rice. This is a striking and to contemporary people in Bhaktapur a mysterious and unexplained reversal of the customary practice. The *ghya: cāku* is also made into sweetmeats that (as well as a certain kind of wild yam) are also traditionally eaten on this day.[4] (Moderate.)

BISKĀ: [20–29]: THE SOLAR NEW YEAR FESTIVAL

Three months after the winter solstice period of Ghya: Cāku Sa(n)lhu, the *saṅkrānti* at the approximate time of the vernal equinox marks the beginning of the solar New Year. The solar New Year comes in the course of a nine-day festival, Biskā: (also sometimes written "Biskā") (see fig. 25). The New Year's Day, which in 1975/76 fell on the fourteenth day of the waxing lunar fortnight of Caulāthwa (Caitra, in March/April), is the fifth, the midday, of the nine-day sequence. Biskā:, which draws spectators from all over the valley, is unique to Bhaktapur,[5] and one of the four annual festivals of focal importance for the city. The beginning of the solar New Year is signaled on the fifth, the central day of the sequence, with the pulling down of a great tree-trunk pole, the *yasi(n)*—also locally called *lya:si(n)*[6]—which had been erected on the previous day. In the course of the nine days themes of division, conflict, and reintegration are represented and enacted. Images of sexuality and images (and realities) of physical struggle embody these themes, which ultimately have as their reference the city as a whole. The themes are expressed through a pattern of interlocking im-

Figure 25. Biskā:. The struggle to pull the Bhairava chariot into the upper or lower city.

ages, stories, and actions with three main foci: (1) the city's major space-protecting deities, (2) the adventures of two of Bhaktapur's dangerous deities (Bhairava and Bhadrakālī) who are dominant during the festival, and (3) the "Yasi(n) God" whose actions mark the end of one year and the beginning of the next.

The chronicles have references to the supposed historical introduction of the Biskā:[7] festival into Bhaktapur (Wright [1877] 1972, 191):

> [Jagajjyotīr Malla, in the early seventeenth century] introduced at Bhatgaon [Bhaktapur] the custom of holding the rath-jatra [a chariot procession] of Adi-Bhairava on the anniversary of the Mēsh [Meṣa] Sankranti when a tall pole was erected in his honor as a flagstaff. . . . Having on one occasion suspected that the Bhairava of Bhatgaon had improper desires regarding a certain Sakti or female deity, he punished him by bringing the rath [chariot] of Kali into violent collision with the Bhairava's rath.

In the two large complex festival sequences, Biskā: and Mohanī, there is some arbitrariness in deciding which of the several component events should be listed as elements in themselves for the purposes of a catalogue of annual events. For Mohanī (chap. 15) we were able to follow the conventional local festival calendar in listing component events. For Biskā:, however, that calendar indicates only the central portions of the nine-day sequence, the raising [21] and lowering [24] of the Yasi(n) God to signal the ending of the old and the start of the new solar year. As the description of the sequence that follows indicates, there are approximately ten major component events,[8] and many minor ones in the course of the sequence. One of these "events," the Bhairava/Bhadrakālī Jātrā, takes place intermittently in a set of component phases throughout most of the nine days of the Biskā: sequence.

There is a further difficulty in comparing the components of the complex focal sequences (and the components of the Devī cycle) with the relatively disconnected events of the remainder of the annual cycle; this is in the evaluation of the importance of individual component events. Components of larger sequences are of varying importance in two ways—in themselves, in some sense, and in the extent and nature of their contribution to the meaning and significance of the larger sequence. For our purposes of providing an approximation of the quantity and significance of calendrical events we are conventionally designating the components of focal events as of "major" importance.

In our descriptions of the "structural focal sequences," here Biskā:, and in the next chapter Mohanī and its associated Nine Durgās performances, we are faced with the descriptive problems produced by a change of the scale that is now of importance to us. In earlier chapters we have tried to filter out unnecessary details, sometimes placing them in appendixes, for the sake of keeping a narrative or an argument relatively clear. However, these focal festivals are not only relatively massive and complex, but their details are particularly meaningful in relation to the organization of the city at its own level. While the preceding chapters were able to build to a large extent on what had gone before, the reader who wishes to follow the meaningful patterning of the focal sequences of this and the next chapter must be faced with large quantities of fairly minute descriptive detail out of which the festivals' meanings slowly arise.

THE PRELIMINARY PREPARATIONS

1. *The yasi(n).* A few days prior to the start of the sequence a group of men from the Sa:mi *thar*[9] go to a forest in the hills, about a two hours walk east of Bhaktapur.[10] They select a tree for the large *yasi(n)* by releasing a goat and waiting to see which tree it rubs its head against. The goat is then sacrificed to the tree, and the tree is cut down. The trunk is cleared, except for selected branches at the top that will represent the Yasi(n) God's hair. A second smaller tree is also selected for a secondary *yasi(n)*, and its limbs are cut off. Ropes are attached to the shorn trees and they are then dragged along the river bed toward Bhaktapur by men chanting a rhythmic work chant to coordinate their efforts. Each evening at sundown the trees are left, the men returning the next day to begin dragging them again. They will finally, after two or three days, be dragged into Bhaktapur, respectively to the field, the Yasi(n) Khya:, where the large *yasi(n)* will be raised, and to the location in the potters' quarter where the smaller one will be raised.

2. *Bhairava and Bhadrakālī.* Eight days prior to the solar New Year's Day, and thus three days before the festival sequence is to begin, the *jātrā* image of the dangerous goddess Bhadrakālī is taken from the inner room of her god-house and brought to a front room where noninitiates may enter. The god-house of Bhadrakālī is the house that also houses the maṇḍalic goddess Vaiṣṇavī, and it is only during the Biskā: festival that the goddess of this location is exclusively thought of as Bhadrakālī,[11] who is in her form, legend and consort quite distinct from the other goddess.[12] Vaiṣṇavī, although a dangerous deity, is a beautiful form of the Goddess. For this particular festival she is trans-

formed into the terrible form of the Goddess as Bhadrakālī, and the *jātrā* image represents this form, with its frightening face, fangs, and multiple arms. Our informants do not know why Bhadrakālī is associated with Vaiṣṇavī rather than another deity. The image of her coprotagonist, Bhairava, is also brought down from its ordinary hiding place in the main Bhairava temple into the public area of the temple, on the first day of the sequence.

During the days prior to the festival the chariot that will carry the public *jātrā* image of Bhairava will have been refurbished.[13] This is the responsibility of several craft *guthi*s, including those of the painters, carpenters, and the Sa:mi, the traditional oil pressers, who have several important support functions in this festival.

3. *The representation of Royalty.* On the day before the beginning of the festival an official of the central government's Guthi Saṃsthān comes to Bhaktapur from Kathmandu. Accompanied by musicians, he walks around the city festival route carrying an ancient sword representing "the king,"[14] which will be used in later stages of the festivals.

THE FIRST DAY: START OF THE BHAIRAVA/BHADRAKĀLĪ JĀTRĀ [20]; THE STRUGGLE BETWEEN THE UPPER AND LOWER HALVES OF THE CITY

On the first day of the Biskā: sequence, four days before the solar New Year's Day proper, some of the festival's central topics are introduced —two of its main actors, Bhairava and Bhadrakālī; the representation and involvement in the festival of important segments of the city's macrostatus system; and the themes of division and struggle.

For this festival (and in Bhaktapur, only in this festival) chariots are used for the *jātrā* procession. There are two of them, one for Bhairava and his high-status attendants, and another, a smaller one, for Bhadrakālī, and her lesser attendants. These chariots, *kha:*s,[15] are of great size; the larger one, that of Bhairava, is about twenty-four feet in height.[16]

The larger of the two, that of Bhairava, is placed in Ta:mārhī Square. This square is just "below" (i.e., to the southwest of) the line dividing the upper from the lower city, and at about the central point on that line (for the movements of the chariots see map 5, above, chap. 7). During Biskā: it is considered to belong to neither the upper nor lower city and, thus, to be a neutral and central point. It is one of the central reference points in the festival sequence, and marks the starting point from which

Bhairava and Bhadrakālī will be displaced and to which, finally, after many adventures and dangers they will return on the ninth day of the festival sequence. The smaller chariot, that of Bhadrakālī, is placed in front of her god-house (the structure usually referred to as the "Vaiṣṇavī god-house" [see map 2]) in the western part of the city.

During the early part of the day the chariots are completed, decorated, and prepared for the *jātrā*. An image of Bhairava's *vāhana* or "vehicle," Betadya: ("Beta God"), is attached to the front of Bhairava's chariot by a member of the Sa:mi *thar*, and its face is painted by a member of the Chathar Dhaubhāri *thar*, who worships the image at this time. Crowds of people come to the square to watch the preparations of the chariot. The *jātrā* images of Bhairava and Bhadrakālī meanwhile are still in their god-houses.

The representative of the central government's Guthi Saṃsthān goes to the Taleju temple and presents the royal sword to Taleju's chief Rājopādhyāya Brahman priest. This priest represents—or rather becomes—the king for the remainder of the festival. He is, in traditional local perspective, the Newar's Malla king. It is said that in the past, when the Malla kings still reigned, it was the Malla king himself and not a surrogate who rode in the Bhairava chariot during Biskā:, as his Brahman representative now prepares to do. Another Taleju Brahman will accompany the "king" throughout the many occasions in the festival sequence when the Bhairava chariot is in use, as the king's special priest, his "Guru-Purohit."

The king, as we will henceforth call him—dressed like all the others who will join him in the chariot in what is now understood in Bhaktapur to be the traditional clothes of the Malla period—and his priest, his Guru-Purohit, go from their royal palace and Taleju temple area, Lāekū, to Ta:mārhī Square by a traditional route.Throughout the day, and whenever they take part in the later festival, the king and the Guru-Purohit are always side by side, the king to the right, the Guru-Purohit to the left. They are accompanied by music, and shaded by a large ornate ceremonial umbrella. One attendant also carries a large and ornate ceremonial oil lamp, a *sukundā*.[17] When the king arrives at the chariot at Ta:mārhī Square, he orders that the *jātrā* image of Bhairava be brought from its temple, and he and his party wait in the square. Messengers go to the Bhairava temple to ask the god's attendants that he be taken out.

At the time the Bhairava image is ready to be taken from the Bhairava temple another group leaves it on an ostentatious "secret mission."[18]

These are men from families at the Jyāpu level that traditionally perform services for the Bhairava temple. One man precedes the group to clear onlookers out of the way. He carries a heavy iron chain that he swings in front of him as he walks. He is silent during the procession, but he has a bell hung on his back that sounds as he walks and swings the chain. The bell's sound and the dangerous chain are warnings to bystanders to stay out of the way of the group. The first man is followed by another man carrying a large oval object wrapped in cloths, called a "Jāki Gwa," a term whose literal meaning is a "ball of uncooked husked rice." This man is surrounded by other men who are conceived of as guards for the Jāki Gwa. The group moves through the crowd on their way to the Bhairava god-house—used only during Biskā:—near the Gā:hitī (map 5) area to which the two gods in their chariots will eventually be brought. These three sites, Ta:mārhī Square, Gā:hitī (and its adjacent Bhairava god-house), and the field just beyond Gā:hitī in which the Yasi(n) God will be eventually erected form the main spatial axis for the festival events. It is generally known to the onlookers that the group is carrying the "secret god," of which the *jātrā* image is a less powerful public representation. It is popularly believed by most bystanders that the major image is wrapped in the attention grabbing Jāki Gwa itself, which, it is believed, contains the head of Bhairava.[19] Some few bystanders suspect that one of the other men in the group, probably the one who follows the man carrying the Jāki Gwa, is carrying what is perhaps the "true" secret image, that is , an image duplicating the form in which Bhairava is represented in his temple's inner and hidden sanctum.

Meanwhile the *jātrā* image of Bhairava is brought from the Bhairava temple out into the adjoining Ta:mārhī Square. This is the beginning of his *kwaphaegu*, his "being taken down"—the term used for the movement of the god out of his temple and "down" from Ta:mārhī Square to the more southerly and peripheral Gā:hitī. This foreshadows the taking out of dangerous deities from temples and god-houses throughout the city, which will take place on the fourth day at the approach of the new year. Now the procession that had left Lāekū, including the king, Guru-Purohit, umbrella, ceremonial *sukundā*, musicians, and attendants—who had been informally awaiting the arrival of the chariot—is reconstituted and now circumambulates the chariot. The Bhairava image is placed in the chariot facing toward its front. The king, doing a brief *pūjā* to the image and carrying the sword that had been brought to him by the representative of the Guthi Saṃsthān, enters the chariot, seating himself to the right of the Bhairava image. The Guru-Purohit seats himself to the image's left. Now the representatives of other crafts and professions station themselves on the chariot in their proper stations. Four carpenters, representatives of the builders and repairers of the chariot, stand at the four corners. Two non-Brahman Taleju priests (a Jośi and an Ācāju), the Ācāju *pūjārī* from the Bhairava temple, the leader of the Bhairava *guthi*, and a member of the Bhairava *bhajana* group (a group of Jyāpu who play music as worship to the Bhairava of the main temple) sit to the rear of the king. Also seated behind the king is a Jyāpu, the representative of the group of farming families who farm the granted land, a portion of whose revenues help support the expenses of the Bhairava *jātrā* segments of the Biskā: sequence. At both the front and at the rear of the chariot stands a member of one of the Mahā(n) *thar*s, representing both charioteers and royal guards.[20] All these personages, like the king and his attendants, are dressed, as we have noted, in what are taken to be the traditional costumes of the Malla period. The chariot is facing south, in the direction in which it must eventually move so that Bhairava, the king, and the other riders of the chariot may witness the fall of the Yasi(n) God and the beginning of the new year.

Now the Bhadrakālī chariot, in which the Bhadrakālī *jātrā* image, taken from its god-house, has been placed, is brought to Ta:mārhī Square from in front of the Bhadrakālī/Vaiṣṇavī god-house. The *pūjārī* of the god-house, who is a Jyāpu Ācāju, accompanies the image in her chariot, and another Jyāpu sits on the front of the chariot, to call out the rhythmic chant that coordinates the joyful efforts of children who have come to the god-house to pull the chariot by means of long ropes attached to its front. When the Bhadrakālī chariot is brought to Ta:mārhī Square, it is placed to the right side of the Bhairava chariot (a reversal of the ordinary relative positions of Tantric couples). It is said that Bhairava has now been able to get a glimpse of Bhadrakālī, and this introduces their later unfolding relations.

In contrast to the Bhadrakālī chariot, the Bhairava chariot has ropes attached both to its front and its back ends. Traditionally, it is said, there were eight ropes attached to the front of the chariot and only six ropes at the back. In more recent years, perhaps because fewer haulers took part, this had been reduced to six at the front, and four in back. The tug of war that will ensue as people pull the unequal number of ropes is thus biased toward the forward direction. This compensates in part for the comparative difficulties of the terrain in the two directions of the tug of war.

The Bhadrakālī chariot is pulled out of Ta:mārhī Square in the direction of the Gā:hitī Square, in whose vicinity it will make an intermediate stop toward its ultimate destination in the "Yasi(n) Field" (map 5). The Bhairava chariot is also to be pulled to that square—but first there will be a major diversion often called the "playing" of Bhairava. The king tells the two Mahā(n) charioteers to start, and after asking the king for a confirmation, the Mahā(n)s, one at each end of the chariot, call out to the men who have come from the crowd of bystanders to take hold of the ropes at the two ends and begin to pull. (These men, usually young men, may come from any of the *thar*s including the Brahmans except the untouchables and the groups just above them.) Men from the lower city take the ropes at the front of the chariot; men from the upper city, at the back. This is congruent with the direction—front to south—in which the chariot is facing. It is now the late afternoon or early evening of the first day. Ta:mārhī Square is full of thousands of spectators, massed shoulder to shoulder in all the available spaces, including the stairs and terraces of the great temples adjoining the Square.

Now a tug of war begins to determine to which half of the city the chariot will go first. It is considered that the presence of the chariot represents a *darśana*, a manifestation or "showing himself" of the deity Bhairava to that city half. The men from the lower half of the city try to pull the chariot out of Ta:mārhī Square into and along the Bazaar street to the south and then west as far as the Tekhāco *twa:*. The people from the upper city try to pull it out of the square along the Bazaar street to the north and east into their half of the city as far as Dattātreya Square. These two terminal goals are roughly equidistant from the central point (map 5). Access from the square to the southern route is much more obstructed and winding than the upper route and this gives the people from the upper city an advantage that balances their fewer ropes and participants. Ideally the main struggle is within Ta:mārhī Square itself, which is the main arena and theater for the struggle, and once the chariot has reached the exit of the square leading to either the upper or lower city, the struggle should become perfunctory. Again ideally, when the chariot reaches its goal in either the upper or lower city, even the perfunctory struggle should be over. Then, when all goes well, the people from the losing half of the city either quit the struggle or join the people from the temporarily winning half, who now pull the chariot back through Ta:mārhī Square into the *other* half of the city as far as the *jātrā*'s traditional furthest point in that half for a *darśana* for the losing half of the city. When the chariot has been to both halves of the city, all join together on the ropes at the front of it, and pull it back to its proper destination, Gā:hitī Square, which ideally should be reached during the course of the first night. During all this the king, the Guru-Purohit, and the other officials and representatives in the chariot are submitted to a long, tiring, bumpy, swaying, vertiginous, and dangerous ride, which at best takes several hours. Although, as we have noted, ideally the chariot should reach Gā:hitī during the first night, this often does not happen, the chariot is delayed. Whatever happens, however, the chariot and its god and riders *must* reach Gā:hitī Square before the time of the raising of the Yasi(n) on the fourth day of the sequence, the *saṅkrānti*, which marks the beginning of the solar New Year.

In chapter 7 in our discussion of Bhaktapur's city halves we noted references to serious conflicts, sometimes bloody ones, in other Newar cities beginning with some ritual event that eventually pitted one half of the city against the other. We argued that ritually organized antagonisms between the upper and lower city halves served to deflect antagonisms from within smaller local areas, particularly between the groups of economically and socially interrelated *thar*s in such areas, antagonisms whose overt manifestations would have been considerably more serious in their consequences. The struggle with the chariot is the major manifestation in Bhaktapur's annual calendar of this conflict.[21] We have emphasized the *ideal* timing and action of the movements of the Bhairava chariot. But the idealized struggle is liable to turn into a ritually uncontrolled one, and other accidents may also delay the movements of the chariot. In the course of the tug of war, fights sometimes break out. These are usually fights between individuals or small groups from the opposing halves of the city. Sometimes these fights may escalate, larger groups may become involved, stones may be thrown. In such cases the bystanders may flee to their homes, and the *jātrā* may be temporarily discontinued. In the years preceding this study the outbreak of fighting was unusual. It is estimated that there were perhaps four or five occasions in the twenty years before this study in which fights broke out, but they did not interfere with the completion of the *jātrā*.[22] But the ever-present possibility of the eruption of dangerous conflict gives this phase of the festival a particular tone of anxiety for observers and participants, particularly for the entrapped riders in the chariot. On the occasions when a fight does break up the tug of war, or if the chariot becomes stuck in the narrow streets, requiring a long complicated process of extrication, the chariot may be left, its riders returning to their homes for the remainder of the night, leaving behind only the deity and its *pūjārī* attendants. In such cases the chariot will be pulled directly to Gā:hitī on the next day, and the excursion into the city halves will be aborted.

Yet, ideally and almost always, in fact, the Bhairava chariot arrives at Gā:hitī on the evening of this first day of the festival sequence. Earlier the Bhadrakālī chariot had been pulled first to Gā:hitī, and then down the road toward the field where the Yasi(n) was to be erected on the fourth day. It was left at a point about half way along this road, where there is a special Bhadrakālī god-house used only during Biskā:. Gā:hitī[23] is an irregularly shaped square into which four crossroads enter. It is a part of the Lākulāche(n) *twa:*, which adjoins the Ta:mārhī *twa:*. It is bordered by shops and religious structures and contains some temples.

On the arrival of the Bhairava chariot at Gā:hitī the king and Guru-Purohit, followed by the other officials and crew of the chariot, take flowers from the Bhairava image as *prasāda* and descend from the chariot. They circumambulate the Bhairava chariot and then walk on in a procession to the Bhadrakālī chariot, take flower *prasāda* from her image, and circumambulate that chariot. Now shaded by the ceremonial umbrella, accompanied by the ceremonial *sukundā*, musicians, guards, and attendants, the king, bearing the royal sword, returns to the Taleju temple, the site of the Malla palace.

Now the god images are taken from their chariots with music and procession each to their respective special *jātrā* god-houses, Bhairava's being some forty yards to the west of Bhadrakālī's.

THE SECOND DAY

The chariots are where they had been left on the previous night. The deities are in the special *jātrā* god-houses. This is a quiet day after the late-night events of the previous night, an interlude before the crowded days that are to follow. People go about their ordinary activities, although many may go to one or both god-houses and offer minor sacrifices.

THE THIRD DAY

The third day of sequence is the occasion for a feast, a *bhwae,* the first feast of Biskā:, with meat eating and the drinking of alcohol. The day is popularly called *syakwa tyā*, a word of uncertain meaning now, but thought to have reference to the eating of large and thus stomach-disturbing quantities of food.[24]

There is an important secret *pūjā* in the Taleju temple on this day, during which several goats and a buffalo are sacrificed to one of the esoteric forms of the goddess contained in the temple.

THE FOURTH DAY

Preliminaries The events of the fourth day fall into three events or clusters of events, which occur sequentially. The first is the raising of the secondary *yasi(n)*. The second is the raising of the primary *yasi(n)*, one of the pivotal events of the Biskā: sequence. The third is the "taking out" of certain god images, in preparation for the local areal *jātrā*s that will follow on succeeding days.

During the morning of the fourth day a *yasi(n)*, the shorter of the two tree trunks that had previously been dragged to Bhaktapur by the Sa:mi, is erected in the Tālākwa area of the Bolāche(n) *twa:*. Tālākwa is the larger of the city's two potters' quarters. This *yasi(n)* is popularly known as the "Yasi(n) God without arms," in contrast to the main *yasi(n)*, which has a transverse crossbar toward its top representing, among other things, arms. The armless Yasi(n) God will remain standing until the final ninth day of the sequence. After the Armless Yasi(n) God is pulled into upright position by means of ropes and pushing, a local man acting as a priest quickly leads the god through the *daśa karma*, the ten basic *saṃskāras* or rites of passage, to bring it to its "mature" form.[25]

Meanwhile the Bhairava chariot has been moved into the proper position for Bhairava's next journey. It is arranged with its front end facing south toward the Yasi(n) Khya, the field where the main Yasi(n) is to be erected. Once again with the same processions and ceremonies as on the first day the king, his Guru-Purohit, and the rest of the chariot crew assemble and wait by the Bhairava chariot. Bhairava is brought from his *jātrā* god-house to the chariot and placed in it and is followed into it by all the riders who take their positions as on the first day. The Bhadrakālī image is then brought from the special *jātrā* Bhadrakālī god-house and placed in her chariot, which is also facing toward the Yasi(n) Khya. Now the Bhairava chariot, with the Bhadrakālī chariot following it, is pulled down the road to the upper end of the Yasi(n) Khya (map 5), "so that the two deities can watch the erection of the main Yasi(n)

God." This brings together the Bhairava/Bhadrakālī pair and the Yasi(n) God, the deities around whom most of the stories, ideas and action of the festival are gathered.

The Raising Up of the Main Yasi(n) God—The Ending of the Old Year
The erection of the Yasi(n) God pole[26] is one of the foci of the festival sequence (see fig. 26). The *yasi(n)* draws to itself, as we will see, diverse legends and meanings. These are, superficially at least, almost entirely separate from the Bhairava/Bhadrakālī story, although there is a very tangential reference in some of the *yasi(n)* stories to Bhairava. The falling of the *yasi(n)* will indicate the coming to an end of the old year, and the beginning of the new. It marks a focal point not only in time, but in space for people throughout the city who, if at all possible, come to witness its raising and its bringing down.

In contrast to other points that are given a focal and central meaning in other events—such as the palace area, Ta:mārhī Square, and the Tripurasundarī *pīṭha*—Yasi(n) Field is in a vaguely defined boundary area. Not far to its east is the area where the Po(n) untouchables live in an area that is clearly outside of the symbolic city (map 4). The position of Yasi(n) Field; the peculiarity of the second Yasi(n) in the potters' area, which seems disconnected from other events and whose existence has no present doctrinal[27] or legendary explanation; the presence of additional, secondary god-houses for Bhairava and Bhadrakālī; and, for some observers, the struggle between the upper and lower city halves, have led to some attempts at historical rather than structural and functional explanations for these phenomena (e.g., Kölver 1980, 168; Gutschow 1984). Such explanation takes these features as indications of residues of old, separate, and antagonistic communities, and witnesses of the locations of now forgotten centers of ancient once unamalgamated towns.[28]

As we have noted, the very tall tree, perhaps seventy feet in height, which will be the Yasi(n) God has been divested of all its limbs, except for the branches at the summit, which represent the god's hair. A straight segment of another tree is attached at right angles some feet below the top of the trunk, giving it a cruciate form. This is said to be the *yasi(n)*'s arms, which, it will be recalled, differentiate it terminologically from the smaller *yasi(n)*. Some small branches and leaves are attached to the ends of the crosspiece to represent the god's hands and fingers. The *yasi(n)*'s form, then, is given an anthropomorphic inter-

Figure 26. Biskā:. A stage in the raising of the Yasi(n) God to mark the solar New Year.

pretation, in keeping with its designation as a deity, the Yasi(n) God. Toward the juncture of the crossbranch and the main trunk two long strips of cloth are tied, one at each side. These are *patā*, banners,[29] of the sort that are sometimes tied to the pinnacles of religious structures and which, like many other aspects of the Yasi(n) God, are given more than one interpretation. Thus, in an echo of the later developments in the Bhairava/Bhadrakālī plot, they are said to represent Śiva and Śakti, and when they move in the wind, this represents their sexual intercourse. The two banners are also related to a legend about the saving of Bhaktapur from two snakes by a Tantric magician who came to a bad end through the weakness of his wife, a story that we will recount below. Sometimes the banners are said to represent the snakes; sometimes the Tantric Ācāju and his wife. A bundle of eight ropes is also tied onto the upper part of the trunk. In one interpretation the eight ropes represent the eight Matṛkās at Bhaktapur's borders, and the *yasi(n)* represents Bhairava. When the ropes flutter in the wind, this represents the intercourse between Bhairava and the Matṛkā.[30]

The stories about the snakes come in different versions, borrowing freely and heavily from widespread and well-known Hindu folk tales. Some versions are quite long and detailed, and are popular local stories recounted by traditional Brahman storytellers in the city. We will paraphrase (and shorten) the two major variants of the stories.

The first version is in itself a cluster of unrelated stories, which rather clumsily gives a legendary warrant to miscellaneous aspects of Biskā:. In the first version of the story, it happened that a long time ago there was a king in Bhaktapur whose daughter married. On her wedding night she and her groom went to their room, "had a friendly talk," and then had sexual intercourse. After that they slept deeply. As they were sleeping a pair of snakes came out of the princess's nose.[31] The snakes grew bigger and bigger. They then bit the prince, who died. The snakes, shrinking to their original size, crawled back into the princess's nose. The princess, who was unaware of the snakes that she harbored, awoke and was distressed to see her dead husband. The king was also sad, and arranged for a funeral procession and cremation. This occurrence was repeated with many new husbands over the years.[32] The local people, therefore, had to arrange for many expensive royal funeral processions and cremations, and they formed a special *guthi* to take care of them.

One day a prince came to a forest. He met an old woman there, at a river that flowed among the trees. He asked her what she was doing there, and she said that she had come to meet him to advise him to marry the princess. He asked what he should do and whether he would have a happy marriage with the princess. The old woman told him about the snakes, and told him to stay awake and kill them with his sword. "Then you will have a beautiful wife, wealth, and a kingdom." She told him to go to the eastern part of the forest and that he would find a sword at a place where three rivers met. The story then recounts his meeting and marriage with the princess. "After the marriage they went to sleep in their room. The young man had great courage. It was a very difficult thing to do. They had a good conversation, then they had sexual intercourse and the princess went to sleep, but the young man did not sleep. He was very cautious. He remembered what the old woman had said." When the snakes appeared, he killed them. But before they died, the snakes said to him "You are a lucky and a great man. We have killed many princes and now we are going to die. That may be good or it may be bad. Please do a memorial for us every year." The story recounts the surprise and happiness in the city the next day at the prince's survival.

The prince established a festival on the last day of the solar month of Caitra. He erected a *yasi(n)*, and attached the two *patās* to it to represent the two supernatural snakes or *nāga*s. The festival is called *bisket* (the Nepali language version of the name), *bi* meaning "snake," and *syat* meaning "he killed." The old woman whom the prince met in the forest was really Bhadrakālī, which is why the festival is dedicated to her. In the forest where they met there were many tall trees and it is a tree taken every year from this forest which incarnates the Yasi(n) God. The *tīrtha*, the place where the prince found the sword, is at the river Hanumante just at the Bhadrakālī (Vaiṣṇavī) *pīṭha*. Because it was Bhadrakālī who helped the prince, it was decided to erect the pole in sight of Bhadrakālī's *pīṭha*, which is just to the south of Yasi(n) Field.

Now the appearance of Bhadrakālī allows another piece of the story to be attached. One day, after the Bhadrakālī Jātrā had been established, Bhairava came from Kāśī (Benares) to see it. This particular Bhairava was called "Kāśī Bhairavanātha," the chief of the Bhairavas. A local Tantric practitioner recognized Bhairava in the crowd and tried to trap him by means of a powerful *mantra*. But Bhairava tried to escape by sinking into the ground. When all of his body except his head had disappeared below the ground, Bhadrakālī recognized him and said, "That is my husband, we must keep him here. At least cut off and keep his head." That was done. The head was placed in the Bhairava temple in Ta:mārhī Square, and the body was returned to Benares (where there is an important headless representation of Bhairava).

Thus, in memory of the meeting of Bhadrakālī and Bhairava, temples throughout Bhaktapur organized *jātrās* for their gods and goddesses.[33]

There is another and different tale told about the Yasi(n) God. This one contains a theme that is echoed in the legends about the origin of the Nine Durgās (chap. 15). This theme concerns a man of great magical power whose power is lost through some error of his wife's, an error that is a sign of her weakness of character. If the story of the prince and the snakes is taken to mean in part that women are dangerous for domesticity until their dangerous "phallic" attributes have been brought under control by male action, then this story suggests that that control is always precarious. In a popular local version[34] told by Brahman storytellers, the protagonist in a long story is Śeṣar Ācāju, a Karmācārya priest with exceptional Tantric powers, who was the *guru* of a Licchavi king of Bhaktapur, Śiva Deva.[35] The story tells how the priest protected Bhaktapur from an attack by the Kirātas by turning himself into one thousand tigers and chasing off the Kirāti army. "But after I have chased off the Kirātas, I will return to you in the form of a tiger," said Śeṣar Ācāju to the king. "Don't be afraid. You must throw rice on me, and I will become a man again." The *ācāju* gave the king some grains of husked rice to which the proper Tantric power had been added. He chased away the Kirātas, returned to the king, and was turned back into a man. The king welcomed him gratefully to his palace. The tale continues:

Śeṣar Ācāju returned to his own house. His wife was very happy to see him, she respected and loved him very much. One day Śeṣar Ācāju talked with his wife of his feats. His wife said, "Can you turn yourself into a python (*aji[n]gar*)?" Śeṣar said, "Yes, I can." His wife said, "I am very curious to see you as a python." Śeṣar Ācāju agreed with her wish, and said "I will show you myself as a python, but don't be afraid." He gave her some magical polished rice (*kiga:*) [given special power by a mantra] and said "I am going to become a python. You can see me as a python for as long as you like, but then you must throw the rice at me and I will become a man again." He showed himself to her as a python but she became frightened and forgot about the rice. She ran away. The python followed her in order to get the rice. While his wife, Nararupā, was running away in her fear she put her hand to her mouth and happening to swallow some of the rice she was carrying she also turned into a python.

The story goes on to say how the two great snakes moved through

Bhaktapur trying to find the proper *kiga:* to change them back into human form. They went to a Tantric temple in the hope that people with Tantric knowledge there could help them, but they had no luck. They then went to the palace in the hope that the king might help. The king did not know who they were, but he announced to the people that the two serpents (referred to at this point as *nāga* and *nāginī*, as supernatural serpents) had come for asylum, and therefore should not be harmed. But the snakes, not understanding this, were in despair and so commited suicide in front of the palace. And now a great famine came to Bhaktapur. The people consulted an astrologer, a Jośi, who told them that the death of the *nāga* and *nāginī* was its cause. The king wished to do something to overcome the difficulties and went to seek Śeṣar Ācāju. But his house was empty and the door was unlocked. The king found the trail of the *nāgas* there, and he followed it to the place where the *nāga* and *nāginī* had killed themselves. He thus finally came to understand the true nature of Śeṣar and Nararupā's suicides. The king felt great sorrow. He remembered Śeṣar's good qualities. He wanted the people to know about and remember Śeṣar Ācāju's great contributions to the city. Therefore the king organized the *jātrā* of Śeṣar and his wife Nararupā, which is called "Biskā:." The two *patās* on the *yasi(n)* represent the two *nāgas*.

The *yasi(n)* has been prepared and is lying in Yasi(n) Field. Earlier in the day ceremonies for installing divinity or "life" into it took place, and an Ācāju administered to it as a newborn (or reborn) deity the entire set of *saṃskāras*, or life-cycle rites, necessary to bring the newborn god to his maturity. The arrival of the two chariots, that of Bhairava and Bhadrakālī, signals the time when people may begin the attempt to raise the *yasi(n)*. At the point where the *yasi(n)* will be erected there is a permanent hole, surrounded by a wall about five feet high, with an opening to the west. The pole is first put through the opening, and maneuvered into the hole. After the pole is raised, the edges of the hole and the wall will support it.[36] The *yasi(n)* is very difficult to manipulate and raise. Scores of people come to coöperate in its raising, pulling on the ropes and pushing with their hands and with long poles. When, on the next day, the erect *yasi(n)* is rocked back and forth in preparation for its lowering as a sign of the beginning of the new solar year, it is said that the god is being rocked to sleep, as he is very tired from having stood up all year. The erection of the *yasi(n)* is to represent that old year—and it is only its taking down that marks a sharply transitional time. Now, at the approach of the transitional point between two solar years, the Yasi(n) Field and the Yasi(n) God have become the focus of attention of the whole city, which has participated in and watched the erection of the pole in a coordinated cooperative act.[37] When the Yasi(n) God has been raised, young men climb the ropes attached to it representing the Aṣṭamātṛkās, and present an offering of small coins at the knots where the ropes are attached to the pole.

Now the two chariots are pulled in front of the standing Yasi(n) God. In Yasi(n) Field there is a temple, the Cyāsi Ma(n)dap, which is only used during this phase of Biskā:, that has a small window in its north side. The Bhairava chariot, facing east, is placed parallel to the Cyāsi Ma(n)dap, and aligned so that the window of the Ma(n)dap is at its right side and exactly in line with the side opening of the chariot. This exact ordering is said to facilitate the movement of the Bhairava image, which is always placed into the chariot from its left side, and removed from its right side. The Bhadrakālī chariot is placed at the other side, the southeastern side of the field, and lined up with similar precision alongside the Bhadrakālī *pīṭha*. Now most of the riders of the Bhairava chariot, who had remained there during the raising of the *yasi(n)*, descend and circumambulate the Bhairava chariot, and take a flower as *prasāda*. They then circumambulate the Bhadrakālī chariot and take *prasāda* there. Finally they circumambulate the Yasi(n) and the Cyāsi Ma(n)dap at the same time. Then this group, including the king and his Guru-Purohit and most of the officials, return with music, *sukundā*, and umbrella first to Gā:hitī and then, after the others leave them there, the king, Guru-Purohit, and the two Mahā(n) charioteers return to Lāekū and the Taleju temple.

Certain priests and officials attached to the Bhairava temple, an Ācāju and some assistants, had remained on the Bhairava chariot. Now they descend and take the *jātrā* Bhairava and bring him to the Cyāsi Ma(n)dap, where he joins the "true" Bhairava image and the Jāki Gwa that had been brought there on the first day of the sequence. Now there are offerings and sacrifices by many people at the temple to the *jātrā* image, and to the enwrapped Jāki Gwa. The true image remains hidden from sight.

The Bhadrakālī *jātrā* image is removed from her chariot by her priest. She is brought to an open building, a *phalcā*, near the Bhadrakālī *pīṭha*, which adjoins Yasi(n) Field, where she will be kept during the night. Up until this point the two dangerous deities have been near each other, but there has been no direct contact.

That evening there are large feasts in people's houses, and guests and extended family are invited.

Taking Out the Gods: The Vārāhī Jātrā After the Yasi(n) God has been raised, the *jātrā* images of certain deities throughout the city are taken from their god-houses and special rooms in temples and placed either on the *cheli*, the open ground floors of the god-houses, or on nearby *phalcā*, open rest houses, each conventionally associated with a particular god-house. They will be left outside of their god-houses and temples for the next four days, to be brought in again on the eighth day of the cycle. The deities so brought out include all the Maṇḍalic Goddesses (except Vaiṣṇavī, who is represented by Bhadrakālī), other dangerous goddess figures—particularly the ones identified as Bhagavatī, some minor Bhairavas, and the major Gaṇeśas. These are, in short, the major dangerous city deities, and Gaṇeśa, who is as much of a Tantric god as he is an ordinary one.[38] Blood sacrifices are routinely offered to these deities during this period, certain of whom become the foci for important local areal *jātrās* that are considered major events, and which draw people from all over the city. Vārāhī is the focus for this night. The next day, the fifth, will belong again to Bhairava and Bhadrakālī. The sixth and seventh days, which echo some of the activities of the fifth day, have Mahākālī and Mahālakṣmī as the central actors (on the sixth day) and Brāhmaṇī and Maheśvarī (on the seventh). The eighth day centers around a form of Gaṇeśa, Chuma(n) Gaṇeśa. Seven of the nine Maṇḍalic Goddesses (if we take Bhadrakālī to represent Vaiṣṇavī) are foci of *jātrās* of city-wide interest (even though their movements are restricted to some limited area of the city), the remaining two, Kumārī and Tripurasundarī, have festivals in their own maṇḍalic areas at the same time as the mass of other deities who have been brought out of their god-houses and are not otherwise emphasized.[39]

The remainder of the deities who have been taken outside have small *jātrās* of only local and sometimes very limited importance.[40] On the evening of this day many people make sacrifices at their local Gaṇeśa shrines and at one or another local temple or shrine of a dangerous deity. Over the next four days the areas in which the various local areal *jātrās* take place are sites for household feasts and sacrifices to the particular local deity who has been "brought outside."

Although there are now, as we have noted, activities at many Tantric temples and shrines, the city's focus is now at the god-house of the Maṇḍalic Goddess, Vārāhī. After the *yasi(n)* has been raised, a procession of some thirty or forty people who are members of the Vārāhī maṇḍalic area, and who belong to the Vārāhī *guthi* (which supervises and arranges Vārāhī ceremonies) or the Vārāhī *bhajana*, or music group, bring clumps of dry reeds, called *ti* or *ti(n)pwā*, to the *cheli* of the

Vārāhī god-house where her *jātrā* image had been placed. Taking some fire from a votive oil lamp that had been set in front of the image, the reeds are set afire as an offering to Vārāhī. Then the image of Vārāhī, placed in a palanquin, is carried, followed by many hundreds of people, across the river to the Vārāhī *pīṭha.* As the procession moves toward the river through the maṇḍalic area it stops many times in front of houses, and householders make animal sacrifices to the goddess in front of their houses. When the procession reaches the river it stops and the Vārāhī Ācāju touches the palanquin with river water, and then offers some water to the *jātrā* image. The people accompanying the *jātrā* drink river water, wash their faces with it, and splash each other with it. This water is *prasāda* from Vārāhī. Now the procession continues to the Vārāhī *pīṭha*, where the *jātrā* image is placed on the *pīṭha* stone.[41] The goddess is worshiped by means of an animal sacrifice. Now the procession takes her back to the open *cheli* of her god-house.

THE FIFTH DAY: TAKING DOWN THE YASI(N) GOD—BEGINNING OF THE SOLAR NEW YEAR

The fifth day of Biskā:, the central day of the sequence, is a *saṅkrānti*, the first day of the solar month, the day that begins the new solar year. Its ceremonial beginning will be at the fall of the *yasi(n)* in the late afternoon toward sunset.

On the morning of this fifth day everyone who can—that is, many thousands of people—go to the Hanumante River at the Cupi(n) Gā, which is the location of the *tīrtha* associated with Bhadrakālī. There, in what is a kind of *melā*, people enter the river for a ritual bath.

During the course of this New Year's Day there are a number of esoteric activities in the Taleju temple. Among these is the worship by the "king" and his Guru-Purohit of the dangerous deity Dui(n) Māju, a deity said by some to be Taleju's own *pīṭha* goddess, and a deity of special historical interest (chap. 8). She is worshiped on this day as a "sister of Indrāṇī," a deity to whom this day makes special reference. On this day, also, those Jugīs who during the year play their special instruments at the Taleju temple come to the temple and are offered food on which the king throws *masalā* (a mixture of betel nut, nuts, cinnamon, raisins, etc.), as a token of gratitude for their work.[42]

This is the day of the Indrāṇī Jātrā,[43] which involves, exactly like the Vārāhī Jātrā of the previous day, the taking of the deity from its outside resting place to its external *pīṭha*. In addition, in the course of this *jātrā* the procession brings the Indrāṇī image to the front outer gate of the Taleju temple, opening on Lāekū Square, where she is met by the king and the Guru-Purohit and worshiped by them.[44]

Now the king, carrying the royal sword, the Guru-Purohit, and the two Mahā(n) charioteers, accompanied by musicians, the royal umbrella, and the ornamental *sukundā*, return to Yasi(n) Field, and meet the remainder of the chariot passengers there. All seat themselves on seats to the north side of the Cyāsi Ma(n)dap. Meanwhile the Bhairava chariot has been turned around to face the west.[45]

The leader of the Bhairava *guthi* makes an offering of yellow pigment to the Yasi(n) God, and then gives some of it as *prasāda* to bystanders. Now the Bhairava *jātrā* image is placed in the chariot. All the passengers and the charioteers mount the chariot and take their proper positions in relation to the Bhairava image. Meanwhile the Bhadrakālī chariot has been readied near her *pīṭha* and her image put into it, and the riders of her chariot have mounted and entered the chariot. The secret Bhariava image and the Jāki Gwa had earlier been returned to the Bhairava *jātrā* god-house (where the *jātrā* image of Bhairava will later join them) by the same group of men running in the same order who had brought the two images down to Yasi(n) Field on the first day.

Now it is the time for bringing the Yasi(n) God down. First the Yasi(n) is rocked back and forth in an east-west direction, in a motion called "rocking to sleep." The god is said, as we have noted, to be tired for "he has been standing up all year." At the time of the rocking the eight ropes representing the Aṣṭamātṛkās and the two *patās* representing the Tantric *guru* and his wife move, and this is interpreted by religious specialists as representing the sexual intercourse of the Aṣṭamātṛkās and the Yasi(n) as Bhairava, and of the two *nāga*s with each other. The pole is slowly rocked back and forth, and finally, after perhaps ten minutes to half an hour of swaying, eased down to the west so that it falls outward through the opening of its retaining wall. People who wish a son try to pull one of the leaves from the *yasi(n)* or its crossbar, and if they get one they will not only have a son, but he will be an important man. When the pole falls, the new year begins.

When the Yasi(n) God is down, the Bhairava Ācāju and *guthi* leader decorate the Bhairava image again with yellow pigment, *bhuisinha(n)*, which is then given as *prasāda* to the other chariot riders. Now there is the beginning of a unique episode—the Po(n) untouchables become integrally involved with the sequence. The Bhairava Ācāju and *guthi* leader, standing on the chariot, place some yellow pigment as *prasāda* taken from the Bhairava image, on the foreheads of Po(n)s who crowd around the chariot to receive it.[46] At any other time this contact would be greatly contaminating to these two men, but at this one time in the year it is not.[47] Now some of the Po(n)s take hold of the ropes at the back of the chariot, and other men, mostly Jyāpus,[48] take hold of the ropes at the front. Again a tug of war begins to determine the direction in which the chariot will move. The Jyāpus are trying to pull the chariot back toward the city, while the Po(n)s are trying to keep the deity in Yasi(n) Field, which adjoins the "Po(n) *twa:*," the area where they live, just outside of the symbolic boundaries of the city. This struggle does not (at least in the memory and expectation of present informants) lead to fights, and gradually the more numerous Jyāpus with the advantage of the two extra ropes at the front of the chariot prevail. At the top of Yasi(n) Field, where the road to Gā:hitī enters it, the Po(n)s let go of the ropes, and return to their own area. The turning back of the Po(n)s indicates that the chariot is now within the symbolic boundaries of the city. The Bhadrakālī chariot, pulled only from the front, is drawn up after the Bhairava chariot is on its way. The chariots are hauled up the road that they had descended at the beginning of the sequence in the direction of Ta:mārhī Square. But when they reach Gā:hitī there is an essential episode, a further interruption to Bhairava's civic journey.

The chariots are arranged in Gā:hitī Square, with the Bhairava chariot facing north toward Ta:mārhī Square and the Bhadrakālī chariot moved in front of him blocking his path and facing south, in the direction from which they had just come. They are placed near the stone deity Swatuña Bhairava, which represents (among other things; see chap. 8) the body of Bhairava, at the place where Bhadrakālī first recognized him, where he sank into the ground in an attempt to escape, and where Bhadrakālī ordered that his head be cut off.[49] Now the two chariots, with their passengers aboard, are pushed toward each other. Most of the movement is by the Bhadrakālī chariot, which is crashed into the comparatively immobile Bhairava chariot. This is in keeping with Bhadrakālī's meaning as a Śaktī, for the banging together represents sexual intercourse, and the Śaktī is the active partner. Each time the chariots crash together the people in and on them throw flowers out into the crowd, and people rush to gather them as important *prasāda*. The chariots are banged together three times. There is a certain hesitation in the interpretation of the meaning of this banging together between sexual intercourse and aggression. It is said by upper-status informants that the esoteric meaning is sexual intercourse. Although, such informants say, lower-status people often understand this meaning, they also may be unaware of this, and may misinterpret it as the two gods fighting. The banging together is, in fact, called *lwākegu*, from a verb meaning "to fight, to quarrel" as well as "to collide, or to hit against each other."[50] Even among those who hold the "correct" interpretation of sexual intercourse, however, it is believed that at the time of the sexual banging together Bhadrakālī becomes angry with Bhairava for reasons that are unclear to present informants. Perhaps, it is believed, her anger is for someting that Bhairava has done wrong—for he will later try to atone for this and quiet her by means of a gift.[51] Now Bhadrakālī "returns in her anger to her home"; that is, her chariot is removed first from Gā:hitī to an area near Bhadrakālī's *jātrā* god-house where she will remain in angry seclusion until the seventh day of the sequence, when Bhairava will have to send her a present to placate her.

The Bhairava *jātrā* image is now taken to its *jātrā* god-house in Lākulāche(n). His chariot is left in Gā:hitī, where it will remain until the ninth day. The evening of this New Year's Day, following the banging together of the chariots, is the occasion of major feasts in most households, with guests from other cities and towns who have come to watch the festival.

THE SIXTH DAY: THE MAHĀKĀLĪ/MAHĀLAKṢMĪ JĀTRĀ

The previous day had continued the themes of struggle and still problematic unification, portrayed in ambiguous sexual and aggressive images. The events of the next two days echo these themes in an imagery which is said to show the "cooperation and friendship" of adjoining maṇḍalic sectors of the city.

The sixth day is the day for the special *jātrā*s of two of the Maṇḍalic Goddesses, Mahākālī and Mahālakṣmī. In the morning of the day there are two important *jātrā*s in two nearby towns that are visited by many people from Bhaktapur. These are at Thimi, where there is a Gaṇeśa festival in which thirty-six chariots are paraded, and Bode, where there is an important Mahālakṣmī *jātrā*. In Bhaktapur, in the afternoon, the *jātrā* images of the two Maṇḍalic goddesses, Mahālakṣmī and Mahākālī, who protect the two adjacent maṇḍalic zones of the north and northeast, are taken from the "outside" placements where all the Tantric deities had been brought on the fourth day of the cycle and taken on a *jātrā* to their respective *pīṭhas*. Their *jātrā*s resemble the Vārāhī and Indrāṇī Jātrās, which we have described above, with an important additional feature. The Mahālakṣmī image is taken on the usual traditional path between her god-house and her *pīṭha,* but the Mahākālī image is taken out of its usual path so that she encounters the Mahālakṣmī image just before they reach the border of the city. On their meeting the palanquins bearing the two deities are bumped together three times. This, it is said, is not considered a fighting, but a mating, signifying the bringing together or unification of the two zones. There is no doctrine as to which of the two goddesses is male or female during their intercourse.[52] The goddesses then part, and continue on their respective *jātrā*s. That evening there are feasts in the households within these goddesses' maṇḍalic zones.

THE SEVENTH DAY: THE BRĀHMAṆĪ/MAHEŚVARĪ JĀTRĀ

During the afternoon of this day, the previous day's encounter of two neighboring Maṇḍalic Goddesses is repeated in exactly the same manner, including the encounter and the bumping together of the palanquins, but this time with the goddesses Brāhmaṇī and Maheśvarī, of the adjacent eastern and southeastern maṇḍalic zones as the foci. That evening there are feasts in those two zones.

Earlier in the day, a member of the Bhairava temple staff has brought a *sāri* to Bhadrakālī in her *jātrā* god-house as a present from Bhairava—an offering to make peace with her and to appease her anger. On the evening of this day the *jātrā* image of Bhadrakālī is brought to a special *phalcā*, an open shed, adjacent to the western side of the Ñātāpwa(n)la temple in Ta:mārhī Square.[53]

Although the Bhairava *jātrā* image is still in the *jātrā* god-house in Lākulāche(n), the main secret portable image, the "true" *jātrā* image of Bhairava, is now in his temple in Ta:mārhī Square, where it had been returned on the fifth day. The bringing of the Bhadrakālī image, now tranquil, to Ta:mārhī Square represents, it is said, the visit of Bhadrakālī to her "husband's"[54] home, and a brief, but in the flow of Biskā:'s imagery significant, movement toward peaceful domesticity.

THE EIGHTH DAY. FEASTING THE GODS—CHUMA(N) GANDYA: JĀTRĀ

On the morning of this day, crowds of people dressed in some of their best clothes and often accompanied by neighborhood music groups, visit the places adjoining those god-houses and temples throughout the city where deities had been taken out to public view on the fourth day of the Biskā: sequence. As most of these places are on or near the main city festival route, the *pradakṣiṇāpatha*, people are able to follow this route for the most part,[55] moving along it in the auspicious clockwise direction. At each place people present symbolic "feasts" to the deity. They offer eggs, *swaga(n)* (a mixture of husked rice, curds, and pigment),[56] sweets, alcoholic spirits, and beer.

One of the many local *jātrā*s of the Biskā: period serves as a focus for the city on this day. This is the *jātrā* of the local Gaṇeśa of the main Coche(n) *twa:*. This particular Gaṇeśa (or Gandya: in Newari) is called "Chuma(n) Gandya:," "Rat Gaṇeśa."[57] The *jātrā* image of this deity is carried on the afternoon of the eighth day in several processions around the *twa:*, and many people come from all over the city to watch. The importance of this Gaṇeśa is suggested by his surviving legends, which seem to reflect important aspects of the city's history. We will sketch two versions known to contemporary storytellers.

A long time ago the Malla king Ānanda Malla (referring probably to the early-fourteenth-century ruler, Ānandadeva Malla) wanted to make Bhaktapur into a larger city by extending its boundaries. It was only a small town then. He walked around the various places outside of the town. He reached a place in a forest, which is the location of the present-day Bhadrakālī. There he saw a very thin old woman who resembled a skeleton. Ānanda Malla was very frightened when he saw her. Nevertheless, he approached her and asked, "Who are you, old woman? Why are you alone in this forest?" "I came here because I wanted to give you advice about making a city," she replied. "If you go north from this place, then you will see a wonderful scene, something which you have never seen before. Then [after seeing this sight] you must go on, and you will see Gaṇeśa. You must worship Gaṇeśa, and then you will be successful." The goddess revealed herself to him, and then disappeared. She was Bhadrakālī.

The king followed the old woman's directions and went to the north. There he saw a wonderful scene. A cat and a rat [or mouse] were fighting. The rat finally defeated the cat, and ran off, carrying the cat in its mouth. The king followed the rat. It ran up into a tree with the cat in its mouth and then disappeared. Ānanda Malla was full of wonder. How did the rat take the cat up into the tree? This was surprising. He went to look but could not find it. But then he saw Gaṇeśa there. The king remembered what Bhadrakālī had said. He thus served [worshiped and respected] Gaṇeśa, and was given effectiveness [*siddhi*] in many things. The place where the cat and the rat fought is called Bholāche(n). The place where the rat ran up the tree is in Coche(n). [These are adjoining *twa:*s in the northern part of the city (see map 11)]. Ānanda Malla built a temple for the rat in that place [where the rat climbed the tree]. Ānanda Malla then divided the city into twenty-four twa:s, and he constructed the Aṣṭamātṛkā *pīṭhas* and god-houses. He established a festival [Biskā:] for Bhadrakālī.

In another version of the story, Ānanda Malla was hunting in a forest at the north of present-day Bhaktapur. There he saw a cat and a rat fighting. The rat vanquished the cat and then ran up a tree. The king went to find the animals, but could not find them. Both the cat and the rat had disappeared. The king thought the rat must be the vehicle of Gaṇeśa, otherwise he would not have been able to win the fight. The king, therefore, prayed to Gaṇeśa. Then Gaṇeśa showed himself to the king and said to him, "Go south from this place. There you will see an old woman. She is my mother [i.e., Pārvatī, but in the form of Bhadrakālī]. When you see her, bow down to her and say that Gaṇeśa sent you. My mother will be pleased. We [Gaṇeśa and his mother] represent the north and the south. You should build a city between us [that is, the positions where the king encounters them] and we will help you." So Ānanda Malla received help from Gaṇeśa and Bhadrakālī. He then built the enlarged city of Bhaktapur.

On the evening of the eighth day all deities are returned back into their god-houses, except the Bhairava and Bhadrakālī images, which are still, respectively, at the Bhairava *jātrā* god-house, and the *phalcā* in Ta:mārhī Square. In the evening households throughout the city have feasts, often preceded by animal sacrifices.

THE NINTH DAY: TAKING DOWN THE SMALL YASI(N) GOD—FINAL PHASES OF THE BHAIRAVA/BHADRAKĀLĪ JĀTRĀ

In the morning of the ninth day the small Yasi(n) God in the potter's quarter, Tālākwa, is pulled down with no special ceremony by the people of the area.

In the afternoon of the day the empty Bhairava chariot, which has been in Gā:hitī Square, is aligned so that it is facing west, with its left side facing in the direction of Bhairava Jātrā god-house, in preparation for the placing of the image into the chariot at its left side. The Bhadrakālī chariot has been left in Ta:mārhī Square, where it had brought Bhadrakālī on the seventh day. Now, exactly as on the first day, the king, Guru-Purohit, attendants, and chariot crew meet at Gā:hitī and circumambulate and enter the Bhairava chariot. At the same time, in Ta:mārhī Square, the Bhadrakālī image is taken from the *phalcā*, and placed in her nearby chariot.

The people from the upper and lower city grasp the ropes at the Bhairava chariot's two ends, as they had on the first day of the festival. This time, though, the men from the upper city are at the front end of the chariot and those from the lower city, at the back. Again, as on the first day but this time because of the slope of the land in Gā:hitī, it is easier for the chariot to be pulled into the lower city, and this is compensated for by the fewer ropes on the lower city end of the chariot. The entire procedure of the first day is repeated, and, again, if all goes well, the struggle supposedly ceases at the exits to the two squares—that is, of Gā:hitī if the chariot is being successfully pulled into the lower city, and of Ta:mārhī if it is being successfully pulled into the upper city. It is then pulled first toward the traditional far point in the victorious half, then brought to the end point in the other half, as it was on the first day. Then, for the last time, it is cooperatively pulled back to Ta:mārhī Square, where the Bhadrakālī chariot has been waiting.

But, as on the first day, all this may not go smoothly. Many people have been drinking on this day, and there may be resentments smoldering from the conflicts and violence of the first day. There is always anxiety that the tug of war may not follow its conventional script and might turn into a fight.

When the chariot is returned to Ta:mārhī Square, after Bhairava has been to the upper and lower cities once again and shown himself again in *darśana*, the chariot is pulled up to the north side of the Bhairava temple and the *jātrā* image is taken from the right side of the chariot and returned to its dwelling within the temple. The Bhadrakālī image, which has been waiting at the Ta:mārhī Square *phalcā*, is taken in its chariot to its ordinary god-house, the Vaiṣṇavī god-house, where it will be kept for the remainder of the year. The two gods are welcomed into their homes with the *lāskusa* ceremony, the traditionally welcoming and sanctifying ceremony for moving a focal participant into a sacred area. While the two gods are being taken back into their homes, bystanders and the Ācāju priest, who greets them in front of the temple to perform the *lasakusa* ceremony, tease them about their recent romantic and sexual adventures.

And now, finally, the passengers and crew of the Bhairava chariot descend. The king, carrying his sword, the king's Guru-Purohit, and the two charioteers, joined by the musicians, the carrier of the umbrella, and the carrier of the *sukundā*, take leave of the others, and, followed by representatives of the central government's Guthi Saṃsthān, return to the Taleju temple, where the king, becoming a Brahman once more, returns the sword to one of the Guthi's representatives, who will take it back to Kathmandu.

This final night is an occasion for feasts throughout the city.

APPROACHES TO MEANING

Biskā: is a complex symbolic enactment. A cast of human and divine actors moves through meaningful city space, in endlessly repeated annual performances in concert with the city's symbolically ordered and ordering time, in a context of legends and traditional interpretations. Against this background the actors do certain things; they enact dramas or, if all the events of the period are considered to have some possible overall pattern, they enact a single theatrical performance, albeit one whose dramatic unity is rather Shakespearian. Biskā:'s significant contexts include the year's other festival enactments. When considered in relation to the entire group of festivals (chap. 16) or in comparison with particular other ones—say, the other great structural focal festival, Mohanī, or the lunar New Year sequence, Swanti—certain of its peculiarities and relations within the larger cycle are highlighted. We can at this point approach the question of its meaning—that is, the meanings bearing on civic integration with which we are concerned—under some general rubrics that can be applied for comparison to still other annual events.

1. *Biskā: as a solar festival.* One of our questions is whether cyclical events that are "outside" the annual festival cycle affect that cycle. With the exception of the minor event Ghya: Cāku Sa(n)lhu [10] and the minor observances of the first days of each solar month, "the events of the solar cycle" (as this chapter is entitled) really means the Biskā: cycle. Biskā: has, of course, some direct "solar" references. It takes place at the vernal equinox and begin a new year at the moment of the

balance between daylight and dark. The raising and lowering of the *yasi(n)* to mark the transition to the new year in an east-west direction has, perhaps, some now forgotten connection with the sun's direction. Otherwise, there is no evident direct reference to the sun and the seasons. In Biskā:'s contrast with the lunar and agricultural Mohanī sequence there is, however, an intriguing, if perhaps fortuitous, contrast, which relates Biskā: to the modes of astral religious action, whose presiding figure is the deified sun. Biskā:'s central narrative (although not all of its subsidiary legends) reflects the kinds of passive and self-adjustive relations that worshipers have with the astral deities and the transcendent macrocosm, rather than the active and manipulative interactions they have in some other annual events with the realms represented by the dangerous and ordinary civic deities. Thus, in Mohanī the king and his Guru-Purohit actively participate in the struggle of the Goddess against forces of disorder, but in Biska: both king and deities are passive, moved by the forces of convention, affected only by a ripple of urban disorder, a thesis of disorder that tends to clarify the subsequent resolution of order. The king and his entourage and the god Bhairava are moved by immemorial ritual order, as the sun moves through the year. Even the tug of war that threatens to disrupt the movement of the chariot and that determines which half of the city it will move to first is in the realm of luck and chance, the neutral nonmoral realm of the astral deities.

There are also marked contrasts in the emphases of Swanti, the lunar New Year's sequence, and Biskā:. However, to anticipate chapter 16, the contrasts are internal to the entire annual cycle, and not in any obvious way semantically urged by the contrasts of the solar and lunar cycles, except perhaps in a contrast in personal effort in Swanti and passive witness in Biskā:. Swanti's emphasis is on the affirmation of the family in the household, Biskā:'s is on the integration of the city as a whole and in its relation to annual time.

2. *Biskā: as a structural focal sequence.* The Biskā: sequence, as we have described it, differs sharply from the majority of miscellaneous annual events in ways that lead us to characterize it as of focal importance for Bhaktapur. The first evident difference is quantitative. It has more events and more deities and consumes more time than do the events we presented in the last chapter; the closest being the Sāpāru events. Biskā:'s mass of events is not just a disconnected collection, however; its actions and themes are woven together and related in var-

ious ways. This adds formal complexity to quantity. In contrast to many other events, the entire city is represented, not just an area, and there is a representative range of actors from king to untouchable, not just some one or some few social segments. Furthermore, the themes and actions of the sequence make use of those representative actors and spaces to make general and basic statements about the city *in itself*, and not about just one *element* of life in the city, a shared anxiety, for example, about disease. We call such elaborated festivals "focal." While Sāpāru with its emphasis on death and carnival may be thought of as an antistructural focal festival, Biska:, like Mohanī (in its own and different way), emphasizes urban order, and thus is a "structural focal festival."

3. *Interactive versus parallel features: bases for solidarity.* The complex pattern of Biskā: means that to the "parallel" relations of simpler festivals, where many of the city's units are doing the same sorts of things at the same time,[58] there is added interactive or "syntagmatic" relations *at the city level.* In the major focal structural festivals—Biskā: and Mohanī—there is a central emphasis on interrelated actions on the public civic level, while parallel actions, such as household feasts and neighborhood *jātrās*, are secondary. This is in contrast with, say, an important major festival sequence like Swanti, in which the major *civic* significance is in the parallel performance of the events within all households (events that may be interactive *within* the unit itself).

In contrast to parallel events—which have static structural significance—interactive events are dynamic, and can express relations, conflicts, dilemmas, resolutions and their failures; in short, they have the quality of narrative and drama. Actors, space, time, and plot combine to say something—if the proper rhetorical devices can be found to capture and hold the attention of the narrative's audience.

4. *Human actors.* In Biskā:'s parallel events individuals throughout the city participate as members of households, of maṇḍalic sections, and (less systematically) as members of *twa:*s and neighborhoods. At the level of the public urban performance, the city's central interactive narrative, *The Adventures of Bhairava and Bhadrakālī*, we have as our cast the Newar king, the chief Brahman, and representatives of the Jośi, Ācāju, Bhā, Jugī, Po(n), Mahā(n), Sa:mi, Ka:mi, and various Jyāpu groups. Many of these personages are gathered into the Bhairava chariot, which is pulled and tugged at by men of various clean *thars*—

subdivided, however, at the chariot's two ends into representatives of the upper city and the lower city. The selection of *thar*s in the interactive public performances effectively samples and represents the city's traditional macrostructural, ritual, and productive structure. The two city halves represent by summation its entire space; but this particular way of representing it (rather than, say, by the sum of the maṇḍalic sections that represent the space of the city in Mohanī) has special implications.

In Biskā:'s action the king, priests, and *thar* representatives do not, in fact, act. They are passively moved. They are moved through the city on fixed routes, at fixed times, at the mercy of the tugs of war that represent the tensions in the city underneath the order that the chariot riders represent. They *represent* order, but they are not the active agents of that order. In Mohanī they act, and the power of the Kṣatriya and of the Brahman as a Tantric practitioner are explored. While in Biskā: the passive adventures of king, Brahman, and their company are in the public routes and spaces of the city, in Mohanī, their actions are for the most part confined to the sacred and royal enclosure of the Taleju temple.

5. *Divine actors.* The central deities in this festival are the powerful dangerous deities Bhairava and Bhadrakālī. The Maṇḍalic Goddesses and the remainder of the city's important dangerous deities are foci of important but secondary parallel activities. The Yasi(n) God has no independent existence in Bhaktapur aside from this special festival use and is rather a focal sacralized collection of important images, signs, and ideas, a kind of *ad hoc* deified object. While other deities *contribute* meaning because their identities transcend Biskā: (although Biskā:, in turn, contributes to their meanings), the Yasi(n) God is no more than a component, albeit an important one, in the festival sequence.

As in Mohanī and in the Devī cycle the divine actors in Biskā: are dangerous, not ordinary, gods. As we have repeatedly argued, they represent—in their contrast to the benign, personal, and familial moral and *dharmic* deities—forces that threaten the moral order on the one hand, but that can be captured through power and made to protect it on the other. In Biskā: the male dangerous deities—Bhairava and the Yasi(n) God)—predominate. In Mohanī the female deities are central. In keeping with the balance of male and female deities, which distinguishes the benign from the dangerous deities (chap. 8)—although here unusually represented within the realm of dangerous deities—Biskā:'s deities are portrayed as powerful but limited beings, rather like humans in the social world, in their irritations, ineffectual attempts to escape, and passivity. Instead of the complex rites that will bring the dangerous goddesses of Mohanī into some useful relation to the city, Bhairava and Bhadrakālī and the Yasi(n) God are, like the chariot's representative social microcosm, simply manipulated and moved through space like puppets. The "deities" at issue here, far below the surface and beyond anthropomorphic gods, are order and chaos.

6. *Space.* Throughout Biskā: city space is carefully made use of to represent the city itself and the narrative movement of the festival sequence. Space, it is important to recall, is only one of the possible ways of representing Bhaktapur—or any community. A community can be represented, for example, by the sum of its citizens, or (as in Swanti) its family units. Furthermore, when spatial units are used in representation, Bhaktapur has various options for demarcating the whole city. In Biskā:'s narrative aspect it is the city halves, areas whose antagonistic potentials are traditionally emphasized, which are used to represent the city. The "neutral" points between them (Ta:mārhī Square and Gā:hitī Square and Yasi[n] Field), and the neutral axis connecting them is played against an axis of struggle between the upper and lower halves of the city defined by that axis. The neutral points and axis are "liminal," out of ordinary space and time. It is here that the adventures of the nonordinary deities Bhairava and Bhadrakālī unfold, and here that the Yasi(n) God waits to start the next year.

Independent of the central narrative other spaces are used starting, for the most part, on the fourth day of the sequence. The goddesses of the maṇḍalic sections are brought beyond the borders of the sectors to their *pīṭha* seats, enacting the essential meaning of these goddesses—their relation to the dangerous, amoral outside of the city. And throughout the city the major dangerous deities are, in a unique movement, taken outside of their "houses" and seated in the public city space. The city is represented through the parallel movement of all these deities, although the movements of two neighboring pairs of the goddesses include an echo of Bhairava and Bhadrakālī's ambiguous enactment of unity and disunity. In another enactment of unification the city's people move on the eighth day in a *jātrā* along the *pradakṣiṇāpatha* to worship all the dangerous deities. This movement, like the movements of the chariot, is *within* the city boundaries in contrast to a similar sequential summating movement to the *pīṭha*s of the Maṇḍalic

Goddesses to the bordering outside of the city, during Mohanī. In the private realm, households—which can be considered either as social units or spaces—are having their feasts on the same designated days throughout the city's larger space and social hierarchy.

In the legend of the Chuma(n) Ganedya: the *legitimate* location and extent of the city itself is emphasized and given a divine charter. In keeping with the resolutions of the festival action itself, this legend is a supernatural warrant for civic unity—a warrant that serves to suppress the autonomy and divisive strife of preexisting and/or persisting smaller communities and segments.

In contrast with Mohanī, the spatial emphasis is primarily on the internal integration of the spatial components of the city. In Mohanī—and in the Devī cycle generally—the emphasis is on the city's defining and unifying contrasts and transactions with its environing outside.

7. *Narrative content.* The festival sequence talks about, so to say, social order and disorder. So do all the major festivals, but with significant differences in the aspect of order and disorder at issue, and in the sources of disorder and the means of rectification portrayed.

The central public enactment is the movement of the king, priests, charioteer-warriors, Jyāpu and craftsmen, and Bhairava in one chariot and Bhadrakālī and her attendants in another. The two chariots allow for an expression of one opposition. The movements of the first, the largest and most important chariot, makes use of the two halves of the city for another opposition directly representing the city and its divisions. The main actors in the hierarchical macrosocial system—including important representatives of the large middle-level and lower-middle-level groups—are gathered into the main chariot as a static unit and moved passively, in conjunction with Bhairava, in a movement along an interstitial axis from one "central" point to another. In the course of this journey they deviate to "show themselves" to the real space (existing in the everyday civic world, in contrast to the transcendent axis and points) of the two halves. This realization is accompanied by struggles between the halves which threaten disruption and danger. Disorder must be enacted so that the processes and forces that overcome it may, in their turn, be dramatically prepared for and meaningful. It must be remembered that in the chariot are real kings (at least they were in the Newar autonomous past), real chief Taleju Brahmans, and real representative citizens all exposed to real discomforts and dangers, to real risks. In the middle of their journey, that is, in the middle of the festival sequence itself, they—in unison with the Bhadrakālī chariot—are brought into contact with the other main symbolic cluster of the sequence, the Yasi(n) God, at the moment when cooperative efforts raise, again with some risk, and then, at the interstitial moment between two years, lower it to mark the beginning once again of a new solar year and the recommencement of annual time.

Biskā: in its central public enactment represents the order that is automatically and ineluctably imposed on the possibility of civic disorder in the ritually ordered movement of traditional forms through time. The chariot does not move through any activity of the king and priests. Mild disorder and reestablishment of order, with the latter emphasized, *happen* to those witnesses.

The achievement of unity is pervasively represented in Biska: through sexual intercourse, with its reminder of the division that the two sexes represent. This action, in the case of Bhadrakālī and Bhairava, reflects underlying anxieties, for it is not sure whether the encounter is in sexual union or in battle.

Although the male deity Bhairava takes precedence in the action of the festival, with Bhadrakālī a faint presence in his shadow, the *legends* associated with Biskā: make her the dominant figure. She is responsible for the site of the city, and Biskā: is in some accounts her festival. She must capture Bhairava—or the part of him that was unable to escape—to keep him in the city. In contrast to the major dramatic enactments of the Devī cycle where the dominant female dangerous deities are on center stage, Biskā: relegates the Goddess to the legends describing the state of things prior to the establishment of the ordered city. She is here a potentially ominous shadow at the edges of social order as the king and Bhairava survey their socially ordered city, a reminder that Bhaktapur's social order is only a precarious clearing in a larger, different space.

The stories gathered around the Yasi(n) God explore the danger to men and the society they are taken centrally to constitute of women—both as sexual beings and as inadequately controlled wives. The domestication of the princess[59] is accomplished by a man, a prince, but through the absolutely necessary aid of Bhadrakālī, who in the ambivalent use of dangerous deities both represents the same sorts of dangers as does the princess and can—and must—be used to bring them under control. But the transformation of the princess into an ordinary wife is—the fatal problems caused to the Tantric expert Śeṣar Ācāju by his wife remind Bhaktapurians—a problem that will never be fully solved, no more than the unity of the city will be. But in the moments of resolution in the Biskā: sequence, at the achievement of the lowering of the Yasi(n) God and the final momentary reconciliation of Bhairava and Bhadrakālī, the problems somehow seem to be resolved. It will all need to be repeated yet again in each revolving year.

The emphasis in the stories that inform Biskā: is on the *legendary* realm where the supernatural once made contact with Bhaktapur—at a particular moment of real historical time and at a point of earthly space—for the purposes of locating or ordering that city. The events of the legends happened only once, although they must be repeatedly memorialized. In Mohanī the explanatory stories of the central narrative take place within a thoroughly transcendent and timeless *mythic* realm—with no relation to terrestrial time and space—where a battle is taking place in which the city must actively and magically participate each year, over and over again. The presence and force of the "supernatural" is quite different in the two structural focal festivals.

8. *Rhetoric.* We are concerned everywhere in this study with those aspects of symbolic form in Bhaktapur that are presumably significant to its citizens. It is not enough for such forms to be meaningful, they must also be *engaging*. For this a sort of rhetoric of symbolic form is necessary. We have noted some miscellaneous engaging devices: the advertised mystery of the Jāki Gwa and the whereabouts of the "true" Bhairava *jātrā* image, the ambiguity and psychic resonances stirred by the princess whose nose (or vagina) hides snakes, the hesitation between sex and aggression in the ambiguous banging together of Bhairava and Bhadrakālī, and the fascination of watching the major figures in the hierarchical order symbolized by themselves. To jeopardize the symbol of a king is one thing; to jeopardize the king himself is something more.

One of the sources of the fascination of Biskā: for the participants and, often the onlookers, is that it involves real risk. In its symbolization of conflict a movement can always occur, a breakdown, into real physical and social danger. Here marked symbolism is in danger of collapsing into real life.

9. *The message.* It is possible to tease out of the drama or dramas of the city's various complex symbolic enactments, a task simplified somewhat when they are compared with each other, something like a central import or message, a message that is simple and redundantly presented. For Biskā: this seems to be something like this: admire and

celebrate the civic order. That order may momentarily and frighteningly sway and lurch, but when the city works together—or refrains, really, from not working together, for the task is not difficult—and accepts the traditional directives of the mesocosmic order, it will all hold together; the space and personnel of the city will remain unified both in itself and in relation to the pulse of annual cyclical time. The main danger to civic order, in Biskā:'s main narrative, and in contrast to other narratives, is civic strife, the danger of something going awry in the balance of those human forces that constitute the city.

Other aspects of disorder, those beyond the moral sphere of the city, are alluded to in Biskā:'s legends. But Biskā: in itself is not centrally concerned with them. That is the concern of the Devī cycle.

CHAPTER FIFTEEN

The Devī Cycle

INTRODUCTION

In our presentation of the miscellaneous calendrical events of the lunar year we set aside a group of events distributed throughout the year for special treatment. This group, closely related to the rice agricultural cycle, makes up a thematically interrelated set in which the meaning of each unit is dependent on the entire group. While the meaning of the other events of the lunar cycle is often affected by their structural similarities and contrasts with other events in the cycle, the events in the Devī cycle are related by a central thread. This thread is a narrative of the states and activities of one group of supernatural beings, the "Nine Durgās," a group of dangerous deities thought locally to be uniquely associated with Bhaktapur (see fig. 27).

The Nine Durgās are, in part, manifestations of Devī, the Goddess. In the course of Mohanī at the time of the climactic harvest of the rice cycle Devī is portrayed in all her complexity. Mohanī brings her transcendent exploits as the conquering Mahiṣāsuramardinī in the mythic realm into concrete representation in Bhaktapur's mesocosm and, in so doing, brings the mythic Devī into empowering contact with the local legendary Nine Durgās.

In our listings of the annual calendrical events of the lunar cycle we were able to use the lunar New Year's Day as a place to enter it and to begin it. The Devī cycle has no conventional beginning, and there is more than one place where a descriptive beginning might be justified.

Figure 27. The Nine Durgās' *pyākha(n)*. Dumā dancing.

One might be with Mohanī itself, in which, with the harvest, the presence and protection of the Goddess is returned to and into the city after a vital sojourn outside in the fields and away in other realms. Another entrée to the cycle, the one we have chosen, is with the departure from the city of Devī's manifestations, the Nine Durgās. The results of that departure conveys the implications of her absence and thus the meaning of her return. We will preface our description of the cycle itself with a necessarily detailed introduction to the legend, membership, and iconography of the Nine Durgās troupe.[1] For the Devī cycle, as they were for the focal Biskā: festival, details are essential.

THE LEGEND OF THE NINE DURGĀS

There are a number of variants of the tale or legend of how the Nine Durgās came to be introduced into Bhaktapur. A familiar version goes as follows: A long time ago during the reign of the Malla king Guṇa Kamanā Deva[2] the Nine Durgās troupe inhabited a forest called Jwala (to the northeast of Bhaktapur).[3] They used to catch people who happened to pass by, and they killed them and drank their blood as sacrifices to themselves. One day an Ācāju whose name was Sunanda was walking through the forest and was captured by the Nine Durgās, who prepared to kill him. Sunanda Ācāju told the deities that if they wished to take him as a living sacrificial offering, they should allow him to worship them first. They agreed.

Now it happened that Sunanda Ācāju was not just an ordinary Ācāju; he was a great expert in Tantric knowledge and *mantras*. So he was able to say a powerful *mantra* that bound the Durgās so that they were unable to move. The Nine Durgās were very ashamed. They asked him to forgive them and to release them from their immobility. They gave him their word that they would not sacrifice him. But Sunanda Ācāju, shrinking them in size, put them in his carrying basket and brought them into his house in Bhaktapur. He kept them in his room in a secure chest and periodically looked at them and worshiped them.

After a certain period of time (which varies in different accounts from the short period of this account to two or three generations in others) Sunanda Ācāju's *guru*, a Rājopādhyāya Brahman with deep Tantric knowledge who lived in the Palisāche(n) neighborhood, came to Sunanda Ācāju and told him that he (the Ācāju) was unable to worship the Nine Durgās properly, but that he (the Brahman) could, and therefore he took them in their chest to his own house and hid them in a room. Then the Brahman, Somarā Rājopādhyāya, worshiped the Nine Durgās in great secrecy with Tantric *bidyā*, or "secret arts," and made sacrifices to them. He made the Nine Durgās dance, telling stories through movements of their hands. (In other versions the Brahman also plays various games of skill with them.) At some point in the stories the Nine Durgās had warned the Brahman, or sometimes the Ācāju before him, that they could only be kept under the spell if no one else saw them. Somarā Rājopādhyāya had warned his wife that she must never look into this particular room. (In some versions he had given her the keys to all the rooms except this one, which was not to be unlocked.) One day he was absent (in some versions having gone by means of his Tantric powers through the air to Benares to bathe in the Ganges), and his wife (as it is significantly phrased in one version, "being a woman and having a small mind") either opened the door or looked through a hole in the door and saw the Nine Durgās, who in some versions were dancing. As the stories emphasize, Somarā had spent most of his time in that forbidden room, and his wife was very curious to know what was going on. In some versions the Nine Durgās kill Somarā's wife at this point as a sacrificial offering "because she had done wrong and Somarā Rājopādhyāya did not keep his oath." In other versions she is only severely scolded by her husband.

Because the conditions of their entrapment and control have now been violated, the Nine Durgās escape the Brahman's house. The stories now give various details that "explain" aspects of the Nine Durgās' present ceremonial activities in Bhaktapur. On escaping from the Brahman's house the band of deities capture, sacrifice, and eat a pig at a place called "Bha: Dhwākhā," which will prevent the Brahman from taking the now polluted gods back into his house. Then, the story continues, Somarā returned to his house and finding the Nine Durgās missing pursues them intending to entrap them again through his Tantric power. He pursues them with *mantras* and the beating of a small drum, and causes them to freeze in their flight. He finds them in the upper part of the city at Swa(n)ga Lwaha(n).

Now, the story goes on, Somarā Rājopādhyāya begged the Nine Durgās to return to his house. He says, "Where are you going now in leaving me? Do not leave me." He cried very much. The Nine Durgās were pleased to hear him but said, we have taken a pig as sacrifice. The pig is polluting, and therefore we cannot go back to your house because you are a Brahman. But you can make a dance-drama (a *pyākha[n]*), and we will enter into the performers. Then everyone will be able to see us and worship us. The Brahman then established a god-house for the Nine Durgās, and gave members of the Gāthā *thar* the authority and duty to perform each year as the Nine Durgās and to embody them.

In a variant of the story, Somarā Rājopādhyāya having heard on his return that the Nine Durgās had eaten a pig, and realizing that he could not take them back into his house, instructed one of his faithful students in the proper spells, and delegated the student, an Ācāju, to capture them. This he did after some difficulty, and he put them in accordance with the Brahman's direction in a god-house in Ga:che(n), the area where the Gāthā live. The Gāthā, whose special *thar* vocation was growing flowers for worship, came to present flowers to the Nine Durgās. Then Somarā Rājopādhyāya came and told the Gāthā that he would be grateful to them if they would care for the Nine Durgās and would learn their dances. Somarā Rājopādhyāya said he would teach them everything they needed to know about the Nine Durgās and about other necessary Tantric procedures as he had taught the Ācāju.

And thus, still following these directions, the Gāthā and the Ācāju still perform their duties for the Nine Durgās.

AN INTRODUCTION TO MEANING

In this chapter, because of the interrelated complexities of the Devī cycle, we will interrupt its description from time to time for essays or remarks on its meaning as introduced or most clearly demonstrated by particular aspects of the cycle. We may start with some comments on these accounts of the introduction of the Nine Durgās into Bhaktapur.

These stories or legends relate the Nine Durgās to a particular period of time and to specific events in the history of Bhaktapur and to particular places in Bhaktapur's space. This quasi-historicity contrasts with the locally and historically transcendent Purāṇic mythlike stories of Devī as Mahiṣāsuramardinī, which, while also contributing secondarily to the troupe's meaning, are central to Mohanī. The themes in the legend are repeated and modulated throughout the Devī cycle. We may well begin with the now familiar distinction of outside and inside. This is in its major emphasis a distinction between outside and inside the city itself with the ritual boundaries of the city being understood as the significant border—thus the Nine Durgās are captured outside of the city and brought into it. But once inside they are still "outside" the city in a sense, for they are in the Ācāju's or Brahman's inner secret room, and still separated from the public space of the city. That inner room is in this sense outside of the house (where wife and family are), as the house itself (with its own secrets guarded from its surrounding neighborhood) is outside of the public space of the city itself. The Nine Durgās move from forest to secret room to the house and then, finally, to the public urban space of Bhaktapur. Both the outside of the city beyond its ritual boundaries and the nested, successively more private realms inside a household or inside a corporate group, are in different ways "outside" the city as a public realm.

The Nine Durgās live outside the city in a forest. They have many of the characteristics of predatory beasts which are reflected in the iconic details of their masks. Like such beasts, they are dangerous in that they kill and eat people. It is essential to note that they kill people not because of their "sins" or violations of the *dharma*, but simply because of accidental encounters. Sunanda Ācāju simply chanced upon them. The Nine Durgās are threats to the *bodies* of those who happen to encounter them. They are not related to people's *souls*, to their moral behavior, and the manipulation of *karma* as are the ordinary gods of the inside of the city. In fact, as we have noted in our discussion of sacrifice, the death of the body in such encounters because it represents a sacrifice to a deity results—as does an animal sacrifice for that animal—in a great reward to the soul, phrased sometimes as *mukti* or *mokṣa*, that is, salvation. The Nine Durgās, like all dangerous deities, are brought under control not through ordinary moral action nor the kind of devotion that influences ordinary deities but by an act of power, the Tantric *mantra* of a particularly skillful practitioner. Ordinary people, as we will see, can control them only through blood sacrifice.

In the legends, the Tantric control of the wild divinities of the outside is first used for the private and secret enjoyment of the Tantrikas. The action is still outside the city in the sense that it is hidden from the public realm and of no consequence to it. This private pleasure is disrupted through the prying of a wife who is pejoratively characterized as curious and small-minded and who in one version is even punished by death. Her violation of her husband's authority, of his injunction "do not look in this room," caused the escape of the dangerous forces and her immediate punishment. Through the wife's meddling an essential transformation takes place, however—the powerful amoral gods move from the private personal realm of the Tantric Brahman to the public space of the city for the use and good of the city as a whole.[4] This legendary transformation reflects the way that Bhaktapur has turned Tantra into a Brahmanically controlled or at least supervised civic religion, although a religion that continues to represent the exterior forces which surround, threaten, and sustain the interior moral and civic life of the city.

There is another story told to explain why the Nine Durgās ate the pig. This second story illuminates an important aspect of meaning of the Tantric gods in general and the Nine Durgās in particular—that is that the Tantric and dangerous deities represent a power that transcends purity and impurity. This power can absorb and neutralize problematic quantities and placements of impurity and thus help to maintain and restore that segment of social order that is differentiated by purity and which is the concern of the ordinary gods who partake of the ordering dependent on purity.

The story goes that in a past age the people of the earth had been polluting the earth with urination and defecation. Everywhere the world was dirty and everywhere there were bad smells. The gods consulted with Viṣṇu and asked him, as he had so often done, to come to the help of the world. The gods did not want to do anything to get rid of the feces themselves for fear of contaminating themselves. Finally Viṣṇu agreed to incarnate himself as a pig and to eat the feces. "But," he said to the gods, "if I do this I will become polluted, and it will be difficult for me to again escape from the world." The Nine Durgās said to him that they would agree to take and eat the pig as a sacrifice, and thus through the sacrifice of that pig make it possible for it (and the incarnate Viṣṇu) to gain salvation.

THE NINE DURGĀS—THE CAST OF CHARACTERS AND THEIR ICONIC REPRESENTATION

We have followed the legends in referring to the group of the Nine Durgās without saying anything about the membership of that group. Whatever meanings that troupe as a whole draws from its legend, its membership and position in Bhaktapur's civic pantheon, and its position and activities in the annual cycle, the Nine Durgās give their local performances as a differentiated cast of characters. (We will discuss the local performances given by the troupe throughout the city during the nine months of each annual cycle, when the Nine Durgās are actively protecting the city, at length at the end of this chapter). Like the conventional characters in the European *commedia dell'arte*, the individual members of the Nine Durgās troupe indicate their significance and relationship in large part by their appearance and their contrasts.

How many Durgās are there in the Nine Durgās group? This is a characteristic civic mystery. There are only seven goddesses or "Durgās" represented by the masks worn by the Gāthā as the Nine Durgās. These goddesses are represented in the Purāṇic text, the Devī Māhātmya, which is one of the mythic bases for the Mohanī sequence, among the benign male deities' Śaktis who join the fully powerful cosmic deity Devī in her battles against the order threatening Asuras (chap. 8). These seven Durgās are also represented in Bhaktapur as seven of the eight boundary-guarding *pīṭha* goddesses of Bhaktapur's borders, the Aṣṭamātṛkās. The eighth of Bhaktapur's boundary goddesses, Mahālakṣmī, is, as we have noted, not derived from the Devī Māhātmya, although she has other Purāṇic representation as one of the "mothers." For the Nine Durgās she is present not as a member of the performing group, but as the Nine Durgās' "own god." She is represented at a shrine carried with the troupe where she is generally known because of her decoration with that plant, as the "oleander deity" or Siphadya:, and she is also represented by an image in the Nine Durgās' god-house. Mahālakṣmī is generally understood to be the eighth of the Durgās. But who is the ninth? At the center of the city's eight bounding "mothers" or Mātṛkās is a ninth goddess (Tripurasundarī) who is not a Mātṛkā, nor a god's Śakti, but who represents the Tantric goddess in her full cosmic and creative form. The "nine" in reference to the Nine Durgās presumably refers to such a maṇḍalic schema (which is reflected in the city's nine Maṇḍalic Goddesses), but it is unclear as to just who the ninth Durgā is. There are various proposals. Some Gāthā believe that she is represented by their musical instruments, which they take to represent Tripurasundarī. Others say that the ninth Durgā is Bhairavī, the Śakti of Bhairava, but who is not represented in the masks or the drama.[5] Like many Tantric secrets, it is probably not known definitely by anyone now, assuming that it was ever clearly known in the past. Everyone assumes that there must be someone who knows the real truth but, as is often the case, it is likely that no such person exists.

The goddesses represented by masks in the Nine Durgās troupe are Mahākālī, Vaiṣṇavī, Brāhmaṇī, Indrāṇī, Maheśvarī, Kumārī, and Vārāhī. These masks are worn as part of the costume of the Gāthā performers who will incarnate the deities. The troupe also includes five other masked dancers, Bhairava, Gaṇeśa, Seto Bhairava, Simā, and Dumā, and is further supplemented by a mask of Śiva, which is carried, but not worn. Thus we have now seven performing Durgās, and five other performing deities, all of whom will be incarnated in Gāthā performers, a total of twelve perfomers in the troupe. These are supplemented by two other nonperforming representations, Śiva and Mahālakṣmī, and perhaps by some esoteric hidden deity, who is added to Mahālakṣī as a Ninth Durgā.

The masks are loaded with iconographic details that allow them to be grouped and contrasted in several different ways (see color plates). Many of these details and the possible categorizations deriving from them are peripheral to their performance meanings. An example is the rotated third eye, which is prominently displayed on the foreheads of Śiva, Mahākālī, Bhairava, Gaṇeśa, Maheśvarī (all thus marked as closely related to Śiva) and also, curiously, the Vaisnavite deity Vārāhī. (On the other hand, the protagonist of the *pyākha[n]s* that are given in the city's neighborhoods, Seto Bhairava, who is conceptually related to Śiva, and is in fact a copy of the mask of Śiva with certain significant transformations, does not have such a third eye.)

The neighborhood dance-drama divides the twelve mask-wearing performers into principal performers and a remainder who act as a kind of chorus and who are restricted to formal geometric dances performed as a group. The masks of the major and individual performers all have jeweled *bindu*s at the bases of their noses. The minor performers (Vaiṣṇavī, Brāhmaṇī, Indrāṇī, and Maheśvarī) do not. Vārāhī, who does have a jeweled *bindu* at the base of her nose, is not a major performer in the dance-drama, but in contrast to the other members of the "chorus" she does perform an independent dance. Gaṇeśa, who also has a *bindu* at the base of his nose, this one painted as part of his harness, like Vārāhī does independent dances.

Within the group of major performers two masks dominate by their larger size, by their intensely saturated dark colors, and by the presence of prominent fangs. One of these is the dark blue Bhairava, the main actor in the ceremonies that are the immediate context of the dance-drama, and the other is the dark clotted-blood-red Mahākālī, who is represented with emaciated flesh, deep-set eyes, and facial bones protruding in a cadaverous way through her skin. Mahākālī is the main antagonistic figure of the dance-drama itself.

Kumārī is visually clearly a transitional figure, and this is consistent with the role she plays. She is the same size and shape as the benign goddesses of the "chorus" (Maheśvarī, Indrāṇī, Brāhmaṇī, and Vaiṣṇavī), and she shares with them the rounded features of a young woman in full sexual attractiveness. Although she is smaller than Mahākālī and full-fleshed rather than emaciated, she is painted in the same deep clotted-blood-red as Mahākālī and has fangs that the other benign goddesses do not have. While Mahākālī is emaciated and skeletal, Kumārī is not—but Kumārī's mask has the same exaggerated frontal protuberances (in anatomical terminology, the "mental tubercles" of the mandible) as does Mahākālī's jaw, which signify and call attention to the underlying skeleton. It is much easier to see at a glance than it is to put it into words that Kumārī is in a marginal position between the maximally frightening representation of the Tantric goddess and her exaggeratedly beautiful manifestations.

Two other masks whose features are very closely related to each other are those of Śiva and Seto Bhairava. Many of their features are identical and do not occur on any other mask. They are represented as young men, with firm full flesh, identical stylized eyebrows, mustaches, and tiny beards. They differ in that the Śiva mask is of a pastel orange color resembling the purely decorative colors of the secondary goddesses of the chorus. Seto Bhairava, as his name implies (*seto*, "white"), is white, and the contrast of his white with the blue-black and clotted-blood-reds of the Bhairava and Mahākālī and Kumārī masks reflects the color contrasts (male versus female, minimal power versus maximal power) of Tantric symbolism. Seto Bhairava lacks Śiva's third eye icon on his forehead. His other obvious differences from the troupe's representation of Śiva in his mask (a representation of Śiva that is locally sometimes said to represent Śiva in his aspect as a "young bachelor") is that Seto Bhairava has small fangs that associate him (even, as we shall see, in a comparatively ineffective manner) with the dangerous aspect of the Tantric gods. The Śiva mask, which is small in size compared to the other masks, has no eyeholes and is not worn. During processions it is carried attached to the costume of the dancer who incarnates Gaṇeśa, and during the local performances the Śiva mask is hung on the Oleander God's portable shrine. This peripheral reference to Śiva is congruent with Śiva's significant but peripheral relationship to the Tantric component of Bhaktapur's religion (chap. 9). Seto Bhairava, as a representation and transformation of the young Śiva, is the protagonist of the neighborhood drama. He is the person who by his social awkwardness causes the drama to unfold as he stumbles into an encounter with Mahākālī and the trouble he gets into and his efforts to get out of it all again provide the main thread of the plot around which the drama develops. Seto Bhairava is the focus for the audience's identification during that part of the drama concerning his conflict with Mahākālī. The things that happen to him also happen vicariously to the audience. The mask's general benignity encourages this identification in the way that, say, the mask of Bhairava strongly discourages it. But Seto Bhairava has another dramatic function in the drama. As Mahākālī is to him, he is to the boys and young men in the audience during one phase of the proceedings. The fangs in his otherwise benign face serve to remind us of his danger to those who are even weaker than he is.

The remaining two divine actors are two masks that are identical except in the color of their faces (one white, the other a reddish-orange), respectively, in Newari, "Simā" and "Dumā"—also known in popular speech as "Si(n)bā" and "Du(n)bā." These are said to be popular names for "Si(n)hinī" and "Vyaghrinī" (variously pronounced). People know that they represent a lion and a tiger, but it is generally not known which is which, nor which mask goes with which name. They are sometimes said to be two goddesses, but sometimes they are thought of as a couple, with the white-faced Simā as the male. Sometimes they are said to be messengers of Yama Rāja, the ruler of the Kingdom of the Dead. Their headbands of skulls identifty them as dangerous Tantric figures, as do their open mouths and sharp teeth. However, their decorative colors and relatively smaller size suggest, as does their action in the dance drama, that they represent a much less serious danger than the maximally frightening masks.

THE ANNUAL CYCLE

The activities of the Nine Durgās are woven into the larger Devī cycle, providing one of the main plots that ties that cycle together. They also have a subcycle of their own, a cycle of performances that takes place during the nine months of their annual life, which we will present in a later section of this chapter. We must now turn to the annual Devī cycle arranged on the thread provided by the Nine Durgās' annual life and death. We may begin after their last annual performance, shortly before they disappear.

SITHI NAKHĀ [36]

Sithi Nakhā[6] falls on the sixth day of the waxing fortnight Tachalāthwa (May/June). The Nine Durgās have to perform their last dance drama[7] on either the Sunday or the Thursday prior to Sithi Nakhā, depending on the day of the week that Sithi Nakhā will fall. Sithi Nakhā, like all the annual calendrical events of the Devī cycle, has a significant connection to the events of the rice producing agricultural cycle, all being related either to the rice planting and harvesting activities themselves or to the phases of the rainy season on which they are dependent. Sithi Nakhā marks the expected end of the dry season, the day when wells and ponds and roads are to be cleaned in preparation for the coming rains.[8] Anderson notes that "Chronicles tell how the city of Bhadgaon [Bhaktapur] was once surrounded by a thick fortifying wall and moat, the maintenance, renovation, and cleaning of which were the responsibility of every citizen of the town, regardless of caste. Any person who failed to complete his assigned section by Sithi Nakhā Day was duly punished" (1971, 70). This day also marks the beginning of the period during which rice seeds are to be planted to produce the rice paddy plants that will be transplanted in the next stage of the rice production. For farmers, this day anticipates the beginning of a long period of hard work and anxiety and traditionally was the (the *only*, it is sometimes said) day in the year when farmers bathed their bodies completely, as a kind of purifying preparation for the period to come. The evening before Sithi Nakhā marks the termination of the seven-week Dewālī [30] period during which, on their particular days, various *phukī*s worship their lineage deities as Digu Gods.

Like most calendrical events, the day has a miscellaneous additional set of references and activities, some being derivations of its wider areal and historical uses. This day elsewhere in South Asia and Nepal commemorates the day on which the god Kumāra was born,[9] but this connection is largely lost for Bhaktapur. On this day a *maṇḍala* containing a six-petal design is made in the Taleju temple and in the homes of the Brahmans associated with Taleju. Although such a *maṇḍala* is in some other Nepalese communities thought of as representing Kumāra, it is locally interpreted as the Goddess Pṛthivī, that is, the earth, a reference that is closer to the agricultural implications of the Devī cycle.[10] In Bhaktapur Pṛthivī is thought of quite concretely as the actual earth, the soil in the fields and beneath human constructions. *Pūjās* to Pṛthivī are held in many homes on this day. In the evening many households have special dinners.

Sithi Nakhā is a threshold day, the ending of some of the year's activities and a preparation for something new. What is being prepared for with the anticipation of the seasonal rains is an encounter with nature vital to agriculturally based Bhaktapur, an encounter full of risks. This "nature" is the environing and supporting realm of Bhaktapur's public moral, civic life.

BHAGASTI [40]

Bhagasti, short for Bhagavatī Aṣṭamī, "Bhagavatī's eighth day," falls on the eighth day of the waning fortnight, Tachalāgā, that is, in June, seventeen days after Sithi Nakhā. In the period between Sithi Nakhā and Bhagasti the seed rice is being planted and the rains are anticipated. During this time many people go to the god-house of the Nine Durgās to do *pūjās* and to offer sacrifices. This is a respectful gesture of farewell. Soon the Nine Durgās will be disappearing.

The disappearance of the gods is signaled by the "cremation" of the masks that had represented them during the previous year. On the Sunday or Thursday before Bhagasti (whichever is the closest) the Gāthās go to each of the major and minor *twa:*s throughout the city where they had performed throughout the course of the year (map 14, below). They wear their masks turned to the side of their heads and thus not covering their faces, as they had done during their previous performances. They visit the *twa:*s by walking around the city's main *jātrā* route, and proceeding to them in the order in which they lie on that route not in the formally prescribed order in which they had visited them during the course of the previous nine months.

When in the course of their procession around the city they reach the Taleju temple, they enter it. A secret ceremony is performed there, indicating that they have completed their work for the year. In the minds of the Gāthā performers and of people in general (cf. Teilhet 1978, 95) it is thought that this represents the withdrawal of some of the power from the masks, a power that had been given to them at the beginning of the yearly cycle, but this is not the understanding of the priests who administer the ceremony. The ceremony is called the "Sījā Nakegu," that is, "feeding the 'death rice.'"[11] The exact meaning of this is not clear now to the priests, but seems to refer to the approaching death of the Nine Durgās. When the Nine Durgās troupe leaves the Taleju temple they continue on the *jātrā* route and finally return to their god-house. When they reach there, in a significant contrast to what had always happened on the occasions of their return after performing earlier in the year, they are not met by their Naki(n), the senior Gāthā woman ceremonially attached to the group, who would have led them into the god-house with a purifying and welcoming ceremony, the *du kāegu*, but they simply and unceremoniously enter the house.[12]

On the evening of Bhagasti the masks are secretly cremated at the Brāhmaṇī *pīṭha*, a *pīṭha* that has a particular importance in the ten-day

Mohanī sequence and in the beginnings of the Nine Durgās' activities at the end of that sequence. Jehanne Teilhet (1978), on the basis of observations of the mask-making process and of interviews with the Pu(n) mask maker who was in charge of making the Nine Durgās masks each year, recorded many details and interpretations concerning the masks.[13] According to Teilhet's informant, the ashes of the masks are collected and stored in a copper vessel that is placed in a secret spot on the river floor near the *pīṭha* (Teilhet 1978, 96f.).[14] This is the "going into the water" of the Gods, *dya: jāle bijata*. The vessel is left in the river until a month before Mohanī, when it will be withdrawn and the ashes then used in the creation of new masks. According to the mask maker, the Nine Durgās "leave their masks and their Gāthās [i.e., their vehicles] to go into the water because the water is necessary for the planting of rice; they help increase the water for the rice crops" (Teilhet 1978, 97). Their disappearance out of the city and back into "nature" underlines one of the important themes of the larger cycle.[15]

The idea of deities going into the earth for a four-month's sleep is a general one in Hindu South Asia (e.g., Stevenson 1920, 59; Kane 1968–1977, vol. V, pp. 110f., 158). Devī herself is traditionally thought to begin her sleep on the eighth day of the bright half of Āṣāḍha, that is, the eighth day of the Newar Dillāthwa, which has no corresponding annual event in Bhaktapur's calendar. As she appears again only three months later in the autumnal harvest festival she must, in some local versions of that festival, be awakened (Kane 1968–1977, vol. V, p. 158; Shastri 1949, 259). The Nine Durgās' "sleep" or death or going into the waters precedes their reappearance in Mohanī by only three-and-a-half months, and although their life will be renewed at that time, there is no overt reference to awakening, *bodhana*, as there is elsewhere in South Asia for Devī, or, as there is, for example, in Bhaktapur for Viṣṇu on Hari Bodhinī [4]. Sithi Nakhā [36] is, in fact, the event that precedes the reappearance of the Nine Durgās by four months, but this span does not seem related, now at least, to the general idea of a divine sleep of exactly one quarter of the year.

THE PERIOD BETWEEN BHAGASTI [40] AND GĀTHĀ MUGA: CA:RE [45], HUMAN SACRIFICE

Bhagasti is the time when the first rains of the summer monsoon are expected. The Nine Durgās are dormant. Now if the city is lucky, the rains will come, the rice fields will be flooded, and the rice seedlings will be replanted into the mud of the paddy fields to begin their growth into mature plants. This is a period of risks—the danger of too much or too little water and of violent storms that may disrupt the planting. It is also a time of illness, particularly the gastrointestinal diseases that are common during the summer. It is said that because of the absence of the Nine Durgās, evil spirits freely enter into the city and are responsible for disease and troubles.[16] Some nine weeks after Bhagasti the spirits will be driven from the city during the vivid and dramatic festival of Gāthā Muga: Ca:re at which time the rice transplanting from the seed beds into the paddy fields is ideally completed—although it often may last for some more weeks depending on the weather conditions.

During the period between Bhagasti and Gāthā Muga: Ca:re is the time when the Gāthās who will later once again incarnate the Nine Durgās are believed to capture the human skullcaps or calvaria that they use as drinking vessels (*pātra*). They need three such skullcaps each year, one for their god-house, one for their dance performance, and one as an extra reserve "in case one of the others break." They take these skullcaps from living men by means of mantras. They are significantly never taken from women. Furthermore, the men from whom they take them must show auspicious signs, similar to the signs that were said to have characterized people who were taken for human sacrifice in earlier periods. When a man's skullcap has been removed by the Gāthā's magic, the person dies within six months. This echoes the legends' Nine Durgās' random murderous activities before they were transformed into servants of the city; the tenuousness of this transformation is, as we will see later, an essential part of their civic use. In one sense, because the Nine Durgās are out of the city and no longer protecting it, the inside of the city develops, during this unprotected period, some of the qualities and dangers of the outside. Yet, these dangers of disease and disorder are the sorts of dangers that the Nine Durgās symbolize as well as protect against, and the Nine Durgās persist as shadowy representatives of dangers in the fantasized magical murderous activities of the Gāthās at this time—who could have such powers only in some still active association with the now "dormant" Durgās.

These magical human sacrifices may very well be an echo of something else. Hamilton, in the early ninteenth century, reported information that he had obtained from a Gāthā informant. According to his informant (Hamilton [1891] 1971, 35 [original parentheses]):[17]

> From those who come to worship at the temple, the Got [Gāthā] that represent these deities [the Nine Durgās] accept of spirituous liquors, which they drink out of human skulls until they become elevated, and dance in a furious manner, which is supposed to proceed from inspiration. In the same manner,

> they drink the blood of animals which are offered as sacrifices. In these temples the priests (Pūjāris) are Achars, who at the sacrifices read the forms of prayer (Mantras) proper for the occasion, but retire when the animal is about to be killed by the Got who represents Bhairavi. The shrine, in which the images of the gods are kept, is always shut, and no person is allowed to enter but the priest (Pūjāri) and the Gots, who personate in masks these deities. Once in twelve years the Raja offers a solemn sacrifice. It consists of two men, of such a rank that they wear a thread; of two buffaloes, two goats, two rams, two cocks, two ducks, and two fishes. The lower animals are first sacrificed in the outer part of the temple, and in the presence of the multitude their blood is drunk by the masked Gots. After this, the human victims are intoxicated, and carried into the shrine, where the masks representing Bhairavi cuts their throats, and sprinkles their blood on the idols. Their skulls are then formed into cups, which serve the masks for drinking in their horrid rites.

Hamilton then goes on to report that other informants denied that such human sacrifices took place. Newars in Bhaktapur do believe that human sacrifices were performed in the past, and may still be performed on certain occasions in remote Newar towns and villages. Whatever Hamilton's story has to do with a possible historical reality (and his other details are quite accurate), they point to the important psychological reality that the Tantric control of the Nine Durgās by no means meant the end of their threat to innocent humans, and that behind the animal sacrifices that are of central importance throughout the Devī cycle is, as we have argued in chapter 9, an essential reference to human sacrifice. We will return to this in our summary discussions of the meanings of the Devī cycle and the Nine Durgās.

During the period beginning after Bhagasti and coming to a climax at Gāthā Muga: Ca:re, obscenity is extensively and publicly licensed and used. Obscenities are called out loudly by male farmers working in the fields and in public areas of the city, and by young men and boys of various social statuses. The remarks are grossly sexual, and at any other time of the year they would be considered (particularly for people of middle and upper status) extremely bad behavior. Obscene remarks are made loudly to others at a distance so that they can be heard by an audience, thus indicating the essential public significance of the behavior. The remarks are made mostly by young men, from roughly sixteen to forty, and only very rarely by a girl or woman, who would be considered to be particularly brazen and uncaring of her status. Like all of Bhaktapur's other ritualized behavior of the special sort that collapses and disturbs ordinary social order and conventions (such as the public role switching that occurs during Sāpāru [48] and the otherwise forbidden activities represented and licensed in Tantric rituals), there are strict limits to the license exhibited. While the obscene remarks are addressed by young men to young women, they would not properly address them to an older woman, a high-status woman, or an acquaintance. Above all, they would not address these remarks to any girl from their immediate or extended family. Within the limits of propriety for obscenities they say such things as "Hello, you girl over there who is holding my penis in your hand" or "A penis put into you is going to make you pregnant and then you will eat a lot of beaten rice (a food that is thought to have special value for pregnancy) and that will give you diarrhea." Sometimes the remarks are directed by young men and boys to other young men and boys (again within the limits of propriety), and they would say such things as "go lick a vagina" or "go lick your mother's vagina," although the latter may be considered too strong, and may well offend the recipient of the insult. There is, then, a "safe" area of conventional obscenities, a forbidden area that would represent a violation of proper behavior, and a risky borderline area where differences in individual daring and judgment operate. There are many more such phrases, and they are usually followed by a conventional phrase "*pae hwa*," which forms a kind of refrain and which is derived from the very strong and shocking term "*paegu*" for the act of intercourse and "*hwa*," which means a hole.

What is being expressed during this period is not only erotic sexuality but also, in the use of obscenity, a violation of status restraints that in other contexts would be extremely aggressive and insulting. This all has a special force in view of Bhaktapur's extensive (in comparative perspective) controls on sexual talk outside of its proper limited familial forms—above all, in public arenas where family *ijjat* or reputation is crucially at issue.

The period of obscenity comes to a climax and conclusion in the events of Gāthā Muga: Ca:re, the day by which the Gāthās' searching for human victims also ceases.

GĀTHĀ MUGA: CA:RE [45]

On the *ca:re*, the fourteenth day of the waning fortnight of Dillāgā in July, a little less than five weeks after Bhagasti, the events of Gāthā Muga: Ca:re (see fig. 28) bring the events of the intermediate period to a climax and to a close. By this day the transplanting of the plants that

Figure 28. The demon Gāthā Muga:.

have been grown from the rice seed into the—if all has gone well—rain-flooded paddy fields has ideally been completed.[18]

Although the Nine Durgaš themselves have departed, the Gāthās whom they will possess again at Mohanī continue their esoteric preparatory activities. On this day, according to some accounts, the Gāthās take some black clay soil from the river bank and make a *liṅga* representing Śiva from it. Some of this soil will later be added to the new Nine Durgās' masks to be made by the mask maker before the reappearance of the Nine Durgās during Mohanī (Teilhet 1978, 86).[19]

The main public activities of this day are related to the expulsion of the dangerous spirits, vaguely characterized as "*bhūt-pret*" (chap. 8), which are conceived to have accumulated in the city and paddy fields at this time, and which can now be chased out of the city and fields and destroyed. The expulsion of the spirits—represented by a particular dangerous being, Gāthā Muga:—comes at the time in the cycle when the complex events of nature necessary for the rice cycle have usually allowed for the firm establishment of the rice plants in the irrigated fields. Now some of the disorder associated with relinquishing control to the dangerous generative forces of the outside can be overcome in the humanly orchestrated expulsion of the demons and in the consequent cessation of the obscenity that mimics those generative and disorderly forces. There will continue to be risk from the weather until the rice harvest is completed, however, and a season of sometimes devastating gastrointestinal diseases is now at its height. In the language of the Devī cycle, the city still lacks the protection of the Nine Durgās. It will not be until Mohanī and their reappearance—at the tension-reducing time of the rice harvest itself—that the danger will be once more fully under control. On this day, Gāthā Muga: Ca:re, most households drive iron nails into the main doorway of their houses to protect them from *bhūt-prets*, and some people put on iron finger rings[20] and keep them on for days to protect their bodies.

The central imagery and legendary references of the day have to do with the giant demonic figure, Gāthā Muga:, whose appearance and story overlap with that of a South Asian Rākṣasa, a giant fairy tale type of ogre, named Ghaṇṭākarṇa. Gāthā Muga:[21] was a dangerous predatory being variously described in different accounts. According to Anderson, "he was so corrupt that he vilified the gods themselves, defiled and destroyed homes and fields, roaming the land, stealing children, maiming the weak, killing and devouring his captives. His depraved sexual orgies and unspeakable excesses with his countless wives horrified the pious people" (1971, 72).[22]

There are, in addition, more human accounts of Gāthā Muga: in Bhaktapur, which suggest its Newar urban complexity. In a story widely known in Bhaktapur, "Gāthā Muga: was a man who believed in *karma*, and not in the power of the gods."[23] The story continues, "he loved the poor people. He sat at the crossroads where he took money from the rich to give to the poor.[24] If rich people refused to give money to him for this purpose, he would kill them. He also lived without concern about pollution. As he lay dying he hung bells on his ears, so as not to hear the gods' names called out.[25] After his death [because of his failure to conform to traditional religion] no one was willing to cremate him, and his body was left at a crossroads. But then [ordinary] people joined together to donate money for his cremation, and they called a low caste man to perform it. Many people followed this procession because he had always protected the ordinary people." This legend throws an oblique light on a number of tensions, contradictions, and paradoxes in Bhaktapur's systems of moral control. For our present purposes, however, the story refers to aspects of the actions of the day, and illustrates an ambivalence, an attraction and repulsion, in what is symbolized by Gāthā Muga:.

The events of the Gāthā Muga: day, as well as the salient legends, differ somewhat in different Newar communities.[26] In Bhaktapur each neighborhood area constructs representations for Gāthā Muga:, interpreted in the neighborhoods as demons who once inhabited the local area. These vary in size, complexity, and elegance from vaguely anthropomorphic bundles of straw to elaborately masked, painted, and dressed figures (see fig. 28). The more elaborate figures have faces with fangs and often with bells at their ears, in reflection of the legends. Most of these figures are larger than life size; some have legs and will be carried, others are hollow papier-mâché constructed over wicker frames that are placed over a man who dances the demon. Some of these figures when carried or worn reach a height of eight or nine feet. Some are given crowns, mustaches, and beards, military jackets with epaulets, and rows of medals. This adds the imagery of a recent (in Bhaktapur's perspective) and alien authority to the demon's complex meanings. Whatever the variations in the figures, all are equipped with very prominent phalluses, often some two feet in length, and a pair of large globular fruits representing testicles. Sometimes red powder and strings of red beads are placed at the end of the phallus to represent ejaculated sperm.

In each neighborhood bundles of wheat straw are prepared which will later be used as torches in the processions chasing the demons, represented by the Gāthā Muga:s, out of the city and, finally, for fire for their cremations. Throughout the city groups of small boys block various roads, in an echo of the legend, and demand coins from passersby before they are allowed to proceed along the road (see fig. 29). In the late afternoon and evening music is played in various neighborhoods, often by Jyāpu music groups, and the giant figures are made to dance. Finally the time comes when the *bhūt-pret*s are to be expelled from the city. Processions form in each neighborhood and men and boys, holding torches in their hands, and shouting the sexual insults that they had been using since Bhagasti, chase the demons out of the city.[27] The processions are called *bha kāyegu*, which refers to processions accompanied by shouting of conventionalized phrases, but this is a travesty of such processions in which the phrase is often "victory" or the like. The figures are taken beyond the boundaries of the city and set on fire. In contrast to other major processions very few women watch the procession from the roadside or other public areas. They go into their houses "to avoid being insulted" and watch through the windows.[28] After the cremation some people wash their faces and eyes in the river as a perfunctory purification. Then the members of the processions and the onlookers drift back to their homes. There are feasts in many households during the evening.

Gāthā Muga: Ca:re culminates in a partial restoration of civic order. Obscenity, which had reached a crescendo on this day, will now cease. The Gāthā Muga: figure in its form and legends combines in itself unsocialized sexual power, wanton destructiveness, and a mockery of authority. But all this is ambivalently viewed. He and his behavior are demonic and dangerous but fun, shameworthy and demonic but praiseworthy, rebellious against the gods and the rich but a support of "poor people" who love him in turn. He is driven from the city and his ashes returned to the bordering outside where the rice plants are growing and where the Nine Durgās had generatively gone to die and to sleep the month before.[29]

Not only does Gāthā Muga: represent various kinds of threats to Bhaktapur's social and cultural structure in his legends, such antistructural emphases are reflected in the day's actions. The day dispenses with deities and with priests, and with references to any of the city's hierarchical roles. The only references to authority are the crowns and

Figure 29. Gāthā Muga: Ca:re. Children holding a phallic representation of Gāthā Muga: block the streets and demand money for passage.

the medals, and military mustaches of Gāthā Muga: himself—and he is destroyed. The city is represented, not in the kind of integrative events characteristic of structuring festivals such as Biskā:, but in the parallel activities of the neighborhoods. But these are only loosely coordinated. Each neighborhood constructs Gāthā Muga: after its own fashion and follows its own funeral routes out of the city.

The disorder mimed here is not the same kind of social disorder referred to in Biskā:. This disorder, like all the disorder of the Devī cycle, has a vitality about it that represents the unruly and generative life—both of individuals and of the environing world—that the moral order must depend on as well as control.

Now for two months, between Gāthā Muga: Ca:re and Mohanī, the climactic festival sequence of the Devī cycle, during the slow growth of the rice plants to maturity, there are no events in the Devī cycle. Agriculture is left now, so to speak, to its own unfolding. The ordinary lunar cycle, however, is crammed with events. There are twenty-one of them in the intervening sixty days (chap. 13).

MOHANĪ, THE AUTUMNAL FESTIVAL SEQUENCE OF THE RICE HARVEST [67–76]

The Mohanī sequence begins on the first day of the waxing fortnight Kaulāthwa (the bright half of Āśvina) in late September. By this time the monsoon rains should have finished[30] and the rice harvest been completed (see fig. 30). As with other complex festivals, it is somewhat arbitrary as to how many discrete calendrical units it may be said to contain. Calendars used by local Brahmans simply list each of the ten days of the festival, each named for its particular focal Maṇḍalic Goddess. We will follow this for our enumeration of festival events although there are more than ten major component elements in the sequence.

Within the Devī cycle the ten days of Mohanī is the time for a concentrated and complex sequence that is the focal point and climax of many of the themes of the annual cycle as well as a summation of the relations and meanings of Bhaktapur's dangerous goddesses. It is also the period during which the Nine Durgās are given a new birth and launched on their annual careers. "Mohanī"[31] is the Newari name for the local version of the widespread South Asian harvest festival dedicated to Devī, which in Nepali and generally elsewhere in South Asia is called "Dasai(n)." It is, by all our criteria, one of the city's major focal sequences.

Figure 30. Standing on the *ka:sis*, the open roof porches of houses, men fly kites during Mohanī, said to be reminders to the deities to bring the monsoon rains to an end.

Bhaktapur, as it usually does in its relation to its South Asian context, selects, builds on, and adds to the materials out of which Dasai(n) is constructed elsewhere. The central thematic thread running through Bhaktapur's Mohanī is the dramatization of, and civic participation in, the story recounting how Devī, represented most centrally as Bhagavatī/Mahiṣāsuramardinī, the conqueror of the great enemy of the gods, the Asura Mahiṣā came into her full strength and achieved her victory,[32] how that strength is amalgamated with the power of Bhaktapur's political goddess, Taleju, in the course of the festival, and then, finally, transferred by Taleju to the Nine Durgās, who will use it to protect Bhaktapur during the following nine months.

Each of the first nine days of the festival begins and ends with visits to the *pīṭha* of one of the nine Maṇḍalic Goddesses, starting with Brāhmaṇī in the east, and proceeding in the auspicious clockwise direction day by day around the periphery of Bhaktapur,[33] ending on the ninth day at the *pīṭha* of the central goddess, Tripurasundarī. On the tenth, the final day of the festival, a day of transition to a new phase, the Brāhmaṇī *pīṭha* once again becomes the focus, with an emphasis now on the newly emerged Nine Durgās.

Mohanī: The First Day On the first day of the festival, as they will again on each succeeding day, people from all over the city go at dawn to the *pīṭha* of the day's Maṇḍalic Goddess. On this day, as they will on each day, people dressed in their better clothes (see fig. 31) walk together in groups, often accompanied by musicians, from the city's neighborhoods to the Brāhmaṇī *pīṭha*, the protective goddess of the east. People move on this day, as they will on all the subsequent ones. That is, they join the main *jātrā* route, the *pradakṣiṇāpatha*, at a point convenient to their homes, and take it in either direction until they reach the god-house of the day's particular Maṇḍalic Goddess (map 2). They then follow the conventional route from the god-house to the *pīṭha*. On their way from god-house to *pīṭha* they go via the *tīrtha*, the sacred spot at pond or river associated with the day's goddess. At the *tīrtha* they sprinkle water on themselves in a ritual bath. They then proceed on to the *pīṭha*, which is always close to the *tīrtha*, and hold a brief *pūjā*, offering coins, grains of rice, flowers, incense, and the like. They bow to the goddess, circumambulate the *pīṭha*, and quickly move on to accommodate the crowds behind them. Most people then go on to the Taleju temple, and circumambulate the inner courtyard, as they will on their return from the *pīṭha*s of the goddesses of the following days.

Figure 31. Mohanī. A group of Ivāpu women going on the twice-daily visit to the day's mandalic *pītha*.

On this first day it is the god-house, *tīrtha* and *pīṭha* of Brāhmaṇī to which the townspeople go.

In most houses, usually on the middle floor of the house, and also in each Tantric temple and god-house, a room or area is selected to be a locus of worship to Bhagavatī (referred to in this setting sometimes simply as the "Mohanī Dya:," the "Mohanī God") during the Mohanī sequence. During Mohanī this room is called the "*Na:lā swā(n)*" room, or simply "*Na:lā* room."[34] A layer of soil that has been gathered at one of the Maṇḍalic Goddesses' *tīrtha*s is spread on an area of the floor of the room. Barley grains are to be planted in this soil in the course of an important *pūjā* later in the day. For the upper *thar*s, Chathariyā, Pa(n)-cthariyā, Brahmans, and those Jyāpu *thar*s that have some special relation to Taleju, the barley will include grains given to them at the Taleju temple on this day, mixed with other barley grains. A connection between the goddess Taleju and Devī as the warrior goddess Bhagavatī is thus established for them at the start.

After the barley has been distributed at the Taleju temple, the Taleju priests gather in that temple's *Na:lā swā(n)* area, which is in one of the temple's inner courtyards or *cuka*s, the Kumārī Courtyard, to begin chanting the verses of the Purāṇic text the *Devī Māhātmya* in Sanskrit. The *Devī Māhātmya* will be read in successive divisions on each of the ten days of Mohanī and completed on the final day. That text, as we have noted in chapter 8, provides many of the images and conceptions on which the forms, meanings, and arrangements of the dangerous goddesses in Bhaktapur are based. The sequences and images of Mohanī follow it particularly closely. During and just prior to Mohanī the stories of the *Devī Māhātmya* are told in Newari by storytellers in the public squares, and read out and recounted throughout the city by elders in many individual homes to assembled family members.

After the reading of the first portion of the *Devī Māhātmya* at the Taleju temple, barley will be planted in the soil in Taleju's *Na:lā swā(n)* area in the course of a *pūjā* to Bhagavatī. The planting must be done within a *sāit*, a proper and auspicious span of time whose beginning and end are based on astrological considerations as determined by the Royal Astrologer of the central government in Kathmandu. The *Na:lā swā(n)* planting in the Taleju temples of all three of the old Malla royal cities, Kathmandu, Patan, and Bhaktapur, will take place during this centrally determined span. There will be other such centrally determined *sāit*s on the seventh and the tenth days of Mohanī.

There are common features in the contents and procedures in the *Na:lā swā(n)* rooms in the Taleju temple, in the other temples and god-houses, and in private homes. We have noted the area of soil in which barley grains are planted on this first day. In the worship of the first day, prior to the time of the planting of the barley, it is also necessary to "establish" (*sthāpana*) the image that will represent Bhagavatī most focally in the Na:lā swā(n) room during the first phases of Mohanī. Throughout most of Mohanī Bhagavatī is represented there by a particular kind of metal pot, a *kalaśa*, or by a clay pot, thought of during Mohanī as a *kalaśa*, on which an image of Bhagavatī as Mahiṣāsuramardinī has been painted on one side with, frequently, a pair of eyes painted on the other. On the eighth day of Mohanī other images of Bhagavatī will be added, usually a painted image on paper, and sometimes a metal image of the deity. As the barley sprouts the blades of the young plants will be a third reference to the warrior goddess. On this first day sacred water is poured into the *kalaśa* and a small clay dish holding rice grains is placed as a cover over it. The *kalaśa* is set on a bed of leaves of five different plants.[35]

Before the *pūjā* to be held in the *Na:lā swā(n)* room to the properly established deity, people, as they always do prior to important household worship, go to their local Gaṇeśa shrine. Some people, in a reflection of the importance of the Maṇḍalic Goddesses during Mohanī, also go for prelimimary worship at the local maṇḍalic areal *pīṭha*. The details of the home *Na:lā swā(n) pūjā* vary for different *thars* and at different status levels. In general, the sequence has the following steps. The *pūjā* equipment and materials other than the *kalaśa* have been gathered in an area in front of the patch of soil.

1. The *sukundā*, the oil lamp that contains representations of Gaṇeśa, Śiva, and of Śakti, is first worshiped.

2. Then the *kalaśa*, representing Bhagavatī, which had been placed on the soil and arranged as noted above, is worshiped.

3. Now the barley is spread on the soil and worked into it.

4. The soil is worshiped.

5. The *kalaśa* and the soil are then worshiped together by means of offerings of the light of an oil-soaked wick and with the smell of incense.

6. As is appropriate in the worship of dangerous deities, and introducing the theme of sacrifice, which is a dominant theme of Mohanī and of the Nine Durgās, the meat-containing mixture *samhae*, as well as

sweetcakes, fruits, and flowers are offered to these combined representations of the Goddess—the *kalaśa* and the mixture of soil and barley grains. There will be no actual blood sacrifice until the climactic ninth day.

7. The family takes back some of the offerings as *prasāda*.

In contrast to Chetri women who, according to Lynn Bennett (1983, 138), are forbidden entrance into their equivalent of the *Na:lā swā(n)* room until the tenth day of Dasai(n), Newar women take part in this worship.[36]

We may note here that the focus of worship is Devī, and not the Tantric Śiva/Śakti relationship (although those upper-status families with Tantric initiations will, as in most *pūjā*s, add some reference to this relationship in a more or less peripheral fashion). The relation of the autonomous Goddess to the earth and to the processes of germination is established from the beginning.

The day introduces an activity that will reach a crescendo on the tenth day. Men, usually young men, from the maṇḍalic area of the first day's Maṇḍalic Goddess, Brāhmaṇī, who have made vows to that deity to perform a *vrata* on her special day during Mohanī, perform a *matā beigu*, "a presentation of lights" at the Brāhmaṇī *pīṭha*. There are two varieties of this *vrata*. In one the man will sit on an armchair, with his forearms supported on the chair's arms. He wears a loincloth, a turban, and sunglasses (the latter two articles generally thought to suggest royalty). Seven oil lamps, small terracotta dishes with wicks floating in them, will be placed on his body,[37] supported by an *āsana*, a "seat" or base of cow dung mixed with mud. The lamps are lit and then kept full of oil by friends and family members. The devotee will sit relatively immobile for at least two or three, and sometimes as long as seven or eight, hours (see fig. 33). In the other major kind of *matā beigu* the devotee will lie covered with a thick mixture of mud and cow dung, on which 108 oil lamps have been placed. The man, also dressed in loincloth and sunglasses (although his position prevents his wearing a turban) will usually lie there for the full eight-hour period. This practice is both more expensive[38] and more strenuous than the simpler *matā beigu*, and thus a greater offering.[39] Both of these *vrata*s are performed adjacent to the Brāhmaṇī *pīṭha*. On each successive day of Mohanī, people of the particular maṇḍalic area that is the focus of the day have their turn to fulfill pledges to perform a *matā beigu vrata* at their area's *pīṭha.* On the tenth, the final day, men from all over the city as well as from hinterland villages outside it, do these kinds of *vratas*—and also, as we shall see, much more dramatic ones—*en masse* at the Brāhmaṇī *pīṭha*, which is once again on the final day the focus of an important part of the day's activities.

In the evening the stone that represents the goddess and its framing arch or *toraṇa*, which together constitute the Brāhmaṇī *pīṭha*, are elaborately decorated with flowers, in patterns that are thought to resemble a flight of stairs. Thus the act of decoration is called *swā(n) taki tānegu*, "erecting a flower stairway." This form does not seem, at least to contemporary knowledge, to have any special significance aside from being a traditional decorative form. These decorations are made by local maṇḍalic area groups, including areal *guthi*s and groups of musicians, in honor of the goddess. Once again in the evening, as they had in the early morning, masses of people, accompanied by music, walk from their neighborhoods in groups to the Brāhmaṇī *pīṭha* following the same routes. They now emphasize flowers in their presentations to the Brāhmaṇī *pīṭha*. In contrast to the morning's procession, in the evening they do not bathe at the goddess' *tīrtha* but go directly to the *pīṭha*. The routes they take through Brāhmaṇī's area had been previously cleaned by the local people in preparation for this day, and now lamps and decorations have been placed on shrines, open sheds, and various buildings along the routes. Arriving at the *pīṭha*, people quickly present their flowers and other offerings. Their offerings are part of the *swā(n) taki tānegu*. They then return to their homes.

The special events in the Taleju temple on this day begin a period of dense activity for that temple, much of which involves the "Malla king" as represented by the chief Taleju Brahman. The king is responsible for the ceremonial management of many temple activities. He is the central worshiper in the temple's *Na:lā swā(n)* worship of this day, and will be important for the later activities that center in the Taleju temple,[40] which also represents, as always when the Malla king is recreated, his palace. These activities require the assistance of representatives of many *thar*s who perform what were their traditional specialities and responsibilities at the time of the Malla court.[41] Mohanī is the time in the annual festival cycle that the segment of Bhaktapur's society centering about the king, palace, and court is ceremonially reconstructed. This is done in large part within the Taleju temple as the "royal palace," and is hidden from the larger city. This represents, as so much symbolic activity in Bhaktapur does, the reconstruction or maintenance of one of the city's cellular components, in this case one whose output was once essential to the traditional organization of the city.

The Second Day through the Sixth Day On each of the next five days of Mohanī the morning and evening processions and worship of the first day are exactly repeated, but on each day a new Maṇḍalic Goddess and her *pīṭha* is the goal of the worship. The sequence continues in its daily movement around the periphery of the city in the clockwise circle of the compass points represented by the *pīṭhas*. The maṇḍalic *pīṭhas* of these next five days are, in sequence, those of Maheśvarī, Kumārī, Vaiṣṇavī, Vārāhī, and Indrāṇī, that is, the *pīṭhas* of the southeast, south, southwest, west, and northwest. On each day, following the morning visits, people return to their household Na:lā swā(n) rooms to worship Bhagavatī. Then, during the rest of the day they go about their ordinary affairs. In the evening they will once again go to the day's *pīṭha*, this time, again as on the first day, with the emphasis on flower offerings to augment the flower "stairway" constructed there by the people of the day's maṇḍalic area. On each day the focal *pīṭha* is a focus for *matā beigu vratas* for people from the local maṇḍalic area.

On the fifth day, the day of Vārāhī—the goddess in the form of a tusked wild boar—the bladed shoots of the barley planted in the *Na:lā swā(n)* room usually begin to appear. The blades, which will eventually be taken to symbolize the sword of the conquering Bhagavatī, are said to symbolize Vārāhī's tusks on this day.

The Seventh Day: Taking Down the Goddess Taleju The systematic daily visits to the Maṇḍalic Goddesses continue on this day with processions to the northern boundary *pīṭha*, that of Mahākālī, as the focal point. But on the seventh day a new phase of the festival sequence begins with events at the Taleju temple in preparation for the special events of the following, the eighth, day. The preparations begin with the "taking down" of the goddess Taleju. Many people go to the outer courtyards of the Taleju temple, which become tightly packed with viewers. Within the limits of the astrologically determined proper time span, the *sāit*, determined—like the *sāit* on the first day for the proper planting of the barley grains in the Na:lā swā(n) room in the Taleju temple—by the central government's Royal Astrologer in Kathmandu, an image of the goddess Taleju, wrapped in cloth decorated with gold and jewels in order to conceal it, is brought down from the room where it is usually kept on the second floor of the temple. It is carried in a procession led by the chief Taleju Brahman, representing both the king and his Guru-Purohit,[42] who carries the wrapped image, followed by a Jośi and three Ācājus from the Taleju staff. They are accompanied by musicians, and seven sword bearers. All these officials are dressed in the costumes of the Malla period. The concealment of the image, leading to speculation among the spectators as to whether the concealed image is the "true image" representing, or more accurately embodying the goddess, or a decoy, and if not, where in the procession that image might be, is part of the use of secrecy and mystery which we have discussed in chapter 9 and which is an important part of the Taleju component of Mohanī. Yet, somewhere in the procession, whether it be the wrapped image or not, is, in fact, the "true" Taleju, the embodying and living form that for the people of Bhaktapur began its career as Indra's personal deity, and was, as recounted in Taleju's legendary history (chap. 8), eventually brought to Bhaktapur by Harisiṃhadeva. This procession, the taking down of Taleju, is thus considered a very powerful *darśana*, the showing herself to her devotees by the deity. Also included somewhere in the procession is Taleju's *jātrā* image, which will be carried in a procession outside of the temple on the tenth and final day.[43]

The procession enters the Taleju temple's main internal courtyard, the Mūcuka ("main courtyard") at its inner end through the inner "Golden Gate," which has access to the upper parts of the temple.[44] It then proceeds into the Kumārī courtyard, which adjoins the main courtyard to the west, where the two Taleju images will be left. As the procession moves through the inner courtyard, the man who is at the head of the procession turns at three points, and the others follow. These turns signify *yantra*s, diagrams of esoteric significance and power, traced out by the movements of the deities in the procession. The Kumārī courtyard is closed off by a door from the main courtyard, and it is there the Na:lā swā(n) worship has been taking place. Now, therefore, the goddess Taleju has been brought together at the Taleju temple with the *kalaśa* representing the goddess Bhagavatī and with the symbolism of the *Na:lā swā(n)* room.[45] Taleju will be left there until the tenth, the final day.

After the procession has brought the images to the *Na:lā swā(n)* room, Taleju is worshiped there by the Taleju priests, and, in an introduction to the great number of blood sacrifices of the following day, a number of male goats are sacrificed to her. These are said to give her strength in preparation for the battles of the next day, and suggest Taleju's identification now with the warrior Devī of the *Devī Māhātmya* myth. The throat of the first goat must be cut by the chief Brahman himself, while the others are then sacrificed by Jośis. The Brahman completes the sacrifice of the first goat by decapitating it. One reason given for this initial sacrifice by the Brahman is his representation here of the Malla king, who is now making a sacrifice to Taleju as his own lineage god. As we have noted, people should, if they have the proper initiation, do their own sacrificing to their Āga(n) gods, and not delegate it to an Ācāju. In addition to this representation, the Taleju Jośis and Brahmans make sacrifices to Taleju during Mohanī in their own right, as they believe their *thar* forbears did during the Malla period. During these sacrifices, the "Malla king" makes a *dakṣiṇā* offering of gold coins to Taleju, as he will also do during subsequent sacrifices to her. The decapitated heads of these goats will be left in the Kumārī court, along with the Taleju images, the *kalaśa*, and the rest of the *Na:lā swā(n)* room materials.

We have noted that the *sāit*s for certain Taleju activities during Mohanī in each of the former Newar royal cities are set by the central government, that is, by the Śāha king's astrologer, following a policy of the Śāha kings from the time of the Valley's first one, Pṛthvī Nārāyaṇa Śāha, to maintain and support Newar festivals in the understanding that reference to royalty in them would now represent the new dynasty. During the "taking down" of the goddess Taleju at the proper *sāit*, central government representatives who have come to Bhaktapur for this purpose and the staffs of the central government bureaus located (for local administrative purposes) in Bhaktapur are in attendance in the inner courtyard. This attendance is mandatory, and a roll call is taken to check their presence by a government official.

On this seventh day of Dasai(n) in Kathmandu, the seat of the central government, there is a procession honoring an image that is said to represent the lineage deity of the Śāha kings[46] (Anderson 1971, 146ff.; G. S. Nepali 1965, 406).[47] This deity is said in Kathmandu to *also* represent Taleju who has become one of the Śāha king's several protective deities. The procession there brings the image to the old royal palace, where it is placed in a *Na:lā swā(n)* room, in the same way as is Bhaktapur's Taleju on this day.

The Eighth Day: Kālarātri The Maṇḍalic Goddess of this day is Mahālakṣmī, at the northeast, and her *pīṭha* is the focus of the day's morning and evening processions. But now additional activities are added to the continuing daily processions to the maṇḍalic *pīṭhas*. On this and the following day in the *Na:lā swā(n)* rooms in individual homes and at the Taleju temple the climactic mythic events will take place which reflect the two days of battle and the eventual cosmic victory of the Goddess over Mahiṣāsura, as recounted in the *Devī Māhātmya*.[48] And on the final tenth day this victory, now completed, will be celebrated.

On this day in most of the Na:lā swā(n) rooms in the city an image of Bhagavatī in the form of Mahiṣāsuramardī, the warrior goddess of the Devī Māhātmya, raised sword in hand, foot on the body of the defeated Asura in his water buffalo form, is introduced into the room. This warrior image is thus brought together in the same room with the *kalaśa*, representing Devī. The Bhagavatī image, usually a painting on paper, often supplemented by a second metal image, is placed not on but in front of the area of earth in which the barley is growing and on which the *kalaśa* had been placed. The Bhagavatī image will be offered a blood sacrifice on this day in temples and Āga(n) houses, and on the next, the ninth day, in homes—and blood cannot be spilled on the soil. At this time Devī as the full creator deity seems in the barley shoots and *kalaśa* on the soil to represent fertility, while her partial manifestation as Bhagavatī represents her ferocious warrior form who protects the gods and the city against their enemies.

If possible one or more swords are also put into the *Na:lā swā(n)* room, and Bhagavatī is decorated with tiny flags. Bhagavatī is preparing for her great battle against the Asuras which will begin during the approaching night. In addition to the worship that has been repeated daily in the *Na:lā swā(n)* room since the first day, the newly introduced Bhagavatī image and the swords are worshiped with an offering of the meat-containing *samhae*. In the Tantric temples and Āga(n) Houses, in contrast to homes, preliminary blood sacrifices are offered on this day. In these Tantric settings blood sacrifices are routinely made and the sacrifice on this day does not have the special meaning that the unusual—and, for many households, unique—domestic blood sacrifice will have in private homes on the following day.

In the course of the evening of this eighth day, fitted in among the evening's other events, large feasts are held in people's homes. This is the first[49] of three major household feasts, which take place on this and the following two evenings. In the feasts on these three days, there is much drinking. People who are drunk sometimes joke that they have become the warrior goddess through their intoxication.

On the approach of the night between the eighth and ninth days the focus of events moves to the Taleju temple. Large numbers of goats and buffaloes are to be sacrificed. A flock of some thirty goats[50] is first brought to the temple. The lead goat, called "Nikhudugu,"[51] must be of an unbroken black color and without physical defects.

A male water buffalo, called "Nikhuthu,"[52] which like the lead goat, the Nikhudugu, must be all black and without blemish or defects, has been kept in a special shelter in the Byāsi area of the Kwāche(n) *twa:*. On this day the buffalo is given alcoholic spirits to drink, and is made drunk.[53] In the Byāsi area local women station themselves along the main road holding lit *sukundā*s, whose oil has been taken from the Taleju temple. At Lāekū Square, a Taleju Brahman dressed in traditional Newar clothes and carrying a sword and who represents the Malla king seats himself at the outer Golden Gate of the Taleju temple. It is now evening, perhaps seven or eight o'clock. The king sends three members of the Taleju staff, one of whom is a Nāe, or butcher, the traditional sacrificers of water buffaloes, to fetch the buffalo and conduct it to him. When the envoys arrive at the house where Nikhuthu has been kept, his Jyāpu keeper worships him and flicking sacred water on his body, asks him for assent to what is to follow, which will lead to his sacrifice and death. The buffalo signals his assent by shaking his body (which is the buffalo's usual response to being splattered with water). Then the staggering buffalo, accompanied by these functionaries and large crowds of people, is run through the streets to Lāekū Square. Twenty-four other water buffalo bulls have also been brought to the square, and the Nikhuthu joins them. Now a formalized dialogue takes place between the king and the Nāe, in which the Nāe, on being queried by the king, swears six times to the identity and proper condition of the Nikhuthu.[54] The lead buffalo is now brought into the temple. Now, one by one, twenty-four other buffaloes are brought by the Nāe to the king. These are said to represent the twenty-four *twa:*s that are believed to have traditionally constituted Bhaktapur.[55] Some of these buffalo are given the names of particular *twa:*s; others are not named. The Nāe is queried by the king about each buffalo in turn, and each time the Nāe swears, six times, to its proper condition. The formula used for Nikhuthu is repeated for each. The lead buffalo, Nikhuthu, represents the Asura king, Mahiṣāsura. Each of the other buffaloes is said to represent one *akshauhiṇī*, or army, of Asuras.

The sacrifice of the goats begins in the Taleju temple on the afternoon of this eighth day. The goats are sacrificed in the various areas of the temple where its host of Tantric deities are located and represented. A major site for goat sacrifices is the *Na:lā swā(n)* area of the Kumārī courtyard, where the true Taleju image is—and where the heads of the goats sacrificed on the previous day had been left. Some goats are sacrificed in the Mūcuka, the main inner courtyard where the principal buffalo sacrifice will later be held. These goat sacrifices are said to provide strength for Bhagavatī in her continuing battle. The buffaloes, meanwhile, are tied to stakes in the main courtyard.

Now the inner courtyard of the Taleju temple begins to fill up as people come to witness the climactic events of Kālarātri. These begin before midnight of this eighth day and last until dawn, thus spanning the ending of the eighth day and the beginning of the ninth day. They represent the two-day battle described in the *Devī Māhātmya.* The preparation for battle starts with the sacrificing of two goats at the threshold of the now open inner Golden Gate that separates the main courtyard from the inner, central and most sacred parts of the temple. After asking for (and receiving a sign of) their permission to be sacrificed, and after then worshiping them and dedicating them to Taleju, the throats of the sacrificial goats are cut and their blood sprayed on, that is, offered to, the *jātrā* image of Taleju. These sacrifices, like the previous ones, represent the strengthening of the Goddess in preparation for her battles, and thus Taleju is here conjoined with Bhagavatī. After each goat dies it is decapitated.[56]

At about this same time throughout the city in the upper *thar*s' Āga(n) houses one member of each *phukī*, or an Ācāju (if there is no one with the proper initiation among the *phukī*) sacrifices a male goat as an offering to the lineage deity. The *phukī's* Āga(n) Goddess is here, like Taleju, identified with Bhagavatī, who herself is identified more and more clearly with Mahiṣāsuramardinī as Mohanī proceeds.

Now in the Kumārī courtyard, first the Nikhudugu, and then the remainder of the goats are being sacrificed. They must be killed by a Brahman or Jośi, and not by an Ācāju surrogate. The sacrifice of the goats takes several hours, the *pūjā* prior to the sacrifice of the Nikhudugu lasting, perhaps, some two hours. Each goat in turn must be asked permission to be sacrificed, and then be dedicated to Taleju and worshiped and then sacrificed with the proper ritual. The preparatory *pūjā* for the first sacrifice is considered to be the true beginning of the Kālarātri, the black night, in which in the mythic time of the *Devī Māhātmya* the goddess battles the Asuras.

In the main courtyard it is now time for the sacrifice of the buffaloes.

Two men from the Mahā(n) Jyāpu *thar*s (which had provided the charioteers of Biskā:), dressed only in short, apron-like loincloths and with their bodies rubbed with oil, stand on the elevated ledge that adjoins the two sides of the inner Golden Gate. These men are called the *Hipha:* men, the "receivers of blood."[57] When these men are performing their ritual actions, they are called the "Hipha: gods." As Gods the two men represent a dangerous goddess and her consort whose names are esoteric secrets. (This goddess is represented elsewhere in Mohanī as a member of the Gaṇa Kumārī and also as a form of the goddess in Taleju's *Na:lā swā[n]* area.) They also represent the "right and left hands" of the Malla king and of Taleju. In their hands each holds a *kalaśa*.

The same procedure will now be followed with each of the twenty-five buffaloes, starting with the Nikhuthu. The Brahman-king is the offerer of the sacrifice, but now the killing is done by the low-status Nāe. This is a public sacrifice and as we have noted in chapter 9, blood sacrifice is only done by Brahmans (and Jośis) in nonpublic settings.[58] The king must ask the assent of the buffalo to the sacrifice.[59] The king throws uncooked husked rice, flowers, and sacred water on their heads and bodies, which usually produces the shaking motion that signals assent. If this does not work, a flower is placed in the buffalo's ear, which invariably causes the necessary motion. The sacrifices begin with the sacrifice of the Nikhuthu. He is led to the open gate leading to the inner temple. The *jātrā* image of Taleju is in front of him, just behind the open gateway. The two Hipha: Gods stand facing the buffalo, at each side of the gate. The buffalo's throat is cut by the Nāe. His blood is sprayed first on the Taleju *jātrā* image, and then into the *kalaśa*s of the two Hipha: Gods,[60] who become splattered with blood. The Nāe then decapitates the animal. Now, in turn, one by one, the remaining twenty-four buffaloes are sacrificed in the same way.

The sequence of sacrifices and their accompanying ceremonies last until dawn. After the last buffalo has been killed,[61] people leave the Taleju temple. The sacrificial area and adjoining parts of the courtyard are now soaked with blood. The purification and cleaning of the temple that now follows is considered to be deeply secret. It is said that if unauthorized people were to see this it would be extremely dangerous to them, that they would die. The Hipha: men go to bathe in a bathing place in an inner courtyard of the temple, said to be a pond associated with the goddess Dui Māju.[62] Taleju representatives from several different *thar*s (particularly from among the Jyāpus) come to do the traditional cleaning up. Also at this time a Po(n) untouchable comes to the temple and "does something" that facilitates purification by transferring some of the impurity onto himself. This is the only time during the year that a Po(n) can enter the inner parts of the Taleju temple.

Now the *jātrā* image of Taleju is just inside the inner Golden Gate, which has now been closed, surrounded by twenty-five water buffalo heads and by two goat heads. The true Taleju image is in the Kumārī court surrounded by more than twenty goat heads, from some of the goats that had been brought in a flock to the temple, plus other ones that had been offered and sacrificed by Taleju priests and by Chathar families descended from Malla kings. All the buffaloes are now considered to be representative of the Asuras, which have now been thoroughly vanquished in the setting of the Taleju temple, although the battle is still to be resolved later in the day elsewhere in the city.

Continuation of the Ninth Day: The Living Goddess Kumārī and Emergence of the Nine Durgās The ninth day of Mohanī, which had been introduced with the events of the previous night, is the climax to the events of the first eight days. On this day the sequence of daily processions to the *pīṭhas* of the Maṇḍalic Goddesses reaches its central focus; the work at the *Na:lā swā(n)* rooms comes to a climax; the living goddess Kumārī makes her first major public appearance;[63] and the Nine Durgās reappear, entering once again into the annual cycle, and preparing to carry forward the powerful meanings of Mohanī.

The Maṇḍalic Goddess of this day is the civic *maṇḍala*'s central goddess Tripurasundarī. As we have discussed in chapter 8, she is not one of the host of goddesses of the *Devī Māhātmya.* In contrast to the peripheral Maṇḍalic Goddesses who are, in their *Devī Māhātmya* versions at least (although not, necessarily, in other Purāṇic treatments), partial and limited goddesses, Tripurasundarī represents the goddess as the full creator deity. Thus, as we have noted, she is not only a local areal Maṇḍalic Goddess in her own right, but as the center of the *maṇḍala* she concentrates and contains the partial forces of the peripheral goddesses in the same way that the Devī of the *Devī Māhātmya* does in that vivid narrative expression of this fundamental South Asian conception. In its focus on Tripurasundarī the ninth day represents a completion of one important aspect of the cycle, while the tenth day, which returns once more to the first peripheral goddess Brāhmaṇī, is an opening out into the succeeding phase. The morning and evening processions to and worship of the Tripurasundarī *pīṭha* is exactly like the worship of the Maṇḍalic Goddesses of the prior eight days. There is a morning procession to her *tīrtha* (which is at the river at Khware),[64] followed by worship at her *pīṭha*. In the evening great masses of people walk to the *pīṭha* again with flower offerings. After the evening pilgrimage people will go to view the new masks of the Nine Durgās, which are the first public signs of their reappearance after their long sleep.

On returning home in the morning from their visit to the Tripurasundarī *pīṭha*, people go to worship in their *Na:lā swā(n)* rooms. This is the one time in the year in which all Hindu Newars in Bhaktapur are expected to perform a blood sacrifice. For the very poorest people it may be the presentation of only an egg; others will offer a chicken or a duck, but, for those who can afford it, the ideal sacrificial animal is a male goat.[65] The sacrificial animal's head is kept and will be presented as *siu*, the hierarchically distributed parts of the head (chap. 9), during the family feast, which will be held on the tenth and final day.

While these sacrifices are going on in households throughout the city there is a sacrifice of a number of goats and buffaloes on Bhaktapur's Lāekū Square. This is done by members of the Nepalese army, with accompanying rituals performed by non-Newar Brahmans.[66] These public ceremonies are considered to have been introduced after the time of the Malla kings. Although the Taleju sacrifices of the Kālarātri and, in fact, of the Mohanī period[67] had previously come to an end, the Na:lā swā(n) room sacrifices, and Lāekū Square sacrifices, are considered to be representations of the ongoing mythic battle.

Associated with the *Na:lā swā(n)* worship of this day is the worship of household members' tools and implements of trade. Some of these may be brought into the *Na:lā swā(n)* room, but the larger implements are worshiped at their usual locations. Potters worship their wheels, women their looms, farmers and dyers their special tools, truck drivers their trucks, and so forth. The implements are thought of sometimes as Devī, sometimes as Viśvakarmā, whom the Purāṇas describe as "the inventor of innumerable kinds of handicrafts, the architect of the gods, maker of all kinds of ornaments, and the most famous sculptor" (Mani 1975, 869). Blood sacrifices are generally made to the tools.[68]

As we have noted (chap. 8), Bhaktapur gives the same name to, and in part condenses,[69] Kaumārī, the Maṇḍalic Goddess derived from the *Devī Māhātmya* and other lists of Matṛkās, and Kumārī, the maiden goddess. Worship of the latter form is commonly associated with the

South Asian Dasai(n) Festival. The *Devī Bhāgavata Purāṇa*, for example, specifies that young girls (in this case at two years of age) should be worshiped during the Navarātri *pūjā*. Traditionally for South Asia—and reflected in the events of the day in Bhaktapur—"there are no hard and fast rules as to how many Kumārīs should be worshiped and as to the manner and method of the worship. . . . Age alone does not render [a] Kumārī suitable for worship. They should be absolutely free from [skin] ulcers, leprosy, ugliness, squint-eyes, dwarfishness, lameness, bad odor, stigma of low birth, etc." (Mani 1975, 439). Chakravarty, however, writing of Kumārī worship, emphasizes the unimportance of the "stigma of low birth." "Maidens of all castes not exceeding sixteen years in age may be worshipped without making any distinction of caste" (1972, 81). He adds that in contrast to the sometimes "hidden ritualistic orgies" that sometimes accompany the Tantric tradition of the worship of adult women "as forms of the Mother Goddess," the worship of the child Kumārī is "quite sober."

Kumārī worship, as the worship of girls who become princess-like "living Kumārīs,"[70] is highly developed in the three old Newar royal cities, and has been a subject of scholarly as well as popular interest.[71] The various major "living Kumārīs" of the Kathmandu Valley are really a heterogeneous group, Bhaktapur's main one differing, for example, in status and conditions of her life from the major Kathmandu Kumārī.

On the morning of this ninth day, after completing the blood sacrifice and worship in the *Na:lā swā(n)* room, most families at some other location in the house worship the young, premenstrual girls in the family. They may worship one girl alone as Kumārī,[72] and, sometimes, if there is more than one girl, as some set of goddesses. Thus three girls may represent the set of goddesses Mahālakṣmī, Mahākālī, and Mahāsarasvatī, or nine girls, the Nine Maṇḍalic Goddesses. However the family girls worshiped, whatever their symbolism as a group, are thought of individually as Kumārī. It is said that the motive of these *pūjā*s on this day is not to honor the girls, but to use them as vehicles to bring the Goddess into the home.

Kumārī as a "living goddess" is worshiped in two representations at the Taleju Temple during the course of the day. In the first and less elaborate representation she is one member of the Gaṇa Kumārī,[73] the "retinue" of Kumārī. This troupe consists of eleven young children of the high-status Buddhist Bāre *thar*, the same *thar* that provides the main Kumārī.[74] These children are selected each year (a child may be reselected in succeeding years) by the Bāre themselves and will have no further ceremonial role to play, at least in the Hindu life of the city, aside from on this day. Two of them are boys representing, respectively Gaṇeśa and Bhairava.[75] The nine girls in the group represent the nine Maṇḍalic Goddesses, with the exception that the girl who represents the ninth goddess is not Tripurasundarī, but a goddess of esoteric importance in the Taleju temple, Ugracaṇḍī. In the course of their preparation and dressing by the Bāre, *monhi* (the pigment derived from lamp black, and which is of Tantric importance for facilitating possession by a deity), which has been sent from the Taleju temple, is placed on the foreheads of the children. Members of the Taleju staff go to the Dīpaṇkara *vihāra*, a Buddhist religious and social community in the northeastern part of the city, to conduct the Gaṇa Kumārī to the Taleju temple. The king waits at an intermediate place along the processional route in the Sukuldhoka neighborhood and joins Kumārī and his envoys there for the return to the Taleju temple. The details of this procession and its membership and procedures are generally the same as the one that will fetch the main Kumārī, the Ekānta Kumārī, later in the day, and will be described below. But in contrast with procedures for the selection of the Ekānta Kumārī, the members of the Gaṇa Kumārī group are selected and inspected for the proper physical state (whose characteristics we will note in connection with the main Kumārī) by members of the Bāre *thar* without having to have any additional examination and confirmation by Taleju priests.

The children are greeted at a special Kumārī god-house in the Kwāche(n) *twa:* by the delegation. Each one of them is taken and carried by a Jyāpu woman (of one of the Jyāpu groups traditionally associated with the Taleju temple) who carries them in her arms in a procession. They are first brought to the outside courtyard of the Taleju temple, and then with a greeting and purifying ceremony, the *lāsakusa*, led into the main inner courtyard. The king welcomes them there and washes their feet, as he would visiting deities. The children are then led to a room within the temple on the northeast part of its upper floor, where they are worshiped by the king and the Taleju priests, and by members of the Malla and Pradhānāṇga *thar*s. These are descendants of the Malla kings, whose lineage goddess is, thus, Taleju.[76] In the course of the worship these living deities are asked to destroy the power of the Asura enemies of the king and the city. The king is considered the main worshiper, and the worship is for his protection as ruler and for the protection of the city. In contrast with the main Kumārī, there is no legendary explanation of this group known to us (although, as we have noted, such groupings of deities are elsewhere in South Asia associated with Dasai[n]), but the gathering of these representatives of the Maṇḍalic Matṛkās into the Taleju Temple signifies not only the gathering together of the areal forces but also their association with and (as the subsequent Kumārī worship indicates more clearly) their incorporation into the power and centrality of Taleju herself.

As they will with the main Kumārī later in the day, the priests watch the behavior of the child deities for omens—messages from the deities. While the later omens from the main Kumārī will be messages for the king himself concerning his own fate, these are considered messages for the people, for the city in general. That is, this group of Maṇḍalic Goddesses, plus Gaṇeśa and Bhairava, speak to and about the city, while the lone Kumārī, who, as we will see later, is a manifestation of Taleju herself, speaks to the king, as the personification of traditional political power. It is the function of the main Taleju Jośi to interpret the signs. In contrast to the main Kumārī, who tends to act seriously in her role as goddess, the child deities of this group usually act like a group of children. They laugh, sometimes fight, tell the priests that they want to go to the toilet or want to go home. The omens are fairly generalized and simple to interpret. If the children fight or cry, it is a bad sign. If they laugh too much or act foolishly, it is also unpropitious, as it would be if they refused food offerings made to them or if they accept them but then eat them too hungrily or with evident greed. The ideal portent, in short, is if they behave properly as guests at a feast.

In contrast to the Gaṇa Kumārī, the main living Kumārī (see fig. 32) has her local legends. She is sometimes called the "Ekānta Kumārī," the lone or solitary Kumārī, to distinguish her from other forms,[77] but more usually just Kumārī. For local informants "Ekānta" implies, in reference to Kumārī, that she is the "sole goddess," that is, the Goddess in her full and complete form, as is Taleju, whom she represents.

The Malla kings of Bhaktapur, the story goes, used to talk freely with the goddess Taleju, who often appeared to them in her divine form. One day the goddess saw the king watching her in the way a spy does when trying to discover something about someone without their knowing about it, something that they may wish to hide. Because of this Taleju became angry at the king, and said she would not return anymore. He pleaded with her to come again to him. She said, "Because of what you did I will never appear to you again. But I will talk to you now in the body of a *caṇḍāla*, an untouchable girl." There are other versions of the

Figure 32. The living goddess Kumārī. People are making offerings and receiving *prasāda*.

story, but they differ principally in the reason given for the anger of Taleju. Thus, in another telling, the king had a diamond that he cherished. Taleju advised him to keep that diamond secret from everyone. But one day the king's daughter somehow saw the diamond. Taleju became angry and the rest of the story followed.[78] These stories go on to say that when the king told the Brahmans what had happened, they said, "We cannot bring a Po(n) girl (Bhaktapur's equivalent of a *caṇḍāla*) here into the temple, but we can choose a Bāre's daughter." Thus the water-unacceptable Bāre became, according to these Hindu legends,[79] a compromise substitute for the truly unclean girl with which the angry Taleju—and the Tantric tradition—threatened priestly Bhaktapur.

The child who is the Ekānta Kumārī always comes from the same Bāre lineage group. She is selected by members of that group among the girls of their *phukī*. She is usually about six or seven years of age (and thus premenarche) and must not yet have had her *Ihī*, mock-marriage, ceremony. She must not have lost any teeth (which is one reason that seven is a critical age), nor have any obvious physical defects or blemishes. In contrast to the living Kumārīs of Patan and Kathmandu, who maintain their role as goddess for several years and who will find themselves in a permanently altered and disadvantaged state after their tenure as goddess (for they will be unable to marry), the Bhaktapur Kumārī plays her part for only a year or two, and lives an ordinary Newar life after it is finished. Furthermore, her only function for the city as a whole is on this and the following day of Mohanī, although she is an occasional focus of worship from time to time in her local area, where she and her family will inhabit the nearby special god-house of the living Kumārī, in a place called "Cāsukhel," during her tenure.[80] Even during this period, however, when not at the center of local worship she can play with other children and go to school.

In contrast with the children of the Gaṇa Kumārī, whose physical propriety was not checked by the Taleju staff, the Ekānta Kumārī is checked three times prior to the ninth day. Three days before the beginning of Mohanī and again on the fourth and sixth day of the Mohanī cycle, a Taleju Brahman—representing the king and the Brahmans—and a Jośi and an Ācāju from the temple go to the Dīpaṇkara *vihāra* to inspect her. They check to see if she has the required physical characteristics. If not, another girl must be substituted. They do not, as a matter of fact, check her completely. She is clothed, and they examine only her face, teeth, and extremities. They ask the responsible Vajrācārya

Buddhist priest to swear an oath that her entire state is proper for her to be Kumārī, which he does on each of the three occasions.[81]

By now the children of the Gaṇa Kumārī have finished their time at the Taleju temple, and have been carried back to the living Kumārī's god-house in Cāsukhel. Now once again, the Brahman-king, the Jośi, and the Ācāju proceed from the Taleju temple to the Sukuldhoka area, to a position along the southern circumference of the city's main processional route as it enters the upper city and wait there. Now members of the Jyāpu Kālu *thar*, thought to have been traditionally messengers for the Malla kings, go, accompanied by musicians, to the living Kumārī god-house, where the girl is now staying. She is now elaborately dressed and decorated to represent the goddess, and her forehead has been marked with *monhi*. The messengers bring her back to the waiting king and priests. The king now takes her in his arms and carries her, accompanied by the other members of the procession, back along the processional route to the Taleju temple. When they arrive there she is met at the entrance to the temple's inner courtyard by another set of priests who welcome her and by means of a *lāskusa* ceremony lead her to the door leading into the Kumārī court. Now the king washes her feet, as the feet of the Gaṇa Kumārī gods had earlier been washed, and bows down to her. He then lifts her again and carries her into the Kumārī court. In that court is the *Na:lā swā(n)* area, the true image of the goddess Taleju, and the decapitated goat heads from the preceding day.[82] The blood, however, has been cleaned from the floor, making the scene less horrible, and the heads have been neatly arranged.[83] Now Kumārī becomes the focus of worship, with the king as the chief worshiper. During the worship, which takes perhaps two hours, the girl's behavior is carefully watched. This is the time of the annual *darśana*, or manifestation of Taleju in the form of the living Kumārī to the king. The staff, under the leadership of the Jośi, will later interpret her actions as a sign of future events, as they had interpreted the actions of the Gaṇa Kumārī. The staff looks for two different things. First they look for some sign in the girl's behavior, something in her action that seems more knowing or mature than the ordinary behavior of a six-year-old girl that will confirm to them that the goddess is present. This is for their own satisfaction, for however the child acts, that action is taken as a manifestation of Taleju, and as a sign. More important (at least it was in the Malla times) is their search for omens. As with the Gaṇa Kumārī, the child's measured acceptance of food and offerings, neither rejection nor gluttony are good signs, as is the quiet, good-natured acceptance of the worship, manifesting neither silliness, tears, nor a desire to go home as soon as possible. Proper or improper behaviors are interpreted as giving some very general indication of the sort of year that is in store for the king. In the days of the Malla kings, it is said, the Kumārī's behavior actually affected the kings' policy. Now if, and only if, there is some particularly dramatic or portentous occurrence, the Śāha king's priest in Kathmandu is informed of it. Although the Ekānta Kumārī, like the members of the Gaṇa Kumārī, is a vehicle for a god, the deity does not possess her in the same way as it will the members of the Nine Durgās troupe, who *become* the deities in an uncanny transformation. She is a child through whose ordinary behavior the goddess manifests herself.

At the end of the worship the priests take *prasāda* from the child goddess, and she is brought out of the Kumārī courtyard into the main inner courtyard. Now the king calls for music, and musicians, who are in adjoining courtyards, begin to play. People, who have come in large numbers and now pack the inner courtyard, bow to her and take *prasāda* from her if they can. In the main courtyard the priests transfer her to her Vajrācārya priest, who conducts her back to her god-house along the main *jātrā* route, where multitudes of people wait to see her and receive *prasāda* from her (see fig. 32).

On the evening of this ninth day and on the following day there are a number of public events that signal the imminent return of the Nine Durgās to Bhaktapur. During the weeks before Mohanī members of that family among the Pū(n) *thar* which has the hereditary right and responsibility to prepare the masks of the Nine Durgās troupe have been making the masks with the proper and traditional ritual and technical procedures (Teilhet 1978). The masks include among their ingredients a mixture of a specially gathered and prepared clay mixed with some of the ashes saved from the cremation of the previous year's masks. Also during this period the members of the Gāthā *thar* who will perform and become the Nine Durgās are engaged in the secret activities that will ensure the successful and proper public effectiveness of their representation of the Nine Durgās.

On their return from their evening procession to the Tripurasundarī *pīṭha* many people pass through the courtyard of a special house in the Yāche(n) *twa:*, where the thirteen masks that will be used by the Gāthā are arranged side by side on a platform. Many of them then wait along the route on which the Gāthās will chase a bull water buffalo, in an echo of the running of the Nikhuthu to the Taleju temple on the previous day. This buffalo is called the "Kha(n) Me:." *Me:* means "water buffalo," and *Kha(n)* is a term of uncertain meaning here, although the same term is used as one name of the Na:lā swā(n) room, where it is locally interpreted to mean "sword." The Kha(n) Me: has been kept in a special room on the *cheli*, the ground floor, of the Nine Durgās' god-house. It has been made drunk, as had the Nikhuthu, and now staggering and lurching toward the bystanders, is chased by the Gāthās—who are in their ordinary clothes and are not yet the Nine Durgās—from the god-house down to Dattātreya Square, where great crowds of people are waiting to watch it, and then on to the Brāhmaṇī *pīṭha*, which will be a focus of secret activities for the Gāthā during the night, and one of the centers of the next, the tenth, day's activities. The Kha(n) Me:, like Nikhuthu, represents the great Asura, Mahiṣāsura. This echo of the previous days' events represents, with the involvement of the low-status, marginally clean Gāthā, a movement of the Devī myth out of the Royal and aristocratic Taleju temple, and into the demotic realm of the city.

Later in the night, when people are asleep, the Gāthā go to "steal" the masks. Those who happen to be abroad in the city during the night avoid the areas on the route from the house where the masks were displayed to the Brāhmaṇī *pīṭha* where the next Gāthā activities will take place, because they fear that to see these things will cause death. The Kha(n) Me: will be secretly sacrificed at the Brāhmaṇī *pīṭha* by the Gāthā during the night. The sacrifice follows the procedures for the Nine Durgās' sacrifices, which we will describe below. The Gāthās as the Nine Durgās are at the same time the sacrificers and the deities to whom the sacrifices are offered, and they will drink some of the blood of the Kha(n) Me:. The drinking of this blood, the "life blood," is appropriate to dangerous deities but would be fatal to humans. This thus signals that the Gāthā have become the Nine Durgās. It is said that at the Brāhmaṇī *pīṭha* on this night the Gāthā, wearing their costumes as gods, do their first dances as deities for the new cycle. They have not yet, however, attained their full power. This is a preliminary stage during which their slowly waxing powers derive from their sacrifice and from their worship of Brāhmaṇī. They will attain their full *siddhi*, or supernatural effectiveness, from Taleju in the course of the events of the final, the tenth day of Mohanī.

The Tenth Day: The Taleju Jātrā, and the Transfer of Power to the Nine Durgās On the morning of this day people dress in their best clothes, the women if possible wearing one of their most beautiful *sāris*, and go for the last time from their neighborhoods along the *jātrā* route, joining in a great mass of people to visit one of the protective Maṇḍalic Goddesses of the city. This time they go once more, as they did on the first day of Mohanī, to the eastern *pīṭha*, that of Brāhmaṇī, stopping as they had on the first day to wash or sprinkle themselves with water at her *tīrtha*. Even people who might not have gone previously join in on this day, and large numbers of people from surrounding villages and towns also join in,[84] so that many thousands of people converge. Seated near the *pīṭha* are scores of music groups, playing—each group its own music—at the same time. At the *pīṭha* the corpse of the Kha(n) Me: is lying. The Gāthā, dressed in their Nine Durgās costumes, which are now splattered with blood, stand close to the buffalo's corpse. Their masks, which have been marked with *monhi* and other sacred pigments lie on the ground. As people file by the *pīṭha* they worship not only Brāhmaṇī as they did on the first day but also the Nine Durgās group, represented by the masks. Each person is given a bit of meat from the buffalo carcass, which they eat as *prasāda*, thus sharing in the killing of the buffalo, and in Devī's victory over Mahiṣāsura.

This morning is the major time for the fulfillment of the pledges for the "offering of lights" *vrata* (see fig. 33). This is the sitting or lying supine of young men for many hours on end, supporting burning oil lamps, which we described in our discussion of the first day. On this tenth day another, a much more strenuous way of fulfilling such pledges is also done. The devotee will move starting from his home, and then join and proceed along the city *jātrā* route to the Brāhmaṇī *pīṭha* in one of two ways. He may move forward by lying on the ground, and then alternately rolling himself up into a ball, then extending his body forward, and then rolling it up again by bringing his legs up toward his head while keeping his most forward position, slowly proceed along the *jātrā* route. Another way of proceeding is by alternatively kneeling, prostrating himself, moving his knees forward, rising on his knees, making a gesture of respect, standing up, and then kneeling again. In this latter method a friend or family member may help support a burning oil lamp on his head as he proceeds. These *vrata*s are performed for the same kinds of purposes as we have described for the much more ordinary offerings of lights, but are usually motivated by more severe problems. The devotees, dressed in loincloths, and wearing turbans, have their knees and elbows heavily bandaged to protect them from injury.[85]

Figure 33. A *vrata*, an offering of light at the Brāhmaṇī *pīṭha* on the tenth day of the Mohanī festival.

As people leave the Brāhmaṇī *pīṭha* and enter the main city festival route again, many of them proceed to the Taleju temple. When they pass Sukuldhoka on their way to that Temple they encounter the living goddess, the Ekānta Kumārī, seated there at the side of the road. People stop and worship her and give her small offerings and take *prasāda* from her (see fig. 32). When they reach the temple they enter the main courtyard. The fifteen buffalo heads have been arranged in three rows of five each just in front of the closed inner Golden Gate behind which is the *jātrā* image of Taleju. The head in the center of the row just adjoining the gate is considered to be the Nikhuthu. People circumambulate the buffalo heads, walking along the raised ledge just in front of the inner gate in order to do so. The people will now return to their homes for their final activities in the household Na:lā swā(n) rooms.

At Taleju the true Taleju image has been in the temple's *Na:lā swā(n)* area, the Kumārī court. The activities that will take place there must take place during the proper astrologically determined *sāit*, one of three such *sāits* that are important to the temple's activities during this tenth day. Two of these *sāit*s are locally determined by the Taleju Jośis; one of them, the taking up of the true Taleju image is, like the two earlier *sāit*s of the Mohanī period, determined by the central government's astrologer. The first event is a *visarjan*, a "taking leave" ceremony. During the proper *sāit* the Taleju priests will now complete their reading of the *Devī Māhātmya*, and do a final *pūjā* to the combined Taleju-Bhagavatī in the Kumārī courtyard. At the end of the worship the goat heads are removed. They will be distributed to members of the Taleju staff, to be cooked and distributed as *siu* in their next household feast.[86] All the other objects in the room are left in place until the second of the day's *sāit*s, the "*tikā sāit*." This may come immediately after the "taking leave" worship, or may be some hours later. At this time the king gives a *tikā* (a pigmented mixture that is placed on the image or specifically on the forehead if the offering is to an anthropomorphic representation or to a person) to Taleju. He also presents her with barley shoots brought from the *Na:lā swā(n)* rooms in the homes of each of the Taleju priests. These shoots, conceived of now in part as swords, represent Devī's great victory. Then each of the priests takes back some of the *tikā* mixture and barley shoots from the Taleju image. They are now *prasāda*. Each priest then gives *tikā* and some of the barley shoots to each of the others. The barley shoots in the temple's own *Na:lā swā(n)* room are left undisturbed for the time being. During this *tikā sāit* the non-priest members of the Taleju staff and members of their families, as well as the families of the priests, wait in the Taleju main courtyard, outside of the Kumārī courtyard. The Taleju priests then leave the Kumārī courtyard and give Taleju *prasāda* to them.

Meanwhile the people who have returned from the Brāhmaṇī *pīṭha*, perhaps via Taleju, go to their *Na:lā swā(n)* room for the final worship there. A *pūjā* is held for the representations of Devī, that is, for the *kalaśa* and the Bhagavatī image. During the course of this last *pūjā* the worshipers do something that is usually restricted to Tantric worship. Using a special oil lamp, often in the shape of a reclining skeleton with the lamp bowl over its genitals, they prepare the lamp-black pigment, *monhi*, which the worshipers then apply to their foreheads in a straight vertical black line. In esoteric Tantric practices, that *monhi* mark is used to facilitate the entrance of a deity into the worshiper's body, but here it is a routine ritual gesture. People take pieces of red cloth, which had been brought into the room on the eighth day, and tie them around their necks in another sign of Devī's victory. The blades of barley are now pulled out of the soil and offered to the Devī images, and then some of them are taken back by the worshipers who decorate themselves with them. On the eighth day a pumpkin-like gourd, a *bhuiphasi*,[87] had been placed in the *Na:lā swā(n)* room to represent the Asura. Now the men and young boys in the household take the *bhuiphasi* out of the *Na:lā swā(n)* room, along with one or more of the swords that had been kept there, and "kill" it by giving it three slashing cuts. They jokingly brandish the swords, pretending to be Kṣatriya warriors. This little domestic victory parade is a forerunner of the goddess Taleju's public victory *jātrā* that will take place later in the evening. Now the men and boys, carrying the swords, return to the *Na:lā swā(n)* room, and they and the other family members take *prasāda* from the goddesses. The *bhuiphasi* will then be cut up and distributed to all people in the household to eat and once again to share in the killing and the victory.

The *Na:lā swā(n)* worship, which has lasted throughout Mohanī, is now over. The remnants of the barley plants are placed on the household *pikhā lākhu*. The soil, the special *kalaśa*, and the Bhagavatī painting are left in the room until the fifth day following the end of Mohanī, that is, until the next full-moon day. Then the soil is sent to be thrown into the river, the painting hung on a wall, the *kalaśa* stored, and any metal Bhagavatī image that might have been used returned to the household *pūjā* area.

On this or one of the immediately following nights many households hold feasts. Married-out household women and their families are invited to the house for these feasts and offered various *prasāda* items from the household *Na:lā swā(n)* room.

Meanwhile in the Taleju temple the priests await the third *sāit* of the day, which will be the proper time for Taleju's *jātrā*. This consists of an internal *jātrā* first within the temple, and a subsequent external one that moves out through the city. In both of these the details of the movements of the goddess Taleju are determined by the position of the moon at the time of the *sāit*. She must be carried in such a way that the moon is either in front of her or at her right in the first movements of her procession.

Just before this *sāit* an esoteric form of Devī[88] in her warrior manifestation, which had been placed on the soil before the barley seeds were planted, is removed and taken to her quarters in the temple, and the remaining barley shoots are taken up. People have come to the Taleju temple and wait in the inner courtyard to watch the "taking up" of Taleju, the internal *jātrā*. At the proper time a procession leaves the Kumārī court. This includes seven people carrying swords, and three others carrying secret objects wrapped in cloth, and covered with flowers, jewels, and barley shoots. Among them is the true Taleju image. The procession goes through the main court and enters the inner Golden Gate. It is led by the king carrying one of the bundles in his hand. He again stops at three points within the main courtyard and turns in a movement that designates a *yantra*. The exact movements are determined by the position of the moon. The procession then proceeds to carry the true Taleju goddess upstairs again to her room, where she will remain until the next year's Mohanī.

The final phase of Mohanī is a literal and symbolic moving outward, both into the city and into the new cycle, which begins at this time of harvest. This is enacted in the public victory procession of the goddess Taleju, and is called "Pāyā(n) Nhyākegu." *Nhyākegu* means to "cause to move," "to be put into motion." The word "*pāyā(n)*" is now used only in this context in Bhaktapur, and its meaning is unknown to our informants.[89]

The procession assembles in the main courtyard of the Taleju temple. The Taleju *jātrā* image is taken from behind the inner Golden Gate, where it had been left since the previous night. The king takes the *jātrā* image, covered with cloths and ornaments, and goes to an external courtyard of the temple, the Bekwa (or "zigzag") courtyard. He stands there holding the goddess, and now there begins a conventionalized little drama which takes its context from the legend of the origin and movements of the goddess Taleju, which we have presented in chapter 8. The king, "played" by the chief Taleju Brahman, now represents Harisiṃhadeva, the exile from Kanauj who—according to local history—became king in Bhaktapur and established his lineage deity Taleju, whom he had brought with him, as the city's protective "political" deity. The king is met in the courtyard by a Jyāpu who plays the part of a merchant visiting from the Indian city of Simraun Gaḍh, the city from which Harisiṃhadeva had come. The merchant has a carrying pole over his shoulder with baskets at either end, which is identified as "the Newar style" of carrying loads. The king asks the merchant where he comes from. The merchant tells him that he has been sent from Simraun Gaḍh by the king Nandideva, who sends his respects and good wishes to the king of Bhaktapur and the goddess Taleju. Now in what is to all local people including the actors an incomprehensible part of the sequence, one that is believed to be a comic interlude, the king asks the merchant whether one can still buy nine *pathi* of rice for a one-*dān* coin in Simraun Gaḍh. The messenger answers that one still can. The king then asks, "Everything is still cheap and untroubled there?" The Merchant answers affirmatively. He answers with a farcical double-meaning phrase. "Everything is fine; things are well up into other things," a sexual reference that makes the king and bystanders laugh. The king then asks him whether he brought anything with him from Nandideva in Simraun Gaḍh. The merchant says he has, and then shows and presents some *ta:syi* fruits, a kind of citron, to the king and to Taleju. The little drama is then over. This episode, although vaguely naturalized into Bhaktapur's legendary history, is a mystery to the people of Bhaktapur.[90]

The Taleju *jātrā* procession forms in front of the temple. First in order are two Jyāpus, who will walk abreast carrying representations of Bhairava. Next comes a Pa(n)cthariyā who carries a sword. He is followed by the two other high-status sword bearers, the second a member of the Chathar Ta:cābhāri *thar*, and the third a Brahman. Each of the three sword bearers represents an esoteric warrior form of Devī. At the center of the procession is the Taleju *jātrā* image carried by the king, and followed by a white horse, Taleju's vehicle. And, now, at the end of the procession come the Gāthā, dressed as the Nine Durgās. The Nine Durgās have their own order in the procession. The portable shrine of their own deity the Siphadya:, identified with Mahālakṣmī, is carried first. It is followed, in order, by Bhairava and Mahākālī, the group's dominant deities, and they, in turn, by Vārāhī. The next group comes in the order of the sequence (in both their position around the city and their respective days during Mohanī) of the peripheral Maṇḍalic Goddesses (except for Mahākālī and Vārāhī, who have already appeared). This sequence is Brāhmaṇī, Maheśvarī, Kumārī, Vaiṣṇavī, and Indrāṇī. These goddesses are followed in turn by Simā, Ḍumā, Seto Bhairava, and finally Gaṇeśa.

The direction that the procession will take was determined by the *sāit*, which also determined the way in which the true Taleju image was carried within the temple. In this case the procession will go to either the upper or the lower part of the city depending on the position of the moon so that, as in the earlier procession within the temple, the moon will in the first out-moving phase of the procession, be either at Taleju's right or in front of her.[91]

Whichever route the procession takes, it loops back via Gā:hitī Square, the spatial focus of much of the Biskā: festival. Here the focal point is the stone deity Swtuña Bhairava. When the procession reaches the stone, the entire procession circumambulates it. The Brahman carrying Taleju then stops at a designated point at the right side of a Śiva temple[92] in the square. It is at this point that the Nine Durgās will demonstrate their submission to Taleju. The members of the group, in the same order in which they have marched in the procession, come to "say farewell" to Taleju. They come to the wrapped image, bow and embrace it twice. In esoteric understanding it is through these embraces the power of the Nine Durgās is raised, each one in its turn, to their full power.[93] Now the Nine Durgās, having said farewell, leave the procession and return to their god-house, stopping to perform formal dances at certain places along the route. Taleju, her work for this elaborate festival being completed for another year with the empowering of the Nine Durgās, returns directly to her temple. On their return there Taleju and her entourage are met just inside the external Golden Gate by a Brahman who had remained behind. He performs a welcoming and purifying *lāskusa* ceremony, and leads the image back into her room in the inner temple, where it will be kept until the next Mohanī.

While Taleju is being returned to her inner chamber, her white horse vehicle, which had left the procession at the entrance to Lāekū Square and had been met there by a Taleju Ācāju, is decorated with an offering of *swaga(n)*. Then it is led by the Ācāju—who runs while leading it by a rope—in three movements, first to the Golden Gate, then back to the entrance to the square, and then, finally, back to the Golden Gate, where it is taken into the temple.

Now the Devī cycle, insofar as it is a set of events within the annual lunar calendar, is finished. The cycle is continued now in the wanderings of the Nine Durgās over the next nine months, as they move throughout the entire city and many of its hinterland communities.

MOHANĪ: APPROACHES TO MEANING

The Mohanī sequence is the complex climax of the Devī cycle. We must pause to discuss it before presenting the succeeding activities of the Nine Durgās regenerated in its course. We will follow the arrangement of issues we used in our discussion of Biskā:'s meaning in chapter 15; the similarities and contrasts in the two focal festivals are often illuminating.

1. *Mohanī and the rice agricultural cycle.* One of our questions about annual calendrical events is their possible relations to cyclical events outside of the festival cycle itself. Such external relations are of paramount importance in the Devī cycle, both in the timing of its events and in a give and take of meaning. The events of the Devī cycle echo the planting of rice seeds and the transplanting of seedlings; the phases of growth of the seeds and of the replanted shoots; the anticipation, onset, and ceasing of the annual monsoon rains; and the cycles of disappearance, latency, and regeneration of the crops. At the successful climax of all this is the harvest, and that is where Mohanī is situated. With the harvest the Nine Durgās are returned to the city to "protect" it yet once again, until they must disappear back into the wilds they originally inhabited as the earth prepares for its next cycle of regeneration.

In a metaphorical flow, symbols that express the relations of agriculture and weather to the city's inner order are extended to the quite similar relations of other vital realms—individuals' passions, the protective and destructive force of Kṣatriyas—to the city's moral order.

2. *Mohanī as a structural focal sequence.* In all the aspects that constitute festival events—time and resources used, extent of participation, extent of the city space that is ritually marked, quantity of symbolic resources put into use, and complexity and importance of the festival themes to the life of the community—Mohanī is clearly of predominant importance in Bhaktapur's collection of calendrical events. Only Biskā:

approaches it in these aspects. Like Biskā:, Mohanī has much to do with the representation and ordering of Bhaktapur as a city—but it does it with a signicantly different emphasis. The primary emphasis in Biskā: is the ordering of the internal, the contained, structures of the city; the primary emphasis in Mohanī is the relations of the city to its sustaining and threatening external environment—the city being delineated by its transactions, contrasts, and boundaries with that external environment. As we noted in our discussion of the legendary origins of the Nine Durgās, the bordering realms external to the orderly public realm of the city are not only in the forest wilderness outside the city boundaries but also in the secret reaches of houses, or (as the obscenities associated with Gāthā Muga: suggest, and the neighborhood performances of the Nine Durgās, which we will discuss below clearly indicate) in the asocial or antisocial areas of the minds and passions of Bhaktapur's citizens.

3. *Interactive versus parallel features.* In Biskā: the dramas of disunity and unification take place in the public space of the city, and are only secondarily augmented by "parallel" household and neighborhood events throughout the city. Mohanī's primary emphasis is also on the public civic dramas, but there is an important additional feature in Mohanī. In addition to its public interactive narrative using socially defined actors, deities, time, and space for a complex dramatic performance, and its parallel household feasts, and its repetition of events on successive days in one internal maṇḍalic segment after another, each individual household also participates throughout the nine days of Mohanī in its own complex and vivid drama echoing the larger civic drama. Thus, individuals busily participate in a drama that takes place in their homes, and again in the larger city, and still again in mythic space and time as the vivid cosmic battle of Devī and the Asura enemies of the gods. In Mohanī individuals do not only watch the performances of other civic actors; they do not only interact with deities in their homes and at temples and along the paths of *jātrās* in relations of honor, respect, and submission and the reaffirmation of vital relationships. In Mohanī ordinary people, like the Taleju priests and the king, *participate* in the work of Devī. They kill with her, they work with her to produce life in their *Na:lā swā(n)* rooms; they become Devī.

4. *Human actors.* The human actors of Biskā: passively represent Bhaktapur's hierarchical social order. Their main location is in a chariot moved through the city's public space and brought to rest at significant points. The king and his Brahman Guru-Purohit appear in Biskā:

from the off-stage Taleju temple and royal palace complex to become passive doll-like figures joined with other representatives of the social hierarchy as static symbols and witnesses of Biskā:'s events. There is very little human action in Biskā: aside from the struggle of the city halves—an action produced by the nameless representatives of those halves—the remainder of the action is an automatic unfolding. In Mohanī people must, as we have noted of the participation of ordinary citizens in household dramas, actively help in the unfolding of the festival's drama. In this the king now conflated into one figure with Taleju's chief Brahman has a central role.

The main arena of their action is the Taleju temple, the temple of the Royal Palace. That action takes place in the inner, often hidden, chambers and courts of that temple. Around the king and the Taleju priests the old Malla court life is recreated in the ceremonial attendance of the councilors, suppliers, and servants of that court.

The king is now an active figure in the encounter with the deities—trying to recreate an intimacy that he once had, but lost—and participating within their realm, or more specifically Devī's realm, through ritual and through blood sacrifices, in mimicry of Devī's battles and her slaughter of the enemies of the heavenly order. The priests, above all Taleju's chief priest, is, insofar as Tantric Brahman and king are differentiated, his ally in all this. This is another striking contrast with Biskā:. The priests in Biskā: are simply representatives of civic order. Here they are Tantric practitioners, joining with royalty in blood sacrifice. A complex of themes—king, court, warrior, Kṣatriya, Brahman as Tantric practitioner, human activity beyond social action and relationships—are amalgamated with those of the agricultural cycle and are explored in Mohanī. They are all themes of power.

5. *Divine actors.* In Biskā: the main public deities are Bhairava and the vaguely deified Yasi(n) God, both masculine figures. Bhadrakālī is a very secondary figure in Biskā:'s action—although in the legends associated with that festival sequence she stands in the shadows as a much more powerful figure than Bhairava. The Goddess must await Mohanī to come from her shadowy presence in the wings to center stage. Both Bhairava and the Yasi(n) God are, like the human actors in Biskā:, passive figures who are manipulated in space and time and, aside from whatever active participation Bhairava may possibly be thought to have in his sexual-aggressive encounter with Bhadrakālī, *represent* much but *do* little.

The deities in the public narrative of Mohanī are Devī and her manifestations and emanations. These forms are very active, indeed. They battle the Asura forces of disorder, cause the rice and barley to grow, inhabit the children of the Gaṇa Kumārī and the Ekānta Kumārī in order to bring oracles to king and city, and eventually embody themselves as the Nine Durgās. Bringing Devī and her forms into useful contact with the city requires the powerful ritual of Tantra, rather than the devotional ritual more or less appropriate to the comparatively tamed Bhairava of Biskā:. Mohanī is about the *capturing* of "natural" forces represented by Devī for civic use; Biskā:, about the *deployment* of these already captured forms.

The *Devī Māhātmya*, tells of the alternating gathering together of components of the Goddess into her forms of maximum power, and their subsequent emanation and differentiation in order to do specialized tasks. In the sequence of Mohanī the nine Maṇḍalic Goddesses of the city, Bhagavatī, Kumārī, several esoteric goddesses, the tutelary lineage Āga(n) Goddesses, and Taleju are repeatedly joined as one goddess, Devī, and then differentiated as special manifestations.

While the *Devī Māhātmya*'s Devī is the focus of Mohanī's mythic realm, in the course of the events of the sequence it is Taleju who becomes progressively established as the central reference point for the gathering in and centralization of forces, and it is through Taleju that the momentum of the festival is handed over—from her point of view, delegated—to the Nine Durgās at its end. Taleju is the Malla king's lineage deity; her home is the united palace/temple complex. The ingathering of powers on the completion of the harvest is a validation and renewal of the power of the king.

Biskā:'s passive Bhairava and Bhadrakālī are powerful but limited, resembling socially limited humans in their irritations and ambivalences, their ineffectual attempts to escape, and their susceptibility to teasing. The goddesses of Mohanī are quite different. They are uncanny and powerful beings, whose transformations and powers belong to some other than ordinary social world. In Hinduism's view of Royalty in its transcendence of the ordinary *dharma* (chap. 9) the king and these goddesses are natural allies.

Devī as the focal deity of Mohanī is not the Śakti of Śiva-Śakti theory, whose symbolism and manipulations are central to Bhaktapur's ordinary Tantric religion. Śiva is here, as he is among the Nine Durgās, a faint, peripheral figure. This Devī, the full, creative Goddess, is in this harvest context the supreme, the only significant deity.

6. *Space.* The public drama of Biskā: moved through and took much of its meaning from the public space of the city. That movement centered on an axis and on points that, in their centrality, transcended and represented the divided components of the city. In Biskā:'s main movement of masses of people—the visits to the dangerous deities of the city on the eighth day of that sequence—the procession moves within the city along the *pradakṣiṇāpatha*. In Mohanī the major spatial emphases are within the Taleju complex, within houses, and—in the mass movement of people to the *pīṭha*s of the Maṇḍalic Goddesses—to the external borders of the city's boundaries and to the city's maṇḍalic center. These areas are all outside of the public spaces of the city and of its public society. In Mohanī, and generally throughout the Devī cycle, the space of the public city is delineated by its edges, its inner and outer boundaries, its hidden cells—households and royal enclave. While Biskā: emphasizes units of city space—city, city halves, maṇḍalic areas, *twa:*s—in themselves and in their relations to each other within the city, Mohanī's main emphasis is on the boundaries of units and refers to what is beyond those boundaries—putting outside and inside in relation and opposition.

It is only at the end, the last day of Mohanī, that there is a movement out of such peripheral spaces. The goddess Taḷeju, that is, her *jātrā* image, is taken out of her temple into the city streets for her one yearly *darśana*. The representative of the Buffalo Asura is taken out of each house's *Na:lā swā(n)* room in a little victory procession to be destroyed. And now the Nine Durgās prepare to move out into the city's neighborhoods and into the ordinary time of the next nine months.

7. *The narrative.* Within the complex movements and events of Mohanī we have suggested the presence of a central theme and narrative, clarified by its context in the Devī cycle and its contrasts with other festival narratives, particularly that of Biskā:. Throughout Mohanī the relation of the city and the outside is explored, and is represented in a coherent way.

The sequence begins with the processions, which continue each morning and evening throughout the sequence, to the *pīṭha*s of the border-protecting goddesses, culminating in the sequence's climactic ninth day at their central representative, and then, on the morning following that climactic day, returning once again to the goddess of the first day, where the mass of moving people encounter the Nine Durgās. Throughout Mohanī this motif—which we first encountered in the

Nine Durgās' legend—is repeatedly represented: a gathering in of external bordering forces to a climactic concentration in a ritually bounded space, and then, in a coda, their socially controlled moving out again into the public city's space and time. On a larger scale the movements of the processions are echoed in the movements of the Devī cycle, with its progressive concentration of the powers of soil, weather, and seed in the generation of the rice, which is now about to be gathered into the city and distributed within it. And in the largest scale of all they are represented in Devī's myth where the gods of the heavenly city generate her to share in the nature of the Asuras at their borders, and thus to conquer them and restore cosmic order. As the *Devī Māhātmya* puts it, after the final victorious battle "favorable winds began to blow; the sun shone with perfect brilliance, the sacred fire burnt in a tranquil manner; and the strange sounds that had filled the quarters of space also disappeared" (X, 27; Agrawala 1963, 127).

In their cumulative movements the twice daily processions mark the outer boundaries of the city and the central point where the protective forces at and just beyond the boundaries are concentrated. The people of Bhaktapur move *en masse* to the *pīṭha*s nineteen times during the course of the sequence. They are active participants as they will be throughout. In the course of their daily processions they include the Taleju temple, the ultimate center for the in-gathering of forces for the city as a whole, in a movement that allies king, court, and temple with the forces of the bordering outside—and with the successful harvesting of their recalcitrant potentiality.

From the first day the agricultural resonances of the festival are made concrete in every household, Tantric temple, and god-house. Earth is placed in them and grain is planted. The Goddess in her aspect as the cosmic creator and here specifically as the genetrix of agricultural life both presides over the earth and grain and is represented in the plants themselves as they develop.[94] But this generative goddess, as the sequence makes increasingly clear, is a warrior goddess, she is Bhagavatī/Mahiṣāsuramardinī, the bloody warrior goddess of the *Devī Māhātmya*. The success of the agricultural cycle, the generative powers of earth, seed, and weather are now allied with the force of the warrior, *kṣatra*, in the battle against the forces of disorder at the boundaries of the heavenly city of the moral gods. The use of Taleju's barley by the upper *thar*s is a further reminder of the connection of *kṣatra*, Taleju, and Bhaktapur's traditional monarchy.

The central package of symbols is in place by the first day—the conflation of agricultural and warrior power, and the relation of that power to the inside of the city, to the moral city. The *matā beigu vrata*s, which begin on the first day, introduce a further active way in which people will participate in and control these forces, that is, through sacrifice, through self-sacrifice and, above all, through the city-wide mass slaughter of represenative and surrogate animals. This sacrifice not only is a mimesis of the death and regeneration of the agricultural cycle but also has as one of its implications (as we will argue in our discussion of the activities of the Nine Durgās later in this chapter) the forceful binding of individuals—who represent another fertile and dangerous outside—to the city's social and cultural order.

Slowly at first and then gaining momentum throughout the sequence the forces of the outside are moved under the direction of traditional enactments and rituals into bounded areas of the city. The barley grain begins to grow in the houses and temples; the processions, after finally visiting all the bounding goddesses in their proper sequence, will move to the maṇḍalic center; and at the Taleju temple the Goddess *herself*—uniquely not a *jātrā* image—is manifest (albeit under wraps) to the spectators, and then brought together with Bhagavatī and the growing grain. For the city as a whole all the forces now begin to amalgamate themselves to Taleju—agricultural growth, Bhagavatī, and the cosmic warrior Devī, soon to be joined by representatives of the Maṇḍalic Goddesses as the Gaṇa Kumārī, by Kumārī herself, and eventually by the Nine Durgās.

All this comes to a climax in the Kālarātri, the "black night," between the eighth and ninth days, when Taleju/Bhagavatī/Devī and the king and his priests participate vividly in the bloody cosmic mythic war of Devī against the disordering Asuras. That battle is replicated in each household on the following day with animal sacrifice. The city's citizens are not just witnesses; they continue to be active participants.

For the court and Taleju there is a further in-gathering. The Devī cycle tells of the moving out of the city of the deities and, then, of their return along with the harvest for the inner uses of the city. The tale of Kumārī tells of how Taleju herself has fled the direct presence of the king, but now with the Gaṇa Kumārī and the Ekānta Kumārī she makes her annual return, once more to advise him.

Taleju's urban hegemony has now been established, but it is a hegemony in alliance with a peculiar collection of forces, the forces that are the concern of king and Tantric expert and farmer and craftsman—the worship of whose tools is an important part of the sequence. These are not the forces, the arena, of concern to the Brahman as Brahman and to his auxiliary and covert priests (with the exception of his Tantric surrogate, the Ācāju). Mohanī is a celebration of the forces that are the support of the moral order, not of that order in itself.

The final episode in the story is the moving out of the concentrated forces from households and palace once again into the city. On the morning of the last day people once again go to the peripheral Brāmaṇi *pīṭha* whence they had started on the first day, but now they find the Nine Durgās there, who have killed a buffalo in their mimesis of Mahiṣāsuramardinī's battle, and are preparing for their full return to the city. In the households boys and men carrying swords storm out of the *Na:lā swa(n)* rooms in a mini victory procession to kill the *bhuiphasi* gourd. And finally—the true Taleju having been returned to the recesses of her temple-palace—the *jātrā* Taleju image, carried by the king, is brought out in a victory procession into the public city where Taleju delegates power to the Nine Durgās so that the manifestation and uses of the powers of Devī may be carried throughout the city for the next nine months until once again they must be returned to their proper and necessary places in the outside order.

8. *Rhetoric and participation.* In our discussion of Biskā:'s meanings we noted some of the rhetorical resources that are used in that festival sequence in attempts to ensure the engagement of people with its meaningful forms. Mohanī uses some of the same ones. It uses mystery, pageantry, and the revelation of wonders as deities become manifestly embodied in living forms. However, Mohanī's emphasis on participation shifts the problem of engagement from the engagement of an audience—the traditional problem to which rhetoric is devoted—to the engagement of the performers themselves. People become participants in the drama—in a participation with "magical" implications. Centrally in the Taleju temple, and throughout the city in the Na:lā swā(n) rooms, they participate in the transformation of seeds into "weapons," and through the one annual blood sacrifice expected of all the city's citizens, in Devī's conquest of the antigods. They share in the killing—and eating—of the sacrifice, privately in the household sacrifice and publicly in the eating of the Kha(n) Me: Buffalo, sacrificed by the Nine Durgās at the festival's final day.

In Mohanī, deities, king, priests, and householders all participate in Devī's battle, and in so doing partake in Devī's victorious—and necessary—power. As is everywhere evident in the worship of the dangerous deities, but above all in the Devī cycle, they achieve a limited influence or control over that power by being *like* the gods. In a manner reminiscent of ancient Indian sacrifice, this participation in the restoration of cosmic order involves a necessary, active, and effective solidarity in action with the gods.

Through their active participation in Devī's battles people *become*, in a sense, Devī. In other festivals, or in other parts of Mohanī itself they may *relate* themselves to a deity by visiting it, by watching a procession, following it, taking *prasāda*, worshiping the deity through gestures or more elaborate *pūjās*. Participating in the work of a deity, becoming in a sense that deity, has quite different social and personal implications than simply observing it, worshiping it, respecting it, interacting with it, fearing it, worrying about the values implied by it, and in part, identifying with it. It is the difference between (in the first case) participating in the protective and environing forces surrounding, protecting, threatening, and sustaining the moral civic order and (in the second case) acting properly within that order. It is the difference between the realms of Kṣatriya and of Brahman.

THE PERFORMANCES OF THE NINE DURGĀS

We have been concerned in the earlier sections of this chapter with the legend and membership of the Nine Durgās and with the Devī cycle within which they are a major component as well as a thread binding the individual calendrical events of that cycle into a larger thematic unit. Now with Mohanī the Nine Durgās have emerged again to carry Devī's power and significance out into the city throughout the succeeding nine months of their annual life cycle until their disappearance once again at the following Bhagasti. We may now turn to a consideration of their performances throughout the city.

The dance drama, or *pyākha(n)*, which the Nine Durgās troupe performs throughout the city, comes to each of the neighborhoods in which it is performed as a kind of invasion. The troupe appears in each neighborhood in an order determined by a traditional annual sequence (map 14, p. 233). Local people must prepare for a visit that is beyond their control. Before turning to those systematic, sequential *pyākha(n)*s, however, we must consider another setting and form in which individuals encounter the Nine Durgās.

During much of the period when the Nine Durgās are active they may be invited by a family, a group of extended-family members, or a larger neighborhood group, to come and dance for the "protection of the area," which is how the Nine Durgās' function is usually phrased. This invitation is often in fulfillment of some vow. In the case of these invited performances a messenger is sent from the Nine Durgās to the hosts to say that the Nine Durgās are ready to go to their quarter. Thereupon the men responsible for the invitation and the expenses of the performance go to the Nine Durgās' god-house to conduct the gods to the place where the ceremony will be held. This is in significant contrast with the formal systematic neighborhood sequence when the gods will come by themselves, uninvited and unconducted. In the course of their being worshiped in the local area, usually in the courtyard of a house, a domestic pig, called in this context a *mū vāhā(n)*, or "main offering," is given as an offering to the Nine Durgās. This pig represents the strategic pig of the Nine Durgās' legend.

The pig is killed by Bhairava, who is the only one of the Nine Durgās who performs blood sacrifice, with the important exception of the killing of a cock by Mahākālī during the formal neighborhood dance-drama. He does this by splitting the skin of the young pig's foreleg with his fingernail (in a relatively thin area at the inner part of a joint) and separating the skin until he reaches the thoracic cage. He then forces his hand between two ribs and pulls out the heart and offers it to the Oleander shrine goddess, the Siphadya:. Now first Bhairava and then all the other gods (including demonic skeletal figures representing attendants of the Nine Durgās incarnated by Gāthā children) take blood from the pig's open chest and drink it. The gods now begin to tremble. This is said to be in response to the "force" in the blood, and to be a sign of the Gāthās' possession by the gods, but also to be a kind of intoxication. This image of the goddesses intoxicated with the blood of their Asura enemies, sometimes dancing as a result, is salient in the *Devī Māhātmya*. Now Bhairava gives a mixture of beaten rice and curds, *dhaka baji*, to each god to eat. He then offers *dhaka baji* as *prasāda* to the onlookers, with a particular emphasis on the children, and among the children, especially the boys. It is thought that this offering will protect children from disease. Bhairava's hands are still contaminated with the blood of the pig, and the audience thus share in this sacrifice. (Brahman boys after initiation and adult Brahmans are not allowed to accept this *prasāda*.) Following the sacrifice, the group of Durgās do formal dances. These dances describe certain geometric patterns and are said to be mystical diagrams or *yantra*s that protect the locality through supernatural power. Then the Nine Durgās troupe, taking the body of the pig with them, returns to its god-house accompanied by the important people of the inviting group. At the god-house the Gāthā dancers are said to cook and eat the pig.[95] Occasionally for particularly important offerings the Nine Durgās are offered five kinds of male animals for a major sacrifice called a *pa(n)ca bali.*

In the course of their nine months of life the Nine Durgās troupe dances at twenty-one public squares (map 14) throughout Bhaktapur and in nineteen villages outside of the city (Gutschow and Bāsukala 1987). These villages are generally with a few exceptions within the boundaries of the old Malla kingdom of Bhaktapur.[96] The pattern traced by the sequence of dances both outside and within the city are considered to form protective *yantra*s, in the same way as the detailed patterns of the dance performances within each local area mark out a local protected space. Aside from the Gāthā performers themselves, only a few specialists in the city are aware of the places and sequences in the larger cycle. All that the vast majority of the spectators to the local performance know is that somehow this local performance weaves their locality into a larger pattern of temporal and spatial relationships reiterated during each annual cycle, a pattern whose center is Bhaktapur.

In presenting the local performance, we must make the same choices we have made throughout this study. We will select out of the complex traditional performances, whose detailed description and elucidation would justify a volume in itself, those aspects that are presumptively meaningful in the particular and limited sense of this study. Thus we are here concerned with the "message" delivered by the performance to the neighborhood people and the purposes the performance serve in the symbolic organization of the city.

The relative position in the annual sequence of the visit to each neighborhood and village is fixed, but the Gāthā performers make use of various calculations known to themselves to determine the exact day in which they will come, so that the local people are never sure exactly when to expect them, although the performances always take place on either a Sunday or a Thursday. As we have noted, in contrast to the invited performances the Nine Durgās thus enter the area as a kind of invasion beyond the determination of the local people. These sequential local performances are often referred as the "*Ñā lākegu*" *pyākha(n)*, the "going fishing" *pyākha(n)*, using a reference to one element in the performance to stand for the whole. On the afternoon before the *pyākha(n)* the group of Gāthā—performers, musicians, and attendants—go to the *twa:* or neighborood area in which they will perform. Gutschow and Bāsukala (1987, 152ff.) have described this movement to the performance area in detail, and we will follow their description for the phases prior to the *pyākha(n)* itself. According to Gutschow and Bāsukala, on the occasion of one of the sequential visits the masks are brought from their hidden room in the Nine Durgās' god-house to the courtyard of that house, where the three frightening masks—Bhairava, Mahākālī, and Vārāhī—are separated from the others, and hung facing west. These are the same three deities who preceded the other Nine Durgās in the Taleju procession of the tenth day of Mohanī. Although the troupe itself may take several hours to reach their destination, the palanquin on which the Siphadya: will be placed is first brought directly to the square where the public performance of the following day is to be held. As Gutshow and Bāsukula write, "it [the arrival of the palanquin] is the first sign of the procession of the night . . . [as] the people are never sure when the gods [will] come" (1987, 152). The Gāthā troupe leave the god-house at twilight. First comes a man carrying a human skullcap as a drinking cup[97] in his left hand and a small drum, a *ḍamaru*, in the right. Next comes the man who carries the Siphadya:, accompained by another carrying a ceremonial umbrella to protect and honor that god. Then come three boys who at this point represent the deities Simā, Dumā, and Kumārī. They are followed by the masked men who incarnate Bhairava, Mahākālī and Vārāhī. The goddesses of the "chorus" follow next—Brāhmaṇī, Maheśvarī, Vaiṣṇavī, and Indrāṇī. Finally comes Gaṇeśa, wearing at his waist the mask of Śiva.

On each occasion the group begins its procession in the same way. It goes first to worship at a shrine of Gaṇeśa, Sala(n) Gaṇeśa, in the upper city. Mahākālī does a formal dance there. Now the procession proceeds to the Wā(n)lāekū Taleju shrine near Dattātreya Square. Mahākālī bows to the shrine, and is lifted twice into the air by an attendant. The procession proceeds along a main road that "serves as a kind of backbone from which the individual places are reached," and makes five further stops at various shrines, temples, and god-houses, where the Nine Durgās perform brief formal dances.

When they reach the particular quarter that is the goal of the day's procession, some of their activities are differentially determined according to the particular quarter. On their way to its main square they make from three to nine stops. The *naki(n)*, the senior woman of the troupe, seats herself at each stop with some baskets and pots to receive offerings of food and drink. Often the troupe is invited into individual houses and given offerings.

In eleven of the twenty-one neighborhoods in which they perform there is an additional sequence, the chasing of a pig, as they had done in the legend to protect themselves from recapture by the Brahman Tantric practitioner. This is done, according to Gutschow, in areas peripheral to the various performance squares in the direction of the borders of the city. The pig that is intended for sacrifice to Mahālakṣmī by Bhairava is, instead, stolen by groups of young men and boys. "The youngsters run around carrying the squeaking pig under their jackets and passing it quickly from one to the other. The gods are obviously teased and asked to come and fight for the pig. . . . This kind of teasing may last for an hour or two" (Gutschow and Bāsukala 1987, 156). Finally the pig is released and Bhairava grabs it and carries it back to the main square where he tears its heart out and throws it to the Siphadya:, that is, to the goddess Mahālakṣmī. This teasing ending in a blood sacrifice anticipates the themes of the next day.

These preliminary activities take from two to six hours, when, finally, toward midnight, the troupe reaches the square where they will perform.[98] It is said that the Gāthās do secret dances and rituals on the square. Non-Gāthās do not know what these are—it would be very dangerous to see them—but it is believed that they increase the power and effectiveness of the goddesses in preparation for their next morning's performances.

The next day's sessions are a mixture of formal dances (conceived as *yantras*) and worship, interspersed with dance-dramas or *pyākha(n)*s.[99] Following the first formal dances in the morning, there is a performance by the lion and tiger deities Simā and Dumā (see fig. 27). Although generally conceived as goddesses, and derived from the goddesses Si(n)hinī and Vyaghrinī, Dumā is here considered as a woman and Simā as a man, her husband.[100] Dumā has a cup out of which she will drink beer, but at some point Simā steals it. During this sequence the younger boys among the spectators laugh and make mocking noises directed to Simā and Dumā. Simā now begins to chase the children, occasionally catching one and holding him for a short time. If he catches the child he may bring the child to the shrine of the Sipha: God. If a child is caught, people may say this is the result of adverse planetary influences and his family may worship the Nine Durgās to remove the bad effect. This chase occurs several times during the course of the morning. These

Simā-Dumā sequences are considered to be comic, more concerned with younger children, and less serious than the *pyākha(n)* that is to follow in the afternoon.

This afternoon *pyākha(n)* focuses and conveys much of the meaning of the Nine Durgās and of the Devī cycle, and systematically delivers the message of that cycle to localities and their people. It derives its force and significance from all that has preceded it, and also from certain background experiences and interpretations of its audience in relation to animal sacrifice (chap. 9).

The afternoon performance has as its principal characters Seto Bhairava, the small white-faced young man with a mustache and tiny fangs who is the protagonist; Mahākālī, the largest and most frightening goddess, who is his antagonist; and Kumārī who is, as we have noted, a transitional form between the benign-appearing goddesses of the chorus and Mahākālī, acting as a mediator. These characters are augmented by Simā and Dumā as comic figures.

The *pyākha(n)* begins with Mahākālī doing a formal dance. Seto Bhairava seats himself on a woven straw mat, which he will later use to "go fishing." While Mahākālī is dancing, Seto Bhairava smears himself with a white pigment (a mixture of oil and white powder that is used otherwise in marriage ceremonies as a cosmetic for the bride). He has been given this as well as *ghya:* (clarified butter), brown sugar, and a white shawl by one of the members of the local area who is responsible for local supplies and arrangements. Seto Bhairava puts the white pigment on his face and hands and puts on his mask. He then puts the shawl over his head, approaches the place where Mahākālī is dancing and, seating himself with head still covered, slowly moves his head about in a fashion that is interpreted as a kind of mocking or making fun of the dancing Mahākālī. Keeping one's head covered in this fashion in front of a deity (or in this case a superior deity) is to show disrespect. Mahākālī becomes enraged and shakes her head in a quivering motion, indicating her great anger. She suddenly seizes the shawl from Seto Bhairava's head and holds it in her hand. Seto Bhairava wants to get his shawl back and the next part of the sequence has to do with his attempt to recover it. First he makes a gesture of respect to Mahākālī, but she ignores it and turns her head away. This attempt having failed, Seto Bhairava turns to the onlookers and begs for small coins. Some people in the crowd give coins to him. Seto Bhairava now offers the money to Mahākālī, asking her to take the coins as an offering. (His words now and in later parts of the *pyākha[n]* are spoken for him by one of the musicians.) Mahākālī takes the money from him, but does not return the shawl. All this ineffectiveness is amusing to the spectators. Now this part of the drama comes to a climax. Seto Bhairava takes a cock, which one of the onlookers hands to him, and offers it to Mahākālī. At first she is angry; she keeps her head turned away and will not take it. Then suddenly she grabs the cock, and with an angry gesture throws the shawl back into Seto Bhairava's face. Now Mahākālī bites the head off the living cock and drinks its gushing blood.

The *pyākha(n)* comes to an intermission. Now the *twa:* representatives do *pūjā*s to Kumārī, Bhairava, Mahākālī, Vārāhī, Seto Bhairava, Simā, and Dumā and to the Oleander Goddess, the Sipha: god. The background deities of the chorus are not worshiped at this time. Thus the gods that are worshiped are all frightening forms, with fangs, tusks, or sharp teeth. Now the masks are placed in a specially designated place and only Seto Bhairava remains masked. He takes his mat, which is now to serve as a fishing net. This mat is a rectangle about two or three feet long, with seven or eight tiny dried fish placed in openings of the net. He will use this net to "go fishing," as his chasing of older boys and young men which is about to occur is called. The chase by Simā in the morning is also called "going fishing," although he does not use a symbolic fishing net. As we have noted, the performances of the day with their various scenes and elements are, in fact, often named as a unit in reference to these episodes, and referred to as the "fishing," or "*Ñā lākegu pyākha(n)*," suggesting the central significance of this element. Seto Bhairava now does a formal dance (see frontispiece), as Mahākālī had been doing when Seto Bhairava showed disrespect to her. As he performs, the young men and older boys in the crowd begin to mock and taunt him by clapping their hands together and making sounds, rhythmically covering and uncovering their mouths with their hands to make a wavering noise. These young men are usually youths between fourteen and twenty, and include members of the clean *thar*s, even Brahmans. This is considered to be a brave and daring thing to do, and people are said to admire them for it. Now Seto Bhairava "goes fishing," angrily chasing the offending boys and young men. Sometimes during the course of his chase he will stop and be invited into a nearby house, where he is given an offering of food, including meat and alcoholic spirits. The young men will wait outside and continue their mocking when he comes out. If he manages to catch one of them, Seto Bhairava will drag him toward the Oleander God's shrine, but if he is far away from the shrine, he may let him go after dragging him for a while. This is considered bad luck for the boys and young men, and sometimes the younger ones cry with fear when they are caught. Seto Bhairava then returns to the shrine, and resumes his formal dance, only to be interrupted once more by the taunts and mockery of the boys and young men. The sequence of dancing and chasing occurs three times.

Now a new phase of the *pyākha(n)* begins, a comic phase. Seto Bhairava's stomach begins to hurt him. He is said to have an upset stomach from "eating fish," the boys and young men whom he has been chasing being those fish. He lies down on the mat and begins to rub his stomach. Simā and Dumā, now danced by boys instead of men, come to feel his abdomen "to see where the pain is." Seto Bhairava wriggles around because this tickles him. He is still in pain, however, and he calls for Kumārī (with one of the musicians again speaking for him). Kumārī, now also danced by a boy, comes with a handful of parched beaten rice and holding it first to Seto Bhairava's head, chest, and stomach, throws it to the right and to the left.[101] During these scenes in the dance-drama, Kumārī (as she is danced in this scene by a child, she is now sometimes called Bālakumārī, the "child Kumārī") is considered to be the wife of Seto Bhairava. As Kumārī throws the parched beaten rice to the right and to the left, she throws it into the faces of Simā and Dumā, who have been standing and looking on at either side of Seto Bhairava, and they react with gestures of discomfort. Now Seto Bhairava is cured of his affliction. He gets up and embraces the reluctant Kumārī, which usually provokes much laughter. Now Seto Bhairava gives his shawl to Dumā, asking her (through the Gāthā musician who speaks for him) to wash it for him saying, "It is a little dirty, please wash it." Dumā throws it down on the ground. Seto Bhairava says, "I should hit you," and makes a fighting gesture. He then picks up the shawl and goes through the same sequence, with the other member of the pair—Simā—and with the same results. Finally he picks up the shawl, which Simā has thrown down, and washes it himself in pantomime. He then walks away. The dance drama segment is now finished. All the gods, except Simā and Dumā and Seto Bhairava, perform a set of formal dances. This is the only time that the benign and beautiful forms of the goddesses also dance, and now Gaṇeśa also dances with the group for the first time during this day's proceedings.

Now the true Bhairava, as Bhairava is usually conceived in Bhaktapur, the large blue-black dangerous-looking male figure, comes to the fore.[102] As in the informal invited ceremonies described above, Bhairava is offered a pig to be sacrificed and returns beaten rice with his blood-stained hands as *prasāda* to be eaten by the onlookers, who thus become participants in the sacrifice.

Now the dance-drama is over and the gods making music return to their god-house, now accompanied in their return procession by people from the locality. The locality has been protected.

THE SIGNIFICANCE OF THE NINE DURGĀS' *PYĀKHA(N)*: SOME SPECULATIONS ON HOW THE NINE DURGĀS PROTECT BHAKTAPUR

In Bhaktapur's characteristic "religious" language the Nine Durgās are said to be of major importance in the protection of the city. In our analytic language this is, indeed, what they are doing in their neighborhood *pyākha(n)*s through the significance of their performances to the people of the local neighborhoods. They protect the city by helping to assure the proper relation of individuals to the city's society.

As always, we are concerned with the significance of the Nine Durgās' performance for Bhaktapur's symbolic ordering, that is, with its impact on Bhaktapur's people. Much of the form of the Nine Durgās has no direct significance in this sense—although it would be significant analytically to, say, historians of South Asian culture. We must note, however, that many aspects of the Nine Durgās' form and action are indirectly significant in our limited sense even if the meaning of those forms and actions is, in some sense, unknown to most or all of the Newars who witness and engage in the performances. These aspects are significant in part precisely *because* their meaning is unknown. It is sufficient that the spectators have the conviction that there *is* meaning even if they do not know what it is. Thus the spectators to the Nine Durgās' *pyākha(n)* do not know what the overall sequence of visits by the Nine Durgās is in the spatial *maṇḍala* they create over nine months, but they do know that the visit to their neighborhood is an essential part of this pattern. They do not know what many of the iconic details of the masks signify, nor which of the minor goddesses is which. They do not know what the mask makers or the Gāthā actually do to give proper *siddhi* to the performances. They do not know what the formal *yantra* dances of the Nine Durgās signify. Such unknown matters are in contrast with the very accessible and direct implications of other aspects of the masks, sacrifice, *pyākha(n)*, and so on. But the things they do *not* understand have their own meaningful implications, they contribute to the performance's special *sacred* force.[103]

Although the great majority of the spectators to the local *pyākha(n)* may not understand such matters, they know that they are correct and necessary. The dances, masks, and procedures represent an order that is organized and guaranteed by something beyond ordinary contingent local human action, improvisation, and decision. This helps give the performance, in spite of its sometimes comic style, a deep seriousness and relates it to the sacred realm of Hinduism—a seemingly eternal and transcendent realm beyond the here and now. The forms that spectators do not understand, to a certain degree just because they are not understood, evoke—as do the transcendent ritual and ceremonial forms and sequences and their contexts—this other mysterious world. All that the spectator has to know or believe is that something is being done properly, that it is generated out of a sacred tradition, where it is rooted in myths and legends, and that it is properly passed down from generation to generation of priests, mask makers, and dancers through proper initiation, teaching, and *mantras*. The audience sees a performance that is a manifestation of something beyond the ordinary, something organized in some other order beyond the whims of the Gāthās. These properties of the performance, allied to references to ultimate macrocosmic realms of order, powerfully evoke ideas and emotions characteristic of encounters with the "sacred."

Yet, within this larger frame is the *pyākha(n)*'s drama and the gamelike "fishing" episodes of the pursuit of the mocking boys and young men by the gods. The messages here are direct and specific, completely dependent on peoples' understanding of the *pyākha(n)*'s symbolic forms. The dramas and fishing chases have a central theme or motif, which is elaborated in various ways. This theme is the violation of hierarchy, shown concretely through the violation of proper respect toward a superior. The young boys mime this to Simā and Dumā, the older boys to Seto Bhairava, and Seto Bhairava to Mahākālī. This violation of hierarchy and the response to that violation illustrated in the drama and fishing pursuit does not concern ordinary violations of the moral law, the *dharma* of civic life, any more than the struggle between the gods and the Asuras in the *Devī Māhātmya* concerns ordinary moral relations among deities. Ordinary moral violations, the arena of shame, loss of face, and the generation of bad *karma*, have their own symbols and myths, their own spatial location, their own religious modes and divinities. This *pyākha(n)* and its context does not concern the moral problems of human beings with each other. In its offending of superior dangerous gods it concerns the violation by humans of the very order that makes the moral realm possible, and it shows the consequences of such a disruption.

Hierarchy, the central principle of social order in traditional Hindu societies, is, as we have shown in chapters 5 and 6, greatly elaborated in Bhaktapur's complex urban organization. The violation of the conventions of hierarchical relationship, therefore, strikes at the central organizing principle of Bhaktapur's society. Thus the Nine Durgās' *pyākha(n)* can be interpreted as being about the struggle between disorder and order, about what happens to individuals who violate order, and, finally, about what has to be done to restore that order. The contextual meaning of the Nine Durgās in the larger Devī cycle indicates that although this disorder is dangerous both to the ordinary moral gods and to humans as social beings it is at the same time a source of fertility and energy. Thus the boys and young men who mock the gods are admired for their courage and Seto Bhairava is a sympathetic Chaplinesque figure with whom one must empathize as he struggles against the terrifying Mahākālī. Similarly, the boys and young men who called out order-threatening and immoral obscenities at the proper phase of the annual cycle were also doing something positive, amusing, and vital. The children and young men are pursued by the gods whom they mock and are sometimes caught without particularly serious consequences, but the potential consequences for the acts of rebellion that they have mimed are shown graphically in Seto Bhairava's encounter with Mahākālī. He fails to show respect for the superior deity, who becomes enraged. He tries to restore relationships with her by the kinds of exchanges that are effective with the ordinary, the non-Tantric gods—gestures of respect, the offering of money or *dakṣiṇā*. But only an offering of blood sacrifice appeases this kind of a deity. The biting off of the head of the cock and the drinking of its blood signifies to the onlookers that it was Seto Bhairava who was to be killed, or at the very least castrated, if it were not for this convenient substitution. The sacrifice enables the return of the shawl and some social dignity to Seto Bhairava and atones for his violation of hierarchy.

The Nine Durgās are dangerous deities, and Mahākālī is the dangerous goddess in her most frightening representation. As we have argued throughout, such deities have a special position in the maintenance of order in Bhaktapur, where Tantra and the worship of dangerous deities (as is widely the case in the history of South Asia) has been captured and put to use by the social order as the legend of the origin of the Nine Durgās attests, rather than representing attempts by renouncers, magicians, and peripheral social groups to escape from that order. Like the traditional Hindu ruler in his ideal relationship to the priest, the dangerous deities are responsible for the *protection* of the traditional ritual and moral life, although they are beyond morality themselves. They are ambivalently made use of when that moral order is being threatened either by some internal force or by some external danger. Seto Bhairava's rebellion threatens the hierarchical basis of urban order, and a dangerous deity becomes activated.

The way Mahākālī's threat is both manifested and avoided is in the blood sacrifice of the cock. This is in the context of the massive blood sacrifices of Mohanī, the blood sacrifices by the Nine Durgās at other times, the legend of the Nine Durgās' murder and eating of humans before they were captured by Tantric priests, and the accounts of human sacrifices performed by the Gāthās in the past. We have noted (chap. 9) that animal sacrifices are for some informants, at least, consciously and with deep emotion associated with vivid memories from their boyhoods when they felt that the sacrifices were in fact selfishly motivated murder, that they might be directed toward them if the adults became angry at them, and that the animals were somehow equivalent to themselves. "I could feel the knife on my own throat," as one man said in reminiscence.

The *pyākha(n)* thus makes use of a particularly powerful and complex local constellation of meanings. Its message is directed directly at males.[104] Men are the critical actors in the public social organization of Hindu communities, and the largest component of the civic symbolic system is devoted to the expression and control of their problems, emotions, and orientations in the performance of their social roles. It is striking in view of this male prominence in the public life of the city, that that force which is represented as external to the city but vital to it, both as the energy of nature and as the force that both threatens and which, if properly placated and controlled, will protect the city against disruption, is represented primarily by the nonsocial, dream-like "Mother Goddess" and the images, concepts, and emotions associated with that powerful symbol.

Sacrifice is not only a powerful symbol of a threat, a potential punishment for violation of hierarchy, but as we have argued in chapter 9, an important motivation for accepting the social order, for identifying with and becoming one of the sacrificers, to escape the fate of being one of the creatures that are sacrificed. This acceptance of order under the pressure of sacrifice is manifested in the acceptance, the "understanding," of the particular ideologies and dogmas of the group that would be hypocritical, problematic, and perhaps nonsensical to an innocent eye. Such items requiring faith are vividly represented in the mystifying dogmas about sacrifice itself.

The *pyākha(n)* plays with the theme of the vital impulses of the city's citizens that are socially disruptive and, making use of blood sacrifice, one of the very most powerful symbolic resources for restoring and maintaining individual assent to Bhaktapur's culture and society, restores order both within the drama, and, ideally, in the minds of its spectators. Seto Bhairava is not only the ineffectual protagonist who blunders into trouble with Mahākālī and is saved only through a substitution of a sacrificial animal; in another phase of the *pyākha(n)*, the "going fishing," after which the whole event is significantly named, he is the one who is mocked by his inferiors and becomes, in turn, the agent of punishment. Similarly, the people of Bhaktapur are not only the passive objects of potential destruction in the face of violations of order. They themselves offer the sacrifice, perform them themselves on other occasions, share in the blood by feasting on the sacrificial animal, and, during the course of the Nine Durgās' performances, eating the blood-stained *prasāda*. The people identify, then, not only with the victim but also with the dangerous deities, both in their wildness on the one hand, and as collaborators in slaughter for the sake of social order on the other, which results in a sense of community that psychoanalytically inclined observers might argue not only represents the mastery of switching from a passive to an active role and an identification with the punitive forces but also has something to do with a sense of shared guilt.

The last part of the drama may be thought of as a kind of moving downward from a more cosmic scale to a more domestic one, thus providing another bridge to the audience.[105] Here Seto Bhairava is healed through his wife in a common magical healing procedure known to all people. The grain that he throws in the face of Simā and Dumā has perhaps an added bit of meaning insofar as those two personages are also thought to represent Death's messengers. But in this little episode of healing domesticity, of Seto Bhairava having to turn to his wife for help, the wife, Kumārī, is herself merely an attenuated form of that violent natural force, Mahākālī. This reminder of the danger that persists even in domesticated women, the Kalī that is said to dwell within all women, crops up as we have seen, from time to time in Bhaktapur's stories, as a subdued and faintly comic counterpoint to the grand theme of the cosmic Devī. But with the help of Kumārī Seto Bhairava is cured. Like Somarā, the Tantric Brahman in the Nine Durgās legend, after the escape of the Nine Durgās brought about by the interference of his wife, Seto Bhairava is returned to ordinary civic life. He is safe, but as his inability to get Simā or Dumā to wash his shawl for him reminds the audience, he is without power to alter the conventional order of things, and thus without, in fact, much power at all.

CHAPTER SIXTEEN

The Patterns and Meanings of the Festival Year

The state is concentric, man is eccentric. Thence arises an eternal struggle.
James Joyce, conversation cited in *James Joyce,*
by Richard Ellmann, 1982, p. 446.

INTRODUCTION

In our discussions of Bhaktapur's focal festivals, of the Devī cycle, and of the performances of the Nine Durgās, we have illustrated various ways in which social units, space, actual history and legendary history, gods, and time are woven together in an eternally returning annual cycle. The major festivals are surrounded by a mass of lesser calendrical events whose symbols and activities are more limited, often seemingly unrelated to other annual events or to the larger city order. Our task in this chapter is to examine the entire collection of annual events in a quest for possible order of one kind or another among them.

To facilitate such an overall view we have summarized the year's events, added comments on different phases within the yearly cycle, and placed events and comments in the context of the annual lunar calendar in appendix 5.

DISTINCTIONS AND ENUMERATIONS AND THEIR IMPLICATIONS

We can make a first approach to the year's collection of annual events by summarizing and enumerating, where possible, some of their distinguishing features.

1. In the course of a year there are seventy-nine named annual events, occasionally grouped so that there are more than one in a day, and with

one event lasting two days. The seventy-nine events thus occupy to some greater or lesser extent seventy-four days.[1]

2. These seventy-nine annual events are of greatly differing importance. On the basis of the comparative amounts of city personnel, space, resources, and time devoted to them, as well as our opinion of their significance to Bhaktapur as a city, we have sorted the annual events into those of major, moderate, and minor importance. It is fairly easy to discern at the two extremes major events and the often very trivial minor ones, but the inclusion of an event in the middle category, "moderate importance," is often somewhat arbitrary. At any rate, our sorting gives us twenty-five major events (many of which we grouped into "focal" festival sequences), twenty-eight events of moderate importance, and twenty-six events of minor importance among the year's seventy-nine annual events. Thus we have some fifty-three events that we take to be of some more than minor annual importance to the city.

3. If we sort the annual events by the social-spatial unit, which is emphasized, we find that only two such events are primarily occasions for *individual* activities, that is, *vratas* ([42] and [43]). Twenty of the seventy-nine annual events are of *primary* concern to the *household*—although many other events entail household activities that are *secondary* to some activity in the public city. In contrast to household-centered events (and in contrast to a predominant emphasis in rites of passage), only two events may be said to be directed primarily to the *phukī*, but one of these is the fundamental *phukī*-defining Dewālī [30].[2] The majority of annual events are those fifty festivals of various kinds located primarily in *public city space*. Four annual events have their loci *out of the city*, and there are an additional two such events attended by those whose loss of a parent makes them unable to worship a father or mother in the two annual household ceremonies devoted to their worship. Finally there are two events ([18] and [34]) whose spatial location is ambiguous for this classification, the latter case—not exactly an "event" in the same sense as other days—concerning both the household and the *phukī*.

The "primary" annual household events, in contrast to the household phases of rites of passage and to those household *pūjās* motivated by some specific familial problem, are generally observed by all city households on the same day, and are in this sense "city-wide" events. Thus, almost all the annual events are either such parallel household events or take place in the public city space, and may be amalgamated together into a class of civic events emphasizing the public city and households as units of that city. On closer inspection, as we shall see, these household events and events in public city space are differently related to civic life.

The primary household events insofar as they take place in parallel throughout the city are civic events, but in another distinction they take place below the level of the public city. In such a view, certain annual events—and segments of particular events—are occasionally above the city level, many more are below it, but most are at the level of the city, the fifty events located in public space being, by definition, at that level. Above the city level are the *melā*s where individuals from Bhaktapur join with individuals from other cities and from other ethnic groups in pilgrimages to one or another Valley shrine, all, significantly, located out of the major Valley cities. In *melā*s Bhaktapur's participants escape their city and its particular order. Individuals join in a larger human community, refracting themselves against another context than the city's public order, the city being reflected only in its absence. The characteristic annual events below the level of the public city are the calendrically determined household events, centered, for the most part, on the moral life of the household and its benign deities.

One important difference between household and public events requires a repeated comment. Competent members of a household must (as an index of that competence) participate in its ceremonies, as *phukī* members must participate in rites of passage and other *phukī* ceremonies. But participation in public ceremonies is, for the most part, voluntary for the mass of observers (although not for the central actors). Thus public ceremonies must have their own special ways of motivating attendance.[3] We have discussed some of the sources of the attraction of the important performances in previous chapters. These include their aesthetic qualities, their mystery, their intriguing complexity, their sacred and supernatural auras and, in some cases, the thrill of their dangers. The vivid presence of a deity in human form, its living manifestation in the Kumārī maiden or the Nine Durgās, is an almost irresistible attraction. Many of the stories, dramas, and symbolic forms of the festivals engage and fascinate because they have compelling psychodynamic interest and resonate with the personal psychological forms out of which the public citizen is constructed. The tales of the phallic snakes issuing from the princess's nose and the banging together of the chariots of Bhairava and Bhadrakālī in Biskā:, the blood sacrifices of Mohanī, and the echoes of human sacrifice in the Nine Durgās' *pyākha(n)* are vivid examples.[4]

4. The deities who are foci of the various annual events include all of the major members of the city pantheon, a few quasi-deities or supernatural figures who exist only for the purpose of a particular festival, and some social categories—e.g., father, mother—treated as deities. For the benign deities there are eight events devoted to Viṣṇu/Nārāyaṇa (including here Dattātreya), four devoted to Kṛṣṇa, and one each to Jaganā and Rāma. There are four devoted to Śiva—one as Paśupatinātha, two as Mahādeva, and one (his only primary appearance in a household event) as Maheśvara in conjunction with his consort Umā. Gaṇeśa is the focus of four festivals, Lakṣmī and Sarasvatī of two each. Yama or his representatives have three; *nāga*s, one; the Ṛṣis, one; the deified river, one; and the cow deity, Vaitaraṇī, one. Family members are worshiped as quasi-deities in four events. The family priest is worshiped on one occasion as *purohita*, on another as *guru*.

The dangerous goddess Devī in one form or another is the focus of about twenty-two occasions of which ten are in the Devī cycle. (Three of the events in the Devī cycle do not refer directly to Devī but are essential components of that cycle.) Bhairava—in himself and not as the consort of Devī—is the focus of two festivals and in tandem with his consort, Bhadrakālī, at the center of the Biskā: sequence, which lasts ten days. The dangerous deity Bhisi(n), who is conceptually isolated from the Devī-Bhairava group, is the central deity of one event.

All the city's major deities are thus the subject of one or more festivals during the year; they are all duly honored. But the extent and nature of the festival use of the various deities and types of deities are quite different. The dangerous deities are never the focus of primary household annual events,[5] but they are the center of more than half of the events in the public city, and of *all* the urban structural focal sequences. The remaining minority of the public festivals, those of the benign deities, are divided among those deities, with Viṣṇu having the largest number, eight—or sixteen if his avatars are amalgamated to him. Śiva, the putatively predominant deity of the Shaivite Hindu Newars, is, typically, hardly represented at all for the purposes of the on-the-ground concrete work of the festivals. His major festival Silā Ca:re (Śivarātri [15]) taking place, for the most part, at a pilgrimage site elsewhere in the valley.

While the festivals in the public city of the benign deities, whose exemplary figure is Viṣṇu, are often said to be "in honor of" those morally representative figures, the public festivals of the dangerous deities not only honor and display those figures, but in contrast to the festivals of the benign deities, do something more. These are the public urban festivals, which are sometimes said to be not just for the gods but "for the people." These festivals make use of the special metamoral force of the dangerous deities as guarantors of order.

Not every event has a focal deity—some half dozen events are simply annual occasions for doing something or have some reference to a demonic or legendary figure (e.g., [45] and [65]) with references to major deities only in the far background.

5. Some annual calendrical events are of particular concern to certain categories of people in Bhaktapur—students, women, farmers, upper-level *thar*s, merchants, Brahmans, people who have been bereaved during the previous year. The vast majority of the events concern all of Bhakatapur's people, however, with the traditional exception of the most polluting *thar*s. A different question, however, is the *representation* of the city's various hierarchical macrosocial roles in the cast of characters of the festival enactments. In most cases the human actors on the public stage are simply the *pūjārī* attendants of the focal deities and the musicians (usually from one of the Jyāpu *thar*s) who may accompany the deity in its procession. Thus the vast majority of public festivals do *not* represent the divisions of the city's elaborate differentiated macrostatus system. It is only in the year's two major festival sequences, Biskā: and Mohanī, that there is some complex and differentiated representation of Bhaktapur's macrosocial status system. Yet, even here the representation is sketchy. The king and his chief Brahman are given some centrality, and the court, other priests, farmers, and polluting *thar*s are represented, but for the most part these actors are simply used as a clumped and static résumé of the city's ranks. The focal festivals do not, with one or two trivial exceptions, show any dramatic relations among actors characterized by their social statuses. Whatever the dilemmas, paradoxes, conflicts, and problems that are explored in the annual festivals, the components of Bhaktapur's social system are privileged and taken for granted. The levels and the other components of the macrostatus system are *not* used to provide agonists in the drama, *not* used to illustrate conflict and its possible resolutions. In the midst of all the drama of annual events the hierarchical system of social statuses is protected, represented only as a unified actor, an actor who

Figure 34. Spectators seated on the steps of the Ñātāpwa(n)la temple in Ta:mārhī Square to watch the struggle to pull the Bhairava chariot.

is, sometimes, as is the case pervasively throughout city symbolism, put in contrast with an "external" and oppositional social actor, the untouchable. The potential drama of the interplay and conflicts of macro-statuses is deflected and played out elsewhere—not in the symbolic enactments of the annual events, whose surfaces and middle depths, at least, speak of other dramas.[6]

It has been said of some of the festivals of the Hellenic pagan cities of the second and third centuries A.D. that they "showed off the city in its social hierarchy: people processed in a specified order of social rank, the magistrates, priests and councillors and even the city's athletic victors, if any" (Fox 1986, 80). Those festivals seem to have not only represented the city's statuses but also celebrated the particular citizens who temporarily captured roles in the hierarchy. The particular individuals who occupy the roles in Bhaktapur's largely ascribed—not achieved—status system do not need to be supported by such public advertisement. If Bhaktapur's social system is represented only in its unity, the individuals who happen to hold these statuses are completely dissolved in the immemorial roles they play in the annual festivals.

In summary, most (some 63%) of Bhaktapur's annual events are in the city's public space, with the calendrically coordinated household festivals following in quantity (25%). Almost, but not quite, all of the annual events have direct reference to deities, the annual calendar being largely a "religious calendar." The dangerous deities only appear when the primary or only locus of the event is in public space, but they are then dominant. And, in contrast to the minutely detailed dramatic interactions of various city spaces, of spatially located social units, of deities and times, the macrosocial system is portrayed only as a unified presence in the dramas of the yearly calendar.

A NOTE ON MOVING DEITIES WITHIN THE CITY

When the city's spaces and what they represent are tied together or contrasted in a serial, interactive manner rather than in a parallel summative way, the characteristic device used is the *jātrā*. The deity is either moved systematically so that masses of people may be brought into contact with it, or else—less commonly—masses of people move systematically to encounter a deity or a sequential set of deities. These movements, *jātrā*s, follow traditional routes, variously tying together units of the city and, often, the city as a whole. They explore central points, axes, and boundaries, as people move or as focal deities are carried through space and time. In so doing the procession of people or of the deity is often brought into an encounter with other kinds of dramatic enactments.

By far the most common movement is that of those *jātrā*s that move the deities themselves. Such movements would seem to be a utilization of an unremarkable resource for the enactment of symbols, for putting symbolic forms into effective relations with space and community. Yet, an observation by Walter Burkert suggests that such *jātrā*s are, in fact, problematic in comparative perspective. Burkert writes of ancient Greece that "processions with images of gods—which play a major role in the Ancient Near East—are [in Greece] an exception. . . . *Such a moving of the immovable is an uncanny breaking up of order*" (1985, 92 [emphasis added]). Bhaktapur's gods leave their temples and their fixed positions, and although they do not wander at will in the course of the annual events, their order is a mobile order. The contrast with Greece suggests that the movement of Bhaktapur's gods—or at least of the *jātrā* images they inhabit—out into the city from their fixed bases in the city are invasions, albeit controlled and not chaotic ones, of what in Greece was becoming a safely secular space.

PATTERNS IN THE YEAR

What happens if we reassemble the three cycles that we separated from each other in previous chapters and attempt to examine the narrative movement of the annual cycle as a whole (see app. 5)?[7] We must now look for disjunctions suggesting phases and movements in the year's course, for frontiers indicating some difference in the festivals that precede and follow them. Let us begin by making a cut into the annual cycle after the ending of Mohanī in early October. Although the successful rice harvest had been compellingly represented in the themes of Mohanī, the actual harvesting continues. The work of Devī has now been given over to the Nine Durgās. Taleju returns to the secret inner recesses of her temple, and there will be no more festivals of the Goddess nor of any other dangerous deity (except for the merchants' Bhisi[n] festival)[8] for a span of six lunar months, when the solar festival, Biskā: will reintroduce the Dangerous Goddess and her consort Bhairava. Then, beginning with Biskā:, will come the six months during which all the public festivals of Devī and her various forms and associates and those few of the unaccompanied Bhairava will occur, as well as, in fact, the great majority of the year's festivals. The ending of Mohanī, the symbolic culmination of the cycle of rice agriculture, then, returns Devī to the city in the form of the wandering Nine Durgas̄, but marks the end of her public presence in the annual calendrical events for the next six months.

The first annual event after Mohanī is the lunar new year sequence, Swanti [77-2]. When considered in its contrast to the year's other events, Swanti begins the lunar calendrical year with a turning in and centering on the household and its members. Swanti's interactive solidarity is internal to the household, with a secondary parallel solidarity relating each household to all Hindu (and with Mhā Pūjā to all Newar) households as well as to the households of Bhaktapur itself. The Swanti sequence uses as the antistructure that serves to define the household, not the city in which the household is embedded, but still another realm beyond the household, that of death personified as Yama, at the threshold of an afterlife determined by an individual's moral and ritual activities. The environing city is irrelevant to this opposition and to the resulting dialogue between household and Yama. The lunar New Year thus constitutes still another sort of annual frontier, beginning the voyage through the year that follows it with the positioning of individuals in the basic moral cell of the city, the household.

Swanti is followed first by a pilgrimage and *melā* at a Viṣṇu shrine out of the city [3] and then—nine days after the end of Swanti, and ten days after the New Year's Day itself—by Hari Bodhinī [4], the day of Viṣṇu's awakening from his four month's cosmic sleep, which is celebrated by still another out of the city *melā*. Gaborieau (1982 [summarized above in chap. 12]) had proposed the falling off to sleep and awakening of Viṣṇu as marking off an annual period of four months, dividing off from the rest of the year a special segment, an out of the ordinary time, a period beginning with profound disorder and culminating in regeneration. In Bhaktapur Hari Bodhinī in itself does not mark a shift in the year's activities from the extradordinary to the ordinary—Mohanī did that. Nor does the day of the onset of Viṣṇu's sleep, Hari Śayanī [42]. Yet, aside from its exact timing and duration, Gaborieau's proposals about the year's phases have some relevance to Bhaktapur and we will return to them.

From the end of Mohanī in Kaulāthwa through the lunar New Year some two weeks later and then on through the succeeding nine fortnights there are relatively few annual events, all of them, except for the

Suku(n) Bhisi(n) God Jātrā, focused on the city's benign moral deities. This changes with Pāsā Ca:re on the fourteenth day of Cillāgā (March), when, with an emphasis on protection from evil spirits, the first animal sacrifices since Mohanī—again with the exception of those made by merchants to Sukhu(n) Bisi(n) God—are made to Taleju in the Taleju temple and to some Aga(n) Deities, initiating a "period of anxiety" that will last through the remainder of the year until the end of the following Mohanī. In this period the festivals of the dangerous deities will take place. Thus Pāsā Ca:re is or anticipates still another frontier for the year. That frontier is more clearly signaled in the elaborate public festivals of the Biskā: sequence, which comes (depending on the relation of lunar and solar calendars) some twelve days later. Biskā:, which comes about six months after the end of Mohanī, is the first of the public urban festivals that after the six intervening months center once again around the dangerous deities. Biskā:, the solar New Year festival, contrasts sharply with the lunar New Year sequence. While Swanti emphasizes the household and the relations of individuals in the household, and is characterized by a sort of withdrawal from the city into the household, the solar New Year festival—with its themes of urban division and reunification and of the sacred legitimization of the city's space—emphasizes the city itself. In the solar New Year the household is secondary. The deities emphasized in the lunar New Year's sequence are the benign moral gods—Lakṣmī and quasi-deified family members in the interior of the family and at its exterior and, in fact, continuation, death as Yama, the judge and executor of each individual's morally created and deserved fate. In Biskā:, in contrast, the deities are the amoral dangerous one. In contrast to Swanti, what is contrasted with the household and given primacy in Biskā: is the larger nested set of urban units that surround the household and enable its survival as an element in Bhaktapur's society. Thus, Biskā: begins a six-month phase of the year when the ordering of the household's sustaining "lateral" environment,[9] the public city and *its* environment is explored. This exploration has, in turn, two phases.

In the weeks following Biskā: there are a few heterogeneous events of varying importance—worship of mothers in the household, *jātrās* of forms of Devī, and one especially auspicious day. Three fortnights after the end of Biskā: comes Sithi Nakhā [36], the first event with a reference to the annual rains and the rice growing cycle. Sithi Nakhā is preparatory; it will be the second event in the Devī cycle, Bhagasti [40] in June, which marks the beginning of rice planting, and which is another important transition in the year. The annual festivals of dangerous deities had begun again with Biskā:. Now on Bhagasti, Devī's agents in the city, the Nine Durgās who had begun their cycle nine months earlier with the last of the Devī festivals, the focal Mohanī, disappear—in some versions go into the ground—for seven fortnights.[10] With the disappearance of the Nine Durgās there is a shift of concern among the important "anxious festivals" of the period from the *internal* dangers to the integration of the city to the *external* environing dangers so clearly represented in the successes and failures of the monsoon rains and the rice cycle. These concerns with the city's external and supporting realms will endure for three-and-a-half months, during a period of an increasing density of annual events, until the end of Mohanī. Bhagasti is followed by a five-week period of licensed obscenity, culminating in Gāthā Muga: Ca:re [45]. During this period there is a minor *jātrā* of an *avatar* of Viṣṇu's and then Hari Śayani [42], the beginning of Viṣṇu's four-month cosmic sleep. Like his awakening on Hari Bodhinī, this is not in itself a transitional event in the annual cycle. Hari Śayanī is followed by a minor event, Tulasī Piye [43], related to Viṣṇu (which gives an omen about the length of a worshiper's life), a minor household *pūjā* (Guru Pūjā [44]), and then by Gāthā Muga: Ca:re [45], marking the ideal completion of the transplanting of rice to the flooded paddy fields.

Gāthā Muga: Ca:re is followed by a fortnight with only one event. That one, Nāga Pa(n)camī [41], is intended for the protection of houses and households from dangerous *nāgas*. Then the next four lunar fortnights become filled with events; they contain thirty-one of the year's seventy-nine festivals and thus constitute the most concentrated festival span of the year. This period contains a mixture of types of events—public and household, devoted to both benign and dangerous deities. However, within this diverse group there are two major events. First comes Sāpāru, with its active support of the progression of the spirits of the recently dead into King Yama's realm and its accompanying "antistructural" carnival. Second is the focal structural Mohanī, culminating the year, celebrating and miming the power of Devī in Bhaktapur's supporting world, and drawing her into the city's center of royal power.

The festival cycle as a whole does, then, seem to have some overall patterning. One of its most striking aspects is the division of the year so that in the six months from Mohanī until some twelve days before Biskā: there are relatively few events (twenty of the year's seventy-nine). These are with one exception—the generally anomalous Sukhu(n) Bhisi(n) God Jātrā [8]—devoted only to benign deities and lack the anxious themes of many of the annual events that will follow. Then, after an anticipation in events with reference to dangerous spirits and protection of the body (Pāsā Ca:re [18] and Cika[n] Buyegu [19]), Biskā: introduces the long season of the festivals of the dangerous deities, of the Devī cycle, and of events with primary and central references to protection and to death. Aside from the festivals of the Devī cycle, there are some fifteen additonal such events during this period. Mixed in with these events exclusively characterizing these six months are thirteen "ordinary" festivals, primarily minor ones "in honor of the gods" of the sort found throughout the other half of the year.

Within the span of six anxious months between Biskā: and Mohanī, the death and disappearance of the Nine Durgās during Bhagasti some two months after Biskā: marks a shift in the emphasis on the dangerous deities, primarily Devī, from their roles as the representatives and protectors of urban spatial units (epitomized in Biskā:) to their use in the representation of—and the mediation with—the noncivic encircling enviroment. In this perspective there is a movement from household in Swanti to the public city in Biskā:, and then to the city's vital environment after Biskā:, this final shift having its resolution in Mohanī.

To return finally to Gaborieau's specific suggestions about the structure of the Indo-Nepalese festival year (see chap. 12), the shifts within the six-month Biskā:-Mohanī, period, starting with Bhagasti and ending with the end of Mohanī, three-and-a-half months later, correspond roughly, that is, within a few weeks, to the period of Viṣṇu's cosmic sleep. Viṣṇu's sleep and awakening do not in themselves delineate any shift, however, nor is the period of that sleep (Cāturmāsa) of the same significance in Bhaktapur as an "inauspicious period" as it is, reportedly, elsewhere. The span from Bhagasti to Mohanī can, nevertheless, certainly be characterized (as Gaborieau does for the period of Viṣṇu's sleep) as a time when "the earth is left to the demons." In addition (further paralleling Gaborieau), there are major festivals of "reversal" early in the period (the five weeks between Bhagasti [40] and Gāthā Muga: Ca:re [45], Gāthā Muga: Ca:re itself, and the carnival phase of Sāpāru [48]) and a major festival of "regeneration" (Mohanī itself) toward its end. The span does not divide neatly into a "reversal" half and a "regenerative" half, however, being full of a miscellaneous variety of festivals. It is really only certain events that are clearly (the first ones) reversals and (the last) regenerative. What Bhaktapur seems to show, in contrast to Gaborieau's proposal of an Indo-Nepalese "normal" period of eight months followed by an "out of time" period of four, is an *addition* to the "normal" festival cycle that had held undisturbed for the prior six months of something more in the remaining six, an addition first of the urban ordering festivals of the dangerous deities, and then of a span that is "out of time" in the sense that attention turns to the exterior of the city, and its actors and its order. The last move seems prodded by the obsessions of the rice growing cycle and to be related to that cycle, as much as to the kind of abstract structural considerations argued by Gaborieau.

EXTERNAL INFLUENCES ON THE ANNUAL CYCLE

There are many possible external cyclical features beside the rice agricultural cycle that *might* have influenced the content and forms of the year's various annual events. These are the various aspects of the yearly solar cycle, the monthly lunar cycle with its phases of the moon and its bright and dark fortnights, and the various yearly patterns of weather and agriculture. The annual solar cycle, with its solar year, its seasons, its equinoxes and solstices, its "ascending" and "descending" halves, is almost unreflected in Bhaktapur's annual calendar. The great exception is Biskā:, the focal solar New Year sequence centering on the vernal equinox.[11] In Biskā:'s symbolism, as we have discussed, the possible references to the sun's behavior and to the solar year are minimal or equivocal.[12] There is only one other annual festival in the solar cycle—Ghya: Cāku Sa(n)lhu [10]. It comes at a time which once elsewhere in South Asia traditionally marked the winter solstice and the beginning of the ascending half of the year, but such connections are entirely lost in the events of the day. Aside from a reference to "spring music" in anticipation of a spring still several weeks away in the course of the lunar event Śrī Pa(n)camī [13] there are no other annual events which respond to, symbolize or express the solar year.

The lunar cycle provides, of course, the basic month and the basic structure of Bhaktapur's calendar. For the most part the days of the lunar month simply provide a counting device with no further meaning. Within each month the phases of the moon provide additional materials for possible symbolic elaboration. The full moon and the new moon (to a much lesser degree) are occasions for differentiated events as well as regular monthly ones. Yet, once again these differentiated events seem to have no salient present symbolic reference to the light or the dark of the fortnight's culminating phase of the moon.

The phases of the moon allow, however, for a further differentiation of each month into waxing (or bright) and waning (or dark) fortnights. There is a marked difference in the quantity of events in the two kinds of fortnights. *Thwa*, the waxing fortnights, have throughout the year twice as many annual events as *gā*, the waning fortnights. The waning fortnights all contain a special day, the fourteenth or *ca:re* dedicated to Devī. This and the difference in quantities of events would suggest the possibility of some contrast of ordinary versus dangerous, or auspicious versus inauspicious between the two types of fortnights. Ancient Hindu South Asia was explicit regarding differences in the two half-months *(pakṣa)*. "The general rule is that the *śukla pakṣa* [bright half] is recommended for rites in honor of gods and rites for prosperity; while the dark half is recommended for rites for deceased ancestors and for magic rites meant for a malevolent purpose" (Kane 1968–1977, vol. 5, p. 335). Bhaktapur's festivals do not sort neatly in such a way. There are festivals of the benign deities, of the dangerous deities and *twa:s*, and *melās* in both. Worship of living mothers and fathers is in the dark half, the Biskā: sequence spans light and dark fortnights, and so does the Swanti sequence. Yet, the major festivals with reference to death, to the loss of order, and to "antistructure" are, in fact, found in dark fortnights, where they represent a large segment of those fortnights' relatively few events. These include Bālā Ca:re [7], Silā Ca:re [15], Pāsā Ca:re [18], Bhagasti [4], Gāthā Muga: Ca:re [45], Sāpāru [52], Śmaśāna Bhailadya: Jātrā [64], Pulu Kisi Haigu [65], Dhala(n) Salā(n) [66], Kwa Pūjā [77], and Kicā Pūjā [78]. The events with reference to death in the bright fortnights are either secondary to the celebration of the household (as on the fifth day of Swanti),[13] or very minor (as in Yama: Dya: Thāigu [59] and Yau Dya: Punhi [62]).

The patterning of festival events by light and dark fortnights is not discursively salient. That is, although this patterning presumably gives a sense of meaningful order to the year, can be recognized by people when pointed out, and is probably known to some scholarly citizens, it must be pried out for the most part by an inspection of the distribution of annual events. The rice agricultural cycle and its enabling conditions, in contrast, is a salient and overt influence on the annual cycle. It not only influences the distribution and sequence of various events (as the bright and dark fortnights do) but also enters into the content, stories, and symbolism of those events in direct and obvious way. Images of fertility and generation, of cyclical appearance and disappearance, of protection and destruction in an equivocal balance, and of capricious vital forces just beyond the urban order and just beyond the social selves of its citizens—all this expresses, responds to, and builds on the implications of the rice and monsoon cycle and their phases.

The annual rice agricultural cycle has reflections elsewhere in the calendar beside in the Devī cycle itself. One event, Ya: Mārhi Punhi [9], comes when the annual consumption of the newly gathered rice harvest is about to begin. The benign goddess Lakṣmī is asked on this day to ensure that the rice consumed by the household will eventually be replaced. With the successful gathering in of the harvest, the emphasis has moved from the dangerous goddess of fertility to the benign goddess of the household stores. A major reflection of the agricultural cycle is in the shift that we have discussed at length in the kinds of events that occur in the segment of the year between the beginning of the rains at Bhagasti [40] and the symbolic end of the harvest at Mohanī. The concentration of all kinds of events during this period in a sort of crescendo of symbolic effort and the large number of events related to death and antistructure are congruent with the problematic nature of this period of the year.

A VIEW OF THE ANNUAL EVENTS WITH THE CITIZEN AT THEIR CENTER

The symbolic forms, events, sequences, narratives, and structures of narratives of the year's cycle comprise a substantial library of South Asian forms and ideas transformed and modulated so as to place Bhaktapur at their center. Yet, the yearly events from their humblest members to their most developed sequences of interrelated events speak to each of Bhaktapur's people not only of the universe as refracted and centered in Bhaktapur but also of the auditor-actor himself or herself in an attempt, so to speak, to deal with their eccentricity. The annual events, along with the city's other symbolic enactments, speak of being a "person" in Bhaktapur, a socially defined and placed and judged to be competent individual, a proper citizen. The annual cycle talks to the person of his or her relation to the household and its contained family, to the extended family, to the city and its significant components, to a moral world beyond the city, and to still another world, an amoral or meta-moral world, beyond that.

The household within its arena, the physical house, is represented in the contrasting perspectives of the mass of annual events as the place of affectionate solidarity. Relations with supportive, affectionate women (mothers, sisters, wives)—absent from the symbolism of the public city—are emphasized. Other primary household festivals are occasions for worshiping mothers and fathers and the benign deities, foci of human ideals, affection, and identifications—Lakṣmī as guardian of the storeroom, Śiva and his benign consort, Gaṇeśa, Viṣṇu, the Ṛṣis. In the movement of women among households, the household and its persons are related to a particular larger network of households, those of the "mother's brothers," of the women's *tha: che(n)*s, their "own homes." This network, as we have discussed in chapter 6, is a nexus of warm personal support when seen in contrast to the austere patriarchal network, the *phukī*, which must ensure proper lineage, *thar*, and civic behavior. When the household in this thematic mode of affectionate relationship spills beyond its boundaries, it is primarily into the neighborhood, the *twa:*, with its neighborhood Gaṇeśa shrine, which acts as a kind of fringe of family-like relationships around the household.

The household person lives in a sort of tube within the walls of the household, a tube that is open at both ends into time. One is born into the household from some previous incarnation—a vague idea that is not represented in the festivals. One will finally leave it to move on, keeping much of one's household self, into Yama's realm and to a pleasant rebirth or social heaven beyond. Death—ordinary death[14] within the household—is the threshold within this open-ended tube of personhood to a next moral stage, the stage where the person's morally earned soterial rewards or punishments will affect the conditions of his or her new life. Annual events comment on this threshold. They explore ways of holding on to household existence for as long as possible in the face of a humanized god of death, Yama, who honors his promises and whose messengers can be distracted and deceived. Household events also ensure the remembrance of the household's personal dead (not the distant unknown patrilineal "fathers" of the rites of passage) and, in conjunction with the public Sāpāru festival, ease their passage into Yama's realm. Thus the annual household events represent the career of the individual in his or her intimate personhood through a span of time encompassing both sides of death.

The household is a place of familiar refuge at the center of the systematic displacements an individual experiences in the course of the annual cycle. It is the here and now position within the "tube" of personhood extending from distant past into the postmortem future. The annual events also explore the limits and the phases of the person in another direction, "laterally," through the walls of ordinary household personhood. They probe downward into the person's body, outward into the city, and beyond. The lunar new year begins on Mhā Pūjā [1] with the worship of the "*mhā*"—a word indicating both body and self—of each individual. In the course of its worship the *mhā*'s elements, the *mahābhuta*, "of which the body is supposed to be composed and into which it is dissolved" (chap. 13), are represented. The body is given a meat-containing offering, and thus treated as if it were a meat-eating dangerous deity. This offering is not to the benign "indwelling god," usually thought of as Viṣṇu, who is or who inhabits an individual's soul, a soul habited somewhere in the body. This offering is to a deified something else, the supporting matrix that houses the soul, a matrix that exists everywhere beyond the bounds of the person and the household, and which represents everywhere in Bhaktapur's symbolism the threatening and sustaining amoral forces at the boundaries of the moral world.

Another move away from the household and household personhood, that from household to *phukī*, is little represented in annual festivals, although it is an aspect of all rites of passage and of all Tantric worship of upper-status lineage deities. There is a radical shift when an individual moves from household to *phukī*, as there is when he or she moves from the self to its bodily support. The move is from the affectionate moral order of household relations supported and represented by the benign deities to an order whose more burdensome morality is sternly enforced by means of the fear-inducing meanings, emotions, and practices associated with the dangerous deities and their sacrificial religion. *Phukī* worship makes use of symbolic resources similar to those used in urban festival integration, but in the annual cycle it is not represented so much as a nested unit of the city but as a kind of parallel to it. The locus of its main annual ceremony is not the Āga(n) House within the city, but the Digu God shrine beyond the city's boundaries. The *phukī* and the city are both in their own, different, ways at the perimeter of the household and share the same kinds of order-ensuring forces. It is in the rites of passage that the *phukī*'s force over the household is centrally emphasized, and in those rites the *phukī*'s relation to the organization of the larger city is also not particularly emphasized, but only sketched in movements to the maṇḍalic *pīṭhas*.

Outside of the household people are reminded that the family-based moral order, the order of love and respect and of the forms of valid shame and guilt based on intimate family experience, is shared throughout the city where it is written large in support of king, Brahman and the social hierarchy as members of a great family. The festivals of the benign deities—primarily in the *jātrā* processions along the main city festival route, the *pradakṣiṇāpatha*, and secondarily in visit to temples of benign deities—display and honor these moral values. In this group of civic enactments the ordinary person of the houehold extends his or her imagery of the household to the larger city.

But this extension of household imagery is a minor move in Bhaktapur's festivals. For the most part the festivals in public space deal with something else, paralleling the shift in the move from household to *phukī*. The festivals which use dangerous deities to designate civic areas and their relations make use of forces and images different from those used by the household and its extensions. Here imagery and implications played down or hidden in the annual cycle's imagery of household and household person are brought forth, elaborated, shaped, distorted, and given a social placement in the representation of the fertile, dangerous, and enforcing borderlands of social order and personhood.

When people move still further out of the household, beyond the borders of the city, they encounter a new realm of a quite different kind. There are eight events ([3], [4], [7], [15], [33], [39], [46], and [51]) during the annual cycle where a shrine far outside of the city (as opposed to just outside of its borders) is the focus, sometimes for all who choose to go, or (in three cases) for those who have had a death in their family within some designated period of time. Women also may make pilgrimages to valley shrines during the period of the Swāthanī Vrata. The principal deities of these pilgrimage sites are, with one only apparent exception,[15] once again benign deities. These out-of-the-city events bring people from Bhaktapur into crowds of Nepalis and, sometimes, North Indians from many different ethnic groups. They are movements out of Bhaktapur's particular order into a larger, less differentiated humanity. In these far out-of-the-city activities, Bhaktapur is represented negatively, as it were, in leaving it. What is found "out there" is a larger community of fully human beings—albeit on vacation from various kinds of local social orders—in a context of references to moral orders beyond Bhaktapur's civic order, the cosmic realms of Viṣṇu and Śiva, their heavenly cities and the realms of the remembered and beloved dead. Similar in meaning to the *melās*, and associated, as several of the annual *melās* are, with the fate of the souls of Bhaktapur's recent dead, is the Sāpāru carnival.

Melās and carnival are thoroughly *within* the moral realm. Here, in a familiar anthropological phrasing (Victor Turner 1969), there is a movement toward a generalized human "*communitas*" that is substituted for local division and categories of social ordering. In Bhaktapur's example of *carnival*, a characteristic universal genre for an escape from ordinary civic order, the carnival associated with Sāpāru [48], some privileged men playfully divest themselves of their roles and take on other familiar roles. Presumably in the process of shedding one role and pretending another—including some nonhuman ones—they enjoy for a few hours the brotherly excitement of shared being and omnipotentiality rather than the restrained pleasures of the security of social order. However, this escape from structure in Bhaktapur remains for the most part carefully within the bounds of the deeper categories of social order. Men switch roles, but do not reject the reality of role itself, nor, for the most part, of familiar culturally designated roles. Even in the farthest reaches of *communitas* the social category of "humanity" and its varieties is still kept. As Turner (1969, 131f.) puts it, suggesting the horizon of *communitas*, but going far beyond what Bhaktapur's *melās*, carnival, and other annual moral antistructural moves achieve:

> Essentially, communitas is a relationship between concrete, historical, idiosyncratic individuals. These individuals are not segmentalized into roles and statuses but confront one another rather in the manner of Martin Buber's "I and Thou." Along with this direct, immediate, and total confrontation of human identities, there tends to go a model of society as a homogeneous, unstructured communitas, whose boundaries are ideally conterminous with those of the human species.

Some of the pleasures of the Sāpāru carnival are quite different from the escape from society into an unsegmented pan-human I-Thouness. There is also a darker possibility seen in some few of its images—those of demons and powerful beasts—of a more radical escape, this time from human identity itself. "*Communitas*" versus "social-structural order" is a tension, as the quotation from Turner points out, within "the social," a tension between "models of society," of aspects of "human identities." The tension here is between two *moral orders*, a "social-structural" one and a "communal" one. This particular dichotomy of "structural" and "antistructural" within the human realm is contained and represented in Bhaktapur in the terms of individuals' relations to the moral deities and to morally ordered death. In myth its prototypical mediating figure is Śiva, who is a marginal moral actor within the realm of the gods and who is easily duped into giving morally unmerited rewards, familiar from many traditional stories, rewards that are misused by the unworthy recipients. Thus, during Silā Ca:re [15] people mimic a legendary "accident" in which a preoccupied Śiva was deceived into taking someone directly and totally undeservedly into his heaven. Playing with chance and luck in festival gambling [Swanti] and the use of deceits and manipulations that distract and delay Yama's death-announcing messengers during the same sequence are examples of other *human* practices rehearsed in the course of the annual cycle that allow people to get around the heavy moral pressures of Bhaktapur's structured world.

Turner's 1969 treatment of structure and antistructure has a second antistructural option besides *communitas*, the Hobbesian "war of all against all" (1969, 131). Bhaktapur's festivals and symbolic resources also explore another kind of opposition to "structure" than *communitas*, bringing a subsidiary theme of carnival—its demons and beasts—to the fore. This opposition places yet another world in opposition to the realm shared by both *communitas* and social structure; it opposes a meta-moral or amoral world to a moral one. This is the nonsocial world around the city and within the individual, a realm in which *communitas* is irrelevant as the very categories of community and human are themselves dissolved. For Bhaktapur, however, this realm is not Hobbes's antisocial world. Life for humans within Bhaktapur's amoral realms might indeed have been conceived as "solitary, poor, nasty, brutish, and short"—or even worse, for the predatory dangers portrayed in Bhaktapur's civic environs are perhaps more ingeniously terrrible even than Hobbes's "nature." But Bhaktapur's antisocial realm is not the near chaos Hobbes feared if the then recently achieved balance between newly individualized citizens freed from a restraining medieval world view and the equally new nation-states were to be disturbed. The realm of the amoral in Bhaktapur—neither social-structural nor *communitas*—is extensively represented and encountered as consisting of underlying and environing forms and forces that have their own kind of mysterious, vital, often demonic order out of which the moral order draws its energies, whose forces the moral order depends on and uses to protect itself, against which it provides its own peculiar kind of order. This balancing and restorative tension is clearly represented in the stories of the *Devī Māhātmya* and the festivals of the Devī cycle. The internal tension and oscillations between the benign (moral) and dangerous (amoral) deities is at the service of a larger order, which in its moments of exact balance is congenial to gods and humans, if not to that larger order's enemies, the Asuras. When the moral order *and* its context are in proper balance, as they become periodically as the result of Devī's bloody victories against the Asuras, then, as the *Devī Māhātmya* puts it, "favorable winds began to blow; the sun shone with perfect brilliance, the sacred fire burnt in a tranquil manner; and the strange sounds that had filled the quarters of space also disappeared" (X, 27; Agrawala 1963, 127). As represented in the imagery of the annual cycle, Bhaktapur's moral world and amoral worlds together assure, ultimately, a higher ordering. The "Asuras" are vague notations for still another, more radical, antiorder set against this balanced system, notations for some Nibelungian revolution that would plunge both gods and humans into chaos for the alien purposes of some other class of beings. And even this is only chaos from the limited point of view of gods and men.[16]

The annual cycle of events systematically defines certain aspects of their city and their personhood to individuals, but it does not celebrate a unified "individuality."[17] In their relation to individuals, the different kinds of events in the cycle have to do with the different aspects of the person that are realized in the various arenas that are the concern of the annual cycle. The individual is portrayed as a dynamic and delicate interface, as constructed of constituent elements that can dissolve into something else, as shifting according to (and thus as being dependent on) his or her relation to different civic arenas, as located in, generated out of, and defended against the environing amoral worlds found outside of the various urban units and, in their internal relation to an individual's body and mind, beyond the inner boundaries of the individual's self.

In the course of the annual cycle individuals rehearse their membership in most of the nested units that define their complex citizenship in Bhaktapur—the city's beyond, the city itself, the city half, the maṇḍalic section, the *twa:*,[18] the *phukī* and the household family. For the most part they do this directly, not via representatives. The use of representative actors to indicate the hierarchy is exceptional. In the course of the annual cycle Bhaktapur moves each of its citizens into each of the arenas that are the essential units and varieties of their social experience and of phases of their selves. Positioned successively in each arena, citizens find the appropriate forms of the city's symbolic world rotating around them, engaging them in contemplation and action.

Bhaktapur's other symbolic enactments, driven by other tempos than the annual cycle, have other centers than the city itself, and from the points of view of their participants are local and private affairs. They concern the cellular components of the city that the larger public order of the city presupposes and with which it must deal, components whose outputs are necessary for the order of the larger city.[19] It is the annual cycle that describes and, in part, makes the integrated civic order of city and citizen in which these smaller symbolic enactments find their place.

CHAPTER SEVENTEEN

What Is Bhaktapur that a Newar May Know It?[1]

> Theseus. *And as imagination bodies forth*
> *The forms of things unknown, the poet's pen*
> *Turns them to shapes, and gives to aery nothing*
> *A local habitation and a name.*
>
> Shakespeare, *A Midsummer Night's Dream*

STRUCTURES OF THE IMAGINATION

We have been most centrally concerned in this book with one particular aspect of Bhaktapur's communal life, its poetic imagination, and we have emphasized, for the most part, only one of the subjects of that imagination, the city itself. Bhaktapur's imagination has worked over a span of several centuries, making use of the opportunities and constraints of its history and its context in the building of a world. As its citizens, at the same time poets and audience, strove to build a coherent civic world out of the opportunities provided by history, tradition, and accident, they became progressively enveloped in and shaped by what they were building.

Shakespeare's Theseus discovered a midsummer night's dream that he found "more strange than true," in contrast with the unstrange truths of Athens. Yet, as Puck reminds us at the end, Theseus, his dream and his truth, all is our dream. We have been concerned for the most part with Bhaktapur's dream within a dream—those particular aspects of Bhaktapur's order that were "marked," that is, precisely, *made strange* to Bhaktapurians, although as Hindus and not Athenians Bhaktapurians find them to be members of an order that is both strange *and*, in some sense, true. That order, the "religious realm," which is where most of Bhaktapur's marked symbols are situated, is there generally sharply distinguished from the "ordinary," the unstrange. As we characterized the marked realm (for the sake of considering its margins in chap. 11) its "proper spaces are the temple or shrine, the purified, bounded and isolated *pūjā* areas in houses, the ideal spaces of the city carved out through the positions and festival movements of the deities; its expert workers are the priests; its time is the calendrically determined eternally recurring times of festival or that of rites of passage or of crisis-generated or prophylactic *ad hoc* worship; its proper action is in ritual and the traditionally specified actions of the festivals."

Bhaktapur's referral of most of its marked symbolic forms and enactments—myth, legend, drama, literature, poetry, and music—to the realm of the gods is one of the city's most striking features to a secularized Westerner. It is the city's way of making all these forms *both* strange and true, and thus giving them great seriousness and force. Not as is sometimes said of religious matters, "ultimate" seriousness and force, for there is in some of Bhaktapur's thought, particularly in the implications of its Tantrism, something else more profound beyond the realm and reality of the city's gods. But it is that system of deities that puts Bhaktapur at the center of a cosmos and that provides the characteristic emblems of the realm of strange symbols.

Alongside the strange world of marked symbols Bhaktapur has also constructed, as all communities do—sometimes yielding to, sometimes molding, sometimes denying recalcitrant "physical facts"—a world of self-serving common sense, a world meaningful in its "embedded symbolism." This world, illustrated in this book in our discussions of the city's larger and smaller social orders and by the ideas, feelings, and actions of the "purity complex," is the kind of order that Theseus confidently set as truth against dream. The strange and the ordinary are united in Bhaktapur's urban mesocosm in a common world mediating between the microcosm of each of its citizens and the macrocosm.[2]

We have been occupied throughout with details of that mesocosm. We wish now, in summary, to consider some of the most general aspects of Bhaktapur's order, the arrangements that give some overall coherence and characteristic style to Bhaktapur's multilayered and segmented world. We will make a working distinction between two interrelated issues. First we will consider some very general aspects of the city's symbolic forms that contribute to the particular *meaningfulness*, the particular coherence, of Bhaktapur's life. Then we will consider some of the arrangements of symbolic forms that serve to make, under Bhaktapur's special circumstances, potentially meaningful forms *intelligible*, and thus, ultimately, *significant*. Both are aspects of our orienting question, "What is Bhaktapur that a Newar may know it?"

"Meaningfulness" and "intelligibility" are really proposals toward an explanation for why, once many other features are in place, Bhaktapur is the way it is. We will in the final section of this chapter make some further probes at distinguishing the necessary from the contingent in Bhaktapur's order in a search for that city's typological and explainable features.

SPHERES, STRUCTURES, AND OPPOSITIONS

If it seems unproblematic to characterize Bhaktapur's strange order as mostly "religious," the symmetrical characterization of its ordinary, everyday order as "secular" *is* problematic. Louis Dumont approached this asymmetry by characterizing for Hindu societies one particular component of our strange order as a religious *sphere* within a larger religious *universe*, a universe that also encompasses a "secular" sphere.

Dumont was specifically trying to distinguish the functions of the king and the Brahman. He thus proposed (1970, 68) that Hindu religious universes were characterized by a royal, secular, *political sphere* of the king, a sphere characterized by power or force, opposed to a *religious sphere* of the Brahman, a realm of "values and norms." We argued in chapter 10 that this particular phrasing was problematic and even misleading for Bhaktapur.

We have in the course of this book encountered many contrasting terms, emphasizing some and touching on others. Among them are dangerous deities and benign deities; Tantric religion and ordinary religion; "secular" and "religious"; conventional and ritual; king (and court, merchants, farmers, craftsmen) and Brahman (and other kinds of priests, and polluting *thar*s); worldly power and other-worldly force; unclean (epitomized by the Po[n]) and clean (epitomized by the Brahman); orders where purity is irrelevant and orders where purity is central; amoral realms and moral realms; the bordering outside of the city (and of each of its component units) and the inside of the city (and of each of its component units); life stages for males prior to the *Kaetā Pūjā* ceremony and subsequent life stages. Among these heterogeneous oppositions, for any particular contrast the right hand term is that of the ordinary dharma and/or of one of the functions of the Rājopādhyāya Brahman as highlighted by the contrast. The collection of contrasts and oppositions to "Brahman" are not as a whole unified, at least not in their surface characteristics. Taken together, however, they help anatomize Bhaktapur's larger traditional ordering of meaning.

That order is more complex than a secular royalty versus a sphere of Brahmanical religiosity expressing the *dharmic* world of values and norms. Let us review some of the aspects of that order which are in some ways peculiar to Bhaktapur and South Asian places that are or were like it.

1. As we have noted in chapters 8 and 9, in many Hindu communities in South Asia the religion of the dangerous deities is thought by the upper-status Hindus in those communities (and by many modern Indians) as an inferior, illegitimate, superstitious folk religion, alien to true Hinduism and its Aryan roots. The legitimate religion of such communities is held by these elites to be the moral Brahmanical religion concerned with benign deities, representatives of an ideal patriarchal social order. In Bhaktapur, in contrast, the dangerous deities are fully legitimate, and not only legitimate but at the focus of aristocratic and royal Tantrism. Bhaktapur thus has two equally legitimate religious spheres within its religious universe, a religion of moral order (ordinary Brahmanical religion) and a religion of power (the cult of the dangerous deities both as Tantrism and as the practices of noninitiates). The religion of power variously supports, evades, and transcends the moral order.

We have repeatdly characterized the dangerous deities and their religion as representing the environing forces that both threaten and sustain the moral religion of the city. So viewed, the dangerous deities are at a systematically "higher" level than the benign ones in the sense that they provide the context for the moral religion, respond to problems that the moral system cannot deal with, and in so doing protect the moral realm. The polytheistic separation and discrimination of deities makes such a two-tiered representation possible, this being one aspect of the complex ordering of the city's pantheon into a fundamentally useful system of signs (chap. 8).[3]

2. Bhaktapur's splitting of religious spheres within the religious universe makes untenable a simple opposition of a *religious* sphere concerned with values and a secular, political sphere, that of the king, concerned with power. For there is a special religious precinct concerned with power and those who use it within the "secular" sphere. That secular power in Bhaktapur's world view includes much more than the political power of the king and *kṣatriya;* it includes all direct operations

on the world that are not fully produced by the assent to the system of *dharmic* values. The religion of power is the proper religion of kings, *kṣatriyas*, merchants, farmers, and craftsmen—not as individuals who must follow the *dharma*, must worry about rebirths, and whose priest, serving them as generalized individuals is the Brahman as *purohita*—but in their particular functions as specialists in the "direct" manipulation of the world, through what Dumont calls "force" and places in opposition to the ordering of "values and norms."

3. The use of force in this sense thus characterizes not only the king's activities but also the activities of a large segment of the city's hierarchy cutting through from its top almost to its bottom. This vertical segment of Bhaktapur's social system is defined against a large group of what we have called (in chap. 10) "priests," "auxiliary priests," and "covert priests," who are united most saliently as manipulators of purity. The manipulation of purity characterizes this latter segment of Bhaktapur's organization, as the manipulation of force characterizes the former.

Tantric priests and Brahmans in their particular functions as Tantric priests (and, for different reasons, the Jośi astrologers) do not belong with the group of purity manipulators and thus to the religion of "values and norms," but to the sphere of the manipulators of power. They deal with power in the universe through attempts at understanding, alliance, avoidance, and forceful coercion in close metaphorical alliance with the city's other technicians of power.

It is the Brahman as Brahman and the various sorts of purity manipulators who derive from him and support him who deal with that segment of Bhaktapur's life which is constituted through definitions of what persons and systems of persons are and should be. They manipulate that particular system of symbols that is effective because it shapes and helps constitute the arena of definition and value. They are primarily technicians of those symbolic forms that *constitute* actors and community in Bhaktapur.

The contrasting segment of Bhaktapur also makes use of symbols to represent and support their functions. But their primary functions, no matter how important their symbolic component, work directly on the world in a different way—through direct manipulation of materials and physical forces and of those psychological forces that make political threats and promises effective. They are thus allied with the priests of Tantrism who in local conception use power and who, viewed from outside the phrasings of Hinduism, make use of mental forces beyond the self and the social person constituted with the aid of the religion of the benign gods to serve, sustain, control, or dissolve that person.

4. The symbolic forms and enactments of both the religion of power and the religion of norms and values are within the realm of the extraordinary. The roots of each in the ordinary are different. The moral religion augments, resonates with, and puts to social use images of ideal and tolerable social behavior; the religion of the dangerous deities augments, resonates with, and transforms for social purposes forms that are suppressed in ordinary awareness, that are unnamed and unspoken in ordinary discourse with others and within the self, that are relegated to and express the non-social aspects of the mind, alien to the person and to the proper logic and categories of everyday life.

This suppressed realm is represented with suitable transformations within the realm of dangerous religion, where its forces are tentatively captured for the purposes of social order itself. The original nature and dangers of these forces and their capturing and social transformation into tentatively domesticated forms are vividly portrayed in Bhaktapur's myths and, most concretely, in its legends,[4] as well as in the city's symbolic enactments.

Legends bring together dangerous deities and heroic figures in a realm of the marvelous. They suggest that even the secularized sphere of power has, in fact, a certain uncanny quality, for it represents—as does the associated order of the dangerous deities—a violation and transcendence of the central dharmic moral order. Techniques of power, political force, magic, Tantra, wish and dream, dangerous deities, and demonic forces all inhabit—from the viewpoint of the morally organized city life—one metaphorically unified sphere. That sphere is not exactly what the modern world wishes to mean by the secular.

Yet, in Bhaktapur's world of shifting viewpoints the Brahman's religious sphere, at least as exemplified by the Brahman himself, is not always seen as an unproblematic heightening of the banal and ordinary. From some viewpoints the entanglement in the manipulation of the system of purity and impurity of the Brahman and his allies has something suspect about it, something encumbering and unpleasant, something that is not represented in contrast but, rather, directly by the state of the untouchable. The sphere of the Brahman's operations has in such perspectives, where the "secular" is privileged, a displacement from the banal quite different from the displacement, from another viewpoint, of the realm of power.

5. It is not only the "sphere of power" that uses force. The realm of norms and values and its religion has, of course, characteristic "forces" at its disposal. These are the familiar forces that sustain the unity of any moral community—a great miscellaneous variety of agreements on what is real and what is sane, of definitions, identifications, values, goals, concerns for face and reputation and being loved or admired, and the wish to avoid guilt and shame and ostracism.

These forces are internal to the community. They help constitute it and keep it going from moment to moment. They are made, to a considerable degree, to seem ordinary and naturalized forces. This naturalization, generating the force of the taken for granted, is, as we have asserted in chapter 2, much more difficult to achieve in Bhaktapur than in some other simpler communities, and people often become potentially subversive skeptics who must be kept in line by the emergence of the superordinate forces of the marked realm.

6. Bhaktapur places most of its marked symbols in the religious sphere, which is the realm of the gods, a bounded domain of a still larger Hindu religious universe, a great mind in which gods along with all living, sentient things participate, out of which they are generated, whose immutable moral laws they are subject to, and whose ultimate nature they can come to glimpse. Other complex civilizations whose citizens shared the "symbol hunger" (chap. 2) of Bhaktapur's citizens have elaborated realms of marked symbols, but came to place them elsewhere. Thus, in the West, secular drama, literature and art, are marked as extraordinary—by setting, cadence, presentation, and other devices—but have come to represent a class of communication that is in some sense "imaginary," "*only* symbolic," not to be taken literally. Until its contemporary transformations most of Bhaktapur's extraordinary statements have not called themselves imaginary, but as belonging to another sort of reality, the reality of the gods' divine sphere. In a different bounding than the Western one, both Bhaktapur's everyday reality and the reality of the gods can be seen as imaginary, as *māyā*, when grasped by the highest intuitions of religious awareness. But, for the most part, gods and Bhaktapurians are content to remain in their divine illusions and by putting the imagination of the extra-

ordinary in a religious subsphere to give it and its representations the strongest possible position in the life of the community and its citizen's minds.[5]

7. The ordinary masquerades as simple reality. Bhaktapur sometimes attempts to make problematic things natural by forcefully anchoring them in the sensually perceived world. The lives of the Po(n)s, in a vivid example, are manipulated so that their connection with real feces and the taking of life and their degraded living conditions become the perceptually based evidence for the reality of the system of pollution and purity and of the effects of bad (and thus, in contrast, good) *karma*. It is the problematic aspects of *karmic* and pollution theory, debatable and rethinkable in the terms of the other doctrines and viewpoints common in Bhaktapur, that makes such anchoring in the apparently objective useful.

8. Bhaktapur's sphere of the religious and of the ordinary have boundaries, boundaries of a peculiar permeability (see fig. 35). We have commented on the crossing of boundaries—the movements of the gods in their processions out of their temples into a carefully designated city space, and of the Nine Durgās in their somewhat more chaotic forays into the city's neighborhoods. These moves cross the boundaries of sacred enclosures and allow the usually isolated marked realm to spill, within some limits, over into the ordinary. The closeness to the ordinary of Bhaktapur's religious sphere—in contrast to the self-banishment of the Judeo-Christian-Islamic transcendent deity—as well as the air of autonomy and reality of those deities in their on-the-ground manifestations in comparison with the "imaginary" and "conventional" status of latter-day Western art and literature, give the boundaries between the ordinary and the strange realms a special and problematic permeability and make urgent the problem of defining places for the gods, keeping them in those places if possible, and dealing with them if they leave them. For Hindu deities, at least in Bhaktapur, do not need the force of a Western *miracle* to enter the secular realm.

9. Not only do symbolic constructions occasionally cross boundaries to invade the realm of the ordinary but, in another direction, the "real" may be thought of as occasionally crossing what in the West is often taken as an inviolable boundary into the symbolic. Westerners, as represented by Freud, expect the "overt" content of a symbol of emo-

Figure 35. Problems on the boundary between the ordinary and the extraordinary. The living goddess Kumārī has her running nose wiped by her attendant.

tional importance ideally to be a disguised transformation of some powerfully disruptive complex of ideas and emotions that is its latent meaning or reference. A censor holds the two kinds of meaning apart and helps accomplish the bowdlerization of the overt form. If the symbolic form seems to stand for itself, especially if it is as fearsome and unpalatable as the raw unconscious form is thought to be, then Westerners sense a problem, something has collapsed, some reference has disappeared.[6] Bhaktapur uses many "symbolic forms" that are directly in themselves powerfully meaningful, representing exactly the sorts of things that are—or were—presumably relegated to Western unconsciousness. In one dramatic example, human sacrifice, Bhaktapur once used the actual murder/sacrifice of its citizens to "represent" murder/sacrifice. It has had to give up this resource and the actual sexual intercourse of nonspouses in Tantrism, but it still uses direct and powerful images of sexual arousal (e.g., Tantric images of Bhairava with an erect penis, a wild look and a flaming halo [see fig. 17, above]), of sexual intercourse (for example in temple images and in the banging together of the chariots in Biskā:), of cannibalistic women, of women who change from images of sexual desire to images of death, of murder and dismemberment of human bodies. It uses these images not so much to *represent* or *symbolize* something, as to *do* something.

Bhaktapur's symbols of this sort do not take their power from their references and latent meanings, they are directly meaningful in themselves. Their disguise is not in a transformation of form—sword or umbrella for penis—so much as in an isolation of such powerful forms from their experiential bases, above all their bases in the life of the family,[7] and a new placement in the religious sphere.

10. As we noted in chapter 16, some matters of what might seem to be of great potential interest in Bhaktapur are ignored in the city's symbolic enactments. We have commented in previous chapters on the privileged status of certain solidarities—the family, the *phukī*, the internal membership of the *twa:*, and the hierarchically ranked *thar*s—whose members are not represented as antagonists in the year's many representations of conflict and antagonism. In this light, conflict and antagonism within these essential units is "not thought about" in the annual enactments, and is displaced to safer realms. Intrafamilial conflict is illustrated in some of the *pyākha(n)*s of Sāpāru, typically where two men represent a farmer and his wife fighting, and is amply and presumably safely represented in tales about unfaithful and dangerous

wives, wicked stepmothers, and weak kings usually set in a magical, fairy tale mode.[8] These relatively permissive realms are more playful, less real, than the religious spheres of the city. They are only stories; in them fantasy may be taken to be just fantasy.

RESOURCES FOR MAKING MEANING INTELLIGIBLE

We have reviewed here, and throughout this volume, some of the arrangements of forms that contribute to the style of Bhaktapur's symbolic organization and make it seem familiar, coherent, engaging, meaningful, and important to many, most probably to most, of its people. Still more is required, however; that organization must be apprehensible. The mass of symbolic forms must be organized so that people can grasp and remember and understand something about them and find their way about in them. We introduced the problem of intelligibility in our discussion (in chap. 8) of the city's pantheon as an organized "system of signs." The pantheon is sorted into classes of supernaturals distinguished by simple oppositions, oppositions that are not arbitrary but are semantically related to the meaning of the class. Those oppositions distinguish the classes with the same sort of didactic efficiency as the opposition of the dangerous and forbidding, fiery and bloody red to the encouraging living green of traffic signals. The contrasts that distinguished the classes are further arranged in the form of a successively branching tree, leading step by step ultimately to the closest and most familiar class of deities, the benign deities. *Within* each class of supernaturals members are distinguished by family differences based on a complex variety of differentiated features requiring a concrete familiarity with the class, for some classes a specialist's knowledge, in order to distinguish one member from another.

These particular features of the city pantheon can be thought of as attempted solutions to Bhaktapur's considerable problem of the intelligibility of its hypertrophied symbolic world. Let us recall—and comment further on—some of the resources for intelligibility we have emphasized in our discussions of Bhaktapur's complexity, bearing in mind that these prevalent resources have implications in themselves not only for intelligibility but also for meaning.

1. *Levels.* We have repeatedly encountered hierarchical arrangements of classes of forms—for example, among *thar*s, supernaturals,

spaces, systems of behavioral control, and aspects of "the person," into discontinuous, successively more inclusive, "higher" levels. Bhaktapur uses levels extensively for distinguishing and ordering classes (and, often, subgroupings within classes) of phenomena and ideas. The levels have both formal and semantic implications. Higher levels, by definition more inclusive, are also usually less specialized, have more potential and generative (in contrast to concrete, specialized, and applied) power, are corrective of the errors and problems of the next lower level, and thus are activated when the low level's autonomous self-controls do not work or are insufficient for that lower level's own purposes. But the higher levels have purposes of their own and are thus ambivalently viewed. Sometimes they are helpful and their resources are sought; sometimes they are punitively corrective or simply destructive, and they must be avoided.

In an exemplary contrast that we have repeatedly emphasized, the dangerous deities are related to the benign ones as being more powerful, as being on the outside, as actuated when the powers of the benign deities are insufficient, as being further away than the benign deities from the concrete, human, and ordinary. We have usually called them "amoral," but they are more precisely "meta-moral," related to but "above" the urban system of morals. They protect it while being alien to it; that is, in a way typical of successive levels, they are intimately related to lower levels without sharing their characteristic qualities.[9]

Within the moral realm the behaviors and categories related to purity and the avoidance of shame and loss of face are similarly discontinuous from those related to power and the avoidance of danger, punishment, sin, guilt, and fear. This latter complex of moral forces is at a different, higher level, insofar as those forces come into operation when the controls of the purity system are not sufficient or are breached. These dangerous forces are closely related to the world of magic and of meta-moral power that lies at the edges of the ordinary world. In a way charactertistic of adjoining levels, the moral world organized through adherence to the *dharma* and through concerns with purity and proper behavior is a bulwark against these other forces and in the normal run of things prevents them from emerging.

There are hierarchical characteristics differentiating the stories told of deities in their existence in transcendent space and time, "myths," on the one hand from their appearances in the ordinary world, "legends," on the other. We have had many examples of both throughout the book. The myths are for the most part standard and ancient South

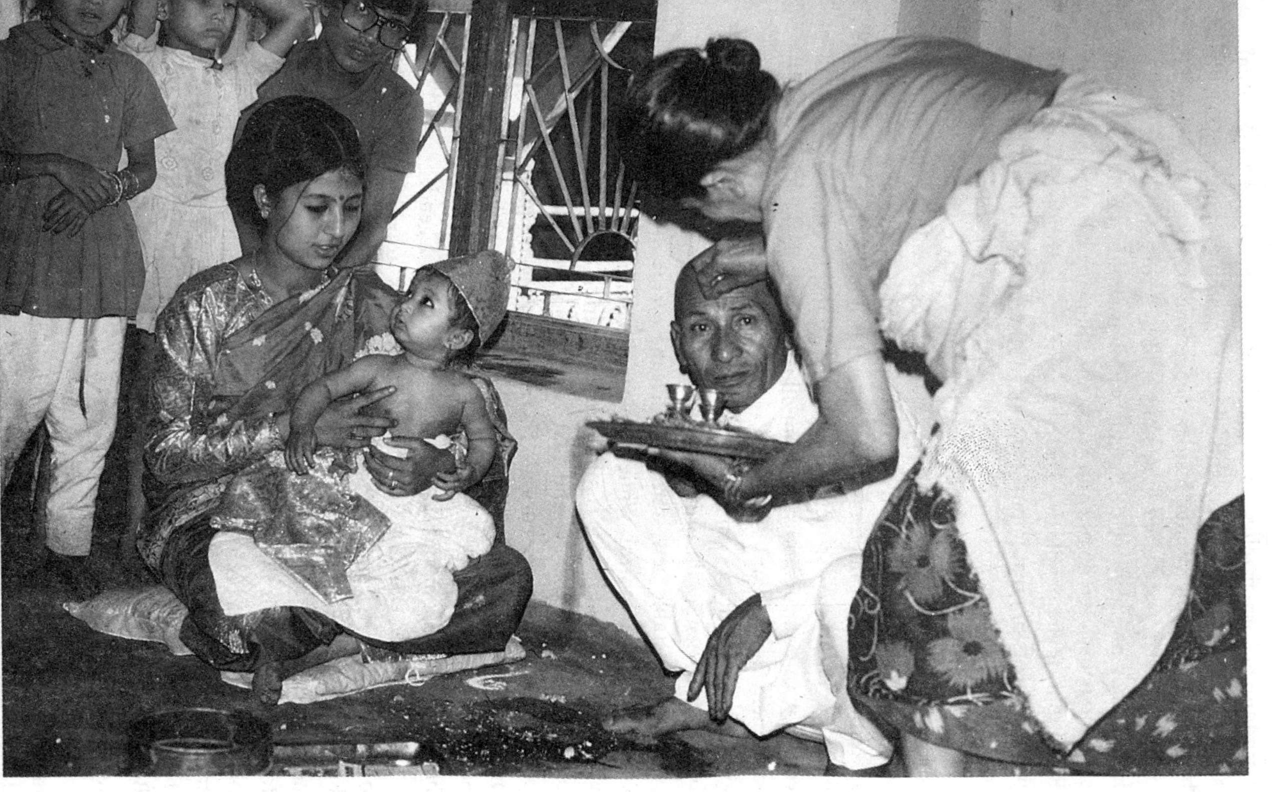

Figure 36. Rites of passage. A young mother, her first son, and the family's Brahman *purohita* at the child's *Macā Ja(n)ko*, the "rice feeding" *saṃskāra*.

Asian forms. They are often formally told or read at some given point in a traditional formal religious sequence where they relate some ritual action to transcendent time and space. Legends, in contrast, usually have to do with the specific history, space, and social arrangements of Bhaktapur. They are often informally told by professional storytellers in the city's public space or by elders in households. Legends recount encounters between deities and high status humans who are citizens of Bhaktapur or else people of essential importance in its history, and they portray events of great importance not for the cosmos, as in myths, but for Bhaktapur. Legends border on another group of stories, "wonder tales" (the story of the princess and the snakes has qualities of both), that are more purely "recreational," but legends recount events that are supposed to have taken place in real time and real space, a time and space that take their importance from—and that are central to—Bhaktapur's special history, space, and location. Myths, in contrast, are concerned with events equidistant from all times and places. The essential movement in Bhaktapur's legends is the transition from an uncanny encounter with deities on the ground—a marginal and fleeting event belonging to neither the order of the transcendent world nor to the civic world—to a stable new state in which the events of the legend have come under civic control. While people may temporarily participate in a myth (as in Mohanī), this is a kind of celebration of a juncture of two orders, civic and cosmic, and that celebration must be cyclically repeated in a continuing renewal. The events of legend produce a once and for all transformation into ordinary time, space, and order. Rarely, notably in the complex story of Taleju's origin and history, a story begins in a mythic mode and then modulates into a legend.

The unstable situations portrayed in legends are resolved by the overcoming of the uncanny transitional state through the actions of high-status figures—Bhaktapur's ambivalently viewed version of the hero—resulting in the transformation and civic "capturing" of the forces portrayed in the legend. The resolution of the legend thus explains and fortifies both city order and traditional high status. The high status justified in legends is always a status of power, a prince, king or Tantric practitioner, and not the high moral status of the Brahman as Brahman. Legends are thus related to the protection of the moral order rather than its internal operation.

There is thus a movement from a most abstract and general level in myth, to a more concrete and local mode in legend, and then a further descent into the present concrete symbolic enactments of the city. In that final move there is a passage from a "mere" recounting of events to a fuller symbolic enactment in which much more than speech is involved, a participation through complex action as well as through listening and imagining.[10] The deities are transformed as they move from myth to legend to their embodiment in plastic forms and their controlled engagement in the symbolic enactments of the city.[11] Thus myth-legend-symbolic enactment represent, in many aspects, successively descending levels—cosmic, transitional, and civic.

The shared implications of steps in hierarchical classification allow for cross-cutting metaphorical bridges among particular classes in either the same or different hierarchies that can be made to seem to be at the same level. We noted in our discussion of the genealogies of various goddesses that forms considered to have the same level of abstraction, inclusiveness, and, thus, potential power, could be seen as in some sense equivalent, as being "sisters." King and total city and the full goddesses and behavioral controls related to power are all tied together through the shared implications of the equivalent level of each item in its particular hierarchy, and one can find other bridges both at humbler and at still higher levels.[12]

2. *Redundancy and filtering.* We have commented, especially in chapter 16, on the redundant portrayal of a limited set of particularly significant statements throughout the myriad forms of symbols and symbolic enactments. Repetition in a sense creates the significant statements that are being repeated by filtering out through comparison and contrast a selected and simplified sample of the very complex cluster of meanings attached to many of the city's symbolic forms.

Śiva in himself is, as we discussed in chapter 8, an enormously complex figure, but his position in any particular domain or context of Bhaktapur's gods selects and simplifies, for the purposes of that domain, his impact. The Nine Durgās' *pyākha(n)* is a very complicated performance, dense with meaning, full of historical and areal residues and of psychological resonances, but its psychosocial significance is much simpler when considered in comparion and contrast with the city's other symbolic enactments. The multitude of other meanings carried by the *pyākha(n)* contributes to its ability to fascinate and to engage a heterogeneous variety of community members, but this is another aspect of effectiveness of symbolic forms than their specific contribution to the construction of an urban order. In a Western analogy, returning once again to our simplistic traffic light, if we are concerned with the particular integrative relation of such lights to the urban order we are concerned solely or primarly with that particular aspect of the redness of a light that means generally and powerfully "Stop!" in its contrast to that aspect of greenness that means "Go!"

3. *Discrete categories.* Redundancy and filtering produce relatively simple and effective symbolic elements. Those symplified elements are for the most part "discrete" or "digital." For the purposes of the public order a Brahman is or is not a Brahman, a deity is Śiva or not Śiva. Thus they can be unambiguously recognized and do their work, and be placed in the domains and hierarchies that amplify and transform their meaning. The "more or less" and "sort of" calculations of the private realm are not adequate here.

It is this digital definition of elements in the public realm that is achieved through rites of passage, iconic criteria for icons, rituals of bringing effective life into statues, and by the emphasis on purity in the public realm of humans as social types. A polluted Brahman is not a Brahman in the dynamics of the public social realm whatever he may be known as concretely to family, friends, and neighbors.

4. *Membership in a domain.* The discrete units of Bhaktapur's public system are, like all units of meaning, largely meaningful in their relationships and not in themselves. But those relationships are not the limitless shifting contexts of private experience, they are rather a matter of membership in clearly delineated domains and hierarchies whose other members are also discrete units. In Bhaktapur it is taken for granted that meaning accrues from such relationships. There is no attempt to escape from context dependency through doctrines of individuality and essence. Thus when the context changes a unit changes in meaning and may ultimately loose all its public meaning. A great deal of effort in Bhaktapur is devoted to maintaining the contexts of definition, particularly the definition of public social actors who are what they are not so much because of their private history nor of some inherited biological essence, but because of their ongoing contexts.

In those cases where a unit may belong to different domains or levels, its different positions and, thus, meanings are always clearly designated by some "context marker" that signifies whether, for example, killing an animal is murder or a sacrifice.

5. *Boundaries.* Bhaktapur's proliferation of discrete categories, domains, and levels in the construction of an intelligible symbolically ordered public world requires the construction and maintenance of var-

ious different kinds of boundaries. We have been much concerned with boundaries throughout this study. The maintenance and breaching of boundaries relates many different ideas—purity, contagion, the carefully encircled realm of sacred power, the power of gods and powerful men to cross boundaries, secrets, initiation, magic, and so on. What is peculiar about Bhaktapur is the sheer quantity of such boundaries, the richness of the conceptions, emotions and operations associated with them and their particualr problematics. For not only are there many of them, not only are they problematically anchored in the more fixed qualities of perceivable nature, not only are objects and events located in shifting classes and hierarchies, but there is, as we have discussed above, a traditional and frequently used emphasis on their openness under certain conditions and on their illusoriness to a higher knowledge. Bhaktapur as a symbolically constituted social order must always strive through action to keep these boundaries and the categories they bound from dissolving, to protect through constant vigilant action an order that is not otherwise guaranteed in seemingly hard reality or in codes of laws.

6. *Systematic ordering.* A further way that Bhaktapur's mesocosm responds to the demands of intelligibility is through attempts to fit as many symbolic bits and pieces as possible into larger and larger patterns of coherence, to strive to construct an aesthetic and philosophical unity, a Wagnerian multidimensional artwork. The few disconnected pieces (such as the little drama in the course of the tenth day of Mohanī between the king and the merchant from Simraun Gaḍh discussed in chap. 15) are striking in their very disconnectedness.

Insofar as a community's representations are coherently organized those phenomena that are represented but that do not fit easily into that order stand out against it. It is in such orders that paradoxes and mysteries—rather than just chaos—are able to appear. Such paradoxes and mysteries, any unexpected disconnectedness, motivate further elaborations of ideas and symbolic forms in attempts to save coherence. The striving for coherence in itself necessarily generates rococo elaboration.

BHAKTAPUR'S ORDER, STABILITY, AND STASIS

Bhaktapur has emphasized a certain way, one way among others, in which a community tries to hold flux, tries to make it seem meaningful and knowable. In an essay on the relations of History and Anthropology Bernard Cohn (1980, 218) wrote:

> We write of an event as being unique, something that happens only once; yet every culture has a means to convert the uniqueness into a general and transcendent meaningfulness through the language members of the society speak. To classify phenomena at a "commonsense" level is to recognize categories of events coded by the cultural system. An event becomes a marker within the cultural system. All societies have such markers, which can be public or private. The death of a ruler may be mourned by rituals which turn the biographic fact of a death into a public statement relating not only to a particular ruler but to rulership per se. In many societies ritual transforms uniqueness into structure.

Bhaktapur's system of marked symbols, its mesocosm, has been a powerful device for turning accident and history into structure, for trying to escape the contingencies and consequences of history, for trying to capture change, to make change seem illusory within an enduring order.

The very attempt to capture change, to deny a meandering history, to deny the effects of political will is—like the city's striving for coherence—in itself a fertile source of intellectual problems. Contact with a modern world is bringing problems of another order, much more difficult—and finally impossible—for Bhaktapur to absorb within its traditional order. For the implication of the ideas and the economic imperatives of that new world denies the city's central orienting value of birth-determined and fixed social hierarchy, assigns power and rewards by new principles, defines and values individuals in new and different ways, and treats a religiously anchored marked symbolism and its enactments as radically alien to a new and valued mobile secular order.

WHY IS BHAKTAPUR THE WAY IT IS?

Why is Bhaktapur the way it is? Much that exists in Bhaktapur is a result of its long history and its location in a South Asia whose areal forms are the products of several millennia of creation and reaction. Thus one explanation of much that exists and goes on in Bhaktapur is historical and diffusionist. Yet, as we have emphasized repeatedly, throughout its history Bhaktapur selected among and shaped to its own purposes the offerings of history and the inventions of its neighbors. Its growth and its day-to-day life were determined by its internal structures, tensions, and requirements, internal forces that influenced the city's response to history and environment. From the city's own point of view, "history" was only a disturbance for better or worse of its natural order, only a contingency to be dealt with until its effects became rejected or else transformed and worked out within the order of the city. When we consider the city's inner order it becomes possible to discern not only the effects of Bhaktapur's historical and areal character as a "South Asian" or "Hindu" city, but also its characteristics—in a different sort of classification—as one of a limited number of possible forms of human community, in this case an "archaic city."

The settlements that became Bhaktapur and the conditions of its Valley context were propitious—"preadapted" in particular ways for the formation and efflorescence of Bhaktapur's peculiar order. Bhaktapur, in a mnemonic shorthand, ascribes its ordering to a particular transformative time and to the efforts of a particular heroic man, Jyasthiti Malla. What facilitated and made possible the transformation that the city ascribes to him was an enabling partial destruction of a previous haphazard spatial order, a destruction which at the same time spared the Valley's great wealth and its Newar culture and society—that relatively homogeneous areal "folk tradition" where, in the phrasing of Redfield and Singer (1954, 57 [quoted in chap. 2]) a long established local culture or civilization could be carried forward, developed, and elaborated. Yet—it is necessary to add to Redfield and Singer's schema—not all local cultures are able to facilitate such developments. There was something peculiar and fortuitous about the Kathmandu Valley's "folk culture." It was derived in large part from a medieval Hinduism that, as a result of its own historical genesis, was remarkably suitable for the purposes of the construction of Bhaktapur's order and, equally important, able to fortify it against the disorganizing stimulation of foreigners, who were, literally, put in their places and enveloped in an isolating pollution rather than welcomed into the transformative dialogues of Redfield and Singer's secular, heterogeneous cities where under the stimulus of competing and initially disconnected ideas "new states of mind [arise]. . . indifferent to . . . states of mind associated with local cultures and ancient civilizations" (1954, 57).[13]

It was also critical for what Bhaktapur was to become, that rather than develop, like many other cities, in concert with the control of a very large area whose administrative or imperial center it was, it expanded, essentially, in place. Bhaktapur's significant space could be walked and directly experienced and made use of in ways impossible in such very large areas, and the city did not need to develop the modes of integration, such as force and abstract law, necessary for the management of states, nations, and empires controlled from a central city, modes of integration that might have flowed back to affect the inner life of the city itself.

It became possible, with all this, to construct an urban order in which naked force was secondary (or superordinate) to other systems of controls, secondary to the ordering force of a symbolic urban order—in a context in which the external uses of force and law for control of a heterogeneous large state, nation, or empire were minimal. The symbolic order was compelling in itself, and was much more than a mystifying support for and mask of another, somehow more basic, coercive power. It is emblematic of this order that within the civic arena the king was secondary to the priest.

In such an order there is a peculiar and necessary tension between the dominant sphere of symbolically constituted order and the sphere of more direct force. The king and the other technicians of power must look to an empirical reality which is resistant to symbolic manipulation if they are to adapt to changing conditions. They must understand this aspect of the world, and they must try to do what is necessary to deal with it. The priests worry about the moral implications of the power technicians' transcendence of the city's order, while those technicians sense that the priests and their allies are unpleasantly tangled up in something that they, the power technicians, have difficulty defining, something which clings to and encumbers the priests, something that is not quite clean. A balance is necessary. If the closed order of the constitutive symbolic system paralyzes the corrective perceptions and operations necessary for the proper uses of power, the city becomes vulnerable to decadence and decay. But if, on the contrary, pragmatism defeats the forces of the constitutive symbolic system, or alters it so that such symbolism becomes no more than a mobile mystifying ideology, then the old order collapses. For the city to be viable both systems have to work in difficult concert, a task for which Hinduism has exhibited considerable genius.

Let us recall Hinduism's fateful encounter with a differently constructed order, an order with its own and different necessities. It was, of course, Islam that was the particular variant of the Judeo-Christian-Islamic world revolution which made the first great iconoclastic invasion into South Asia, one of its furthest raids touching Bhaktapur itself in the fourteenth century. These invaders, unlike earlier ones, did not become

Kṣatriyas and fit themselves into a preexisting hierarchy and society—one of the classic ways in which South Asian kingdoms repeatedly changed accident and history into structure—but struggled to build a new and quite another kind of imperial and urban order.

Their iconoclasm was fundamental to their vision. The "idols" that they destroyed, that they sensed they had to destroy, were the seats of those immanent gods who, dancing civic order as Śiva danced the universe itself, anchored each South Asian royal city at the center of the universe—thus generating innumerable local universes. In irreconcilable contrast, however, "the basic objective in the expansion of Islam was to acquire political control over an area and to set up the symbols of the Islamic sovereignty" (Halil Inalcik in an unpublished paper on the transformation of Constantinople into Islamic Istanbul [1984, p. 10]). Within this expanding and universal Islam, the Islamic world view "determined the physical and social landscape of the city. The city was supposed to become a space where the prescriptions of the Islamic religion could be performed fully and appropriately" (ibid., 9). Instead of the city being a center transcending secular history and geography in order to center itself in a mythic history and space, it became an off-center marker in a universal and presumptively objective and real grid of mundane space and history whose presiding god was incorrigibly transcendent. The tasks of symbols—and thus their form and nature—in such a transformed city are altered. They become thinned out, more universal, easier to read by the various kinds of people who were to belong more to a universal Islam than to a particular city. Law, standardized Islamic law interpreted and enforced by a bureaucracy, became central to the regulation of such cities, a law that "included not only those things related to ritual, social relationships and conduct, but also food, habitation and environment" (ibid., 18). Local symbolic forms—including local spatial constructions—had to be made to represent an abstract, rational, and universal political, social and ethical order. As far as possible local mesocosms had to be dissolved.

Bhaktapur seems to us to be representative of the kinds of places Islam tried to transform in India, having held out for still a few more centuries against the new kind of world that Islam represented. In one of the "conceits" that we entertained in chapter 2, we imagined that Bhaktapur and the kind of Hinduism it represents belonged to an untransformed "preaxial" world in its use of a mesocosmic construction in the service of social and personal order, a construction with profound implications for individuality, for change, for the meaning of history itself.

Thus, a kind of an answer to "why is Bhaktapur the way it is," the problem of its particular form in comparison with other communities, is that when its economy and agricultural surplus and situation permitted, it grew into a city by making use of and transforming what it had at hand in the local settlements of the time. It was natural for its builders to assume that a community is a collection of people who share and are rooted in a coherent local world, and it was natural for them to make extended use of the powerful and relatively easy to craft marked symbols that small communities use for more restricted purposes. Bhaktapur—like the other Newar cities—following Indian models, elaborated a long-established local culture, converting it into its civilized dimension in the simplest and most self-evident way. In this conversion to a city and a civilization marked religious symbols became elaborated for the special tasks of the burgeoning community. It worked for a long time.

Most of its precursors in type were long gone when Bhaktapur was founded. The kind of wealth that made them possible attracted barbarians and empire builders, and thus they contained the seductions to their own often violent transformations. South Asian communities held out longer than most. As they, finally, under long and intense pressures began their transformations, accidents of location and history and, eventually, of national Nepalese policy allowed Bhaktapur to drift on for a while, a witness.

Appendixes

APPENDIX ONE

Transliterations Used in the Text

TRANSLITERATION OF SANSKRIT AND NEPALI

Vowels

Initial	Medial	Equivalent
अ, अ		*a*
आ, आ	ा	*ā*
इ	ि	*i*
ई	ी	*ī*
उ	ु	*u*
ऊ	ू	*ū*
ऋ	ृ	*ṛ*
ॠ	ॄ	*ṝ*
ऌ	ॢ	*ḷ*
ए	े	*e*
ऐ	ै	*ai*
ओ, ओ	ो	*o*
औ, औ	ौ	*au*

Consonants

	Equivalent		Equivalent
क	*k*	प	*p*
ख	*kh*	फ	*ph*
ग	*g*	ब	*b*
घ	*gh*	भ	*bh*
ङ	*ṅ*	म	*m*
च	*c*	य	*y*
छ	*ch*	र	*r*
ज	*j*		
झ	*jh*	ल	*l*
ञ	*ñ*	व	*v*
ट	*ṭ*	श	*ś*
ठ	*ṭh*	ष	*ṣ*
ड	*ḍ*	स	*s*
ढ	*ḍh*		
ण	*ṇ*	ह	*h*
त	*t*		
थ	*th*		
द	*d*		*ḥ*
ध	*dh*		*ṃ*
न	*n*		

TRANSLITERATION OF BHAKTAPUR NEWARI

The transliteration of the Bhakatpur dialect of the Newari language is based on the local scribal conventions for recording that dialect in Devanāgarī script. These conventions are not entirely consistent, and we have made some arbitrary choices. Where possible, Newari phonemes are represented in scribal Devanāgarī by their approximate Sanskrit equivalents. Spoken Newari lacks the retroflexed consonants of Nepali, *ṭ*, *ṭh*, *ḍ*, *ḍh*, and *ṇ*, and the Sanskrit spirants represented as *ś* and *ṣ*. The written language sometimes, but not invariably, keeps these written—but not so pronounced—forms in some words of Sanskritic or North Indian origin. Many of them will be found in the lists of *thar* names. Newari has a short high phonemic midvowel [*a*], a long high midvowel [*a:*], a short low frontal vowel [*ā*], and a long low frontal vowel [*ā:*]. Our transcriptions, using the macron to indicate position and the colon (representing the Devanāgāri *visarga*) for length, follow scribal conventions. For other vowels where it is thought necessary to indicate long vowels scribes use, sometimes erratically, the Sanskrit convention, which we have rendered (as is done for Sanskrit and Nepali) by the macron. Scribes hesitate between the written alternatives *ay'* (the apostrophe indicating that the consonant *y* is not followed, as the Sanskrit transcription would otherwise suggest, by a short a) and *e*; and between *āy'* and *āe*. We have followed the second usage in each case. To avoid having to place two diacritical marks over vowels that are both long and nasalized, we use (*n*) following a vowel to show nasalization of that vowel. Bhaktapur has a dorsovelar nasal that is not present in Kathmandu Newari which we represent by *ñ*. We follow the convention of transcribing the Devanāgāri व, used in Newari for the bilabial glide [*w*], as *w*. (See K. P. Malla [1985] for Kathmandu Newari.)

APPENDIX TWO

Bhaktapur's Newar Hindu *Thar*s Ranked by Macrosocial Status

We list here Bhaktapur's New Hindu *thar*s by the names usually used by others in reference to those *thar*s. In some cases members of a *thar* may use a different form of the reference name or a completely different name, or set of names, as surnames. Where we have some information about variant surnames, we have listed them in parentheses. Sometimes differences in surnames may indicate different sections of a particular *thar*, sometimes simply optional alternative names. Many *thar*s use Sanskrit or North Indian spelling for names of Indian derivation, even though the pronunciation has been changed.

PART 1. *THARS* LISTED BY STATUS LEVELS

I. Newar Brahmans
   a. Brahman (Rājopādhyāya) (group 1)
   b. Lākhae Brahman (Rājopādhyāya) (group 2)

II. Chathar
   Jośi; Malla; Pradhānāṇga; Hāḍā; Hoḍā; Amātya (also called "Mahāju"); Bhau (Bhaju); Kasaju (Kāyaṣta); Ta:cābhāri (Talcābhaḍel); Muna(n)karmi; Mulepati; Bhāri (Rajbhaṇḍāri); Ujhā(n)ṭhāche(n); Jo(n)che(n);[1] Go(n)ga:; Sa(n)gāmi; Dhaubhāri (Dhaubhaḍel); Pakwa(n); Timlā; Sāe(n)ju; Koṇgāsyo; Khe(n)dhaumāku; Baidhya (Rājbaidhya); Rāya; Palikhel; Khaeguli (Khayargoli); Kapa:ta:go; Piyā; Khwākhāli; Bāsi; Pula(n)che(n)

III. Pā(n)cthar
   a. The "Cārthar" section
      Māka:; Bramhalawat; Anu; Boche(n); Batās; Jaekāma; Khumjajy; Jhanga; Ulak:; Sacinyā; Bhadrā; Baḍiyā; Pasakala

b. The remainder
Ācāju (Karmācārya); Māske; Baidhya; Māḍhika:mi (Maḍhikarmi); Banepāli; Bhāri (Ca[n]gubhāri, Pujābhaṇḍāri, Bhaṇḍāri); Nāeju; Phaiju; Dristi; Jośi; Bhaju; Hoḍā; Bijukche(n); Go(n)ga:; Hyeju; Tapol; Yaucā; Kachipati; Piyā; Rājba(n)si; Mulmi

IV. Tini (Śivācārya)

V. Jyāpu (group 1)
Suwāl; Bāsukalā; Koju; Dholāju; Lawa; Lāgeju; Dumaru; Twāti; Ācāju; Byā(n)ju; Bake; Kharbujā; Dhukhwā; Chukā(n); Māka:; Cawa: (Cawāl); Gusāi; Colekhwa:; Khāemali; Lākha; Twāenā; Kawā(n); Kusi; Gwāchā; Deśemaru; Lāsiwa; Laghuju; Nāgāju; Khātākho; Nhinaeṅāemasa; Yākāmi; Khotejā; Dho(n)ju; Khaeguli; Duwāl; Dhaugwārā; Delā; Dupo(n)la; Gya(n)maru; Hyā(n)goju; Hyāu(n)mikhā; Jyākhwa; Kibānāyo; Kisi; Khināo; Ku(n)pākā; Khusu; Khorjā; Macāmasi; Mākhāsyā; Nhisutu; Nhuche(n); Nhemāphuki; Pāu(n); Phasikebā; Pya(n)tago; Sitikhu; Simātwā; Sujakhu; Tacamoga; Talāsi; Tadyoyā; Tagorā; Thike; Twānabāsu; Twi(n)twi(n); Tyāta; Wāsaba(n)jār; Wā(n)gāeyo; Yākāduwa; Dekānā; Do(n)ju; Chusyābāga; Colekhwa

VI. Tama: (Tāmrākār)

VII. Kumha: (Prajāpati); Awa: (Awāl); Malekār (Malkaju, Nepāli)

VIII. Jyāpu (group 2)[2]
Rājacal;[3] Caguṭhi;[4] Muguṭhi;[5] Dhauba(n)jār; Da(n)degulu; Galaju; Khāitu; Kutuwa:ju; Phelu; Khwālepālā; Da(n)dekhyā; Pachiju; Hyāu(n)wā; Ka:mi (Silpakār); Kutuwā; Kusāthā; Chu(n)ju; Pahi; Khitibaku; Kāsulā; Gojā; Dhusu; Kulluju; Bajiko(n); Bakhādyo; Kaiti; Datheputhe; Māka:; Twāenā; Bidya; Loha(n)ka:mi (Lo[n]halā); Bakānani; Dhatuchā; Machi; Boḍel; Dwārā; Jha(n)galthaku; Pampu; Bāga:; Basuju; Bhilla; Bhele; Bhāiju; Bhuyo; Biao; Cho(n)ju; Dāiju; Dhalapāmāga; Dhampo; Dhobwā; Dhi(n)griju; Gasucā; Gaṇapati; Gāisi; Ghāru; Gopi; Gopa; Gāṭhe; Gorkhālī; Guche(n); Gwāe(n)maru; Gwāe(n)masyu; Jugiju; Hāmo; Hā(n)ju; Hāleyojośi; Hāmonāyo; Hā(n)chethu; Jatādhāri; Jaidaju; Jhā(n)ga; Joharju; Joti; Jotisuwāl; Ka(n)pā; Khaju; Khāiju; Khi(n)ju; Khwāiju; Khuju; Kila(n)bu; Kisa(n)kari; Ko(n)dā; Kusmā; Lākhemaru; Lāchimasyā; Libi; Ligiligi; Lu(n)ba(n)ja:; Mātā(n); Mārikhu(n); Malākasi; Mathyā; Mogaju; Nakhetri; Nailā; Naramuni; Nāemasaphu(n); Ne(n)che(n); Pakā; Pa(n)ca; Pā(n)kā; Pakha(n)ju; Pā(n)gulu; Phitiju; Puwa; Pyātha; Sa(n)dha; Si(n)kedathe; Si(n)kemanī; Sibahari; Si(n)khwa; Si(n)ba(n)jār; Syāmā; Sulu; Sukhupāyo; Swa(n)gamikhā; Swanapā; Tākrā; Tāhāmatī; Tajalā; Tamakhu; Tālāche(n); Thakulawaṭ; Thakuba(n)jār; Thuyāju; Tusibākhyo; Twa(n)ju; Tyochi(n)a; Wātā(n)kachi; We(n)ju; Bhenātwā(n); Dubche(n); Da(n)dekhu; Cokāmi; Chusyākhi; Cho(n)ju; Che(n)gutalā; Cākumani; Bakhu(n)che(n); Bweju; Bholā(n)dyo; Bhokhāju; Gorā; Hākuduwa; Tulādhar

IX. Jyāpu (group 3)
Kastī; Dhanachwā; Gane, Phā(n)ju; Hyā(n)goju; Pāluba(n)ja:; Khicāju; Kuchumanī; Lākhe; Mātā(n)gulu; Nālāmī; Ṇākhusi; Bāthu; Gulmī

X. a. Chipī (Śreṣṭha; Śākha:karmī; Balla; Bhuju; Nāebhā; Dyoju)
b. Debabhandārī; Khāwāju

XI. Cyo (Phusikawā[n])

XII. Dwi(n)

XIII.[6] a. Gāthā (Bānamālā)
b. Bhā (Kārāñjit)
c. Kata: (Sudhdakār)
d. Cāla(n) (Diwākar)
e. Khusa:
f. Nau (Nāpit)
g. Kau (Nakarmi)
h. Pu(n) (Citrakāri)
i. Sa:mi (Mānandhar, Sāhu)
j. Chipā (Rāñjitkār)

XIII. Pasi

XIV. Nāe (Kasāi, Śāhī, Khaḍgi)

XV. a. Jugī (Darśandhārī, Kapālī, Kusle)
b. Danyā[7]

XVI. Do(n)

XVII. Kulu

XVIII. Po(n) (or Poḍe or Pore) (Mātaṅgī)

XIX. Cyāmākhala:

XX. Hālāhulu

PART 2. NEWAR HINDU *THARS* IN BHAKTAPUR LISTED ALPHABETICALLY

Ācāju (Karmācārya) [IIIb];[8] Ācāju [V]; Amātya (also called "Mahāju") [II]; Anu [IIIa]; Awa: (Awāl) [VII]; Baḍiyā [IIIa]; Bāga: [VIII]; Baidhya [IIIb]; Baidhya (Rājbaidhya) [II]; Bajiko(n) [VIII]; Bakānani [VIII]; Bake [V]; Bakhādyo [VIII]; Bakhu(n)che(n) [VIII]; Balla [Xa]; Banepāli [IIIb]; Bāsi [II]; Basuju [VIII]; Bāsukalā [V]; Batās [IIIa]; Bāthu [IX]; Bhā (Kārāñjit) [XIII]; Bhadrā [IIIa]; Bhāiju [VIII]; Bhaju [IIIb]; Bhāri (Rajbhaṇḍāri) [II]; Bhāri (Ca[n]gubhāri, Pujābhaṇḍāri, Bhaṇḍāri) [IIIb]; Bhau (Bhaju) [II]; Bhele [VIII]; Bhenātwā(n) [VIII]; Bhilla [VIII]; Bhokhāju [VIII]; Bholā(n)dyo [VIII]; Bhuju [Xa]; Bhuyo [VIII]; Biao [VIII]; Bidya [VIII]; Bijukche(n) [IIIb]; Boche(n) [IIIa]; Boḍel [VIII]; Bramhalawat [IIIa]; Brahman (Rājopādhyāya) [Ia]; Bweju [VIII]; Byā(n)ju [V]; Caguṭhi [VIII]; Cākumani [VIII]; Cāla(n) (Diwākar) [XIII]; Cawa:

(Cawāl) [V]; Che(n)gutalā [VIII]; Chipā (Rāñjitkār) [XIII]; Cho(n)ju [VIII]; Cho(n)ju [VIII]; Chu(n)ju [VIII]; Chukā(n) [V]; Chusyābāgā [V]; Chusyākhi [VIII]; Cokāmi [VIII]; Colekhwa [V]; Cyāmākhala: [XIX]; Cyo (Phusikawā[n]) [XII]; Dāiju [VIII]; Da(n)degulu [VIII]; Da(n)dekhu [VIII]; Da(n)dekhyā [VIII]; Danyā [XVb]; Datheputhe [VIII]; Debabhandārī [Xb]; Dekānā [V]; Delā [V]; Deśemaru [V]; Dhalapāmāga [VIII]; Dhampo [VIII]; Dhanachwā [IX]; Dhatuchā [VIII]; Dhauba(n)jār [VIII]; Dhaubhāri (Dhaubhaḍel) [II]; Dhaugwārā [V]; Dhi(n)griju [VIII]; Dhobī [XVII]; Dhobwā [VIII]; Dho(n)ju [V]; Dholāju [V]; Dhukhwā [V]; Dhusu [VIII]; Do(n) [XVI]; Do(n)ju [V]; Dristi [IIIb]; Dubche(n) [VIII]; Dumaru [V]; Dupo(n)la [V]; Duwāl [V]; Dwārā [VIII]; Dwi(n) [XII]; Dyoju [Xa]; Gāisi [VIII]; Galaju [VIII]; Gaṇapati [VIII]; Gane [IX]; Gasucā [VIII]; Gāthā (Bānamālā) [XIII]; Gāṭhe [VIII]; Ghāru [VIII]; Go(n)ga: [II]; Go(n)ga: [IIIb]; Gojā [VIII]; Gopa [VIII]; Gopi [VIII]; Gorā [VIII]; Gorkhālī [VIII]; Guche(n) [VIII]; Gulmī [IX]; Gusāi [V]; Gwāe(n)maru [VIII]; Gwāe(n)masyu [VIII]; Gwāchā [V]; Gya(n)maru [V]; Hāḍā [II]; Hākuduwa [VIII]; Hālāhulu [XX]; Hāleyojośi [VIII]; Hāmo [VIII]; Hāmonāyo [VIII]; Hā(n)chethu [VIII]; Hā(n)ju [VIII]; Hoḍā [II]; Hoḍā [IIIb]; Hyā(n)goju [V]; Hyā(n)goju [IX]; Hyāu(n)mikhā [V]; Hyāu(n)wā [VIII]; Hyeju [IIIb]; Jaidaju [VIII]; Jatādhāri [VIII]; Jaekāma [IIIa]; Jhanga [IIIa]; Jhā(n)ga [VIII]; Jha(n)galthaku [VIII]; Jo(n)che(n) [II]; Joharju [VIII]; Jośi [II]; Jośi [IIIb]; Joti [VIII]; Jotisuwāl [VIII]; Jugī (Darśandhārī, Kapālī, Kusle) [XVa]; Jugiju [VIII]; Jyākhwa [V]; Kachipati [IIIb]; Kaiti [VIII]; Ka:mi (Silpakār) [VIII]; Ka(n)pā [VIII]; Kapa:ta:go [II]; Kasaju (Kāyaṣta) [II]; Kāsulā [VIII]; Kastī [IX]; Kata: (Sudhdakār) [XIII]; Kau (Nakarmi) [XIII]; Kawā(n) [V]; Khāiju [VIII]; Khāitu [VIII]; Khaju [VIII]; Kharbujā [V]; Khātākho [V]; Khāwāju [Xb]; Khaeguli (Khayargoli) [II]; Khaeguli [V]; Khāemadli [V]; Khe(n)dhaumāku [II]; Khi(n)ju [VIII]; Khicāju [IX]; Khināo [V]; Khitibaku [VIII]; Khorjā [V]; Khotejā [V]; Khuju [VIII]; Khumjajy [IIIa]; Khusa: [XIII]; Khusu [V]; Khwāiju [VIII]; Khwākhāli [II]; Khwālepālā [VIII]; Kibānāyo [V]; Kila(n)bu [VIII]; Kisa(n)kari [VIII]; Kisi [V]; Koju [V]; Ko(n)dā [VIII]; Koṇgāsyo [II]; Kuchumanī [IX]; Kulluju [VIII]; Kulu [XVII]; Kumha: (Prajāpati) [VII]; Ku(n)pākā [V]; Kusāthā [VIII]; Kusi [V]; Kusmā [VIII]; Kutuwā [VIII]; Kutuwa:ju [VIII]; Lāchimasyā [VIII]; Lāgeju [V]; Laghuju [V]; Lākhā [V]; Lākhe [IX]; Lākhe Brahman (Rājopādhyāya) [Ib]; Lākhemaru [VIII]; Lāsiwa [V]; Lawa [V]; Libi [VIII]; Ligiligi [VIII]; Loha(n)ka:mi (Lo[n]halā) [VIII]; Lu(n)ba(n)ja: [VIII]; Macāmasi [V]; Machi [VIII]; Māḍhika:mi (Maḍhikarmi) [IIIb]; Māka: [IIIa]; Māka: [V]; Māka: [VIII]; Mākhāsyā [V]; Malākasi [VIII]; Malekār (Malkaju, Nepāli) [VII]; Malla [II]; Mārikhu(n) [VIII]; Māske [IIIb]; Mātā(n) [VIII]; Mātā(n)gulu [IX]; Mathyā [VIII]; Mogaju [VIII]; Muguṭhi [VIII]; Mulepati [II]; Mulmi [IIIb]; Muna(n)karmi [II]; Nāgāju [V]; Nailā [VIII]; Nakhetri [VIII]; Ṇākhusi [IX]; Nālāmī [IX]; Naramuni [VIII]; Nau (Nāpit) [XIII]; Nāe. (Kasāi, Śāhī, Khaḍgi) [XIV]; Nāebhā [Xa]; Nāeju [IIIb]; Ñāemasaphu(n) [VIII]; Ne(n)che(n) [VIII]; Nhemāphuki [V]; Nhinaenāemasa [V]; Nhisutu [V]; Nhuche(n) [V]; Pachiju [VIII]; Pakā [VIII]; Pakha(n)ju [VIII]; Pakwa(n) [II]; Palikhel [II]; Pāluba(n)ja: [IX]; Pampu [VIII]; Pa(n)ca [VIII]; Pā(n)gulu [VIII]; Phā(n)ju [IX]; Pā(n)kā [VIII]; Pasakalā [IIIa]; Pasi [XIII ?] Pāu(n) [V]; Phaiju [IIIb]; Phasikebā [V]; Phelu [VIII]; Phitiju [VIII]; Piyā [II]; Piyā [IIIb]; Po(n) [or Poḍe or Pore] (Mātaṅgī)

[XVIII]; Pradhānāṇga [II]; Pula(n)che(n) [II]; Pu(n) (Citrakāri) [XIII]; Puwa [VIII]; Pyātha [VIII]; Pya(n)tago [V]; Rājacal [VIII]; Rājba(n)si [IIIb]; Rāya [II]; Sacinyā [IIIa]; Śākha:karmī [Xa]; Sa:mi (Mānandhar, Sāhu) [XIII]; Sa(n)dha [VIII]; Sa(n)gāmi [II]; Sāe(n)ju [II]; Sibahari [VIII]; Simātwā [V]; Si(n)ba(n)jār [VIII]; Si(n)kedathe [VIII]; Si(n)kemanī [VIII]; Si(n)khwa [VIII]; Sitikhu [V]; Śreṣṭha [Xa]; Sujakhu [V]; Sukhupāyo [VIII]; Sulu [VIII]; Suwāl [V]; Swanapā [VIII]; Swa(n)gamikhā [VIII]; Syāmā [VIII]; Ta:cābhāri (Talcābhaḍel) [II]; Tacamoga [V]; Tadyoyā [V]; Tagorā [V]; Tāhāmatī [VIII]; Tajalā [VIII]; Tākrā [VIII]; Tālāche(n) [VIII]; Talāsi [V]; Tama: (Tāmrākār) [VI]; Tamakhu [VIII]; Tapol [IIIb]; Thakuba(n)jār [VIII]; Thakulawaṭ [VIII]; Thike [V]; Thuyāju [VIII]; Timlā [II]; Tini (Śivācārya) [IV]; Tulādhar [VIII]; Tusibākhyo [VIII]; Twānabāsu [V]; Twa(n)ju [VIII]; Twāti [V]; Twāenā [V]; Twāenā [VIII]; Twi(n)twi(n) [V]; Tyāta [V]; Tyochi(n)a [VIII]; Ujhā(n)-ṭhāche(n) [II]; Ulak: [IIIa]; Wā(n)gāeyo [V]; Wāsaba(n)jār [V]; Wātā(n)kachi [VIII]; We(n)ju [VIII]; Yākāduwa [V]; Yākāmi [V]; Yaucā [IIIb]

APPENDIX THREE

Kinship Terminology

Bhaktapur's kinship terminology is a variant of the terminology used in other Newar communities (cf. Toffin 1975*a*; Nepali 1965). Newar kinship terminology is closely related in both its structure[1] and in much of its vocabulary[2] to what Karve (1968) has called "North Indian" systems of kinship terminology. The details of Bhaktapur's kinship terminology and classification are not relevant to the concerns of this present study, but we will list here the terms and note some of their features for reference purposes.

We will first present Bhaktapur kin terms as arranged by generation and will then note some special terms for relations acquired by an individual through marriage.[3] These terms are in relation to "ego," the conventional designation for an imagined individual on whom the various relations of another individual ("alter") or category of individuals designated by the terminology are centered. Each term's "focal" or "primary" genealogical referent, the individual or group of kin to whom it centrally refers, is given first,[4] followed by terms used in address. Most Newar kin terms have extended references, sometimes to a very large group of "classificatory kin."[5] Thus, for example, *ajā*, whose focal genealogical referent is Father's Father[6] and Mother's Father, is extended to all consanguineal male kin of the second generation senior to "ego," and also to a further group of men related to "ego" through marriage to his extended group of "grandmothers." The exact limits of the extension of these categories and an adequate statement of the principles on which that extension is based is beyond the scope of this study. Extension is similar in many respects to other North Indian systems and is treated in some of the works referred to above. Toffin (1975*a*) deals in a summary way with the principles of extension of Newar terms in the communities he studied. We may note that the nuclear set of kin terms *abwā* (Father), *amā* (Mother), *kāe* (Son), *mhyāe* (Daughter), *bha:ta* (Husband), and *misā* (Wife) are *not* extended beyond their focal reference, although related extended terms (e.g., for Mother's Sisters) may be variations of the core term.

I.

A. Two or more generations senior to ego.

1. a. *Ajā.*[7] Genealogical referent: FF/MF.[8] Address: *bājyā*, and (rarely) *ajā*.

   b. *Tapā ajā.*[9] Genealogical referent: FFF, MFF, FMF, MMF. Address: same as for *ajā*.

   c. *Aya: ajā.*[10] Genealogical referent: FFFF, MFFF, FFMF, MFMF, FMFF, FMMF, etc.

   d. *Ghāe(n)ghāe(n) ajā.* This term includes for those speakers who use *aya: ajā* all male members of those consanguineal and affinally related kin of the fifth and higher ascending generations. For those who do not use *aya: ajā*, this term begins with the fourth ascending generation.

2. *Aji.*[11] Genealogical referent: FM/MM.[12] Address: *aji, baje*. Subsequent generations are designated as for *ajā*, with the addition of *tapā:*, *aya*: (for some speakers), and *ghāe(n)ghāe(n)*.

B. One generation senior to ego.

3. a. *Abwā.* Genealogical position: F.[13] Address: *Bā, Yabā, Abwā.*

   b. *-bwā.* Genealogical position: FeB (tarhibwā, etc.); FyB (cicārhibwā, etc.).[14,15] Address: same terms of address as for *abwā*. One may use if older than Father or else Mother,[16] *taribwā, tarhibwā*, etc.; if younger than Father or else Mother, *cicārhibwā*, and related terms. If alter is considered as Father's youngest Brother, or as significantly younger than Father, special terms for "youngest Brother" may be used, such as *akā*, *pui(n)cābwā*, or *kanchābwā*.[17]

4. *Jicā pāju.*[18] Genealogical position: FZH. Address: *pāju* or *jicā pāju*.

5. a. *Amā.* Genealogical position: M. Address: *amā, mā(n), yamā.*

   b. *Māmā.*[19] Genealogical position: MZ. Address: *Māmā, Māmācā*, or terms used for *amā*.

   c. *-mā(n)* or *-amā.*[20] Genealogical position: FBW. Address: the term of reference itself, or terms used for *amā*.

6. *Pāju.* Genealogical referent: MB. Address: Pāju. Sometimes terms designating older or younger than Mother are added.

7. *Maleju.* Genealogical referent: MBW. Address: *Maleju, Malju.*[21]

8. *Nini.* Genealogical referent: FZ.[22] May be qualified optionally for older or younger than Father. Address: *nini*, with optional additions indicating age relative to Father.

C. Ego's generation.

9. *Arā.* Genealogical referent: eB. Address: *Arā, dai, dāju.*

10. *Kijā.* Genealogical referent: yB. Address: *kijā, bhaicā.*

11. *Jicā dāju.*[23] Genealogical referent: eZH. Address: same as for *arā*, older Brother.

12. *Jicā bhāju.*[24] Genealogical referent: yZH. Also for DH, SDH, DDH.

Address: For ySH, addressed by name, or term for *kijā*. For DH, etc., *jicā bhāju*.

13. a. *Atā*.[25] Genealogical referent: eZ. Address: *atā*, *tatā*, *didi* (from Nepali).
    b. *Tatā:ju*.[26] (also *ta:ju*). Genealogical referent: eBW. Address: same as for *Atā*.
14. *Kehe(n)*. Genealogical referent: yZ. Address: name, *kehe(n)*, and various affectionate, diminutive terms.[27]
15. *Bhau*.[28] Genealogical referent: yBW, also SW, SSW, etc. Address: name, or *bhau*, etc.

D. One generation junior to ego.

16. a. *Kāe*. Genealogical referent: S. Address: name or affectionate terms such as *Bābu* and *bābucā*.
    b. *Kāecā*.[29,30] Genealogical referent: BS (man speaking) or ZS (woman speaking). Address: same as for *kāe*.
17. a. *Mhyāe*. Genealogical referent: D. Address: name, Affectionate terms, *Nani*, *Māyā(n)*, etc.
    b. *Mhyāecā*.[31] Genealogical referent: BD (man speaking), ZD (woman speaking). Address: same as for *mhyāe*.
18. *Bhe(n)cā*.[32] Genealogical referent: ZS/ZD (man speaking) or BS/BD (woman speaking).[33] Address: Addressed to a male, *bhe(n)cā* or one of the terms of address for *kāe*. In the case of female alters *bhe(n)cā* is not usually used for address, but one of the terms of address for *mhyāe* is used.

E. Two or more generations junior to ego.

19. *Chay*. Genealogical referent: SS, SD, DD, DS. Address: same as for *kāe* or for *mhyāe*.
20. *Chui*. Genealogical referent: SSS, SSD, SDS, SDD, DDS, DDD, etc. Children of *chay*. Address: same as for *kāe* or for *mhyāe*.
21. *Ui*. Genealogical referent: Children of *chui*.
22. *Kui*. Genealogical referent: Children of *ui*.
23. *Jhui*. This term is reported by some informants but is unknown to others. Genealogical referent: Children of *kui*.

II. Terms for kin generated through ego's marriage.

24. *Bha:ta*.[34] Genealogical referent: H. Address: kin terms and proper name are avoided.
25. *Misā*. Genealogical position: W. Address: kin terms and proper names are avoided.
26. *The remainder of acquired affinal terms*. Other affinally acquired terms of reference are usually based on the spouse's relation to alter, with the addition of prefixes or suffixes indicating the affinal relationship.

The husband uses the prefix *sasa*, indicating "Wife's family," and adds the kinship term derived from his Wife as ego. Thus Wife's Mother is *sasa mā(n)*, Wife's younger Brother is *sasa kijā*, and so on. Toffin (1975*a*) reports the term *sasa* in another Newari dialect as being used also by Wives for referring to members of the Husband's family. In Bhaktapur, however, a Wife tends to use the term *bhata*[36] suffixed to a kin term based on the Husband's position as "ego." Thus the Husband's youngest Brother is *kijā bhata*, Husband's Mother's Brother is *pāju bhata*, and so on.[37] A Wife, however, does not refer to her Husband's parents by means of the *bhata* form. Instead, the honorific suffix *-ju* is used. Husband's Father is referred to as *ba:ju*, and Husband's Mother as *māju*.

Terms of address used for spouse's kin may be the term of reference, but they are usually the same term of address used directly to one's own kin. Thus, for example, *Pāju bhata* may be addressed as *pāju*. A Wife is more likely to refer to her Husband's Sisters' Children (to whom she is *maleju*) as *bhe(n)cā* rather than *bhe(n)cā bhata*, but a Husband will be more likely to refer to his Wife's Brothers' Children (for whom he is the ritually and socially less important FZH or *jicā pāju*) more formally as *sasa bhe(n)cā*. Such differences, like the Wife's use of the terms *ba:ju* and *māju* (rather than *sasa mā* and *sasa bwā*) for her Husband's Father and Mother, reflect the implication that for women marriage entails the acquisition of new kin—particularly her Husband's core kin, or *syāphu(n)*—through her radical transformation in that marriage and that these kin who are not supposed to be essentially different from the kin of her natal household, *phukī*, and *tha:thiti*. The Husband, in contrast, uses an affinal terminology that emphasizes that the new kin acquired through his marriage are, essentially, his Wife's kin.

Like other North Indian systems, the Newar kinship system names certain core family members unambiguously and without extension—Mother, Father, Son, Daughter, Husband, and Wife. In contrast, again as in other systems, there are extremely extended categories of Brother, Sisters, Father's Brothers, and Mother's Sisters, and of ascending and descending "Grandparents" and "Grandchildren." The Newar system goes beyond some other North Indian systems in lumping together both matrilineal and patrilineal ascendents. In contrast to most other North Indian systems, Newar systems amalgamate Mother's Sister's Husband to Father's Brother, and in some Newari dialects (but not Bhaktapur's) Father's Sister's Husband is also amalgamated to this category. In contrast to other North Indian systems, Mother's Brother's Wife is given a specific name (of both reference and address) of her own, *maleju*, and not just a feminine form of Mother's Brother. Finally, in contrast to most other North Indian systems, Father's Sister's Husband is given a name (*jicā pāju*) that terminologically connects him to Mother's Brother (*pāju*) and to the "bridegrooms," *jicā*, who marry into the patriline.[38]

The Newar system deals with the reciprocal terms to Mother's Brother and Father's Sister—a woman's Brother's Son and Daughter, and a man's Sister's Son and Daughter—in what is on the surface a radically different way from the North Indian systems. The Newar system calls all cross-nephews and nieces by the same name, *bhe(n)cā*, and calls parallel nephews and nieces "Sons" or "Daughters," adding, however, the diminutive particle *-cā*, to distinguish them from "focal" sons and daughters. The North Indian system, in contrast, simply separates Brother's Children from Sister's Children, independently of the sex of ego, and does not provide a reciprocal term to Mother's Brother and Father's Sister, although when the sex of the speaker is known there is no ambiguity. These differentiations of cross and parallel uncles and aunts, and of cross and parallel nephews and nieces disappear, as they do in other North Indian systems in the next ascending and descending generations where they become amalgamated as "grandparents" and "grandchildren."

Most terms are strictly generational, with the equivocal exception of the affinal terms *jicā bhāju*, which includes younger Sister's Husband and Daughter's Husband, and *bhau*, which includes younger Brother's Wife and Son's Wife. Generational terms include a wide range of consanguineal and affinal kin.

APPENDIX FOUR

Types of Worship and Materials Used in Worship

We have said something of the worship of the dangerous deities in chapter 9 but have not discussed personal and household acts of worship directed to benign deities.

"Worship" in its most general sense is often phrased as *sewā yāgu*, "to serve," a term used to designate service to a superior, an employer, or a king as well as a deity. Specific, relatively formal, and circumscribed acts of worship are called, as generally in Hinduism, *pūjā*s. In formal *pūjā*s and in most of the more informal gestures of worship, the worshiper acts out respect, subordination, hospitality, and honor to the deity—implicitly giving the deity, in turn, responsibilities to the worshiper. Various kinds of daily worship are considered to be a duty, part of following the *dharma*, a way of maintaining relations with the deities. Many special acts of worship and special kinds of *pūjā*s are required or advisable or available options in various circumstances.

In addition to the daily *pūjā*s performed in households without the aid of Brahman *purohita*s (family priests), and the minor optional household and personal *pūjā*s that are also done without the assistance of Brahmans, Rājopādhyāya Brahman *purohita*s are able to list more than seventy specifically named *pūjā*s that they perform for their middle- and upper-status employers under various circumstances.

The offering of pure and unbroken husked rice, *kiga:*, is considered an elementary *pūjā*. People knowing that they will pass some favorite temple or shrine may carry some *kiga:* with them to offer to the deity. Other *pūjā*s add to and elaborate on this offering. Within more complex *pūjā*s there is often a climactic offering of *kiga:* in a component act that is specifically called (as is the larger sequence of which it is a part) *pūjā yāgu*, "doing a *pūjā*."

We will sketch some different *pūjā*s in a summary and incomplete way, using local terms for some materials and implements that will be defined and described in later sections of this appendix.

PŪJĀS NOT CONDUCTED BY A BRAHMAN *PUROHITA*

TEMPLE VISITS

We have remarked the minimal *pūjā* act, the offering of *kiga:*, which may be added to respect gestures and circumambulation when passing temples and shrines. Purposeful visits to temples and shrines for worship, most commonly visits to the local Gaṇeśa shrine necessary before most other family worship, entail a more elaborate procedure that is essentially the same as the basic daily household *pūjā*. Women bring the necessary materials (*kiga:*, flowers, incense, a wick, which has been soaked in oil or purified butter, and other optional offerings) on a shallow metal dish, a *pūjā bha:*, or in a shallow bamboo container, a *swalyācā*, a grain winnowing basket. Men bring the supplies in a small box, a *kiga: battā*, a "*kiga:* box." The worshiper first washes himself or herself—ideally at the river—and then proceeds to the temple (or temples). First he[1] presents *kiga:* and, usually, flowers, ideally visualizing the deity as seated or standing in his chest. Then he may offer other offerings—burning incense, a burning wick, and so on. Then, if it is spatially possible, the worshiper circumambulates the temple or shrine.

HOME *PŪJĀS*

Daily Worship. Nitya Pūjā The household deities who are the focus of daily worship have been listed in chapter 8 and the location of the worship area in houses noted in chapter 7. The worship area is purified each morning. Household members (including girls after their mock-marriage ceremony, and boys after their *Kaetā Pūjā* ceremony) come to worship at the household shrine before they have taken any food. They come in no particular order, depending on their daily schedules. Worship is usually done rapidly, and takes only several minutes. In contrast to other kinds of household *pūjās* where there is usually one deity who is the central focus of worship, this *pūjā* is directed to all the household gods. The necessary equipment and supplies are arranged near the worshiper and in front of the god images. In a typical sequence the worshiper pours one kind of pure water, *nina:*, on his right hand, and using the dampened fingers of his right hand, washes the images' faces. He then applies either a white or yellow *sinha(n)* pigment to the forehead of each image, using the ring finger or little finger of the right hand and then, using the same finger, applies a red pigment. Then he places some grains of *kiga:* on the *sinha(n)* spot. Next flowers or flower petals are placed on the images' heads, or a sprig of flowers long enough when placed on the ground to touch a deity's head may be leaned against the statue. Next burning incense is offered. The incense is constructed of fragrant materials twisted into a cord. The cord is folded in the middle and twisted again, so that one end is now constituted by the fold and the other by the two cut open ends. Newars, at least those with Brahman family *purohitas*, burn the rounded end, which quickly splits and separates to produce two flames, representing Śiva and Śakti. This is thought to be a specifically Newar (i.e., non-Indo-Nepalese) custom. When the incense is lit a bell is rung, and the incense is held in turn toward each god as an offering of a pleasant smell. The bell, an offering of music, also captures the attention of the god who is meditating or whose attention is elsewhere. Next the wick is lit, the bell is rung again, and the lit wick, as an offering of light, is held in turn toward each god. The incense and the wick are then placed on a mound of *kiga:* in front of any of the god images. A small bowl containing *baji* and sweetcakes is taken and, held in joined hands, presented to each deity in turn. This represents a feeding of the deities, who are said to be hungry in the morning. The bowl is then placed somewhere in front of the images.

The next step is the climax of the *pūjā*. The bell (or sometimes a small drum, or a conch trumpet, instruments more usually used in Brahman-assisted *pūjā*s) is sounded, then a respect gesture is made with joined palms, some grains of *kiga:* being held between the palms. If the worshiper knows an appropriate Sanskrit phrase or verse he will say it, otherwise he will say the god's name, trying to visualize the deity as present in his chest. The worshiper may call all the gods' names, he may just say *bhagavān*, "god," or may just name Viṣṇu or Śiva as representing all the deities. He may add, "be happy," or "protect us," or mention some personal concern. He will then do the elemental *pūjā yāgu* act, flicking some *kiga:* at the deity.[2]

Now the worshiper takes some of the water that had been offered to the deities and sprinkles it on his own head. He takes some of the pigments on the tray—which had been touched by his finger as he decorated each deity in turn, and puts it on his own forehead. He takes some of the flowers that have fallen to the feet of the gods and places them on his own head. If there had been a food offering he would also take a bit of the food and eat it. This taking of "*prasāda*"[3] concludes the *pūjā*.

Optional Household Worship When a household or one of its members feels that they should do some special worship beyond temple visits or daily *pūjā*s, but one that will not require a Brahman's participation, the *pūjā* variously named *apāsa(n) cwanegu, brata cwanegu*, or, simply, *dya pūjā*, "god *pūjā*," is done. The first two terms (the first term, derived apparently from the Sanskrit *upavāsa*, "fasting," and the second from *vrata*, "austerity") mean to undergo a fast or an "austerity" of some kind. Typical motivations for such *pūjā*s might be to overcome an illness, to seek an improvement in farming or business affairs, for success in an upcoming school examination, so that a household girl will find a good husband, and so forth. These are usually done by the person concerned or by a household woman for the household. Often the supplicant vows to do a regular series of such *pūjā*s, once a week, twice a month, and so on, during a given period. Occasionally the family *purohita* may assist in the *pūjā*, but this is optional and does not make it equivalent to the more elaborate and costly *pūjā*s, which require a Brahman's participation. In contrast to the daily morning *pūjā*s, these *pūjā*s are principally addressed to a particular deity, usually Viṣṇu/Nārāyaṇa or, sometimes, Gaṇeśa.

The *pūjā* is usually held in the late afternoon, and participants cannot eat or drink before the *pūjā*; hence the nominal fast or austerity suggested by the name. After the *pūjā* is completed the participants eat a meal usually constituted of rich, sweet foods, such as milk, curds, sugar, and sweetcakes. For this kind of worship additional steps or elements are added to the sequence of the basic daily household *pūjā*, essentially by adding more elegant offerings. These vary somewhat, but typically include the following. The gods' faces are washed in addition to the usual *nina:* with "five nectars" (milk, clarified butter, honey, curds and sugar), then with milk, then again with *nina:*, and finally with *Ga(n)-gā jal*. Instead of simple *kiga:*, a mixture of *akye*, barley, and sesame seeds, is added to the *sinha(n)* spot on the deities' foreheads. Before flowers are presented to the deities, white threads representing sacred threads are put over the shoulders of the images, and after the flower presentation flower garlands may be placed around their necks. If men are doing the *pūjā*, they are more likely to blow a conch shell or rattle a drum than they would be in a simple household *pūjā*. Fruit is always added to the food offerings. The light offering now will be not just wicks, but oil lamps and burning sticks of camphor, and an offering of small coins is added to other offerings. At the end of the *pūjā*, just before taking *prasāda*, the worshiper will rise and circumambulate the *pūjā* area, or if the spatial arrangements make this impossible, he visualizes the act, or stands and rotates his body in the auspicious direction.

PŪJĀS CONDUCTED BY A BRAHMAN *PUROHITA*

The basic and most common Brahman-assisted household *pūjā* is usually called a *dhala(n) danegu*, or sometimes an "important" or "great" (*tarha[n]gu*) *apā-sa(n) cwanegu* or *brata cwanegu*, to distinguish it from the non-Brahman-assisted special household *pūjā*s. The etymology of the term *dhala(n) danegu* is variously explained. In what may be folk etymology it is locally related to the term *dhala:*, a list or inventory, and said to mean to perform rigorously by following a list of procedures.[4]

These are the most elaborate *pūjā*s that a household without Tantric initiation (and thus all households at the Jyāpu or lower levels) will usually do. Households in those upper-level *thar*s who can do Tantric *pūjā*s often do *dha-la(n) danegu pūjā*s rather than Tantric *pūjā*s for many purposes, because such *pūjā*s are easier to arrange and people within the family without Tantric initiation can participate. In contrast to simple household *pūjā*s, in *dhala(n) danegu* and other Brahman-assisted *pūjā*s groups of people, household members, relatives coming from outside of the household and, sometimes, friends often participate.

There are certain days in the annual calendar in which a *dhala(n) danegu* may traditionally be offered to one or another of the focal deities of the day (chaps. 13 to 15). The noncalendrical *dhala(n) danegu pūjā*s are generally directed to Viṣṇu/Nārāyaṇa. The expressed motives for such *pūjā*s are various. They may be in fulfillment of a pledge, or more vaguely as an expression of thankfulness because the family's life has been going well, or to "support the *dharma*," or for a good next life for the participants, and so on.

The Brahman's *paddhatis*, written guides for the performance of various kinds of *pūjās*, give sixty stages in the sequence of *dhala(n) danegu pūjās*. The first seventeen are the preliminary work to be done by the Brahman *purohita*, the remainder are for the client, the *jajmān*, as instructed and sometimes aided by the *purohita*. The *pūjā* takes place in the late afternoon or evening. The participants must fast from the morning, and must have a *bya(n)kegu* purification (chap. 11). This was formerly a major purification, but in recent years it is often a minor one. The clothes worn by participants must all have been washed since their last use. As many people may attend, the *pūjā* will be held in an open area, not the crowded and restricted area of the household shrine. It may be given in the open area of the *cwata* floor or, sometimes, in a courtyard outside of the house. Depending on the number of people who participate and its optional elaborations, the *pūjā* may take from roughly two-and-one-half to five hours to complete.

MATERIALS AND EQUIPMENT

The equipment and supplies used in *pūjās* in Bhaktapur are collectively called *pūjā jola(n)*. There are some thirty items of equipment used in addition to the *mūrtis* or god images. With the exception of two conch shells (one used as a container for water, the other as a trumpet) the other items are made of metal—of copper, iron, brass, "bell metal" or *kāe(n)*, and other alloys.[5] Most items must be made from the proper specific type (or a selection among limited specific types) of metal. Most of the thirty items come from the standard Hindu inventory of ritual equipment, but some of them are locally considered specifically Newar, which is to say that they are not used by the Indo-Nepalese Hindus. The equipment includes bowls and dishes of various sizes and shapes, spoons, containers for water or other fluids (some with spouts for pouring, some without), a funnel, tripods, oil lamps, containers for colored pigments, bells, a mirror, a conch shell container, and a conch shell trumpet. About half these items are used in ordinary *pūjās*, the remainder in various types of specialized *pūjās*. Ordinary Brahman-assisted household *pūjās* use about ten items; ordinary Tantric *pūjās* use some sixteen pieces of equipment.

Nine items are locally considered to be specifically Newar. The most prominent of these is an oil lamp, *sukundā* (a variant shape with the same usage is called *mukundā*). This is an elaborate lamp of complex symbolism, much of it representing the various relations of Śiva and Śakti. We have discussed it in chapter 9. The other special Newar items are the *salāi*, a metal dish; the *nyā(n)thālā*, and the *thāpi(n)cā*, flasks; the *dhaupatu*, a cup; the *sinhamu*, a container with a removable top used to hold one kind of pigment (*bhui sinha[n]*); and the *arghapātra*, a container in the shape of a human skullcap.

Rājopādhyāya Brahmans list more than 200 materials that are necessary for various *pūjās*. These include cleaning materials, leaves and grasses, pigments for decorating the deities and the *pūjā* equipment and other pigments for marking out the worship area with elaborate diagrams, flowers, various forms of rice, foodstuffs of many kinds (including sweetcakes of various shapes and ingredients), alcoholic spirits and sacrificial animals (for Tantric *pūjās*), products of the cow, threads of various sorts, oil-lamp wicks, cosmetic kits as gifts to the goddesses, small unglazed clay dishes, and other disposable pieces of equipment. Such materials are used in the preparation of the *pūjā* and in its course as offerings to various deities and to the officiating priests.

Some of the materials that are referred to in this volume warrant some special comment.

PURE WATER

There are three kinds of progressively purer water.

1. *Na:nā* is used (along with red clay and cow dung) for preparing the *pūjā* area for ordinary, non-Brahman-assisted *pūjās*. It is used for washing the face and hands and rinsing the mouth in the morning, after excretion and before meals, and before *pūjās*. It is used for a first rinsing of *pūjā* equipment, which is then washed with water of a higher degree of purity. It is the proper water for boiling rice. *Na:nā* must be drawn on the same day it is used from the river, a well, or a tap, and it must not be touched by a menstruating woman, polluting animal, or member of the lowest-status *thars*. Household women collect it in the early morning after they have swept the houses. When she returns home a woman will call out a warning to make sure that no one is above her on the stairway (which would pollute the *na:nā*) as she brings the water up to the floor of the house on which the *pūjā* is to take place or the cooking is to be done.

2. *Ninā* is used for preparing *pūjā* areas for Brahman-assisted *pūjās*. It is used for washing the images of deities, for mixing with pigments to be presented to deities, for cooking sweetcakes presented to the deities, as the water offering presented to deities for "drinking," and for rinsing *pūjā* equipment after it has been first washed with *na:nā*. On the day that *ninā* is to be collected, the women first clean the house and then purify the area in front of the front door with *na:nā*, cow dung, and red clay. When the woman who is to carry the water reaches the source, she cleans her feet, legs, and hands and then washes her mouth and face. She scours the vessel that is to carry the water and then cleans the tap, edge of the well, or stone at the edge of the river with ashes or the proper kind of soil. She then once again cleans herself as she had before and draws the water, which is now considered *ninā*. She returns home being careful that no one else touch the container or the water unless they are similarly purified. At home she calls out a warning, as she had done with the *na:nā*, and for the same reason. Before placing the water container on the ground near the *pūjā* area she will pour out some of the water, and place the container on the wet area to prevent contamination.

3. There is water of still higher purity called "Ganges water" or *Ga(n)gā jal*. This is mixed with *ninā* in the more elaborate *pūjās* for washing the gods and giving them water offerings, and is used in death ceremonies. It is drawn with

the same precautions used for gathering *ninā* from areas in the river that are considered to be *tīrtha*s, where the water is considered to be of special purity and potency.

PIGMENTS

Various pigments and fragrant woods are used in marking deities and individuals in the course of *pūjā*s. The marks made (and by extension the materials so used) are called *sinha(n)* (*sinḣa:* in Kathmandu Newari). Traditionally white and red pigments derived from fragrant white and red varieties of sandalwood were used, but now cheaper substitute pigments are often used. These are a saffron yellow pigment, *mhāsusinha(n)*, and an orange pigment, *bhuisinha(n)*, used respectively as replacements for the white and red sandalwood pigments. A red powder derived from red sandalwood, called either *Hyausinha(n)* or *Hikusinha(n)*, is used as a cosmetic to be presented in a small box—along with such items as a comb, bracelet, a necklace, and mirror—to goddesses in certain *pūjā*s. The same red pigment was traditionally used as *sinha*(n) where *bhuisinha(n)* is now used. For Tantric *pūjā*s, *monhi*, a black pigment derived from lamp black, is also used.

Not only god images but also ten other pieces of equipment used in one or another *pūjā* are given *sinha(n)* markings. All objects so marked are considered as deities. Some of the pigment is taken back from the deities and placed on the heads of the officiants and worshipers as *prasāda*. The white or yellow pigment is applied first, followed by orange or red pigment. Then three kernels of husked rice (*jāki*) are placed on the worshiper's *sinha(n)* mark. The pigments and rice are given various exoteric and esoteric interpretations.

A vermilion pigment, *abhir*, is the pigment thrown during Holi festival in India, and in recent years on that occasion in Bhaktapur. Mixed with "popped" rice, *tāe(n)*, it is given as an offering during joyful rites of passage, and is sprinkled on the heads and shoulders of the central participants in some processions and ceremonies.

RICE

Various forms and mixtures of rice are used in *pūjā*s. These are *wā*, uncooked, unhusked rice;[6] *jāki*, uncooked husked rice; and *ākhye*, husked rice selected so that it includes no broken grains. *Ākhye* purified by prewashing in *nina:* and presented as an offering to deities is called *kiga:*.[7] *Matāki* is a mixture of husked and unhusked rice (also called in nonreligious terminology *wākijāki*, "*wā* and *jāki*"). Other forms of rice are of secondary importance. *Baji*, rice that is cooked in oil and then flattened by beating, is, in contrast to rice boiled in water, acceptable by a superior if cooked or touched by a clean inferior. It is offered as a food offering to deities. *Jā*, boiled rice, is offered to deities in household *pūjā*s once a year, when it is acceptable because it has been cooked, on that occasion, in milk.

Tāe(n) is "popped" rice, which is mixed with the red pigment *abhir*, and given as an offering in joyful rites of passage and some major *pūjās*.

Matāki is used for the base on which two items of equipment—the Sukunda and the Kales (or Kalas)—are placed. Both these items represent Śiva and Śakti (chap. 9). The husked rice in the *matāki* mixture represents Śakti (the potential force in the rice grain), and the unhusked rice, the combination of covering and kernel, represents Śiva as the integration of form and energy. This use of *matāki* is considered specifically Newar, in contrast to Indo-Nepalese practice. Some other items of equipment, such as the main god image in non-Tantric *pūjā*, are placed on a base of unhusked rice.

SAMHAE

Samhae (in Kathmandu Newari, sometimes, *samae*) is a "mixture of beaten rice [*baji*], popped rice [*tāe(n)*], dried fish, roasted [water buffalo] meat, eggs, soybeans and raw ginger pieces" (Manandhar 1976, 566), or some modification of such a mixture. It is presented to the meat eating dangerous deities, but is not equivalent to an animal sacrifice to such deities.

SWAGA(N)

This is a mixture of *kiga:*, *tāe(n)*, curds, and *abhir*, which is placed as a mark on a deity's forehead, and then taken back as *prasāda*, and placed on the worshiper's forehead. The mixture is also presented to individuals who are the main subjects of auspicious rites of passage, and of some other household ceremonies. It is said to confer good luck, and protect against evil. In some interpretations the *swaga(n)* mark represents the moon, which should be in front of a person as an auspicious sign for a journey.

APPENDIX FIVE

A Catalogue of Annual Events and Their Distribution throughout the Lunar Year

In this appendix calendrically determined annual events are placed within the consecutive fortnights of the lunar calendar. The numbers in square brackets represent the sequential numbering of events that is used throughout the book. Events within the solar calendar are designated "solar" and placed within the lunar calendar as they occurred in 1975/76. Events within the Devī cycle, a subset of the lunar cycle, are designated "Devī cycle."

Kachalāthwa (October/November)
The year's first two events [1, 2] complete the five-day Swanti sequence, which began three days previously with Kwa Pūjā [77], Khicā Pūjā [78], and Lakṣmī Pūjā [79]. Swanti is the lunar New Year sequence. It is a "focal" sequence concerned with the integration of city households.

1 [1] Mhā Pūjā. The first day of the lunar New Year. Primarily concerns the household and individuals in it. Special focus is worship of self/body. (Major importance.)

2. [2] Kijā Pūjā. Primarily concerns the household and individuals in it. Worship of individuals, with their household roles emphasized. Reconstitution of household with return of married-out women. Defense of members through deception against "moral death." (Major importance.)

In Swanti, the lunar New Year sequence, the household, its boundaries, and the relations of its members are emphasized and put in contrast with a larger moral world—the larger city and "moral death" as represented by Yama—beyond the household. The household deity emphasized is the benign goddess Lakṣmī. All city households do the same kinds of things at the same times in a "parallel" integration.

3.

4.

5.
6.
7.
8.
9. [3] Jugāri Na:mi. Out-of-the-city pilgrimage and *melā* at a Viṣṇu shrine. (Moderate importance.)
10.
11. [4] Hari Bodhinī. This day traditionally commemorates Viṣṇu's awakening from his four-mouths cosmic sleep. There is an out-of-the-city pilgrimage and *melā* at a Viṣṇu shrine. (Moderate importance.)

This day is the traditional end of the four-month Caturmāsa vrata which had begun on [42] Hari Śayanī on the eleventh day of Dillāthwa (June/July) in the previous lunar year.

12.
13.
14.
15. [5] Saki Manā Punhi. Worship of Viṣṇu at city temples. Many households throughout the city eat special food. (Moderate importance.)

Kaulāgā (November)

1. [6] Gopīnātha jātrā. A *jātrā* of Kṛṣṇa on the *pradakṣiṇāpatha*. (Minor importance.)
2.
3.
4.
5.
6.
7.
8.
9.
10.
11.
12.
13.
14. [7] Bālā Ca:re. An out-of-the-city pilgrimage and *melā* to the Valley Paśupatinātha shrines by those who have had a death in the family during the previous twelve months. (Moderate importance.)
15. [8] Sukhu(n) Bhisi(n)dya: Jātrā. (Begins with preliminary events on the evening of previous day). *Jātrā* of Bhisi(n) God (Bhīmasena) on the *pradakṣiṇāpatha*. Special to shopkeepers and merchants for whom Bhisi(n) is a patron deity. They offer blood sacrifices to Bhisi(n). (Moderate importance.)

Thi(n)lāthwa (November/December)

1.
2.

3.
4.
5.
6.
7.
8.
9.
10.
11.
12.
13.
14.
15. [9] Ya: Mārhi Punhi. Concerns household. Worship of rice representing Lakṣmī to ask for replenishment of the grain that, having been supplied by the harvest, will now be consumed. (Moderate importance.)

This event is related to the final completion of the rice harvest. It is an event with agricultural implications not included in the Devī cycle.

Thi(n)lāgā (December)

1.
2.
3.
4.
5.
6.
7.
8.
9.
10.
11.
12.
13.
14.
15.

Pohelāthwa (December/January)

1.
2.
3.
4.
5.
6.
7.
8.
9.

10.
11.
12.
13. [10] Ghyo cāku sa(n)lhu. **Solar cycle.** Middle-status and upper-status households make special food offerings to their *purohita*. Most households have special food and feasts. Focal deity is Viṣṇu. (Moderate importance.)

This is the local version of the calendrical event traditionally associated in South Asia with the winter solstice and the beginning of the ascending bright half of the year.

14.
15. [11] Chyālā Punhi. Unusable clay kitchen pots are discarded at the *chwāsa*. Special foods are eaten in some households. (Minor importance.)

Pohelāgā (January)

1.

The thirty-day period of the Swāstanī Vrata begins here.

2.
3.
4.
5.
6.
7.
8.
9.
10.
11.
12.
13.
14.
15.

Sillāthwa (January/February)

1.
2.
3.
4. [12] Sarasvatī Jātrā. A *jātrā* of Sarasvatī on the *pradakṣiṇāpatha*. (Minor importance.)
5. [13] Śrī Pa(n)camī. People, particularly students and farmers, worship Sarasvatī at her major temple for help in the acquisition of skills. (Moderate importance.)
6.
7.
8.
9.
10.
11.

12.
13.
14.
15. [14] Mādya: Jātrā. *Jātrā* of Śiva on the *pradakṣiṇāpatha* and other activities devoted to Śiva. There is a secondary reference to the Viṣṇu temples in the upper and lower cities. (Moderate importance.)

This is the last day of the period of the Swāsthanī Vrata. The Mādya: Jātrā has some thematic connections to it.

Sillāgā (February)

1.
2.
3.
4.
5.
6.
7.
8.
9.
10.
11.
12.
13.
14. [15] Silā ca:re. Out-of-the-city Śivarātri *melā* at the Paśupatinātha shrine complex. Within the city some men sit by fires along the roadside all night chanting the name of Śiva and sometimes smoking cannabis. An "anti-structural festival" in which "the borders of the domestic moral realm are represented by means of the ideas and images associated with benign deities." (Moderate importance.)
15.

Cillāthwa (February/March)

1.
2.
3.
4.
5.
6.
7.
8. [16] Cīr Swāegu. The first day of the Holi period devoted to Kṛṣṇa. Important elsewhere but of very minor importance in Bhaktapur. (Minor importance).
9.
10.
11.
12.

13.
14.
15. [17] Holi Punhi. End of Holi period. An image of Kṛṣṇa is carried around the *pradakṣiṇāpatha*. (Minor importance.)

Cillāgā (March)

1.
2.
3.
4.
5.
6.
7.
8.
9.
10.
11.
12.
13.

All the annual events to this point, with the equivocal exception of Sukhu(n) Bhisi(n)dya: Jātrā, a deity of relatively independent status as the patron deity of one specialized group, have been associated with benign moral deities. The next festivals introduce a long segment of the year when the dangerous and nonmoral deities become of major importance. Pāsā Ca:re comes at a time as Anderson (1971, 264) puts it "when typhoid, dysentery, cholera, and smallpox flourish with the advent of hot weather, prior to cleansing monsoon rains. It is a time of uneasiness."

14. [18] Pāsā Ca:re. An animal sacrifice is made to Taleju in the Taleju temple. Farmers' *guthi*s make animal sacrifices. Aga(n) deities are asked for protection against *pisāca*s, ghoulish evil spirits. Pollution-consuming stone deities in courtyards are cleaned. (Moderate importance.)
15.

Caulāthwa (March/April)

1. [19] Cika(n) Buyegu. Farming *thar*s and some lower *thar*s rub oil on household members' bodies to protect them against illness. (Minor importance.)
2.
3.
4.
5.
6.
7.
8.
9.
10.

The following nine-day period is Biskā:, the solar New Year sequence. The main deities are Bhairava, Bhadrakālī, the Yasi(n) God, the Maṇḍalic Goddesses, and Gaṇeśa, with secondary references to other dangerous deities. This is a "focal" sequence concerned with the division and integration of the city's spatially based units.

11. [20] Bhairava/Bhadrakālī Jātrā. Continues through the fifth day of Caulāgā. **Solar**. (Major importance.)
12.
13.
14. [21] Raising the Yasi(n) God. **Solar**. (Major importance.)
    [22] Taking the Dangerous Deities outside of their temples. **Solar**. (Major importance.)
    [23] Vārājī Jātrā. **Solar**. (Major importance.)
15. [24] Taking down the Yasi(n) God. **The beginning of the solar New Year**. (Major importance.)
    [25] Indraṇī Jātrā. **Solar**. (Major importance.)

Caulāgā (April)

On the first day of this fortnight the fifty-day Dewālī *period begins during which each phukī has a traditional time and place for its worship of its Digu God lineage deity. We list these collectively as one calendrical event, Dewālī [30], as it is for any particular phukī. (Major importance.)*

1. [26] Mahākālī/Mahālakṣmī Jātrā. **Solar**. (Major importance.)
2. [27] Brāhmaṇī/Maheśvarī Jātrā. **Solar**. (Major importance.)
3. [28] Procession to worship the dangerous deities that were taken out on the fourth day. **Solar**. (Major importance.)
   [29] Chuma(n) Gandya: Jātrā. A *twa: jātrā*. **Solar**. (Major importance.)
4. [30] The conclusion of the nine-day Bhairava/Bhadrakālī Jātrā and of the Biskā: sequence. (Major importance.)
5.
6.
7.
8. [31] Cait Dasai(n). In many households animal sacrifices are given to Bhagavatī. Sacrifices to Āga(n) deities and dangerous deities are made in temples. The day commemorates Devī's aid to Rāma. The emphasis in Bhaktapur is on Devī rather than Rāma. (Moderate importance.)
9. [32] Rām Navamī. Special worship of Rāma in his temples by the temple *pūjārī*. Recent worship at Rāma temples by devotees. (Minor importance.)
10.
11.
12.
13.
14.
15. [33] Mā(n) yā khwa: swaegu. Primarily concerns the household. Household members worship mother as a deity. Married-out daughters and absent sons try to return to the natal household for this. Those individuals

whose mother has died more than one year before this date join other Kathmandu Valley Hindus at a pilgrimage site out of the city. (Moderate importance.)

Bachalāthwa (April/May)

1.
2.
3. [34] Akṣaya Tṛtīyā. An annual auspicious day in which rites of passage can be performed without considering the proper astrological *sait*. (Minor importance.)
4.
5.
6.
7.
8.
9.
10.
11.
12.
13.
14.
15. [35] Caṇḍeśvarī Jātrā. A local *twa: jātrā*. (Minor importance.)

Bachalāgā (May)

1.
2.
3.
4.
5.
6.
7.
8.
9.
10.
11.
12.
13.
14.
15.

Tachalāthwa (May/June)

1.
2.
3.

4.
5.

On the day before Sithi Nakhā, the period for Dewālī worship of the lineage Digu deities comes to an end. Sithi Nakhā signals the preparation for the ending of the year's relatively uneventful phase, and introduces an anticipatory period of about one month until Bhagasti [40]. It designates a day safely located at the end of the dry period before the onset of the coming monsoon rains. It is the first event related to the rice agricultural cycle in the Devī cycle.

6. [36] Sithi Nakhā. **Devī cycle.** Wells, ponds, and roads must be cleaned in preparation for the coming rains. Beginning of the planting of seed rice. The Nine Durgās must complete their nine-month dance cycle prior to this date. There is worship of the earth as the goddess Pṛthivī in the Taleju temple and in many homes. (Moderate importance.)
   [37] Caṇḍi Bhagavatī Jātrā. A local *twa: jātrā.* (Minor importance.)
7.
8.
9.
10. [38] Dasa Harā. People bathe in the river and worship it to prevent misfortune. (Minor importance.)
11.
12.
13.
14.
15. [39] Panauti Jātrā. Out-of-the-city pilgrimage to attend a focal festival at another Valley town. Focal deities are Brāhmaṇī and Bhadrakālī. (Moderate importance.)

Tachalāgā (June)

1.
2.
3.
4.
5.
6.
7.

Bhagasti marks the time by which the rains should have begun and replanting of rice seedlings into the paddy fields begins.

8. [40] Bhagasti. **Devī cycle.** The Nine Durgās disappear. The masks are cremated and the ashes placed in the river. (Moderate importance.)

In the period between Bhagasti and Gāthā Muga: Ca:re [45] the rains should be under way and the rice fields and irrigation ponds flooded. The Gāthā magically take calvaria from human victims. Conventionalized obscenity is used in the fields and public areas of the city.

9.
10.

11.
12.
13.
14.
15.

Dillāthwa (June/July)

1.
2. [41] Jaganā God Jātrā. A *jātrā* of an *avatar* of Viṣṇu on the *pradakṣiṇā-patha*. (Minor importance.)
3.
4.
5.
6.
7.
8.
9.
10.
11. [42] Hari Śayanī. The beginning of Viṣṇu's four-month cosmic sleep. People may perform special worship or *vrata*s directed to Viṣṇu starting on this day. (Minor importance.)

This is the beginning of the four-month Caturmāsa period of Viṣṇu's sleep, which ends on Hari Bodhinī [4] in the next lunar year.

12. [43] Tulasī Piye. Individuals plant *tulasī* seedlings representing Viṣṇu. The plants are omens about the length of the person's life, and their dried leaves are used in death ceremonies. (Minor importance.)
13.
14.
15. [44] Guru Pūjā. A few families worship their family *guru*s on this full-moon day. (Minor importance.)

Dillāgā (July)

1.
2.
3.
4.
5.
6.
7.
8.
9.
10.
11.
12.
13.

The following day marks the period by which the transplanting of rice into the flooded paddy fields should be completed. The Gāthās have by now taken their calvaria from human victims. The period of licensed obscenity will cease on the following day.

14. [45] Gāthā Muga: Ca:re. **Devī cycle.** Demonic figures are chased out of the city's neighborhoods and then out of the city and cremated. (Major importance.)
15.

Gu(n)lāthwa (July/August)

1.
2.
3.
4.
5. [46] Nāga Pa(n)camī. Worship and propitiation of dangerous *nāgas* (supernatural serpents) for the protection of the house and household. (Moderate importance.)
6.
7.
8.
9.
10.
11.
12.
13.
14.

The four lunar fortnights beginning with Gunhi Punhi contain thirty-one of the year's seventy-nine annual events. This period is a quiet one for farming work. The rice transplanting has been completed, and the harvesting will not begin until the last days of the period.

15. [47] Gunhi Punhi. Purification and renewal ceremonies by the Rājopādhyāya Brahmans. Farmers worship frogs inadvertently killed during farming work. Introductory events anticipating the carnival of the next day. (Moderate importance.)

Gu(n)lāgā (August)

1. [48] Sāpāru. A procession, the Cow Jātrā, is held representing all people who have died in Bhaktapur during the past year to enable them with the help of the "Cow Goddess" to enter Yama's kingdom to be rewarded or punished according to their *karma*. Interspersed with the procession is a carnival. The procession moves around the *pradakṣiṇāpatha*. (Major importance.)

The events of this day constitute the city's major public festival of its dead and its most extensive antistructural festival.

2.
3.

4.
5.
6.
7.
8. [49] Kṛṣṇa Janmāstamī. A Kṛṣṇa image is carried in a procession around the *pradakṣiṇāpatha*. Visits by Kṛṣṇa devotees to his city shrines. (Minor importance.)
9. [50] Śītalā Pūjā. Visits by household members to the shrine of the goddess Śītalā, traditionally for protection against smallpox. (Minor importance.)
10.
11.
12.
13.
14.
15. [51] Gokarṇa Au(n)sī. Primarily concerns the household. Household members worship their father as a deity. Married-out daughters and absent sons try to return to the natal household for this. Those individuals whose father has died more than one year before this date join other Kathmandu Valley Hindus at a pilgrimage site out of the city. (Moderate importance.)

Ya(n)lāthwa (August/September)

1.
2. [52] Sūrya Vināyaka Jātrā. A *jātrā* of a Gaṇeśa image—brought from an important shrine at a neighboring village—on Bhaktapur's *pradakṣiṇāpatha*. (Minor importance.)
   [53] Vārāhī Jātrā. The *jātrā* image of the Maṇḍalic Goddess Vārāhī is taken around the *pradakṣiṇāpatha*. (Minor importance.)
3. [54] Dattātreya Jātrā. *Pradakṣiṇāpatha*. (Minor importance.)
   [55] Bhairava Jātrā. *Pradakṣiṇāpatha*. (Minor importance.)

On this day Tij is celebrated by Bhaktapur's non-Newar Hindu neighbors, but not by Bhaktapur.

4. [56] Cathā Gaṇeśa. Household worship of Gaṇeśa and avoidance of the dangerous seeing of the crescent moon on this day. (Minor importance.)
5. [57] Ṛṣi Pa(n)cami. Household worship of Ṛṣis, particularly by women. (Minor importance.)
6.
7. [58] Umā/Maheśvara. Worship in households of a manifestation of Pārvatī and Śiva as an affectionate conjugal couple. (Minor importance.)
8.
9.
10.
11.

The following eight days are the integrated focal sequence of Indra Jātrā in Kathmandu. Certain of the otherwise independent events ([59], [61], [62], and [65]) in Bhaktapur during this period have thematic echoes of Kathmandu's sequence, but are not, for Bhaktapur, a connected sequence.

12. [59] Yama: Dya: Thānigu. Poles are erected in each *twa:* representing Yama, and worshiped during the next eight days to protect the local *twa:* people from death. (Moderate importance.)
13.
14. [60] Ananta Nārāyaṇa Pūjā. Visits to the city's major Viṣṇu temples. (Minor importance.)
[61] Indrāṇī Jātrā. The maṇḍalic deity Indrāṇī is carried around the *pradakṣiṇāpatha* and then left out in an open shelter near a pond overnight. (Moderate importance.)
15. [62] Yau Dya: Punhi. The name of this day refers to lights that will be carried around the city for three days, the sight of which will enable people to go to heaven when they die. People from Bhaktapur and surrounding villages go to the pond where the Indrāṇī image had been left on the previous night to worship it and bathe. (Moderate importance.)

Ya(n)lāgā (September)

1.
2.
3. [63] Chuma(n) Gandya: Jātrā. A local *twa: jātrā.* (Minor importance.)
4. [64] Śmaśāna Bhailadya: Jātrā. A funeral mat representing the Bhairava of the cremation grounds is carried around the *pradakṣiṇāpatha.* (Moderate importance.)
[65] Pulu Kisi Haigu. An elephant made of funeral mats, associated with Indra's vehicle and with death, is carried around the *pradakṣiṇāpatha.* Sometimes this is an occasion for violence, including fights between the upper city and the lower city. (Moderate importance.)
5.
6.
7.
8.
9. [66] Dhala(n) Salā(n). (May be optionally observed on the fifteenth day of the fortnight instead of on this day.) The ceremony is for the "*pitṛ*," in this case all deceased ancestors of a *phukī* group who have been dead more than two years, and the ceremonies are done ideally at the river side by large groups of associated *phukī* members. (Moderate importance.)
10.
11.
12.
13.
14.
15.

Kaulāthwa (September/October)
The next ten days are the complex focal sequence Mohanī. Rather than attempting to enumerate here individually its complexly interwoven events, we follow the local practice of listing it by its successive days during any of which more

than one major event may be taking place. Mohanī marks the period in the rice cycle when the rains should have finished and the rice harvest completed. The festival enacts the victory of Devī over forces of disorder, the gathering together of the forms of the goddess in central association with the political goddess Taleju, and the movement of Devī's powers into the Nine Durgās group that will move out into public city space during the next nine months. During these ten days important household events take place in the context of city-wide public events marking a large variety of significant city spatial elements. The full goddess Devī and her various subordinate forms are the central deities of the sequence.

1. [67] Mohanī. **Devī cycle.** (Major importance.)
2. [68] Mohanī. **Devī cycle.** (Major importance.)
3. [69] Mohanī. **Devī cycle.** (Major importance.)
4. [70] Mohanī. **Devī cycle.** (Major importance.)
5. [71] Mohanī. **Devī cycle.** (Major importance.)
6. [72] Mohanī. **Devī cycle.** (Major importance.)
7. [73] Mohanī. **Devī cycle.** (Major importance.)
8. [74] Mohanī. **Devī cycle.** (Major importance.)
9. [75] Mohanī. **Devī cycle.** (Major importance.)
10. [76] Mohanī. **Devī cycle.** (Major importance.)
11.
12.
13.
14.
15.

Kaulāgā (October)

1.
2.
3.
4.
5.
6.
7.
8.
9.
10.
11.
12.

The last three events of the year [77, 78, 79] are the first three days of the five-day Swanti sequence.

13. [77] Kwa Pūjā. Primarily concerns the household and individuals in it. Placation of Yama, the god of death. (Moderate importance.)

14. [78] Khicā Pūjā. Primarily concerns the household and individuals in it. Placation of Yama. (Moderate importance.)
15. [79] Lakṣmī Pūjā. Primarily concerns the household and individuals in it. Worship of Lakṣmī for good fortune for the household. (Moderate importance.)

APPENDIX SIX

Rites of Passage and Death Ceremonies

In this volume one major aspect of Newar religious life has been neglected—the sequence of *saṃskāras*, the rites of passage that each individual traditionally undergoes on passing from one culturally defined stage of life to the next. A consideration of these ceremonies with their emphasis on such matters as birth, maturation, menstruation, initiation, marriage, old age, and death is of central importance for the study of aspects of intimate individual experience and family organization to cultural tradition—matters that we hope to deal with more extensively elsewhere.

The timing of the rites of passage is generated by the tempos of each individual's life cycle, in contrast to the annual events that have preoccupied us in this volume which submit the entire city to the seemingly impersonal tempos of regular cosmic events, affecting all in the same way, bringing everyone's life into a common synchrony. Each citizen of Bhaktapur—and the family group clustering for the occasion around him or her—undergoes, in contrast, each of the *saṃskāras* in his or her own unique turn. In resonance with this individually determined tempo the *saṃskāras* are most centrally concerned with aspects of the representation, formation, and maintenance of certain of those urban "cellular units"—individuals, households, and components of the extended family—whose outer faces, whose specialized outputs and inputs, constitute and are integrated by the mesocosmic integrative processes of the larger city. The individual at the focus of the *saṃskāras* moves through them—or more precisely is moved by them—into larger and larger networks of other people, into more and more developed and responsible moral "personhood," and into wider and wider spaces. While there is some minor reference to the constituting spaces of the city, the movements marked by the *saṃskāras* are primarily those that we have designated in chapter 16 as within the "tubular" life of the family, a life whose main movement is from an opening into this present lifetime from a previous birth, then to a progression through the stages of the moral life of the family and extended family, and finally on to an elaborately conceived postmortem state at the other end. In all this the family is central and the city only a peripheral environment.

Throughout the sequence of the *saṃskāras* there is first a gradual separation from the mother, a successive movement into larger sets of relations and spaces, an increase in the definition of personhood, and an associated emphasis on increasing purity and moral responsibility. Then in the later *saṃskāras* there is a movement toward a transcendence of ordinary personhood and responsibilities, and a preparation for postmortem life. Yet, underneath this theme of progressive growth and eventual transcendence there is an important common theme or implication running through all of the *saṃskāras*, an implication that is consonant with the implications of the annual festivals on the one hand and with the general shape of the experience and the informal and formal education of people in Bhaktapur on the other. This is the absolute dependence of the individual undergoing the rites of passage on the precise and often difficult work of others. In the *saṃskāras* the essential workers are family members, who are necessary for the individual's development, beginning with the enabling *mantra* that will produce his or her ability to speak and ending with the collective work of forming a body for his or her spirit after death and moving it on to its place of judgment in Yama's kingdom. The subject of the *saṃskāra* rites is dependent on the strenuous, traditionally specified activities of the performers of the *saṃskāras* to form his or her very self—and those responsible workers, for the most part members of household and *phukī* (abetted in the more complex rites such as cremation by specialists), must commit themselves over and over again to the performance of the traditional practices of the rites in the service of the rite's subject individual. As the subject of the *saṃskāras* needs the family workers and their assistants and comes to learn to depend on them, so do they in turn need the forms provided by tradition, and reiterate that dependence on tradition in the course of the mass of *saṃskāras* they perform for others in the course of a normal life cycle.

Not only is the locus of the *saṃskāras* in the matrix of household and extended family different from that of the annual festivals but the nature and place of the deities is also different. The deities involved are not the deities emphasized in the major city festivals, deities who are, to a large degree, both special and central to Bhaktapur as a city. In most rites the reference to deities—aside from the lineage gods who, in keeping with the emphasis on family, are emphasized—are minimal and peripheral. Where deities are present and emphasized they are the old major gods of the central Hindu tradition, the sun, Sarasvatī, Viṣṇu, Śiva as a *liṅga*, gods from a time and place beyond the city. In the *saṃskāras* people are more Hindus than they are Newars or citizens of Bhaktapur.

However, there are certain exceptions to this within the group of *saṃskāras*. While most of Bhaktapur's *saṃskāras* are variants of traditional South Asian *saṃskāras* (cf., e.g., Pandey 1969) there are some (and some aspects of others) that are considered to be specifically Newar; that is, they are not performed by the Indo-Nepalese. Of these the most significant "Newar" rite is the *Ihī* or mock-marriage. Because of the implications of mock-marriage, aspects of menarche rites and of "true" marriage must also be modified in ways locally thought to be distinctively Newar. The *Ihī* ceremony does have, not surprisingly, a local deity. This is Pārvatī as the patroness of the Kathmandu Valley. There are also included among the special Newar *saṃskāras* a set of old-age celebrations not performed by the Newar's Hindu neighbors.

Bhaktapur's *saṃskāras* are sufficiently complex in themselves, in their social distribution, and in their relations to traditional South Indian versions, that they would warrant a full study in themselves.[1] We will list here the total collection of rites identified as Bhaktapur's Hindu *saṃskāras* by local Brahmans. We can only sketch some of their dimensions for reference purposes, giving relatively more details of the specifically Newar *saṃskāras* and of those aspects of others that are particularly relevant to the concerns of this study. While a few *saṃskāras* are done only by upper segments of the macrostatus hierarchy, and are thus socially differentiating, many of them are reportedly performed by all ranks, including the untouchables.[2] We have no systematic information, however, on differences in the *form* of the procedures at different levels and among different *thars*, nor on when various *saṃskāras* may have been introduced into middle or lower *thar* practices in a possible relatively recent gesture of "Sanskritization."

Bhaktapur does not have prenatal *saṃskāras*. The first *saṃskāra*, the Jihvāśodhan, takes place after birth. Cremation is considered to be the final *saṃskāra*, and the many death ceremonies that follow cremation—and that we discuss in this appendix—are not included in the term. Some of the *saṃskāras* are usually given their traditional Sanskrit names, by upper-status speakers, at least, for others alternate or exclusively Newari names are used.

1. *Writing a mantra on the tongue: Jihvāśodhana.* The particular Hindu postnatal *saṃskāra* emphasized in Bhaktapur by upper-level *thars*, at least, is a variant of the traditional *medhājanana*, the "production of intelligence." Following birth, after the infant has been cleaned and before it is put to the mother's breast, a *mantra* representing the goddess of learning Sarasvatī is written on the infant's tongue in honey, often by means of a silver stylus, by the infant's father. This is said to ensure that the child will be able to talk and to learn well.

2. *Application of lamp black to the child's eyes by the father's sister.* On the sixth day after birth the father's sisters, the infant's *ninis*, and members of the *phukī* group come to the house. The *ninis* bring small gifts for the infant. Six oil lamps (usually small unglazed clay dishes with oil and two wicks in each of them) are placed on beds of unhusked rice and lit. Each *nini*, in turn, prepares lamp black by holding a metal container over each of the six flames sequentially to collect lamp black, which she then places on the infant's eyelids. This is said to strengthen the eyes, and to protect them from disease and blindness. The naked infant is rubbed with oil by each of the *ninis* in turn. When each has done her part, the infant is dressed in a shirt-like garment.

3. *Name giving: Nāmakaraṇa.* This takes place on the twelfth day after birth. The time of the cutting of the infant's umbilical cord, when it is thus separated from its mother, is considered the moment of birth, and is made note of. On the sixth day after birth the child's astrological status is supposed to be supernaturally inscribed on its forehead by the divine record-keeper Citragupta. On the sixth day (the day that lamp black is placed on the infant's eyes) a Jośi, an astrologer, comes to the house and is told the time of birth—the day, hour, and minute. He tells the family something about the infant's astrological condition, and then returns to his house to prepare a written account, a *jāta:*, which will be presented to the child on this twelfth day.[3] At this time the child is given a secret name known to household members but not ordinarily used. This name is chosen by the household, but must begin with the proper first letter determined by the Jośi from his reading of the infant's horoscope. The name is written on the birth record, the *jāta:*, by the Jośi, and is whispered into the infant's ear at this time by the head of the household.

In upper-status families, those who have the right to Tantric initiation, just after the *phukī*'s purification following the ten-day period of birth contamination the infant is taken to be presented to the family lineage deity, the Āga(n) God.[4] As the place where this deity is kept, the Āga(n) House, is usually separate from the family house, among these families this is the first occasion on which the child is ceremonially taken out of the house.

4. *The rice feeding ceremony: Ja(n)ko.* This ceremony takes place for girls when they are either five or seven months of age and for boys when they are six or eight months. The earlier time is the usually preferred date; the later one is used if there is some polluting condition in the family, or if the earlier date is considered astrologically inauspicious. This is (in the nomenclature used by the upper-level *thar*s) a *macā* ("child") *ja(n)ko*; the term "*ja(n)ko*" is also used for certain old-age ceremonies. There is an alternate term used by many upper-status people (although seldom by Brahmans), and used as the ordinary term among Jyāpus and lower *thar*s, *jā cipa(n) thiyekegu*, "feeding [the infant] with boiled rice."[5] The elements of this ceremony common to the various *thar*s are the "rice feeding" itself and the taking of the child out of the household to the neighboring Gaṇeśa shrine. Upper-level *thar*s add further elements.

In the first focus[6] of the ritual, at the proper astrological time, the *sāit*, the infant is fed boiled rice and other food (such as bread, fruit, curds, milk) by the *phukī* leader, the *phukī nāya:*. In a common interpretation the mother's milk is not sufficient to feed the infant any more and it must be "taught" to eat other foods. The infant's diet had been mother's milk, typically supplemented by honey, rice flour, milk from other sources, and clarified butter. Now boiled rice and other mashed-up foods are added. It is said that with this shift in its diet the infant can now be taken care of by people other than its mother.

After the rice feeding and before the next major phase of the sequence other elements may be added to the ceremony. In upper-status families at this point the beak of a live and carefully held gander may be introduced into the infant's mouth so that it touches the tongue "in order to give the infant strength in digesting its food as Agni (the fire deity) was able to digest the sacrifice." In a practice followed in many *thar*s (many more than do the gander ceremony) the child is now surrounded by various objects that represent interests and professions that would be appropriate given its gender and status, as well as by objects that would be inappropriate. These might included a book, a pen, soil, rice, ornaments, and items representing some particular trade. The child is now watched to see which objects seem to interest it. It is said that if it is interested in the wrong kinds of things it must be watched and guarded against the development of that interest.

In the next major movement of the *saṃskāra*, done by all the *thar*s who do it at all, in another movement of separation from the mother the child is taken by its *pāju*, one of its mother's brothers, and carried out of the house in a procession preceded by musicians and followed by men of the infant's father's *phukī*.[7] Women will not join the procession, although young girls may join it. The *pāju* carries the infant to the local Gaṇeśa shrine or temple—introducing the child, it is said, to the neighborhood—and then to other temples that are important to the family. Each temple is circumambulated and offerings are given in behalf of the infant (symbolized by being first held to the infant's head in mimicry of a respect gesture) to the temple or shrine deity. The procession then returns to the house where the *pāju* returns the infant to its mother.

While in the previous *saṃskāra*s the household and the patrilineal *phukī* members—the groups who had shared in the pollution of the infant's birth—were the ritual actors, in this *saṃskāra* a new kind of participant is introduced, the mother's brother, the *pāju*, representing the matriline. The *pāju* will be of central importance in many of the subsequent *saṃskāra*s. The *pāju* now gives a symbolic gift of money to the mother "to compensate her for having taken the [paternal] household's child out of the house." Then as representative of the mother's natal household he gives substantial and valuable presents to the child, the mother, and other household members. (The *pāju* will return again, echoing this first visit, with gifts at the time of a boy's second birthday, and of boys' and girls' fourth birthday.) Members of the *phukī* and affinally related kin and friends then present *swaga(n)* (app. 4) and other gifts to the infant.

The ceremony is followed by a major feast, a *bhwae* (which characteristically is attended by guests from a group wider than *phukī*). This is the first of the *saṃskāra*s in which such feasts are given. If a family is able to do it, in some cases, such as the birth of a first son, this feast may include hundreds of invited guests.

Now the sequence of *saṃskāra*s separates for a while for boys and for girls. The boys will go on to the *Busākhā* and *Kaetā Pūjā* rites; the girls, to the *Ihī* and *Bārhātaegu* rites.

5. *Boy's hair shaving: Busākhā.* The *Busākhā*, or hair-shaving ceremony, like the following (and often intimately associated) rite for boys, the *Kaetā Pūjā*, not only moves the boy from one "Newar" or Hindu stage to the next but also, in so doing, differentiates him from the people of other *thar*s and, much more saliently, other status levels. At the same time it differentiates him from females.

Not only do girls not have these two ceremonies, but there are emphases on the boy's maleness within them.[8] The *Busākhā* represents the beginning of a boy's moral responsibility for the *dharma* of his *thar*, a responsibility that, however, is most clearly and fully introduced in the next *saṃskāra*, the *Kaetā Pūjā*.

The *Busākhā* and the *Kaetā Pūjā* are often associated conceptually and among many *thars* are approximated in time. The Rājopādhyāya Brahmans separate the two widely. Among them the *Busākhā* is often done when boys are five years of age; the *Kaetā Pūjā* (associated for the Brahmans with the traditional *Upanayana* initiation) comes much later, at eleven or thirteen years of age. For those other *thars* who do the *Busākhā* as well as the *Kaetā Pūjā*,[9] however, the *Busākhā* may be done only three days prior to the *Kaetā Pūjā*—as is often the case with the Chathariyās and Pa(n)cthariyās—or immediately prior to the *Kaetā Pūjā*, on the same day, in a combined ceremony (as is the case with the Jyāpus). The *Busākhā* and the *Kaetā Pujā* must be done when a boy is at an odd-numbered age, and is usually done at the ages of five, seven, or nine.[10]

The core act in this *saṃskāra* is the shaving of the boy's head with, as is the traditional custom of "twice-born" Hindu men, the exception of an occipital queue of hair, called in Newari the *āngsā*.[11] Boys do not have their hair cut before this ceremony, and it is said that after the *Busākhā* the boy, because he has had his hair cut, no longer looks like a girl. In the course of the elaborate ceremony the key moment of transition comes when the *pāju* at the proper astrological *sāit* shaves four patches of hair on the boy's head, representing, in sequence, east, south, north, and west, conventionally the front, right, left, and rear of his head, respectively. The *pāju* will also touch the boy's right and left earlobes with needles, to symbolize ear piercing, another traditional Hindu *saṃskāra* that is done in Bhaktapur along with the hair shaving. A Nau, a member of the barber *thar*, does the full shaving of the head and the actual piercing of the ears. After the barber's work the boy is stripped naked in front of the onlookers and helped by family members in bathing.

In the course of the day representatives of the *phukī* go to worship at the maṇḍalic *pīṭha* as they will, starting with this *saṃskāra*, at the time of all subsequent auspicious ones.

Ideally the *Busākhā* is the first of the rites that ceremonially mark an increasing social responsibility—the others, for a boy or young man, being the *Kaetā Pūjā* and marriage. Traditionally in the course of South Asian *saṃskāras* "after the *Cūḍākaraṇa* or tonsure when the child grew into a boy, his duties were prescribed and his responsibilities explained . . . without encumbering his mind and body with book-knowledge and school discipline" (Pandey 1969, 33). Those disciplines were to follow later.

For most *thars* it is the *Kaetā Pūjā* that almost immediately follows the *Busāhkhā* (and that in the lower *thars* may be done without a *Busākhā*), which is the *saṃskāra* most clearly associated with a change in the behavior expected of the boy, a change defined with *Kaetā Pūjā* as the boy's new status as a fully privileged and responsible member of his *thar*. Among the Rājopādhyāya Brahmans and the upper-status priestly *thars* who emulate them (Jośi, Tini, and Ācāriya) where there is a separation of some years between the two *saṃskāras*, a boy after his *Busākhā* is expected to begin to be cautious and responsible about polluting contacts in his play and other activities outside the family. It is said that he should now begin to represent the Brahmans and to act like one outside the family.[12]

6. *Boy's full membership in their thar: Kaetā Pūjā.* This is one of the major *saṃskāras* and, in contrast to most of the preceding ones, is done by *thars* throughout the macrosocial system, including the Po(n) untouchables. It takes its name from the giving of the *Kaetā*, a loincloth, and derives from the traditional Hindu *Upanayana* ceremony, that initiation into the knowledge, responsibilities, and full membership of one's *jāt* or "caste" which entailed the "new birth" of the sacred thread-wearing, twice-born non-Sudra castes whose sacred threads were presented to them in this ceremony.

The *Kaetā Pūjā* varies in its timing, its elaboration, and its details among different *thars*. But the presentation of the loincloth is always of focal importance. That presentation, like all the focal moments in *saṃskāras*, must be made at the astrologically proper *sāit*. Those *thars* that wear the sacred thread (Tini and above) have a second climactic *sāit*, the proper moment for the presentation of the thread.[13]

The *Kaetā Pūjā* must be done in an odd-numbered year of age. It is usually performed by non-Brahmans at a relatively early age—five, seven, or nine. The Brahman customarily do the *Kaetā Pūjā* at the age of nine or eleven, their boys' *Busākhā* having been done at the age of five or seven. Those upper-level *thars* whose members have priestly functions, and who wear the sacred thread (i.e., Jośi, Tini, and Ācāriya), usually follow the Brahman pattern of having the *Busākhā* at an early age and the *Kaetā Pūjā* several years later. For non-Brahman nonpriestly upper-level *thars* the *Kaetā Pūjā* usually follows on the fourth day after the *Busākhā*. For Jyāpus and other middle-level and lower-level *thars* who do the *Busākhā*, it is usually combined with the *Busākhā* in one continuous sequence.

For the Brahmans the *Kaetā Pūjā* ceremony is part of a complex set of events called *Burā(n) taegu*,[14] which represent the traditional Brahmanical initiation, the *Upanayana*, which is followed by a now abbreviated period lasting for three months of further study and ritual activities representing the traditional period of Brahmanical studies, the *Brahmacārya*.

For Jyāpu and other middle-level *thars* served by Brahmans the *Kaetā Pūjā* (with its immediately preceding introductory *Busākhā*) is usually the first of the *saṃskāras* that employ Brahman *purohitas*.[15,16] The *thars* that combine the two *saṃskāras* begin by the shaving of the boy's head, starting with a gestural cutting by the *pāju* completed by the Nau.

Now among the middle-level *thars* after the hair shaving, and among upper-level *thars* at the beginning of the independently held *Kaetā Pūjā*, a special purification of the boy takes place. A Naunī, a woman of the barber *thar*, pares the boy's finger and toe nails, For the higher-level *thars* this is done at an astrologically determined *sāit*. The nail paring represents a further degree of purification than the boy has previously had, and thus a further degree of resulting purity. While in the case of *phukī* pollution, prior to the *Busākhā* children only need a simple purification and following it upper-status boys must have their hair shaven, now, following *Kaetā Pūjā* boys must also have their nails pared in a full participation in adult male major purification. They are now full "persons" in the sense defined by considerations of purity and impurity.

After the nail paring the boy is washed and brought naked to the previously prepared and purified *pūjā* area, where the ceremony will proceed under the direction of a *purohita*. In its course a ceremonial loincloth is presented to the naked boy and tied on him by the senior active male *phukī* member, the *phukī nāya:*. The *pāju* has, in this phase, only a secondary role; he brings additional loincloths as gifts to the now mature boy. After the *kaetā* is given, the upper-level non-Brahmanical *thar*s may then give the boy his sacred thread.[17] But for all *thar*s, whether they have rights to wearing the sacred thread or not, it is the *kaetā* itself—the *Kaupīna*, an important part of traditional Hindu *Upanayana* rites—which marks the transition of the boy into full membership in his *thar*.

The *Kaetā Pūjā* is also a *dekhā* (Sanskrit *dīkṣā*), an initiation (chap. 9). The family *purohita*, now acting as the boy's *guru*, reveals to him one or more of the *mantra*s that the *phukī* gives to its boys in the course of various initiations (chap. 9). Among the upper *thar*s this is done at the time of the presentation of the sacred thread, and is the first of a series of *dekhā*s that the upper-status boy and young man will be given—the later ones being related to the Tantric worship of the lineage gods and to the special knowledge that may be acquired in preparation for death. At the time of the *Kaetā Pūjā* the boy is also instructed about morning and evening worship and about ritual cleanliness, and—in the upper-level *thar*s—may be told about elementary meditation techniques using the *mantra*s he has been given.

After the *Kaetā Pūjā* the boy is theoretically a responsible and full member of his *thar*. He can now perform all the rituals, most importantly the death ceremonies for his parents, with the exception of those upper-status Tantric rituals that will need further initiation.

The *Busākhā* and *Kaetā Pūjā* are devoted to the social and psychological formation and definition of boys.[18] During childhood there are also two *saṃskāra*s for girls, the mock-marriage and the menarche ceremony. Then, with the marriage ceremony, both men and women will again undergo the same *saṃskāra*s.

7. *Mock-marriage: Ihī.* The Newar *saṃskāra*s in Bhaktapur are for the most part closely modeled on the traditional Hindu *saṃskāra*s. The most dramatic exception is the *Ihī*, the mock marriage ceremony for girls.[19] The implications of the *Ihī* require major changes in traditional menarche rites, and some changes in the traditional "true" marriage.[20] *Ihī* and the related modified menarche and marriage rites were traditionally not done by the Rājopādhyāya Brahmans,[21] nor, for different reasons, by the unclean *thar*s from level XIV, that is, the Nāe, and below. "*Ihī*" is an old Newari word for marriage, but it is now used only for the mock-marriage, not the "true" marriage, the *Byāhā*.[22] The *Ihī saṃskāra* must be done before the onset of menstruation, and can take place at any time between, approximately, five and eleven years of age. At the core of the *Ihī* is a traditional Hindu ceremony of marriage, but the spouse is

Viṣṇu/Nārāyaṇa.[23] The premenstrual virgin girl is given in marriage to the deity as a gift or offering in the traditional Hindu marriage act called *kanyā dāna*, "the giving of a virgin daughter." Because of this prior gift in the Newar mock-marriage, the *kanyā dāna* segment of the marriage ceremony is, in contrast to traditional South Asian practice, omitted in Bhaktapur's true marriage ceremony.

The legends told to explain the *Ihī* ceremony emphasize one of its central implications. Pārvatī was the daughter of Himavān, the deity of the Himalayas. When she was to be married to Śiva, Himavān gave Nepal (that is, the present Kathmandu Valley) to her as her dowry. One day as Pārvatī was walking through the Valley she heard an old woman crying. Pārvatī asked her why she was crying. "My husband is dead. A husband is necessary for a woman; without a husband a woman's life is terrible." Pārvatī pitied her and asked Śiva for a boon. "Can you do something for the women of my natal home so that they will not become widows?" Śiva answered, "Nārāyaṇa and I will arrange it so that there will no longer be any widows in Nepal." Thus the Newars were given the *Ihī* ceremony. Nārāyaṇa was the groom, and Śiva the witness.

The legend not only emphasizes a maneuver for avoiding the ritual disabilities of widowhood but places the scene in the setting of Pārvatī's natal home, her *tha: che(n)*, the setting where a woman is a relatively indulged child and daughter, rather than being in the greatly contrasting condition of wife and mother in the home of her husband's family and in the circle of his *phukī*. The women of "Nepal," that is, the Newar women of the Kathmandu Valley, are Pārvatī's sisters, not her sisters-in-law.

The *Ihī* ceremony is, as a marriage had to be in Hindu tradition, a premenarche marriage. This means that the second marriage, the one to a mortal, can be delayed as all second marriages can, until after menarche—often long after it. Thus both the necessity of child marriage[24] and the full force of widow disability are ameliorated by the invention of this Newar *saṃskāra*. The *Ihī* ceremony is, as we shall see, in some aspects of its form as well as in its legendary intent, somewhat subversive of the Hindu patriarchal and hierarchical principles that are central to other *saṃskāra*s.

Ihī ceremonies involve a group of girls, often a large group. There are several *Ihī* ceremonies in Bhaktapur during the course of a year. Each is sponsored by a well-to-do man who has a (biological or classificatory) daughter, granddaughter, or younger sister to be given the *saṃskāra*.[25] The sponsor will gain religious merit and social prestige through his sponsorship. Traditionally sponsors were Chathariyā and Pa(n)ctharivā, but in recent years Brahmans and Jyāpus (the latter made relatively wealthy through land reforms and beginning to follow upper-status religious practices) have also become sponsors. The exact range of *thar*s taking part in a particular ceremony is determined in part by the status level of the sponsor; thus the lower-level clean *thar*s are more likely to be found at a Jyāpu-sponsored ceremony than at a Brahman-sponsored one.

In the days preceding the *Ihī* ceremony each girl who is to take part receives invitations from her *tha:thiti* (the kin acquired through out-marriages of the *phukī* women) and from her *pāju*'s (mother's brother) households in

Bhaktapur—and sometimes in nearby towns—to visit them. She spends several days in these visits and is offered *swaga(n)* and food in each household. On the day before the main *Ihī* ceremony there are various preliminary activities. During the day the main Ācāju priest who will join with other priests in the ceremonies sacrifices a goat at the sponsor's local areal Gaṇeśa shrine, and then visits each of the city's nine maṇḍalic *pīṭha*s to make offerings of *samhae* and alcoholic spirits to the goddesses. He begins, as is always the case in such sequential visits, with Brāhmaṇī to the east, ending after a circuit of the periphery in a clockwise direction with Tripurasundarī at the center. He worships, making the proper sacrificial offerings, at each *pīṭha* in turn. While there are visits to the particular maṇḍalic areal *pīṭha* of *phukī* groups in the course of most of that *phukī*'s *saṃskāra*s, this movement to all the *pīṭhas* reflects the amalgamation of the *Ihī* girls into a spatially and socially heterogeneous and at the same time integrated group.

During this preliminary day—as they would before any major *saṃskāra*—the members of each involved household will have preparatory purification ceremonies, and those families with Āga(n) deities will make offerings of *samhae* to them. In the latter part of the day before the ceremony the sponsoring household, the one where the ceremony is to take place, performs a *Duso* (or *Duswa*), "a looking in" ceremony, that is, a preparation for the visit of the deity. This is thought of as a notice and "invitation" to the deity to attend the ceremonies. This ceremony is done by Brahmans for all their own major auspicious *saṃskāra*s, but by other *thar*s only in this preparation by the sponsor of the *Ihī* ceremony. The *Duso* begins when the main Brahman *purohita* (there are usually two or three Brahmans involved in the ceremony), and the two auxiliary priests (a Tini and a Jośi), the sponsor of the *Ihī*, and, often, other senior males of his household, go in a procession accompanied by musicians to a location near the Jyāthā Gaṇeśa shrine in the potter's quarter, where a purified *pūjā* area is prepared. A member of the Kumha: (potter) *thar*, accompanied by members of the procession, brings black clay to the ritual area. The black clay is formed into a ball, the "Ali(n) God," said to represent "Śiva and all the (benign) gods." The Ali(n) God is now worshiped along with a clay pot, a *Brahmākalaśa*, on which there is an image of Brahmā, representing the *trimūrti*—Brahmā, Śiva, and Viṣṇu. Another piece of black clay is set aside to represent Gaṇeśa in the next day's ceremony.[26] Carrying the Ali(n) God, the Brahmākalaśa, and the clay that will represent Gaṇeśa, the group returns to the house of the sponsor in a procession and is met at the house's *pikhā lākhu* by the wife of the main *purohita*. She now performs a *lāskusa*—a formal ceremony greeting the deities and the members of the procession and chasing off evil influences in a formal exorcism, followed by her leading the central participants into a sacred area, in this case the area in the house where the formal ceremonies will take place.[27] Now the main *purohita* goes through the proceedings for ritually "establishing" (*sthāpana*) the Ali(n) God.

The girls who are to have the ceremony the next day are waiting at the house, and are each attended by at least one representative (either male or female) of their *phukī*. The *Ihī* girls are dressed in red, sometimes in a special red-and-yellow *Ihī* dress resembling a traditional marriage dress. One girl—

usually the sponsor's daughter, or perhaps niece or granddaughter—is chosen as the *naki(n)*, the "leader of the brides." A complex series of events follows, many of which mimic procedures from Brahmanical marriage ceremonies, which indicate in various ways the binding together of each girl with her divine groom and the divine witness.

These ceremonies are followed by a feast for the *Ihī* girls at the sponsor's house in which boiled rice, here called *duso jā*, prepared by the wives of the Brahman *purohita*s who are officiating at the ceremony, is eaten. This partaking by a group of mixed *phukī*s, *thar*s, and macrostatus levels of boiled rice is unique. In other feasts where there are representatives of non-*phukī* groups, and above all, members of other *thar*s it is essential that boiled rice *not* be served—*baji*, beaten fried rice being served instead. Nevertheless, this apparent opposition to ordinary proper procedures is limited. First, the girls are not yet full members of their *thar*s. Second, the girls are separated into "eating groups" by floor space—so that some group separation is maintained. As in all ritual feasts, the leftover food is taken to the areal crossroads deity, the *chwāsa*, and discarded. At the end of the ceremony the girls return to their homes. They are now considered to be in a state of purity. They must now fast until the next day.

The main events occur on the next day in an elaborate sequence requiring the services of Brahman, Jośi, Tini, and Ācāju priests. In the events of the day, as in those on the preliminary day, the *Ihī* mirrors many of the elements of South Asian upper-status traditional true marriage ceremonies, as well as having its unique aspects. The ceremony has three astrologically determined *sāit*s, indicating the core transformative elements. This is the time for the preparatory purification by a *naunī*;[28] for the application of *bhuisinha(n)*, orange-red pigment, to the parting of the girl's hair;[29] and for the presentation of the girls as gifts of a virgin, a *kanyā dāna*, to the deity.

In the course of the day's preparatory phases the Ācāju does a *pūjā* called *desa bali*,[30] which is an offering to the gods of all the Tantric temples in the city, represented in the *pūjā* by grains of polished rice. There is nothing like this in ordinary *saṃskāra*s.

The main images at the wedding—provided separately for each girl—are the *byā* (in Nepali, *bel*) which is the fruit of the Bel plant (*Aegle marmelos*), and a small gold image (or flat piece of gold with an image engraved on it). The *byā* represents Śiva; the image represents Viṣṇu/Nārāyaṇa. Each girl is accompanied by her father (or, if he is not available, an elder brother or one of her father's brothers). He will offer her as a *kanyā dāna* to Viṣṇu/Nārāyaṇa. At the proper *sāit* for the *kanyā dāna* each girl stands with her hand linked to her male donor's and the girl's mother (or, if necessary, a surrogate) pours ritually pure water and milk over their joined hands. The donor says his name and (in the case of the upper-level *thar*s) the name of his *gotra*, his daughter's name, and the name of his father and grandfather. The daughter is to be presented "in the name of" these lineage members. At the exact astrological time—called out by a Jośi—the donor gives his daughter to the god as manifested by pressing her thumb against the golden image. The image is held against the *byā* representing Śiva as the witness to the marriage. The focal marriage is followed by a sequence of closing ceremonies, and ends with a supper of rich, sweet foods.

Many girls customarily establish bonds of fictive kinship with other girls during the *Ihī* ceremony by exchanging *sinha(n)* pigment and *kisalī*, small pots containing husked rice grains. The pots and the rice are then used in offerings to a ceremonial sacrificial fire that had been made and worshiped at the beginning of the *Ihī* sequence by the attending priests. The bond friend or fictive sister is called a *twāe* (chap. 6). During later life two young women may make themselves *twāes* in special ceremonies as men do, but the *Ihī* is the setting in which young girls characteristically form these bonds. It is noteworthy that in congruence with other implications of the *Ihī* ceremony, *twāe* relations extend kinship beyond the *phukī*, and frequently beyond the *thar*, and, sometimes, even beyond the two girls' status levels.

The *Ihī* ceremony stands in a coherent contrast to the other city *saṃskāras*—all others (except the old-age ceremonies) variants of traditional Hindu rites of passage. In its main import it rationalizes an avoidance of premenarche marriages and of certain aspects, at least, of the stigmatization and disabling of widows in a society where, in consonance with its Himalayan roots, the status of women had long been relatively less constrained than in Indo-Nepalese and Indian Hindu societies. In keeping with its legendary reference to the Newar's homeland as Pārvatī's natal home and to Parvatī as its tutelary goddess, the *Ihī* ceremony in itself has elements suggesting social integration blurring the central patriarchal order and differentiation of the *phukī* and its satellite alliances—an order emphasized or taken for granted in other *saṃskāras*. Such gestures of blurring of patriarchal order are the joining together in one ceremony of members of different *phukīs*, *thars*, and status levels, the worship of all the city Tantric shrines and all the maṇḍalic *pīṭhas* in concert—in a representation of, among other things, all the city's lineages—and the creation of trans-familial, and sometimes trans-status-level fictive sororal bonds. These gestures are made within the context of a traditional Hindu marriage ceremony. In Michael Allen's epitome, "the mock marriages may be said to constitute a formal show of commitment to orthodoxy in Brahman dominated communities within which key values are still strongly unorthodox—especially as regards the status of women and female sexuality and reproductivity" (1982, 203).

It is usually said that a Hindu boys' transition to full adult "ritual" status begins after *Upanayana*—which means in Bhaktapur his *Kaetā Pūjā*—while a girl's transition begins after her marriage. Thus, for example, in traditional South Asia "the death of a boy after his *Upanayana* entails full fledged defilement, but a girl before her marriage is still regarded as a child and her death causes defilement for a period of three days only" (Pandey 1969, 258). The transformation made by marriage in a Newar girl's ritual life stage is more complex, for she has two marriages. After the first one, the *Ihī*, she is still a full member of her natal family, while the second one, her "real" marriage, brings membership in a new, a conjugal family.

In some ways the *Ihī* ceremony does have the same implications for a girl that the *Kaetā Pūjā* has for a boy. After her *Ihī* ceremony, the girl would receive full adult death rites if she were to die. She is now said to belong fully to her *thar* and to be responsible for not becoming polluted by sharing vulnerable foods with children of lower *thars* and for purificatory cleaning before eating. For middle-level *thars* after *Ihī* a girl is presented to her *phukī* lineage deity, the Digu God, as a sort of initiation into the *phukī* at a special ceremony of initiation held at the time of the following Dewālī Digu Pūjā[31] (chap. 9).

While girls are notionally said to be fully responsible after the *Ihī*, many of them are still very young, and in fact it is at the time of their menarche ceremony that they are really expected to be able to understand and follow the *thar* rules for separation and purity, and it is that *saṃskāra* that signals a girl's passing beyond some aspects, at least, of childish lack of responsibility.

8. *Menarche ceremonies: Bārhā taegu and Bārhā cwa(n)gu.* The menarche rite differs significantly between those *thars* who perform the *Ihī* ceremony and the Rājopādhyāya Brahmans, who traditionally did not. The contrast illustrates the influence of the mock-marriage on the Newar menarche *saṃskāra*.

For the Brahmans, marriages were until a few years prior to this study necessarily completed ceremonially before the bride's first menstruation. Although the child bride continued to live in her natal home until after menarche, sometimes well after it, she was brought—usually temporarily, returning to her own home after the rite—to her husband's house in anticipation of the onset of her first menses so that her menarche rite would be held at her husband's home. If menses started unanticipatedly at her natal home, she was immediately brought to her husband's home, her head and face covered with a shawl. For the Rājopādhyāya Brahmans it was in accordance with standard Hindu traditions considered to be a serious violation of the *dharma* if (1) a girl was not married before menarche and (2) once so married, the married girl's first menstruation took place in her own home. In the Brahmanical (and traditional Hindu) case the menarche *saṃskāra*, a ceremony lasting for twelve days, took place not only in the husband's home but at the time of actual menstruation.

For all the other *thars*, those whose girls had *Ihī* marriages and who were thus "married" before menarche but who did not have a human husband's home to be brought to, the *saṃskāra* takes place in the girl's natal household—or in a related *phukī* household. These ceremonies can be performed at the actual time of a girl's first menstruation—in which case they are called *Bārhā cwa(n)gu*, or prior to, often long before, menstruation, as a mock-menarche *saṃskāra*, the procedure in these latter cases being called *Bārhā taegu*.[32] There are various combinations of *Bārhā taegu* and *Bārhā cwa(n)gu* procedures. Upper-status *thars* usually do a *Bārhā cwa(n)gu*, that is, a ceremony at the time of menarche, although this may be a relatively recent change from earlier *Bārhā taegu*, premenarche, practices.[33] Traditionally middle-level *thars*, that is, for the most part Jyāpus, would link a group of premenarche girls in what was for those girls a *Bārhā taegu* to the *Bārhā cwa(n)gu* ceremonies for an actually menstruating girl. In recent times, among such middle-level *thars*, the connection to actual menstruation has been often ignored and often only premenarche girls participate in a group ceremony. All these arrangements are considered effective menarche ceremonies, in that girls who have a premenarche *Bārhā taegu saṃskāra* will have no further ceremony at the time of their eventual first menstruation.

Traditionally the girls who were to have their *Bārhā taegu* had completed their *Ihī* marriage, and were perhaps seven or eight years of age, although now, it is said, there is some tendency at least for some of the girls to be older. While the *Bārhā cwa(n)gu* must be done at the time of actual menstruation, the optional range of timing of the *Bārhā taegu* calls for an astrological decision as to the auspicious timing. In contrast to other *saṃskāras*, the decision does not determine the *sāit* for some focal action within the ceremony but, in this case, the proper lunar fortnight in which the twelve-day rite should take place.

The menstruating girl, or the group of premenstrual girls (who are usually sisters or girls of the same *phukī*) are to be isolated for twelve days in a room in which the windows are covered so that no sunlight will enter.[34] The *Bārhā taegu* girls are dealt with as if they were actually undergoing their first menstruation, that is, as if they were *Bārha cwa(n)gu* girls. During this time the "menstruating girls" must not be seen by males (as the girls are within the house, this taboo primarily concerns male kin and, perhaps, their friends) who are beyond their *Kaetā Pūjā saṃskāra*. The sight of the girls is said to be somehow dangerous to them. It was, reportedly, traditionally said that men would turn to ashes and die if they glimpsed the girls, and it is still said that it would, at the least, bring some sort of misfortune to a man who happened to see them. After twelve days of seclusion the girls are brought to the upper open porch, the *ka:si*, of the house to see and be seen by the sun. It is said that the girls are still full of power at this time, and that only the sun can resist their force, although it is said that, if the day is cloudy, even the sun resists seeing them. The isolation, then, is said to protect men and the sun from seeing the girls—not to protect the girls. During the girls' isolation from men household women enter the girls' room, and girl friends and young female relatives from other houses visit the girls. These visits, during which the girls play and laugh, are particularly important in the *Bārhā cwa(n)gu*, as the single girl would otherwise be relatively isolated. The visiting women and girls who are not *phukī* members are not polluted by these visits—in contrast to the household and *phukī* members, both male and female, who may share group impurity during this period (see below).

During the first four days the *Bārhā* girls have a restricted diet. On the fourth day they have the first of the two ceremonial purifications associated with the *saṃskāra*. The girls go to the *ka:si* or *cheli* (chap. 7) of the house and bathe in a minor purification procedure. This marks the traditional end of actual menstruation. They then return to the room. Now, and for the remaining days, the girls are given rich foods to eat, including milk, meat, and beaten rice. On the fourth day in all *thars* served by Brahman *purohitas* the families of the girls send traditional substances—twelve betel nuts, twelve cloves, *bhuisiha(n)* pigment, rice powder, and mustard oil[35]—to the family *purohita*. This is said to be a notification to the *purohita* that the girl has completed her first menstruation.[36]

On the twelfth day the confinement ends with the *Bārhā pikāegu*, "the taking outside," which is a ceremonial climax of the *saṃskāra*. On this day, in preparation, the Nau and Naunī come before sunrise to purify the girls in a house courtyard or on the *cheli*. Household members are also purified before sunrise but separately from the girls.[37]

After dawn the *purohita* does a *Kalaśa Pūjā* on or near the open porch. The girls, their heads and faces covered with a cloth, are brought by household women to the edge of the *pūjā* area, where the *purohita* sprinkles sacred water and other purifying substances that had been used in the *pūjā* on them. The girls are then brought to the *ka:si*, where the cloths covering their heads are removed so that they can see—and be seen by—the sun (or, on a cloudy day, the sky). The girls' special power/contamination[38] is now considered to be removed. The girls worship the sun with *kiga:* in an elementary *pūjā* (app. 4). They then do a second *pūjā*, this time a formal and elaborate one, to the sun with the help of the *purohita*, during which they worship the "twelve suns" of the twelve solar months. In the course of this *pūjā* the girls make offerings using a conch shell for the first time and will now be able to do so in subsequent worship on other occasions.

After the *pūjā* to the sun the household senior woman, the *naki(n)*, does a ceremonial act that anticipates a similar act occurring toward the end of the sequence of ceremonies in the "true" marriage sequence, and which on that occasion is said to signify that sexual intercourse has begun. This is the *sā(n) pyākegu*, the hair-parting ceremony. The *naki(n)*, as will the husband in the marriage ceremony, places a ceremonial cosmetic mixture (rice flour and oil) in the supine hands of each girl. The girls then rub the cosmetic mixture on their faces. The *naki(n)* then combs each girl's hair and braids it into three plaits, which are then woven together. Then for each girl in turn, the *naki(n)* places black pigment on the girl's eyelids and puts a spot of decorative *bhuisinha(n)* pigment on her forehead. Now the *naki(n)* holds up a mirror so that the girl may see herself, a gesture that has added force in that during the twelve days of seclusion the girls were forbidden to look at their reflections in a mirror.

The *sā(n) pyākegu* is followed by other *pūjās* and offerings. In contrast to other auspicious *saṃskāras*, there is no worship of the maṇḍalic areal *pīṭha*. The ceremony is followed by a small feast for close *phukī*, affinal, and feminal kin, but there is no large feast for the larger *phukī* group as there is in many other *saṃskāras*. The *phukī* group in some *thars* has been polluted during the twelve days. That pollution is lifted at the time of the *Bārhā Pikāegu*, without any need for major purification procedures.

This *saṃskāra*, as the *sā(n) pyākegu* makes clear, alludes to the traditional implication of the menarche ceremony as a married girl's transition to active sexuality. The delayed true marriage and, also, the inclusion of the *Bārhā taegu* preadolescent girls alters this meaning. But the implication of incipient sexual passions, if not active sexuality, is still there.

The *Bārhā Pikāegu*, the ceremonial exit from seclusion, represents the reintegration after a period of "liminal" isolation (during which the major danger is to the household males) of the now actually or notionally sexually mature girl with religious and social forms and controls. In the traditional context this all takes place within a girl's husband's family, and represents a significant addition to her role as the family's daughter-in-law to now also being her husband's sexual partner. All these implications of the menarche ceremony have been transformed for the Newars by the introduction of the *Ihī* mock-marriage.

9. *Marriage: Byāhā.* With the "true" marriage we begin the remainder of the sequence of *saṃskāra*s that are now once again common to males and females.

The complex marriage sequence for the middle and upper *thar*s is a variation of traditional Indian marriage patterns with adjustments made for the mock-marriage. Those Brahmans who do not perform the mock-marriage do not make these adjustments. There has, however, been some shift in recent decades even among non-Brahmans away from the traditional Newar sequence—which was adjusted to the mock-marriage—toward more ordinary South Asian marriage ceremonies.

A complete description of Newar marriage would have to take into account not only first marriages (that is, for the Newars, first "true" marriage) but also secondary marriages. It is only possible here to outline some of the major features of these complex sequences of ceremonies. Many descriptive details for other Newar groups are given in P. H. Bajracharya (1959), Nepali (1965, 198–231), and Toffin (1984, 401–420).

After the preliminary informal decisions about a marriage have been made (chap. 6) the betrothal is formalized in the first ceremonial act of the marriage sequence by a gift of ten betel nuts, *gwae(n)*,[39] and secondary gifts that are presented by the prospective groom's father to the prospective bride's father in a visit to the bride's household. The *phukī naki(n)*, representing the prospective groom's *phukī*, accompanies the groom's father. She puts two decorations on the girl's forehead—one a mark of *swaga(n)* and below it a gold decoration, which often has an image of Nārāyaṇa on it. Before these visits the prospective marriage could have been called off by either household without any impropriety, now the betrothal is considered formal and definite.

Sometime during the month prior to the wedding ceremony the prospective groom's family (but not the groom himself) will visit the betrothed girl's household to present gifts. In upper-level *thar*s—and now also in many middle-level ones—this visit is formalized as the "*lākhā*" visit, during which sweetcakes, *lākhāmari*, and other presents are given. The members of the bride's household will eat some of the cakes; after the wedding they will return the remainder, supplemented by presents, to the groom's household. In some upper-level *thar*s other traditional gifts are sent in the course of the month to the prospective bride's household.

In the four days preceding the wedding itself the prospective bride, echoing the visits of her long-ago *Ihī* marriage, visits the households of her *phukī* as well as of her mother's brothers, her *pāju*s, where she is given ceremonial foods.

On the day before the wedding ceremony both the bride's and groom's households in middle-level and upper-level *thar*s hold *śrāddha* ceremonies (see death ceremonies, below) to the lineage ancestors, "notifying" the ancestors of the event. Upper-level *thar*s also worship at their maṇḍalic *pīṭha*.

For Newar Brahmans who do not have *Ihī* marriages, the core of the true marriage is the *kanyā dāna*, the gift of the virgin girl. This must be done at the bride's home at the proper astrological *sāit*. But among the other *thars* the *kanyā dāna* has already been given in the *Ihī* ceremony. For these *thars* the essential act of marriage union, which must be done at the auspicious *sāit*, is a ceremony done at the groom's home, a ceremony called *ho(n)kegu*, "causing to be joined together." Among some families in recent years an additional South Asian marriage custom that did not exist among the Newars of Bhaktapur in previous decades has been adopted by some upper-status families and those Jyāpu families who now emulate them. This is the *swayambar* (Sanskrit *svayaṃvara*), in which—again at the proper astrological *sāit*—the bride is ceremonially given to the groom at the bride's household in a first phase of the marriage on the evening of the day preceding the *ho(n)kegu*. The traditional absence of the *swayambar* ceremony among the Newars is sometimes speculatively explained as not being necessary because "the girl was already married," that is, she has already been given away by her natal household. Several of the ceremonial acts in the *Ihī* ceremony, in fact, are versions of acts that are done among Indo-Nepalese (and traditionally in South Asia) in the course of the *swayambar*.[40]

In the traditional Newar sequence there is a ceremony at the prospective bride's household on the evening before the wedding. The groom's father and other representatives of his family, but not the prospective groom himself, attend the ceremony. The prospective bride presents sets of ten betel nuts, first to the family *purohita*, then to senior members of the household, and then to other assembled relatives and household members[41] with the exception of her mother and father. After the bride has presented the betel nuts the household or *phukī* senior woman (other than her mother) decorates the bride and gives her offerings. Now her father presents her with a ceremonial mirror, a *jyalānheka(n)*, and she, in return, gives him a set of betel nuts. Her mother then gives her an ornate container for ceremonial pigment, a *sinhamu*, and the daughter, in return, gives ten betel nuts to her mother. The girl now takes pigment from the *sinhamu* and applies it to her own forehead. In some families at this point the groom's father places an anklet on each of the bride's legs. He must bend down and touch her feet to do it, reversing the usual action of respect of child to parent and, even more poignantly perhaps, bride to parent-in-law. Finally her mother's brother, the bride's *pāju*, takes her on his back and carries her out of the house to the *pikhā lākhu* of the house, its symbolic outer boundary, where he delivers her to the groom's representatives. In the past she was then taken—covered over and hidden from view—in a carrying sling carried by men from the Gāthā *thar*.[42] A procession is formed. Musicians come first, then the bride, next people carrying her dowry, and finally the representative of the groom's family. The bride is taken first to the neighborhood Gaṇeśa shrine, and (if carried) carried three times around it. Her family members have followed. Now there is a formalized exchange between representatives of the two households, in which the representative of the groom's family is asked to promise to take care of the new bride. Her family now leaves her and returns to the household.

The groom's representatives and the bride now proceed to the groom's household. The bride is met at the house *pikhā lākhu* by the *phukī* or household *naki(n)* and is ceremonially "taken in" (*du kāegu*) to the house in a ceremony in which evil forces and spirits are driven from the new bride.[43] The bride has had her head and face covered with a shawl since she left her parents' home, and it is still covered. On entering the house the women of the household may look under the shawl to see her face[44] and will talk with her informally.

The next step is the actual marriage ritual, the *ho(n)kegu*. At the proper *sāit* the bride, holding ten betel nuts and a garland, circumambulates the groom and presents him first with the garland and then the betel nuts. The transfer of the betel nuts is the focal moment of marriage. The groom then presents traditional presents to the bride. She then gives a set of ten betel nuts to each of the ritually adult members of the groom's household and to his family *purohita*. She is introduced to each of these, and bows to their feet as she presents the nuts. Each family member puts small coins in a dish kept near the bride in exchange for her presentation to them. The bride bows to each member superior in status to her, but those of inferior status[45] bow to her. All this is done under the directions of the *purohita*.[46] Throughout the *ho(n)kegu* he directs the actions of others and makes some offerings to the bride and groom, but he does not conduct a *pūjā* or perform formal worship to deities himself.

Now the *naki(n)* places a *Swaga(n) sinha(n)* mark on the bride's forehead and gives her presents of clothes. The *naki(n)* then gives the bride and groom water for washing their hands and purifying their mouths. According to various reports, in Newar marriages in other Valley cities and towns the bride and groom now take food offerings from a common metal dish—a *thāe(n) bhu*—signaling through the eating of each other's *cipa*, a nonhierarchical sharing of substance. In the upper-level *thar*s in Bhaktapur (and among those other *thar*s that emulate them), however, two *thāe(n) bhu* are used, as it is said that because the bride is no longer a *kanyā* and has menstruated it is not proper for her husband to eat from her dish.[47] The food in the two dishes and the sequence of eating is ascribed complex symbolism, and is associated with offerings and worship to the sun and the collective deities. After these offerings have been made the groom eats half of a hard-boiled egg and gives the other half to the bride. He does the same thing with a portion of fish and of meat that he has tasted and (in most families) of alcoholic spirits that he has previously sipped. The groom puts food into the bride's hands, and sometimes (often in response to joking requests from the onlookers) puts food directly into her mouth. The active feeding has overtones of erotic play and female receptivity and intimacy, as well as indicating the bride's subordinate and dependent status signaled by her sharing in the groom's *cipa*, that is, in his substance (chap. 11). The *ho(n)-kegu* concludes with other ceremonial actions. The focal and essential elements in the *ho(n)kegu* are the bride's giving of betel nuts to the groom and her eating of his *cipa*. These are found in the variations of the ceremony among various *thar*s. Thus the Jyāpu ceremonies, which may dispense with most of the features of the upper-status *ho(n)kegu*, keep these two elements.

Following the *ho(n)kegu* the groom and males of the *phukī* go to the maṇḍalic *pīṭha* with an Ācāju for worship to the Maṇḍalic Goddess. In the evening there is a large feast in the groom's household and family and friends of the household come to "see the bride."

There are various activities which may follow in the days after the wedding.

In Brahman and some upper-status non-Brahman families the bride will be brought to the groom's Digu God shrine and presented to that lineage deity a few days after the wedding. In families at most status levels, however, the new bride will be brought to the Digu God shrine for the first time during the *phukī*'s collective worship to the Digu God during the next Dewālī period.

Usually within four days after the wedding members of the bride's family come to "see their daughter's face" in a visit to the groom's house. They bring gifts, including clothes and, perhaps, money. In the presence of women from the groom's household who offer them sweets and other hospitality, the members of the bride's family present the gifts and decorations of *swaga(n)* to the bride. After this visit the bride's family may conduct her back to her natal home, where other members of her own family and friends and neighbors visit. The bride's family may now send a representative to invite the groom to visit his new wife's natal home. The groom returns to the bride's house accompanied by a friend (rarely a *phukī* member). The bride's mother or the household *naki(n)* gives gifts of clothes and decorations of *swaga(n)* to the couple. The husband, the wife's household's new *jicā bhāju*, is introduced to the assembled guests and household members, traditionally meeting the family for the first time. At each introduction to household members and other relatives the husband presents a gift of ten betel nuts, and they, in return, make an offering of money to the couple. There are other ceremonial offerings and exchanges, and then a feast, during which there may be some teasing of the couple, and some mild practical jokes may be played on the *jicā bhāju*.[48]

Now the husband, his accompanying friend, and the wife return to the husband's house, often led by someone (traditionally for the upper *thars*, a *jyāpu* with a client relationship to the husband's household) carrying a very large and ornate oil lamp, a "marriage *sukundā*."[49]

10. *Tantric initiation: Dekhā.* The initiation (*Dekhā* or *Dīkṣā*) of upper-status males into their *phukī*'s Āga(n) God worship (chap. 9) is sometimes considered as a Newar *saṃskāra*.

11. *Old-age ceremonies: Burāburī ja(n)ko.* Another set of *saṃskāras* that are not done by the Indo-Nepalese and are thus identified as Newar *saṃskāras* are the old-age ceremonies called the *Burāburī ja(n)ko*.[50] They are done by lower-middle-level, middle-level, and upper-level *thars*. These are first celebrated by a married couple when the husband reaches the age of "seventy-seven years, seven months, seven days, seven *ghaus* and seven *palās*."[51] If a man or woman is widowed, the *ja(n)ko* takes place when he or she[52] has reached that age. There are preliminary phases of purification and other preparatory ceremonies that may, for the upper-level *thars*, be elaborate, lasting for several days and requiring the work of several priests. The core of the ceremony comes when the couple (or the widow or widower) dressed in "royal" clothes (the man wearing a turban) enter a small chariot at the proper astrological *sāit* and are pulled by their children and grandchildren around the coutryard adjoining the house. Sometimes the chariot is pulled around the *twa:*. The ceremony, called the "*Bhīma rathārohan*," the Bhīma chariot ride, takes its name from this epi-

sode. When the chariot ride is finished, the couple leave the chariot and family members and friends make offerings to them, take *prasāda* from them, wash, and bow down to their feet. All this treats the man and woman not only as royalty but as gods. They are considered as quasi-divine after the ceremony—progressively so if they live to undergo the subsequent ones—and this divinity is ideally associated with the relinquishing of active control over family affairs. Three more ceremonies, all making use of a chariot, may follow, one at the age of eighty-one years (at which time it is said that a person has seen the full moon 1,000 times) one at eighty-eight years, eight months, eight days, eight *ghaus* and eight *palās*, and again at ninety-two years. These three *ja(n)kos* are called, respectively the Candra, Deva, and Mahā *Rathārohans*.

These *ja(n)kos* progressively move individuals out of ordinary social "personhood," allowing others in the family to assume positions of authority, while compensating the old people with an increased ceremonial status. The ceremonies may also be thought of, in part, as a disentanglement from ordinary life in a preparation for dying and death, a preparation that culminates in the procedures immediately prior to death.

12. *Dying and cremation*. The ceremonial aspects of dying and the subsequent cremation is considered the last of the *saṃskāras*. There are a long set of rituals following death that are not considered to be *saṃskāras*. The sequence of ceremonies associated with dying and death are very elaborate, are related to various and sometimes contradictory doctrines about the fate of the soul after death, and vary somewhat in extent and detail among different *thars*. These ceremonies are closely related to other South Asian death practices, and we will treat them in a somewhat summary way here.[53]

Dying. Among middle and upper *thars* when an individual is thought to be in danger of dying, various ceremonies may be performed. These include *dāna*, offerings, sometimes very substantial ones, to a Brahman. These ceremonies and their accompanying offerings are made in the hope of healing or, if that fails, of facilitating dying and the fate of the individual after death.

When death is considered to be imminent, the dying person and his or her family have an option as to where the death will take place. This should be either on the *cheli*, the ground floor of the house (considered for this and other purposes to be outside the house), or at one of the sets of steps, *ghāts*, descending into the river.[54] It is said that most people prefer to die on the *cheli* of their own home, and that the great majority do so. An Ayurvedic physician is often in attendance, and when he decides that death is imminent, an area purified with cow dung and scattered with black barley grain is prepared. The dying person is placed on the purified area with his or her head facing toward the south, the direction of Yama's kingdom. Shoots of certain plants (*tulasī*, a variety of basil, and *kusa* [Sanskrit *kuśa*] grass, *Demostachya bipinnata*) are placed under the body.

There is an emphasis on Viṣṇu/Nārāyaṇa at the time of dying.[55] The *tulasī* leaves placed under the person's body represent him.[56] Water touched to a *śālagrāma*, a representation of Viṣṇu, is flicked into the dying person's mouth.

He or she is reminded (and this is done even if the person appears to be unconscious) to repeat the name of Nārāyaṇa over and over again.

If the person is dying at home, a vessel containing pure water, representing a *tīrtha*, an area usually associated with a river or other body of water that has power to give merit, is placed near his or her feet. At what is presumed to be the moment of death, an attendant splashes water from the bowl on the person's feet, which may also be placed into the bowl. Some of the water is also poured into his or her umbilicus. When someone dies at the river, the feet, or sometimes the entire lower half of the body, may be plunged into the river. This act, represented during dying at home by the action with the "*tīrtha* water," is said to be to prevent the vital principle, the *prāṇa*, which leaves the body at the moment of death, from leaving it inauspiciously through one of its lower openings.[57]

Preparation of the body. After death the body is prepared for cremation. (If the person has died at the river, the body is brought first to the top of the *ghāṭ*.) The body is prepared by *phukī* members and members of the death *guthi*—an association of fellow *thar* members who will assist the family of the dead person with the subsequent stages of preparation, funeral procession, and cremation (see Toffin 1975*b*). The corpse's eyes are closed, its clothes removed, and the body washed. A piece of clay from the river is placed as a ceremonial mark, a *tīrtha si(n)ha*, on the corpse's forehead. The individual's birth horoscope, or *jāta:*, which was prepared at the time of the *Nāmkaraṇa saṃskāra*, is placed on his or her forehead and fastened with a thread. The corpse's genitals are covered with a white cloth, which will be left in place during the subsequent cremation, when all other coverings are removed from the body. Four small clay dishes, containing oil and burning wicks, are placed at the body's right and left shoulders, head and feet. The body is now covered by two additional white cloths—one covers it from the waist to the neck, and the other is placed over the head and tied under the chin, leaving the face exposed. A burning wick from the dish at the corpse's head is given to a member of the Cāla(n) *thar* (level XIII; see chap. 5), who uses it to light a twisted oil-soaked cloth supported in a bowl of oil to make a flaming torch that he will carry in the funeral procession, which is about to begin.

The clothes worn at the time of death (or under some conditions other clothes that had belonged to the person) are brought to the neighborhood crossroads *chwāsa*. A member of the Jugī *thar* who has a traditional client relationship with the family and who will be used again during the mourning ceremonies of the fifth or seventh day after death, is notified, and then expected to go to the *chwāsa* and take the clothes "for his own use."[58]

The funeral procession. The body is now lifted by members of the death *guthi* and carried to the *pikhā lākhu* boundary stone in front of the front door of the house. A bamboo carrier for the body, a *kūta:*, has been placed there, and covered with a woven reed mat, a *pulu*. The body is placed on the *pulu*, and the *pulu* is folded to wrap and enclose the body. Finally a colored cloth is placed over the *pulu*, and garlands of flowers and uncolored popped rice are placed on the cloth.

The *kūta:* is carried by four *guthi* members. The procession is headed by a member of the *guthi* who throws unhusked rice and small coins along the road, in a procedure that mimics the *jātrā* of a deity being carried in a procession in order to be housed for the first time in a temple, the corpse being likened to the god and the afterworld to the temple. Following the leader of the procession is the Cāla(n) carrying the flaming torch in one hand, and a pair of small cymbals in the other, which he clangs together as he approaches each road crossing the funeral route to prevent anyone crossing in front of the funeral procession, which would be an ill omen for all concerned. Following the Cāla(n) is the litter of the corpse, followed, in turn, by the chief mourner, ideally the eldest son of a man, or among some *thar*s the youngest adult son of a woman. The chief mourner, generally referred to by the Sanskrit term "*kriyā putra*," "the son who does the [death-related ceremonial] work," is called at this stage the "fire setter," the one who will ignite the funeral pyre. Wearing only a loincloth (for the upper *thar*s the traditional South Asian loincloth, the *dhoti*), with his upper body naked, he walks with the support of two helpers who are client Jyāpus for the upper *thar*s, or friends or neighbors for the middle or lower ones. The *kriyā putra* is followed by male *phukī* members, neighbors, friends, and affinal male relatives.[59] The body is carried along the *twa:*'s traditional route to the particular cremation ground, where it is to be burned (chap. 7).

The cremation. When the cremation ground is reached, the activities preliminary to the cremation itself are begun. This phase of events is called the *liko kriyā*, "the [death] work done at the feet." For the upper *thar*s a member of the Cyo *thar* (level XI) acts as, it is said, "a sort of a priest" to direct the activities during the *liko kriyā*. For the other *thar*s the work is directed by a *phukī* or death *guthi* member. The *kūta:* is placed on the ground so that the head of the corpse is to the south. A paste made of water and *mā baji*—fragments that are residues of the beating of fried rice to make *baji*, and which is used only on this occasion—is formed into three mounds at the feet of the body by the *kriyā putra*, who, facing the body, kneels to its feet. The three mounds are considered to be sacrificial offerings, *bali*, to, respectively, crows (the mound to the left), to the *preta* (the spirit form that the soul of the dead person will take; the mound at the center), and to dogs (the mound to the right). The crow and the dog are considered as representatives or messengers of Yama, and are so represented in later death ceremonies. Now, as part of the offering, water is poured near each of the three mounds.

Four clumps of grass with soil still clinging to the roots are placed at the borders of the area on the cremation ground where the funeral pyre is to be erected. They are arranged so as to be at the head, feet, and right and left shoulders of the body, as the clay oil lamps had been at the time of death. The funeral pyre is assembled by the death *guthi* members. The cremation is considered by Brahmans to be a "Vedic fire sacrifice," a *yajña*. The four clumps of grass and earth are said to represent the four Vedas. When the pyre is completed the *kūta:* is lifted and carried three times around it. The *pulu* and the cloths covering the body (except for the cloth covering the genitals) are removed, and the body is removed from the *kūta:*, placed on the funeral pyre, and covered with dry straw. Now the chief mourner takes a torch and, igniting it from the flame of the torch held by the Cāla(n), circumambulates the body three times. An inflammable mixture of sandalwood, camphor, and clarified butter is placed at the corpse's mouth, and it is here that the *kriyā putra* applies the flame to begin the cremation. Now a bundle of straw is ignited at the flames at the mouth and then used to set fire to the pyre itself.

As the pyre and corpse burn, the climactic moment comes with the cracking of the head of the corpse, at which time the soul of the corpse leaves in the form of a *preta* to begin its postmortem journey and transformations.[60] The *kriyā putra* throws offerings (which may include barley, parched rice, *kiga:*, clarified butter, and leaves of the *Ficus religiosa*) into the fire at the time of the cracking of the skull.[61] When the body has been reduced to ashes and bone fragments, the fire is extinguished. The ashes and bone fragments are brought to a *tīrtha* in the river near the cremation grounds. The *kriyā putra* enters the water and throws some of the ashes in the four cardinal directions. He then puts some of the ashes and bone from the head into the clay soil at the river bottom.

The return to the house. The men now return to the house where the procession had begun. A Po(n) will go to the cremation grounds to take the funeral cloths and mat and the *kūta:*.

The women of the household have remained at home during the procession and cremation. If a dead man leaves a widow, she breaks her bangles and they will be thrown away at the neighborhood *chwāsa*. Women who are related to the family begin to come to the house at this time, as they will throughout the succeeding period of mourning, and conventionally begin to wail loudly as they approach the house.[62]

The members of the funeral procession return to the house, where the family members enter the upper floors. The *kriyā putra* cannot enter the house. He goes to the *cheli*, the ground floor, which is in such situations considered to be outside of the house.[63] He will remain there during the following period of mourning.

The activities of the mourning period. The cremation is considered the last of the *saṃskāras*. What now follows continues the effect of the *saṃskāras* in effecting and signaling an individual's movement from one culturally defined stage of being to another, but now the locus of the individual's life, now his or her life in death, is removed progressively further and further from house, household, and city.

Following the cremation there is an elaborate cycle of postdeath ceremonies and procedures. Those taking place in the ten days immediately following the death and ending when the family is purified of its postdeath pollution are called the *dasā kriyā*, the "ten works."[64] In the subsequent months and years there is another series of special ceremonies on various anniversaries of the death, as well as the special observances incumbent on or optional for bereaved people during the course of the festival year, which we have noted in our discussions of the annual cycle. We will only outline these ceremonies here, noting some details that bear on other aspects of this study.

The *dasā kriyā* period revolves around the activities of the *kriyā putra* and the evolution of the spirit of the deceased person. The *kriyā putra* remains on the *cheli* alone or, sometimes, accompanied by a male member of the household. During this period the *kriyā putra* wears only a loincloth, wrapping himself in a shawl if it is cold, cooks his own food, sleeps on a straw or wool mat on the ground, and does not shave. He is unable to touch anyone except the man who may keep him company, and is thus even more polluted than the household and *phukī* members who also have been polluted by the death.

On each day of the mourning period the *kriyā putra* boils rice at home and carries it to the river, taking care not to touch anyone. In upper-level *thar*s the *kriyā putra* is accompanied in his trips to the river by a man from the borderline clean Bhā *thar* who will later, on the tenth day, consume rice that has been in contact with the corpse to ensure that the spirit will take a human form (chap. 10). The Bhā carries flowers, colored pigment, and other materials that are to be used in worship. The Bhā is also supposed to instruct the *kriyā putra* at the riverside in the proper steps of the worship.[65] The Bhā makes a *liṅga* out of a kind of clay that comes from some distance below the earth to represent Śiva as the deity "Hāṭakeśvara,"[66] a god said to dwell under the earth. Offerings of milk and water are poured into small terracotta dishes placed on either side of the *liṅga*. A clay waterpot with a hole in the bottom is placed on a tripod over the *liṅga* and an "umbrella" formed from *kuśa* grass is placed in the pot. Each morning the *kriyā putra* takes river water and puts it into the clay pot, where it slowly drips through the hole onto the *liṅga*. It is said that the Śiva *liṅga* represents the deceased person. The water is said to cool the spirit of the dead person, which is in its *preta* form.[67] Now the *kriyā putra* forms the rice into three balls—called *pya(n)* in Newari or *piṇḍa* in Sanskrit[68]—as offerings to (in the following order) the crow, the dog, and, finally, the *preta*. The *piṇḍa* offered to the *preta* is both an offering to and a representation of the dead person, as is the case with *piṇḍa*s in all the subsequent death ceremonies.[69] The three *piṇḍa*s are then given various offerings. Finally, the *kriyā putra* throws the crow *piṇḍa* across the river as food for the crows, puts the dog *piṇḍa* on the near river bank as food for the dogs, and throws the *preta piṇḍa* onto the mud in the center of the river (if the river is low as it is during much of the year), where it is supposed to be picked up and supposedly eaten by the same Po(n) who was also responsible for taking the funeral cloths from the cremation grounds.

The *kriyā putra* then returns to his home. He cooks his own food, restricting himself to one meal a day. He is supposed to spend his time there reading sections of the Garuḍa Purāṇa dealing with life after death.

On the fourth day of the mourning period close friends, relatives, and members of the death *guthi* come to the *cheli* to talk with the *kriyā putra*.[70] A focal day in the course of the *dasā kriyā* is, depending on the *thar*, the fifth or seventh day.[71] On this day a married-out daughter of the household (or, if there is none, of the *phukī*) returns to the house, and goes to the *cheli*, where she boils rice. She forms the rice into three portions, and places them in three bamboo baskets. Two of the portions are simply lumps (in contrast to the variously shaped *piṇḍa*), but the third is often formed into the shape of a body. This third portion is given to a Jugī who will come to the house on this day, the same Jugī who earlier gathered the death clothes at the *chwāsa.* This offering is called the "giving of the fifth-day (or seventh-day) body." The three portions of rice are offerings, but the portion offered to the Jugī, which is called the *preta bali*, the *preta* sacrificial offering, also represents the *preta* itself. The Jugī's act might be thought to represent an agent in the forming of the *preta*'s body, as are in that case explicitly, the activities of the Bhā on the tenth day after death. One of the other two portions is brought by the daughter to the riverside, where it is left as an offering to the crows. Late at night the third portion, called the *pākhā jā*, or the "boiled rice of the roof eaves,"[72] is brought from the *cheli* and placed outside of the house at the *pikhā lākhu* boundary. It is left there for a while, sometimes only a few minutes, and sometimes throughout the night. It is said that the hungry *preta* is waiting outside the house to be fed. Household members keep watch in order to prevent dogs from disturbing the rice. Then, in a further distancing movement, the *pākhā jā* is brought to the river—for upper-status *thars* by a Jyāpu client—and thrown into it.

The *kriyā putra* continues his daily *dasā kriyā* activities on the fifth or seventh day, and on the following days. On the tenth day following the cremation a ceremony is held at the riverbank, an elaboration of the *kriyā putra*'s daily morning offering. The ceremony, which includes offerings of food and drink to the spirit and the construction of *piṇḍa*s, is the first of a long series of such ceremonies called *śrāddha*s,[73] rites characterized by offerings and the making of *piṇḍa*s.[74] For the upper-level *thar*s the Bhā who has attended the *kriyā putra* on each morning is again present to help prepare and (traditionally) to direct the offerings. All members of the *phukī* are supposed to attend this tenth-day *śrāddha.*

Now, in part because of the successful performance of the *dasā kriyā*, the spirit of the dead person is said to have its full human form, and to be no longer a *preta.*[75] The purification procedures that terminate the period of the *dasā kriyā* begin at this point. These purifications are called *du bya(n)nkegu*, the "*du*" purification.[76] At least one man and woman representing each of the *phukī* households is supposed to come to the river for purification. After they have all purified themselves, the *kriyā putra*, finally, does his own purification. Other members of the *phukī* will be purified at home or at the house of a Nau.

After the *du bya(n)kegu* at the river there is a ceremony during which the *kriyā putra*, facing west toward the setting sun, makes an offering of water and *gūta* grass (*Cynodon dactylon*) to the sun. The *kriyā putra's purohita* stands in front of him, and thus also, to his west, and the *kriyā putra* circumambulates him three times, "being careful not to step on the *purohita*'s shadow." A Nau stands near by with a ceremonial mirror. He hands it to the *purohita*, bowing in respect, and the *purohita* presents it to the *kriyā putra*, who shows the mirror to the sun, and then looks into it at himself.[77] The other *phukī* members now worship the sun. Now, having become purified and having worshiped the sun, they will be able to worship (but still not touch until the time of the still-to-come *sapiṇḍa śrāddha*) other deities.[78] Now the *purohita* hands the *kriyā putra* a set of white mourning clothes that he will wear during the following year until the first annual anniversary of the death.[79]

At sunset on this tenth day, the *du bya(n)nkegu* purification having been completed earlier in the day, the *kriyā putra* accompanied by two or three *phukī* members goes to the river. They place on the riverbank on the river's *far* side, fragments of beaten rice (the same material that was offered to the *preta* just prior to cremation), two oil-lamp wicks, and some sprigs of *kuśa*. These are offerings to the dead person who is now beginning a journey to the realm of Yama, where his or her *karma*-based post-death transformation will be effected. On the fifth or seventh day after death the *preta* had been given offerings in the cremation grounds, outside the house, and at the near bank of the river. It now moves still further off in its more human, less uncanny, ethereally embodied state.

After the river offerings have been made, substantial gifts[80] are given to the Bhā. These include the item of food that he is to eat that will aid the human formation of the spirit's ethereal and, in some accounts, its eventually reincarnated body.

Death related activities following the dasā kriyā mourning period. There will be further offerings to the humanoid spirit in the next few days, and the house itself must be further cleansed of its death pollution. During the year following a death, men who have lost a parent will wear white and will not wear leather shoes or belts. If a mother is lost, men are not supposed to drink milk for one year; if it is a father, they are not supposed to eat curds.[81] If a male *phukī* member other than a man's father dies, men are supposed to wear a white cap for forty-five days; if it is a female household member other than a man's mother, the household men are supposed to wear white caps until the twelfth day after the death.[82]

The end of the ten-day mourning period is the beginning of a long series of *śrāddha* ceremonies, centering on offerings to the spirit, whose condition is now variously understood. The exact number, timing, and details of procedures vary according to the level and Brahmanical orthodoxy of various *thar*s.[83] Some of these are considered to be of predominant importance, and thus are more generally done. These are the ceremonies of the eleventh, twelfth,[84] and thirteenth days, the forty-fifth day, the sixth month, the first yearly anniversary of the death, and each subsequent yearly anniversary of the death. In the same way as the events of the *dasā kriyā* period helped form the *preta*'s body, the *śrāddha* ceremonies of the first year aid the formed spirit's movement through its ensuing adventures.

On the eleventh day after death there is a ceremony called *swamā lhuyegu*, the "washing away of sorrow." Males of the household and of the *phukī* go to the river, where the *kriyā putra* offers a single *piṇḍa*[85] made of wheat flour, to which other substances are added, to the dead person. Although the spirit is supposed to be in its human form by this day, this offering is still called a *preta piṇḍa*, and this procedure is a kind of redundant coda to the *dasā kriyā*. The *piṇḍa*s formed on the next, the twelfth (or for many *thar*s the forty-fifth) day will have a different name and significance, and the ceremonies associated with them will be within the city.

In this eleventh-day ceremony the *kriyā putra*, facing south, worships an oil lamp said to represent the deity "Siddhikeśvara." In the course of the worship the *preta piṇḍa* made by the *kriyā putra* is worshiped and given offerings including flowers, cloths, *sinha(n)* powder, fruits, incense, and an oil wick. When the *pūjā* is finished, the *kriyā putra* places the *piṇḍa* on a patch of exposed soil in the river, whence a Po(n) is supposed to come and take it. Now the attending family and *phukī* members wash in the river. Then in an act of purification the family *purohita* sprinkles water and milk, which had first been poured over a Śiva *liṅga*, on each person in turn, starting with the *phukī nāya:* and ending with the *kriyā putra*. The *kriyā putra* takes water of high purity, *Ga(n)gā jal*, and purifies the area where the daily morning *dasā kriyā* worship had taken place. The men now return to the *kriyā putra*'s house on the path he had used each day during the *dasā kriyā*. As they go, the *kriyā putra* sprinkles *Ga(n)gā jal* along the path. On reaching his house he walks around it, continuing to sprinkle the water.

These acts of purification of the residues of the death are followed later in this day or on the next, the twelfth day,[86] by another important act of purification called the *gha:su yajña*[87] or, in ordinary Newar reference, the *lhā pānegu*, "hand drying." The *gha:su yajña* is done among the upper-level *thar*s in Bhaktapur by a special class of priests, the Tini (chap. 10).[88] Lower *thar*s perform this ceremony with the aid of a daughter who had married out of the house (and whose household had thus not been contaminated by the death), who returns to the household to light the fire, and so now do many upper-level families because of a shortage of Tini priests in Bhaktapur in recent years.

In the course of this ceremony the Tini performs a simplified fire sacrifice, or *yajña*, on the *cheli* of the house, in the course of which, in contrast to ordinary fire sacrifices, a meat-containing offer of *samhae* is made. The focal deity of the offering is Śiva.[89] People of the household, joined by a man or woman representing each of the *phukī* families, hold their hands toward the fire—the act of *lhā pānegu* itself. The fire, or its smoke, is thought to purify them and—through the medium of the representative—each of their households. The smoke of the fire moves up through the *kriyā putra*'s house, thus purifying it of dangerous influences.[90]

Brahman households, and a few upper-level Chathariyā households, perform a complex set of additional ceremonies on this day. These are thought to be "Vedic" ceremonies, and include a fire ceremony, offerings of the five auspicious products of the cow, and a *Vṛṣotsarga* ceremony, the setting of a cow and a bull "free to roam." These ceremonies are thought to enhance the dead person's chances of going to a "good place" after reaching Yama's realm.

If there is time on the eleventh day, and if not, then on the twelfth day, a ceremony called an *apadutāegu* will be done. An *apa* is a small clay waterpot with a spout.[91] In the course of the ceremony five or (for upper-level *thar*s) seven *apa*s are made use of. One, dedicated to Sūrya, is placed in the sunlight; one in the neighborhood Gaṇeśa temple; one at a nearby well; one, dedicated to Śiva, at the side of the river; and one within the house. Upper-level *thar*s place two additional *apa*s, one at their Āga(n) House, and one "dedicated to all the deities" outside of their houses in the courtyard of the house.

During the *apadutāegu* fourteen *preta piṇḍa*s are made. These fourteen *piṇḍa*s are conceptually grouped with the *preta piṇḍa* made on the eleventh day, and with one that will be made during the *sapiṇḍa śrāddha* (which will be held later either on this day or else on the forty-fifth day) as a set of sixteen *preta piṇḍas*. The sixteen *preta piṇḍas* are said to make a full body for the deceased person's *preta*, the body being completed with the making of the last *piṇḍa* during the *sapiṇḍa śrāddha*. The *preta piṇḍas* are also said to represent the stage of the journey of the *preta*, a journey that in one sense or version ends at the time of the *sapiṇḍa śrāddha* when the *preta*'s body is complete and—no longer a *preta* as it is now in its ethereally embodied form—joins with the *pitṛ*s, the "ancestors." While these ideas are not consistent with the doctrine that this formation had been completed during the *dasā kriyā* period, they reflect not only some general inconsistency in doctrines about details of postmortem happenings but also, perhaps, an effort to ensure that the formation and progress of the spirit be in accord with all the various ambient doctrines about the spirit's whereabouts, forms, and tasks.

The work of the first twelve days is said to summarize what was in some distant past a full year of death work, during which the *kriyā putra* had to remain on the *cheli* and perform mourning ceremonies. Each day in this view represents a month.

The essential ceremony of the twelfth or forty-fifth day[92] is the *sapiṇḍa śrāddha*. "*Sapiṇḍa*" refers to a group of living and dead kin who are thought to share the same body (*piṇḍa*) or body particles.[93] The "*sapiṇḍa śrāddha*" is a variant of the traditional South Asian *sapiṇḍīkaraṇa śrāddha* ceremony (cf. Kane 1968–1977). This is the time when, in one of the parallel conceptions of the fate of the soul, the soul changes from its *preta* form and enters into the community of the *pitṛ*s, the "fathers" or "ancestors." In the course of the *sapiṇḍa śrāddha* a *piṇḍa* representing the dead person—a *piṇḍa* considered still to be a *preta piṇḍa*, the final one in the series of death ceremonies—is, in the course of an elaborate and largely traditional ceremony, physically joined with three *piṇḍas* representing the ancestors of three ascending generations.[94] This represents the transformation of the *preta* not only into an embodied spirit but also into an ancestor—the spirit of the deceased person having now reached the *pitṛ loka*, the realm of the ancestors.[95] The *śrāddha* ceremonies that will follow the *sapiṇḍa śrāddha* during the first year also represent a journey, the journey of the soul now in its ethereal body, its second, "*bhogadeha*," form, toward Yama's realm.

The timing of the subsequent *śrāddha* ceremonies depends on when the *sapiṇḍa śrāddha* had been done. When it is done on the twelfth day, it is followed by another *śrāddha* ceremony on the thirteenth day, and then subsequent ones at one month, forty-five days, six months and one year after the death.[96] For those who do the *sapiṇḍa śrāddha* on the forty-fifth day, the sequence of subsequent *śrāddhas* begin with the sixth-month ceremony.

The spirit's journey to Yama's realm continues during the first year. In the ceremonies of the annual Sāpāru festival [45] activities by the community and the relatives of the deceased person help the spirit to cross over the river bounding that kingdom on its eventual arrival there. Finally, safely arrived in King

Yama's realm, the person's fate will be announced, the reward or punishment not only for his or her own moral and ritual actions during this and previous lives but, in a somewhat uneasy relationship to this idea, also for the adequacy of the enormous ritual efforts of *kriyā putra*, household, extended family, and the people of Bhaktapur.

Notes

CHAPTER 1: INTRODUCTION

1. Many of Bhaktapur's local forms of behavior (like its material artifacts) are of great historical and theoretical importance for South Asian studies, and some of those forms will provide bases for possible future changes in the life of the city. They are not immediately relevant for the kind of place Bhaktapur was at the time of the study, however, and are either neglected or treated summarily in this report.

2. Nepali belongs to the Pahari group of Indo-Aryan languages; Newari, to the Tibeto-Burman division of the Sino-Tibetan language family. For the conventions used in this text for transcriptions of these languages, as well as Sanskrit, see appendix 1. I was able to use analyses of the Kathmandu dialect of Newari by Austin Hale and his associates of the Summer Institute of Linguistics (Sresthacharya, Maskey, and Hale 1971; Hale 1970*a*, 1970*b*; Hale and Hale 1970) as a basis for approaching the quite different Bhaktapur dialect. To facilitate my work in Bhaktapur, with the help of Rama Pati Raj Sharma I prepared a dictionary of Bhaktapur Newari, beginning with the Newari translation of Nepali terms in a Nepali-English dictionary, and supplemented by terms derived from the transcription of my tape-recorded interviews in Bhaktapur Newari. This dictionary eventually contained about 5,000 entries. At the end of my fieldwork I obtained a draft manuscript of an extensive and scholarly Kathmandu Newari-English dictionary by Thakurlal Manandhar (1976), which was of great help in my later study of interview transcripts and which I have used extensively in the course of this volume. The first comprehensive grammatical analysis of Newari in English is that by K. P. Malla (1985).

3. I am, as the sequel will show, particularly indebted to the work of Gopal Singh Nepali, Sylvain Lévi, Colin Rosser, Christoph von Fürer-Haimendorf,

Lynn Bennett, D. R. Regmi, Niels Gutschow and his associates, Gérard Toffin, and Mary Slusser.

4. Readers who know Sanskrit will remark that the majority of "Newari" terms used in this study are Sanskrit or of Sanskritic origin. This is because we are dealing most centrally here with religious and philosophical terms that are for the most part Sanskritic. The vocabulary of everyday lanuage is largely of Tibeto-Burman derivation. In the cases where the Bhaktapur Newari form is a modification or "corruption" of Sanskrit, as it is, for example, in the names of many of the city's deities, we use the classical Sanskritic form to facilitate recognition and comparison.

CHAPTER 2: ORIENTATIONS

1. Tahitian villages are only one kind of "simple traditional community." Like many other Polynesian communities, they are characterized by a relative self-sufficiency and a location in isolated undifferentiated aggregates of almost identical communities. Simple or, as they were once characterized, "primitive" communities elsewhere, such as those of Melanesia, which are embedded in complex areal relations with dissimilar communities, seem to have as a function of this areal complexity some of the same sorts of cultural and psychological differences from Tahitian villages, in both epistemology and the uses of symbolic forms, that Bhaktapur does.

2. In chapter 17, we will discuss the problem of what "religious" means in relation to Bhaktapur.

3. In addition, there are a centrally important series of performances in the city's neighborhoods by a major set of embodied deities, the Nine Durgās, which are partially determined by the lunar calendar and days of the week. There are twenty-one of these performances.

4. Toffin (1984, 271) makes use of a similar characterization of "city" by Braudel (1967, 370) to support his definition of another Newar Valley community, Panauti, as a city.

5. This distinction between "intelligentsia" and "literati" is, as we will suggest later in this volume and elsewhere, of considerable importance in the characterization of Bhaktapur's public and personal order.

6. Some modern scholars, noting its disregard of the work of Fustel's own contemporaries, its cavalier use of his sources, and the untrustworthiness of its conclusions on Fustel's own evidence, have treated *La Cité Antique* mostly as an interesting and influential event in the history of ideas (Momigliano, 1977; Fustel de Coulanges 1980, preface; Finley 1977). Finley (p. 314) criticized Fustel, whose subsequent work he greatly admired, for replacing "the mode of subsistence by religion as the focus of attention and the key to the formation and change of institutions" in this study.

7. J. C. Heesterman (1985) argues that India had its "axial breakthrough" even before the heterodox challenges in Vedic *ritualism* which was "unmythical, rational and individualistic" (see also Inden's [1986] review and criticism of

this argument). Yet, it was, as Heesterman says in an aside, Buddhism with its legitimation of the universalistic imperial claims of the Mauryas that had an impact on the *mundane* order. The impact of Buddism in India was historically limited and countervailed by a developing Hinduism. It is the relation of "transcendence" to forms of mundane order, and not to elements of ritual order, which concerns us here.

8. "With the modern knowledge . . . of the major role played by symbolic systems in shaping the individual understanding and, indeed, in shaping the very perception or cognition of the subject's world . . . [the problem of the relation of individuals to social action] becomes the problem of the relationship between individual (or group) interpretations of events in the light of a collective or encompassing symbolic code; and the problem now goes to the heart of our understanding of belief and symbols: in a word, culture" (from the introduction to a collection of readings on "symbolic anthropology" by Dolgin, Kemnitzer, and Schneider [1977, 16]).

9. The Tantric and Vajrayāna Buddhism of the Himalayas also functions in the support of archaic cities. This Buddhism is, in fact, a regressive Buddhism from the viewpoint of the transcendence of the "axial age" and is in its structure thoroughly Hindu. In its Newar form it has castes, married hereditary priests and no renouncers of society, and a pantheon of gods who are involved with special segments of space, time, and social structure—in short, all the immanent structures of the Hinduism of the city.

10. I (R. L.) am indebted to Antony Hooper (1975) for pointing out this indispensable phrasing for the problem of the conception and actualities of "self" and "role," "personality" and "culture" in psychological anthropology.

11. As the matter of "self" has a bearing on our argument about Bhaktapur's peculiarities, some further remarks may be useful here. Tahitian response to the peculiar question from an interviewer who has known him or her for a long time, "Who are you?," is puzzlement at the question. If an answer is given, it is usually the person's name. The same question asked of a Newar is very liable to elicit an elaborate and self-conscious discussion. Newar informants sometimes said that the question of self or identity was an interesting problem for them and that they had discussed it with their friends. They characteristically define themselves discursively in terms of relationships, occupation, and descent, in terms of sometimes conflicting definitions that various segments of society hold about them, all in motion and dependent on context. As one respondent put it, "There is a saying in the Gita, I do not know it by heart, the verse where Kṛṣna talked to Arjūna, but I understand the meaning of what he said. He said that he [Kṛṣna] was everything other. And so, to a great extent, it seems that I am everything other also, because whenever I cook, I am a cook; whenever I love some girl, I am a lover; whenever I have a son or a daughter, I am a parent, I am a father; whenever I am with my father, I am a son; whenever I am alone with a friend, I am a friend; whenever I am with foes, I am an enemy." Self in such examples is treated as a problem, a problem which generates discourse, a problem that has something to do with a multitude of situations and roles. In this example the "solution" to the problem, namely, "I am

everything other," is taken from a literary-religious text in the Hindu canon, from the available universe of marked symbolic resources, in this case the "extraordinary" conversation between the god Kṛṣṇa and Arjūna.

12. The differences in the experiences of mature Tahitian villagers and Bhaktapur's citizens are augmented by great systematic differences in the household experiences and education of children in the two places, as well as by cultural doctrines such as *māyā*.

13. The studies of individuals chosen from all ranks of the status system that we will present elsewhere all show the intellectual ferment generated by their understanding of contrasting urban perspectives.

CHAPTER 3: NEPAL, THE KATHMANDU VALLEY, AND SOME HISTORY

1. For geographic background, see Karan (1960), Gurung (1973), His Majesty's Government Nepal (1969), Shrestha (1968), and Hagen (1971). For Nepalese ethnic groups, see Bista (1972). For language groups, see Malla (1973) and INAS (1976). Werner Winter, director of the Nepal Research Program's Linguistic Survey in Nepal, estimates that there may turn out to be as many as one hundred languages in Nepal (personal communication). It is possible to group many of the languages and cultures into larger groups, with respect to northern (Tibeto-Burman) and southern (Indic) affinities.

2. The major work on the foundation of the modern Nepalese state in the eighteenth century is Stiller's *The Rise of the House of Gorkha* (1973). See also Stiller (1968) and Gewali (1973).

3. We will now shift to the "ethnographic present" and speak of the situation in the early and mid-1970s, when this study was done, in the present tense.

4. These gross figures for Bhaktapur include "noncitizens" (e.g., prisoners from surrounding areas), and will be modified in our discussion of the demography of Bhaktapur in chapter 4. Patan is referred to in government census data as "Lalitpur."

5. Census data bases ethnicity on the language spoken. There is good reason to believe that this underestimates the percentage of Newars (cf. K. P. Malla n.d., *Newar Ethnicity*, 96).

6. Most of the Valley villages and towns are primarily Newar settlements, the other Valley people live in small hamlets and scattered farmsteads. There are some thirty-five Newar villages and towns in the Valley, aside from the three main centers (Slusser 1982, 12).

7. Historical works in European languages are D. R. Regmi (1965–1966, 1969), Lévi (1905), and Slusser (1982). For materials on the Licchavi period, see Jha (1970). English translations of some of the Nepalese Chronicles are Hasrat (1970) and Wright [1877] (1972). Summaries of political and cultural history can be found in Gewali (1973), P. R. Sharma (1973), and K. P. Malla (1979*a*). Hasrat also has an extensive bibliography of source materials and works on Nepalese history. His book contains a critical "prolegomena" with a detailed summary of Kathmandu Valley history.

8. There is some evidence for a still earlier population of Austro-Asiatic speaking people, perhaps Munda-speaking peoples from Assam. The evidence for this is noted by Malla (1979*a*, 1981*a*). Malla rejects an Austro-Asiatic influence on the non-Sanskrit nominals found (among the dominant Sanskrit terms) in ancient Nepalese epigraphy, but notes that although "The Newari language belongs to the Sino-Tibetan family, . . . it betrays several features, particularly syntactic, which are, in all likelihood [a] Muṇda substratum. . . . If the Newari language is any clue to the identity of [the] early settlers, the language has been definitely influenced by features which are not shared by other Tibeto-Burman languages" (1979*a*).

9. There are various spellings, Lichchavi, Licchavi, Licchivi, Lecchavi, and others (Jha 1970, 3). We will here, and elsewhere where there are alternative spellings of historical terms, follow the usage of the *Historical Atlas of South Asia* (Schwartzberg 1978). According to Slusser, "as a conservative estimate it seems reasonable to assume that the beginning of the Licchavi Period in Nepal is no later than A.D. 300. Most likely it is earlier" (1982, 23).

10. Although they were culturally North Indian, it has been suggested that the Licchavi themselves might have been of Mongoloid origin, in which case, as Slusser remarks, the "major penetration of the Valley by Caucasoid peoples took place only in late historic times" (Slusser 1982, 8). According to Majumdar, Pusalker, and Majumdar (1951, vol. II, p. 7), however, the view that the Licchavi were of "foreign origin" is not supported by evidence.

11. References to canals using a Tibeto-Burman term in Licchavi epigraphy suggest that some canal irrigation was begun prior to the Licchavi period.

12. Some Nepalese scholars believe that it was another Nepali king, Udayadeva (622–623 A.D.). Other scholars believe the tradition may be legendary.

13. "Vishnuism may have flourished in Licchavi Nepal because of its preeminence in Gupta India, where the sect received liberal patronage from the imperial Guptas. Viṣṇu seems always to have appealed to the martial caste, and particularly to conquering monarchs, for whom the heroic god has remained a symbol of regal valour" (Pal 1974, 11f.; Pal 1970). "The great popularity of Saivism [in Licchavi Nepal] was mainly because discrimination of sex or caste or birth had no place in it" (Jha 1970, 182).

14. See Jha (1970) and Pal and Bhattacharyya (1969) on these minor deities.

15. There has been disagreement and confusion on the date and on the ruler who established Bhaktapur. Ānanda Deva has been confused with a later king Ānanda Malla (or Ānanda Deva II) who reigned from 1308 to 1320. Furthermore, Wright ([1877] 1972), in a miscalculation of the Western equivalent of the various systems of dating in the chronicles, puts the founding of Bhaktapur and "Ānanda Malla's" reign into the ninth century. This error is reflected in recent literature, for example, Maskay (1962) and Auer and Gutschow (1974), who give dates for the founding of Bhaktapur of 889 and 865 A.D., respectively.

16. According to the chronicle, Ānanda Malla at the same time founded seven villages, which should be noted for their relation to the Nine Durgās cycle that will occupy us later, specifically, "Banepa, Panauti, Nala, Dhulikhel, Khadpur, Choukot, and Sanga."

17. For a discussion of the various chronicles, see D. R. Regmi (1965–1966, part 1, pp. 21–37).

18. These "Navadurga" images refer to what we will call the "Maṇḍalic Goddesses" (chap. 8) and not to Bhaktapur's Nine Durgās troupe, who are also referred to in the chronicles.

19. These earlier settlements may still be reflected in aspects of one of Bhaktapur's major festivals, Biskā: (chap. 14); one of whose themes is the founding and unification of the city.

20. Bhaktapur, in the time of the Mallas, "got in exchange [for various traded commodities] silver and gold bullion from Tibet and this placed it in a special position of advantages compared to the [other] two cities in the Valley. Minting of coins for Tibet was the crowning advantage of all, which also provide an exclusive source of income" (D. R. Regmi, 1965–1966, part 1, p. 512).

21. It was believed that there was occasionally a paramount ruler during this period at Patan. Slusser (1982, 54 n., 87) claims this is a misconception. "It seems almost certain that Patan, the almost universally accepted site of both the capital of the Licchavis and their successors, did not enjoy this prestige. If before the seventeenth century it was a capital city at all, it may have so served the Kirata, whose associations with that city are particularly evident" (1982, 87).

22. The area of Mithilā or Tīrabhukti (modern Tirhut) influenced Malla Nepal. A kingdom was founded there by Nanya Deva, who according to some chronicles "captured" Bhaktapur. He was of the Karnataka dynasty, and had been an officer under the Palas, who had had the control of Tīrabhukti (see Majumdar, Pusalker, and Majumdar 1957, vol. 5, p. 47f.). "This kingdom comprised most of present day Nepal's eastern Terai and a portion of the present Indian state of Bihar. Little is known yet about the full cultural significance of this kingdon. Its sculptural art had reached a highwater mark judging from a fine group of icons found in Simraungarth and several other regions of the eastern Terai. The rise of Tirhut posed a new political threat to Nepal, but at the same time it opened fresh avenues of cultural exchanges between the two states. No other language after Sanskrit has made such a valuable contribution to the literature of the Nepal Valley as Maithili, the language of this kingdom. Many dramas were written in Maithili or Maithili and Newari by the late Malla rulers of Bhaktapur. Maithili scholars were held in great respect in Nepal. The Maithili Jha Brahmans [chap. 10] were given high positions in the hierarchy of the Nepalese priesthood. Far more important than this, the two houses of the Mallas and the Karnatakas were actually joined by blood when Rajalla Devi became the wife of Jayasthiti Malla. Thus the late Malla rulers trace their ancestry to the Karnataka dynasty. Lastly, goddess Taleju, the highly venerated goddess of the Mallas, and still a prominent deity of the Valley, is believed to have been introduced from Tirhut" (P. R. Sharma 1973, 73). The Pala and Karnataka dynasties both had important cultural and religious influences on the Valley. Pal, however, argues against the assumption of "most scholars. . . that the Pala style exerted a strong influence on [the arts] of Nepal" (1974, 164).

23. Gewali (1973, 51) has 1350 as the date. Hasrat (1970) states that there were two invasions, one in 1346 and a second in 1349. Recent scholarship suggests that there was only one, in 1349.

24. There had earlier been five attacks on the Valley by the Hindu kings of Maithilī between 1244 and 1311 A.D. In one raid (in 1299) the Tripura palace in Bhaktapur was reached (Slusser 1982, 56). Slusser believes that more important than the Muslim raids in the destruction of Valley monuments were "the successive raids of the Maithilī and the constant natural calamities of earthquake and fire" (ibid., 58).

25. Different commentators on the evidence give different accounts of the establishment of Jayasthiti Malla's reign. For a summary of the recent scholarly consensus, see Slusser (1982, 58ff.).

26. For comparison with contemporary groups in Bhaktapur, "Kasai" is Nāe; "Podhe" is Po(n); Kulu is Kulu; and "Charmakara" is Hālāhulu.

27. A *birta* is "an assignment of income from the land by the state in favor of individuals in order to provide them with a livelihood. In a society such as Nepal's, we generally find groups which, by virtue of religious tradition or their social or political function, cannot participate in economic pursuits. Their maintenance, generally at the cost of the agrarian class, is a primary responsibility of the state. Divestiture of ownership rights in the land through *birta* grants in favor of priests, religious teachers, soldiers, and members of the nobility and the royal family was thus the pivot on which rested the social and political framework of the state. *Birta* ownership not only insured a stable and secure income to the beneficiary, but also symbolized high social and economic status. *Birta* was in fact regarded as a form of private property with a clearly defined right vis-à-vis the state" (M. C. Regmi 1976, 16f.).

28. Similar considerations may illuminate his new "rule that Brahmans might follow a profession" (Wright 1972, 187). These professions, judging by the later history of Newar Brahmans who pride themselves on not having to do "non-Brahmanical" work such as farming—as many non-Newar Nepalese Brahmans do—were probably limited to a narrow range of activities (scribal work, storytelling, administrative and advisory work to the court) thought to be consonant with Brahmanical status, but that gave them a wider influence in the city.

29. The extent and placement of Bhaktapur's wall is relevant to our later discussion of the city's symbolic boundaries. Mary Slusser, who was able to trace the location of the city walls of Patan and Kathmandu, was able to discern only a few vestiges of the Bhaktapur wall as earthworks along the western perimeter, and "a fragment of the moat and several stone thresholds that mark former gateways" (1982, p. 102 and maps 7, 8, and 9). There is at least one religious painting on a cloth scroll in one of Bhaktapur's Buddhist *vihāras* (a photograph of which is contained in the collection of Stephen Eckherd), which shows Bhaktapur as a completely walled city. Father Ippolitio Desideri, writing in 1722, after describing the three Valley cities, remarked that there were also, "a few *other* towns surrounded with the walls, all the rest are poor villages consisting of huts," implying that all the three Valley cities were surrounded by walls (Desideri [1932], as quoted in D. R. Regmi, [1965–1966, part II, p. 1013]). The Bhasha Vamsavali says that the Gorkhāli attackers entered the city of Bhaktapur by breaking through the eastern and northern gates of the city (Stiller 1973, 129). It seems likely that Bhaktapur had a complete wall around

its boundaries, but it did certainly have at least large extents of bounding wall with gates at the main roads that crossed the boundaries of the city, all dating in large part from Yaksa Malla's reign (see also D. R. Regmi [1965–1966, part I, pp. 420, 438]).

30. According to Niels Gutschow (personal communication), this Bhairava, in fact, faces south.

31. His estimates of numbers of households for the three cities is of interest. He was told that Kathmandu was supposed to have had 22,000 houses at the time of the last Malla king, and that it had been augmented under the Gorkhālis "not without some consequent decrease in the numbers of Patn [Patan] and Bhatgong [Bhaktapur]." He notes that the figures he was given for Kathmandu must have included an estimate of houses in Kathmandu's pre-conquest-dependent Valley villages and towns, as in his estimation the city itself could not have had more than 5,000 houses. He estimated ten persons to a house and thus a population for the city of Kathmandu of about 50,000 at the time. He estimated the population of the rest of the Malla kingdom of Kathmandu (at eight people to a household, the village house being smaller) as having consisted of about 186,000 people. These figures seem to be of the right order. For Patan "and its dependencies" under the late Mallas there were said to have been 24,000 houses; and for Bhaktapur "and its dependencies" 12,000 (Kirkpatrick 1969, 160–163).

32. There is a large literature on the various aspects of political modernization in Nepal. For the Tribhuvan restoration, a sketch of the Rana polity that proceeded it, and the political changes that followed it, see the work of Leo Rose and his associates (Rose and Fisher 1970; Joshi and Rose 1966; Rose 1971).

CHAPTER 4: BHAKTAPUR'S OTHER ORDER

1. It is, however, the site of an important shrine, a *pīṭha*, of one of the city's "Maṇḍalic Goddesses," Mahākālī.

2. A demographic sample survey conducted by the United Nations fund for Population Activities in 1976 (cited in Acharya and Ansari [1980, 104]) reported an annual growth rate based on differences in the birth and death rates of 1.88 percent per annum for Bhaktapur, which will, if it were to keep up without a large increase in emigration be another of the many foreseeable problems for a future Bhaktapur.

3. The urban population of Nepal as a whole has been calculated by the Central Bureau of Statistics as having a 12.95 per hundred excess of males; Kathmandu has 15.42. Most of this seems to reflect differential male migration into cities, as rural Nepal as a whole has a male/female excess of only 0.66 per hundred males, and the total Nepalese population has an excess of 1.35 per hundred males.

4. These functions are enumerated in the Nepal Nagar Panchayat act of B.S. 2019 (1961): (1) to construct, maintain, and repair roads, bridges, drains, public latrines, and to keep them clean; (2) to provide drinking water; (3) to keep

the lanes and roads clean; (4) to arrange and maintain the cremation grounds; (5) to keep census, birth, and death records; (6) to construct and repair the shelters for religious pilgrims; (7) to take measures against rabid dogs; (8) to provide treatment and preventive measures against epidemics; (9) to establish and manage schools, in accordance with the policies and regulations of the central government; (10) to keep records of the number of houses and their distribution in the town wards; (11) to provide parking places; (12) to encourage and aid activities for cultural development; (13) to provide assistance to district projects; (14) to provide street lighting; (15) to arrange for exhibitions, fairs, and markets; (16) to plant trees along the sides of the access roads into the town; and (17) to provide social and health services (adapted from Krishna Prasad Pradhan 1968, 120ff.).

5. These wards have been the focal units for several economic surveys. They are newly created modern administrative units and are not related to the traditional city spatial units with which we will be concerned.

6. A detailed general economic study of Bhaktapur has not yet appeared. Partial studies that give useful statistical and survey data include, in addition to census data, the Nepal Rāṣtra Bank (1978) on household budget surveys, Acharya and Ansari (1980) on the "basic economic needs" of Bhaktapur, and Wachi (1980) on the economy of farming households. Important materials on land ownership and use in a large traditional Newar town, Thimi, with presumptive similarities to Bhaktapur, are in Müller (1981). Details on agricultural techniques in a Newar village are given in Toffin (1977). Toffin also treats the economy of a Newar town in 1984, chapter 11. For aspects of agricultural economies, see also Pant and Jain (1969), M. C. Regmi (1971, 1976, 1978), and Müller (1981, 1984).

7. Data cited in Müller (1981, 62) gives the extent of land devoted to various crops as well as their yields for the Bhaktapur district in 1972/73. Note that because of the high yield of rice its actual production has even more relative importance than the land devoted to it would indicate. Rice: land, 5,653 hectares, yield, 20,135 tons; wheat, 5,500 hectares, 9,810 tons; maize, 2,528 hectares, 4,425 tons; millet, 850 hectares, 1,452 tons; potatoes, 438 hectares, 3,920 tons; oilseed, 360 hectares, 216 tons; sugarcane, 7 hectares, 90 tons; barley, 4 hectares, 4 tons.

8. One source (His Majesty's Government Nepal, 1969, 85) gives an intensity index (cropping in relation to land in cultivation) of 127 percent for the Bhaktapur district. Müller reports on the basis of detailed studies in Thimi that "the degree of intensity with which the land is farmed is always over 200 percent [for example, for fields used for both rice and wheat]. In the case of vegetable and potato growing it can be as high as 300 percent. The highest degree of intensity is reached in all year round vegetable cultivation. The Newar farmers never leave the land fallow longer than one to two months a year" (1981, 61).

9. The use of hand digging tools by the Newar farmers is associated with a rejection of the use of animal-drawn ploughs. The rejection of such ploughing is explained by Newars in terms of religious taboos about yoking and using cows, bulls or oxen, thought to represent a goddess or Śiva to plow the earth. There has been some discussion about whether this represents in fact an ideological

rejection of what would otherwise have been a superior method of farming (Webster, 1981). The digging of fields at the start of the rainy season in preparation for rice planting is done with the short-handled hoe, or *ku*. As Müller (1981, 57) states the problem, "as ploughing is generally regarded as a criterion for an advanced civilization in connection with wet rice growing, it is strange that in an area termed as the center of an 'advanced civilization' in Nepal, ploughing is not done, whereas it is common even in the smallest, terraced fields outside the Kathmandu Valley. It is not possible to give an explanation for this phenomenon, especially as the plough is known to the Newars. Nevertheless, its use is punished with expulsion from the caste. As human labor is not highly valued as a production factor and as the Newars believe that they obtain more yield with their own, traditional methods of working the land the farmers regard the work with the Kodali [or *ku*], which seems archaic to us, as something very positive." Webster argues (1981, 129) that "the plough was not used by the Newars to any significant extent because of practical, economic and ecological reasons." Subsequently, later events, perhaps "related to a Newar fixation on status, led to a prohibition on ploughing. The preference for the *ku* crystallized into a taboo."

10. We are talking here of families who actually farm. This is not necessarily the same as the large section of the city's hierarchical system who are locally referred to as *Jyāpu*s, that is, "farmers." Most, but not all, of the *thar*s (see chap. 5) within the Jyāpu group farm, but not all of the families within a farming *thar*, nor all of the working members of a farming family farm. Furthermore there are members of other nominally non-Jyāpu groups who *do* farm. Farming, in fact, as everywhere in South Asia, is one of the activities least restricted by caste prescriptions.

11. The contributions of the exchange of goods and services to household income and the payment of debts is of importance throughout the Bhaktapur economy.

12. One kind of land that tenants rent and farm is "Guthi" land. Guthi land is land that was set aside in the past, often by the Malla kings, with the purpose of providing income through a portion of its produce for maintaining a variety of religious and charitable institutions (including the maintenance of temples and the support of festivals) and, for the support of various social services such as "schools, hospitals, orphanages and poor houses" (M. C. Regmi 1976, 17). These lands are administered now through a central government agency in Kathmandu.

13. In the 1964 Land Act the ceiling on land ownership for the Kathmandu Valley was 2.67 hectares (6.6 acres). The rents for agricultural land were also limited depending on the quality of the land. For the Kathmandu Valley as a whole rents are estimated to amount to about one-third the value of the total produce (Pant and Jain, 1969; M. C. Regmi 1976).

14. Note that *sāhu* is linguistically distinguished from the "trader," the *banjā*, who travels to sell his merchandise.

15. Membership in the hereditary status system affects trades or professions followed by members in various ways. Some economic activities are more likely to be followed by members of certain *clusters* of hereditary status groups. Thus

commerce and trade are most likely to be followed by Pa(n)cthar and Chathar groups, farming by the members of the Jyāpu cluster. These clusters have many aspects of social class. In contrast, there are a number of professions specified entirely by one's status group membership, particularly by one's membership in the clan-like unit called a *thar*. A *thar* member does not have to follow the *thar*-specific trade, although he often—in many cases almost always—does. If he does not, he cannot perform the *thar*-specific profession or trade of another *thar*; he must follow a profession or trade (mostly farming, commerce and trade, government service, or unskilled labor) not specialized by *thar*. His access to these other kinds of work may be informally restricted by the "classes" that already have and that tend to control these jobs. Membership in *thar*s determines some twenty-one specific crafts or professions (chap. 5). There are also certain hereditary professions (laundering, shoemaking, knife sharpening, some kinds of healing, and certain priestly activities) that are traditionally done in Bhaktapur by "non-Newars."

16. Acharya and Ansari remark that the percentage of the economically active population in Kathmandu that is involved in services is 77.5 percent (according to the 1971 census materials), and note that employment in the services sector for Bhaktapur Town Panchayat is not only the lowest among the towns of the valley but also includes a considerable number of persons who actually work in Kathmandu (1980, 109).

17. The Household Budget Survey of the Nepal Rāṣtra Bank showed that Bhaktapur households had the lowest level of externally produced manufactured goods of the three valley cities. For example, in Kathmandu in 1972, 71 percent of the household had kerosene cookers; 4.7 percent, kerosene heaters; 43.6 percent, radios; and 15.9 percent, bicycles. For Bhaktapur, for the same items, 13.8 percent of the households had kerosene cookers; 1.0 percent, kerosene heaters; 9.1 percent, radios; and 0.3 percent, bicycles. Even for locally produced modern items Bhaktapur households had very few. Only 8.6 percent of the households had chairs, 6.8 percent tables, and 14.3 percent beds (1974*b*, 15).

18. Of 18 representative town panchayats and market centers surveyed in the early 1970s by the Nepal Rāṣtra Bank, Bhaktapur had the lowest household income and the second lowest per capita income but also (with the exception of two towns in far western Nepal) had the highest percentage of household income in kind, some 46.54 percent. (Nepal Rāṣtra Bank [1978], from a table reprinted in Acharya and Ansari [1980].)

CHAPTER 5: THE DISTRIBUTION OF ROLES: THE MACROSTATUS SYSTEM

1. There is frequently a difference between the name that members of a *thar* use to refer to and to identify themselves, and the name by which outsiders refer to it. When it differs, the name used by outsiders may refer to a professional or occupational category, or it may be a name that has some pejorative connotation in the judgment of the *thar* members themselves. In the presence of mem-

bers of a *thar* outsiders may often use a third, an honorific, name. For the most part in this work we use the ordinary names used by outsiders in references to a *thar*.

2. In Bhaktapur, in contrast to its common use in Kathmandu and other cities, Śrestha is used by only one traditionally low group, the Cipī, whose traditional status is below the farming groups, but who are now engaged mostly in upper-level socioeconomic activities.

3. Fürer-Haimendorf also notes that Chetri *thar*s are not unilineal descent groups "in the narrow sense of the term. All members of the Bista clan [for example] no doubt consider each other as linked in an undefined way, but the fact that those who are of different lineage are not debarred from intermarriage excludes a fiction of patrilineal descent from a common ancestor" (1966, 30).

4. Different *thar*s may have internal differences in details of their religious practices, styles of life, and internal political organization, which in part derive from the *thar*'s origins and history and in part, for many of them, from the effects of the position and functions forced on them by their position in the macrostatus system.

5. Dumont (1964) had suggested that by his own criteria for caste structure, the Newars do not have a true caste system. This was probably based on limited information on the Newars. Greenwold, using Dumont's criteria, has argued that "the Newars in fact possess a caste structure that conforms most stringently to Dumont's definition" (1978, 487). Toffin also argues in the face of Dumont's statement that the Newars at least in the larger towns and the cities do have a "caste system" in Dumont's terms, "en ce sens qu'elles sont fondées sur un modèle religieux qui donne à la société une grande cohérence et qui lui sert de fondement intellectuel" (1984, 222). We will return to Dumont's conception of the caste system in chapter 11 in conjunction with a discussion of Newar uses of purity and impurity in social hierarchy.

6. "A *jāti* is an endogamous, hereditary social group that has a name and a combination of attributes. All members of a *jāti* are expected to act according to their *jāti* attributes, and each member shares his *jāti*'s status in the social hierarchy of a village locality in India" (Mandlebaum 1970, 14). For the *jāti* members themselves, Mandlebaum notes, the *jāti* has a position in a ranked hierarchy of groups. A "*jāti* cluster" is a set of separate *jāti*s, classed together under one name, whose members are treated by *others* as having the same general status (ibid., 19).

7. The designation "*sāhu*" or "*jyāpu*" may indicate either the groups of *thar*s and status levels whose members usually engage in these professions, or in other contexts it may designate all those who actually engage in the profession, irrespective of *thar* or status level.

8. At a more abstract level there is, as we will touch on again below and discuss in later chapters, a *vertical* division of groups into two hierarchies, those whose members are "technicians of marked symbolism" and those who deal with other kinds of power and production.

9. These distinctions have, however (as we shall note), one significant structural usage in Bhaktapur, in the separating of the *thar*s grouped as a unity

elsewhere among the Newars as "śreṣṭha" or "sesya:," into two strata, Chathar and Pa(n)chthar, distinguished as being "kṣatriya" and "vaiśya," respectively.

10. Starting in the midnineteenth century the Ghorkāli state, following the Malla practice of written legal codes, began efforts to codify the entire heterogeneous population of the new multiethnic state into a traditional hierarchical system in a document called the *Muluki Ain*, "the law of the country." This intriguing imperial expansion of the Hindu ordering of small states underwent a number of stages and versions and was considered as "official" until the 1960s (Höfer 1979).

11. The many status lists for Bhaktapur in the chronicles and other Malla documents (some of which are in the Hodgson collection at the India Office Library in London) and reports by later foreign visitors also provide an invaluable basis for an understanding of the historical changes that the system has undergone under various historical, economic, and demographic pressures. A very valuable attempt at collation of reports for Newar Nepal is Chattopadhyay (1923).

12. Endogamy must be outside of the extended patrilineal kin group, the *phukī* (chap. 6). For the Rājopādhyāya Brahmans the lack of non-*phukī* kin in Bhaktapur requires that they marry Rājopādhyāyas from one of the other major Valley Newar cities.

13. The Lākhe do not, apparently, exist in other Newar cities. Early accounts have noted similar lower-status Newar Brahman priests such as the "Lawerju" mentioned by Oldfield ([1880] (1974), vol. I, p. 177).

14. The term "*śresṭha*" is from the Sanskrit *śreṣṭha*. In classical Sanskrit its meanings included "best," "chief," "first," "best among," "oldest, senior," and in the form *Śreṣṭin*, "a distinguished man, a person of rank or authority" (Monier-Williams [1899] n.d., 1102). "*Syesya:*" derives, according to Manandhar (1976), from an old Newari term "*sista*," "a king's man" which may, in turn, be derived from "*śresṭha*."

15. Although the Brahmans are not "renouncers," this terminology may suggest an idea of a contrast between the worldly professions and situation of the Chathariyā and Pa(n)cthariyā and an "other-worldly" profession of Brahmans and other priests. Most of the city's *thar*-specified activities can be sorted into one or the other of these "worlds," the realm of the "ordinary" on the one hand and of marked symbolism on the other.

16. "*Thariyā*" means member or members of a *thar*. Thus Chathariyā are members of the Chathar level. We will use this form frequently.

17. The Nepali coding of statuses, the *Muluki Ain* of 1854, divides the *Śresṭha* into two levels, "cord wearers" and "non-enslavable alcohol drinkers" (Höfer 1979, 137f.). Höfer speculates that these two divisions may be equivalent to Chathariyā and Pa(n)cthariyā.

18. Early accounts of Newar *thars* note groups written "*jaisi*" or "*jausi*." In some accounts (e.g., Hamilton [1819] 1971) and those derived from some of the chronicles (e.g., Basnet 1981; Lévi 1905) the *jaisi* are described as a high mixed group "derived from a Brahman by a Newar woman," who have subsections variously doing divination, astrology, medicine, and some priestly work.

Hamilton ranks them above "Shreṣṭa" (i.e., Chathariyā) as some middle- and low-ranked people still do.

19. Some early accounts (e.g., Oldfield [1880] 1974; Hodgson n.d.) similarly report "classes" of Jyāpu (three [Oldfield] or six [Hodgson] in number), which, however, in contrast to the present status-level "classes," were said to intermarry.

20. "*Jyā*" means "work," or "task" in a very general sense. "*Jyāpu*" (female "*Jyāpunī*") means one who farms. It is used in two different ways. One is for anyone who belongs to a traditional farming *thar*, even if that person has some other profession. The other usage specifies "farmworker" and can also be used for someone from a nonfarming *thar* who does farmwork, although it would not usually be said that they *are* Jyāpu, but rather that they "do Jyāpu work." Even though farming is permissible to a large range of middle-level and upper-level *thar*s it is not, in fact, done by upper-level ones and was traditionally forbidden to the lower "unclean" ones. Thus "*Jyāpu*" also has implications of both "class" and a certain level of purity.

21. The Chipī consider themselves to be of a higher status. It is said that there was a court case during the Rana period on the question of their ranking when their present low status was confirmed or determined. Our informants did not know why they have low status.

22. Chattopadhyay (1923, 525) collates some of the early accounts of the Dwi(n). He notes that they were described as having originally been hunters and fowlers who worshiped both Śiva and Buddha. They were said to have been elevated to the pure castes because they saved Pṛthvīnārāyana Śāha's life. Chattopadhyay speculates that the Dwi(n) were originally a "more or less wild" jungle tribe. Niels Gutschow has interviewed the only Dwi(n) in Bhaktapur who follows the traditional *thar* activities, and notes that he has some special tasks during two annual festivals, Biskā: and Pāsā Ca:re (personal communication).

23. Our reasons for qualifying such uses of "ritual" are discussed in chapter 11.

24. It is said that under the Rana regime the Sa:mi, whose *thar* name is Mānandhar, petitioned the Rana regime for a reclassification and were subsequently classified as being "water-acceptable" for the higher levels. This reclassification was "not accepted" in Bhaktapur (cf. Nepali 1965, 171). Oil pressing is generally associated in South Asia with low status. "The pressing of seeds . . . is stigmatized as a degrading occupation in the Code of Manu because it destroys life by crushing the seed" (Hutton 1961, 89).

25. Several of the earliest accounts of Nepal, summarized in Chattopadhyay (1923), include a "caste" of Newar "washermen" variously given as "sanghar," "songat," "sangat," "sughang," and "pasi." Aside from Pasi (which we have placed at level XIII), these or similar names are not known now. These washermen were listed in some accounts as being at the bottom of the status hierarchy, below "sweepers."

26. According to Hodgson (n.d.), all these *thar*s (with the exception of Cāla[n], which he does not list) were "a class of Newars called Ekthureea [Ekthariyā] or outcaste, or 'single body,' distinguished by their profession or trade." As Chattopadhyay (1923, 534) points out in a comment on this passage,

they were certainly not "outcastes" but were placed just above the clearly polluting levels. Earle, in the 1901 Census of India (cited in Chattopadhyay [1923]), includes Cāla(n) in the list and lists the group as a whole as "intermediate castes." Earle's and Hodgson's lists both have some additional *thar*s at this level not known in contemporary Bhaktapur. Lévi (1905, vol. I, p. 242) writes of this group that they "only form a group by opposition to the previous groups, and are subdivided into true castes." The polluting status of this group in earlier accounts is somewhat ambiguous. Hamilton writes, "All the castes yet enumerated are considered as pure, and Hindus of any rank may drink the water which they have drawn from a well; but the following castes [our level XIII] are impure, and *a person of any considerable dignity will be defiled by their touch* (Hamilton [1819] 1971, 36 [emphasis added]). This comment corresponds to Hodgson's "outcastes." Oldfield, however, includes them among the "heterodox Buddhists" and says that "from their hands any Hindu will, or may, drink water" ([1880], 1974, vol. 1, p. 187). Nepali (1965, 168ff.) includes them among the clean *thar*s. These differences, and the consequent differences in reports about them by differently placed informants, suggest their marginal status.

27. The Nāe slaughter only the water buffalo. Other animals whose flesh is eaten in Bhaktapur are slaughtered by the households and other groups who will subsequently eat them as sacrifices to one of the "dangerous" deities (see chap. 9).

28. The Do(n)s may be related to the Doms of Kumaon (Srivastava 1966, 194). According to Niels Gutschow, the remaining traditionally active Do(n) in Bhaktapur play a drum during certain festivals and other occasions (personal communication).

29. They are often referred to as "Po(n)," and refer to themselves as "Pore" (which is probably an older Newari form).

30. In 1974 Niels Gutschow interviewed a Hālāhulu who lived in Bhaktapur at that time, and who later moved to the nearby town of Timi.

31. On Newar Buddhism, see Lewis (1984), Snellgrove (1957, 1961*a*), Locke (1976), Lévi (1905), and Greenwold (1973, 1978).

32. David Snellgrove expresses the same opinion with an evaluative turn, "Whereas in India Buddhism was ruthlessly destroyed, in Nepal it has to be forced into conformity with other traditions, which represent the negation of all its higher striving, so that it has died of atrophy, leaving outward forms that have long ceased to be Buddhist in anything but the name" (1957, 106).

33. The "Urāe caste," according to Colin Rosser, was "a composite caste of merchants and craftsmen of generally high economic status through their predominance in the trade with Tibet, and of all Newar castes the one which is by far the strongest in devotion to Buddhist beliefs and practices according to the Tibetan model, largely, of course, through their close and continuing association with Tibetans in the course of trade" (1966, 106). For a study of a Urāe group in Kathmandu, the Tulādhars, see Lewis (1984).

34. The Urāe were, as Hodgson (n.d.) put it, "traders and foreign merchants," and could draw their members from different *thar*s. Associated with the Urāe by various authors are both trading and craft *thars*, including

Tulādhar, Loha(n)ka:mī, Sika:mī, Tāmrākār, Awa:, Kumha:, Mādhika:mī, and "Kassar" or "Kasa" (workers in bell metal alloy). Hodgson (n.d.) also lists carpenters associated with the Matsyendranāth festival in Patan, "red lead makers," and doorkeepers.

35. For a study on the Muslims in Nepal, see Gaborieau (1977). The Malla courts, influenced by Indian Mughal court styles, invited Muslims to settle in the valley as manufacturers of perfume and bangles and as court musicians from at least the early eighteenth century. See also Slusser (1982, vol. 1, p. 68f.).

36. There is a section on the Gāine and their music in Hoerburger (1975). According to Niels Gutschow, the Gāine play music throughout Bhaktapur in the weeks before Mohanī (chap. 15) according to a fixed schedule, each family having the right to play in certain quarters (personal communication).

37. Priestly and para-priestly roles are often *covertly* stigmatizing (chap. 10).

38. It is worth noting that the estimates made by our informants were usually very close, sometimes identical to Gutschow and Kölver's survey findings.

39. In general, there seems to be some correspondence between the numbers of households needed for many of the city functions and the actual numbers of households, although this does go wrong and provide problems in some cases. It would be of importance to attempt a study of the adjustive mechanisms involved.

40. This varies from the census figure of 6,484 because of distortions in rounding numbers in the adjusted table.

41. One can get a rough idea of the number of *individuals* who are members of different classes of *thar*s by multiplying the number of households by the mean number of individuals per household for the city, which is six. The number of individuals per household, however, varies significantly by status level (chap. 6).

42. Thus the total number of households in the group of occupational *thar*s is misleading because of the large numbers of Kumha: households that are engaged only in farming and not in the traditional *thar* craft of pottery-making. Similarly, the number of households in the group of *thar*s associated with Taleju is artificially enlarged by the inclusion of the large number of Suwāl households, only a few of which have traditional Taleju functions.

43. We will use the term "boiled rice," as the Newars do themselves, to denote both boiled rice and boiled pulses.

44. "Each jāti closes its boundaries to lower jātis, refusing them the privilege of intermarriage and other contacts defined as polluting to the higher jāti. Each jāti, in turn, is excluded by the jātis ranking above it in a local caste hierarchy. Thus, differences in degree of pollution create closed segments, as each segment tries to preserve its own degree of purity from contamination by lower castes" (Kolenda 1978, 66; derived from Dumont 1980 [1966]).

45. Not only were "pure" levels forbidden to take water from "impure" levels, but traditionally and to a considerable degree now, members of the water-unacceptable levels did not take water from what they considered to be still lower levels, and this was sometimes true of *thar*s *within* a water-unacceptable level. As Höfer has noted, the *Muluki Ain* of 1854 formally for-

bade "pure castes" as a group from taking water from "impure castes" as a group, and no "impure caste" was allowed to take water from a still lower ranking "impure caste" (1979, 56). That is, the first sorting of "pure" and "impure" on the city level was replicated within successive divisions of "impure castes." However, these further divisions were of no importance, or of a different sort of importance, for the larger city organization.

46. D. R. Regmi (1965, vol. II, p. 696), remarking that the conception of two types of polluting groups is found in the classical Dharmaśāstras attributed to Manu and other writers, stated that the two classes, those who were water-unacceptable but not polluting by touch and those who could not be touched, were probably present in Malla Nepal. These two levels, "impure but touchable" and "untouchable," are present in the official codification of the caste Hierarchy of Nepal, of 1854, the *Muluki Ain*, which codified existing social regulations (Höfer 1979, 45). Rosser (1966, 88f.) divided status levels among the Newars into a simple opposition, water-acceptable and water-unacceptable, equivalent to "pure" and "impure," "dominant" and "subordinate," respectively. His separation begins with the Jugī and does suggest the strong symbolic emphasis on the special polluting status of *thar*s at this level and below. It does not, however, correspond directly to the actual categories of purity and impurity. The water-unacceptable group begins for upper-level people above the Jugī, and the separation between simple water-unacceptability and untouchability cuts through his "subordinate" group. Stephen Greenwold (1978, 458f.), in a study of Newar castes in Kathmandu, tries to incorporate both the Hindu and Buddhist *thar*s there into one system. He divides the resulting combined status levels into two ranked groups with a "great divide" between them—those who have *either* Brahmans or Vajrācārya Buddhist priests as household priests, and those who do not. By so doing, he incorporates our level XIII *thar*s into this upper division. He then further separates the households in his "clean" category served by priests into two ranked subgroups, whose purificatory services are done in the upper section by the barber *thar* (Nau) and whose lower section is purified by the low-level butcher *thar*, the Nāe. The designation of a lower section of the status hierarchy which has purificatory services, specifically nail cutting, done by women of the butcher *thar* is reported in some of the chronicles of early Nepal (see D. R. Regmi, part I, p. 642). In Bhaktapur the barber *thar* does purification only for those levels above XIII (and for themselves), and some of the other *thar*s do have certain ritual purification performed by women of the butcher *thar*. Greenwold's "lower-clean" division represents those who are water-unacceptable (but not untouchable) in the Hindu system, and who are not served by Brahmans, even though they are served by Vajrācāryas and other auxiliary priests. In the Hindu system of Bhaktapur the first separation in terms of cleanliness comes between level XIII and those above it. Greenwold's system works from the Vajrācārya priest's point of view in which all the levels that he serves are necessarily "clean," but not from the point of view of upper-level Hindus.

47. Newar Brahmans do eat mutton and goat meat.

48. As Dumont has argued, in order to clarify the significance of "caste" endogamy in Hindu marriage, "the first marriage must be distinguished from

subsequent freer marriages and, *a fortiori*, from illegitimate unions" (1980, 113). Newar marriage, as we shall see later, has special features because the woman's first marriage is not precisely (in Dumont's terminology) a *primary* marriage, as she was previously married to the god Nārāyaṇa in a ritual mock-marriage.

49. In contrast to Indo-Nepalese marriages Newar primary marriages are not optionally hypergamous, nor do they have hypergamous implications (see chap. 6).

50. Höfer notes that in the *Muluki Ain* "a hypergamous union is prohibited only if it implies a transgression of the demarcation lines (a) either between pure and impure castes or (b) between touchable and untouchable castes within the category of the impure castes" (1979, 81).

51. In the *Muluki Ain* of 1854 the Bāre are listed below the Chathariyā with a middle group of castes (Höfer 1979, 137f.).

52. Now, as in Nepali, the term "Bhote" is used for Tibetans and distinguishes them from the Sāe(n) hill peoples of northern origin.

53. The equivalent Nepali term is "*Parbate*" or "*Parbatiya*:." Some informants tend to use the Nepali term to include both Sāe(n) and Partyā.

54. The Sāe(n)/Khae(n) contrast has a dubious relation to the historical origins of the Khas group, which may well have had Mongoloid, as well as North Indian, components (K. B. Bista 1972, 13).

55. According to Slusser's summary of scholarly opinion, the Muslim conquests of North India at the end of the twelfth century which caused orthodox Brahmans from Mitilā and Buddhists from Bihar to flee into the Kathmandu Valley also forced other refugees into the western hills of Nepal: "The latter belonged to well-defined Hindu castes, particularly the Brahman priesthood, the Kṣatriya military aristocracy (known as "Chetris" in Nepal), and, at the bottom of the social scale, occupational castes such as tailors, shoemakers, and blacksmiths. . . . This influx fortified other Indian immigrants who had long filtered northward, and had mixed in various measure with the established local population. The latter essentially issued from two streams: the Khasa, Indo-Aryans who spoke a Sanskritic language ancestral to Nepali, and who for centuries had drifted eastward through the Himalayan foothills; and the Mongoloid tribes, particularly the Magar and Gurung. . . . By the sixteenth century, an ethnically mixed military aristocracy, who often claimed Rajput descent and emulated the latter's preoccupation with military chivalry and the purity of Hindu religion, had carved out numerous petty hill states. Gorkhā, immediately west of the Valley was one of these" (1982, 8).

CHAPTER 6: INSIDE THE *THARS*

1. "Sixty percent of all Bhaktapur households lived in multi-unit structures, thirty-six percent occupied single-family houses, three percent lived in commercial buildings and a smaller number were in temporary quarters" (Nepal Rāṣtra Bank 1974*a*).

2. This distribution is very similar to that found in the other valley cities,

Kathmandu and Patan, studied in the same survey. There is a somewhat larger percentage of the largest-sized households in Bhaktapur.

3. See Mandlebaum (1970, vol. I, part II) for a summary of studies on family, family roles, and the family cycle in Indian societies.

4. The male/female sex ratio for Bhaktapur is 102.6 males per 100 females in 1971. The figures for Nepal as a whole—with its mix of Himalayan and Indo-Nepalese communities—were about the same.

5. The relationship is symbolized in an annual Newar ceremony, the *Kijā Pūjā* (chap. 13), a variant of a widespread Hindu ceremony in which sisters worship their brothers.

6. In the lower *thar*s, whether the wife returns to her natal home and the length of the stay is limited by the need for the woman to return to help in household and other economic tasks. Among the Jugī, for example, the wife returns to her parents' house only if there are other women in her conjugal household to help with household tasks, and among the Po(n) sweeper families the wife does not return to her natal home at all.

7. The *nakhātyā*s generally take place after the main day or days of the festival or rite of passage. On the main days there may be feasts for the patrilineal kin, the *phukī*.

8. A similar system of precedence characterizes the hierarchical sharing of the head of a sacrificial animal among wider male kin groups (chap. 9).

9. In some farming families in Bhaktapur, a father will stop accepting a daughter's *cipa* once she has been married out of the family, a practice that has been reported elsewhere in South Asia. Thus, in the central provinces of India, "some castes will not take food from their own daughters once these daughters are married, even to men of their own caste (Hutton 1961, 73; citing Russell and Lal [1916] 1975, vol. 1, p. 179).

10. The great majority of *thar*s marry within Bhaktapur.

11. Newar girls are kept out of the sun during their menarche ceremonies (app. 6).

12. In contrast to its reported use elsewhere in South Asia, menstrual blood is not reportedly used in esoteric Tantric rituals in Bhaktapur.

13. See the discussion of menarche rites in appendix 6.

14. During the course of a wedding, at the end of the first phase representing the separation of the bride from her parental household, it is not her brother but her own maternal uncle, *her pāju*, who plays a key transitional role. He physically carries her out of her natal house and hands her over to the groom's representatives.

15. It may also be referred to in relation to the child, simply, as grandfather's or grandmother's house while those kin are alive, but it will always be the *pāju*'s house.

16. A young husband wishing to give his wife a present, say, cloth for a *sāri*, without it appearing that the money was withheld from the common household pool, may sometimes claim that the *sāri* is a gift to his wife from his *pāju*, with some assurance that the lie is plausible and, furthermore, that the *pāju* will back him up.

17. As there has been some liberalization of marriage rules in recent de-

cades, particularly a prohibition of child marriage, among all Nepalis, the Newars now are not as different from other Nepali Hindus as they formerly were in these particular aspects of marriage.

18. Among the Newar Brahmans after the marriage of a girl of perhaps nine or ten to a Brahman boy of perhaps twelve to fifteen (or sometimes older), the girl would go to her husband's household for important household ceremonies. She was also brought to her husband's household in anticipation of her first menstruation and its associated rite of passage which should take place there, but she would then return to her natal home and not return to live at her husband's house until sometime after menarche—in some cases not, in fact, until she was seventeen or eighteen.

19. A younger wife may also, it is said, be flighty and may run off, either back to her home or to another man.

20. There are some rough statistics on actual ages of first marriage for other Newar communities at a period some fifteen years before this study. In 1957 and 1958 Gopal Singh Nepali surveyed 206 Newar families in Kathmandu and fifty-one in the village of Panga. He reported that about 35 percent of the women in his Kathmandu sample married at less than fifteen (the majority were thirteen or fourteen years of age). About 41 percent of the women married when they were between fifteen and eighteen years of age, and another 15 percent married between nineteen and twenty years of age. The remaining 9 percent married at more than twenty years of age. For the men, some 12 percent married below the age of fifteen years, 39 percent between fifteen and eighteen years, 30 percent between nineteen and twenty-four, and the rest, about 19 percent, above age twenty-four. Most girls, he concluded, married between thirteen and twenty years of age and most boys between fifteen and twenty-four. The village statistics showed slightly earlier ages for the marriage of girls in Panga. He attributed this to the high value of labor among the farmers of Panga but commented that in contrast to some agricultural villages in India none of the Panga girls were below ten at the age of marrigae (Nepali 1965, 201ff.).

21. G. S. Nepali found that because, he was told, of a comparative scarcity of brides, people had "started marrying a woman from the third or fourth generation, if the relationship is traced through the female links only" (1965, 205). This is probably true now for many of the *thar*s of Bhaktapur who are faced with similar scarcities. Nepali and others have written that the patrilineal restriction is limited to seven generations. For many, perhaps the majority of Bhaktapur's *thar*s, however, it applies as long as common membership in a *kul* is recognized, whatever the number of generations.

22. There are a few groups, such as the Brahmans, who consider all Bhaktapur Rājopādhyāya to belong to the same *kul*, who must marry outside the city. In recent years there seems to have been a tendency for some of the wealthier, more educated people involved in business or trade to take wives from a larger area.

23. Although it is possible to object to a particular arranged marriage, it is greatly harder for either to reject marriage *altogether*. Girls, for example, are told, "All right, you do not have to marry this man, but remember you are going to have to marry someone."

24. *Hilābulā* marriages are not uncommon among Brahman families because of the restriction of available brides to a relatively few families.

25. That the girl is married to the Bel fruit is a frequently repeated error. See appendix 6 under discussion of the *Ihī* ceremony.

26. G. S. Nepali (1965, 239) quotes the 1911 *Census of India* in a reference to the Newar custom of placing betel nuts on the bed to signify divorce. Nepali writes that it still persisted at the time of his study, but was confined to the "Udas [Urāe] and Manandhar castes." I [R. L.] did not hear of its use in Bhaktapur, although it may be practiced by some *thars*. Nepali also quotes the 1911 Census of India to the effect that a Newar woman "could undo her marriage bond by placing two betel-nuts on the chest of a dying husband." He found cases of this practice among some women who were young and without children. This removed from the young widow obligations for a prolonged mourning period, and for the deceased husband's family it removed the widow's claims to a share of his property.

27. These statistics are derived from Nepali's tables I and II, not from his discussion, which seems to be in error in regard to the extent of divorce and separation among his own sample.

28. Failure to produce children would be an important contributing reason, but this, as we will see, may lead to a multiple marriage (or, very rarely, adoption) rather than separation if the wife's relation to the household is otherwise satisfactory.

29. According to Brahmans, a woman who left a previous marriage with a divorce *could* by customary law have a full marriage ceremony, but it is not done because of "social (*sāmājik*) custom." On the other hand, they say that a woman who leaves her husband without a divorce is not entitled to a major marriage ceremony, which requires the participation of Brahmans. Nevertheless, a minor ceremony—*gwe(n) kaegu*—which does not require the participation of a Brahman, gives the new wife full ritual as well as social membership in the family, and she may subsequently participate in the other Brahman-led rituals of her new conjugal family.

30. "Misā," the Newari term for "woman," is used for "wife" in Bhaktapur. "*Kala*" is used in other Newar towns for "wife," and as an elegant usage in Bhaktapur.

31. In this case the second marriage, in fact, *permits* the first wife to be kept in the husband's home. Otherwise, there would be a necessary separation.

32. Having more than two wives in a multiple marriage is reportedly extremely unusual in Bhaktapur. Nepali's discussion suggests that each of the eight cases in his sample involved only one additional wife.

33. For a theoretical interpretation of Newar isogamy, and a review of often conflicting statements about Newar marriage patterns in relation to status, see Quigley (1986).

34. See also Gray (1980) on Chetri hypergamy. Among Chetris, status differences "are created during, and do not exist prior to, the marriage ceremony. As a result of the performance of a Vedic wedding, the affinal rule becomes relevant to and structures the relationships between the members of the households newly linked by marriage [with the]. . . superiority of the wife-taking

household and the inferiority of the wife-giving household. . . . Through kinship contagion, these status attributes emergent in marriage become part of the substance of all members of the giving and taking households" (Gray 1980, 27).

35. The Newar avoidance of adoption is in marked contrast to the situation in Polynesian and Micronesian societies where adoption is extremely frequent (Carroll 1970), and is an index of structural differences affecting, among much else, the experience and education of children.

36. For the neighboring Indo-Nepalese Brahmans and Chetri an important maximal indicator of lineage is the *gotra*, which relates individuals to one of the seven mythical Vedic Ṛṣis or "seers." Among them a concept of *gotra* exogamy creates an exogamous group much larger than the patrilineal kinship involved in *kul* exogamy. See Bennett (1977, 38ff.) and K. B. Bista (n.d.). Bista claims (p. 39) that notions of endogamy and exogamy among the Chetri are fundamentally based on *gotra* exogamy. Only upper-level Newars know their *gotra*s, which they must specify in the course of certain rituals. All Rājopādhyāya Brahmans may use the alternative *thar* name Subedi, which indicates, they say, that they belong to the Bharadvāja *gotra*. Most Chathariyā are said to belong to the Kaśyapa *gotra*. For the Newars the *gotra* has no special ceremonial entailment, aside from identifying oneself ritually, and has no exogamous entailment at all, even the Brahmans intermarrying within the same *gotra*.

37. As has been noted above, nonpatrilineal marriage restrictions that apply to *tha:thiti* become annulled after several generations.

38. Toffin (1978) found these "clans" in the Newar town of Pyangon. The unit there was named *gwoha(n)*, a designation apparently not used among Newars elsewhere. As in Bhaktapur the *phukī* in Pyangon was a subunit of the "clan."

39. For decisions affecting a larger section of the *thar* or the entire *thar*, for example, the Brahmans' decision as a group to abandon child marriage, a matter of litigation over a *thar*'s proper status, or a decision about ostracizing a member from a *thar*, the heads of various *phukī*s may meet in a council. The council may or may not represent one *kul*, depending on the constitution of the *thar*.

40. Steven Parish found an average of 4.5 familes per *phukī* among Bhaktapur's Jyāpu Suwāl *thar* (1987, 86).

41. "*Thakaki*," "elder," "*nāya:*," "leader," and "*naki(n)*," "eldest or leading woman," are used as titles in various kinds of groups. Thus, there is both a household *naki(n)* and a *phukī naki(n)*.

42. For a sketch of *phukī* organization in the Sa:mi (Kathmandu Newari Sāemi) *thar*, see Fürer-Haimendorf (1956).

43. This term may derive from *tha:*, "one's own," and "*thiti*," from the Sanskrit *sthiti*, "rule, regulation, decree," thus meaning related through ritual arrangement (e.g., marriage) in contrast to descent.

44. The daughter of the *phukī* who marries out is in herself not a member of an individual's *tha:thiti*, although her husband, children, and husband's own *phukī* members and their spouses are. She has, as we will see in connection with lineage rituals and rites of passage, ritual and social connections with both her

kul and her husband's *kul*, as she has continuing social relations with her natal and affinal households.

45. "*Bhata*" is a term used by a woman to refer to members of her husband's family (e.g., *kijā bhata*, a husband's younger brother). It was not clear to Bhaktapur informants why this term is used, but it might conceivably derive from the context in which girls traditionally form *twāe* relationships, which is while both girls are part of a group of girls being given in mock-marriage to the god Nārāyaṇa. Each would be to the other a *twāe* from her divine husband's family. It is also possible that historically cowives in real marriages at times formed these ritual relations.

46. Most people only have one *twāe*. A businessman or trader with connections in several communities may have several *twāe*s representing his interests or major connections in various communities.

47. For an extensive discussion of *guthi* land tenure, see Mahesh C. Regmi (1971, 1976, 1978).

48. Most of the important temples and larger festivals (chaps. 12 to 15) are now funded from a centralized bureau of the Nepalese government that controls major *guthi* funds. There are still, however, many smaller temples and festivals supported by local *guthis*.

49. When the *guthi* has a professional membership, it seems to echo the traditional South Asian professional guild, the *sreni*.

50. For an extensive discussion of Newar guthis, see Toffin (1975*b*).

CHAPTER 7: THE SYMBOLIC ORGANIZATION OF SPACE

1. Niels Gutschow and his associates, and Mary Slusser (in the works cited in this and other chapters) have been particularly concerned with persisting material forms, including aspects of urban space, as evidence for the history of the Newar cities and of the Kathmandu Valley. We will cite such materials and their work insofar as they have a persisting active reflection in Bhaktapur's ongoing life.

2. For another representation of Bhaktapur as a *yantra* or *maṇḍala*; see Kölver (1976) and Auer and Gutschow (1973).

3. These shrines are *pīṭha* or "hypaethral shrines," which we will discuss in chapter 8. Each of the nine goddesses is also associated with a *tīrtha*, a sacred area in a body of water, usually the river but in some cases a pond.

4. The names of the individual goddesses and their order at the circumference of the city will be given below in the section on Bhaktapur as a *maṇḍala*. The mythological sources of that particular order is discussed in chapters 8 and 15.

5. Hadigaon (or Harigaon) was a major settlement in the Licchavi period and afterward and was the site of a Licchavi royal palace (Vajrācārya 1985, 9). This provides an intriguing possible connection with the folk tale that the original site of the Digu God worship was once Hadigaon.

6. Fustel de Coulanges quotes "ancient authors" on the founding of Rome

to the effect that at the founding of that city Romulus dug a small circular trench and then he, followed by each of the settlers, threw a clod of earth from their previous home city into it. "A man could not quit his dwelling-place without taking with him his soil and his ancestors. This rite had to be accomplished, so that he might say, pointing out the new place which he had adopted, 'This is still the land of my fathers . . . for here are the *manes* of my family. . . . These souls, reunited there, required a perpetual worship, and kept guard over their descendants'" (1956, 136).

7. Throughout the book we will generally use the Sanskrit rather than the Newari form of the names of major Hindu deities when the Newari variation is closely related to the Sanskrit form.

8. In the classical Hindu period there were funerary prescriptions separating the four *varṇa*s into at least two divisions. The corpses of "twice-born" men, the three highest *varṇa*s, were to be carried out of the western, northern, or eastern gates of a town, while the corpses of Sudras, the lowest, were to be carried through the southern gate (*Manu*, Book V, 92 Bühler 1969, p. 184). The division here simply separates a lower segment from the amalgamated upper one.

9. Fustel de Coulange believed that this division was pervasive in the ancient Indo-European world: "We find this class [plebeians] around almost all the ancient cities, but separated by a line of demarcation. Originally a Greek city was double; there was the city, properly so called—*polis*, which was built ordinarily on the summit of some hill; it had been built with the religious rites, and enclosed the sanctuary of the national gods. At the foot of the hill was found an agglomeration of houses, which were built without any religious ceremony, and without a sacred enclosure. These were the dwellings of the plebeians, who could not live in the sacred city" (1956, 231). He goes on to describe a similar arrangement in ancient Rome.

10. Mary Slusser stated that the butchers as well as the sweepers, traditionally lived outside of the city boundaries. She cites Oldfield and Sylvain Lévi (1905, vol. I, p. 56) on this. As Lévi wrote (vol. I, p. 238 n.), however, as he did not have time during his visit to Nepal to do his own research on castes, he followed Hamilton and Oldfield, and in doubtful cases Oldfield, who was "more recent and more complete." Gutschow and Kölver accepting the Oldfield statement about the butchers, or Nāe, proposed that Bhaktapur's *pradakṣiṇā-patha*, the major city-wide processional route, on whose outer perimeter the Nāe and many other city groups live, was the actual ritual boundary of the city at one time (1975, 21). If the butchers ever lived outside the Newar city's walls it was already no longer the regulation at the time of Jayasthiti Malla's fourteenth-century codification of Bhaktapur's tradition, and we may take the Oldfield-Lévi remark as, perhaps, at the most some reflection of some very ancient arrangement.

11. See the analysis of the neighborhood dance performances of the Nine Durgās troupe in chapter 15 for a detailed description of this usage of the symbolism of the outside.

12. The names of these deities are given here in their Sanskrit form, not in

their local Newari pronunciation. We will discuss their relevant characteristics and their relations to other divinities in the next chapter.

13. As we will see in chapter 8, Taleju has her own *pīṭha*, that of the goddess Dumāju.

14. Untouchables living outside the city's borders belong neither to the upper or lower city, nor do they belong to a maṇḍalic segment.

15. Kauṭilya and other writers quoted in Dutt use the eight compass directions as the basis for the ideal placement of occupations and castes, an arrangement that, although possibly having some echoes in Bhaktapur in, say, the untouchables' southern location, is not an organizing principle there.

16. According to Lewis (1984, 560), the royal Taleju temple in Kathmandu is at that city's highest point.

17. Dutt emphasizes the classical "technical" use of the term "*grāma*" for an urban component. "It should be noted here that this *grāma* is not a modern village. It is a technical term for a locality with certain definite measurements and corresponds to the *insulae* of an ancient Greek town as well as to the municipal wards of a modern city" (ibid., 188). This does not take account of the functional analogy of the ward to the village.

18. D. Vajrācārya (1985, 13) also identifies *twa:* and *grāma*. D. R. Regmi suggests another village/*twa:* analogy for Malla Nepal in which, "the village must have been the lowest unit of administration in the rural [areas] as was the *ṭol* in urban centers" (1965–1966, part I, p. 514).

19. A legend ascribing the establishment of the city's twenty-four *twa:*s to the fourteenth-century king Ānanda Malla is given in chapter 14 in connection with the Chuma(n) Ganedya: Jātrā.

20. Slusser believes that the Licchavi *grāma* in Nepal must have been considerably smaller than the Indian *grāma* (1982, vol. 1, p. 85).

21. For descriptions of the construction, structure, and symbolism of Newar houses, see Auer and Gutschow (n.d.), Toffin (1977), Barré, Berger, Feveile, and Toffin (1981), Korn (1976), and Vogt (1977).

22. Gutschow notes that the brick walls, not wooden posts, bear all the structural loads of the house. The inner face of the wall may be of unbaked, sun-dried bricks (personal communication).

23. This idea is closely reflected in ideas about the protective pollution and danger accumulating functions of the lowest *thar*s, particularly the Po(n) and the Jugī.

24. According to Katherine Blair (1975), cited in Vogt (1977), there are some villages in Nepal where every house is oriented in traditional directions.

25. Vogt's informant, Mangal Raj Josi, added some ideal compass placements, which seem to be very often ignored in practice. Thus the household shrine should be to the northeast "because north is the direction of the Himalayas, home of the gods, and east is the direction of the rising sun." The area or room for household "treasures" should be to the north, the home of Lakṣmī the patron of household wealth; the kitchen area should be to the southeast, the home of Agni, god of fire (1977, 89f.).

26. In 1986/87 Gutschow attempted a complete survey of Bhaktapur's

chwāsas. He found 108 *chwāsas* where clothing of dead people is left to be picked up by Jugīs (app. 6). He notes that not all *chwāsas* within the city are at crossroads, and was unable to find why they were located at particular places (personal communication). They may, in fact, represent what were once crossroads in the past, or there may be some other historical or legendary basis for their uncanny significance.

27. Most potentially polluting materials are disposed of outside the city boundaries, often in the river, and in the case of dead bodies, by cremation at the cremation grounds. There are some places near the river where polluting materials such as placentas are traditionally disposed of, that are also thought of as *chwāsas*.

28. In a work summarizing his studies in several Newar communities of various sizes, Toffin notes the general location of *chwāsas* at crossroads in those communities (1984, 488).

29. See, for example, S. Stevenson, (1920, 425). Victor Turner (1968, 580), in a discussion of "tricksters" as "liminal figures," notes as a sign of their liminality that the Yoruba spirit Eshu-Elegba and the Greek god Hermes both inhabited crossroads as well as thresholds of houses and open public places. The Tantric-like Greek goddess Hecate is also a goddess of crossroads (Burkert 1985, 171).

30. One of these *twa:s* in the extreme west of the city is a relatively new addition to the city.

31. Veena Das, in a review of studies of Hindu cooking practices, noted that in some aspects, at least, Hindu space was not abstract Western Newtonian space, in which it was once hoped everything else could be fixed. "The most interesting idea that emerges from these descriptions is that one cannot define the characteristics of a space independently of the characteristics of time as a logical category" (1981, 140). Thus "In the context of a marriage, when the time governing the event is described as auspicious, the [sacred, household] cooking space may expand to include many more areas than the kitchen, and ritual injunctions would be applied to all these areas. In contrast, a death in the domestic group . . . results in the shrinking of the cooking area till it becomes nonexistent" (1981, 140). In contrast, however, the city spaces we have been considering here are quite fixed in their extent, and are used to help anchor other shifting aspects of the city's organization.

CHAPTER 8: BHAKTAPUR'S PANTHEON

1. For Newar religious and art history in relation to representations of divinities, see Pal (1970, 1974, 1975, 1978), Pal and Bhattacharyya (1969), Slusser (1982), M. Singh (1968), Macdonald and Stahl (1979), and Ray (1973).

2. Compare the discussion of Viṣṇu's avatars below.

3. There is some correspondence between the shape of the main body of the temple—square, rectangle, circular, octagonal—and its particular deity (Slusser 1982, vol. I, p. 142).

4. This unemphasized reference to Brahmā is one of the very few times where this divinity is represented in Bhaktapur.

5. For Indian Vaishnavites, *śālagrāmas* are a particular species of fossilized mollusk thought to embody Viṣṇu's presence.

6. This is of particular interest in regard to Kṛṣṇa. His cult is of great importance in India and elsewhere in Nepal, but it has not developed in Bhaktapur's traditional religion. This probably is related to the conflict that the personal *bhakti* religion centering around Kṛṣṇa represents in relation to the civic priestly religion of Bhaktapur. Kṛṣṇa devotion is beginning in certain groups in Bhaktapur and represents a transformation and "modernization" of Bhaktapur's religious organization.

7. Vārāhī is generally conceived as one of the forms of the Tantric goddesses derived from Śiva. She is also the Śakti of Varāha, however, the boar *avatar* of Viṣṇu, and this gives her a connecting thread to Rāma, another *avatar* of Viṣṇu.

8. See Pal (1970). Some of these representations represent the Vaishnavite emphases of earlier Newar dynasties.

9. "Some works differentiate the divine essence in the several human incarnations thus: Kṛṣṇa, full incarnation; Rāma, half; Bharata, Rāma's Brother, one quarter; Rāma's two other brothers, one-eighth; and other holy men, various appreciable atoms" (Atkinson 1974, 709).

10. In spite of their marked contrasts to the imagery and uses of the dangerous deities, particularly the Goddess (below), some of Viṣṇu's *avatars* share with the Goddess her ability to overcome the Asuras, and people may occasionally pray at their shrines for protection against exterior dangers such as earthquakes, evil spirits, and destructive weather as they would, and most usually do, to the Goddess. These *avatars* represent a "semantic" potential use that is not important in Bhaktapur because, in a sense, the dangerous goddesses fill the need.

11. Śiva is in a different way a bridge to the Tantric gods but he is worshiped as an "ordinary" deity.

12. The ambivalent nature of Gaṇeśa is sometimes signaled elsewhere in South Asia by the position of his trunk to the right or left. "The trunk . . . may turn either to the right or to the left, and it is most important to notice in which direction it is turned, for Gaṇeśa with his trunk turned to his own right hand is a dangerous god to worship. Only a Brahman in a state of the utmost ceremonial purity dare attempt it. . . . The god with his trunk turned toward his left hand, however, is in quite a different mood; even a Sudra dare approach him, and he can be worshiped quite informally, and even though his worshiper be not ceremonially pure" (Stevenson 1920 [1971], 292–293).

13. In Bhaktapur (and generally for the Newars) Gaṇeśa's vehicle is a shrew, *techu(n)*, (Kathmandu Newari *tichu[n]*) rather than his usual South Asian vehicle, a mouse or rat. He is only rarely represented in Bhaktapur in his one tusk, *ekadanta*, form.

14. "The idol of Gaṇapati is installed at the gateways of villages and forts, under the fig tree, at the entrance of temples, and at the southwestern corner of Śiva temples" (Mani 1974, 273). This last placement is also represented in

Bhaktapur, when Gaṇeśa is placed along with Viṣṇu, Sūrya, and Bhagavatī, as one of the four protectors at temples of Śiva as the supreme god.

15. "Inar" derives from the Sanskrit Ina, one of the names for the sun and the sun god, (Sūrya is another). Worship, *pūjā*, to Gaṇeśa is called *ina pūjā* in Newari. There is a legend regarding the founding of the Inar Dya: temple in which the dead son of a Brahman is brought back to life through the agency of Gaṇeśa, who had previously taken the boy's life out of jealousy because of the excessive love of Gaṇeśa's father Śiva for Nepal. The boy's life was restored at a spot in a forest where the first rays of sunlight at dawn touched the ground, which thus became the site of the present shrine.

16. Niels Gutschow and his associates were shown a complex drawing of Bhaktapur as a *maṇḍala* showing concentric arrangements of various deities (Kölver 1976; Auer and Gutschow n.d., 38). They have designated this as a "ritual map" and made attempts to locate the divinities in Bhaktapur's actual space. The deities include eight Gaṇeśa locations, ten Mahāvidyās, eight Bhairavas, and eight "Mothers" (Aṣṭamātṛkās). The painting was made in the 1920s, and provides considerable difficulties in its evaluation and interpretation in relation to the present and past realities of Bhaktapur's religious practices and existing shrines. The location and function of the Aṣṭamātṛkās is clear in relation to present practices, the rest problematic. The eight Gaṇeśas, ten Mahāvidyās, and eight Bhairavas located in the "ritual map" have no clear location or representation in Bhaktapur's present religious life, with the possible exception of certain Tantric initiations where their location and function may, perhaps, be referred to in a trace of some traditional esoteric knowledge.

17. Brahmā has no important representation nor significance in religious action in Bhaktapur. He is represented, as we have noted, as one of the three gods, the Trimūrti, represented in the Dattātreya temple, which has its major importance as a Shaivite pilgrimage site for non-Newars during the annual Śivarātrī festival. As Slusser writes, "In the Kathmandu Valley there are no temples of Brahmā, his images are few, and his role in Nepalese affairs minor" (1982, 263f.). Slusser, while noting that Sarasvatī, like Lakṣmī, is an independent goddess, says that she may be considered as having a relation to Durgā, the Tantric goddess. She notes early Newar representations where she is "Durgā's daughter, and one of Viṣṇu's consorts," and is the "Kumārī aspect of Durgā herself" (1982, 320f.). Such interweavings are sometimes significant in Tantric esoteric doctrine, but for her meaning and action in Bhaktapur's city organization, Sarasvatī, like Lakṣmī (who has similar esoteric connections), is an independent and benign divinity.

18. There is a month-long period of devotion to Pārvatī (the Swasthānī Vrata; see chap. 13) which is important to all Valley Hindu women. For Bhaktapur's women the spatial foci of this devotion are the household and together with other Hindu women in *melās*, mass pilgrimages at out of the city Valley sites.

19. This reflects a traditional South Asian distinction in the *form* that a particular deity as well as kinds of deities may take between "peaceful" forms and (in the conventional Sanskrit terms) *ugra* "mighty, violent, grim, terrible" or *krodha*, "angry," forms.

20. It is possible to offer an "ordinary" *pūjā* to the dangerous gods, but it is not the properly effective *pūjā* required for most of the purposes that their worship serves. The legend of Taleju, discussed below, indicates the importance of the "proper" worship of such deities through meat and alcoholic offerings.

21. Fustel de Coulanges long ago suggested that the "*pater*" and "*mater*" as used in relation to the classic Mediterranean gods had more to do with titles of respect and authority rather than of ordinary (biological) parẹnthood, which was expressed in terms such as "*genitor*" and "*genitrix*" (1965, 89f.). Sanskrit also has these two contrasting Indo-European terms for mother, *Mātṛ* and *Ñanitṛ* (the latter, related to the term for "birth"), which are cognate with "*mater*" and "*genitrix*."

22. Each of the Maṇḍalic Goddesses was sometimes popularly referred to as "Ajimā," the respect title for grandmother, preceded by a differentiating term. Indrāṇī, for example, was called "Ili Ajimā," and Vaiṣṇavī was called "Naki(n)-ju Ajimā." These names seem to be going out of ordinary usage.

23. The *pīṭhas* of the Maṇḍalic Goddesses are worshiped in the same order by an Ācāju priest during the course of the mass mock-marriage ceremony, the *Ihī* (app. 6).

24. Bhaktapur, like the Newars generally (Slusser 1982, vol. 1, p. 322n.), has given this name to two historically distinct forms. One of these is the Matṛkā proper (Kaumārī in Sanskrit), considered as the Śakti of the god Kumāra. The other historically different goddess given this name is the Goddess as a young virgin (Sanskrit Kumārī). While the Maṇḍalic "Kumārī" is derived from Kaumārī, Bhaktapur's "living goddess" Kumārī is partially derived from the virgin Kumārī, and her representations as young daughters in households during Mohanī is entirely derived from that virgin form. Other Bhaktapur Kumārīs, preeminently the Kumārī of the Nine Durgās, combines *both* precursors in one figure.

25. The order of the Aṣṭamātṛkās at Bhaktapur's periphery seems to reflect another cosmic sequence. Pal and Bhattacharyya (1969, 39) give a diagram taken from the Pūjāvidhi chapter of the Agni Purāṇa. This diagram presents the Aṣṭamātṛkās with the same membership and in the same order as they are arranged in Bhaktapur, beginning again with Brāhmaṇī. But here the Matṛkās are associated with corresponding heavenly bodies or *grāhas*. Seven of the *grāhas* are associated, in a tradition shared with the west, with particular days of the week. With one exception, that of Vaiṣṇavī associated with the sun and hence Sunday, who appears in the fourth and central position, the other deities in the list as they are arranged in Bhaktapur are exactly in order of the days of the week; Brāhmaṇī, for example, is associated with the moon, and thus Monday, and so on in order. The goddess in the eighth position, Mahālakṣmī is associated with a *grāha*, Rāhu, which does not preside over a day of the week. Mahālakṣmī is the deity who does not occur in the *Devī māhātmya* list either, and is from the point of view of both correspondences added to the seven basic Matṛkās to yield an eighth.

26. Guhyeśvarī is primarily represented in Bhaktapur in a hidden and restricted shrine within the Taleju temple. A second representation is a hole in

the ground in the western part of the city, next to a rest shelter, where people entering Bhaktapur in that direction from a pilgrimage were customarily met by their family priest and family members and where they would stop and pray.

27. This is in contradiction to the belief held by some in the Valley that it was Satī's anus that fell to earth at the place marked by the Guhyeśvarī shrine (G. S. Nepali 1965, 307; Slusser 1982, vol. I, p. 326).

28. The eighth Durgā is the Sipha goddess, or Mahālakṣmī. We will discuss the "mystery" of the ninth Durgā in chapter 15.

29. These forms are historically related to the Nepalese tiger- and lion-headed goddesses Vyāghriṇī and Siṃhinī (D. R. Regmi 1965–1966, part II, p. 590; Hamilton [1819] 1971, 34.) Slusser writes of them that they derive from "the lion-headed Siṃhavaktrā and her tiger-headed companion, Vyāgravaktrā, Buddhist *ḍākinīs* who are the fearful psychosexual partners of yogins" (1982, 326).

30. There have been a number of architectural studies of the Kathmandu Valley Malla palaces (Nippon Institute of Technology 1981, 1983; Sanday 1974; Korn 1976). Korn (1976, 59) and Slusser (1982, vol. II, fig. 3) present sketches of the ground plan of the Bhaktapur palace and its adjoining temples. See also Slusser (1982, vol. I, chap. 8).

31. Some of the inner structures' sculptures and frescoes, superb examples of Newar art of the Malla period, have been photographed and reproduced in Singh (1968, 192–193, 198–199).

32. "In A.D. 1097, Nānyadeva, a chief from the Karṇātaka country (the western part of southern India) proclaimed himself King of Mithilā and established a new capital at Sīmaramāpura, referred to in Nepali sources as Simraongarh [Simraun gaḍh]" (Slusser 1982, vol. I, p. 46).

33. This buffalo sacrifice amalgamates Taleju in Bhaktapur with the warrior goddess Bhagavatī as Mahiṣāsuramardinī (below).

34. In contrast to other sacrificial animals, which are supposed to be killed by the person who offers the sacrifice whatever his status, the killing of water buffaloes including the major sacrifices to Taleju is the special function of the low Nāe, or "butcher" *thar*. This part of the legend is connected with this.

35. At present the Taleju temple still has esoteric ritual relations with the Indrāṇī *pīṭha*. The Taleju temple is within Indrāṇī's maṇḍalic section.

36. Slusser has made the suggestion that Taleju was associated with and eventually absorbed the cult of the ancient Licchavi tutelary goddess Maneśvarī (1982, vol. 1, p. 317). In Bhaktapur there is a stone within the Taleju temple which is worshiped as Maneśvarī.

37. D. R. Regmi states that in the Kathmandu Taleju temple, "There is no image of Taleju at the main shrine, only a finial with certain symbolic marks engraved in a plate of bronze stands in its place as is the case with similar patterns in other temples of the type in Nepal." (1965–1966, part II, p. 593). The "finial" is a metal ritual waterpot, the *kala*s.

38. A Brahman, a Tantric priest (Ācāju), and an astrologer (Jośi) are necessary for all of Taleju's internal rituals. At the time of this study the Taleju staff had four Rājopādhyāya Brahmans, six Ācājus, and three Jośis. Among the Brahmans one is considered Taleju's chief priest. This is a title and function that

is inherited within one segment of the Rājopādhyāya *thar*. It is noteworthy that in contrast to both Malla royal inheritance (D. R. Regmi 1965–1966, part I, p. 485; part II, p. 394) and current Nepalese law, where succession to title is by primogeniture, the Taleju chief priest title passes on the death of a holder to his next oldest brother, even if the eldest son of the deceased title holder is elder than the next eldest brother. However, this principle is limited to brothers dwelling in the deceased title holder's extended household. If the brothers live in a separate household, the title will usually pass to the deceased title holder's eldest son if he is of age.

39. These rituals are perfunctory. The priests read an oath in Sanskrit, which is translated into Newari. The person being initiated takes the oath while making an offering of a mixture of rice, nuts, and coins to the goddess.

40. It is said that there is only one group in Bhaktapur's civic religion whose Tantric initiation does not depend ultimately on Taleju mantras, namely, the Jugīs.

41. Only a failure to consider the esoteric and structural aspects of her role or perhaps an emphasis on the comparatively fragmented religious system of Kathmandu may explain Slusser's remark that "today, except for a brief annual resuscitation at Dasai(n) [Mohanī], the Taleju—Maheśvarī temples are closed and her cult is virtually extinct" (Slusser 1982, vol. I, p. 319).

42. As Slusser remarks, Bhagavatī "is the name most commonly invoked to identify any image that is iconographically puzzling to the Nepalese, particularly gods or goddesses that remind them of the familiar multiarmed Durgā" (1982, vol. I, p. 310).

43. Dui Māju has another entirely different legend in another context. On the fifth day of the Biskā: festival sequence (chap. 14) she is worshiped as the "younger sister" of the Maṇḍalic Goddess Indrāṇī. According to the legend told about this day's worship the Goddess Devī had gone in the form of a low-caste Dwi(n) maiden to the market where she was recognized and captured by a Malla king with Tantric power and placed in the Taleju temple. This story may have been generated entirely by the resemblance in sound of Dui and Dwi(n).

44. Bacchalā's temple image is variously described as an anthropomorphic image in the embrace of Śiva as the Lord of the Dance, and as a *yantra* on a Kalaśa. Her temple is next to a temple of Śiva as Paśupatinātha and seems to represent his consort.

45. The story goes that a Malla king of Patan, jealous of the king of Bhaktapur, sent a merchant to sell Ku Lakṣmī's image (and thus the goddess herself) to the Malla king of Bhaktapur, who was famous for accepting all new things offered to him. The king bought her and placed her near his palace with the result that she drove out the other protective goddesses, who did not want to be associated with her. So she was moved to a different area, and people went there to worship her.

46. The practice of going on the twelfth day meant that most of the children who might die from smallpox had already died, thus protecting the goddess's reputation.

47. The *Devī Māhātmya* is an independent text that was once a part (chaps. 81–93) of the Mārkaṇḍeya Purāṇa. According to Vasudeva Agrawala, that

Purāṇa was a product of the Gupta Age and its final version was completed by the time of Chandragupta Vikramāditya at the end of the fourth century A.D. (1963, p. iv).

48. The version of the *Devī Māhātmya* we are using here is a translation of a thirteenth-century Nepalese palm-leaf manuscript (Agrawala, 1963, p. xiii).

49. In Bhaktapur, Taleju, Bhagavatī, and the Devī of the *Devī Māhātmya* are sometimes addressed as "Bhavānī," a title that would be inappropriate for lesser Tantric goddesses, or for ordinary goddesses such as Lakṣmī. Bhavānī, "the popular name of Devī in the Śakti cult" (Stutley and Stutley 1977, 44), connects the goddess for Shaivite purposes to Bhava, a title of Śiva, a title stressing his creator functions. According to Bhaktapur Brahman informants, Pārvatī is not properly called "Bhavānī" until she becomes transformed into Pārvatī Devī, or Bhagavatī, that is to say, the fully powerful manifest goddess. Bhavānī sometimes is held to mean Śiva's consort, stressing the Shaivite connection, but sometimes to mean the "*naki(n)*" of "mistress" of existence, which emphasizes the goddess as the supreme creator.

50. Bhisi(n) is only one of the protective deities choosen by Newar tradesmen and shopkeepers in other places. In other Newar communities Lakṣmī is said to be the most popular of their deities. Bhisi(n)'s central status for them in Bhaktapur is special to that city.

51. As Toffin notes Nāsa Dya: and some other figures in the Newar pantheon "clearly have non-Indian roots. These autochthonous elements represent that part of the religious heritage that is authentically Newar. . . . Unfortunately our knowledge of the pre-Indian substrate is too limited to determine precisely its role in contemporary Newar religious life" (1984, 422 [our translation]).

52. Ākāśa Bhairava, in Bhaktapur a severed head, is described in Purāṇic accounts as having cut off the head of Brahmā who had enraged Śiva. In some of the versions Bhairava was forced to continue to carry Brahmā's severed head with him because of his great sin. He was finally able to purify himself and get rid of Brahmā's head (which in some versions had become stuck to his palm) in Benares, at a place that is still commemorated (Mani 1975, 115; Sahai 1975, 119, O'Flaherty 1973, 124).

53. These eight Bhairavas (for their names, see Kölver [1976, 69–71]) are those eight forms traditionally designated as the "leaders" of the eight major groups of Bhairavas, each group containing, in turn, eight lesser Bhairavas (Sahai 1975, 121).

54. The slits in the walls of houses, which allow supernatural serpents, Nāgas (and other vague spirits), to enter and, more importantly, to leave the house, are sometimes identified with Bhairava. These slits are called "Dya: lā(n)," or god paths, and are also identified with a dangerous form of Hanumān as Hanumān Bhairava, and variously called "Hanumān," "Bhaila Dya:," "Nāsa Dya:," or "Nāga" holes.

55. Among the non-Newar Hindu Chetri the lineage gods are also represented by stones generally found outside the village (K. B. Bista 1972, 66).

56. *Toraṇas*, which commonly are placed behind or over figures of divinity, are in Bhaktapur often carved with a demonic protective figure at their apex. This figure, Che(n)pha: God, represented with a lion's head, sometimes with

horns, is said to be the brother of Garuḍa, to whom he is related in local legends. He is iconographically related to the demon-like South Asian form Kīrtimukha. Some arches have Garuḍa himself as the protective figure at the apex.

57. Niels Gutschow remarks (personal communication) that there are some particular stones in the city that represent (or are) *nagās* and that can be worshiped and placated.

58. According to Toffin (1984, 488), the *chwāsa* is identified in some Newar communities "by women" as the goddess Ajimā. "Ajimā" is a respect title for "grandmother" and is used in Bhaktapur with additional qualifying terms, as we have noted, to refer to various major dangerous goddesses.

59. According to Manandhar (1976, 37), Buddhist priests similarly believe that the *chwāsa* is "the location of an image of Śiva."

60. For the Biskā: festival Swatuña Bhairawa represents the place where Bhairava descended into the ground in an attempt to escape his angry consort Bhadrakālī. The attempt was only partially successful in that she seized his head and cut it off; the headless body escaped. This movement is consonant with the idea of the stone deities as transitions to the underground.

61. These are the sun, the moon, Mercury, Venus, Mars, Jupiter, and Saturn, plus two more (Rāhu and Ketu) representing the ascending and descending nodes of the moon where it crosses the ecliptic and, thus, the "dangerous" points where eclipses may occur.

62. The various particular kinds of influence—neutral, auspicious, and inauspicious—of each of the Navagraha are also reflected in the auspiciousness or inauspiciousness of particular days of the week for various activities, each day of the week having its particular presiding *Graha*.

63. Bhaktapur's shrines of Jagannātha, Rāmaśvara, Kedarnātha, and Badrinātha "were conceived as substitutes for four famous Indian *tīrtha*s, to which the king's subjects could more easily repair in their own city square" (Slusser 1982, vol. 1, p. 207). She has some notes on their construction.

64. "Annāpurṇā, 'Giver (or possessor) of food.' A household goddess who is a beneficent form of Durgā. Her worship ensures that the household and the world shall never lack food" (Stutley and Stutley 1977, 14).

65. In South Asia the persisting *preta* is generally associated with greediness and a hunger and thirst that cannot be assuaged. For example, "to linger as a *preta* is the most dreaded of all states, for a *preta* has a throat as narrow as the eye of a needle, so it can neither drink water nor breathe, and its shape is such that it can never stand or sit, but it is for ever flying in the wind." Stevenson, from whom this quotation is taken (1920, 191), goes on to say that, the *preta* "continues in that terrible state not . . . owing to any bad *karma* it has acquired, but, generally, owing to the way in which its Śrāddha [death ritual] has been either omitted or bungled. There is, however, another thing that may hold a spirit in this terrible condition, and that is the force of its unfulfilled desires."

66. The *bhūta*/*preta* distinction is vague and varies for different people, and in different communities. In his Kathmandu Newari dictionary Manandhar (1976, 409) defines "*bhūta*" as "a ghost, spirit of a dead person." Stevenson (1920, 161) says that the *preta* may become a *bhūta*, "a malignant spirit."

Stutley and Stutley (1977, 47) indicate that *bhūta* were a special class of created malignant beings, who later became assimilated, in part at least, with the malevolent qualities of "particular *pretas* such as those who have met with violent deaths, or who have died without the performance of the correct funerary rites."

67. D. R. Regmi believes that the *khyā* is derived from the ancient Indian forest spirit the Yakṣa (1969, 31).

68. The numbers of deities in household pantheons are of the same order, however, as Roberts, Chiao, and Pandey's numbers.

69. As we have seen, differentiations based on "elementary family groupings" only—and significantly—apply to one component of Bhaktapur's pantheon, the benign major deities.

70. Some of the historical residues that are represented in a "religious" object or event may in a global way give it its canonical validity. They give force to the object or event from the very fact that they are "traditional" yet not presently understandable. Compare Rappaport (1979) on the "sacred" implications of traditional invariants in ritual.

71. The epitome is St. Paul's Epistle to the Romans (i. 20–24). "Ever since the creation of the world his invisible nature, namely, his eternal power and deity, has been clearly perceived in the things that have been made. So they are without excuse; for although they knew God they did not honor him as God or give thanks to him, but they became futile in their thinking and their senseless minds were darkened. Claiming to be wise, they became fools, and exchanged the glory of the immortal God for images resembling mortal man or birds or animals or reptiles . . . they exchanged the truth about God for a lie and worshiped and served the creature rather than the Creator."

72. "Horror stories," as exemplified by *Dracula*, are familiar modern examples. See Levy (1985), which contrasts *horror stories* as explorations of the moral periphery of a community with *tragedy* as portrayals of their moral centers.

73. The iconographic features of Hindu gods are discussed in the books on Nepalese art history mentioned above and exhaustively for South Asian icons in Rao (1971), Banerjea (1956), and Sahai (1975).

74. Totagadde's terms for this "*dēvates*" group includes "*būta*."

75. Both these terms refer to a sort of general deity, which has successively differentiated concrete forms that add specific attributes and functions to the general characteristics of the term. Each level of differentiation is a being, a *deva* in itself. Wadley notes the contrast between what we have called the "generative powers" of the more abstract beings to the concrete, embodied powers of the more and more specialized manifestations: "We move from the least differentiated beings (with the broadest powers) in the first deity class to the most differentiated beings (the most marked beings with the most defined powers) in the last class. The more differentiated, more marked beings are most likely to be found acting in the world of men or to have derived mythologically from the world of men. Related to the amount of specification (differentiation) of deities is the ideas of powers as embodied. *Bhagavān*, only vaguely anthropomorphized, represents largely unembodied powers—and the least differentiated powers" (1975, 145).

CHAPTER 9: TANTRISM AND THE WORSHIP OF THE DANGEROUS DEITIES

1. They had capured a pig and drunk its blood, thus making it impossible for the Brahman to take them back into his home.

2. One upper-status interview respondent, a noninitiate, described such uses of Tantrism as "traditional Hindu science," which was falling into disuse because it was being replaced by Western alternative techniques of power such as medicines.

3. The low Jugī *thar*, which has some customs and traditions relating it to an historical yogic sect (chap. 10), has some rudimentary Tantric aspects in its initiations. Some of the Jugī's public functions, notably their performances as Śiva, are interpreted by upper *thar*s as having some Tantric meaning and power, and members of the upper *thar*s imagine that the Jugīs have private Tantric knowledge.

4. There are Tantric elements or references in Bhaktapur's ordinary *pūjā*s. The *sukundā* (see below) with its references to Śiva and Śakti is used in many Newar *pūjā*s, and aspects of the diagrams on which *pūjā* equiment is placed, some of the hand gestures used in the *pūjā*s, and so on, are understood by the priests, although not by uninitiated participants, to have some Tantric references. This is thought by local Brahmans to represent a difference between Newar ordinary *pūjā*s and Indo-Nepalese ones.

5. Beyer (1973) devotes an entire long volume to a detailed description and exegesis of a Tibetan Tantric *pūjā*. Van Kooij (1972) provides a detailed discussion of Hindu Tantric worship. For other sources on Tantric procedures, see Gupta, Hoens, and Goudriaan (1979).

6. "*Ailā*" is renamed "*nyā(n)*" in Tantric ritual contexts.

7. A "right-handed method" was associated with the "purely internal worship" of Śakti. Such worshippers "abhorred the use of wine and other unconventional ritual items. The term Vāmācāra... became established for the time-honored Śākta use of wine and meat, and perhaps also other antinomian elements in their ritual" (Gupta et al. 1979, 44).

8. The significance of *mudrā* as one of the five *makāra*s is generally assumed to be in reference to the supposed aphrodisiacal power of the substances usually used as *mudrā*, parched grain and kidney beans (see Stutley and Stutley 1977, p. 195). They note that in Buddist Tantrism, the word may be applied to a female adept. In Gupta et al. (1979), Hoens has a comment on this latter use. "*Mudrā* sometimes denotes the *sādhaka*'s female partner or [the] wife of a deity but in that sense it is almost exclusively confined to the Buddhist Tantras. *Mudrā* is the fourth of the five *makāra*s used in Kaula types of Tantric rituals, where in modern times it stands for parched rice, some other cereal or savory titbit. Nevertheless one wonders whether originally it did not mean a female partner" (Gupta, Hoens, and Goudriaan 1979, 117).

9. "Kaula Tantrics always follow the most orthodox form of esoteric rites involving the practice of drinking alcohol, eating meat and fish, and having sexual intercourse with a chosen partner during *pūjā*. The partner is sublimated to the position of the goddess and is called "Śakti." She is initiated in the sect and, at the time of*pūjā* is consecrated and worshiped. Her face, breasts and sex

organ are specially revered. The Tantric exerts himself to please her with food, drink and gifts" (Gupta, Hoens, and Goudriaan 1979, 147n.).

10. As we will see in a later section, there is evidence that human sacrifice probably once existed in Bhaktapur as part of the worship of the dangerous deities. The killing would have been a sacred act, having been done in the correct ritual context, and the victim would have received liberation, or *mukti*. This is the sort of transformation of what would otherwise be a crime or a "great sin," a *mahāpāpa*, into a positive religious action that otherwise illicit sexual practices in a Tantric context would have represented, and suggests a climate in which they may have been more likely than in recent decades or perhaps centuries.

11. Gopal Singh Nepali remarked that the Indo-Nepalese Brahmans of Nepal refused to accept the Newar Brahmans as their equals because they are priests to the Newars "whose domestic ceremonies are similar to those of the Sudras. An additional reason is purported to be the influence of Tantrism on them, involving use of liquor" (1965, 152).

12. A Tantric *pūjā* may, for example, be required, on the advice of some religious expert, in response to some offense to a Tantric deity, particularly to the Āga(n) God itself.

13. Non-Tantric *pūjās* are not necessarily less expensive than Tantric ones, and some of the Brahman-assisted *dhala(n) danegu pūjās* (app. 4) may be quite expensive.

14. The shift from Tantric to non-Tantric *pūjās* seems to be part of the weakening of the *phukī* group and a consequent emphasis on the household, and is allied with other recent shifts toward a more "modern" type of Hinduism.

15. When the maṇḍalic *pīṭha* is a center of worship, people first go to the *twa:* Gaṇeśa temple, then to the Āga(n) God to make a perfunctory offering, and finally to the *pīṭha* for the main *pūjā*. In the case where Āga(n) House *pūjās* are at the center worshipers again go first to the *twa:* Gaṇeśa temple, but then to the maṇḍalic *pīṭha* to make a perfunctory offering, and finally to the Āga(n) House for the main worship. An Ācāju can be delegated to do the early parts of the sequence.

16. The comparative meanings and uses of Digu Gods and Āga(n) Gods are different in Newar villages, which lack the social complexity of Bhaktapur (cf. Toffin 1984, 76–81).

17. The people who in legend brought Tantric forces into the city, such as Harisiṃhadeva, who brought Taleju, and the Brahman Tantric expert, who introduced the Nine Durgās, are very high-status people. The presence of Tantric Āga(n) Gods within the city in the possession of high-status families is consonant with this association of high status and legitimate Tantric power.

18. In the case of need a family section of a relatively poor *phukī* sometimes moves into the Āga(n) House, relegating the worship area to an isolated section.

19. The expenses of the Āga(n) House are sometimes supported by the proceeds from family-owned farmland set apart as a special land grant. The farmers who farm the land pay rent or give some of the land's yield to the *phukī*. The famers also have some responsibilities toward the protection and mainte-

nance of the Āga(n) House. This system of support, like others based on upper-status land ownership, has begun to disappear because of land reform and the changes in the famers' socioeconomic status.

20. Some texts on the Newars refer to the Āga(n) Room as the "Agama Room," and the Āga(n) House as the "Agama House." This is said in Bhaktapur to be a "Nepali" or a "foreign" usage and is not used locally. The Āga(n) image itself is reportedly sometimes called "Āga(n)mā," said to be a contraction of Āga(n) *māju*, "*māju*" being an honorific appellation of some dangerous goddesses. The term Āga(n)mā has been confused with the term "Āgama", which designates traditional Tantric and non-Vedic texts.

21. Slusser gives as alternate names "Degu," "Deguli," "Dehuri," "Digu," and "Devālī *pūjā*." "Dugu," meaning "goat," refers to the animal often sacrificed to the Digu God. It is a common "vulgar" term for the deity in ordinary usage in Bhaktapur.

22. There are some *thar*s whose members believe they all have a common ancestor and thus must marry into other *thar*s at the same status level. Such a *thar* may have only one Digu shrine for the entire *thar*. There are other *thar*s whose members believe that they are in the same *thar* because their ancestors although unrelated shared some common trade or historical origin. It is for this latter group and for those *thar*s who believe that their common ancestor is now so distant in time as to no longer require *thar* exogamy that the Digu God shrines are significant markers. In Bhaktapur's cultural mosaic all this is further complicated in that among some, at least, of the low *thars* the deity they call their "Digu God" is of a different significance. The Jugī, for example, say that they all have the same Digu God, but they have intermarrying sections.

23. Building a new Āga(n) House is an expensive undertaking, and sometimes the same Āga(n) House may continue to be used for some period of time by two or more split-*phukī* groups who use it at different times.

24. In some South Asian contexts *iṣṭadevatā* implies a personal deity in a modern sense, often in the context of Bhakti religion. Thus, the choice a person makes of an *iṣṭadevatā* "is a radical, ultimate choice, an act of faith involving his total person and life. It also has the aspect of a 'voluntary association,' and he enjoys a 'freedom' to make his choice in worshiping a deity, regardless of group, family, caste, and other ties, including the kuladevatā" (T. K. Venkateswaran 1968, 159). This description is alien to traditional Bhaktapur, however, where one's *iṣṭadevatā* is one's family deity.

25. Those Rājopādhyāya Brahmans who are attached to the Taleju temple usually become initiated into this stage at much younger ages than other high-status candidates. In addition to the three levels of *dekhā*, the Taleju Brahmans must undergo further initiations to understand and participate in Taleju worship. These are not properly *dekhā*, but are called "elevations" or *thā taegu* (see chap. 8 on Taleju).

26. This is not to say that there may not be some individuals in Bhaktapur who may have this belief and who, indeed, may not know more profound Tantric meditative techniques, and who may not have experienced the more profound personal experiences that are the ideal goals of the practice. However, such virtuosi, if they exist, are hardly representative of what, to all accessible

evidence, seems to be experienced and believed even by advanced Brahman practitioners.

27. Their main images are at the household shrine near the cooking area on the top floor.

28. Goudriaan, in listing the constituents of Tantrism, includes as one of them the "realization of the supernatural world by specific methods of meditations *(dhyāna),* involving in the first place the creation of mental images or pictures of gods and goddesses who may be worshiped internally. The deity thus created may be invoked for social, especially medical, aims" (Gupta, Hoens, and Goudriaan 1979, 8).

29. We will consider the royal and aristocratic implications of Tantrism for Bhaktapur in conjunction with the relation of king and Brahman in later chapters.

30. The last *chemā pūjā* prior to this study had been some ten years earlier, in 1962, when the astral *grāha*s had all been in conjunction, a sign of great danger portending perhaps a major earthquake. Ceremonies lasted about two weeks throughout the entire city.

31. The various specialized craftsmen who contribute to the masks and other images of the Devī cycle and the people who are possessed by and who perform as the Nine Durgās (chap. 15) are enabled to do this because of the powerful Tantric *mantra*s that are (or were in the past) transmitted to them by high-status, initiated Brahmans.

32. When considered in relation to function the clapper of a bell may be considered as *śakti* in relation to the bell itself; when considered in relation to sexual imagery, the clapper would be male, Śiva, and the enveloping bell itself would be Śakti.

33. All this is related to the issue of the differences in the relations between male and female deities among the benign deities and the dangerous deities, which we discussed in chapter 8.

34. They cannot be ranked by some unifying scale of purity, for the benign gods are supremely pure, while the dangerous gods belong to a realm where conditions of purity and impurity are irrelevant.

35. As we will see later, in the public religion of the city most vividly and clearly in the Nine Durgās performances (chap. 15), much of the "message" of sacrifice is specifically directed to male citizens of the city. The preferential sacrifice of male animals was general in South Asia. Kane quotes the Kālikā Purāṇā, which after an extensive listing of animals proper to be sacrificed to Devī (the list including human beings and "blood from one's own body"), adds that "females of the species specified . . . were not to be offered as *bali* and the person who did so would go to hell" (1968–1971, vol. V, p. 164). Whatever additional meanings that Hindu or Newar emphases on male sacrifice may have, since neolithic times the sacrifice of male rather than female animals has been everywhere more prevalent in large part because of the critical relation of the number of female livestock to the quantity of births and thus new stock.

36. As Kane puts it, "The convenient belief from very ancient times has been that a victim offered in sacrifice to gods and *pitr*s went to heaven. . . . Hemādri quotes verses saying that all the animals such as the buffalo that are employed

for (gratifying) Devī go to heaven and those that kill them incur no sin" (1968–1977, vol. V, 168).

37. Stevenson reported of Kāṭhiāwār that when "non-Brahmans are about to offer a goat at Daserā [the Newars' Mohanī] the shaking and quivering of the goat is a clear sign that it is acceptable" (1920, 122). She implies that this is associated with an idea of the possession of the goat by the deity.

38. In some Bhaktapur households which are relatively modernized, secularized and, therefore, closer to general Nepalese culture, animals that are sacrificed primarily for feasts—and therefore with perfunctory ritual—are sometimes decapitated.

39. In contrast to the killing of animals for food, the killing of wild "game" for sport by Kṣatriyas has generally in South Asia been considered a nonstigmatizing aristocratic activity, like the killing of foes in warfare (compare the discussion of king and Brahman in chap. 10).

40. The highest-status public sacrificer is the Ācāju, who performs the sacrifice for, "in the name of," the leading client. Sometimes when an animal is dedicated and offered at a maṇḍalic *pīṭha*, or at a local temple of Gaṇeśa, the killing may be done by some member of one of the low castes, a Po(n), Jugī, or Nāe, who may be attached to the temple as a "guardian," a *dya: pālā*.

41. K. B. Bista notes, without giving details, "festivals of the head" among at least two non-Newar Chetri groups, in which the head of the sacrificial animal is shared at a special feast for the leading male members of the family group (1972, 104, 107).

42. Among the Po(n)s there are occasions, such as following the birth of a child, when a pig sacrifice is made and the *siu* is distributed in hierarchical order among family women only.

43. This and the following quotations are from tape-recorded interviews. R. L.'s questions in the interviews are given in parentheses.

44. As Kierkegaard put it in relation to Abraham's imminent sacrifice of Isaac, unless Abraham doubted the meaning of his act and thus suspected that the sacrifice of his son might possibly be only a common murder—and of an exceptionally reprehensible sort—his faith had no significance. "The ethical expression for what Abraham did is, that he would murder Isaac; the religious expression is, that he would sacrifice Isaac; but precisely in this contradiction consists the dread which can well make a man sleepless, and yet Abraham is not what he is without this dread" (Kierkegaard [1843] 1954, 41). I have previously used this quotation (1973, 352) to suggest the kind of ethical dilemmas that Tahitian village society tries to avoid, and is generally able to avoid, but which, in contrast, proliferate in complex societies such as Bhaktapur's, giving rise to new problems, solutions, and sensibilities.

45. The secret religion of the cellular groups corresponds to Fustel's conception of the cellular aspects of family religion in the ancient Indo-European city. "Each family has its religion, its gods, its priesthood. Religious isolation is a law with it; its ceremonies are secret" (Fustel de Coulanges 1956, 113).

46. This cellular privacy also greatly reduces the number of things that any competent citizen must know about. Thus, aspects of information management in a complex traditional society are also at issue here.

47. In other kinds of societies and historical conditions full secrecy may, of course, exist (alongside of groups who will, like the groups in Bhaktapur, advertise that they have secrets), and its symbolic implications will be directed entirely toward the members within the unit which holds the secrets.

48. Of course, the danger is also to the holders of the secret, who, like the Wizard of Oz, may lose the power of the secret if it becomes public knowledge. Insofar as this brings about the collapse of the sociocultural system organized through secrets, however, it is also a genuine threat to the violator.

49. The loss of the secrets of an urban unit with a resulting loss of the differentiation of information is analogous in part to the social uses, conceptions, emotional implications, and metaphorical extensions of "purity" and "impurity" (chap. 11).

50. As we have discussed, this escape from the constraints of ordinary logic and fixed social relations and physical forms is an important part of the legends, classification, appearance, and behavior of the dangerous deities in contrast to the ordinary ones.

51. Newar Brahmans, because they are both "ordinary" priests and Tantric *gurus*, embody the opposition of being guardians of the moral realm and guides to its proper violation.

CHAPTER 10: PRIESTS

1. A classic attempt to explore and resolve the moral paradoxes of the king's responsibilities is the Bhagavadgītā.

2. Some Rājopādhyāya Brahman individuals or families now use for some purposes the surname "Subedi" or "Śārma," a generalized Brahman name that does not distinguish them from other Nepalese Brahmans.

3. The Rājopādhyāya Brahmans contrast themselves with the Partyā Brahmans, among other ways, in that they, the Rājopādhyāya, are engaged only in proper Brahmanical activities. The Partyā Brahmans' farming indicates for the Newars a fallen status.

4. This displacement of the old Kānyakubja Brahmans and the building of the "substitute house" is referred to in the legend of the bringing of Taleju into Bhaktapur (chap. 8).

5. This reference to the shortage of families from which the new Rājopādhyāya Brahmans could take wives suggests the possibility that the two groups of Valley Brahmans although supposedly both from Kānyakubja may have refused to intermarry, and that the earlier Brahmans were in fact displaced by the later ones.

6. D. R. Regmi, discussing the Brahmans in Malla Newar society, notes that some of the chronicles state that the Valley Brahmans were divided into two groups, one made up of "five divisions" of North Indian Brahmans and the other of "five divisions" of South Indian Brahmans. He goes on to say, "There is no trace of... [these] Brahmans [within organized Newar society] other than those belonging to one branch, those known as the Kānaujiyas. It was true that some Brahman families came from South India. There were [also] many families

who came also from Mithilā and Bengal. But these never rendered priestly functions to the community. As such they were kept outside the pale of the Nepalese caste structure" (1965–1966, part 1, p. 679).

7. There is another inferior group of Brahmans, usually referred to as the "Lākhae Brahmans," who although they use the *thar* name "Rājopādhyāya," are at present an entirely different group than the dominant Rājopādhyāya Brahmans. (See the next section in the text.)

8. These *thar*s are Malla, Hāḍā, Hoḍā, Pradānāṅa, Ujha(n)ṭhache(n), Gwa(n)ga, Jo(n)che(n), and Bijukche(n).

9. Pressures of modernization and economics have caused changes in recent years. Many Rājopādhyāya Brahmans are now seeking some position in the modernized Kathmandu Valley society commensurate with their traditional status.

10. The Rājopādhyāya Brahmans are well aware of the stigmatizing implication of *dāna* offered them in connection with death and illness in other contexts, and some say that they do not accept such offerings. We will return to the implication of payments to Brahmans below.

11. Taleju's focal festival, Mohanī, requires three astrologically determined *sāit*s or proper times, but these, which coordinate the timing of Taleju's activities in each of the old Newar cities, are made by the central government's Royal Astrologer, a non-Newar. Only some comparatively minor astrological determinations are made in relation to Taleju's activities by the Bhaktapur Temple's own Jośis during this festival (chap. 15).

12. Astrological work for the lower-middle and marginally clean *thar*s is often done by Buddhist Vajrācārya priests.

13. The word "*dasā*," when used without a context specifically meaning "good," implies "bad fortune."

14. It is possible by a secondary use of Karmic theory to say that the reason that a person has a bad relation to the astrological forces is because of his or her bad *karma*. This is a more abstract, theoretical use of "*karma*."

15. In some early accounts and later chronicles (e.g., Hamilton [1819] 1971; Basnet [1878] 1981; Lévi 1905) the Jośi (written "Jaisi" or "Jausi") are described as a high-status mixed group derived from the marriage of a Brahman and a non-Brahman Newar woman who had subsections variously doing divination, astrology, medicine, and priestly work. Hamilton ranks them above "Shresta," that is, above Chathariyā, as some middle-ranked and low-ranked people still do.

16. In the other Newar cities some, at least, Ācāju families are at the Chathar level.

17. Characteristically, the term "Tini" is not used in their presence, where its use would be considered disrespectful. In their presence they are referred to as "Śivācārya" and addressed as "Pūjārī."

18. We only know of one passing reference to the Tini in older lists of Newar status groups (Chattopadhyay 1923, 506).

19. The *gha:su: jagye* ceremony is said to be a shortened version of a fire offering to Bhairava (called a *Bhairavāgni*) made once a year in the main Bhairava temple.

20. Members of the Cyo *thar*, which is at level XI, officiate as a "sort of a priest" during one phase of the ceremonies at the cremation grounds just prior to the cremation itself in the death ceremonies of upper-level *thars*.

21. There are, in fact, still three Pasi families living in Bhaktapur, but they no longer do this traditional and stigmatizing work.

22. One of these is a *liṅga* representing Śiva as Hāṭakeswar, "a god who comes from under the earth," made of special clay dug from deep under the surface, a kind of *liṅga* that can be properly made only by a Bhā.

23. In a very significant contrast to the untouchable and near untouchable *thars* who have been forced to remain in their traditional positions and to perform their traditional functions through various social and economic sanctions, the members of the marginally polluting *thars* find it much easier to drop the status-depressing, polluting, and embarrassing traditional functions of their *thar* for other kinds of work, often in farming or the modern sector of Bhaktapur's economy. Thus many Bhā families have farms, shops, or small restaurants, and have members who are in government service or are school teachers.

24. Toffin describes this service by the Bhā for the high Hindu *thars* of Panauti where a bit of bone from the dead persons skull is mixed with a food offering presented to the Bhā. Toffin says that this practice is for the purpose of evicting the spirit of the dead, of chasing it from the house by "identifying" it with the Bhā (1984, 290).

25. This is said to have been done by a Partyā Brahman in connection with the death ritual of the last king of Nepal. The Brahman is said to have had to leave Nepal and to have gone to India.

26. Hamilton, in one of the earliest Western accounts of the Newars, presents a passage that bears on the activities and status of the Tini, Bhaṭṭa Brahmans, and Bhā. "The Achars [by whom he seems to mean Newar Brahmans *and* auxiliary priests] have among them certain men who perform the ceremonies necessary to free from sin the souls of those who die on certain unfortunate days. This ceremony they call Hom. The [non-Newar] Brahmans perform similar rites, which they call Pushkarasanti. The Hindus believe that if this ceremony is neglected all the relations of the deceased will perish. By this ceremony the officiating priest is supposed to take upon himself the sin of the departed soul; and if, in its performance, he commits any mistake, he incurs certain destruction from the wrath of the Deity. The office is therefore shunned by men of high rank, both as sinful and dangerous. The Achars who perform this ceremony are calculated Gulcul, and cannot intermarry with those of the first rank" ([1819] 1971, 31).

27. Todd Lewis, in his study of the Newar Buddhist Tuladhars of Kathmandu, writes that "most" of them believe that the Newar Brahmans are at the top of their (the Tuladhars') caste system (1984, 148). A survey of Bhaktapur's various Buddhist *thars* on this issue would be of considerable interest. Insofar as Lewis's findings might hold in general, the elevation of the Brahmans in the conceptions of nonpriestly Newar Buddhists may reflect an inference by Buddhist laymen that the status of the Vajrācārya unprotected by an allocation of contaminating functions to others is lower than the Brahmans, an inference

deriving from the logic of the purity-based status system—which the Newar Buddhists accept.

28. This "permanent attachment" is in many ways problematic, and must be reinforced by ensuring often through physical and economic force that the low *thars* continue to perform clearly polluting functions and live in polluting circumstances.

29. As we have noted in chapter 9, the Kṣatriya groups could kill (and eat) animals in the course of war-like hunting and could kill human beings in the course of war without its having a lowering effect on their status. They were following their special kind of Kṣatriya *"meta-dharma."*

30. In popular (and erroneous) folk explanation it refers to "eating the God's meat" (*lā*), that is, the offering to the Tantric Aṣṭamātṛkās.

31. According to Niels Gutschow (personal communication), the main source of temple-caring income for the Po(n)s comes from their assignment to Sūrya Vināyaka temple (chap. 8), which, like the *pīṭhas*, is outside the city's boundaries.

32. The Po(n) have one uniquely nonpolluting role to play in Bhaktapur on the fifth day of the solar New Year festival Biskā: (chap. 14).

33. "Jugī," "Ḍarśaṇdhārī," and "Kapālī" are terms derived from that group's yogic tradition; "Kusle" or "Kusale" is a Nepali term referring to hereditary tailoring groups, one of the Jugīs' professions.

34. D. R. Regmi, however, characterizes the first Jugīs in Nepal as "Nepalese mendicants" of the Gorakhnāth school and contrasts them with the Kāṇphaṭa *yogis* themselves who arrived later in Nepal and became associated with the Valley Matsyendranātha cult, and "who do not belong to Newar society" (1965–1966, part II, p. 756). Briggs (1938), supporting a possible origin of those "mendicants" in the yogic order, gives many examples of descendants of Kāṇphaṭa yogis whose occupations and status resemble those of the present Newar Jugīs.

35. In their musical performances they use other instruments—drums and cymbals—as well, but these instruments are not special or restricted to them.

36. This is on the fifth day for a Brahman, on the fifth or seventh day for various Chathariyā and Pa(n)cthariyā *thar*, and generally on the seventh day for Jyāpu-level *thar*s.

37. The Jugī who goes to a particular *chwāsa* may live anywhere in the city. "One Jugī may own rights at five different *chwāsa*s, and three Jugīs may have divided their rights at one *chwāsa*. These rights are occasionally sold to others" (Gutschow, personal communication).

38. The Bha: also, in the case of high-status clients, incorporates part of their body substance. This magical gesture is only tangentially related to the symbolism of the flow of impurity, and in some cases, as we have noted, previously required the exile of the Bha:.

39. In fact, as we will discuss elsewhere, this is a matter of very vestigial forms used in the course of initiations into certain *thar* activities, such as the beginning of the study of the musical instrument, the *mwāli*. The Jugī now, in Bhaktapur at least, do not know or use traditional yogic practices, and, in contrast to upper *thar*s with Tantric initiation, do not perform meditation. This is,

in fact, characteristic of even those who remained fully in the Kāṇphaṭa tradition. As Briggs wrote in the early decades of this century, there seemed to be little knowledge of their texts and only limited practice of Yoga among them ([1938] 1973, 251).

40. That is, we are excluding here those religious structures that are Newar Buddhist and whose attending priests are the Vajrācārya, and the Maṭhas, the centers for visiting Shaivite ascetics from elsewhere in South Asia, whose presiding priests, or *mahantas*, are Ja(n)gam, Giri, and Puri of Indian origin.

41. For the three or four temples that had more than one priest, only the major *pūjārī* is listed.

42. For example, "The Brahmans, being in principle priests, occupy the supreme rank with respect to the whole set of castes" (Dumont 1980, 47).

CHAPTER 11: PURITY AND IMPURITY: ON THE BORDERS OF THE SACRED

1. A similar point was made earlier by Gabriel Campbell, who adds the observation that the transcendence of the categories of purity and impurity may characterize children as well as ascetics, and thus be prior to social differentiation. "Children are buried [rather than being cremated] because they are social and ritual non-entities; they have not completed the transition into human society... although the child is born in relative impurity, his nakedness and innocence is relative purity.... In the burial [rather than cremation] of saints [that is, Hindu ascetics] exactly the same structural relation to society holds as in the burial of children. Thus the saint is also outside of society both socially and ritually. He is casteless, without a family, and although in a state of basic purity, really exists outside the system of purity and pollution as it affects normal householders.... Cremation is necessitated by 'separateness,' by a social and ritual 'individuality'; whereas the relationship of the child and the saint to Brahman, the pervading Soul, is precisely one of non-separation, or non-individuality" (1976, 118–119). Burial rather than cremation is done in Bhaktapur for infants and young children and for Bhaktapur's historically renouncer group, the Jugī. It should be noted, however, that infants and young children who would not be cremated if they died are nonetheless purified in many *thars*, albeit in a perfunctory manner, following death and birth pollution in the family.

2. As Veena Das remarks, Van Gennep (1909) had in his seminal *Les Rites de Passage* already "emphasized the threatening nature of all liminalities—intellectual, social, and cosmic. He pointed out that being unclassifiable, these liminalities have the potential of disrupting the particular classifications imposed by man on his given reality" (Das 1977, 117).

3. See the discussion of these theorists in Douglas (1968, 336f.).

4. "Even those who have incurred impurity (on death, etc.) are enjoined to do certain religious acts such as offering water to the deceased" (Kane 1968–1977, vol. IV, p. 268). We noted in chapter 6 (in the discussion of menstrual disabilities) that menstruating women—and polluted men—may worship the

Tantric lineage deity and do daily household worship, but in areas away from the shrines, and by making use of imagined images of the deities.

5. "Thus the precise rules for the purification of the body have been declared to you; hear now the decision of the law regarding the purification of the various inanimate things" *Laws of Manu* V, 110 (Bühler 1969, 188).

6. The radical possibilities of the escape from the Brahmanical *dharma*-supported status system when "inner impurity" is not only taken into account but given greater significance than "external impurity" is evident in the way that low castes can and do make use of the altered emphasis. Barnett and Barnett quote a South Indian untouchable, who argues "The caste man [a member of the clean castes] says if you touch a person who is not in the caste system, you will be polluted, but we deny caste. . . . Bathing is for external cleanliness only. . . . Our view of bathing and pollution is rational, theirs is traditional. . . . The caste man is not clean in heart while Adi-Dravidas [untouchables] are, since [we] . . . do not retaliate after mistreatment, and therefore surface dirt is irrelevant. . . . Brahmanical culture emphasized cow worship and sacrifice, not character" (1974, 387f.; cited in Sara Dickey 1984).

7. A person may have "impure" or "dirty" thoughts. These are one particular sort of disturbed and disturbing thoughts, about which people feel variously shame or guilt or concern, but these are distinguished from, and are different sorts of problems than, physical impurities.

8. The Po(n) and Jugī, like all *thar*s, high and low, have their own necessary purification procedures prior to rituals, and their *own* still lower status, and relatively degraded, eaters of *cipa* and collectors of impurity. In their own conception and action some, at least, and perhaps all of their own pollution might also be removed. But, they say, the conditions of their life make it impossible to avoid contamination as well as to devote themselves properly to religious activities. They may ascribe their fallen social condition to an act of a *thar* ancestor (the Jugīs have an elaborate account of this), but this does not explain any "indwelling impurity," only the inherited conditions of life that render each generation and individual impure as a secondary consequence.

9. Veena Das, emphasizing the relation of symbols of impurity to liminality, writes that "In the case of the symbolism of impurity, it is the peripheries of the body which are emphasized. Thus hair and nails, which figure prominently in this, have a peripheral position in relation to the body as they can both belong to the body and yet be outside it. It is significant that both the hair and nails are allowed to grow in a natural state to symbolize impurity" (1977, 127).

10. There are three ritualized life-cycle events: birth, death, and menarche, which cause group pollution—which must be removed by purification at the end of the *saṃskāra* proceedings. However, while the entire *phukī* is polluted by birth and death of its members—the shared pollution being one of the defining characteristics of a *phukī* group—the extent of pollution connected with menarche and menarche rites (see app. 6) varies according to the custom of individual *thar*s. In some *thars* all the *phukī* members are polluted; in others, only the parents of the girl.

11. Compare the discussion by Veena Das (1977, 128f.) on the many problems in attempts to identify birth and death pollution with "caste pollution."

12. The various "purificatory" acts that follow in the days after the main purification, which ends the official ten-day period of mourning after death—which is the purification referred to in this statement—can be seen as purging individuals and various places of dangerous, nondisgusting influences, that is, of "clean contaminants" (see app. 6).

13. One metaphorical connection between "dirt" and birth and death is liminality. "The impurity of death marks off the mourners for the period when they are dealing with the liminal category of the *preta*; similarly, birth impurity marks off the relatives of the new-born, till the child has been incorporated as a person, within the cosmic order" (Das 1977, 125).

14. The idea of the effective transfer of a dangerous "substance" is general in South Asia as it is everywhere in the world. Stevenson noted that on the birthday of a Brahman boy in Kāṭhiāwār a "lucky woman" is brought to wave her arms toward him, and then, cracking her knuckles against her forehead takes on herself his ill luck" (1920, 26).

15. *Manu* lists various procedures for cleaning inanimate objects according to their constituent materials, using ashes, earth, water, fire, Kusa grass, hot water, mustard-seed oil, cow urine, and cow dung (Bühler 1886, 188ff.).

16. This is part of a general understanding that to *be* impure is a matter of discomfort and possible social embarrassment, but to *cause* someone or something (including oneself) to become polluted is a moral error, in the sense that it is a matter of personal responsibility.

17. Lower thars, depending on their status and *thar* customs, make use of other personnel and procedures for purification.

18. The Tulsi plant itself, associated with Viṣṇu, has various ritual uses.

19. *Nanā* is water that must be drawn on the same day it is used from a river, well, or tap, which must not be touched by a major source of contamination such as a menstruating woman, member of an unclean *thar*, or unclean animal. It is used for washing the face and hands in the morning, washing before *pūjā*s, the initial cleaning of *pūjā* equipment, and so forth. It is the least "powerful," the most ordinary, of the various kinds of pure water (app. 4).

20. In most major purifications now only some nuchal hair is shaved off. Total shaving of the head (sparing an occipital tuft of hair) is generally restricted now to the closest male relatives in the purification following a death in the family. In some elaborate Tantric or ordinary *pūjā*s performed for some special purpose, however, both the officiating priests and the sponsor of the *pūjā* may have their head shaved during the preparatory purification.

21. This may have been in part to prevent their use by a witch, a *boksi*, in "contagious magic." This possibility is known about but is considered a trivial risk.

22. Although the Nau is not an untouchable, the minor *bya(n)kegu* after the Nau procedures may reflect to some degree a response to the Nau's borderline clean status as well as the completion of purification. Elsewhere, such as among the Coorgs as reported by Srinivas, "contact with a barber defiles a Coorg, and every Coorg has to take a purificatory bath after being shaved by a barber" (1952, 41).

23. Veena Das's remarks cited above regarding the liminality of hair and

nails, which both belong to the body and are at the same time outside of it, suggest that hair shaving and nail paring serve to delineate anew the clean boundaries of the body by dealing with the peripheral aspects of hair and nails as exuviae, first separating them and then distancing them from the body.

24. Theoretically according to karmic theory the individual who has become polluted would be being punished for some past violation of the *dharma*, but, in fact, such theory is only made use of in special, and usually extreme and rare cases.

25. Marriott and others (e.g., Marriott 1976, 1980; Marriott and Inden 1977) have interpreted some aspects of South Asian thought and behavior as based on conceptions of "dividuals" as open to a flow of substances which continually affect and constitute their individuality. These conceptions are widely represented in Bhaktapurian doctrine and ordinary discourse about the self.

26. Disgust has something to do with powerful motivations for rejection of the ingestion of food or food-like substances. Only some kinds of substances that should not be ingested are disgusting; broken glass, for example, is not. "Disgusting substances" are organic and have some of the properties of food and thus represent some potential *temptation* for ingestion. "Disgust" implies a powerful blocking of a temptation for incorporation. In Bhaktapur the temptation to be "equal to all" has, for middle-status and upper-status people, a strong implication of being free to be equal to those *lower* on the scale. Dirtiness, rejection of hierarchical separations from lower-status people, and rejection of the special restrictive responsibilities associated with middle and upper status, are strongly tempting as well as threatening for middle-status and upper-status people in Bhaktapur for various reasons. Such temptations are associated, particularly for men, with a long period of freedom of association and action during childhood before the extensive differentiation, restrictions, and responsibilities that result from a sudden transition after initiation into full *thar* membership with the *Kaetā Pūjā* rite of passage. The temptation is countered by obsession with the lowest *thar*'s contacts with dirt, particularly with feces, their evident dirtiness, and their "disgusting" moral behavior.

27. An important element in the marriage ceremonies of many *thar*s that also implies a unification of bodies is the ceremonial sharing by the bride and groom of food from the same dish, the sharing of each other's *cipa* (as it is phrased), which symbolizes the unification of the bridal pair. In upper-level *thars* this is the only time that the husband takes the wife's *cipa*; that is, following this unification, she, by taking his *cipa*, incorporates his and his lineage's substance, but he will not incorporate hers.

28. In practice the persons who are concerned with contamination by contact with low-status people are mostly men—particularly Brahman men whose priestly activities would be compromised. Upper-status women's relatively domestic, household-centered life traditionally limited their chances of coming into contact with members of low *thar*s.

29. The purification of ritual equipment and settings is, like individual purification, done through cleaning and washing with various pure substances and varies, as does ordinary purification of the body, from perfunctory to elabo-

rate. The condition to be achieved by such purification is usually phrased as making the area or equipment *śuddha* or (more rarely, and mostly in Brahmanical usage) *pavitra*. "*Śuddha*" means clean or pure in a general sense. "*Pavitra*" adds an additional meaning, it has been glossed as "pure, holy, sacred, sinless, etc." (Monier-Williams [1899] n.d.). Ritual equipment and areas not only are pure but also have supernatural power concentrated within the boundaries delineated by purification—and concentrated further in other smaller maṇḍalic circles drawn within the larger purified *maṇḍala* in which the supernatural aspects of the *pūjā* are located. "*Pavitra*," as "sacred," means both pure (i.e., clearly delineated) *and* powerful. Once the area and equipment are purified, the supernatural power is brought into them through additional procedures such as mantras and entreaties to the deities.

30. This is complicated in Bhaktapur by the Rājopādhyāya Brahmans' esoteric functions as Tantric priests and the fact that they can eat certain meat. But when they are functioning as priests of the ordinary deities they share the purity and food restrictions which apply to those deities.

CHAPTER 12: THE CIVIC BALLET: ANNUAL TIME AND THE FESTIVAL CYCLES

1. The events that take place in multiple numbers of years are *melā*s, in which people from Bahktapur join masses of other Nepalis in a visit to some shrine elsewhere in the Kathmandu Valley or in wider Nepal. Most *melā*s are annual events that are only tangentially connected with the city order. There are four prominent nonannual ones, three of these taking place every twelve years, and one every thirty-three months. Calendrically determined or encouraged events with monthly, fortnightly, or weekly cycles are primarily matters of household and individual worship. Thus, Tuesdays, for example, are proper for Gaṇeśa worship, particularly if they fall on the fourth day of a lunar fortnight. The first day of each lunar fortnight is particularly proper for the worship of Viṣṇu, the full-moon day for worship of the moon, the fourteenth day of the dark lunar fortnight for worship of the dangerous goddesses, and so on.

2. Manandhar defines "*nakha:*" as "a festival in which the central event involves a feast called *nakhatyā* put on at home," and notes in his definition of "*nakhatyā*" that it entails an invitation to women married out of the household (1976, 244). There are, in fact, some *nakhā cakhā* in which married out women are not, properly speaking, "invited" in that they *must* return to their natal homes as an integral part of the ceremony.

3. There are, approximately, seventeen annual *melā*s in which some or many of Bhaktapur's citizens might participate. Among these six are intimately connected with the annual cycle, and are listed in the city's annual festival calendars. These are the events [4], [15], [32], [33], [35], and [51], discussed in the following chapters. (Please see chap. 13, last paragraph in "Introduction" section, for an explanation of these bracketed numbers.) Two of these take place at the same time as events within the city, but are not particularly connected with them. The remainder of the *melā*s, including those four that take place in multiple numbers of years, are not connected with city events.

4. For an extended description of Nepalese and Hindu calendars and eras, see Slusser (1982, vol. 1, pp. 381–391). See also D. R. Regmi (1965–1966, part I, p. 49; part II, p. 793ff.), Gaborieau (1982), Freed and Freed (1964), and Kane (1968–1977, vol. V).

5. For non-Newar Nepalis of Indian origin, the "Indo-Nepalese," and in some other parts of South Asia the lunar month begins on the day following the full moon (Gnanambal 1967, 4).

6. These are, respectively, *timilā* and *khimilā* in Kathmandu Newari; *milā*, according to Manandhar (1976, 452), deriving from an old Newari term for moon.

7. In practice, the Nepali term *au(n)sī* is usually used for the new-moon day.

8. Traditionally the names of the solar months were those of the corresponding signs of the zodiac. Basham writes that the solar calendar was imported with ancient Western astronomy and is known to have been used since Gupta times onward, "although it did not oust the old luni-solar calendar until recent years" (1967, 495). He remarks that the Sanskrit names of the signs of the zodiac from which the names of the solar months were derived are almost exact translations of the Greek originals.

9. Gnanambal's report (1967) on Indian "festivals" includes fourteen festivals (some of which have more than one component part and lasts more than one day) celebrated generally throughout India, in contrast to the many festivals restricted to one or to a group of states.

10. The sequences and events of greatest integrative importance are Swanti, in relation to household organization, Biskā:, Mohanī, and the larger Devī cycle—within which the Mohanī sequence is an element—in relation to the structure of the city and its environment, and Sāpāru as a central "antistructural" festival.

CHAPTER 13: THE EVENTS OF THE LUNAR YEAR

1. As the Swanti sequence includes the lunar New Year's Day, its numbering contains the last and first days of the annual cycle.

2. The ambiguity of the reference of many terms for this period (e.g., Divāli, Dīpāvalī, Tihār, Tiwār) as referring to a three-day or five-day span is more general than in the Newar case. Sometimes the terms designate a five-day period, sometimes they are applied to a three-day core period to which two additional days of events are added (e.g., Kane 1968–1977, vol. V, p. 194; see also "Tiwār," R. L. Turner 1965, 286).

3. There are Purāṇic references to gambling during this festival, which in some other parts of South Asia takes place on the fifth day of the sequence (Kane 1968–1977, vol. V, p. 203). According to Kane's reference, the gambling is conceived as an omen, forecasting whether the gambler would gain or loose his wealth during the course of the year.

4. During the Rana period tents were set up in the city where large groups of townspeople could join together in gambling.

5. Lakṣmī is called "Lachimī" in Bhaktapur, but we are following the con-

vention for the festivals that we used in our discussion of the deities of using Sanskrit names for the major pan-Hindu deities.

6. Certain upper-status families most closely derived from the Malla kings and their priests make a food offering to Taleju before the house *pūjā* to Lakṣmī, and they take an oil lamp from the Taleju temple to the household as one of the lights to be presented to Lakṣmī during the course of the household *pūjā*.

7. The Brahmans and a few high-status Chathariyā families who emulate them are an exception. They use Ācājus rather than the household *naki(n)* to perform the worship.

8. In G. S. Nepali's account of this ceremony for another Newar community, he was told that the *maṇḍalas* represent Yama, the deity of death. This is not the interpretation of our informants, but the symbolism of Yama is central to the Swanti sequence. Nepali also reports that the lamp wicks offered were as long as the height of the person to whom they were presented, and that their length symbolized the length of the life of the individual (1965, 381). The wicks offered in Bhaktapur are commonly about a foot in length, but very much longer than ordinary oil-lamp wicks.

9. In some Jyāpu families the custom is, in fact, restricted to the worship of younger brothers by elder sisters. In the traditional Hindu account of the origin and practice of the *pūjā* in India, the sister is primarily a younger sister, modeled on Yama's younger sister Yamunā (e.g., Kane, 1968–1977, vol. V, p. 2207f.).

10. From here on our estimates of the importance of events for Bhaktapur will be given in a parenthetical note.

11. Many of these days apparently had in the past, different names throughout the year for each one of their successive occurrences. Only a few such special names are known now, and even fewer of them now have any special differentiated current significance.

12. The main temple image, considered the essential one and a form that is often hidden from the view of all except initiated priests, is never removed from the temple.

13. Bhaktapur's main annual festival directed to the same purpose is Sāpāru [48].

14. The local tale goes that Kubera, the god of wealth, came to a house disguised as a beggar. The householders asked him in and offered him Ya: Mārhi cakes to eat. The god revealed who he was and told his hosts that on that day henceforth their grain storeroom would always be filled.

15. Iltis (1985) includes a full translation of one version of the collected stories.

16. This is a peculiar combination of Newar and non-Newar traditions. The girls past the *Ihī* ceremony are always married in that they have had a mock-marriage to a deity. One of the purposes of this is to prevent the traditional Hindu stigmata of widowhood, as the social marriage is (in a restricted way) a secondary remarriage. The nonparticipation of Newar widows in the Swasthānī ceremony implies, in this case, the acceptance of the ritual status of widow.

17. The representation of Śiva as a *liṅga*, or phallus, is a major theme in the

Swasthānī story, where it is an object of worship by Pārvatī, and a dangerous force that had to be controlled by Viṣṇu (Bennett 1983).

18. Iltis, on the basis of discussions with Newar women reported that the large majority of women, in contrast with Bennett's reports on Chetri women, said that they did not participate in the *vrata* in order to overcome some particular problem, but rather "for merit and to help others, as well as to assure a continued good future" (1985, 611). There may well be problems here in the difference between local conventions about expressing a motive for a religious proceeding and the generally understood private motives.

19. In connection with the reference to Lhasa it may be noted that Sarasvatī is associated in some versions of this tale with the Vajrayāna Buddhist deity Mañjuśri.

20. As we will see when we discuss the spatial arrangements of the solar Biskā: Festival, the Khware-Gā:hitī axis is part of the line dividing the city into lower and upper sections, which are marked and placed into opposition during that festival. The use of this route here adds to the sparse evidence for the association of the city's two major Viṣṇu/Nārāyaṇa temples with city halves.

21. If the woman was a widow she would present the eight cakes to her son, and if she had no son they were sent to the river and discarded there.

22. The name of the Ca:re, "Silā," is in folk etymology, at least, associated with *Silā*, stone, which, in turn, is said to stand for Śiva's *liṅga*, usually represented in stone. It is also alternatively said to derive from the name of the month, Sillā. All *ca:res* are in Saivite Hindu tradition associated with Śiva. Kane notes that "The 14th *tithi* of the dark half of a month is called Śivarātri" but that this particular one is the Śivarātri *par excellence* (1974, vol. V, p. 225). The association of the other *ca:res* with Śiva is played down in Bhaktapur's emphasis on the Goddess.

23. Hunting is a Kṣatriya activity, and the hunter in Kane's version is a king. As we have seen in the discussion of Tantra, the transcendence or manipulation of the ordinary *dharmic* realm is a necessary characteristic of Kṣatriya religion.

24. In Patan, in contrast, the Kṛṣṇa image carried in procession on this day is housed in one of the city's major and most imposing temples, a temple specially devoted to that deity.

25. See Anderson (1973, chap. 34) for a description of the events of this day elsewhere in the Kathmandu Valley.

26. In parts of India where the year began with the month of Caitra, this day was often in honor of Brahmā. Kane notes, in passing, in a description of Caitra New Year events that in their course the worshiper should anoint his body with oil and take a bath (1968–1977, vol. V, p. 83).

27. The previous day, the fourteenth is called "Mātāti Ca:re," the *ca:re* of the Mātā Tīrtha, but there are no special activities in Bhaktapur on this day beyond those of an ordinary *ca:re*. For some of the legends told about the pilgrimage site, see Anderson (1971, 51).

28. As in many calendrical events, this requires planning and coordination for the movements of a woman who is both a daughter and a mother.

29. According to Toffin, Caṇḍeśvarī is the protective deity of the Newar town of Banepa (1984, 481). In Banepa and in Tokha, another town in which

there is a festival involving Caṇḍeśvarī, the festivals take place at about the same time of the year as the Bhaktapur festival.

30. Lewis (1984) has a detailed account of the annual festival calendar of the Newar Buddhist merchant group, the Tuladhars, in Kathmandu.

31. Although the Buddha can be amalgamated to Hinduism as a minor avatar of Viṣṇu, the general doctrine, overt among Brahman theorists, is that *any* form that is believed to be divine by anyone and that is worshiped may be considered as a deity.

32. The four deities of the Panauti Jātrā are Bhadrakālī, Brāhmaṇī, Bhairava, and Indreśvar Mahādeva. For a description of this event, "the culminating point of the religious year" at Panauti, see Toffin (1984, 509–520).

33. The day of Hari Śayani in itself is a minor event.

34. *Gu* means "nine," and the compound *gunhi* means "nine days," referring to the period of special activities initiated by this day. Manandhar (1976, 87) gives the form "Gunu Punhi."

35. In the years subsequent to this study the younger and more modernized Brahmans began to resist this annual hair-shaving.

36. In other Newar cities the Rajopādhyāya Brahmans during the course of the day also tie such bags with yellow thread around the wrists of their *jajamāns*. In Bhaktapur, however, the custom is for the non-Rājopādhyāya Brahmans, the Jhā and Bhaṭṭa, to tie the bags on the wrists of men of upper-status and farmer families who are not otherwise the clients of these "non-Newar" Brahmans.

37. As is the case with both these sources for many of the festivals we are describing in these chapters, some of the details and versions of the stories they report are unfamiliar to us for Bhaktapur.

38. This is a traditional South Asian belief. "Vaitaraṇī. The name of the foetid river which flows between the earth and the nether regions, and over which the dead pass to Yama's realm. . . . Vaitaraṇī is also the name of the cow presented to the priest during the funerary rites, in the belief that it will carry the dead man safely across the dreaded river" (Stutley and Stutley 1977, 318).

39. There is, as we shall note, a variation in this ordering in the last segment of the procession.

40. Whatever the situation may have been in the past, there is some uncertainty as to when the shift from a child to an adult representation should be made. It is not simply a matter of level of rites of passage now (i.e., *Ihī* mock-marriage for a girl, *Kaeta Pūjā* for a boy), but a decision each family must make within an uncertain age span. The fact that the large image is considerably more expensive than the small one influences this decision.

41. In other competing accounts of the fate of the soul after death, one would have long before passed through one's *preta* state.

42. The variants "Ghi(n)tā" for Ghe(n)tā(n) and "Ghisi(n)" for Ghesi(n) are also used.

43. As Newar women do not dance now, with the one exception noted in the discussion of the period just following the day of Sāpāru, it is generally assumed that these dances represent dances once done in the past at some period when women still danced in public.

44. Although young Brahman men participate in most dance types, they are said never to do obscene dances.

45. Some people "carry placards decrying social ills—real, exaggerated or entirely imaginary. Local newspapers participate in Gai Jātrā satire, with stories announcing a great increase in salary for the superfluous masses of government workers. Others tell of the release of all political prisoners, who are now to be absorbed into the ranks of officialdom. Again it is reported that the abolished caste system has been replaced with rank 'according to wealth.' On this day, supposedly, citizens are free to express themselves without fear of reprisal" (Anderson 1971, 103).

46. "*Au(n)sī*" is the Nepali term for "new-moon day" and is used not only for this general Nepali festival, but usually for new-moon day in general, rather than the Newari term *āmāi*.

47. See Anderson (1971, chap. 12) for the legend associated with this *melā*.

48. There is another Bhairava Jātrā of great symbolic importance in the course of the solar New Year festival, Biskā: [20–29]. The *jātrā* image used in that festival is a different one from the one used in this festival, although it is housed in the same temple.

49. Compare Toffin (1984, 530). Lewis (1984, 373), remarking that the Buddhist Newar Tuladhars of Kathmandu, whom he studied, did not observe Tij, says that "shreṣṭhas and other Newar Hindu women" do observe it. This may have been a misreporting by his Newar Buddhist informants. It is also possible that some Newar groups who have assimilated to Indo-Nepalese culture may have introduced the practice.

50. In South Asia the *vrata* proper to this day was traditionally practiced mostly by women. According to the Brahmāṇḍa Purāṇa "if a woman performs this *vrata* she enjoys happiness, becomes endowed with good bodily form, beauty and sons and grandsons" (Kane 1968–1977, vol. V, p. 150).

51. According to Niels Gutschow, most of these poles are placed along the main festival route, but may be located anywhere else in the *twa:*. Certain families, mostly Jyāpus, erect the poles year after year.

52. According to Niels Gutschow (personal communication), an image of Indra is painted on the neck of the Kisi.

CHAPTER 14: THE EVENTS OF THE SOLAR CYCLE

1. "*Saṅkrānti*" refers to the passage of the sun from one sign of the zodiac to the following one, which constitutes the basis for the sequential progression of the twelve solar months (Kane 1968–1977) vol. V, p. 210).

2. The numbers in brackets refer to the position of solar events within the sequence of lunar calendrical events in 1975/76.

3. Major offerings to Brahmans were traditionally done in South Asia on all *saṅkrānti* (Kane 1968–1977, vol. V, p. 212).

4. G. S. Nepali (1965, 386) presents some details on the observations of the

day, presumably among village Jyāpu families, which are unfamiliar to us for Bhaktapur.

5. It is unique, that is, in its particular combination of elements at a particular time. Some of those elements are reflections of Kathmandu's Indra Jātrā (see festivals [59–65], chap.14); others are closely similar to aspects of a festival in the Newar town of Panauti about two months later (Barré, Berger, Feveile, and Toffin 1981, 45).

6. According to Gautam Vajracharya (personal communication), this is an echo of the form of the term in classical Newari, *yalasi(n)*. "*Si*" here means "pillar" as well as "tree." Vajracharya glosses the word "*yalasi(n)*" as "sacrificial pillar." Variants of the term are found in other religious forms, such as the central pillar of Newar stupas. The poles that are erected to represent Indra during Kathmandu's Indra Jātrā are also *yasi(n)*.

7. According to D. R. Regmi (1965–1966, vol. II, p. 650), the term "Biskā:" (in its Nepali form, Bisket) derives from Visvaketu, the "universal flag," which was the name given to banners that are attached to the "arms" of the *yasi(n)*. Bhaktapur has its own folk etymology, which we will note below.

8. The major components of the Biskā: festival sequence in our treatment are the Bhairava/Bhadrakālī Jātrā [20] from the first to the ninth day, the raising of the large Yasi(n) God [21] on the fourth day, the "taking out" of the Tantric gods [22] on the fourth day, the Vārāhī Jātrā [23] on the fourth day, the taking down of the Yasi(n) God [24] on the fifth day, Indrāṇī Jātrā [25] on the fifth day, Mahākālī/Mahālakṣmī Jātrā [26] on the sixth day, Brāhmaṇī/Maheśvarī Jātrā [27] on the seventh day, the procession worhiping the gods that had previously been taken out [28] on the eighth day, and Chuma(n) Ganedya: Jātrā [29] on the eighth day.

9. According to G. S. Nepali (1965, 344), it was traditionally the responsibility of the Sa:mi (or Manandhar) *thar* to select, cut with the proper ritual, and supervise the dragging of the tree to Bhaktapur. This is the same *thar* whose members in Kathmandu are responsible for selecting and bringing the tree used for the *yasi(n)* in Kathmandu's Indra Jātrā.

10. The location where the tree is to be cut is "explained" by one of the legends about the *yasi(n)*,which we will present below.

11. In the course of the Biskā: festival Bhadrakālī is generally referred to by her honorific title, "Naki(n) Ajimā," "the leader of the mothers (or grandmothers)," that is the dangerous goddesses. Bhadrakālī is a name occasionally given Śakti in the Tantric tradition. It is used a very few times as an appellation of the Goddess in the Devī Māhātmya.

12. During the Mohanī festival the goddess of the maṇḍalic area is sometimes called "Bhadrakālī" rather than "Vaiṣṇavī," but in that case they are simply two names for the goddess of that area.

13. For some notes on this and other Newar ritual chariots, see Gutschow (1979*b*).

14. This sword, carried at this point by a representative of the central government, is taken by it to represent the contemporary central authority. When Pṛthvīnārāyaṇa Śāha conquered the Kathmandu Valley, he maintained tradi-

tional Newar festivals, but for those that had important political implications, references to the new regime were understood to have been substituted for references to Malla kings. Although the sword represents to the political authorities themselves and to other Nepalis the sign of the superordinate authority of the central regime, to many local people in Bhaktapur this symbol, and many other such symbols still represent the traditional Malla kings; hence, the significance of the carrying and the handing over of the sword in this preliminary event becomes significantly altered in its local implications.

15. In other *jātrā*s images of deities are usually carried in palanquins called *kha:cā*, or "little chariots."

16. For some detailed photographs of the Bhairava chariot, see Gutschow (1982, 82–85).

17. According to Gutschow's account (1984), the musicians are from the low Jugī *thar* and the man who carries the *sukundā* is from the marginally clean Bhā *thar*.

18. This is an important example of the "advertised secrecy" that we discussed in chapter 9.

19. The head of Bhairava separated from his body is an element of one of the legends associated with the festival, which we will recount below.

20. The Mahā(n) constitute a category, now containing two *thar*s (Caguthi and Muguthi) within the middle-status segment of the Jyāpus. According to Manandhar, who has the name Māhā:(n), the word derives from the old Newari term *mahātha*, "a military commander, a very important military post in Malla days. . . . From this the term Maharjan was taken as a caste name or surname by a section of Jyāpus to avoid the contempt associated with the name Jyāpu." He notes also that "those who were in military service during the days of the Malla kings were called *māhā:(n)*." (1975, 444). The military commanders (as opposed to the soldiers) have their *thar* descendants, as Manandhar notes, in the Chathar Amātya (alternately called "Mahāju") *thar*.

21. As we noted in the previous chapter, the Pulu Kisi Haigu [65] is another, but comparatively minor, occasion when confiict between the city halves is expressed.

22. In the years of social change and breakdown of traditional patterns just after the study, some of the fights initiated by the tug of war were very severe, extensive, and difficult to control, and threatened the performance of the *jātrā* itself.

23. A *hiti* is a traditional water fountain. A *gā: hiti*, according to Manandhar, is "the old type of fountain located in a depression in the earth" (1976, 627). Bhaktapur Newari, like Kathmandu Newari, has the form "*hiti*," but has a long final "i" for this particular place name.

24. The Kathmandu version of the term (*syāku tyāku*) refers to another occasion "the main day of the Dasain [Mohanī] festival, involving a feast and a visit to the goddess Durgā. The word is popularly reinterpreted . . . [to mean] 'However much you kill you don't have to repay as retribution; what is killed [and eaten] is for the goddess and is not for self-interest, thus the killer is exempt from the blood-guilt of the animals slaughtered'" (Manandhar 1976, 606).

25. The sequence of Daś Karma signifies for a deity its birth or more accurately rebirth, and is characteristic of deities who reappear during each annual cycle.

26. The erection of a pole, or a pole with banners, on the solar New Year's Day is (and was) found elsewhere in South Asia (e.g., Underhill, 1921; D. R. Regmi, 1965–1966, part II, p. 650).

27. The *yasi(n)*s are symbolically connected in a very minimal way by saying they are consorts, with the larger central *yasi(n)* being the male, the smaller secondary one the female.

28. A quotation from Gutschow illustrates this historical, archaeological approach to cultural features. "We do not know the reason behind the apparent. . . [parallelism] of the two poles [the two *yasi(n)*s]. The clue might again, [as] in so many cases, lie in the spatial development of the town. We also do not know why Bhairava and Bhadrakālī 'take residence' in temporary 'houses' in Lākulāche(n). . . . All these activities point to a former center with its New Year ritual. With the unification of a number of villages, the construction of new temples and the installation of a more elaborate and grander ritual the needs of an enlarged community was served. Older places of reference were then incorporated; . . . modification of rituals and a change of the spatial setting tend to incorporate preceding patterns. The present ritual might well reflect the existence of a more ancient setting, thus telling us in a hidden form about the history of the place" (Gutschow 1984, 17). The legends of the Chuma(n) Ganedya: Jātrā (see text below) refer, in fact, to an enlargement or founding of Bhaktapur in connection with the establishment of Biskā:.

29. It is these banners, as we have noted above, which may have provided Biskā: with its name.

30. As we have noted in chapter 8, each of the eight Matṛkās traditionally has a specific Bhairava consort, independent subforms of that deity. This particular iconic feature of the Yasi(n) God unites the diverse couples into one.

31. In other Newari and South Asian versions of this tale, only one snake appears. The extra snake adapts Bhaktapur's version to the two banners on the *yasi(n)*.

32. Anderson's version of the story (1971, 41f.) has an important variant. Here the sole and "excessively passionate" daughter of the Bhaktapur king takes a different *lover* each night, the duty of providing a lover rotating among city households. Each morning the lover is found dead, until the arrival of the successful prince puts an end to the danger. It is of interest to compare different published versions of this story. In the episode of the snake, D. R. Regmi (1965–1966, part II, p. 650) and Hale and Hale (1970, 248ff. [a direct transcription of a Newari verbal account]) describe one snake coming out of the princess's nose. Anderson (1971) tells of two "dark threads" coming one each from the princess's two nostrils, which "rapidly expanded into monstrous serpents writhing about in search of their usual victim." The version of the story given by Punya Ratna Bajracharya, a Newar, in the Nepalese newspaper "Rising Nepal" (April 18, 1974) is "as he [the soon to be victorious prince] kept awake he saw a very tiny snake coming out from the womb [i.e., vagina] of his queen and it assumed a terrible form and tried to attack him, but he took out his

sword and slew it." It was only after the slaying of this serpent, or serpents, that marriage to the princess was possible.

33. This refers to events that will take place subsequently.

34. D. R. Regmi recounts a similar story (1965–1966, part II, p. 651).

35. There were two Licchavi kings of that name noted in inscriptions who reigned in the sixth and seventh centuries A.D. (Slusser 1982, vol. 1, p. 397).

36. Gutschow and others have made the plausible suggestion that as the *yasi(n)* is often interpreted as a *liṅga*, the hole must represent a *yoni*, or vagina, and that "the erection of the pole can be understood as a reenactment of primal procreation" (Gutschow 1984, 16). Although sexual union is clearly understood in cultural doctrine to be symbolized by other subsequent aspects of the Biskā: cycle, this meaning does not seem to be overtly associated by religious experts, at least, with the placing of the *yasi(n)* into its base.

37. If it were to fall, as it sometimes does, it would be not only dangerous to the people working to lift it but also taken as a sign of danger for the city.

38. Gutschow has studied this phase of Biskā:. He notes that individual deities may be added (and presumably discontinued) from time to time, and notes examples of two deities who were added, at least one of which was brought from a village outside Bhaktapur. In 1983 he counted twenty-nine imags that were brought out at this time (1984, 20).

39. In the course of their *jātrās* the images of Kumārī and Tripurasundarī are carried to their *pīṭha*s outside of the city as are the other Maṇḍalic Goddesses whose *jātrās* are emphasized (see below).

40. Gutschow (1984) observes that the movement of these Tantric deities out of their god-houses and to the outside area where they are exhibited resembles, in part, the movement of the Maṇḍalic Goddesses from their god-houses to their *pīṭhas* outside of the city in the major *jātrā*s of this period.

41. This conjunction of the internal representation of a dangerous deity and its external *pīṭha* or natural stone representation is also enacted, as we have noted (chap. 9), in lineage deity ceremonies.

42. The Jugī also have another connection with this day. Some five-and-a-half months previously, on the lunar day of Bālā Ca:re [7], one of their members had begun dances in the city representing Śiva as Mahādeva. On this day, the fifth day of Biskā:, with the falling of the Yasi(n) God, the period proper to this representation comes to an end.

43. Indraṇī and some of the other deities who have *jātrā*s during the Biskā: period also have *jātrās* during the lunar cycle. These are Indrāṇī Jātrā [61], Vārāhī Jātrā [53], and Chuma(n) Gandya: Jātrā [63].

44. It is not clear why it is Indrāṇī who receives this special royal greeting rather than the other *jātrā* gods of Biskā:. This emphasis is a reminder of the various connections between Biskā: and Kathmandu's Indra Jātrā.

45. This alignment of the chariot, like the direction in which the Yasi(n) God will soon be swayed, would seem plausibly to be related to the sun's east-west path. However, such a connection is not known now to our informants.

46. On the evening of this day the Po(n)s have feasts in their houses and invite other Po(n)s from other communities.

47. Whatever the significance of the lack of contamination of the two men

who touch the untouchables while giving the *prasāda* on this day may be, the others on the chariot are protected from contamination because the chariot is a temple. This protects the riders of the chariot from pollution in the next phase when the Po(n)s pull at the ropes at the back of the chariot.

48. It is noteworthy that the upper-status *thar* men, including Brahmans, who participate in the pulling of the chariot on the first and last days of the cycle, do not do it on this day when the Po(n)s are also involved.

49. This Bhairava stone also marks the place where during the Mohanī festival Taleju gives full power to the Nine Durgās troupe and takes leave of them as they begin their annual mission.

50. Manandhar notes that "this verb requires plural actors and originally meant 'to meet at one place.' This meaning is still current in the causative form of the verb [as found in the phrase] dya: lwākala. 'The deities were made to meet at one place'. . . [this] does *not* mean that the deities were made to fight" (1976, 529). However, whatever its original implication may have been, in the present generalization of the meaning of the term from its use in other contexts, it now seems to convey the meaning of fighting, at least in Bhaktapur.

51. These hesitations between interpretations of sexual intercourse and aggression represent familiar psychodynamic forms as modified by Bhaktapur's special ways of dealing with these problematic passions. For our present purposes it is sufficient to note that these are critical ambiguities that hold the attention, intellect, and passions of the spectators and participants, and help make this element of the festival sequence—like so many others—compelling, significant, and "alive."

52. There are other examples when for some limited purpose one of a pair of goddesses is interpreted as male so that they can be conceived of as a husband and wife, or man and woman. One is Brāhmaṇī and Maheśvarī on the following day, another is Simā and Dumā during the Nine Durgās performances (chap. 16). In that latter case it is generally agreed that Simā is male and Dumā female, probably as an accident of color contrasts in their images.

53. The N̄ātāpwa(n)la temple contains, as we noted in chapter 8, an esoteric form of the Goddess that was placed there to act as a restraining influence on the Bhairava of the main Bhairava temple, also located in the square, who is also the Bhairava of Biskā:.

54. The dangerous deities are not considered to be married in the domestic sense that the benign deities are (see chap. 8).

55. Gutschow (1984, 24) remarks that people must leave the ordinary route to include visits to Bhairava in his *jātrā* god-house in Lākulāche(n) and at two other places.

56. These offerings are called "giving *Swaga(n)* to the gods."

57. *Chu(n)* means both rat and/or mouse. As we have noted, this same Gaṇeśa has another *jātrā* [63] during the course of the lunar year. The rat or mouse is the traditional vehicle of Gaṇeśa. In Bhaktapur's representations the vehicle is usually a *tichu(n)*, a shrew.

58. Theoretically parallel events may be significantly contrastive. This is the case in the presence or absence among various *thars* during a festival of the Āga(n) God worship that characterizes upper-level *thars*. With that exception,

however, contrastive parallel events among otherwise similar units are not salient during Bhaktapur's annual festivals.

59. The princess is unaware of her destructive nature, and can be treated as an innocent wife after her indwelling serpents have been destroyed. This is reminiscent of Pārvatī's relation to her Durgā emanation as suggested in the *Devī Māhātmya* stories (chap. 8).

CHAPTER 15: THE DEVI CYCLE

1. We use the theatrical term "troupe" to refer to the group of men who traditionally embody and act the Nine Durgās as well as the group (or troop) of divinities who become embodied.

2. This probably refers to one of two kings called elsewhere Guṇakāmadeva, who reigned in the tenth and twelfth centuries (Slusser 1982, vol. 1, p. 45). The "Wright chronicle" puts the events of the legend in the realm of one "Suvarna Malla" (placed in that chronicle in the early sixteenth century), who "introduced the dance of the Nava Durgā, having heard that they had been seen dancing at night" ([1877] 1972, p. 189).

3. In some version they just happen to be there; in others they were forced to stay in the forest through the power of still another Tantric expert.

4. We have seen variations on this theme in the legend of Śeṣar Ācāju's wife in Biskā:, whose meddling led, according to one of its legends, to Biskā: as a civic festival (chap. 14). The function of the Brahman's wife in the Nine Durgās legends has interesting psychological and mythic resonances elsewhere. Like Eve and Bluebeard's wife she destroys the paradise of man's childlike, self-absorbed, and selfish pleasures, but in so doing reroutes forces to the service of civilization. In the Yasi(n) God legend of the princess inhabited by snakes and in Purāṇic stories of a benign Pārvatī inhabited by the Dangerous Goddess, we are reminded that the woman not only domesticates but also can represent the very dangers against which domestication protects. Bhaktapur tries, not always successfully, to isolate and separate these meanings.

5. This Bhairavī is thought by some religious experts to be associated with an esoteric goddess represented in the Gaṇa Kumārī, in the Hipha: gods of Mohanī, and in the Taleju temple (see text below).

6. The numbers in brackets refer to the sequence of calendrical events of the lunar year as presented in chapter 13.

7. This last dance-drama or *pyākha(n)* is of the kind called a *ñā lākegu*, or "fishing" *pyākha(n)*. It takes place in the Rājopādhyāya Brahman's neighborhood where they had danced before beginning their circuit of the city and its environing communities some nine months before and closes the spatial circle of the *ñā lākegu* performances by bringing them back.

8. Of course, the relation of these ritual markers of the agriculture and weather cycle to the actual events of that cycle is variable. In the case of Sithi Nakhā, the day occurs early enough in the year to probably well precede the rains. Such markers have to be placed so that they are safely prior to the changes they anticipate and prepare for.

9. For references to Kumāra on this day and at other times during the year elsewhere in Nepal, see Anderson (1971, chap. 5).

10. During the Pṛthivī *pūjā* six sweetcakes are offered to the Goddess in the *maṇḍala*, and six different kinds of pulses are also offered. The name of Kumāra is recited during the *pūjā*, but this is locally thought of as a secondary reference.

11. The rice is prepared at the Taleju temple by members of the high Jyāpu *thar*, the Suwāl. This is one of the many special duties at the Taleju temple assigned to specific *thar*s, which are often residues of ancient *thar* functions during the Malla period.

12. According to Niels Gutschow (personal communication), one of his associates reported seeing the Nine Durgās when they reached their god-house on this day first banging against its closed door, and then falling to the ground and lying there as if dead.

13. Teilhet's paper has important details on the making of the masks, their iconography, on other aspects of the Gāthā's costumes, and on the Gāthā performers themselves. It reflects, however, the limited perspective of Teilhet's informants in their speculations on other aspects of the Nine Durgās' activities other than the ones with which they were most closely concerned.

14. The practice of putting cremation remains "in a small earthen pot and throw[ing] them into the water" in Purāṇic times is noted in Pandey (1969, 261). Following cremations in Bhaktapur now, some of the ashes and bone fragments from the head of the cremated corpse are placed in the soil of the river bed just after the cremation (app. 6).

15. The Nine Durgās may be thought to increase not only the amount of water but also its fertile potency. Niels Gutschow remarks that Bhaktapur's farmers have a strong belief that the Nine Durgās are present in the water in the rice fields during the summer. They say that they should not urinate in the flooded fields in order not to offend or hurt those deities (personal communication).

16. It is important to note for the distinction between the Nine Maṇḍalic Goddesses and the Nine Durgās (chap. 8) that the Maṇḍalic Goddesses remain actively in their fixed locations throughout the entire year. However, neither they nor the ordinary moral gods of the city are fully sufficient to protect the city when the Nine Durgās are dormant.

17. Hamilton writes that the sacrifice was supposed to have taken place on the eighth day of Āśvina, which would have been during the Mohanī sequence. It is Bhairava not Bhairavī who now performs animal sacrifices—with the exception of the killing of a cock during the Pyākha(n) (see text below). In Hamilton's list of the Nine Durgās ([1819] 1971, 35) Bhairavī seems to represent the Mahākālī of the present troupe, and Mahākāla seems to represent the present Bhairava. If it were Bhairavī who did, in fact, perform the human sacrifices, this would be congruent with her later meanings in the Nine Durgās dance-dramas.

18. When farmers have finished the transplanting they have a purification ceremony on this day called *syinā jyā byenkegu*, with feasts later in the day. If the transplanting cannot be completed until after Gāthā Muga: Ca:re, the ceremony will be held when the actual transplanting is completed.

19. It is also said that on this day the Nine Durgās' Gaṇeśa appears and will give the Gāthās ritual effectiveness, *siddhi*, in their preparation for the new cycle.

20. Iron is widely believed to have the power to repel spirits, and is used for this purpose in certain household rituals.

21. His name has no apparent connection with the Gāthā *thar* name.

22. The versions of the legend given by Anderson (1971, 73) and D. R. Regmi (1965–1966, part II, p. 661) tell of an heroic frog who alerted the valley people to an attack of the demon and helped trap and thus destroy him. This part of the legend seems not to be salient in Bhaktapur.

23. That is to say, a consistent and profound belief in *karma*, the automatic and certain rewards and punishmens for moral activities, can produce contradictions with other belief systems, such as the power of devotion or of ritual practices directed to the gods to alter one's fate. This sort of belief in *karma* would be subversive of the priest-mediated ritual order of traditional Newar cities.

24. This detail is related to one of the customs of the day, as we will see below.

25. This is a transformation of the Ghaṇṭākarṇa legend. That name means "bells [at the] ears," and in a Purāṇic legend refers to an Asura who being an enemy of Viṣṇu wore bells at his ears so as not to hear the mention of his name (Mani 1975, 289). This creature later became a devotee of Viṣṇu and an ally of the Gods.

26. One striking difference from some of the descriptions of events in other Newar communities is that Po(n) untouchables are said elsewhere to play important roles in representing Gāthā Muga:. "The main character in the festival is a Newar man of the untouchable Pode [Po(n)] caste who has the dubious honor of impersonating Ghanta Karna, his near-naked body painted with lewd symbols and pictures depicting all types of sexual depravity (Anderson 1971, 74; see also D. R. Regmi 1965–1966, part II, p. 661; G. S. Nepali 1965, 378). This use of a Pore or Po(n) is not made now in Bhaktapur, and we have no information on it having been made there in the past.

27. This reflects a similar practice described in at least one Purāṇic text for the final day of Dasai(n) (Mohanī). "The sending away of Devī should be made . . . by throwing dust and mud, . . . with indulgence in words and songs referring to male and female organs and with words expressive of the sexual act. The Devī becomes angry with him who does not abuse another and whom others do not abuse and pronounces on him a terrible curse" (the Kālikāpurāṇa, quoted in Kane [1968–1977, vol. V, p. 177]). Kane goes on to comment that the purpose of this was to emphasize that "before Devī the highest and the lowest were of equal status . . . [and] to show that all men were equal at least one day in the year."

28. In traditional Newar houses the carved wooden open worked windows are so constructed that it is possible to look out without being visible from the outside.

29. Although there would seem to be a strong metaphorical connection of

Gāthā Muga: and fertility, there is no local doctrine about this nor of any relation to the Nine Durgās or Devī who *are* related to fertility in the Devī cycle. Devī is, in doctrine, fully and self-sufficiently generative in herself.

30. The Newars of Bhaktapur, as Nepalis do in general, fly kites at this time. These are usually flown from the *ka:sis*, the open porches of the upper stories of houses. One of the several accounts given of this practice is that it sends messages to the gods to remind them not to send any more rain (see fig. 30).

31. Mohanī (in Kathmandu Newari, also Moni or Monhi), according to Gautam Vajracharya (personal communication), is derived from the Sanskrit, *mahānavamī*, the "ninth great day." The ninth day is one of the climactic days of the cycle. There are similar words that have close thematic relations to the term. *Monhi* (*monī* in Kathmandu dialect) is a mark made using the soot from a special oil lamp that allows for possession by a deity and which is an important part of the worship of the Mohanī period for all worshipers. *Mohani* (Sanskrit, *mohini*), meaning "enchantment," is an important theme and term in the scriptural account, the *Devī Māhātmya*, which is a major source for the imagery of the period. The two latter words are probably connected, the *Monhi* mark inducing *Mohanī* or the state of being "enchanted."

32. Our discussion of Mohanī refers throughout to aspects and interpretations of Devī and the dangerous goddesses that are treated at length in chapter 8.

33. As we have noted in chapter 8, the position of the goddesses around Bhaktapur and the sequence of their special days during Mohanī correspond closely to the sequence in which they are introduced in the *Devī Māhātmya*, the Purāṇic text that contains much of the mythological account on which Mohanī is based. The *pīṭhas* are visited during Mohanī on each successive day in their exact circumferential sequence around the periphery of Bhaktapur. Starting with (1) Brāhmaṇī to the east on the first day, the successive days' focal *pīṭhas* are (2) Maheśvarī to the southeast, (3) Kumārī to the south, (4) Vaisṇavī to the southwest, (5) Vārāhī to the west, (6) Indrāṇī to the northwest, (7) Mahākālī to the north, and (8) Mahālakṣmī to the northeast. On the climactic ninth day the focal *pīṭha* is Tripurasundarī at the maṇḍalic center. On the tenth day the focus is once again on the beginning position, Brāhmaṇī.

34. Manandhar proposes that "*Na:lā*" is derived from the Sanskrit *Nava Rātra*, the "nine nights," the first nine nights of Dasai(n) (1976, 242). Others think that it has the meaning of "new and delicate." "Swā(n)" means flower. The Na:lā swā(n) is the name given in this context to the barley plant that is grown in soil placed in the room. This room is also sometimes called the "*Kha(n)*" or "sword" room. Swords will be an important symbolic element in the room later in the sequence.

35. G. S. Nepali (1965, 405 ff.) gives details on this and other Mohanī procedures, many of which differ sharply from the common Bhaktapur ones.

36. Girls born into the family take part, as do wives married into it after their introductory initiation into the household rituals and deities. In those upper-status houses with Tantric practices some portions of the *Na:lā swā(n)* ceremonies on the eighth, ninth, and tenth days of Mohanī require initiation,

and only those women with special Tantric "half-initiation" take part. Nepali says (1965, 409) that married-out women can no longer enter the *Na:lā swā(n)* rooms of their parental homes. Although this may be true for some *thar*s in Bhaktapur, it is not, reportedly, generally true for most of them.

37. The lamps are placed on his head, his right and left shoulders, his right and left knees, and the palms of his hands, which are held in a supine position.

38. The lamps may be filled with the particularly expensive fuel, clarified butter, but even the more ordinary mustard or sesame oils are expensive for families in these quantities.

39. In the past there was a more dramatic version of these procedures during the first nine days. The devotee would wrap cloths around each of his fingers and, dipping the cloths in oil, set them afire. This practice has disappeared in recent years. The motives given in explanation of all these *vrata*s are various, but they typically represent gratitude for help in overcoming some difficulty, or in hopes that it will be overcome in the future. In certain extended families the *vrata* had been pledged at some time in the (sometimes distant) past, and various families within the *phukī* take turns in designating one of their members to perform it. These hereditary *vrata*s are sometimes conceived as protection against the flooding of the *phukī's* fields, or against illness in the family. It is mostly members of the farming *thar*s who perform these *vrata*s. This reflects, perhaps, the agricultural emphasis of the Mohanī and the dangers of improper agricultural conditions as well as the special economic vulnerability of the farming *thar*s in Bhaktapur's traditional economy.

40. The major Taleju activities of Mohanī are the daily Na:lā swā(n) worship; various activities concerning the "living goddess" Kumārī; the special activities of the ninth night, the Kālarātrī; the moving ("taking up" and "taking down") of the goddess Taleju within the temple; and, on the final day, the procession of the goddess Taleju.

41. The lower *thars* (such as the butchers, Jugīs, and Po[n]s) still associated with Taleju have kept their traditional functions there, as they have in the wider city society, as have the priestly *thar*s. Shifts since Malla times away from their traditional functions are for the most part among the Pa(n)cthariyā and Chathariyā (whose *thar* names usually signify their traditional functions in the aristocratic court-centered segment of Malla society) as well as among a few of the Jyāpu *thars* who previously had some specialized servant or military function (e.g., guards, charioteers, cooks) for the court. The particular *thar*s who had traditional Taleju Malla court functions are listed in chapter 5.

42. This is in contrast to Biskā:, where the king and the Guru-Purohit are represented by two different Brahmans.

43. The true Taleju image may be moved *within* the temple, but cannot be taken out of it. The *jātrā* image, like all such images, is specially designated for processions outside of the temple. These two images are the only images of Taleju in the Taleju temple.

44. Taleju temple also has an elaborate external Golden Gate facing on the Lāekū or "Durbar" Square. Access to Taleju's inner courtyard is forbidden to non-Hindus. The inner Golden Gate and the adjoining areas in the Mūcuka are

shown in a color photograph in M. Singh (1968, 192–193). This photograph is of particular importance in that photographing of the interior areas of the Taleju temple is, in principle, forbidden.

45. This conjunction of two forms of the Goddess is reflected on the following day, the eighth day, in the other *Na:lā swā(n)* rooms throughout the city, where an additional image of Bhagavatī—in those cases an anthropomorphic one—is brought into the *Na:lā swā(n)* rooms and placed in conjunction with the *kalaśa*.

46. As G. S. Nepali dryly remarks, "This is a state event and all Government officials, even if they are Newars, have to be present in the procession" (1965, 407).

47. Nepali erroneously places these events on the eighth day of Mohanī.

48. There are some references in the literature to Mohanī's connections (particularly the victory celebration of the tenth day) with the Rāmāyaṇa's account of Rāmā's victory over the demon king Rāvaṇa (e.g., D. R. Regmi, 1965–1966, part II, p. 673; Anderson 1971, p. 152). That story is still told in Bhaktapur, and sometimes informally associated with Mohanī, but is more closely associated in Bhaktapur with the minor spring festival, Cait dasai(n) [31]. None of the mass of symbolic events of Bhaktapur's Mohanī period seem to refer to the Rāmā story.

49. Like many calendrically connected feasts, this one has a humorous name. It is called the "Ku chi," the "one-*ku*" feast. A *ku* is a measure equivalent to about a quart, and the name indicates that people will eat at least this much beaten rice, along with all the other foods they will eat at the feast, and that, thus, they will consume enormous quantities of food.

50. The exact number does not seem to have any traditional significance, in contrast with the number of sacrificial water buffaloes.

51. "*Dugu*" means goat. "*Nikhu*" is said to mean solidly colored in the sense of an unspotted or unblemished color. The morpheme *nī* in other compound words has the sense of "uncontaminated," which is part of the sense of *nikhu* here.

52. "*Thu*" comes from "*thumẽ*," male water buffalo.

53. This is done by a member of one of the farming *thars*, who lives in the house where the buffalo has been kept, and whose family has this traditional responsibility.

54. The king, seated, asks, "What is this buffalo's name?" The Nāe answers, "Nikhuthu." King: "Is this Nikhuthu proper (i.e., does it have the required characteristics as a sacrificial offering)?" Nāe: "Yes." King: "Do you swear to it?" Nāe: "Let there be victory to the king and to Taleju and destruction to myself (if I am not telling the truth)." [He repeats this oath three times.] King: [Again.] "Do you swear to it?" Nāe: "Let there be victory to the king and to Taleju and destruction to myself." [He again repeats this oath three times.]

55. It is said that in the past each *twa:* paid for the buffalo that represented it. Now they are paid for by the central government's, Guthi Saṃsthān.

56. Animal sacrifice during Mohanī is done in the same way as it is at other times during the year (see chap. 9).

57. *Hi* means blood; *pha* comes from *phayegu*, meaning to receive in out-

stretched supine hands held joined together as a cup, or in a container so held in the hands.

58. Buffaloes, in general, are killed only by Nāe butchers in Bhaktapur, and are not used for ordinary householders' sacrifices. The exception is the killing of buffaloes by the Nine Durgās during Mohanī and later in their cycle.

59. At this point the buffaloes, like the goats, are soul-bearing creatures, who are being offered salvation through sacrifice to the Goddess. Their subsequent meaning as Asuras does not affect this interpretation.

60. It does not make any difference whether this sacrificial blood is offered first to the right or to the left.

61. The meat from the bodies of the buffaloes and goats will be cut up and distributed to members of the Taleju staff and to members of the government's Guthi Saṃsthān.

62. It is said that anyone who, following this bath, sees blood in the water at the ancient water fountain and bathing tank associated with Indrāṇī will die within six months. The Indrāṇī bathing tank was historically within the old court complex and drew from the same water supply as the tank where the Hipha: gods bathe, and this may, in part, account for the belief.

63. Kumārī has been seen by people in the northern part of the city throughout Mohanī in a daily procession from her god-house to the nearby *vihāra*, from which on this day she will be brought to the Taleju temple.

64. The *tīrtha* of Tripurasundarī is the only one of the Maṇḍalic Goddesses' *tīrtha*s that (necessarily, because of her central location) is not close to the corresponding *pīṭha*.

65. The demand for sacrificial goats is so great at this period that many people who would be able to afford one are unable to procure one and must offer a lesser sacrifice.

66. The sacrifice is done in "Nepalese" style, that is, by decapitation of the animal in one blow from the back of the animal's neck without a prior cutting of the throat. The Newar Nāe does not sacrifice the buffaloes. The ceremony, furthermore, although taking place on Lāekū Square, is said to have no reference or relevance to Taleju.

67. There will be no sacrifices anywhere in Bhaktapur on the tenth day.

68. It is said, amalgamating these tools with a characteristic of the dangerous deities, that if a sacrifice is not given them they may cause an accident, thus taking the sacrifice by themselves.

69. The condensation is, perhaps, most evident in the "Kumārī" of the Nine Durgās group.

70. The Newari term for such a deity, is Mwāmhā Dya:, literally "living deity."

71. The most extensive general survey and detailed accounts of the Newar Kumārīs is Michael Allen's *The Cult of Kumārī* (1975). See also Allen's article on virgin worship in the Kathmandu Valley (1976).

72. Kumārī in Sanskrit means simply "girl, virgin, daughter."

73. This is a form in which Kumārī the maiden and Kumārī as Kaumārī, the Maṇḍalic Mother Goddess, are represented together.

74. It is important to note here that for the upper-status Hindu Newars in

Bhaktapur, even the high Buddhist *thars* are not water-acceptable (chap. 5). This is significant here in connection with the legend of the Ekānta Kumārī (see text below) and the Tantric aspects of Kumārī.

75. He is identified by the Taleju priests as Bhairava, but the Bāre themselves, it is said, think of him as Kumār.

76. They will not participate in the later main Kumārī worship in the temple. This is restricted to the "Malla king" himself, that is, the Brahman who represents him.

77. In addition to the Gaṇa Kumārī, there is still another "Ekānta Kumārī," who is selected from the same Bāre *phukī* as the main Ekānta Kumārī. She is connected with a now minor temple of Taleju in the Wā(n)lāekū area in the northeast of Bhaktapur near Dattātreya Square. It is thought by some that this temple may have been the royal Taleju temple at an earlier time when the royal palace may have been located in that area and that this Kumārī may represent some residue of that situation. At any rate, the temple is now supervised not by a Brahman but by an Ācāju, and its Ekānta Kumārī is of significance only to the local neighborhood.

78. These stories resemble those of Śeṣar Ācāju (in connection with Biskā:) and Somarā Rājopādhyāya (in the Nine Durgās legend), which we have discussed above—in the loss of direct contact with a deity and/or the loss of supernatural power through a minor and almost inevitable human error. In those stories the blame was put on a weak woman, as it is in the second of these stories. In the first story it is the king's own fault. The Goddess's realm, like the realm of all the dangerous deities and the realm of Tantra, is beyond the civic moral order—and curious prying into this realm, by either the king or some unauthorized woman, is a particularly dangerous violation. On the basis of accounts gathered apparently for the most part from Buddhist Bāre informants, Michael Allen writes that "there is always the implication, which is sometimes made explicit, that the king developed a strong desire to sexually possess the goddess" (1976, 302).

79. For the quite different Buddhist accounts of the origins of the practice of using a Bāre girl as Kumārī see Allen (1975, 1976).

80. According to Niels Gutschow (personal communication), the present (1989) Kumārī lives at her parental home. This may have been true of some previous Kumārīs.

81. Allen (1975, 63) presents a list given him by a Vajrācārya informant of thirty-two ideal characteristics for a Kumārī, including, for example, "blue-black eyes," "skin pores small and not too open," "hair whorls stiff, turning to the right," and "long and well-formed toes."

82. The water buffalo heads at this time are within the inner gate of the Taleju temple's main courtyard, along with the Taleju *jātrā* image.

83. It is commonly said by people in Bhaktapur and is repeated in many descriptions of the Ekānta Kumārī that she is placed among the decapitated heads and left alone there to see if she is without fear as a test of her validity. For Bhaktapur, at least, this is false.

84. Most of them will remain in Bhaktapur to watch the remainder of the day's events.

85. These procedures stand out in Bhaktapur as uniquely extreme and "Dionysian" procedures. However, they are limited in both extent and discomfort and in the very minor bodily injuries, if any, that result, in marked contrast to the much more severe and self-injuring procedures often found in such *vratas* elsewhere in South Asia.

86. The buffalo heads, which are never used as *siu*, are given to non-Brahman members of the staff who will use them for food in feasts.

87. Manandhar notes of the *bhuiphasi* (which he gives in Kathmandu dialect as *bhuyu: phasi*) that it is "a variety of pumpkin which can be offered in lieu of an animal as a sacrifice to a deity (used especially by vegetarians who do not sacrifice animals or eggs)" (1976, 407). This usage is not salient in Hindu Bhaktapur.

88. This same deity is referred to throughout Mohanī. She is included in the Gaṇa Kumārī, the Hipha: gods are her manifestations, and she represents Bhagavatī here. She is sometimes taken to be the mysterious Ninth Durgā, as the unrepresented Śakti of the Nine Durgās' Bhairava.

89. According to Manandhar, "*pāyā(n)*" derives from the old Newari word for sword, "*pā*" (1976, 295). There are descriptions of Newar "sword processions" elsewhere on this day, which differ from Bhaktapur's Taleju-centered procession (e.g., D. R. Regmi 1965–1966, part II, p. 678; G. S. Nepali 1965, p. 411; Anderson 1971, 153).

90. In her description of the activities of this, the tenth day of the Dasai(n) harvest festival in Kāṭhiāwār in Gujarat in western India during the early part of the century, Stevenson reports that toward the end of a ritual centering on the Rajput princes of Kāṭhiāwār, the "chief summons four of the leading grain merchants of the State and asks them what the price of grain is likely to be during the next twelve months. They give a rough estimate, but, in order not to be held to it too closely, say: 'It is in God's hands'" (1920, p. 233). The two episodes, with their references to the price of grain, which is dependent on the extent of the harvest, must obviously have some common historical ancestor.

91. When it goes to the lower part of the city, the procession goes in a counterclockwise loop rather than in the usual auspicious clockwise one. This is apparently determined by spatial constraints, and is the unique occasion when this occurs in a city calendrical procession.

92. The temple has no identifying iconic features now. Niels Gutschow has been told (personal communication) that it is—or was—a temple of Jagannātha.

93. In some popular accounts it is incorrectly said that a *mantra* is given in a whisper by the Taleju priest to the Durgās at this time.

94. The fertility aspect of the warrior goddess of the *Devī Māhātmya* is overt in a verse where foretelling an extended period of drought in a future *yuga* she promises "at that time, O Gods, I shall support the whole world with life sustaining vegetables, born out of my own body, until the rains set in again" (*Devī Māhātmya* XI, 45; Agrawala 1963, 141).

95. The Gāthā do not eat pork except in their ritual capacity as incarnated deities.

96. The reason that some of these locations are outside of the present Bhak-

tapur district is unclear to our informants. These must reflect both boundary changes and special invitations in the years after the inauguration of the dances in, presumably, the sixteenth century.

97. According to Gutschow and Bāsukala (1987), this skullcap represents Guhyeśvarī.

98. Some of the old public squares that were part of the organization of every major *twa:* and every sub-*twa:* neighborhood have been disturbed by patterns of building so that they have now become inner courtyards and/or reduced in size. New areas have to be found now in such places for activities attracting large crowds of local people.

99. Our description of the *pyākha(n)*s is based on observations of segments of it, on descriptions given by local people, and on observations by Steven Parish, who was doing research in Bhaktapur at the time this chapter was being revised.

100. The basis for the differentiation is the only feature in which the two masks differ, their color. Simā's mask is white and Dumā's reddish orange, which reflects a white/red contrast that sometimes designates male/female in Tantric symbolism.

101. This is the same procedure by which Tantric physicians try to chase away the spirits that cling to people and cause diseases. This procedure is also used in other contexts to drive away evil influences. New brides, for example, entering a household for the first time are similarly freed of evil influences at the *pikhā lakhu*, the symbolic boundary of the house.

102. This last sacrificial sequence, which is described on the basis of informants' reports, does not occur in all performances of the *pyākha(n)*. Niels Gutschow reports that he has never seen it done (personal communication).

103. This idea and its development in the following paragraph is indebted to the work of Roy Rappaport (1979).

104. The form that the sacrifice takes within the *pyākha(n)*, the biting off of a cock's head, adds the imagery of the threat of castration to the general sacrificial threat of bodily destruction.

105. This also replicates on a smaller scale the narrative movement in Mohanī, where cosmic forces are represented, then gathered together in a bounded, concentrated and maximized form, and then moved out into the life, space, and time of the larger city.

CHAPTER 16: THE PATTERNS AND MEANINGS OF THE FESTIVAL YEAR

1. Recall (see chap. 12) that we have included in our discussions and enumeration only those particular weekly, fortnightly, or monthly events that have some important differentiated annual significance. The remainder are generally of relatively minor civic importance, of concern only to particular individuals or households. We have also not included here ten *melā*s not associated with the city's annual calendar, and four taking place in multiple numbers of years. If

these events were listed, they would augment the number of days in any given year that are the occasion for some sort of calendrically determined event.

2. The other is a memorial service for patrilineal ancestors held at the riverside during Dhala(n) Salā(n) [66].

3. This comparative optionality also means that public festivals are particularly vulnerable to social change, to alternative forms of entertainment and new pressures on the use of time and capital.

4. These symbols are good examples of what Victor Turner called "bipolar" symbols. "At one pole [there is]. . . a set of referents of a grossly physiological character, relating to general human experience of an emotional kind . . . at the other . . . a set of references to moral norms and principles governing the social structure" (1967, 54). Thus in the Biskā: story what is focally celebrated is the prince's overcoming of the potentially fatal snakes that issue from the princess's nose in order to establish a royal—or any other kind of—marriage.

5. We have arbitrarily included optional annual visits [50] to the dangerous goddess Śītalā by household members for protection against smallpox in our enumeration of "household" rather than "public" events. *Śītalā Pūjā* does not entail worship within the house, and is not really an exception to this observation. The annual worship of Bhagavatī during Mohanī is a *secondary* participation in and reflection of the public worship of the period. It is a sort of invasion of the Goddess into the family circle, which is usually bounded against her.

6. This nonrepresentation is similar to the way potential conflicts of the social groups within a *twa:* are deflected to the less consequential ritualized struggles of the city halves (chap. 7).

7. The summary of the festival year, including its events, themes, and temporal relations given in appendix 5, should make the following discussion somewhat easier to follow.

8. Bhisi(n), although a dangerous deity, is uniquely isolated from the other dangerous deities in both concept and use.

9. The term "lateral" environment is meant to suggest a contrast with the bordering enviroment of the household in a different direction or plane, that is, the realms just beyond birth and death, beyond thresholds that individuals cross as they enter and leave the household in the flow of a lifetime. For individuals and households the city is "lateral" to this direction.

10. The dormant period of the Nine Durgās is not the usual four-month absence characteristic of the periods of "sleep" of many other Hindu deities in South Asian tradition.

11. The lunar harvest festival Mohanī, coming about six months after Biskā:, is thus an autumnal festival and the two focal sequences have a seasonal symmetry, but there is no reference in Mohanī to the autumnal equinox equivalent to Biskā:'s reference to the vernal equinox.

12. We have commented on the "astral" qualities of Biskā:'s symbolism in contrast to Mohanī in chapter 14.

13. Swanti, with the lunar New Year Day at the beginning of a bright fortnight as the fourth of its five days, thus includes a movement from a dark fortnight to a light one.

14. Recall that this "ordinary death" contrasts with the violent destruction of the body at the hands and teeth of the dangerous deities, a destruction due to accidental encounter or some ritual error, a destruction which, once initiated, can only be avoided through instruments of power, not through exemplary social behavior.

15. The exception is the Panauti Jātrā, which is a mass visit to a focal festival of a town that previously was within the Bhaktapur kingdom. The main deities of that festival are dangerous ones. The *jātrā* is a calendrical formalization of the visits to a focal festival of some nearby community that are common throughout the valley and that Bhaktapur does less formally to focal festivals of other nearby places on other occasions.

16. According to the Śatapatha Brāmaṇa, both the gods and Asuras sprang "from the Creator Prajāpati, [and] inherited speech—both true and false, but . . . finally the gods rejected untruth, whilst the Asuras spurned truth which led to their downfall. Another tradition states that though the gods and Asuras were equally powerful, their power was divided, the gods exercising it by day and the Asuras by night. . . . Later the term asura denoted the hostile native rulers and tribes opposed to Āryan religious and political expansion" (Stutley and Stutley 1977, 23).

17. The optional *vrata*s of Mohanī, of the Swāsthanī period, of Cāturmāsa and of some other customary occasions during the year are individual performances, but are most often regarded, as we have seen in our discussion of the *vrata*s of Swāsthanī and Mohanī, as being immediately or ultimately for the good of the family. The individual *vrata*s thus serve to enable an individual to overcome some obstacle in his or her full contribution to the family or to some larger unit. Similarly, the emphasis in acquiring personal skills during the Sarasvatī festivals ([12] and [13]) is on the learner's dependence on the deity for acquiring a socially defined and useful skill, rather than as a quest for self-sufficiency. Learning in general in Bhaktapur is structured to emphasize the profound dependency of individuals on family, deities, and society as the originators and teachers of skills and knowledge.

18. *Thar* membership is only differentially signaled in the course of the annual cycle for those particular *thars*, of particular importance in the symbolic order of the city, that have special ritual symbolic functions in the city (see chap. 5).

19. We deal with the most important of these, the *saṃskāra*s or rites of passage that center on individual, household, and extended family, at some length in appendix 6. A consideration of the *saṃskāras* provides a useful perspective on the peculiar features of the urban mesocosmic enactments.

CHAPTER 17: WHAT IS BHAKTAPUR THAT A NEWAR MAY KNOW IT?

1. The title of this chapter derives from the title of a lecture by Warren McCulloch, "What is a Number, that a Man May Know It, and a Man, that He May Know a Number?" (1965). The second phase of the dialogue—in the form

of "what is a Newar that he or she may know Bhaktapur?"—will occupy us more centrally elsewhere.

2. It should be noted that the idea of a mediating mesocosm with its own particular characteristics implies that Bhaktapur's relation to the great cosmos is not that of, say, a medieval monastery, which was sometimes conceived of as simply a faithful map of the heavenly city.

3. Polytheism avoids the strains placed on a monotheistic representation such as Jehovah, who in his symbolically overloaded ineffability must represent, for example, both ideal human moral qualities, including compassion for individuals, and at the same time a contradictory set of para-human disruptive, destructive, protective, and controlling forces.

4. We will consider some formal relations between myth and legend in the next section.

5. The religiosity of Bhaktapur's marked symbolism is perhaps only a "problem" when looking back on it from later secular perspectives, perspectives where the sacred, to recall St. Paul (whose pronouncement we used in a discussion of the "problem of idols" in chap. 8) has been exiled from the creation to the distant and thus unencumbering realm of the Creator.

6. For example, from James Joyce's story, *The Dead*, "There was grace and mystery in her attitude as if she were a symbol of something. He asked himself what is a woman standing on the stairs in the shadow, listening to distant music, a symbol of."

7. It should be noted that sexuality in civic symbolism is disconnected from ideas of family, procreation, love, or the normally erotic—its symbols are nonhuman and uncanny. This is a sexuality outside of the realm of the social person.

8. For some vivid examples, see Hale and Hale (1970).

9. The transformations in organization and meanings that characteristically occur as levels change highlight the peculiarity of those systemic patterns that are occasionally reiterated at different levels. A characteristic example in Bhaktapur is the Po(n) untouchables who mimic the larger macrosocial system in having their own "Brahmans," as they sometimes put it, and their own "untouchables."

10. Compare Rappaport (1979) on the central importance of action and bodily involvement in ritual in an attempt to overcome the limits of ordinary language—in which lying is possible—for social commitment.

11. The ontological status of deities in these three forms, and the truth claims of the forms themselves, differ. People may doubt a legend that, as we noted in the legend of the Yasi(n) God in chapter 14, often has different and contradictory forms, in a different way than they might doubt the presence of an embodied deity.

12. Classification by levels generates mysteries when a particular entity is placed at different levels in different hierarchies. Within the class of dangerous deities females are more inclusive, more powerful, more independent, and more paradigmatic of the class than are males. This relation is reversed in the class of the benign deities. Women are differently ranked in these and still other classification and thus "femaleness" considered as a united, unsplit, category has a

certain peculiarity about it. The goddess Bhaktapur condenses as Kūmarī derives some of her fascination from being a concrete and differentiated deity, a "maiden," in one series, and a relatively full goddess in another. King, Brahman, and untouchable, in their own different ways, have different positions in hierarchies of purity on the one hand and of power on the other, and so become interestingly and generatively paradoxical.

13. We have sketched, in chapter 2, some aspects of what we take to be the "states of mind" necessarily associated with orders such as Bhaktapur's. We suggested that they were both induced by experience within the city and, at the same time, motivated aspects of the city's order as ways of dealing with those particular states of mind. We hope, as we stated there, to deal with these topics at length elsewhere.

APPENDIX 2: BHAKTAPUR'S NEWAR HINDU *THARS* RANKED BY MACROSOCIAL STATUS

1. This *thar* includes four named subsections: Dho(n), Bajimayo (also called Wo[n]) and Bātā.

2. Two of the *thars* included here among the Jyāpus are craft *thars*—Ka:mi, woodworkers, and Loha(n)ka:mi, stoneworkers. Tulādhar, a merchant group, is sometimes considered separately from this group, but at about the same level. We have included it here.

3. This *thar* is also referred to as "Kālu."

4. This *thar* and the following one, Muguṭhi, are grouped together for some purposes as Mahā(n), and have important ceremonial functions. The history and functions of this group are discussed in connection with the Biskā: festival.

5. See note 4, above.

6. This section consists of ten *thars*, all of which are considered at the same level by the higher *jats*, but each of which considers itself higher than the other groups in the section. They do not interdine or intermarry. Pasi is now sometimes said to belong as an eleventh at this level, but it was lower in the past.

7. Although considered at the same level as Jugī by many people at higher levels, Danyā is considered by both the Jugī and the Danyā themselves to be at a level just below the Jugī.

8. After each *thar* name in this list, its macrostatus level is given in square brackets.

APPENDIX 3: KINSHIP TERMINOLOGY

1. Examples of a wide range of North Indian systems are presented in Karve (1968), Berreman (1963), Dumont (1962), Vatuk (1969), and Fruzzetti and Östör (1976).

2. As Gérard Toffin (1975*a*) has remarked, almost all of the terms used to designate Newar kin categories are of North Indian origin, and have cognates in Nepali and/or in other North Indian Sanskritic languages. A few terms (he is

following Benedict [1941] here) seem to be of Tibeto-Burman origin, and some others having no obvious connection with either Tibeto-Burman or North Indian vocabulary may be taken to be of local origin. Benedict lists as terms of Tibeto-Burman origin: *ma* for Mother, *ba* for Father, *ni* for Father's Sister, *ta* for Older Sister, and a somewhat dubious term, *ca*, for Son. Assuming this list to be exhaustive, Toffin is left with some residual terms, *pāju*, *kāe*, and *chui*, among others, which he takes to be of local origin. Toffin observes that the terms of non-North Indian origin are found only among the Newar terms for consanguineal kin.

3. We follow here the presentation of kinship categories used for other North Indian systems by Vatuk (1969) and Fruzzetti and Östör (1976).

4. The following conventional abbreviations will be used here: F, father; M, mother; B, brother; Z, sister; S, son; D, daugther; H, husband; W, wife; y, younger; and e, elder. Thus, FeBW stands for "Father's elder Brother's Wife.

5. Newar usage permits the distinction of focal kin from extended kin in ambiguous contexts by terms such as "true brother", etc. in distinction to a "*phukī* brother," or a "*tha:thiti* brother," etc.

6. We follow here the convention of using capitalized English kinship terms as approximate glosses for the Newari terms whose extent and boundaries usually differ from those English terms.

7. The term *bājyā* is used in some other Newari dialects and in Nepali.

8. In some North Indian systems FF and MF have different terms of reference; in others they have, as in Newari, the same term of reference.

9. *Tapā*: (or *Tāpā*: in some Newari dialects) means "distant."

10. For some speakers *aya: ajā* is not used, and members of this generation are included with group 1d. Nepali (1965, 263) cites an "archaic term" for *aya: ajā*, "*iya ajā*." The source he gives, Wright ([1877] 1972), seems misattributed.

11. The term *bajye* (cognate with the Nepali term *bajei*) is used in some Newari dialects.

12. Referents MM and FM have separate terms in some other North Indian systems.

13. Mother's Husband other than *Abwā*, ego's presumptive biological father, is referred to and addressed as *bwāju*. *Ju* is an honorific particle.

14. Terms deriving from *ta-*, large, and *ci-* and *cā-*, small, are generally used in Newar kinship terminology to designate older and younger. The terms have many variants. Father's elder Brother may, for example, be referred to as *tharhibwā*, *tarhibā*, *taribwā*, *dhwabwā* (from another root), etc. In some forms the particle *mhā*, or "person," can be incorporated into the term, giving *tarhimhāabwā*, *tarhikamhāabwā*, etc.

15. In Bhaktapur the wide extension of these terms to a large class of male kin of the generation senior to ego does not include Father's Sister's Husband, *jicā pāju* (see item 4, below, this list), who is classified as *-bwā* in some other Newar communities. In contrast to most other North Indian systems, but like Nepali, Mother's Sister's Husband is included under this term and thus classified as a *-bwa*. This is reflected in further Newari extensions, MZHBW, for example, being classified with Father's Sister (*nini*) rather than with Mother's Sister as it is in some other North Indian systems such as Bengali.

16. The elder/younger differentiation of those male kin of the first ascending generation related through Father is based on their relative ages in relation to Father's age, those related through Mother are designated as "elder" or "younger" in relation to Mother's age.

17. Father and his siblings may be referred to as ranked in an absolute (rather than relative) order using Nepali ordinals, such as *jethābwā*, "the eldest Father in my Father's household" or *mahilābwa*, the "next eldest." A similar ranking can be used for ego and his or her same-sex siblings, for ego's Mother and her Sisters, ego's Mother's Brothers, etc.

18. This term is a compound of *jicā*, "bridegroom," implying men married to the out-marrying women of the *phukī*, and *pāju*, whose genealogical referent is Mother's Brother. In some Newari dialects FZH is called *bwā* (Toffin 1975*a*). In some North Indian systems FZH is a masculine form of the term for FZ, and is thus not amalgamated terminologically to either FB or MB.

19. *Māmā* is a homophone of the unrelated North Indian and Nepali term for Mother's Brother.

20. These terms are preceded by terms for older or younger: *tarimā(n), tarhikhāmhā, cicārhi-amā(n)*, etc. The qualification is based on whether the Father's Brother to whom alter is married is older or younger than Father.

21. As Toffin (1975*a*) has remarked, in contrast to other North Indian kinship systems the term *maleju* is not simply a feminine form of the term for Mother's Brother but an independent term.

22. In some North Indian kinship systems one of the extensions of this term, MZHZ, is said to be grouped, as it is by Newars, with Father's Sister (e.g., in Uttar Pradesh [Vatuk 1969]). In other North Indian kinship systems it is said to be grouped with Mother's Sister (e.g., in Bengal [Fruzzetti and Östör 1976]).

23. This term is a compound of *jicā*, "bridegroom," a man married to the out-marrying women of the *phukī*, and *dāju*, a term for older Brother used also in Nepali

24. This term is a compound of *jicā* and *bhāju*, a term of respect, usually used for an older or higher-status male. In some other Newari dialects *jicā bhāju* is *jilāja(n)*.

25. *Tatā* is used in some other Newari dialects and by some of the Chatha-riyā in Bhaktapur.

26. From *Tatā*, "Elder Sister," plus *-ju*, an honorific suffix.

27. People who are junior to ego are often referred to or addressed by their given names without any qualifying kin term. People senior to ego are some-times referred to or addressed by their given names plus their kin term (e.g., Kamela *ta:ju*) when it is necessary to differentiate them from other kin in the same category.

28. Variants include *bhaumacā, bhaumasta*, and *bhamacā*. The latter term is usually used to refer to or address a new wife in the household.

29. This term is a compound of *kāe*, Son, plus the diminutive particle *-cā*.

30. The use of the terms *kāecā, mhyāecā*, and *bhe(n)cā* involve significant differences from other North Indian systems, including Nepali. See *Bhe(n)cā* (item 18, below).

31. This term is a compound of *mhyāe* plus the diminutive particle *-cā*.

32. The term *bhi(n)cā* is used in some other Newar dialects.

33. *Bhe(n)cā* is the reciprocal term and relation to *pāju* and *nini*. The discriminations made by the terms *kāecā*, *mhyāca*, and *bhe(n)cā* among children of ego's cross-sex and same-sex siblings is not made in most of the other North Indian systems in the sources we have listed. The other systems make a distinction between Brother's Children and Sister's Children which is independent of the sex of ego. Thus in Bihari (Karve 1968) for either a male or female speaker a Brother's Son is *Bhatijā*, a Brother's Daughter is *Bhatijī*, a Sister's Son is *Bhānjā*, and a Sister's Daughter is *Bhānjī*. While the Newar terms emphasize the cross-sex relationship, the North Indian terms emphasize patrilineal versus nonpatrilineal (feminal) links. In both systems, however, the nonemphasized aspect is made clear through knowledge of the sex of the speaker.

34. In some other Newari dialects this is *Bhā:ta*. Occasionally in farming and lower *thar*s *mijā(n)*, "man," is used for Husband rather than *bha:ta*.

35. *Misā* means "woman." In some other Newari dialects the Sanskritic term *kalā:* is used for Wife. *Kalā:* is used occasionally in Bhaktapur as an elegant term for Wife, as is the Nepali term *jahān*, which also means "household."

36. This must be differentiated from the term for Husband, *bha:ta*.

37. There are some minor alterations in a few kinship terms when combined with *sasa* or *bhata*. Thus HeB, who is *ara* for Husband, becomes *darā bhata*. Wife's elder Brother, who is referred to as *ara* by the Wife, is *sasa daju*. Certain secondary forms of kinship terms are sometimes conventionally used as primary forms for some of the affinal terms.

38. Toffin (1975*a*) discusses this compound term, *jicā pāju*, at some length. It "opens a breech in the North Indian or Nepalese system in which a person cannot be at the same time a consanguineal and affinal relation; [the term] reflects a rule of marriage with a double cross-cousin" (ibid., 144). Note that the Pahari system of Sikanda also uses a single term, *mamā*, (elsewhere restricted to Mother's Brother) for both Mother's Brother and Father's Sister's Husband (Berreman 1968, 413).

APPENDIX 4: TYPES OF WORSHIP AND MATERIALS USED IN WORSHIP

1. We will use "he" throughout for simplicity of description of *pūjā* procedures. In temple visits and daily worship the worshipers are both men and women. For the more elaborate *pūjā*s the principal worshiper is almost always male.

2. At this point in the household worship of a dangerous deity a sacrifice would be made (chap. 9).

3. The term "*prasāda*" used by itself implies an edible offering taken back from a deity. Other offerings taken back after being offered to a deity unless their nature is clear from the context are specified as "flower *prasāda*," "*sinha(n) prasāda*," etc. *Prasāda* is often shared with others who did not perform the ritual themselves, or who may not have been present. The taking of *prasāda* is popularly explained as a way of keeping the deity in a continuing

presence with an individual. *Prasāda* has connections with the idea of *cipa* (chaps. 6 and 11).

4. Manandhar (1976, 230) derives the term from the Sanskrit *dharaṇa*, "keeping, maintaining," and defines the term as "fulfilling a vow."

5. The clay dishes and pots that are also used are listed by our informants with the expendable materials noted below.

6. "Unhusked" is used throughout this book to mean "with the husk removed," and not "still in the husk."

7. *Kiga:* is, as we have noted, presented to the deity at the climax of a *pūjā*. It is regarded not as a food offering, but as the presentation of a pure and valuable material.

APPENDIX 6: RITES OF PASSAGE AND DEATH CEREMONIES

1. Toffin (1984) and Nepali (1965) deal with Newar *saṃskāras* in some detail among the communities they studied.

2. The hair-shaving rite, the *Busākhā*, was traditionally only done as as an independent rite, that is separate from the following *Kaetā Pūjā* rite, by the macrostatus groups I through IV, who also have Tantric *Dekhā*, sometimes considered in itself to be a *saṃskāra*. The Jugī do not have the *Busākhā*, but they do have the *Dekhā*. The macrostatus levels from XIV and below do not do the *Ihī* mock-marriage, nor for other reasons did the Rājopādhyāya Brahmans in the past. The other *saṃskāras* are said to be performed by all levels. The Rājopādhyāya Brahmans perform, in addition, some extra traditional Brahmanical *saṃskāras*.

3. The *jāta:* will be placed on a person's forehead at the time of cremation, and is supposed to represent the record of the *karma* he or she has accumulated during his or her lifetime.

4. This is done among the Brahmans on the twelfth day after birth.

5. The phrase literally means causing an infant to touch or to be brought in contact with *cipa* (contaminated food, in this case boiled rice) fed to it, and thus contaminated, by a superior member of the family. For the significance of this see chapter 11.

6. Most of the *saṃskāras* (like certain *pūjās*) have one or more critical moments that are astrologically calibrated to a definite moment, the *sāit*. These *sāits* are indicated by some, often dramatic, emphasis in the ceremony and often represent the instant of some change of status.

7. This phase derives from another traditional *saṃskāra*, the *Niṣkarmaṇa* or "first outing," which was traditionally sometimes combined with the rice feeding ceremony. The use of the mother's brother to take the child out of the house was one of the traditional procedures (Pandey 1969, 87f.).

8. The girls' special rites of this period are the menarche rites, thus emphasizing *their* differentiated gender characteristics.

9. All *thars* in Bhaktapur do some version of the *Kaetā Pūjā*, but many of the lower *thars* do not, it is said, do the *Busākhā*.

10. In local counting an infant is "one" (or more precisely in his *first* year) at birth, and thus each of these numbered ages represents one year less than it would be in the Western system. We follow Newari (and Nepali) usage.

11. "*Āngsā*" is said by local Brahmans to mean *āga(n) sā*, "secret hair." Its "secrecy" is indicated by keeping the head covered with a cap in ordinary public settings after the *Busākhā*. The uncut tuft of hair is said to be a remnant of "birth hair" and to represent the lineage and the lineage deity. In this conception the Buddhist monk (and the monk's derivative in Bhaktapur, the Vajrācārya priest) with his completely shaved head and the Sadhu with his uncut hair—and thus no distinguishing *āngsā*—both negate the image of orderly descent and *phukī* solidarity and, thus, the defining solidarities and oppositions symbolized in the queue. The *āngsā* was previously not cut at all, but rather worn long and twisted into a coil. Now it is trimmed and kept short.

12. Following the *Busākhā* Brahman boys must now have their heads shaved in each of the subsequent major purification ceremonies that are required after a birth or death in the *phukī*.

13. Brahman ceremonies have two additional astrologically determined *sāits* in the course of their *Kaetā Pūjā* or *Upanayana*. One is for the proper time for cutting the boy's nails. The other is at the stage of the Brahmanical sequence when a Jośi must touch the boy to release him from his condition of hyperpurity.

14. *Burā(n)* is used in various phrases, for example, in *burā(n) jya*, ritual activities done by farmers at the proper astrological time in connection with the rice harvest. Its derivation is not known to our informants, but is used in phrases suggesting some major and important traditional work. *Taegu* (sometimes written *tegu*) means to persist in doing something.

15. In recent years wealthy middle-level families had begun to employ Brahman *purohitas* for some of the earlier *saṃskāras*.

16. For the Chathariyā and Pa(n)cthariyā, who had completed the *Busākhā* four days previously, the *Busākhā* is given more social emphasis than the *Kaetā Pūjā* itself—the preparations may be more elaborate, it may be attended by more guests, and in contrast to their *Kaetā Pūjā* celebration, it is followed by a large feast.

17. When the Kaetā Pūjā is done at an early age, say, five or seven, as it is sometimes by the nonpriestly upper-level *thars*, the sacred thread is not given, as the boys are considered to be too young. In these cases the thread is given at a special ceremony, a *Dya: Dekhā*, or "God initiation" (the god in question being the family lineage god) when the boy is eleven or thirteen years of age. Some Chathariyā and Pa(n)cthariyā individuals never formally take the sacred thread. This does not prevent them from having advanced Tantric initiations.

18. The *Kaetā Pūjā* is often remembered later as an emotionally significant time of transition, when the freedom of a boy's earlier life is suddenly lost. He must be careful in his contacts with lower-caste children, cannot share food with most of them, and cannot touch those of the lowest ranks. He must now wash ritually before eating, and must become more involved in family worship. He can now attend cremations and can see some of the forms of the lineage deities. In some *thars* with special professions it is now that he may begin to

learn the rituals associated with the profession, and may have more formal instruction in the profession itself. In discussions and reminiscences, the association of nakedness now covered by the loincloth and the growing urgency for control of sexual feelings is salient. Local Brahmans comment on the traditional and persisting importance of this, "Now the time for study has arrived. One must not have sexual intercourse during this time, because if one has become sexually aroused by a woman one is unable to study." The covering of the genitals with the loincloth is also associated with the idea of proper modesty and shame. From this time on being seen naked—as one was during the *Busākhā* and *Kaetā Pūjā* ceremonies—eating improperly, becoming dirty or ritually polluted, are matters of salient shame and embarrassment.

19. Other "Newar *saṃskāras*" are the old-age rites (see text below).

20. Because of the presence of the mock-marriage, we must differentiate the later marriage ceremony with a human spouse as "true," "genuine," "real," etc., marriage.

21. The Rājopādhyāya Brahmans still include the *kanya dāna*, the gift of the premenarche virgin daughter, as part of their true marriage ceremonies. However, as marriage of premenarche girls is now legally prohibited and as in orthodox *dharma* the Brahman girls must nevertheless marry before menarche, the Brahmans now use a simple form of mock-marriage. It is usually called *sinha(n) chāekegu*, "the offering of *sin(ha)* pigment" and, occasionally, *Ihī*. *Sinha(n)* pigment is applied to the foreheads of a group of young Brahman girls in the same way as it is given during a true marriage, in conjunction with a simple *pūjā*. The girl is then said to be married to the gods.

22. On formal written invitations to true marriage, however, the word "*Ihī*" is used as an anachronistic formal form to refer to the *Byāhā*.

23. The divine spouse is often erroneously given both in written and popular accounts as Śiva, who, represented as a *bel* fruit, is for Bhaktapur the "witness" to the marriage. Another deity, Suvarṇa Kumāra, is referred to in one of the traditional names used elsewhere for the mock-marriage, "Suvarṇa Kumāra marriage." This name, also known in Bhaktapur, does not at present reflect any actual reference to that deity in the *Ihī* ceremony itself. One phase of Bhaktapur's ceremony is called a "Suvarṇa Kumāra *pūjā*" but refers primarily to Viṣṇu. In relation to the Newar Buddhist *Ihī* ceremonies observed by Michael Allen (1982, 184), Allen was told that Suvarṇa Kumāra himself was the divine bridegroom.

24. *Ihī* in itself does not prevent optional marriage of premenarche girls, but premenarche marriages are and seem to have been for some time at least, in fact, rare (chap. 6).

25. An exception to this is the occasional sponsorship of the ceremony by a Brahman whose daughters would not have participated in the ceremony.

26. This sequence may be related to the traditional Mṛdāharaṇa ceremony, the "bringing of earth or clay. . . . [to be used] for growing sprouts" [in a pot] performed in South Asian tradition a few days before weddings (Pandey 1969, 209). Stevenson (1920, 65f.) describes for weddings in Kāṭhiāwār clay pots brought by a potter to a temple where they will be used in the subsequent wedding ceremony. "Some Hindus," she comments, "consider this a fertility

rite, and if the child born of the marriage is deformed, they say the potter's thumb must have slipped" (ibid., 65).

27. When there are many girls, a purified public area may be used for the ceremonies and the procedures modified slightly.

28. The Naunī, a woman of the barber *thar*, will paint their nails, as she will in subsequent major purifications. This represents a transition in the girls' purification procedures to the adult form and corresponds to a similar change for boys at the time of their *Kaetā Pūjā*.

29. The placement of the *Bhuisinha(n)* is done in the *Ihī* before the *kanya dāna* ceremony signifying the marriage; in the actual Newar marriage this ceremony is done after the ritual action that signifies the moment of transformation into the married state.

30. *Desa* means "city" and *bali*, "sacrificial offering."

31. This initiation is not necessary for the upper-status *thar*s who present their children to the family lineage deities in the form of the Āga(n) Deity at the time of the *Nāmakaraṇa* ceremony on the twelfth day after the birth of a child.

32. *Bārhā* (Kathmandu Newari, *Bārāe* or *Bārhāe*) has the sense of "ritual restrictions." *Cwa(n)gu* means to continue in a state or activity; *taegu*, an auxiliary verb of many uses, also has the sense of continuing an activity, with a somewhat more active nuance than *cwa(n)gu*.

33. G. S. Nepali remarked in his study made in the late 1950s that the *Bārhā cwa(n)gu* was gradually being adopted among his informants, replacing the premenstrual *Bārhā taegu* (1965, 113).

34. According to Bennett (1983, 215) Indo-Nepalese women were previously "hidden in a dark room away from the sun . . . and out of the sight of all males for the first three days of [all] their periods," and thus not only for their menarche ceremony. Such subsequent menstrual isolation is not done by Newars in Bhaktapur now, nor is it known to our informants as a previous practice.

35. The rice powder and oil represent cosmetics. The girls had applied the mixture as a cosmetic during the *Ihī* ceremony. Now this gift symbolizes that they can wear cosmetics like a married woman.

36. Betel nuts are widely used as messages about changes in ritual status. See the discussion of marriage in the text below.

37. There are three life-cycle events—birth, death, and the menarche ceremonies—which cause a group pollution. However, while the entire *phukī* is polluted in birth and death—a shared pollution that is one of the defining characteristics of the *phukī* group—the extent of pollution in *Bārhā cwa(n)gu* or *Bārhā taegu* varies according to the custom of the particular *thar*. In some *thar*s all the *phukī* are polluted; in others, only the parents of the girl.

38. The interpretive emphasis on the dangerous power of the girls at menarche, rather than the dirty contamination that might be assumed to be associated with menstrual blood, is noteworthy. The emphasis seems to be (directly for the menstruating girls, and by a metaphorical extension for the preadolescent girls) on the danger to others of the girl's nascent sexual feelings and the feelings they may now arouse in men as (for the true menarche girl) legitimate sexual objects. Compare the discussion of menstruation in chapter 6.

39. Betel nuts were used traditionally in Bhaktapur on several occasions as the formal notification sent to others of ritualized changes in status. They were also used at birth (in different forms for boys and girls), menarche, marriage (in various ways), divorce, and various death ceremonies.

40. In the most significant contrast, it is during the *swayambar* in Indo-Nepalese marriages that the *kanyā dāna* is presented. At the climactic *swayambar* act of marriage (the placing of a garland of flowers around the groom's neck by the bride), the groom places *bhui sinha(n)* pigment on the bride's head in exactly the same fashion as the *naki(n)* does to the girls in the *Ihī* marriage.

41. The ten betel nuts that the prospective bride gives to each household member may include five specially packaged nuts that had been sent from the groom's household.

42. Now she is likely to be taken in an automobile waiting at some nearby accessible road.

43. The *naki(n)* holds a handful of *baji phoyā(n)*, beaten fried rice which has been soaked in water, and moves it down the bride's body from top to bottom. After each descending movement she throws the rice away. She doe this three times to the bride's left, and then three times to her right.

44. As most marriages in Bhaktapur are from *thar*s at the same level, usually from within the city and often living near the groom's house, it is likely that the household women know or have seen the bride, and this and the following "viewing" of the bride may well be less embarrassing to the bride than is the case in the similar viewing of the bride in Hindu marriages in other settings where the bride usually comes from a distant community.

45. The status is that designated by the household *cipa* system (chap. 6).

46. In Jyāpu and other middle-level marriages a *purohita* may not be present.

47. In Brahmanical *kanyā* marriages one common dish is used.

48. We may note the careful balancing of the exchanges and activities—and in this case even the discomforts—between the bride's and groom's sides in all these activites. This is related to the emphasis on the equality of the giving and receiving families and the lack of an implied hypergamy, which we discussed in chapter 6.

49. In former times the same person, carrying the marriage *sukundā*, had gone earlier to fetch the groom.

50. A *burā* is an old man: a *burī*, an old woman. "*Ja(n)ko*" is the same term applied to the infant's rice feeding ceremony.

51. A *ghau* is one-sixtieth of a day, and a *palā* is one-sixtieth of a *ghau*.

52. This is another example of the relative lack of stigmatization of widows among the Newars.

53. We will sketch the sequence for adults. Girls who die before their *Ihī* ceremony and boys who die before *Kaetā Pūjā* have rites similar to those of adults at the time of dying, but are carried to the cremation grounds in the arms of a man, rather than on a *kūta:* carrier. The mourning ceremony that follows their death is shorter than for ceremonial adults (individuals past their *Ihī* and *Kaetā Pūjā saṃskāras*), the *phukī*'s purification occurring on the fourth day rather than the eleventh after the death. Infants who die before the age of three months are not cremated, but are buried in an area to the north of the city. In

the case of infants, only the immediate household members incur death impurity. Among upper-level *thar* families following the death of children who die before *Ihī* or *Kaetā Pūjā*, a ceremony called the "feeding of the *jwa:*" (*jwa:*, "a pair of animate beings," in this usage designates a contemporary of the dead child) may be held on the fifth or the twenty-first day after cremation. A Brahman *purohita's* child of the same sex as the deceased child is ceremonially fed and given presents. It is said that this child now in some sense continues the life of the dead child. After this ceremony there is no further special relation between the household and this child.

54. It is considered by some to be more devout to die at the river. Some few people are brought to a *ghāṭ* at the central Kathmandu Valley shrine of Paśupatinātha. Note that all these places, including the *cheli*, are—as are the cremation grounds—outside of the ordinary ordered space of the house or of the city.

55. For the great majority of people the most desired auspicious fates after death is to go to Viṣṇu's special heaven.

56. Compare Tulasī Piya Day [43] (chap. 13). The leaves of the plants grown starting on this day are kept for use at the time of dying.

57. In the association of the river with death there is, added to the idea of the force of the *tīrtha*, an idea of the *flow* of the river, which is said to carry the person along with it to the next world.

58. This introduces a double emphasis reflected in many of the death procedures, a *circulation* of aspects of the dead person, but a circulation that at the same time safely *distances* those aspects by, as here, a movement down the social hierarchy or, as in some other ceremonial elements, a movement into progressively more and more distant spatial regions.

59. In some few *thar*s, notably the Jugī, women are members of funeral processions. For the great majority of *thar*s only men and those boys who have undergone *Kaetā Pūjā* are members of the funeral procession.

60. It is popularly believed that until this moment the mind of the corpse is still active within the body, and thus that the person is aware of what is happening and can feel the heat and pain of the fire.

61. Brahmans, for cremations within their own *thar*, perform a separate traditional "Vedic" *yajña* sacrifice at this time.

62. It is said that the women of the upper *thar*s do not begin to wail until they approach the house, while women of lower *thar*s may begin wailing as they cross the boundary of the city or of the neighborhood. Women cry out such phrases as "Why did you leave us?," "Take me with you," "I did not see your face enough in this life; where can I go to see you now?"

63. In upper *thar* families, the member of the Cyo *thar* who has accompanied the funeral procession and who helps direct the first phase of the cremation takes a position at the *pikhā lākhu*, the stone marking the symbolic front boundary of the house, and swings a flaming clay oil lamp to chase off evil spirits from the *kriyā putra* as he enters the house.

64. The full set of activities are done by Brahmans. Chathariyā, Pa(n)cthariyā, and Jyāpus have more abbreviated versions. The crucial activities, done by all *thar*s, are those—depending on the particular *thar*—of either the fifth or seventh day.

65. As the Bhā, in fact, often does not know the proper worship procedures,

he is sometimes accompanied by the *kriyā putra*'s family *purohita*, who reads out the instructions from the proper *paddhati* (manual of instructions).

66. This appellation is listed as one of the sixty-eight "Svāyambhuva Lingas" in Rao (1971, vol. 2, p. 85).

67. It is sometimes said that the *preta* is, like the clay and the deity it represents, now below the surface of the earth where it is hot, and that this libation cools it. This is another example of the various parallel versions of the spirit's whereabouts and conditions referred to in the course of the death ceremonies.

68. We will use the more familiar Sanskrit term in the following discussion.

69. Compare Pandey, "The dead is regarded as still living in a sense. The efforts of the survivors are to provide him with food and guide his footsteps to the paramount abode of the dead. . . . The Sūtras . . . prescribe that a *piṇḍa* or a 'ball of rice' should be offered to the dead on the first day. The ball was called '*piṇḍa*' [body, person individual] because it was supposed to constitute the body of the *preta*" (1969, 265).

70. They typically talk of the illness and death of the deceased, and of his or her virtues. They urge the *kriyā putra* to continue to do his "death work" well.

71. This is held on the fifth day after the cremation for the Brahmans, and on either the fifth or the seventh day for Chathariyā and Pa(n)cthariyā, and, for the most part, on the seventh day for Jyāpu and lower-ranked *thar*s. For those upper-level *thar*s that identify themselves as descending, like the Brahmans, from one or another particular *gotra*, the day for this ceremony is supposed to depend on the *gotra* to which the *thar* members belong. If they belong to the same *gotra* as the Rājopādhyāya Brahmans, it is on the fifth day. Note that in all such enumerations the day of cremation is counted as the first day.

72. The *pikhā lākhu*, where it will be first deposited, is under the front edge of the overhanging eaves of the house.

73. *Śrāddha* is often written *sarādha* in Newari.

74. Although the elements of the *śrāddha* exist in the earlier offerings to the spirit as a *preta*, the *śrāddha* in its full form becomes possible with the formation of the spirit's ethereal body on this day.

75. The body is said by local Brahmans to form day by day over ten days as follows: (1) top of head; (2) eyes and ears; (3) nose; (4) shoulders and arms; (5) chest and upper abdomen as far as the umbilicus; (6) from the umbilicus to the thighs; (7) knees, fingernails, and hair; (8) lower legs; and (9) feet. On the tenth day the body as a whole is able to eat, drink, and function. "Some of the Purāṇas and medieval digests assert that after a man dies, the soul or spirit assumes what is called an *ātivāhika* body consisting of three of the five elements (viz., fire, wind, and *ākāśa* [space, vacuity]) that rise up from the dead body (while two—viz., earth and water—remain below), that such a body is obtained only by men and not by other beings, that with the aid of the *piṇḍa*s that are offered to the departed at the time of cremation and during ten days thereafter, the soul secures another body called *bhogadeha* (a body for enjoying the *piṇḍa*s offered) and that at the end of a year when *sapiṇḍīkaraṇa* is performed, the soul secures a third body wherewith the spirit reaches heaven or hell according to the nature of his actions" (Kane 1968–1977, vol. IV, p. 265).

76. *Du* is locally thought to derive from *dukha*, "sorrow, trouble, mourning."

77. During the previous ten days the *kriyā putra* and the other *phukī* members were not supposed to look into mirrors.

78. The avoidance of mirrors during the period of impurity and the worship of the sun at the end of the period as an act of purification and a sign of transformation echoes some of the sequence of the menarche rites.

79. Traditionally on this day among higher *thar*s the clothes that were worn by the *kriyā putra* during the *dasā kriyā* period were sent after the *du bya(n)-kegu* to a special group of washermen, members of the Pasi *thar*, to be washed. The few remaining members of this *thar* do not do this now, and the clothes are now given to a member of the Nau, or barber *thar*, for disposal.

80. These may include clothes, mattresses, pillows, kitchen pots for water and milk, drinking vessels, food offerings, and money. There is an emphasis on the number eleven. The Bhā is given eleven milk pots, eleven waterpots, and eleven pieces of meat, the latter representing aspects of the spirit's body.

81. It is said that men of upper *thar*s are not supposed to have sexual intercourse for one year after a parent dies.

82. If the deceased person is the household head, the *nāya:*, avoidable *saṃskāra*s should not be performed during one year; for other deaths in the household, they should be deferred for forty-five days.

83. The extended list of anniversaries of death that may require *śrāddha*s includes the eleventh, twelfth, thirteenth days, the end of the first month, the forty-fifth day, and all monthly anniversaries during the first year, as well as extra commemorations at five and one-half months and eleven and one-half months. There is a *śrāddha* on the first year's anniversary, and then at each yearly anniversary of the death.

84. For some upper-level *thar*s and for all middle-level *thar*s the *śrāddha* performed by Brahmans and some upper-level *thar*s on the twelfth day is done on the forty-fifth day after death.

85. The singleness of this *piṇḍa*s is emphasized in accounts of this event in contrast to the multiple *piṇḍa*s, characteristically three, which are used in other *śrāddha*s.

86. It is done on the eleventh day by upper-level *thar*s, who perform a *Vṛṣotsarga* ceremony (see text below). If a *Vṛṣotsarga* is not done, then the *gha:su yajña* will be done on the twelfth day after the death.

87. *Gha:su* is thought to derive from the Sanskrit *ghara* or *gṛha sudhi*, the cleaning of a house. The essential cleansing agent is the smoke of a fire, which is suggested in *yajña* (locally spelled and pronounced *jagye*), referring to a Vedic fire sacrifice.

88. In other Newar cities the Tini *thar* does not exist, and the *gha:su yajña* is done by a *thar* at the Pa(n)cthariyā level called, in some communities, "Gha:su Ācāju."

89. The *thar* name by which the Tini refer to themselves is Śivācārya, "priests of Śiva."

90. While the *du bya(n)kegu* purification is a typical act of restoration of "ordinary purity" following a condition of temporary impurity, these subsequent acts deal with a wider range of dangerous forces and substances than those central to the "purity complex" (chap. 11).

91. "*Dutāegu*" means "to keep (something) inside."

92. The day depends on the particular *thar* and its status level. "The ceremony of the *sapiṇḍīkaraṇa* 'or uniting the *preta* with the *pitaras*' takes place either on the twelfth day after the cremation, at the end of three fortnights or on the expiry of the year. The first day is prescribed for those who maintain the sacrificial fire, the second and the third for the rest" (Pandey 1969, 267). *Sapiṇḍīkaraṇa*s at the end of the first year apparently do not take place in Bhaktapur.

93. These *sapiṇḍa* relationships are essential in considerations of marriage prohibitions, the corporate sharing of birth and death impurity, and inheritance (Kane 1968–1977, vol. II, p. 452ff.).

94. Exactly whom the three *piṇḍa*s represent varies according to who the principal mourner is in relation to the dead person.

95. People of clean *thar*s can touch other people, including Brahmans, after the *du bya(n)kegu* purification. They are not supposed to touch deities, however, until after the *sapiṇḍa* ceremony of the twelfth or forty-fifth day.

96. There are also optional *śrāddha*s on each monthly anniversary of the death and also after five months and one fortnight and eleven months and one fortnight. The entire series is done by the Rājopādhyāya Brahmans but increasingly rarely by other upper-level *thar*s.

Glossary

We list those Newari and Sanskrit terms that are used frequently throughout the book. Although many of these terms have wider historical and contemporary meanings, we gloss them here in the way they are usually used in Bhaktapur and in this book. The other Newari, Nepali, and Sanskrit terms used in the book are defined as they are used, or are made clear by their contexts.

Ācāju. An auxiliary priest specializing in Tantric ritual. Their *thar* name is Karmācārya.

Āga(n) Dya:, or Āga(n) God. One of the two forms of the lineage deity of upper-level *thar*s. See "Digu Dya:."

Aṣṭamātṛkās. The eight "mother goddesses" placed in a protective ring around Bhaktapur.

Asuras. A class of powerful supernatural beings who are the enemies of the gods.

Ātmā. The soul, the divine element in each individual.

Bhajana. Music played as an act of worship to a deity.

Bhakti. Loving devotion to a particular deity.

Bhe(n)ca. A man's sister's son or daughter. See "*Pāju*."

Bhūta. A spirit, usually one that is not the ghost of a dead person (see "*Preta*").

Bya(n)kegu. A purification procedure.

Ca:re. The fourteenth day of the dark fortnight of a lunar month.

Chathar. A group of *thar*s originally consisting of the royal family, related families, and the families of high court officials.

Chathariyā. A member of one of Chathar *thar*s (see "Chathar").

Cheli. The bottom story of a house, for many purposes considered to be outside of the house.

Che(n). House.

Chetrapāl. A deified stone acting as the protector of a spatial area.

Chetri. The upper-level, non-Brahmanical, section of Indo-Nepalese society.
Chwāsa. A deified stone, usually found at major crossroads, on which certain polluted materials are discarded.
Cipa. Food that has been contaminated by contact with some source of pollution.
Cwata. The third story of a house counting from the ground.
Darśana. An epiphany. The showing of itself by a deity to its worshipers.
Dega:. A temple.
Dekhā. Initiation. See "*Dīkṣā.*"
Devī. The name of the Goddess as the supreme Creator deity.
Dewālī. The annual ceremony of worship by a *phukī* group to its Digu God.
Dharma. Religion, law, proper conduct.
Digu Dya: or Digu God. A form of the lineage deity. See "Āga(n) Dya:."
Dīkṣā. Initiation. See "*Dekhā.*"
Dip. Cremation ground. Sanskrit *dīpa.*
Dya:. A god.
Gāthā. The *thar* whose members incarnate the deities of the group of the Nine Durgās.
Ghāṭ. Steps leading down to the river.
Grāha. A heavenly body having an astrological influence.
Guru. A teacher of esoteric knowledge.
Guthī. A formal association formed for some special purpose.
Ihī. A girl's mock-marriage to Viṣṇu.
Ijjat. Respectability, public reputation.
Jajamān. A patron.
Jātrā. A religious procession.
Jonā. The sacred thread worn by upper-status, "twice-born" men.
Jośi. An astrologer and assistant priest.
Jugī. One of the lowest *thars*, whose members are musicians, tailors, and have various pollution-removing duties.
Jyāpu. A farmer.
Kaetā. A ceremonial loincloth presented to boys during the Kaetā Pūjā rite of passage.
Kalaśa. A flask-like vessel used in worship.
Karma. An individual's condition or destiny as affected by that individual's actions in his or her current or previous lives.
Kiga:. Purified uncooked husked rice grain, a basic material used in worship.
Karmācārya. The *thar* name of Ācājus.
Ka:si. An open porch attached to an upper story of a house.
Kṣatriya. The ruling and warrior class.
Lāekū. Royal Palace. In Bhaktapur the "Lāekū" or "Durbar" Square is the square in front of the Royal Palace and the adjoining Taleju temple.
Lāskusa. A welcoming ceremony in which a person or deity is met and conducted into a sacred area.
Liṅga. A representation of Śiva in an abstract phallic form.
Mahiṣāsuramardinī. A representation of the Goddess Devī in the form of the slayer of the "King of the Asuras" in his buffalo form.

Maṇḍala. A circle, often thought to have special power concentrated within it.

Maṇḍalic Goddesses. The eight Aṣṭamātṛkās plus an additional ninth, centrally located, goddess, who as a group protect Bhaktapur's inner space.

Mantra. A sound, word, or phrase having special power.

Masān. Cremation group. See "*Dīpa*."

Māta(n). The second story of a house counting from the ground. It is just above the *cheli* and is the first interior story of the house.

Maṭha. An ornate building used as a shelter and gathering place for Hindu wandering ascetics.

Māyā. Illusion.

Melā. A mass religious gathering, attracting pilgrims from distant places.

Mhā. Body or self.

Mokṣa. Release from the cycle of rebirths. See "*Mukti*."

Mukti. Release from the cycle of rebirths. See "*Mokṣa*."

Mūrti. A material image of a god.

Nāe. The *thar* whose members slaughter and butcher water buffaloes.

Nāga. A supernatural serpent.

Nāginī. A female *nāga*.

Naki(n). A female leader.

Nau. A *thar* whose members are barbers and who perform purification procedures.

Naunī. A female Nau.

Nāya:. A male leader.

Pāju. A person's mother's brother. See "*Bhe(n)ca*."

Pa(n)cthar. A high-status group of *thar*s just below the Chathar group.

Pa(n)cthariyā. A member of the Pa(n)cthar group of *thar*s.

Pāpa. A violation of the *dharma*, a sin.

Phukī. A group of patrilineally related households which acts as a ritual, moral, and social unit for many purposes.

Pikhā lākhu. A deified stone marking the front symbolic boundary of a house.

Pīṭha. An open shrine lacking an image of a deity. For Bhaktapur the *pīṭha*s are primarily the shrines of the Maṇḍalic Goddesses.

Po(n). The untouchable *thar*.

Pradakṣiṇāpatha. A traditional processional route. "The Pradakṣiṇāpatha" refers to Bhaktapur's main, city-wide, processional route.

Prasāda. A portion of food, or other materials, which had been offered to a deity and then taken back by a worshiper and eaten, or applied to his or her own body.

Preta. A ghost. A stage in the transformation of a person's spirit after death. See "*Bhūta*."

Pūjā. Worship.

Pūjārī. A priest acting as an attendant to a deity at a shrine or temple.

Punhi. The full moon. The day of the full moon.

Purāṇa. A class of Hindu texts, dating from the first millennium A.D., recounting stories of deities.

Purohita. A family priest.

Pyākha(n). A dance-drama.

Rājopādhyāya. The family or *thar* name of Newar Brahmans.
Sādhu. A Hindu ascetic.
Śāha. The present dynasty of Nepalese kings.
Sāhu. A merchant or shopkeeper.
Sāit. The astrologically determined proper time for something to take place.
Śakti. Power. An emanation of god's power conceived as an independent female deity.
Samhae. A mixture of foods, including meat and fish, presented to meat-eating deities.
Saṃskāra. A rite of passage.
Śāstra. A treatise specifying proper action in accord with the *dharma*.
Siddhi. The power to be effective, of a deity or religious procedure.
Sinha(n). Pigment used in religious ceremonies or for personal decoration.
Śrāddha. A ceremony commemorating deceased ancestors that includes offerings to them.
Swaga(n). A mixture of curds, rice, pigment, etc., used as a decorative mark for the foreheads of deities and worshipers.
Thar. A clan-like social unit whose members share the same surname.
Tīrtha. A place in a body of water where the water has special power.
Twa:. A village-like spatial segment of a Newar town or city.
Twāe. A ritually created fictive brother or sister.
Vajrācārya. A Newar Vajrayāna Buddhist priest.
Vajrayāna. A type of Buddhism that is similar to Tantric Hinduism in its pantheon, concepts, and practices.
Vaṃśavalī. A chronicle.
Vihāra. A building or group of buildings acting as a center for Newar Buddhist religious and social activities. Derived from ancient Buddhist monastic buildings and activities.
Vrata. An austerity, such as fasting.
Yantra. A complex diagram of mystic significance and power.

References

Acharya, Rajeshwar, and Hamid Ansari. *Basic Needs and Government Services: An Area Study of Bhaktapur Town Panchayat, Nepal.* Kathmandu: Centre for Economic Development and Administration, Tribhuvan University, 1980.

Agrawala, Vasudeva. *Devi-Mahatmya: The Glorification of the Great Goddess.* Varanasi: All-India Kahiraj Trust, 1963.

———. *Ancient Indian Folk Cults.* Varanasi: Prithivi Prakashan, 1970.

Allen, Michael. *The Cult of Kumārī.* Kathmandu: Tribhuvan University Press, 1975.

———. "Kumari or 'Virgin' worship in Kathmandu Valley." *Contributions to Indian Sociology* (n.s.), 10, 2 (1976): 293–316.

———. "Girl's Pre-Puberty Rites amongst the Newars of the Kathmandu Valley." In *Women in India and Nepal.* Eds. Michael Allen and S. N. Mukherjee. Canberra: Australian National University, 1982.

Anderson, Mary M. *The Festivals of Nepal.* London: George Allen & Unwin, 1971.

Atkinson, Edwin T. *Religion in the Himalayas.* (Reprinted from the Himalayan Gazetteer. vol. II. chaps. VIII–X.) New Delhi: Cosmo Publications, 1974.

Auer, Gerhard, and Niels Gutschow. *Bhaktapur.* Darmstadt: Technische Hochschule, 1974.

Babb, Lawrence A. *The Divine Hierarchy: Popular Hinduism in Central India.* New York: Columbia University Press, 1975.

Bajracharya, Purna Harsha. "Newar Marriage Customs and Festivals." *Southwestern Journal of Anthropology,* 15 (1959): 418–428.

Banerjea, Jitendra Nath. *The Development of Hindu Iconography.* Second edition. Calcutta: Calcutta University Press, 1956.

Barnett, Marguerite Ross, and Steve Barnett. "Contemporary Peasant and Post-peasant Alternatives in South India: The Ideas of a Militant Untouchable." *Annals of the New York Academy of Sciences*, 220 (1974): 385–410.

Berré, Vincent, Patrick Berger, Laurence Feveile, and Gérard Toffin. *Panauti; Une Ville au Nepal.* Paris: Berger-Levrault, 1981.

Basham, A. L. *The Wonder that was India.* London: Sidgwick and Jackson, 1967.

Basnet, Buddhi Man Singh. *Vaṃśāvalī.* [1878.] Translated by Kamal P. Malla. Manuscript, 1981.

Beck, Brenda E. F. "The Vacillating Goddess: Sexual Control and Social Rank in the Indian Pantheon." Paper presented at the Association for Asian Studies Meetings, Boston, March 1969.

Benedict, P. K. "Kinship in Southeastern Asia." Cambridge, Mass.: Harvard Universtiy, Department of Anthropology, Ph.D. thesis, 1941.

Bennett, Lynn. "Mother's Milk and Mother's Blood: The Social and Symbolic Roles of Women among the Brahmans and Chetris of Nepal." New York: Faculty of Philosophy, Columbia University, Ph.D. thesis, 1977.

———. *Tradition and Change in the Legal Status of Nepalese Women.* Vol. I, part 2 of *The Status of Women in Nepal.* Kathmandu: Centre for Economic Development and Administration, Tribhuvan University, 1979.

———. *Dangerous Wives and Sacred Sisters: Social and Symbolic Roles of High-Caste Women in Nepal.* New York: Columbia University Press, 1983.

Bernier, Ronald M. *The Temples of Nepal: An Introductory Survey.* Kathmandu: Voice of Nepal, 1970.

Berreman, Gerald. *Hindus of the Himalayas.* Berkeley and Los Angeles: University of California Press, 1963. (This first edition includes an appendix on Sirkanda kin terms, which is not included in the second edition, 1972.)

Beyer, Stephan. *The Cult of Tārā.* Berkeley, Los Angeles, London: University of California Press, 1973.

Bharati, Agehananda. *The Tantric Tradition.* Garden City, N.Y.: Anchor Books, 1965.

Biardeau, Madeleine, and Charles Malamoud. *Le Sacrifice dans L'Inde Áncenne.* Paris: Presses Universitaires de France, 1976.

Bista, Dor Bahadur. *People of Nepal.* Second edition. Kathmandu: Ratna Pustak Bhandar, 1972.

Bista, Khem Bahadur. *Le culte du Kuldevata au Nepal en particulier chéz certains Ksatri de la vallée de Kathmandu.* Paris: Editions Nové, 1972.

Blair, Katherine. *The Relationship between Traditional Housing and Traditional Settlement Patterns and Urban Housing in Nepal.* Nepal: Fulbright-Hays Scholarship report, 1975.

Bouglé, Célestin. *Essai sur le régime des caste.* Paris: Alcan, 1908.

Bouillier, Véronique. "Si les Femmes faisaient la fête. . . . A propos des fêtes féminines dan les hautes castes Indo-Népalaises." *L'Homme* XXII, 3 (1982): 91–118.

Braudel, F. *Civilisation matérielle et capitalisme.* Paris: Armand Colin, 1967.

Briggs, George W. *Gorakhnāth and the Kānphaṭa Yogīs.* [1938.] New Delhi: Motilal Banarsidass, 1973.

Bühler, George. *The Laws of Manu.* [1886.] Reprint edition. New York: Dover, 1969.

Burkert, Walter. *Greek Religion.* Oxford: Basil Blackwell, 1985.

Campbell, J. Gabriel. *Saints and Householders. A Study of Hindu Ritual and Myth among the Kangra Rajputs.* Kathmandu: Ratna Pustak Bandar, 1976.

Carroll, Vern, Ed. *Adoption in Eastern Oceania.* Honolulu: University of Hawaii Press, 1970.

Central Bureau of Statistics. *Statistical Pocket Book, Nepal.* Kathmandu: Central Bureau of Statistics, 1974.

Chakravarty, Chintaharan. *Tantras, Studies on Their Religion and Literature.* Calcutta: Punthi Pustak, 1972.

Chattopadhyay, K. P. "An Essay on the History of Newar Culture." *Journal of the Asiatic Society of Bengal* (n.s.), XIX (1923): 465–560.

Cohn, Bernard S. "History and Anthropology: The state of play." *Comparative Studies in Society and History*, XXII (1980): 198–221.

Daniélou, Alain. *Hindu Polytheism.* Bollingen Series, Vol. LXXIII. New York: Pantheon. 1964.

Das, Veena. *Structure and Cognition, Aspects of Hindu Caste and Ritual.* New Delhi: Oxford University Press, 1977.

———. "The Culinary Codes of the Hindus." *Reviews in Anthropology* 8, 2 (Spring 1981): 138–145.

Das Gupta, Shashibhusan. *Obscure Religious Cults.* Calcutta: Firma K. L. Mukhopadhyaya, 1969.

Deo, S. P. "Glimpses of Nepal Woodwork." *The Journal of the Indian Society of Oriental Art* (n.s.), III (1968–1969).

Desideri, Ippolito. *An Account of Tibet. The Travels of Ippolito Desideri of Pistoia, S.J. 1712–1727.* Translated and prepared by Janet Ross. Ed. Filippo de Fillippi. London: Routledge, 1932.

Dickey, Sara. "Differential Attraction to the DMK: Scheduled Castes Backward, Castes and Contradictions in Ideology." San Diego: Department of Anthropology, University of California, unpublished Master's thesis, 1984.

Dolgin, Janet L., David S. Kemnitzer, and David M. Schneider. *Symbolic Anthropology.* New York: Columbia University Press, 1977.

Douglas, Mary. *Purity and Danger.* London: Routledge & Kegan Paul, 1966.

———. "Pollution." In *The International Encyclopedia of the Social Sciences*, vol. 12. Ed. David Sills. New York: Macmillan and the Free Press, 1968.

Dubois, Jean Antoine. *Hindu Manners, Customs and Ceremonies* [1906.] Third edition. Oxford: Clarendon Press, 1968.

Dumont, Louis. "Le vocabulaire de parenté dans l'Inde du Nord." *L'Homme*, II (2) (1962): 5–48.

———. "Marriage in India: The Present State of the Question." *Contributions to Indian Sociology*, VII (March 1964): 77–98.

———. *Religion, Politics and History in India.* The Hague: Mouton, 1970.

———. *Homo Hierarchicus, The Caste System and Its Implications.* Complete revised English edition. Chicago: University of Chicago Press, 1980.

Dumont, Louis, and David Pocock. "Pure and Impure." *Contributions to Indian Sociology*, III (1959): 9–39.

Dutt, Binode Bihari. *Town Planning in Ancient India.* [1925.] New Delhi: New Asian Publishers, 1977.

Faherty, Robert I. "Sacrifice." In *Macropaedia*, vol. 16, *Encyclopaedia Britannica.* Fifteenth edition. Chicago: Encyclopaedia Britannica, 1974.

Finley, M. I. "The Ancient City: From Fustel de Coulanges to Max Weber and Beyond." *Comparative Studies in Society and History*, 19, 3 (July 1977): 305–327.

Fox, Robin Lane. *Pagans and Christians.* New York: Viking, 1986.

Frazer, James. *The Golden Bough: A Study in Magic and Religion.* [1890.] New York: Macmillan, 1955.

Freed, Ruth S., and Stanley A. Freed. "Calendars, ceremonies and festivals in a North Indian Village: Necessary Calendric Information for Fieldwork." *Southwestern Journal of Anthropology*, 20 (Spring 1964): 67–95.

Fruzzetti, Lina, and Akos Östör. "Is There a Structure to North Indian Kinship Terminology?" *Contributions to Indian Sociology* (n.s.), 10 (1976): 63–95.

Fuller, C. J. *Servants of the Goddess.* Cambrige: Cambridge University Press, 1984.

Fürer-Haimendorf, Christoph von. "Elements of Newar Social Structure." *The Journal of the Royal Anthropological Institute of Great Britain and Ireland*, 86, 2 (1956): 15–38.

———. "Unity and Diversity in the Chetri Caste of Nepal." In *Caste and Kin in Nepal, India and Ceylon.* Ed. Christoph von Fürer-Haimendorf. London: Asia Publishing House, 1966.

Fustel de Coulanges, Numa Denis. *The Ancient City.* (Translation of *La Cité Antique*, 1864.) Garden City, N.Y.: Doubleday Anchor Books, 1956.

———. *The Ancient City.* (Translation of *La Cité Antique*, 1864.) With a foreword by Arnaldo Momigliano and S. C. Humphreys. Baltimore: John Hopkins University Press, 1980.

Gaborieau, Marc. *Minorités Musulmanes dan le Royaume Hindou du Nepal.* Nanterre: Laboratoire d'Ethnologie, 1977.

———. "Les Fêtes, le temps et l'espace: Structure du calendrier hindou dans sa version indo-népalaise." *L'Homme* XXII, 3 (1982): 11–29.

Gellner, Ernest. *Legitimation of Belief.* Cambridge: Cambridge University Press, 1974.

Gennep, Arnold van. *Les Rites de Passage.* Paris: Nourry, 1909.

Gewali, Surya Bikram. "Political History." In *Nepal in Perspective.* Eds. Pashupati S. J. B. Rana and Kamal P. Malla. Kathmandu: Centre for Economic Development and Administration, 1973.

Gnanambal, K. *Festivals of India.* Calcutta: Anthropological Survey of India (Government of India), 1967.

Goffman, Erving. *Asylums.* Garden City, N.Y.: Doubleday Anchor Books, 1956.

Gould, Harold A. "The Hindu Jajmani System: A Case of Economic Particularism." *Southwestern Journal of Anthropology* 14 (1958): 428–437.

———. *Caste and Class: A Comparative View.* A McCaleb Module in Anthropology (pamphlet series). Reading, Mass.: Addison-Wesley, 1971.

Gray, John N. "Hypergamy, Kinship and Caste among the Chettris of

Nepal." *Contributions to Indian Sociology* (n.s.), 14 (1980): 1–34.
Greenwold, Stephan. "Monkhood versus Priesthood in Newar Buddhism." *The Anthropology of Nepal*. Ed. C. von Fürer-Haimendorf. Warminster, England: Aris and Phillips, 1973.
———. "Buddhist Brahmans." *Archives Européenes de Sociologie*, XV (1974): 101–123.
———. "The Role of the Priest in Newar Society." In *Himalayan Anthropology*. Ed. James Fisher. The Hague: Mouton, 1978.
Gupta, Sanjikta, Dirk Jan Hoens, and Teun Goudriaan. *Hindu Tantrism*. Leiden and Cologne: E. J. Brill, 1979.
Gurung, Harka. "The Land." In *Nepal in Perspective*. Eds. Pashupati S. J. B. Rana and Kamal P. Malla. Kathmandu: Centre for Economic Development and Administration, 1973.
Gutschow, Niels. *Bhaktapur/Nepal-Development Project; Kasten: Hierarchie und Standort*. Darmstadt: Gesellschaft für Stadtsanierung, 1975.
———. *Die Städtebaulich—Räumliche Structure der Newar-Städte im Kāṭhmāṇḍu-Tal/Nepal*. Münster: unpublished dissertation. 1979*a*.
———. "The Ritual Chariots of Nepal." In *Mobile Architecture in Asia*. Art and Archeology Research Papers, vol. 16. 102 St. Paul's Road, London. 1979*b*.
———. *Stadtraum und Ritual der newarischen Städte im Kathmandu-Tal*. Stuttgart: Kohlhammer, 1982.
———. Bhaktapur. "The Urban Symbolism of a Traditional Nepalese Town." Unpublished paper prepared for a Wingspread Conference, *The Meanings of the City*. Racine, Wisc., October 1984.
Gutschow, Niels, and Ganesh Mān Bāsukala. "The Navaduragā of Bhaktapur—Spatial Implications of an Urban Ritual." In *Heritage of the Kathmandu Valley*. Sankt Augustin: VGH Wissenschaftsverlag, 1987.
Gutschow, Niels, and Bernhard Kölver. *Ordered Space, Concepts and Functions in a Town of Nepal*. Wiesbaden: Kommissions Verlag Franz Steiner, 1975.
Hagen, Toni. *Nepal, The Kingdom in the Himalayas*. Third edition. Chicago: Rand McNally, 1971.
Hale, Austin. "Newari Higher Levels." In *Tibeto-Burman Linguistics*, vol. III. Occasional Papers of the Wolfenden Society. Ed. F. K. Lehman. Urbana: University of Illinois, 1970*a*.
———. "Newari Segmental Synopsis." In *Tibeto-Burman Linguistics*, Vol. III. Occasional papers of the Wolfenden Society. Ed. F. K. Lehman. Urbana University of Illinois, 1970*b*.
Hale, Austin, and Margrit, Hale. "Newari Texts." In *Tibeto-Burman Linguistics*, Vol. III. Occasional Papers of the Wolfenden Society. Ed. F. K. Lehman. Urbana: University of Illinois, 1970.
Hamilton, Francis Buchanan. *An Account of the Kingdom of Nepal*. (Reprint edition of 1819.) Bibliotheca Himalayca Series I, vol. 10. New Delhi: Mañjuśrī, 1971.
Harper, Edward B. "A Hindu Village Pantheon." *Southwestern Journal of Anthropology*, 15, 3 (1959): 227–234.

Hasrat, Bikrama Jit. *History of Nepal, as Told by Its Own and Contemporary Chroniclers*. Hoshiarpur: V. V. Research Institute Press, 1970.

Heesterman, J. C. *The Inner Conflict of Tradition*. Chicago: University of Chicago Press, 1985.

Hiebert, Paul G. *Kondura: Structure and Integration in a South Indian Village*. Minneapolis: University of Minnesota Press, 1971.

His Majesty's Government, Nepal. *The Physical Development Plan for the Kathmandu Valley*. Kathmandu: Ministry of Public Works, 1969.

Hocart, A. M. *Caste. A Comparative Study*. [1950.] New York: Russell and Russell, 1960.

Hodgson, Brian Houghton. The Hodgson Collection. Miscellaneous manuscripts bound into numbered volumes. Written and collected while Hodgson was British Resident in Nepal Between 1820 and 1844. In the collection of the India Office Library. London, n.d.

Hoerburger, Felix. *Studien zur Musik in Nepal*. Regensburg: Gustav Bosse Verlag, 1975.

Höfer András. *The Caste Hierarchy and the State in Nepal, A Study of the Muluki Ain of 1854*. Innsbruck: Universitätsverlag Wagner, 1979.

Hooper, Antony. "Review Article of *Tahitians*, by Robert Levy." *The Journal of the Polynesian Society*, 84, 3, 1975, pp. 369–378.

Hutton, J. H. *Caste In India*. Third edition. London: Oxford University Press, 1961.

Iltis, Linda. *The Swasthani-Vrata: Newar Women and Ritual in Nepal*. Ann Arbor, Mich.: University Microfilms International. 1985.

Inalcik, Halil. "Istanbul as an Islamic City." Unpublished paper for a conference, "Meanings of the City," Wingspread Conference Center, Racine, Wisconsin. October 25–27, 1984.

INAS (Institute of Nepal and Asian Studies). *Seminar Papers in Linguistics*. Kathmandu: INAS, 1976.

Inden, Ronald. "Tradition against itself. Review of Heesterman (1985)." *American Ethnologist*, 13, 4 (November 1986): 762–775.

James, Edwin Oliver. "Priesthood." In *Macropaedia*, vol. 14, *Encyclopaedia Britannica*. Fifteenth edition. Chicago: Encyclopaedia Britannica, 1974.

Jha, Hit Narayan. *The Licchavis (of Vaiśali)*. Varanasi: Chowkhamba Sanskrit Series Office, 1970.

Joshi, Bhuwan Lal, and Leo E. Rose. *Democratic Innovations in Nepal*. Berkeley and Los Angeles: University of California Press, 1966.

Kane, Pandurange Vaman. *History of Dharmaśastra*. Second edition. Five volumes. Poona: Bhandarkar Oriental Research Institute, 1968–1977.

Karan, Pradyumna P. *Nepal, A Cultural and Physical Geography*. Lexington: University of Kentucky Press, 1960.

Karve, Irawati. *Kinship Organization in India*. Third edition. Bombay: Asia Publishing House, 1968.

Kermode, Frank. *Essays on Fiction*. London: Routledge & Kegan Paul, 1983.

Kierkegaard, Søren. *Fear and Trembling*. [1843.] Revised edition. New York: Doubleday, 1954.

Kirkpatrick, Colonel. *An Account of the Kingdom of Nepaul*. (Reprint of 1811 volume.) Bibliotheca Himalayica Series I, vol. 3. New Delhi: Mañjuśrī, 1969.

Kolenda, Pauline. *Caste in Contemporarty India: Beyond Organic Solidarity.* Menlo Park, Calif.: Benjamin/Cummings, 1978.

Kölver, Bernhard. "A Ritual Map from Nepal." *Folia Rara.* Eds. H. Franke, W. Heissig, and W. Treue. Weisbaden: Franz Steiner Verlag, 1976.

———. "Aspects of Nepalese Culture: Ancient Inscriptions and Modern Yatras." In *Proceedings cf the First Symposium of Nepali and German Sanskritists, 1978.* Kathmandu: Institute of Sanskrit Studies, Tribhuvan University, Dang, Nepal Resarch Center, 1980.

Korn, Wolfgang. *The Traditional Architecture of the Kathmandu Valley.* Bibliotheca Himalayica, Series III, vol. II. Kathmandu: Ratna Pustak Bhandar, 1976.

Kosambi, Damodar Dharmanand. "At the Crossroads—Mother Goddess Cult Sites in Ancient India." *Journal of the Royal Asiatic Society of Great Britain and Ireland* (1960): 17–31, 135–144.

Kramrisch, Stella. *The Hindu Temple.* Two volumes. Calcutta: University of Calcutta, 1946.

Landon, Perceval. *Nepal.* (Reprint of 1928 edition.) Bibliotheca Himalayica Series I, vol. 16, 1976.

Lévi, Sylvain. *Le Népal, Étude Historique d'Un Royaume Hindou.* Paris: Ernest Leroux, 1905.

Levy, Robert I. *Personality Studies in Polynesia and Micronesia: Stability and Change.* Working Papers, No. 8. Honolulu: University of Hawaii, Social Science Research Institute, 1969.

———. *Tahitians: Mind and Experience in the Society Islands.* Chicago: University of Chicago Press, 1973.

———. "Tahitian Gentleness and Redundant Controls." In *The Socialization of Aggression.* Ed. Ashley Montague. New York: Oxford University Press, 1977.

———. "Horror and Tragedy: The Wings and Center of the Moral Stage." *Ethos* 13, 2 (Summer 1985): 175–187.

Lewis, Todd. *The Tuladhars of Kathmandu: A Study of Buddhist Tradition in a Newar Merchant Community.* Ann Arbor, Mich.: University Microfilms International, 1984.

Lingat, Robert. *The Classical Law of India.* Berkeley, Los Angeles, London: University of California Press, 1973.

Locke, John K. "The Cult of Avalokitesvara—Matsyendranath in the Valley of Nepal." Kathmandu: Tribhuvan University, Ph. D. dissertation, 1976.

Loomis, Charles P. "Geselleschaft." In *A Dictionary of the Social Sciences.* Eds. Julius Gould and William L. Kolb. New York: The Free Press, 1964.

McCulloch, Warren. *Embodiments of Mind.* Cambridge, Mass.: Massachusetts Institute of Technology Press, 1965.

Macdonald, A. W., and Anne Vergati Stahl. *Newar Art.* New Delhi: Vikas. 1979.

Macdonell, Arthur A. *A Practical Sanskrit Dictionary.* [First published in 1924.] London: Oxford University Press, 1974.

Majumdar, R. C., A. D. Pusalker, and A. K. Majumdar, Eds. *The Age of Imperial Unity*. Volume 2 of *The History and Culture of the Indian People*. Bombay: Bharatiya Vidya Bhavan, 1951.

———. *The Struggle for Empire*. Volume 5 of *The History and Culture of the Indian People*. Bombay: Bharatiya Vidya Bhavan, 1957.

Malla, Kamal P. "Language." In *Nepal in Perspective*. Eds. Pashupati S. J. B. Rana and Kamal P. Malla. Kathmandu: Centre for Economic Development and Administration, 1973.

———. *The Newars, Their Formation and Future*. Manuscript. Kathmandu: Nepal Research Center, 1979*a*.

———. *Classical Newari Literature: A Sketch*. Manuscript. Kathmandu: Nepal Study Center, 1979*b*.

———. "Linguistic Archeology of the Nepal Valley, a Preliminary Report." *Kailash*, VIII, 1–2 (1981*a*).

———. *Contemporary Newari a Working Outline*. Manuscript. Berkeley: University of California, Department of Linguistics, 1981*b*.

———. *The Newari Language: A Working Outline*. Tokyo: Institute for the Study of Languages and Culture of Asia and Africa, 1985.

———. *Newar Ethnicity*. Manuscript. Kathmandu, n.d.

Manandhar, Thakurlal. *A Brief Newari-English Dictionary*. Prepublication draft. Kirtipur, Nepal: Summer Institute of Linguistics, and Institute of Nepal and Asian Studies, 1976.

Mandlebaum, David G. *Society in India*. Two volumes. Berkeley, Los Angeles, London: University of California Press, 1970.

Mani, Vettam. *Purāṇic Encyclopaedia*. First English edition. New Delhi: Motilal Banarsidass, 1975.

Marriot, McKim. "Hindu Transactions: Diversity without Dualism." In *Transaction and Meaning: Directions in the Anthropology of Exchange and Symbolic Behavior*. Ed. Bruce Kapferer. Philadelphia: Institute For the Study of Human Issues, 1976.

———. "The Open Hindu Person and Interpersonal Fluidity." Unpublished paper presented at the meeting of the Association for Asian Studies, Washington, D.C., March 21, 1980.

Marriot, McKim, and Ronald Inden. "Toward an Ethnosociology of South Asian Caste Systems." In *The New Wind*. Ed. Kenneth A David. Chicago: Aldine. 1977.

Maskay, P. L. *Guide to Bhaktapur*. Kathmandu: Maskey, 1962.

Momigliano, Arnaldo. "The Ancient City of Fustel de Coulanges." In *Essays in Ancient and Modern Historiography*. Ed. Momigliano. Middletown, Conn.: Wesleyan University Press, 1977.

Monier-Williams, Monier. *A Sanscrit-English Dictionary*. [London: Oxford University Press, 1899.] New edition. New Delhi: Oriental Publishers, n.d.

Morris, Charles. *Foundations of the Theory of Signs. International Encyclopedia of Unified Science*. Vol. 1, no. 2. Chicago: University of Chicago Press, 1938.

Müller, Ulrike. *Thimi, Social and Economic Studies on a Newar Settlement in the Kathmandu Valley*. Giessen: Selbstverlag des Geographischen Instituts der Justus Liebig-Universität Giessen, 1981.

———. *Die ländlichen Newar-Siedlungen im Kāṭhmāṇḍu-Tal.* Giessen: Selbstverlag des Geographischen Instituts der Justus Liebig-Universität Giessen, 1984.

Mus, Paul. *Barabuḍur. Les origines du stupa et la transmigration. Essai d'archéologie religieuse comparée.* Paris: École Française d'Extrême-Orient, 1932–1934.

———."Symbolism á Ankor Thom. Le 'grand miracle' du Bayon." *Académie des Inscriptions et Belles-Lettres: Comptes-rendus des Séances* (1936): 57–68.

———. "Angkor in the time of Jayavarman VII." *Indian Art and Letters* (n.s.), 11 (1937): 65–75.

Nepal Rāṣtra Bank. *Draft Report on Household Budget Survey, Bhaktapur.* 1974*a*.

———. *Draft Summary Report on Household Budget Survey, Kathmandu, Lalitpur, Bhaktapur.* 1974*b*.

———. *The Household Budget Survey.* Kathmandu: The Nepal Rastra Bank. 1978.

Nepali, Gopal Singh. *The Newars, An Ethno-Sociological Survey of a Himalayan Community.* Bombay: United Asia Publications, 1965.

Nippon Institute of Technology. *The Royal Buildings in Nepal.* Saitama-Ken (Japan): Nippon Institute of Technology, 1981.

———.*Cities and Royal Palaces of Nepal.* Saitama-Ken (Japan): Nippon Institute of Technology. 1983.

O'Flaherty, Wendy Doniger. *Aesceticism and Eroticism in the Mythology of Siva.* London: Oxford University Press, 1973.

Oldfield, H. Ambrose. *Sketches from Nepal.* [Original edition, 1880.] Two volumes. New Delhi: Cosmo, 1974.

Ortner, Sherry. "Purification Rites and Customs." In *Macropaedia*, vol. 15, *Encyclopaedia Britannica*. Fifteenth edition. Chicago: Encyclopaedia Britannica, 1974.

Pal, Pratapaditya. *Vaisnava Iconology in Nepal: A Study in Art and Religion.* Calcutta: Asiatic Society, 1970.

———. *The Arts of Nepal.* Part I, *Sculpture.* Leiden and Cologne: E. J. Brill, 1974.

———. *Nepal. Where the Gods are Young.* New York: Asia Society, 1975.

———. *The Arts of Nepal.* Part II, *Painting.* Leiden and Cologne: Brill, 1978.

Pal, Pratapaditya, and Dipak Chandra Bhattacharyya. *The Astral Divinities of Nepal.* Varanasi: Prithvi Prakashan, 1969.

Pandey, Raj Bali. *Hindu Saṃskāras.* Second revised edition. New Delhi: Motilal Banarsidass, 1969.

Pant, Y. P., and S. C. Jain. *Agricultural Development in Nepal.* Bombay: Vora and Company, 1969.

Parish, Steven M. "Hierarchy and Person in the Moral World of the Newars." La Jolla: University of California, San Diego, doctoral dissertation in anthropology, 1987.

Petech, Luciano. *Medieval History of Nepal.* Serie Orientale Roma X. Materials for the Study of Nepalese History and Culture, vol. 3. Rome: Instituto Italiano per il medio ed exremo oriente, 1958.

Pradhan, Krishna Prasad. *Government and Administration and Local Govern-*

ment of the Kingdom of Nepal. Kathmandu: New Printing Press, 1968.

Pradhan, Prachanda. "Political Institutions since 1951." In *Nepal in Perspective*. Eds. Pashupati S. J. B. Rana and Kamal P. Malla. Kathmandu: Centre for Economic Development and Administration, 1973.

Quigley, Declan. "Introversion and Isogamy: Marriage Patterns of the Newars of Nepal." *Contributions to Indian Sociology* (n.s.), 20, 1 (1986): 75–95.

Rao, T. A. Gopinatha. *Elements of Hindu Iconography*. Two volumes. [1914.] Reprint edition. Benares: Indological Book House, 1971.

Rappaport, Roy. "The Obvious Aspects of Ritual," In R. Rappaport, *Ecology, Meaning and Religion*. Richmond, Calif.: North Atlantic Books, 1979.

Ray, Amita. *Art of Nepal*. New Delhi: Indian Council for Cultural Relations. 1973.

Redfield, Robert. *The Primitive World and Its Transformations*. Ithaca, N.Y.: Cornell University Press, 1953.

Redfield, Robert, and Milton Singer. "The Cultural Role of Cities." *Economic Development and Cultural Change*, II, 1 (1954): 53–73, 1954.

Redman, Charles L. *The Rise of Civilization*. San Francisco: W. H. Freeman and Company, 1978.

Regmi, D. R. *Medieval Nepal*. Issued in four parts. Calcutta: Firma K. L. Mukhopadhyay, 1965–1966.

———. *Ancient Nepal*. Third edition. Calcutta: Firma K. L. Mukhopadhyay, 1969.

Regmi, Mahesh C. *A Study in Nepali Economic History, 1768–1846*. Bibliotheca Himalayica Series 1, vol. 14. New Delhi: Mañjuśrī Publishing House, 1971.

———. *Landownership in Nepal*. Berkeley, Los Angeles, London: University of California Press, 1976.

———. *Thatched Huts and Stucco Palaces, Peasants and Landlords in 19th Century Nepal*. New Delhi: Vikas Publishing Company, 1978.

Ricoeur, Paul. "Existence and Hermeneutics." In *Contemporary Hermeneutics*. Ed. Josef Bleicher. London: Routledge & Kegan Paul, 1980.

Roberts, J., C. Chiao, and T. N. Pandey. "Meaningful God Sets from a Chinese Personal Pantheon and a Hindu Personal Pantheon." *Ethnology*, XIV, 2 (April 1975): 121–148.

Rose, Leo E. *Nepal, Strategy for Survival*. Berkeley, Los Angeles, London: University of California Press, 1971.

———. "The History of Nepal." In *Macropaedia*, vol. 12, *Encyclopaedia Britannica*. Fifteenth edition. Chicago: Encyclopaedia Britannica, 1974.

Rose, Leo, and Margaret Fisher. *The Politics of Nepal, Persistence and Change in an Asian Monarchy*. Ithaca, N.Y.: Cornell University Press, 1970.

Rosser, Colin. "Social Mobility in the Newar Caste System." In *Caste and Kin in Nepal, India and Ceylon*. Ed. Christoph von Fürer-Haimendorf. London: Asia Publishing House, 1966.

Russell, R. V. and Lal, R. B. H. *The Tribes and Castes of the Central Provinces of India*. [1916.] Reprint edition. New Delhi: Cosmo Publications, 1975.

Sahai, Bhagwant. *Iconography of Minor Hindu and Buddhist Deities*. New Delhi: Abhinav Publications, 1975.

Sanday, John. *The Hanuman Dhoka Royal Palace Kathmandu*. Art and

Archaeology Research Papers (AARP). Building Conservation and Local Traditional Crafts. London: AARP, December 1974.

Schwartz, Benjamin I. "The Age of Transcendence." *Daedalus. Proceedings of the American Academy of Arts and Science*, 104, 2 (Spring 1975): 1–7.

Schwartzberg, Joseph E., Ed. *A Historical Atlas of South Asia*. Chicago: University of Chicago Press, 1978.

Shaha, Rishikesh. *An Introduction to Nepal*. Kathmandu: Ratna Pustak Bhandar, 1975*a*.

———. *Nepali Politics: Retrospect and Prospect*. London: Oxford University Press, 1975*b*.

Sharma, Babu Madhav Prasad. *Swasthānī Vrata Kathā*. Varanasi: Dudhvinayak, 1955.

Sharma, Prayag Raj. "Art and Architecture." In *Nepal in Perspective*. Eds. Pashupati S.J.B. Rana Kamal P. Malla. Kathmandu: Centre for Economic Development and Administration, 1973.

Sharma, Pushpendara Kumar. *Sakti Cult in Ancient India*. Varansai: Bhartiya Publishing House, 1974.

Shastri, Ashokanath. "Durgā-pūjā." *Bhar Vidya*, 10 (1949): 241–262.

Shrestha, S. H. *Modern Geography of Nepal*. Kathmandu: Educational Enterprise Ltd., 1968.

Singh, Lalan Prasad. *Tantra*. New Delhi: Concept Publishing Company, 1967.

Singh, Madanjeet. *Himalayan Art*. Greenwich, Conn.: New York Graphic Society. 1968. (Reprinted 1971, Macmillan, New York.)

Sinha, U. N. *Panchayat Democracy of Nepal*. Kathmandu: Department of Information, Ministry of Communications, His Majesty's Government, Nepal, 1972.

Slusser, Mary Shepherd. *Nepal Mandala, A Cultural Study of the Kathmandu Valley*. Two volumes. Princeton: Princeton University Press, 1982.

Smith, William Robertson. *Lectures on the Religion of the Semites*. [1889.] Third edition. New York: Macmillan, 1927.

Snellgrove, David L. *Buddhist Himalaya, Travels and Studies in Quest of the Origins and Nature of Tibetan Religion*. Oxford: Bruno Cassirer, 1957.

———. *Himalayan Pilgrimage*. Oxford: Bruno Cassirer, 1961*a*.

———. "Shrines and Temples of Nepal." *Arts Asiatica*, VIII, 1–2 (1961*b*): 3–10, 269–270.

Sresthacharya, Iswaranand, Jagan Nath Maskey, and Austin Hale. *Conversational Newari*. Kathmandu: Summer Institute of Linguistics, Institute for Nepal Studies, Tribhuvan University, 1971.

Srinivas, M. N. *Religion and Society Among the Coorgs of South India*. New York: Asia Publishing House, 1952.

Srivastave, Ram P. "Tribe-caste Mobility in India, and the Case of Kumaon Bhotias." In *Caste and Kin in Nepal, India and Ceylon*. Ed. Christoph von Fürer-Haimendorf. London: Asia Publishing House, 1966.

Stevenson, Sinclair. *The Rites of the Twice-Born*. [1920.] London: Oxford University Press, 1971.

Stiller, Ludwig F. *Prithwinarayan Shah in the Light of Dibya Upadesh*. Bihar, India: Catholic Press, 1968.

———. *The Rise of the House of Gorkhā*. New Delhi: Mañjuśrī, 1973.

Stutley, Margaret, and James Stutley. *A Dictionary of Hinduism*. London: Routledge & Kegan Paul, 1977.

Teilhet, Jehanne. "The Tradition of the Nava Durga in Bhaktapur, Nepal." *Kailash*, VI, 1 (1978): 81–98.

Toffin, Gérard. "La Terminologie de Parenté Newar." *L'Homme*, XV (3–4) (1975*a*): 129–153.

———. "Études sur les Newar de la Vallée de Kathmandou: Guthi, Funérailles et Castes." In *L'Ethnographie* (Revue de la Société d'Ethnographie de Paris) (n.s), no. 70, 1975*b*.

———. "Le *sī kā bheāy*, festin de la tête chez le Néwar." *Kailash*, IV, 4 (1976): 329–338.

———. *Pyangaon, Communauté Newar de la Vallée de Kathmandu. La vie Matérielle*. Paris: Éditions du Centre National de la Recherche Scientifique, 1977.

———. "L' organisation social at religeuse d'une communauté Néwar (Népal)." *L'Homme*, XVIII, 1–2 (1978): 109–134.

———. *Sociéte et Religion chez les Néwar du Népal*. Paris: Éditions du Centre National de la Recherche Scientifique, 1984.

Turner, Ralph L. *A Comparative and Etymological Dictionary of the Nepali Language*. Corrected edition. London: Routledge & Kegan Paul, 1965.

Turner, Victor. *The Forest of Symbols*. Ithaca, N.Y.: Cornell University Press, 1967.

———. Myth and Symbol. *International Encyclopedia of the Social Sciences*, vol. 10. Ed. David Sills. New York: Macmillan and the Free Press, 1968, pp. 516–582.

———. *The Ritual Process. Structure and Anti-Structure*. Chicago: Aldine, 1969.

Underhill, M. M. *The Hindu Religious Year*. London: Oxford University Press, 1921

Vajrācārya, Dhanavajra. "The Development of Settlements in the Kathmandu Valley—an Historical Introduction." Paper presented to the conference, "Heritage of the Kathmandu Valley." Lübeck, Germany, 1985.

Vajrācārya, Dhanavajra, and Kamal P. Malla. *The Gopālarājavamśāvalī*. Wiesbaden: Franz Steiner Verlag, 1985.

Van Kooij, K. R. *Worship of the Goddess According to the Kālikāpurāṇa*. Leiden and Cologne: E. J. Brill, 1972.

Vatuk, Sylvia. "A Structural Analysis of HIndi Kinship Terminology." *Contributions to Indian Sociology* (n.s.), 3 (1969): 94–115.

Venkateswaran, T. K. "Rādhā-Krishna *Bhajanas* of South India: A Phenomenological, Theological, and Philosophical Study." In *Krishna: Myths, Rites, and Attitudes*. Ed. Milton Singer. Chicago: University of Chicago Press, 1968.

Vernant, Jean-Pierre. *Myth and Thought among the Greeks*. London: Routledge & Kegan Paul, 1983.

Vogt, Jay Woodworth. *The Religious Dimension in Newar Domestic Architecture*. Amherst, Mass.: Hampshire College, Master's thesis, 1977.

Wachi, Yasuko. "The Newar Peasants of Bhaktapur Nagar, Kathmandu Valley,

Nepal." *The Journal of Social Science* (International University Publications) (Mitaka, Toyko), No. 199-(1) (October 1980).

Wadley, Susan Snow. *Shakti: Power in the Conceptual Structure of Karimpur Religion.* The University of Chicago Studies In Anthropology. Series in Social, Cultural and Linguistic Anthropology, No. 2. Chicago: Department of Anthropology, University of Chicago, 1975.

Webster, Peter. "To Plough or Not to Plough? A Newar Dilemma, Tabu and Technology in Kathmandu Valley, Nepal." *Pacific Viewpoint* 22, 3 (October 1981): 99–135.

Weil, Eric. "What is a Breakthrough in History?" *Daedalus. Proceedings of the American Academy of Arts and Science*, 104, 1 (1975).

Weisner, Ulrich. *Nepalese Temple Architecture: Its Characteristics and its Relations to Indian Development.* Leiden and Cologne: E. J. Brill, 1978.

Wheatley, Paul. *The Pivot of the Four Quarters.* Chicago: Aldine, 1971.

Witzel, Michael. "On the History and the Present State of Vedic Tradition in Nepal." *Vasudha*, XV, 12 (October–November 1976): 17–39.

Wright, Daniel. *History of Nepal.* [1877.] Kathmandu: Nepal Antiquated Book Publishers, 1972.

Zimmer, H. *Mythes at symboles dans l'art et la civilisation de l'Inde.* Paris: Payot, 1951.

General Index

The numbers in square brackets are annual festival calender numbers, as listed in Appendix Five. Please see Appendix One for an explanation of the transliteration characters used for the Newari and Sanskrit words appearing in this index.

Names Index